Politics in North America

Politics in North America
Redefining Continental Relations

edited by Yasmeen Abu-Laban, Radha Jhappan, and François Rocher

broadview press

NORTH AMERICA
Post Office Box 1243,
Peterborough, Ontario,
Canada K9J 7H5

Post Office Box 1015,
3576 California Road,
Orchard Park, New York,
USA 14127
TEL: (705) 743-8990
FAX: (705) 743-8353

EMAIL:
customerservice@
broadviewpress.com

UK, IRELAND, & CONTINENTAL EUROPE
NBN International, Estover Road,
Plymouth, UK PL6 7PY
TEL: 44 (0) 1752 202300
FAX: 44 (0) 1752 202330

EMAIL:
enquiries@nbninternational.com

AUSTRALIA & NEW ZEALAND
UNIREPS University of New
South Wales
Sydney, NSW 2052 Australia
TEL: 61 2 96640999
FAX: 61 2 96645420

EMAIL:
infopress@unsw.edu.au

LIBRARY AND ARCHIVES CANADA CATALOGUING IN PUBLICATION

Politics in North America : redefining continental relations / edited by Yasmeen Abu-Laban, Radha Jhappan, and François Rocher.

Includes bibliographical references and index.
ISBN 978-1-55111-642-6

1. Canada—Politics and government—20th century. 2. United States—Politics and government—20th century. 3. Mexico—Politics and government—20th century. 4. Comparative government. I. Abu-Laban, Yasmeen, 1966– II. Jhappan, Radha III. Rocher, François

JJ1010.P64 2007   320.3   C2007-904001-2

BROADVIEW PRESS is an independent, international publishing house, incorporated in 1985. Broadview believes in shared ownership, both with its employees and with the general public; since the year 2000 Broadview shares have traded publicly on the Toronto Venture Exchange under the symbol BDP.

We welcome comments and suggestions regarding any aspect of our publications—please feel free to contact us at the addresses below or at broadview@broadviewpress.com

www.broadviewpress.com.

Broadview Press acknowledges the financial support of the Government of Canada through the Book Publishing Industry Development Program (BPIDP) for our publishing activities.

Copy-edited by Betsy Struthers
Cover & Interior design by Em Dash Design, www.emdashdesign.ca

Printed in Canada

This book is printed on paper containing 100% post-consumer fibre.

Contents

Acknowledgements 7

Abbreviations 9

Introduction, *Radha Jhappan and Yasmeen Abu-Laban* 11

PART I: HISTORY AND THE POLITICS OF DEFINING AND REDEFINING NORTH AMERICA

Introduction 25

CHAPTER 1: The "New World": Legacies of European Colonialism in North America *Radha Jhappan* 27

CHAPTER 2: Nation-building and Regionalism in the US, Canada, and Mexico *Claude Couture* 51

CHAPTER 3: The Roots of North American Economic Development *Teresa Gutiérrez-Haces* 71

PART II: REDEFINING INSTITUTIONAL RELATIONS: CONTINENTS, STATES, AND FEDERALISM

Introduction 97

CHAPTER 4: The Governance of North America: NAFTA's Complex Institutional Structure *Stephen Clarkson and Roopa Rangaswami* 101

CHAPTER 5: Birth of a Union: Lessons for North America from the European Union *Vincent Della Sala* 115

CHAPTER 6: Globalization and the Democratic Deficit: Challenging Times for Canada's Political Institutions *Samuel A. Bottomley* 133

CHAPTER 7: Political Institutions in the United States *Ross E. Burkhart* 157

CHAPTER 8: Political Institutions in Mexico *José A. Crespo, Norma Borrego, and Ana Luz Ruelas* 175

CHAPTER 9: National Institutions in North America: US, Canadian, and Mexican Federalism *François Rocher and Gordon DiGiacomo* 195

PART III: REDEFINING ECONOMIC AND SOCIAL RELATIONS: PUBLIC POLICIES AND HUMAN RIGHTS AFTER NAFTA

Introduction 221

CHAPTER 10: North American First Peoples: Self-Determination or Economic Development? *Julián Castro-Rea and Isabel Altamirano-Jiménez* 225

CHAPTER 11: Default Convergence?: Human Rights and Fundamental Freedoms in North America *David Schneiderman* 251

CHAPTER 12: Under Pressure: The Impasses of North American Labour Movements *Gregory Albo and Dan Crow* 273

CHAPTER 13: Ragged Cruelty? Social Policy Transformations in North America *Lois Harder and Marcus Taylor* 295

CHAPTER 14: Ten Years After: Continental Free Trade and Environmental Policy in North America *Luc Juillet* 315

PART IV: REDEFINING SPATIAL RELATIONS: POST-9/11 BORDERS, MIGRATION, AND NATIONAL SECURITY

Introduction 337

CHAPTER 15: Migration in North America *Yasmeen Abu-Laban* 339

CHAPTER 16: From the 49th Parallel to the Río Grande: US Homeland Security and North American Borders *Christina Gabriel and Laura Macdonald* 353

CHAPTER 17: North American Security and Foreign Policy: Does a Trilateral Community Exist? *Athanasios Hristoulas and Stéphane Roussel* 371

PART V: REDEFINING CULTURAL RELATIONS: TOWARDS A NORTH AMERICAN COMMUNITY?

Introduction 389

CHAPTER 18: Economic Integration and North American Political Cultures *Stephen White and Neil Nevitte* 393

CHAPTER 19: Civil Society Organizing Under Continental Integration: The Promise and Limits of Community-Building "From Below" *Jeffrey M. Ayres* 423

CHAPTER 20: Performing North America as Community *Janine Brodie* 441

CHAPTER 21: Beyond NAFTA: The Emergence and Future of North America *Robert A. Pastor* 461

Notes on Contributors 477

Index 483

Acknowledgements

A book such as this one reflects the impact each of our contributors has had on the study of North America. This is a work that requires thinking across languages, across countries, and across continents in ways that challenge much traditional training in political science. We feel, however, that this kind of thinking is critical in the twenty-first century, and we are pleased to offer this volume to the new generation of political scientists training today. We thank all of our contributors for their commitment to this vision and in particular for their work for this volume. This synergy was central to making a book of this nature happen.

We would also like to thank our publisher, Broadview Press, especially Michael Harrison, for his enthusiasm from the beginning for the idea of studying North America and for his patience and support at each and every step along the way. We also thank Betsy Struthers for her prompt and careful copy-editing, Tara Trueman for skilled production, and Greg Yantz for his expert advice as Politics editor.

Y A-L
RJ
FR

Abbreviations

The following abbreviations are commonly used throughout the book.

9/11	The hijacking of planes and subsequent attacks on the Pentagon (Washington, DC) and the World Trade Center (New York City) on 11 September 2001
CUFTA	Canada-US Free Trade Agreement
EU	European Union
GATT	General Agreement on Tariffs and Trade
GDP	gross domestic product
IMF	International Monetary Fund
NAFTA	North American Free Trade Agreement
NGOs	non-governmental organizations
OAS	Organization of American States
OECD	Organization for Economic Cooperation and Development
TNCs	transnational corporations
US	United States of America
UN	United Nations
WTO	World Trade Organization

Introduction

Radha Jhappan and Yasmeen Abu-Laban

> Humanity committed a grave error by constructing the Berlin Wall, and I
> am sure that today the United States is committing a grave error in con-
> structing a wall along our border.
> —Felipe Calderón, Mexico's President-elect (CTV.ca 2006)

Just prior to scheduled Congressional elections, and reflecting the politicization of migration from Mexico, on 26 October 2006, US President George W. Bush signed the Secure Fence Act, 2006. Proclaiming that it would "protect the American people" (Fox News 2006) the Act provides for reinforcing barriers over 700 miles of portions of three US states—California, Texas, and Arizona—that border Mexico. In the mid-nineteenth century, much of the territory of these three modern US states was considered to be part of Mexico; the redrawing and fortification of these boundaries by President Bush in the twenty-first century drew mixed responses. Mexican President Vicente Fox, as well as his scheduled successor, Felipe Calderón, immediately condemned the move. Indeed, Calderón encouraged other leaders, including Canadian Conservative Prime Minister Stephen Harper, to oppose the reinforced fencing. Harper declined, however, declaring that "we share the Americans' concern for safe and secure borders" (CTV.ca 2006). Nonetheless, Harper did "caution against things that can cause unnecessary barriers, not just to trade but to the ordinary exchange of tourism and social relationships between our countries" (CTV.ca 2006). This caution gave implicit recognition to the vociferous opposition being articulated by the Chamber of Commerce in Canada's largest province, Ontario, which was opposed to the Secure Fence Act on the grounds that it authorized studying the possibility of erecting a new security fence along the northern border with Canada and that such a fence might interfere with trade (Godfrey 2006).

The Secure Fence Act, 2006, and the many responses to what it may portend, serves to highlight a key feature that animates this book: North American relations—whether geographic, cultural, economic, or institutional—are historically specific, and political. As such, any attempt to preserve, undo, or reconfigure existing relations will almost inevitably involve debate, contestation, and power struggles.

Politics in North America focuses on the politics infusing the shifting economic, institutional, geographic, and cultural relations on this continent. For example, "North America" is an entity whose imagined geographic boundaries have been variable. Indigenous peoples have long referred to "Turtle Island" as encompassing territories now referred to as Canada, the US, and Mexico, but until the 1990s, for many Canadian citizens and politicians "North America" in the popular imaginary really meant only Canada and the US. In addressing the study of literature, Winfried Siemerling (2005: 1–2) notes that framing analysis in relation to "North America" brings with it a distinct set of foci:

> In the collocation "North America," the second word refers clearly to a continent, not a country, and it includes cultures in North (of) America like those of Canada. North America is a relational designation that marks it as the Northern part of a larger entity, which it does not claim to stand for or represent—yet which it could certainly draw on for contextual and differential self-understanding ... Not associated with any particular nation, North America sheds light on "America's" shadows by evoking the limits of "nation," and the liminal spaces of its borders.

In other words, for Siemerling, thinking about "North America" forces a new and interlinked consideration of national cultures and the diversity both within and across these national cultures. Her pertinent observation could be extended into considering dimensions other than literature.

This book deals with the contemporary politics and economics of North America as a continental region, as well as some of the key historical, economic, political, institutional, and cultural particularities of the three countries within it. In the twentieth century political scientists were content to divide the discipline between domestic/comparative politics and international relations. However, today it is no longer sufficient to examine discrete states in isolation from international political, economic, social, and cultural forces. Our central thesis is that the study of politics in the twenty-first century cannot be approached as in the past, but rather requires simultaneous attention to local, national, and international levels as well as, increasingly, to continents.

While the European invasion of the Americas after 1492 signaled the initial globalizing impulse of imperialism on the continent of North America, the 1988 Canada-US Free Trade Agreement (CUFTA) and the 1993 North American Free Trade Agreement (NAFTA) created the largest free trade area in the world and ushered in a new phase of continental economic integration between Mexico, the US, and Canada. The US is the central pillar in the relationship, literally as well as figuratively, as the most important trading partner for both Mexico and Canada, receiving at least 85 per cent of their exports. Since 1989, bilateral trade between Canada and the US has tripled, so that by 2004 it was close to $680 billion, with over $1.5 billion worth of goods and services crossing the border each day. Indeed, trade with the US is responsible for more than half (52 per cent) of Canada's gross domestic product (GDP), representing roughly four-fifths of Canada's exports and two-thirds of its imports. Canada, on the other hand, accounts for 23.5 per cent of US exports and 17.4 per cent of its imports. Moreover, the US is the largest foreign investor in Canada (worth over $228 billion in 2004) and the most popular destination for Canadian investment (approximately $165 billion in 2004), making Canada the seventh largest investor in the US (Canadian Embassy in Washington 2006). Mexico is the US's second largest trading partner, with a volume of $268 billion in 2004 (the US exported $111 billion in goods and services to and received $158 billion in imports from Mexico). Over 40 per cent of all foreign direct investment in Mexico in 2004 came from the US ($7.3 billion), although Mexicans resident in the US sent home more than twice as much ($16.6 billion) in remittances. Trade between Canada and Mexico has tripled from $4.1 to $12.6 billion since NAFTA was passed, although this accounts for less than 5 per cent of total trade for either country (Davy and Meyers 2005: 2).

In addition to trading in finance, goods, and services, the three states have been vigorously "trading" people as well. Foreign-born Mexicans, for example, constituted 3.3 per cent of the total US population in 2000 (or 29.5 per cent of the total foreign-born population), and in 2004, 18.5 per cent of new US legal permanent residents (175,364 in number) came from Mexico (Office of Immigration Statistics 2004: 12). In contrast, only 2.6 per cent of the foreign-born population of the US is comprised of Canadians. A higher proportion of Canada's foreign-born residents are US nationals (4.6 per cent), while 63.2 per cent of Mexico's foreign-born nationals came from the US, many the US-born children of Mexicans (Consejo Nacional de Poblacion 2001). And while in the US the "illegal immigration problem" is targeted by national and state legislation as well as by US citizens mobilizing at the border (see Chapter 15), Canada is attracting Mexican professionals who are "turned off" by vigilantism, stricter entry requirements, and various iterations of national and/or state legislation aimed at curbing "illegal" immigration from Mexico (Hawley 2005). In Canada there was a 68 per cent increase in the number of legal, temporary workers from Mexico between 1998 and 2003 (from 13,261 to 22,344), compared with only an 18 per cent increase in the number admitted legally to the US from Mexico in the same period (from 110,075 to 130,327). Moreover, as the US accelerated border fortification post-9/11, the number of Mexicans applying for refugee status in Canada almost doubled, making Mexico Canada's third largest source of refugee claimants (Hawley 2005).

In part as a response to increased migration and in part due to the US's security worries after 9/11, a series of accords has committed the three countries to establishing common policies regarding issues such as migration and border security (as found in the US-Canada Smart Border Declaration of 2001 and the US-Mexico Partnership Agreement of 2002, as well as the trilateral Security and Prosperity Partnership of 2005). However, in contrast to the European Union (EU), North America has not created a thick and ongoing network of intergovernmental and even supranational political institutions for developing, implementing, and monitoring common policies. Instead, bilateral and trilateral agreements in discrete policy areas mean that North America is increasingly shaped by constitution-like restrictions on national governments in an asymmetrical relationship, given that the region contains the global hegemon (the US), a middle power (Canada), and a developing country (Mexico).

A brief snapshot of some major indices of wealth amply demonstrates the unequal power relations endemic within and between the three states. Although aggregate statistics can only be suggestive in the absence of a full explanation of the formulae and values used in their calculation, as well as a full contextualization and analysis of their causes, Table 1 nevertheless shows some very significant differences between the three states. For example, although the population of the US is three times that of Mexico, its annual budget is 11.56 times larger. Mexico's per capita income is one-fourth that of the US; in other words, on average, the GDP per capita purchasing power of residents of the US is four times greater than that of Mexicans (US$41,800 vs. US$10,000) and significantly higher even than that of Canadians (US$32,800).

These numbers are, of course, averages, which conceal the great disparities of income and wealth within each state, as shown by the acute inequalities in income between the lowest and highest 10 per cent of income groups in each country, most pronounced in Mexico (1.6 per cent/35.6 per cent), and somewhat flatter in Canada (2.8 per cent/23.8 per cent) than in the US (1.8 per cent/30.5 per cent). The minimum wage in Mexico is 40 pesos (US$4) per day, and there is little or no welfare state and no unemployment benefit. Mexico is one of the four worst countries in Latin America for income distribution. These figures are related (among other things) to the nature of the economy and of the labour force, the types of jobs available, and unemployment rates. For example, 28 million Mexicans labour in the agricultural sector, a much higher percentage than in Canada (2 per cent) and the US (less than 0.7 per cent); many Mexican agricultural workers toil on a subsistence basis producing corn, maize, and squash on small plots of land or communal village holdings, as opposed to the large-scale high-technology/low labour agribusiness that dominates the other two states (King 2001).

Moreover, according to official figures (which may underestimate the actual situation for a variety of reasons), 40 per cent of Mexicans live below the poverty line, compared to 15.9 per cent of Canadians (for 2003) and 12 per cent of Americans (in 2005). Of course, poverty is a relative concept and is both defined and experienced differently in each national context: in terms of access to goods, food, shelter, health care, education, and other essential services, poverty in Mexico is more severe in absolute terms than it is in Canada and the US, where low income groups at least have access to universal state-funded primary and secondary education, as well as health care and some income support programs, even if these have been declining over the last two decades of neo-liberal public policies (see Chapter 13).

Statistics such as infant mortality rates are indicative of a host of social problems, especially in Mexico, where the high rate (20.91 deaths per 1,000 live births, compared with 6.5 for the US and 4.75 for Canada) is related to such factors as lack of access to medical services (especially in rural areas and among low income groups) and the subordinate position of women, which makes it more difficult to challenge poor pre-natal education, uneven pre- and post-natal care, and nutrition. Trade liberalization is likely to provide disproportionate benefits to higher and middle income than to low income groups: subsistence farmers, for instance, are now subject to competition from heavily subsidized US corn being dumped on the Mexican market (Henriques 2003). Despite the often explicit promises advanced by proponents of free trade, there are more, not fewer, poor people in each of the three countries since NAFTA was passed, and the situations of poor Americans and Canadians are likely to be worsened by the erosion of welfare state provisions in the face of neo-liberal restructuring. As such, any equalization stemming from trade liberalization may well be more in the nature of downward equalization for low-income groups in all three countries.

If the profound economic disparities between the three states were not enough to underscore the differences within North America, the US has positioned itself as the lone remaining "superpower," if not the "policeman" of the world. The preoccupation of successive US leaders with global geopolitical and security matters beyond trading relationships with relatively insignificant (on a world scale) neighbours make it extremely unlikely that the relationship between the three states of North America can ever be one of equals. Even so, understanding contemporary North American politics requires considering other questions of interest to political scientists, and drawing on more of what the discipline may offer to the study of the region.

Table 1: Statistical Comparison of Mexico, Canada, and the US, Assorted Data

	MEXICO	CANADA	US
POPULATION IN MILLIONS (2005)	106,202,903	32,805,041	295,734,134
BUDGET: REVENUES EXPENDITURES	$173.2 billion $175.4 billion	$159.6 billion $152.6 billion	$2.119 trillion $2.466 trillion
GDP (PURCHASING POWER PARITY) (2005 EST.)	$1.066 trillion	$1.077 trillion	$12.37 trillion
GDP—REAL GROWTH RATE (2005 EST.)	3%	2.8%	3.5%
GDP—PER CAPITA PURCHASING POWER PARITY (2005)	$10,000	$32,800	$41,800
UNEMPLOYMENT RATE (2005)	3.6% (plus underemployment of perhaps 25%)	6.8%	5.1%
LABOR FORCE, INCLUDING UNEMPLOYED (2005)	37.38 million	17.35 million	149.3 million
LABOR FORCE, BY OCCUPATION	agriculture 18%; industry 24%; services 58% (2003).	agriculture 2%; manufacturing 14%; construction 5%; services 75%; other 3% (2004).	farming, forestry, & fishing 0.7%; manufacturing, extraction, transportation, & crafts 22.9%; managerial, professional, & technical 34.7%; sales & office 25.4%; other services 16.3% (2005). Note: figures exclude the unemployed
HOUSEHOLD INCOME OR CONSUMPTION BY % SHARE: LOWEST 10% HIGHEST 10%	1.6% 35.6%	(1994) 2.8% 23.8%	1.8% 30.5%
POPULATION BELOW POVERTY LINE	40% (2003 est.)	15.9% (2003)	12% (2005)
LIFE EXPECTANCY AT BIRTH FEMALE MALE	78.1 years 72.42 years	83.63 years 76.73 years	80.67 years 74.89 years
BIRTH RATE: BIRTHS/1,000 POPULATION	21.01	10.84	14.14
TOTAL FERTILITY RATE: CHILDREN BORN/WOMAN (2005 EST.)	2.45	1.61	2.08
INFANT MORTALITY RATE PER 1000 LIVE BIRTHS	20.91	4.75	6.5

Sources: CIA World Fact Books for Mexico, Canada, and the US, updated 10 January 2006. <http://www.cia.gov/cia/publications/ factbook/geos/ca.html>; <http://www.cia.gov/cia/publications/factbook/geos/mx.html>; <http://www.cia.gov/cia/publications/ factbook/geos/us.html>.

Major Themes

This book stresses the importance of applying both an historical and a continental lens to the study of domestic/national state and international politics. It examines some of the key ways in which the legacies of colonialism in "The New World" affect contemporary politics, and it situates the historical and contemporary interdependence and points of conflict and cooperation between Canada, the US, and Mexico in relation to the geopolitical positions of each. Several chapters analyze, from different points of view, the implications of NAFTA and contemporary globalization processes for national sovereignty, nationalism, and democracy and representation through national political institutions. Others explore the effects of NAFTA on human rights and citizenship, especially in the areas of Indigenous rights, social policy, labour, and the environment—fields in which the organization and impact of social movements is particularly notable. Finally, the exploration of national security, border, and migration issues underscores new challenges to North America as a community, especially in the post-9/11 world. The debates and controversies surrounding five major themes are woven throughout the volume (though some are more relevant in certain sections and chapters than in others, and these themes are not necessarily mutually exclusive). These are: 1) the role of the state; 2) globalization and challenges to state sovereignty; 3) democracy, representation, and legitimacy; 4) human rights; and 5) community. The conflicts surrounding each theme will be discussed in turn.

1. THE ROLE OF THE STATE

The inequalities within and between the three North American countries discussed above are tied not just to their political, economic, and social histories, but also to their political cultures and dominant ideologies, which condition responses to long-standing questions of interest to students of politics. Indeed, the contemporary era of globalization has coincided with a widespread acceptance of neo-liberal policy prescriptions among policy-makers. Since neo-liberalism promotes the market as an efficient allocator of goods and services, a limited role for the state in the realm of social policy, and a greater emphasis on individual self-sufficiency (Abu-Laban and Gabriel 2002: 21), this trend obliges political scientists and citizens alike to re-engage the big questions of traditional Western political science. What is the purpose of society? What is the purpose of government? Why do we come together, in the classical terms of liberal theory, and agree to give up certain of our liberties and/or control over many aspects of our lives? In the latter half of the twentieth century, most leaders and citizens in Western countries had rejected the spare classical liberal answer to those questions—that the need for mutual security and law and order required both limited government and some curtailment of individual liberties. They took instead a social view wherein a more activist government corrected some of the imperfections of the market by providing not just civil and political rights but social goods in the form of publicly funded education, income support for the needy, health care, and some regulation of the private sector in the public interest. Membership of the political/economic/social community, it was recognized, should have its privileges, which reinforce notions of solidarity and belonging.

The rise of neo-liberal ideology in the late twentieth century, however, especially in North America, has led to a shrinking state and deregulation of the economy. This in turn has necessitated fresh inquiries into not only the purpose of government but also, critically, the purpose of the economy, production, and consumption. Who should make decisions about how these activities are organized and in whose interests? Governments? Corporations and their World Economic Forum? International bodies such as the World Trade Organization (WTO), the G8, the IMF (International Monetary Fund)/World Bank? NAFTA panels? Or citizens?

These questions are far from settled either among publics (as exemplified by the massive demonstrations surrounding discussions of a "Free Trade Agreement of the Americas" in Québec City in 2001) or among politicians. In fact, leaders in the three states that comprise North America have historically taken significantly different approaches to some of these questions, and their competing visions were well illustrated at the Special Summit of the Americas held on 12 January 2004 in Monterrey, Mexico. In his speech to 33 other elected leaders of the Americas, for example, US President George W. Bush reiterated the "Washington consensus" of the 1990s, the proposition that the market, and specifically free trade, could drive democracy forward and promote good government. In order to "to bring all the hemisphere's people into an expanding circle of development," Bush argued, the Organization of American States (OAS) must "chart a clear course toward a vibrant free market that will help lift people out of poverty and create a healthy middle class … increase the credit available to small businesses that generate the majority of jobs in all our economies, and … strengthen property rights so that land can be leveraged as a source of capital to start businesses or hire new workers." Trying to appeal to an audience of heads of governments largely hostile to the US's desire for a Free Trade of the Americas Agreement, Bush maintained that "trade is the most certain path to lasting prosperity" and the Americas would "show the world that free societies and free markets can deliver real benefits to our citizens" (Bush 2004).

In contrast to Bush's free market mantra of property rights, free trade, and market-led decision-making, Canadian Prime Minister Paul Martin (as he then was) focused more on what governments could do to alleviate poverty. While agreeing on the goals of comprehensive trade liberalization, fiscal prudence, and economic and investment reforms, Martin took a more social democratic view of the role of government, stressing that "we maintain our commitment to the social safety net, knowing that a successful society depends upon a healthy, well-educated population." He suggested that the priority for the OAS was to find ways "to improve equity, to reduce the gap between the rich and the poor, create opportunities for all, and finally, reduce corruption in our hemisphere"—these were the keys to building "growing, open, and equitable societies" (Martin 2004).

President Vicente Fox of Mexico, meanwhile, after having alienated President Bush the year before by refusing to support the US-led invasion of Iraq, focused on the issue of illegal migration of Mexicans to the US and welcomed Bush's proposal to create temporary work permits (though not permanent citizenship rights) for undocumented workers (Weiner and Bumiller, 2004). This focus also reflected the important role played by remittances in the Mexican economy. Thus, the differing priorities expressed by the three leaders illustrate not just the particular ideological commitments of their three ruling parties but some of the key conflicts that arise from their relative positions in the world and their different national interests. When the global hegemon speaks, the world listens in a way that it does not listen to Canada or Mexico; this is why the 2004 US presidential election was widely regarded by publics in many countries outside the US as a global election. Of course, only US citizens could vote in the election; nonetheless, in a sense it was a global election both because the Republican and Democratic parties conducted worldwide campaigns to secure the votes of the many thousands of expatriate US citizens abroad (the largest numbers in Canada, Mexico, and Israel), and because of the significance of US foreign and economic policy for the world.

2. GLOBALIZATION AND CHALLENGES TO STATE SOVEREIGNTY

In recent years, distinctive debates on the meaning of state sovereignty have been sparked by new forms of globalization that take on cultural, technological, and economic dimensions, as well as challenges that have global implications and seem to require world-level responses. Some such challenges include environmental degradation, HIV-AIDS, drugs, and poverty (George and Page 2004). Here, the focus is on NAFTA, a major international trade agreement, and its three member countries—Canada, the US, and Mexico—in order to examine globalization and state sovereignty within the continent of North America.

Many political analysts suggest that by their very nature, international trade agreements limit the scope of action of their signatories in discrete policy fields, and from this perspective NAFTA is no exception (Grinspun and Cameron 1993; Cameron and Tomlin 2000). The rules established by international trade instruments mean that governments are denied the flexibility to respond to changing conditions, especially those not anticipated by negotiators. Moreover, the shift in decision-making authority to international bodies such as trade panels that are neither responsible to voters nor mandated to consider the broader long-term needs and interests of any particular country means a net loss of state sovereignty, particularly for the weaker signatories who are under more pressure to abide by the panel rulings.

On the other hand, NAFTA is viewed by many political and business elites (as well as economists) in Canada, the US, and Mexico as either having been of benefit or, at the very least, laying the foundation for greater benefits. Thus, for example, since 2000 there has been a growing push from some business sectors in all three countries, as well as certain political elites and academics (particularly in Canada and Mexico) for even greater continental integration in North America. Dubbed as "NAFTA Plus" in Mexico, and "deep integration" in Canada, the vision inspiring such terms was also articulated in a 2005 Task Force sponsored by the US Council on Foreign Relations (an independent non-partisan organization devoted to foreign policy), the Canadian Council of Chief Executives (Canada's main business lobby), and the Consejo Mexicano de Asuntos Internacionales (an independent non-partisan organization financed in part by business). To quote from the ensuing report's foreword, written by the Council on Foreign Relations President, Richard N. Haass:

> The Task Force offers a detailed and ambitious set of proposals that build
> on the recommendations adopted by the three governments at the Texas

> summit of March 2005. The Task Force's central recommendation is establishment by 2010 of a North American economic and security community, the boundaries of which would be defined by a common external tariff and an outer security perimeter. (Council on Foreign Relations 2005: xvii)

From the vantage point of defenders of trade agreements such as NAFTA and/or proponents of greater integration, worries about a decline in state sovereignty are met with assertions, such as that from Canadian economist, Thomas Courchene, that certain provisions in the agreement can be "'sovereignty enhancing' or at least 'sovereignty preserving'" (2005: 20). However, the meaning of "sovereignty" is being radically reconfigured in relation to the power of business to act in the global economy, rather than in relation to traditional understandings (both in political science and the law) based on the legal equality of states, which view sovereignty as flowing from the idea that the state is the highest authority; that is, the state can act freely since it recognizes no higher authority either within its borders or internationally. Reflecting an altogether novel conceptualization of sovereignty, for instance, is economist Wendy Dobson, a leader in calling for Canada to accept the "Big Idea" of deeper integration: "sovereignty is not just about what a country gives up but also about what it gains in more efficient production, larger markets, freer flow of investment, swift resolution of disputes, and greater protection of intellectual property, to name a few examples" (2002: 3). Within such a market-oriented vision, political/state sovereignty thus morphs into corporate sovereignty.

Notably, however, debates over (free) trade and state sovereignty have virtually ignored other challenges to the state that are particularly pertinent in light of the fact that each of the three states in North America were formed by expropriating land from Indigenous peoples. Several chapters in this volume (Chapters 1, 2, and 10) directly consider the manner in which the ongoing claims made by Indigenous nations challenge a key feature associated with the Westphalian state system and sovereignty: the territorial integrity of the state.

Although possible limitations on state sovereignty are not inherently objectionable in and of themselves, they need at least to be understood and evaluated in light of differing understandings of sovereignty, to which these debates and analyses point, as well as differing values. Central in this regard is consideration of democratic values, a third related theme addressed in this text.

3. DEMOCRACY AND LEGITIMACY

For political scientists, issues relating to democracy and legitimacy (the degree to which people both feel that those in power represent them and accept existing decision-making bodies) have been central to the discipline's inquiries. This has especially been the case in the field of comparative politics, which emerged after World War II as the discipline's central site of empirical theory-building in its exuberant embrace of studying not only countries of the West (as had traditionally been done) but all countries. There is no clear consensus on what constitutes "democracy" (hence the long-standing debate, inspired by Marx, over whether capitalism is anathema to true democracy). However, for many comparativists, a basic working definition has emphasized the necessity of regular, free, and competitive elections; the rule of law; and respect for individual rights. Yet, even using the most narrow criteria of free and competitive elections, it is notable that not only was the 2006 presidential election in Mexico marred by charges of electoral fraud and unfairness, but so too was the 2000 presidential election in the US, along with the 2004 gubernatorial race in the US state of Washington. In other words, even in countries that are frequently described by comparativists as "consolidated democracies" (the US being a key example) actual practices may counter the description. This is what gives rise to ongoing discussions about the nature of democracy within polities such as the US and the nature and functioning of national political institutions (see Chapters 6, 7, and 8).

Free trade in the form of CUFTA and NAFTA has necessitated new ways of considering institutions, legitimacy, and democracy at both national and continental levels. The design and functions of national political institutions affect the processes and kinds of international agreements that are negotiated, but institutions are also affected by those agreements. In the case of the three North American states, all are federations; trade agreements negotiated by national executives potentially affect provincial/state jurisdictions and even circumscribe the powers of central governing institutions by imposing rules that are adjudicated by international panels rather than domestic courts. Alongside challenges to state sovereignty, several chapters in this volume (Chapters 4, 5, and 9) assess the contemporary challenges to the democratic and representative capacities of national and provincial/state political institutions in the face of continental economic integration. These examinations in turn reflect ongoing conflicts concerning the meaning of "democracy" and regarding instances of perceived democratic deficits, giving rise to a new set of questions both political scientists and publics confront. Do supranational organizations exercising authority vis-à-vis domestic economic and social policies damage democracy? Should the citizens of member states be able to demand accountability of them? Should voice go beyond the national voting booth? Several chapters in this volume (Chapters 1, 4, 10, 12, 14, and 19) take up these questions and focus in particular on the transnational mobilization of civil society in response to CUFTA and NAFTA.

While respect for individual rights is key to many definitions of democracy and many national constitutions, the idea of "human rights" is one that has had global impact and that has been central to the discourses of international organizations such as the United Nations.

4. HUMAN RIGHTS

Human rights emerged as a major international discourse in the years following World War II and spurred on some of the most vibrant movements of the twentieth century: those relating to anti-colonialism, national minorities, and women. Although human rights were not on the formal agenda of NAFTA, they were nevertheless part of the public debate around the agreement. Assuming the moral superiority of "the West" and its liberal ideals, some of NAFTA's advocates asserted that trade would liberalize and democratize Mexico, a country burdened by decades of one-party rule, a host of repressive policies to neutralize dissent, and major human rights abuses perpetrated by the armed forces and the police.

Yet, issues relating to human rights are also on the agenda of the US and Canada, especially following 9/11, since in this period the question of whether security should trump human rights remains unsettled. New legislation passed in the wake of 9/11, especially the US Patriot Act, 2001 and to a lesser extent, Canada's Anti-Terrorism Act, 2001, are seen by many legal scholars to involve the violation of civil liberties and individual rights long regarded as constitutive of consolidated/liberal democracies (Cole 2002–03; Daniels, Macklem, and Roach 2001). Additionally, international human rights norms have been violated as exemplified by the US Naval Station at Guantanamo Bay, Cuba, used since 9/11 to imprison indefinitely and without trial hundreds of suspected al-Qaeda and Taliban prisoners who are denied access to any court, legal counsel, or visits. Such detentions are in violation of the Geneva Convention, as are the documented human rights violations (Amnesty International 2006).

Such gross and internationally controversial violations, however, do not exhaust the human rights issues involved in contemporary North American politics; multiple issues arise in different contexts, from the treatment of illegal migrants at work and in US society, to poor living and working conditions for workers deployed in the maquiladoras in Mexico, to the rights of Indigenous peoples to self-determination, to the question of whether property rights should trump human rights. These issues are explored in Chapters 1, 10, 11, 12, and 13. Such human rights issues also take us to the heart of another major theme: community.

5. THE NATURE OF COMMUNITY

The formation of regional/continental trading blocs in various parts of the world has also generated new twists on old questions, such as, what is the nature of community? The political science literature dealing with the emergence of the European Coal and Steel Community and the European Economic Community (the origins of the EU) has long prompted the idea that through initial steps in the sphere of economics there would be "spillover" in other spheres, leading ultimately to the emergence of a new political community beyond the state (Haas 1957; Pentland 1973). Given this, it needs to be asked whether, and if so how, North America can plausibly be understood as a community of any sort, beyond the economic arrangements of CUFTA and NAFTA. This question is directly addressed in Chapters 18, 19, 20, and 21, but this whole book examines the historical and contemporary social, economic, and political forces that have created competing visions of what it means to belong to a political community. It demonstrates how localizing, nationalizing, and internationalizing forces shape the political space of "North America."

While the media tend to cover high-profile conflicts between the North American states, such as the long-running softwood lumber dispute between Canada and the US, or border security issues such as "illegal immigration" from Mexico to the US, there are many other levels of relations between the three states, especially in the lived experiences of transnational communities. Aside from the overwhelmingly corporate nature of contemporary globalization, increased communications and transnational organizing among various civil society groups have reoriented and refreshed what used to be defined as purely domestic questions. As similar patterns of economic, social, and political organization have been identified between states, social movements, individuals, and scholars have been refocusing debates about the possibilities and limits of accommodation in multinational states, especially in relation to ethnic collectivities. These issues take on special significance in Canada, Mexico, and the US since all three countries were formed as settler-colonies with pre-existing Indigenous communities; all three countries are ethnically, "racially," and culturally diverse; and minorities in all three countries continue to demand equality, fairness, and sometimes even political autonomy.

Note on the Text

Given the complexities of the entity of "North America," and the ongoing manner in which this space is being enacted as well as envisioned (see, for example, Courchene 2005 for an overview), no single volume could hope to cover all the possible themes or specific topics of interest. For example, there is much to be said about matters not specifically addressed here, including cultural policy; energy policy; trade and economic policy in general terms and beyond North America, especially relations with the WTO and interactions with NAFTA, the FTAA, and other agreements; relations with other countries, regions, or regional trading blocs; or suggestions for a common currency. We do not presume to offer an exhaustive account of all that is or could be discussed about North American integration. Rather, by introducing a regional unit of analysis and buttressing discussions in relation to history and some key themes, we aim to highlight some of the most important and persistent issues and to inspire further study and debate about North America among political scientists, especially in international relations and comparative politics.

References

Abu-Laban, Yasmeen, and Christina Gabriel. 2002. *Selling Diversity: Immigration, Multiculturalism, Employment Equity, and Globalization.* Peterborough, ON: Broadview Press.

Amnesty International. 2006. "Guantánamo: Lives Torn Apart—The Impact of Indefinite Detention on Detainees and their Families." <http://web.amnesty.org/library/Index/ENGAMR510072006>.

Bush, G.W. 2004. "Address by the President of the US, George W. Bush at the Special Summit of the Americas Ceremony, Monterrey, Mexico, 12 January 2004." <http://www.whitehouse.gov/news/releases/2004/01/20040112-9.html>.

Cameron, Maxwell A., and Brian W. Tomlin. 2000. *The Making of NAFTA: How the Deal was Done.* Ithaca, NY: Cornell UP.

Canadian Embassy in Washington. 2006. "The Canada-US Trade and Investment Partnership." <http://www.dfait-maeci.gc.ca/can-am/washington/trade_and_investment/default_139-en.asp>.

Cole, David. 2002–03. "Their Liberties, Our Security: Democracy and Double Standards." *Boston Review* (December/January). <http://bostonreview.mit.edu/BR27.6/cole.html>.

Consejo Nacional de Poblacion, M. 2001. "Situacion demografica de Mexico, 2004." <http://www.conapo.gob.mx/publicaciones/2004/sdm2004.htm>.

Council on Foreign Relations. 2005. Building a North American Community: Independent Task Force Report No. 53. New York: Council on Foreign Relations.

Courchene, Thomas J. 2005. "Thinking North America: Pathways and Prospects." In Thomas J. Courchene, Donald Savoie, and Daniel Schwanen (eds.), *The Art of the State*, Vol. II No. 1: Thinking North America. Montreal: Institute for Research on Public Policy. 3–48.

CTV.ca News Staff. 2006. "Mexico Urges Canada to Help Oppose Border Fence." (26 October). <http://www.ctv.ca>.

Daniels, Ronald J., Patrick Macklem, and Kent Roach (Eds.). 2001. *The Security of Freedom: Essays on Canada's Anti-Terrorist Legislation*. Toronto: U of Toronto P.

Davy, Megan, and Deborah Meyers. 2005. "United States-Canada-Mexico Fact Sheet on Trade and Migration." Fact Sheet #11. <http://www.migrationpolicy.org/pubs/fact_sheets.php>.

Dobson, Wendy. 2002. "Shaping the Future of the North American Economic Space: A Framework for Action." C.D. Howe Institute Commentary No. 162 (April).

Fox News. 2006. "Bush Signs US-Mexico Border Fence Bill." (26 October). <http://Foxnews.com>.

George, Vic, and Robert M. Page (Eds.) 2004. *Global Social Problems*. Cambridge: Polity Press.

Godfrey, Tom. 2006. "Bush Eyes Fence on Canadian Border." (27 October). <http://www.TorontoSun.com>.

Grinspun, Ricardo, and Maxwell A. Cameron (Eds.) 1993. *The Political Economy of North American Free Trade*. Montreal and Kingston: McGill-Queen's UP.

Haas, Ernst. 1957. *The Uniting of Europe*. Stanford, CA: Stanford UP.

Hawley, C. 2005. "Canada Is Wooing Mexican Immigrants." Republic, Mexico City Bureau.

Henriques, Gisele, and Raj Patel. 2003. *Agricultural Trade Liberalization and Mexico*. Oakland, CA: Food First/Institute for Food and Development Policy.

King, John L. 2001. "Concentration and Technology in Agricultural Input Industries." Agriculture Information Bulletin No. AIB763. Washington, DC: US Department of Agriculture.

Martin, P. 2004. "Address by Prime Minister of Canada Paul Martin On the Occasion of the Inauguration Ceremony of the Special Summit of the Americas." <http://www.pco-bcp.gc.ca/default.asp?Language=E&Page=archivemartin&Sub=speechesdiscours&Doc=speech_20040112_24_e.htm>.

Office of Immigration Statistics. 2004. *Yearbook of Immigration Statistics*. Washington, DC: Department of Homeland Security.

Pentland, Charles. 1973. *International Theory and European Integration*. London: Faber and Faber.

Siemerling, Winfried. 2005. *The New North American Studies; Culture, Writing and the Politics of Re/Cognition*. New York: Routledge.

Weiner, Tim, and Elisabeth Bumiller. 2004. "Expectations are Low for Progress at Americas Conference." *The New York Times* 12 January. [University of Alberta Library Systems: Proquest Newspapers].

PART ONE
History and the Politics of Defining and Redefining North America

This first section outlines the historical context underpinning contemporary North American political, economic, social, and cultural development to highlight how these features have been defined and redefined since the invasion of the Americas in 1492. In Chapter 1, "The 'New World': Legacies of European Colonialism in North America," Radha Jhappan discusses Mexico, the US, and Canada in relation to their historic foundation as settler-colonies. Jhappan reminds readers that prior to contact with Europeans, Indigenous nations throughout the continent traded goods, ideas, and technologies, suggesting that there is a much older idea of an integrated continent than is acknowledged by contemporary calls for "deep integration."

Jhappan traces the impact of European colonization on North America from competition for territory, resources, and power, to the unequal social and economic development within and between Canada, the US, and Mexico, to varied reactions to trade (re)liberalization today. In particular, Jhappan shows how the legacies of slavery and the expropriation of lands from Indigenous peoples have produced enduring divisions (especially along racial, class, and gender lines) that are playing out in the way contemporary forms of regional (continental) integration are received. In this, the still unresolved land and political rights claims made by Indigenous peoples challenge the territorial integrity (and thus sovereignty) of each of the three existing states in a way that finds no parallel in the older states of Europe. At present, this challenge to the territorial integrity of states is even finding expression in Indigenous claims directed at WTO and NAFTA tribunals.

Claude Couture, in Chapter 2, "Nation-Building and Regionalism in the US, Canada, and Mexico," considers region in relation to subnational jurisdictions rather than to continents. Couture both brings front and centre, and challenges, the portrayal of "American exceptionalism" in much historiography, as well as in many theoretical treatments of nationalism. The thesis of "American exceptionalism" suggests that the US is both unique and united in accepting the values associated with "modernity" (especially liberalism, secularism, and cosmopolitanism) over those associated with "traditionalism" (especially conservatism, religiosity, and particularism). Many theoretical accounts of nationalism also suggest that the claims of subnational minorities are mired in traditionalism and directed at a "centre" expressing values of modernity.

Against these claims permeating historical accounts and nationalism theory, Couture's use of recent (revisionist) historiography demonstrates that the US is neither completely nor uniquely modern, and in fact in recent times its "political centre" has embraced traditional values. Moreover, the claims made by subnational and regional minorities within Canada (e.g., those made by the Québécois or by Indigenous peoples), the US (e.g., Puerto Rico) and Mexico (e.g., the South and Indigenous peoples) are often claims for equality and fairness that have much in common with the values associated with modernity. Couture suggests that a more accurate understanding of Canada, the US, and Mexico—particularly in light of national electoral outcomes in all three since 2000—would acknowledge the growing division within all three countries between those communities that express modern tendencies and those that express tradition. His analysis therefore underscores the importance not only of history but of how we interpret history to understand the similarities and the differences in claims and values within and across "national cultures."

In Chapter 3, "The Roots of North American Economic Development," Teresa Gutiérrez-Haces addresses the historic economic development of Mexico, Canada, and the US to account for the asymmetries in power evident in the former two in comparison with the latter. Rooting her analysis in the colonial period and extending into the twentieth century, she illustrates how the economic development of each weaker country was interconnected not only with the US but also with European powers (Spain in the case of Mexico and Britain in the case of Canada). Her main argument suggests that imperialism and capitalism have worked historically to make both Mexico and Canada resource hinterlands and, more contemporaneously, to make these two countries seek to (re)negotiate trade reciprocity with the US. In accounting for the unequal character of the three countries economically, this chapter simultaneously serves to underline the long-standing economic interdependence of the US with Canada as well as Mexico. As such, it stresses that NAFTA did not mark a "new" relationship but rather redrew the terms of a long-existing relationship. The exact nature of this relationship is taken up in the second section of this book, which deals with institutions.

CHAPTER ONE

The "New World"
Legacies of European Colonialism in North America

Radha Jhappan

More than a thousand years ago, long before the Vikings landed in the territory of the Beothuk nation (now called Newfoundland) circa AD 1000, long before the most recent phase of globalization that began in 1492 with the "discovery" of the "New World" by Christopher Columbus, the great city of Cahokia was the centre of an economic and cultural network that linked the territories known today as Canada, the US, and Mexico. As Jack Weatherford has noted, Cahokia was the largest city in the Americas north of ancient Mexico, boasting more than 120 mound pyramids (some larger than the Great Pyramids of Egypt) and strategically situated in what is now the state of Illinois near a major nexus of the Mississippi River. That location permitted travel by water through the river's tributaries to Alberta and Saskatchewan in the north; Montana and Idaho in the north-west; New Mexico in the south-west; the Appalachian Mountains, Pennsylvania, and the Carolinas in the east; and the Gulf of Mexico in the south. Cahokia was the hub of Native North America, "an ideal place for trade, commerce, and communication," a key link in "a trade empire that surpassed in geographic size the empires of ancient Rome and Egypt" (Weatherford 1991: 14). Items from as far away as Yellowstone have been found at the site, as have copper from the Upper Great Lakes, mica from the southern Appalachians, and seashells from the Gulf of Mexico (Mink 1992).

Cahokia was only one such centre. All over the Americas, where cultural and economic exchange had a long pedigree over at least 30,000 years of human habitation (Francis *et al.* 2000: 2), Indigenous nations conducted international relations and were enthusiastic traders of knowledge, technologies, and goods. Obsidian, a volcanic rock used for tools originating in what is now British Columbia, has been found on the western plains, while "copper from the west end of Lake Superior has been found at Saguenay, Quebec, and abalone from California found its way into the interior in the form of beads and other ceremonial items" (Royal Commission on Aboriginal Peoples 1996: 9). In fact, it was the nation-states fashioned by the descendants of the colonizing powers of Britain and France (for the US and Canada) and Spain (for Mexico) that created the national and regional barriers to trade and to free and open cultural and other exchanges on the continent, barriers that are only now being broken down after a couple of centuries of relatively restricted borders. As expressed by the wide use of the term "Turtle Island" among Indigenous nations (Benton-Banai 1979), the conception of North America as an integrated continent is not new; the vast array of interconnections was and is well understood in Indigenous historical and contemporary worldviews.

This chapter examines some of the enduring effects of the European colonization of North America in this new age of trade re-liberalization. Attention to historical context is critical to an understanding of the contemporary politics of North America as historical events and discourses have had lasting consequences for the three states. The history of competition for territories, power, and resources, together with the form and direction of economic development dictated by the European colonial powers, produced hostile relations within and between the nation-states that succeeded them in the Americas. Even after the severance of their formal colonial status and ascension to the status of independent states, Mexico, Canada, and the US continued to be shaped by the practices of their formative colonial periods. The unequal economic, social, and cultural development, power, and status, both within and between the three states are explained (among other things) by the complex geopolitics of imperialism: the treatment of Indigenous nations; political economies; solutions to labour problems, immigration, and settlement patterns; management of racial/ethnic, class, and gender relations; and historical relations with one another.

Due to spatial limits, this chapter focuses on two crucial themes that have carried forward since the formation of the three states: first, the territorial legitimacy claims of each of the states and contemporary challenges to those claims from Indigenous nations; and second, the legacies of slavery, a set of practices that sculpted both the political economy and the contemporary populations of the three modern states at their formative stages. These practices have produced complex politics of race, class, and gender that are being played out today as differently situated social groups respond in diverse ways to regional economic integration.

Settler Colonial States

The inequalities between and within the three states sketched in the Introduction to this volume are rooted in complex social, economic, and political relations developed over the past 500 years. Although the modern states of Mexico, Canada, and the US differ from each other in many, and even some radical ways, they share some significant similarities, particularly in the historical contexts in which they were forged. All three were established as settler colonies of European imperial powers. Hence, all three were born in violence—that between the European powers that competed to colonize the Americas (principally Spain, Portugal, Britain, France, and, to a lesser extent, Holland and Russia), and the violence directed at the hundreds of diverse Indigenous nations of what became known as North America, whose distinct forms of sovereignty, land ownership, governance, cultures, and relationships to the natural world were to be either eliminated entirely or otherwise subdued and/or assimilated.

After the European invasion of North America, the patterns of colonization followed the primarily economic motives for it. The varying interests of the imperial powers produced different trajectories of economic development in the three territories, from colonial/empire-driven slave and indentured resource/precious metals/staples/agricultural economies early on, to industrialization and the so-called post-industrial economy much later. Moreover, each of the three states deployed a range of techniques for managing or suppressing the class, racial/ethnic, gender, and regional differences arising from their colonial histories.

All three states face sets of issues, problems, questions, and politics that are not raised in the same way in the non-settler states of Europe that have until recently been relatively less affected by immigration and thus able to sustain the idea (however mythic) of having ethnically homogeneous populations. Nor have those states had to grapple to the same extent or in the same ways with outstanding questions regarding the territorial integrity of the nation-state or its claim to sovereignty, such as those posed by the Indigenous nations of the Americas who have occupied the continent since time immemorial. Whereas Mexico, Canada, and the US each disposed of questions of sovereignty somewhat differently, all ignored the requirements of international law (itself forged by Europeans in response to their imperialist rivalries), and, to a greater or lesser extent, all violated their own domestic legal requirements, thus leaving unsettled the sovereignty, land, and political rights of Indigenous peoples. The legacies of history not only shape contemporary domestic politics, economies, and social relations in profound ways, they also complicate the politics and economics of regional/continental integration.

Territorial Integrity

Territorial integrity is *a*, if not *the*, crucial element in a state's claim to legitimate existence. In its absence, a state has no claim to protection from the community of nations against invasion or war, nor to dispose of lands and resources over which others have a just and legal claim. The "discovery" of the Americas had in fact prompted a debate among European scholars and theologians as to the rights and status of the Indigenous peoples and of the European powers who soon after began to compete for the lands and resources. The "doctrine of discovery," based on a series of Papal Bulls (decrees) in the thirteenth century and elaborated by jurists such as Emmerich de Vattel and Francisco de Vitoria, recognized that the Indigenous nations had the natural right to their lands whether they were Christians or not (Anghie 1996: 324). De Vitoria in particular theorized that a "just war" against the Indigenous nations could only be defensible if they attacked representatives of the "discovering" European Crown, refused to trade, or refused to admit Christian missionaries among them (Vitoria 1557/1917: 155–56). Regardless of modern judgements of these criteria of justification, as Ward Churchill notes, there is not one recorded instance of any of these three criteria being met in the entire history of Indigenous-European relations in North America (Churchill 1999: 52). That did not save the Indigenous nations from unjust wars, however.

The doctrine of discovery did not confer rights of ownership of Indigenous lands upon the Europeans. The only right that it did confer upon a "discovering power" was the exclusive right vis-à-vis *other* European powers to acquire the territory, subject to the willing consent of the sovereign, self-governing Indigenous owners. These principles of the doctrine of discovery formed the basis of international law as we know it today, and were indeed recognized in different ways in Mexican, US, and British North American/Canadian law.

From the beginning, the *conquistadores* of the lands that became Mexico took the territories by conquest, although colonial policy, as expressed through the *Leyes de Indias* or "Indian laws," in effect left many Indigenous lands under their own localized control and protected them from invasion by Spaniards as long as they provided tribute to the Spanish Crown. However, the recognition of Indigenous land titles was to be short-lived: when Mexico won its independence from Spain in 1810, "Indian" status was abolished as an anachronism, a move that resulted in the confiscation of much Indigenous land and that fuelled "peasant" support for the Mexican Revolution a century later (see Chapter 10). Although the Mexican Constitution of 1917 recognized communal or *ejido* lands (about half of the farmlands in Mexico), they were regarded as within the gift of the state, not as lands owned by Indigenous communities as of right and recognized by treaties, for there *were* no treaties.

In contrast, the territories that became the US did recognize Indigenous land rights, at least in law, if not in practice. As Churchill notes, in 1793 Thomas Jefferson acknowledged that "the Indians [*sic*] have full, undivided and independent sovereignty as long as they choose to keep it ... this might be forever" (Churchill 1999: 40). Similarly, in a series of US Supreme Court decisions in the 1830s, Chief Justice Marshall noted that the Indigenous nations retained their "original natural rights as the undisputed possessors of the soil since time immemorial." Marshall noted that "The extravagant and absurd idea, that feeble [European] settlements along the seacoast ... acquired legitimate power to govern [Indigenous peoples], or occupy the lands from sea to sea, did not enter the mind of any man," and indeed "[Crown charters could only convey] the exclusive right to purchas[e] such lands as the natives were willing to sell" (quoted in Churchill 1999: 44).

Despite these and other acknowledgments of pre-existing Indigenous rights and sovereignty, however, the US proceeded to extort lands from their natural owners by military force (Brown 1991). Although between 1778 and 1871 the US Senate ratified more than 400 treaties—the internationally recognized mode of agreement between nations—none was entered into voluntarily by the Indigenous nation concerned; all were the result of war, forced removals from traditional territories, land pressures from white settlers, decimation by European diseases, starvation, and the ruin of traditional economies. Oddly enough, US jurists and policy-makers could argue that Indigenous nations were sovereign enough to validate US territorial ambitions through treaties of cession but never sovereign enough to decline them—after 1831, refusals to take treaty were construed as "acts of aggression" requiring military response (Churchill 1999: 61). Moreover, some 800 more treaties had been "negotiated" (in practice, often dictated to the Indigenous nation) but not ratified for various reasons, and many nations never even had the opportunity to sign treaties, coerced or otherwise.

In the end, the presence or absence of treaties did not much matter, as in 1871 Congress simply "declared that Native Americans no longer constituted independent nations with whom the United States would have to negotiate, nor would it honour formerly negotiated treaties" (Janiewski 1995: 141). Instead, unbeknown to themselves, Native Americans had become "wards under the paramount authority of Congress which could alter or abolish tribal governments without regard to treaty promises" (Walter Williams, quoted in Janiewski 1995: 141–42). This declaration meant that the vast majority (if not all) of the Indigenous nations of the territories that became the US never consented to the expropriation of their lands and their rights to govern themselves, as required by international and US law. The US state nevertheless acted as if the Indigenous nations had formally ceded their lands and proceeded to marginalize them through various policies, including the Indian Allotment Act of 1887, which transferred the bulk of the remaining "Indian" lands to non-Indigenous use. Finally, the 1934 Indian Reorganization Act created tribal "governments," which, however, while promoting the appearance of self-determination, were firmly under the control of the Bureau of Indian Affairs (see Chapter 10).

Similarly, in the lands that became known as Canada, Indigenous rights were initially well recognized by the British colonizers through the Royal Proclamation of 1763, though not by the French. Indeed the province of Québec did not recognize Aboriginal title until the 1990s (Stasiulis and Jhappan 1995: 105). Such rights were uncontroversial during the first couple of centuries of relations, dominated as they were by the Fur Trade (1670–1870) in which Indigenous nations and Europeans engaged in a mutually beneficial trade (Van Kirk 1980; Trigger 1985). However, as the number of British settlers in particular increased through the eighteenth century, land conflicts and "great Frauds and Abuses" committed by various settlers and unscrupulous whites against the Indigenous nations led the British Crown to issue the Royal Proclamation of 1763. This instrument decreed that Indigenous lands could only be alienated to the Crown, not to individuals, and then only in a public ceremony in which the consent of the Indigenous nation concerned was secured. Thus, the Proclamation created a constitutional requirement of consent—by treaty— that has not been repealed to this day.

Although 138 treaties had been confirmed by the 1870s, most of the early ones were treaties of peace and friendship, and of the others, most if not all were forced upon the First Nations by military and other pressures such as disease, starvation, and white settlement. Contrary to the assertions of the Crown (whose representatives wrote up their versions of the terms of the treaties after the oral talks) none was or is understood by the First Nation involved either as a deed of sale to its traditional territories or as consent to the marginalizing state policies to which they were subsequently subjected (Hildebrandt, Carter *et al.* 1996). Moreover, treaties were not signed at all with over half of the First Nations of the territories. Thus, no argument that they have somehow ceded their sovereignty and other rights can be sustained.

A further challenge to the territorial integrity of Canada has surfaced with the rise of Québec nationalism since the Quiet Revolution of the 1960s. The conquered French had been formally accommodated in the 1867 Constitution by means of a provincial state and recognition of their language, civil law, religious, and cultural rights. However, the ideological construct of "two founding races" or "two founding peoples" that had emerged around the time of Confederation morphed from the Quiet Revolution of the 1960s onwards into a separatist movement among many Quebecers who felt that the interests of the distinct society of Québec were consistently subsumed by those of the dominant Anglo culture, economy, and politics of the rest of the country. They were supported by the findings of the Royal Commission on Bilingualism and Biculturalism in 1967, which reported that in Québec labour spoke French and capital English, while Francophones were underrepresented in the nation's political and business communities and only Italian and Indigenous

Canadians earned less than French Canadian men (Porter 1965; Royal Commission on Bilingualism and Biculturalism, Dunton *et al.* 1967).

Subsequent federal policies, such as the attempt to make Canada officially bilingual (through the Official Languages Act, 1969), and certain constitutional guarantees (sections 16 to 23 of the Constitution Act, 1982) did not fully address the range of inequalities and the pressures for Anglo-conformity. Two provincial referendums—in 1980 and 1995—very nearly resulted in a vote for "sovereignty-association," or effectively political separation of Québec from Canada. Sovereignty is the central goal both of the party that has been dominant provincially since the 1980s, the Parti Québécois (which promises another referendum in its next mandate), and of the Bloc Québécois (BQ), which runs in the province of Québec for federal office. The BQ won 51 of 75 Québec seats in the 2006 federal election. The BQ's hope is that holding the balance of power vis-à-vis Stephen Harper's Conservative minority federal government will enable the party to leverage some movement towards resolving the fiscal gap between Ottawa and the provinces, especially Québec, and towards further decentralization of power from Ottawa to the provinces (Curry 2006).

Thus, another enduring legacy of Canada's colonial history is yet another ongoing internal ethno-nationalist challenge to its status as a sovereign nation. It is one that sits uncomfortably with the pre-existing Indigenous title, however, and the 11 First Nations whose territories lie within Québec's claimed boundaries have vehemently contested the separatists' agenda (Wherrett 1996). For example, during the 1995 Québec secession referendum, the Cree declared that as a people with a right to self-determination recognized under international law, no annexation of their territories by an independent Québec could take place without their consent and that as citizens of Canada the Cree have the right to remain a people bound to Canada by treaty (the James Bay and Northern Québec Agreement, 1975/1978) (Grand Council of the Crees [of Québec] 1995).

Thus, the circumstances under which Indigenous sovereignties were overthrown in favour of the sovereignty claims of the US, Canadian, and Mexican states have had enduring consequences into the twenty-first century. As North America integrates, at least economically, centrifugal forces in the form of movements for independence or regional autonomy are at work in all three countries (see Chapter 2): there are independence movements in several US states, most notably Hawaii (where the Hawaiian Independence Movement seeks full independence from the US), as well as Puerto Rico, an "unincorporated territory" of the US, and Samoa, a territory of the US; and there are separatist movements in three Mexican states that border with Texas (Coahuila, Nuevo Leon, and Tamaulipas), as well as a regional autonomy movement in Chiapas, where the Zapatista Front for National Liberation seeks to protect the Indigenous population from the forces of neo-liberal trade liberalization that would profit the wealthy and foreign multinational corporations at the expense of the working poor (Clandestine Revolutionary Indigenous Committee 2005). Meanwhile, in Canada, although there are no Indigenous separatist movements per se, several (such as the Six Nations/Mohawks of Québec and Ontario) refuse to accept the jurisdiction of the federal government (via the Indian Act) over their peoples and territories (Mohawk Nation News 1998), and a number of First Nations (such as the Tlingit and Haida Nations, discussed below) continue to assert their inherent sovereignty against that of the Crown.

Slavery

Founded upon the confiscation of Indigenous lands, the economies of all three North American states were also based, to a greater or lesser extent, on slavery. As the dominant solution to the problem of labour in the formative years of Mexico and the US in particular, the set of practices constituting slavery initially produced a particular political economy but was also determinative of the racial/ethnic population mix (notwithstanding more recent influxes of immigrants from all over the world) and the distribution of wealth and opportunities that underpin those societies today.

In fact, slavery was one of the first institutions imposed by Columbus, a former slave trader for the Portuguese. In his diary detailing his first voyage in 1492, Columbus described the extraordinary generosity of the various peoples of the many Caribbean islands on which he landed, who "brought us all they had in the world ... and all so bigheartedly and so happily that it was a wonder" (Columbus, de Las Casas *et al.* 1989: 255). "They are very gentle and do not know what evil is," the Admiral reported, "nor do they kill others, nor steal; and they are without weapons" (143); "they love their neighbours as themselves, and they have the sweetest speech in the world; and [they are] gentle and are always laughing" (281). Yet, it took Columbus only three days from his first meeting with Indigenous peoples of the Americas on 11 October 1492 to suggest to the Spanish monarchs, Queen Isabella and King Ferdinand II, that "all of them can be taken to Castile or held captive in this same island; because with 50 men all of them could be held in subjection and can be made to do whatever one might wish" (75).

True to his word, on the island of Bohío, which he called Hispaniola (today Haiti and the Dominican Republic), Columbus soon instituted a system of slavery and "the systematic extermination of the native Taino population" (Churchill 1997: 86). According to the 1496 survey by the Dominican priest, Bartolomé de Las Casas, over 5 million of the estimated 8 million Tainos had been exterminated within the first three years of Columbus's tenure as "viceroy and governor" of the Caribbean Islands, and by 1542 only 200 remained (de las Casas 1992: 42–45; cited in Thatcher 1904: 348ff).

To Columbus also belongs the title of founder of the Atlantic slave trade, as he took some 1,600 Arawaks as slaves in February 1495 and shipped 550 of them to Spain (though nearly half died en route). Enslavement and trade of Indigenous populations was *de rigueur* for the Spanish *conquistadores* who slashed their way across the length and breadth of Central and South America, murdering and/or enslaving the Indigenous nations they defeated. Such was to be the case for the territory that became Mexico.

Immediately after his bloody defeat of the Mexica-Aztec empire at Tenochtitlán in 1521, for example, Hernán Cortés rewarded his soldiers by means of the *encomienda* system, by which whole towns were assigned to a Spaniard—an *encomendero*—and required to pay tribute and provide free labour in exchange for his "protection" and efforts to convert them to Christianity (Stannard 1992; Wright 1992). The system subjected the Indigenous peoples to "every imaginable abuse" as they were "overworked, separated from their families, cheated, and physically maltreated" (Meyer and Sherman 1987: 131). In many ways, the *encomienda* system was even cheaper for the Spaniards than the system of chattel slavery (where slaves were the legal property of their masters and could be bought and sold), as it avoided the costs of feeding and housing people responsible for providing their own subsistence, while relying on the tribute and unpaid labour of people who could be worked even to death and/or rented out to merchants and others. As importantly, the system was the chief means by which the bulk of Indigenous lands fell under the control of the colonizers, without the inconvenient requirement of any form of treaty or other consent. The *encomienda*, as it turned out, was "the system most responsible for demeaning the native race [*sic*] and creating economic and social tragedies that have persisted in one guise or another into modern times" (Meyer and Sherman 1987: 131).

Although "Indian" slavery was formally abolished in 1542, it was hardly a watershed event, given the continuance of the *encomendiero* system until well into the eighteenth century. Moreover, the Spanish Crown thereafter decreed a novel system of forced labour—the *repartimiento*—under which each adult male "Indian" had to contribute 45 days of labour a year. In practice, they were forced to work long hours under treacherous conditions and were frequently cheated and maltreated. Even when the Spaniards moved to a system of paid work, they still effectively enslaved the "Indians" through debt-bondage by advancing them money against their pay in amounts neither they nor their children (who inherited the debts) could ever hope to pay off. Further, after a series of large silver deposits were discovered in the 1540s at sites such as San Luis Potosí and Guanajuato (still in production today), "Indians" were drafted by the thousands to work in the dangerous mines, where many died or contracted debilitating diseases. Indigenous people were also coerced into working in sweatshops in the textile mills and to some extent in the sugar and indigo industries. However, so obsessed were the Spanish colonizers with precious metals, and so anxious were they to avoid Mexican competition with the Spanish economy, that they did not diversify the economy much (Meyer and Sherman 1987: 176–77).

Through the massacres of the colonization process, waves of plagues and pestilence that arrived with the Europeans, cruelty, and severe exploitation, the 20–25 million Indigenous people of Mexico were reduced to under 2 million in the sixteenth century (Borah and Cook 1963: 46). Due to the rapid decimation of the Indigenous population, as early as 1519 Diego Columbus (son of Christopher) had "beseeched King Charles V of Spain for permission to import African slaves to replace the depleted supply of Indians" in the Caribbean (Weatherford 1991: 138). Thus, from 1521 to 1827 (when all formal slavery was abolished), more than 200,000 Africans were imported into Mexico for use as slaves in the sugar plantations and other industries (Palmer 1976). Although transportation costs made them expensive, Africans were preferred as they were seen to be better able than the Indigenous peoples to withstand harsh working conditions.

The character of contemporary Mexican society was inexorably shaped by these forces and events, as most of the migrants—from the Spaniards to the Africans—were male. This meant a high rate of miscegenation ("interbreeding") between Spaniards, Africans, and Indigenous women and between the various permutations thereby created. What began as a complex racial/ethnic hierarchy (the *peninsulares* or European-born Spaniards at the top, followed by *criollos* or Mexican-born Spaniards, *mestizos* or descendants of European or African men and Indigenous women, *mulattos* born of Spanish men and African women, and *afromestizos*—persons of mixed Indigenous,

African, and Caucasian blood) eventually developed into a "cult of *mestizaje*" or race mixing. Today, 60 per cent of the population is considered *mestizo*, though Mexico's 62 Indigenous peoples (numbering some 10 million) still survive in relatively homogeneous communities in most states. However, as Gutiérrez notes, "the development of an introspective nationalism based on assimilation towards *mestizo* patterns has systematically excluded provisions favouring the cultural development or survival of minorities, whether indigenous or immigrant," yet "[it] has not served to completely extinguish cultural or ethnic identities, or the discrimination deriving from these parameters" (Gutiérrez 1995: 161). The cult of *mestizaje* has been a useful one for the Mexican state to the extent that it denies, for example, ethnically or culturally based claims to land and other rights by Indigenous peoples. Meanwhile, the slave economy established by the Spanish settlers has not only shaped the racial/ethnic composition of the country but also the patterns of economic production, wealth generation, and distribution that persist today.

Following the Spaniards' lead, the other European colonizers of the Americas—the Portuguese, English, Dutch, and French—systematically enslaved Indigenous peoples by the thousands. The early French "explorers," Juan Verrazano and Jacques Cartier took slaves, especially captured Iroquois who were sold as galley slaves for the king (Forbes 1988: 53). As in Central America, the settlement of North America by the British from the early seventeenth century relied on unfree labour, both in the form of indentured labour from Britain and of enslaved Indigenous peoples and enslaved Africans. Of the three states of North America, however, that which became Canada relied least on slave labour, in part because for 200 years the dominant interest of both France and Britain was in the Fur Trade, a commodity exchange system that required that Indigenous peoples be free to hunt and trap in the interior. Even after the British defeated the French in 1759 and British settlement began in earnest, it was decided that the territory was to provide raw materials for manufacture in the mother countries. Apart from the fact that the land and climate were not suitable for a single-crop gang-labour plantation economy like that in the southern US, slavery was simply not profitable in the lumbering, mining, and fishing industries. During the eighteenth century, English and American settlers brought several thousand African slaves to Nova Scotia and the other Atlantic provinces to work as domestics, agricultural labourers, and seafarers. As for farming, in New France for instance, it was "organized in a quasi-feudal fashion where small farmers (*habitants*) worked for landowners (*seigneurs*)" (Stasiulis and Jhappan 1995: 106). Slavery was thus limited mostly to domestic service for military officers, clergy, and merchants in the Montreal, Québec City, and the Trois-Rivières regions, where records of some 2,700 Indigenous and 1,400 African slaves over 150 years were to be found (Knowles 1992: 13). Canada's economy largely remained in the "staples trap," relying more on the export of raw materials to metropolitan centres such as Britain and the US than on manufacturing (Howlett and Ramesh 1992: ch. 4). Even in the twenty-first century, though it has diversified somewhat, Canada's economy is still predominantly resource-based and export-oriented.

Although there was some miscegenation between Indigenous and non-Indigenous peoples, creating a distinct Métis community in the west, it did not become a national ideology or cult as in Mexico. On the contrary, miscegenation was discouraged, especially after white women began to immigrate in the eighteenth century. Moreover, Canada virtually followed a whites-only immigration policy that ranked preferred ethnicities even among "whites" (British and French first, followed by northern Europeans and only much later southern and eastern Europeans) and admitted relatively few Asians and Africans until the 1970s. An impressive range of laws, institutions, and policies was devoted to maintaining a racial/ethnic and gender hierarchy, including specific legislation—the *Indian Act*—to govern virtually every aspect of the daily lives and to control the land bases of the First Nations (Royal Commission on Aboriginal Peoples 1996: Vol. 1, Part 2, "The Indian Act"). These hierarchies persist today, though they have been somewhat modified by decades of social movement activism that have produced, among other things, official policies such as multiculturalism and equality rights recognized by the 1982 Charter of Rights and Freedoms. Yet, while section 15 of the Charter has made unconstitutional formal discrimination by governments against individuals on the basis of their race, national or ethnic origin, colour, religion, sex, age, or mental or physical disability, this does not mean that all discriminatory laws have been excised, as evidenced, for example, by the mixed record of successes and losses women, people of colour, and impoverished Canadians (among others) have experienced before the courts since 1985 (Jhappan 2002; McIntyre and Rodgers 2006). Nor does it mean that discrimination in the private sector on all the listed grounds is now history. Social stratification by race/ethnicity, gender, and class remains a reality in Canada (Abu-Laban and Gabriel 2002), as it does in Mexico and the US.

In the territories that became the US, slavery was instituted soon after settlement began. The "Pilgrim settlers" began from 1614 to raid Wampanoag and Pequot villages and sold their captives in Spain and even Africa, using the proceeds to finance new wars of conquest (Weatherford 1991: 140–41). From 1650 to 1750, the colonial "wars" against the Pequots, Tuscaroras, Yamasees, Susquehannahs, Doegs, Piscattaways, and many other Indigenous nations led to the destruction of nearly 90 per cent of the Indigenous peoples of the Atlantic coast. Weakened by the loss of their lands, population, political autonomy, and economic independence, thousands were enslaved in plantation and household economies as day labourers and domestic servants, while tens of thousands of others were relocated away from their traditional territories (Janiewski 1995: 135–36). By the early eighteenth century, the number of Indigenous slaves in areas such as the Carolinas may have been as much as half that of the African slave population (Nash 1974: 113). However, when the Indigenous peoples proved ill-suited to labour-intensive agricultural practices, susceptible to European diseases, or resistant and apt to escape into landscapes they knew well (Minges 2004), African slaves were soon brought in to fill the vacuum. As skilled labourers and experts in tropical agriculture, "Africans were the final solution to the acute labor problem in the New World" (Francis 1995).

The oldest plantation economies were established in the first-settled Chesapeake Bay area, and Virginia and Maryland became the centre of the tobacco export industry. Towards the end of the seventeenth century, as British dominance of the slave trade increased the available supply of African labour, the states of the south hosted slave plantation economies producing rice, indigo, and later cotton (crops that require tending by many hands) and organized along the lines of the "perpetual servitude" plantation model practiced in the Caribbean (McFarlane 1994: 155). As Akomolafe (1994) notes, the slave trade was induced by the large-scale capitalist mode of production, and "it was the Industrial Revolution in Europe that made it necessary to traffic in human lives on a colossal scale." Moreover, whereas in earlier times slaves had enjoyed certain social and individual rights, chattel slavery from the sixteenth century onwards was a new and more insidious form that stripped slaves of all their rights, including even the right to bear their own names.

Every slave state in the US developed its own slave code, though such codes tended to be more draconian where the numbers of slaves were greater—in the southern states—as whites lived more in fear of insurrection (McFarlane 1994: 178). This was chattel slavery writ large, with slave status being passed on through the mother (to cover children of white fathers and Black mothers), and slaves being unable to own property (being defined as property themselves) and subject to a host of cruel, repressive laws to control every aspect of their lives, especially their movement, capacity to organize, and, of course, to revolt. Slaves were deprived of their civil rights, education, the right to gather together without white supervision, and the right to self-defence (Franklin 1980). Slaves who attacked white persons or property were "hung, burned at the stake, dismembered, castrated, and branded, in addition to the usual whippings. White fear of Black rebellion was a constant undercurrent" (DeFord 1997: H1).

As in Mexico and elsewhere in the Americas, miscegenation of various permutations was a feature of the slave-owning society, despite laws against it. A Virginia statute of 1622, for example, punished inter-racial marriage and was only finally overturned 345 years later in 1967 (Higginbotham and Kopytoff 1989). Nevertheless, the reliance on Black women's bodies to reproduce the slave labour force was a key cost-cutting strategy, as "a master could save the cost of buying new slaves by impregnating his own slave, or for that matter, having anyone impregnate her" (Giddings 1984: 37). Through this means, although some 250,000 Africans were actually brought to the mainland colonies before 1775, the total Black population numbered 567,000. Slavery created "a racial, class, and gender system in colonial America that subordinated the slaves to their masters economically, sexually, and legally" (Janiewski 1995: 138).

So integral and uncontroversial a part of American life was slavery that even leading revolutionaries and future presidents, George Washington and Thomas Jefferson, were wealthy slave-owners. Indeed, in the lead-up to the US Declaration of Independence from Britain in 1776 (drafted by Jefferson), the English essayist Samuel Johnson wondered, "How is it that we hear the loudest yelps for liberty among the drivers of Negroes?" (Johnson 1913: 46). Despite the lofty rhetoric about all men being created equal, the subsequent US Constitution was a study in inequality, as it sanctioned slavery (Article IV, Section 2). Nor did the equality of "all men" include that of women; the Constitution by implication also sanctioned the wide variety of state laws that, among other things, denied women the vote, legal status in their own right, education beyond elementary level, property and inheritance rights, jury service, or the right to initiate a divorce except in dire circumstances.

Slavery was not abolished in the US until 1863, after intense pressure from the National Equal Rights League and other anti-slavery organizations, although

President Abraham Lincoln had made it clear that his main aim in the Civil War was not to end slavery but to get the breakaway southern states back into the union, even if it meant retaining slavery (Hofstadter 1973: 89). Although there is a robust debate as to the economic rationality of slavery in the US (see, for example, the essays in Eltis, Lewis, *et al.* 2004), the US sanctioned its practice for almost three-quarters of its 400-year history (counting the colonial period from 1619 when the first African slaves were introduced), and the unfree labour of Indigenous peoples and Africans surely subsidized the development of the whole country by providing cheaper foods and goods, trade goods, and wealth accumulation for certain classes of whites.

As in Mexico 300 years earlier, however, the abolition of slavery did not signal either the end of racial segregation in the US or the exploitation of Black people, as "tenancy and sharecropping locked African Americans into a system that allowed them few opportunities for escape" (Janiewski 1995: 147). Indeed, Lincoln's Emancipation Proclamation did not apply to Indigenous peoples, whose enslavement was not out-lawed by the US Congress until 1868, and they were not granted citizenship until 1924 (Weatherford 1991: 145–46). Moreover, racial segregation was legally sanctioned (for example, by the famous Supreme Court decision, *Plessey vs. Ferguson* in 1896) until the major Supreme Court decision of 1954 in *Brown vs. Board of Education of Topeka* [347 US 483 (1954)] dismantled the legal basis for racial segregation in schools and other public facilities. The massive social unrest unleashed by the Black Civil Rights Movement culminated in the passage of the Civil Rights Act of 1964. Even then, though the Act prohibited "discrimination or segregation on the ground of race, color, religion, or national origin," gender was notably not included as a prohibited ground. In addition, although the influx of immigrants from all over the world (espe-cially in the latter half of the twentieth century) has complicated the racial and gender hierarchies established in the colonial and early phases of settlement, it has not erased them. Members of subordinated racialized groups have tended to be concentrated in the low and unwaged sectors of the economy.

The reliance on slavery in the formative years of the US and Mexico in particular is critical to an understanding of contemporary North American politics. As noted above, slavery produced a particular political economy in which the coerced, unpaid labour of Indigenous Americans and Africans subsidized the consumption and trade of the Euro-American population, directed the nature and rate of economic develop-ment and diversification, and structured social relations, all with lasting effects into the twenty-first century. The legacies of the race politics played out in the disposses-sion of Indigenous Americans and in the institution of slavery are very much alive in the contemporary US.

The intersections of race, class, and gender are amply demonstrated in pov-erty and income statistics. The US Census Bureau, for example, reported that as of March 2002, 13 per cent of the US population—36 million people—were African American/"Black" (about 55 per cent of them in the southern states). The data show consistently lower educational attainment rates (for example, 29 per cent of all non-Hispanic whites have earned at least a bachelor's degree, compared with 17 per cent of African Americans); higher unemployment (11 per cent for African Americans, 5 per cent for whites); and a poverty rate of 23 per cent versus 8 per cent for whites (McKinnon 2003). The official poverty rate in the US rose from 12.5 per cent (35.9

million) in 2003 to 12.7 per cent (37 million people) in 2004, with 45.8 million people lacking health insurance (19.7 per cent of African Americans, 29 per cent of American Indian and Alaska natives, 32 per cent of Hispanics, compared with 11.3 per cent for non-Hispanic whites). And while the median income for white households was $48,977, for Black households it was $30,134 and for Hispanics $34,241 (interestingly, Asian-origin households boasted the highest median income at $57,518) (US Census Bureau 2004). Income distributions are becoming even more skewed as health care, social security, pensions, and welfare programs are being dismantled at the federal level through privatization and deregulation policies. The 1996 "Welfare to Work" legislation has resulted in major cuts in federal and state assistance to the poor, thus hitting women and ethnic minority groups especially hard. In 2002, households headed by single women comprised half of the families living in poverty (Centre on Budget and Policy Priorities 2003).

Racial and related class stratification in the US have been manifested in myriad ways in US politics, a powerful recent example being the federal government's widely criticized failure to respond promptly and adequately to the devastation wrought upon the southern US, especially the city of New Orleans, by hurricane Katrina in August 2005. As the crisis wore on over the months and television screens around the world exhibited some of the many tragedies visited upon the overwhelmingly Black population (those too poor to exit via private transportation), various hurricane victims and commentators suggested that the official response had been slow because the victims were largely poor and African American.[1] Among the many effects of the disaster—human, economic, social, and political—may well be the re-politicization of race and class as a real force in American congressional and presidential politics in the coming years.

The correlation between race/ethnicity and income inequality has been noted in Mexico and Canada as well. A World Bank report on seven Latin American countries, including Mexico, for instance, found that race and ethnicity are enduring determinants of one's opportunities and welfare in Latin America, and Indigenous and Afro-descended people in particular are "at a considerable disadvantage with respect to whites." Indigenous men earn 35–65 per cent less than white men, who earn the highest wages in the region, and the disparity between white women and "non-white" women was in the same range (de Ferranti, Perry, et al. 2003). Similarly, in Canada, various studies have found that "race" is a determinant of income inequality. First Nations women have the lowest incomes of all, and despite some exceptions, other racialized groups overall have lower incomes. This is true even though, for example, 28 per cent of visible minority men have at least one university degree, which is about 10 per cent higher than for the three categories of European-origin men. Being a member of a racialized minority has a negative "market value." and "Canada displays a 'racial divide' between Whites and non-Whites" (Gee and Prus 2000: 254).

"Ancient History" Haunts Us Yet

It is common for non-Indigenous people in the Americas to take the position that the past is past, there is no point in bringing up "ancient history," and we must all accept the present realities stemming from the colonial histories sketched above. Nevertheless, the legacies of "ancient history" haunt us yet. Public, interest group, and social movement responses to NAFTA in all three North American states are a study in the race, class, and gender politics forged in the colonial era. It is not surprising that opposition to regional economic integration has come largely from anti-poverty and women's groups, small independent farmers, and trade unions, especially those in less secure sectors in all three countries. Indeed, NAFTA has inspired a new transnationalism and cross-border collaboration among labour unions in particular, enabling activists to craft "new movement frames, transnational identities, and coalitions" over the last decade (Stillerman 2003: 578).

Well into the second decade of NAFTA, mounting evidence demonstrates that trade liberalization affects differently situated social groups unequally. People in insecure low income jobs with no benefits have been hardest hit, and because women tend to earn less than men in each of the three NAFTA states and are disproportionately hired for certain kinds of jobs, they are often the first to be laid off when companies downsize or relocate production. As Spieldoch notes, in the US and Canada, "women are more likely to move in and out of the formal and informal sectors as they struggle to balance work and family with little federal support," and women and children are also the most negatively affected when social programs are privatized and/or deregulated (Spieldoch 2004: 2–3). Moreover, "women of colour are even harder hit by negative economic trends than white women, since shifts in the economy have differential impacts based on race and class." Spieldoch (4) notes that in the state of Texas, for example, more than 17,000 garment manufacturing jobs have been lost as firms relocated (first to Mexico, then to China), and that most of the workers affected are first-generation, often illiterate Mexican women whose chances of finding similar work are slim.

Meanwhile, one of the main areas to which US and Canadian jobs have migrated, the *maquiladora* sector in Mexico, consists of foreign-owned factories in Mexico's tax- and tariff-free enclaves or free-trade export-processing zones, usually located near the US border. Low-paid workers, about 70 per cent of whom are women, manufacture cheap goods or assemble imported parts into cheap products, which are mostly exported to the US. Working conditions in the *maquiladoras* are notoriously appalling, featuring dangerous workplace practices with little or no safety equipment or standards, exposure to toxic substances, long hours and forced overtime in unsanitary, unventilated factories for a few US dollars per day (Kamel, Hoffman, *et al.* 1999). Moreover, there is evidence of an ethnic pecking order in the *maquiladoras* such that the worst jobs and conditions are reserved for Indigenous workers. Barndt's study, for instance, found that although Indigenous workers had been recruited with fine promises of good jobs, benefits, and housing, "they arrived to find only shells of homes in camps without running water, sewage, or electricity; disease was rampant, and no health services were provided." In addition, "whereas indigenous women of all ages, from grandmothers to grandchildren, were relegated to the fields, young *mestizas* (women of mixed European and native heritage) got the jobs in the packing plants. The working days in these plants could be longer, stretching to 10 or 15 hours, but the wages were three to five times better, up to 100 Mexican pesos [about US$10] a day" (Barndt 1999: 163–64).

Plummeting prices caused by US agricultural subsidies on corn and other staples have forced many Indigenous women who used to be subsistence farmers off their lands and obliged them to become migrant labourers or salaried workers for agribusinesses. In many respects, the *maquiladora* and migrant worker systems represent a modern form of labour that harkens back to the old days of slavery and the *encomienda* system (except that today the *encomendero* is likely to be a transnational corporation). That "the mobility of international capital is predicated on the politics of race and gender" (Gabriel and Macdonald 1996: 167) seems an inevitable conclusion in the face of the practices of multinational and domestic corporations that "take advantage of deeply ingrained and institutionalized sexism and racism in their constant search for cheaper labour" (Barndt 1999: 164). In such circumstances of a choice between NAFTA-led rural unemployment or super-exploitation in the *maquiladoras*, it is not surprising that more and more poor Mexicans risk their lives to enter the US as undocumented workers in the hope of earning enough money to send home to their families.

Indigenous Lands and Regional Economic Disintegration

In this era of trade liberalization and regional economic integration, unresolved sovereignty and land rights issues have resurfaced in each of the three North American states. Of course, prior to and during the CUFTA and NAFTA negotiations, the governments of the three signatory states acted as if their claims to territorial sovereignty were utterly uncontroversial and hence did not even consider consulting with Indigenous nations whose interests would be affected by trade liberalization. Nor was there any media discussion of such issues, at least not until 1 January 1994, the day NAFTA came into effect.

In 1992, exactly five centuries after the Columbian invasion, the absence of treaties with the Indigenous nations of Mexico undoubtedly allowed the Mexican Congress (under pressure from the US in preparation for NAFTA) to modify Article 27 of the Constitution in such a way as to allow further privatization of communal lands. Many fear that this move will ultimately render "many Mexican farmers landless ... as most of their lands will be taken over by private shareholders who will determine wages, crop substitutions, fertilizer subsidies, and credit ... [and which] could mean the end of the *ejido* system" (Chavez 1995; see also Cornelius and Myhre 1998). The *ejido* reform was identified by the Zapatista movement as one of the leading causes of the Chiapas uprising (Mexico Solidarity Network 2006). This changed the nature of media coverage and public discussion of NAFTA and Indigenous peoples both inside and outside Mexico.

On 1 January 1994, a rebellion of mostly Indigenous Mayan people erupted in Mexico's southernmost state of Chiapas. With the support of Roman Catholic leaders and various civil society allies both in urban areas within Mexico and internationally, some 2,000 armed peasants of the Zapatista National Liberation Army (EZLN; named after Emiliano Zapata, an Indigenous hero of the Mexican Revolt of 1914–15), occupied San Cristobal de las Casas and six other towns in the highlands of Chiapas. After 12 days of gun battles with government soldiers and dozens of casualties, they were driven into the mountains. The Zapatista struggle aimed to highlight the great disparities in wealth in Chiapas as well as their longstanding grievances against wealthy cattle ranchers and coffee growers, who were supported by police and government officials. NAFTA, as an instance of regional economic integration under the umbrella of neo-liberal globalization, would, it was argued, produce regional economic *dis*integration: it would benefit the rich at the expense of the poor by sharply reducing coffee and corn prices, and it would empower a de facto corporate government (Otero 1996).

After intense struggle, the government of Mexican President Carlos Salinas de Gortari agreed to a dialogue, and three years of talks yielded a tentative agreement (based on the San Andrés Accords) that promised to modify the national constitution to grant the right of autonomy to Indigenous peoples, as well as to redistribute illegal large landholdings to poor peasants, begin a public works program, and prohibit discrimination against the Indigenous peoples. Later, a commission of deputies from political parties, called COCOPA, modified the agreement with the consent of the EZLN. However, Congress passed a much watered-down version of the COCOPA Law that had excised the autonomy clauses on the grounds that they conflicted with some constitutional rights including private property and secret voting. Since then, although the Zapatistas have engaged in many acts of protest and civil disobedience, their strategy appears to have shifted to a focus on local development of an autonomous education and health care system, with their own schools, hospitals, and pharmacies in the 32 "rebel autonomous Zapatista municipalities."

Although the Zapatista uprising has not yet accomplished its goals, Neil Harvey concludes that its impact has been "revelatory rather than programmatic," especially through its focus on the social costs of neo-liberal economic reforms and on the discrimination directed against two of the most traditionally marginalized sectors of Mexican society—Indigenous people and women. Moreover, the broader political significance of the rebellion is "the openings it created for popular organizations to contest the meaning and scope of democracy and citizenship in Mexico" (Harvey 1998: 199).

Such contestations were dramatically expressed in the presidential election of 6 July 2006. Felipe Calderón, the candidate from the party of President Vicente Fox, the National Action Party (PAN), garnered a mere 0.58 per cent (less than 244,000) of the 41,791,322 votes cast over Andrés Manuel López Obrador of the left Democratic Revolution Party (PRD). Obrador demanded that Mexico's Federal Election Tribunal (FET) authorize a full recount, offering evidence of electoral fraud in 900 pages of alleged irregularities, supported by various international and Mexican observers (Collins and Holland 2006). In the meantime, millions of López Obrador and PRD supporters, including many of Mexico's poorest citizens, set up protest camps in the *Zocolo* square outside the National Palace in Mexico City and disrupted business and traffic for seven weeks. Over the ensuing months, numerous acts of civil disobedience took place all over the country, especially in southern states such as Chiapas and Oaxaca where PRD support is strongest and Zapatistas have backed Obrador. It is interesting that, without even waiting for the contested election to be certified, US Republican President George W. Bush and Canadian Conservative

Prime Minister Stephen Harper both congratulated Calderón on his win. In a situation eerily reminiscent of the US Supreme Court's rejection of a Florida vote recount in the 2000 presidential election, the FET rejected the request for a full recount, authorizing instead a partial recount of only 12,000 (or 9 per cent) of 130,000 polling stations (Anderson 2006). Two months after the election, Calderón was declared the winner.

The matter was not settled by the FET, however, as millions of Mexicans continued to consider the election to have been fraudulent, and Obrador pursued plans to set up a "parallel government" in further protest. The messy results of this election represent an enormous blow to Mexico's democratic development, and challenges to the integrity of the Mexican state can be expected to accelerate under such conditions, with a high probability of political instability, even political violence, over the next few years.

Meanwhile, in the territories now known as Canada, outstanding land and sovereignty claims of Indigenous nations are also recurring political issues, particularly when they interfere with the exploitation of natural resources by non-Indigenous companies. In fact, renewed Indigenous activism and a number of successful legal challenges since the 1970s (Donovan 2001) have forced the Canadian federal government to recognize and settle some 16 comprehensive land claims (involving unextinguished Indigenous land title), and currently over 70 mandates to negotiate are waiting in the queue. In the province of British Columbia alone, 53 claims have been accepted for negotiation and 40 negotiation tables were at the Agreement-in-Principle stage in 2003 (Minister of Indian Affairs and Northern Development 2003: 13). It is in both the provincial and the federal governments' (not to mention corporations') interests to settle such claims as they not only induce business uncertainty when First Nations contest logging, mining, and other activities on their traditional territories, but as their very existence raises questions about the territorial integrity of the Canadian state, which has not lived up to the imperatives of its own legal system. An account of the many dozens of outstanding land issues is beyond the scope of this chapter. However, one case should suffice to exemplify the connections between Indigenous and nation-state sovereignty, as well as the political economy of North American regional trade.

For many years Canada and the US have been at loggerheads over the US policy of imposing duties on softwood lumber imports (worth up to US$5 billion) on the grounds that Canada's forest management practices (with low stumpage fees for companies cutting trees on Crown lands) amount to a subsidy to logging companies. Lumber exports to the US account for over 2 per cent of Canada's total exports to that country, to the tune of Cdn$8.5 billion (over 21 billion board feet) in 2005. Over 57 per cent of this lumber originated in British Columbia, with 16 per cent from Québec, 9 per cent from Ontario, 8 per cent from the Maritimes, 7 per cent from Alberta, and 1 per cent each from Saskatchewan and Manitoba (Foreign Affairs and International Trade Canada 2006). But while this long-running dispute may have been solved after a series of NAFTA panel and WTO decisions favouring Canada's position led to the Softwood Lumber Agreement signed on 20 September 2006, much larger issues loom in the background that could affect North American trading and political relations in more profound ways.

Although spatial limitations preclude examination of the hundreds of similar cases in each of the three North American states, the case of the Haida Nation versus the US-owned international forest products company, Weyerhaeuser, is illustrative of some of the key issues and future trends to come. The people of the Haida Nation have lived in their traditional territory of Haida Gwaii (named the Queen Charlotte Islands by the colonizers after the wife of King George III) off the northern coast of British Columbia for at least 10,000 years. Like the other First Nations of British Columbia, the Haida have never ceded their title to or rights concerning Haida Gwaii by means of any treaty or other agreement, nor have the colonial or subsequent provincial governments ever passed any statute extinguishing such rights. Indeed, the most the province has offered by way of defence of its practice of alienating Indigenous lands to third parties without their permission, participation, or compensation has been a recurring argument that provincial acts of general application have proceeded *as if* Indigenous rights had been extinguished, and therefore they *have* been extinguished.

After various invocations of this defence in cases involving other First Nations, the Supreme Court of Canada finally rejected it entirely in the landmark decision on unextinguished Indigenous title to date, the 1997 case that upheld the legal claim by Gitksan and Wet'suwet'en hereditary chiefs to 58,000 square kilometres of their traditional territories in northeastern British Columbia. The Supreme Court found that a provincial law of general application cannot extinguish Indigenous rights as such an act would be beyond the constitutional powers of the province. Moreover, it found that Indigenous title is: *sui generis* (unique, in a class of its own); "held communally"; "inalienable and cannot be transferred, sold, or surrendered to anyone other than the Crown"; recognized by the Royal Proclamation, 1763; and protected by "the common law which recognizes occupation as proof of possession and systems of aboriginal law pre-existing assertion of British sovereignty" (*Delgamuukw v. British Columbia*, [1997] 3 S.C.R.: 1010, 1025).

None of the above, however, has stopped the province from alienating large tracts of Indigenous lands to third parties, even to foreign-owned companies such as Weyerhaeuser (the world's largest private owner of timber land and the largest producer of lumber), which assumed rights over timber licences on 33.5 million acres in Canada when it acquired Canada-based MacMillan Bloedel in 1999. The Haida have undertaken numerous protest actions against the clear-cutting and other unsustainable practices of logging companies in their territories over the years (including a seizure of $50 million worth of timber cut by Weyerhaeuser in April 2005) and sought a declaration from the courts that both the Crown and Weyerhaeuser had a duty to consult the Haida Nation with respect to timber harvesting licences.

In 2002, the provincial Court of Appeal indeed found such a duty in both the *Haida Nation* and the *Taku River Tlingit* cases, though the Supreme Court of Canada subsequently found that only the province, not the company, had the duty to consult over land use. "Given the strength of the claims for title and the right to harvest the trees, and the serious impact of Licences on these interests," the Court maintained, "the honour of the Crown might well require significant accommodation to preserve the Nation's interests pending resolution of the claims" [*Haida Nation v. British Columbia (Minister of Forests)* [2004] S.C.J. No. 70-2004 SCC 73; *Taku River*

Tlingit First Nation v. British Columbia (Project Assessment Director), 2004 SCC 74]. The British Columbia Court of Appeal also upheld the Haidas' challenge regarding Tree Farm Licence 39 (*Haida Nation v. British Columbia, et al.*, 2002 BCCA 147; 2002 BCCA 462), resulting in a reduction by half of the total Weyerhaeuser cut level to 255 million board feet.

The patent absurdity of the situation that obliges those who have lived on the islands for thousands of years to tender an ownership "claim" before the courts of those who have occupied the territories now called Canada for only a few hundred years was lost on the Supreme Court in this as in many other cases. Nevertheless, the Court did recognize the likelihood that the "claim," launched a week after the duty to consult decision of the British Columbia Court of Appeal, will ultimately succeed. As well as an order quashing all licences, leases, permits, and tenures that are incompatible with Indigenous title and the exercise of Indigenous rights, the "claim" seeks a declaration that the Haida Nation holds Indigenous title to the "land, inland waters, seabed, and sea of Haida Gwaii" (Taillon 2002). The Haida launched their title claim in part in reaction to the provincial Liberal government's plan to lift the 1989 moratorium on off-shore drilling for oil and gas in the waters off the Queen Charlotte Islands (First Nations Drum 2002). Thus, a new set of players—oil and gas companies—may be added to the mix of third parties able to appropriate for private profit resources over which the Haida claim collective public ownership.

In addition to legal and protest actions, Indigenous nations from the interior of British Columbia enjoyed an enormous breakthrough in April 2002 when a WTO panel in the Softwood Lumber Dispute accepted their unsolicited *amicus curiae* submission. The brief argued that Canada was providing timber from Aboriginal Title lands below fair market value because its laws and policies failed to take Indigenous proprietary interests into account. The panel's acceptance of the submission, as evidenced by its circulation to all parties and third parties for comments (more than it had done for earlier submissions from labour and industry) showed that the WTO has recognized the relevance of Indigenous rights to international trade (Manuel 2002: 1–2). Canada opposed the submissions by Indigenous peoples on the grounds that land rights were a domestic issue that had to be dealt with in Canadian courts on a case-by-case basis. As Manuel surmises, "knowing that traditionally Aboriginal Title cases take decades to litigate, the federal government was relying on having at least a decade to still freely allocate natural resources over crown land." Thus, "a clear benefit is conferred upon companies who do not have to take Aboriginal Title into account and do not even have to compensate for it" (Manuel 2002: 4, 12). Canada has similarly objected to the filing of Indigenous and environmental non-governmental organization (NGO) *amicus curiae* briefs in NAFTA proceedings, in contrast to the US Department of Commerce, which has recognized the role Indigenous people can play in international proceedings and negotiations. This recognition is perhaps due to the 1974 US Supreme Court *Boldt* decision that reaffirmed US tribes' treaty-protected fishing rights and gave them a seat in international negotiations on fisheries such as the Pacific Salmon Treaty of 1985 (Manuel 2002: 15).

In view of these sorts of developments, we can expect Indigenous nations to play an increasingly significant role in international, especially continental, trade issues. In fact, various Indigenous communities in Canada and the US have managed to stall or defeat third-party resource developments on their traditional territories in recent years. For example, in 2003 in the Northwest Territories, the 4,000-member Dogrib band won the right to control fishing, hunting, and industrial development over 15,000 square miles of territory (Taicho 2003); the DehCho band has been able to stall the $6 billion Mackenzie Gas Project pipeline through its traditional lands planned by Imperial Oil, Exxon Mobil, and several other companies until the federal government resolves title and jurisdiction issues (DehCho First Nations 2006); in 2001 the Cree of northern Québec reached an agreement with the provincial government that recognizes their full autonomy and substantial powers to help manage mining, forestry, and hydroelectric energy development; and the Inuit of northern Québec have won a measure of self-government and logging rights over vast forests in Labrador (Krauss 2004).

Even though the courts, certain WTO and NAFTA tribunals, and some governments have been recognizing Indigenous proprietary interests of late, the irony is that certain NAFTA provisions could have very serious consequences for the provinces and for Canada, not to mention for the First Nations concerned. For instance, as a foreign investor, Weyerhaeuser could invoke Chapter 11 of NAFTA to claim millions of dollars in compensation if changes to British Columbia's forestry or land use policies reduce the company's access to trees on "public" lands. Chapter 11 requires that investors from other NAFTA countries be treated similarly to domestic investors of a particular NAFTA country and that a NAFTA country must provide a minimum standard of treatment to an investor of another NAFTA country. Such Chapter 11 actions could multiply the costs to governments of land claims settlements. Indeed, such costs could be prohibitive and may well provide another excuse for governments, under pressure from foreign and domestic corporations, either to refuse to negotiate modern treaties with First Nations or to layer even more delays onto what is already a glacially slow land claims process. Alternatively, and worse still, if and when land claims and self-government agreements *are* concluded, Chapter 11 actions against *Indigenous* governments that attempt to shield their lands and resources from exploitation by external private interests could bankrupt those communities and destroy their capacity for self-determination. Up to now, it has not been customary for trade agreements such as NAFTA to exempt Indigenous lands and resources from articles of general application, as Indigenous interests and rights were not considered as limits to states' authority to enter into agreements that bind everyone within the claimed national boundaries. This situation may well change as community activism backed by legal and tribunal decisions shift the matrix of power.

Conclusion

This chapter has traced a number of critical residues of the colonization process in North America with a view to demonstrating some of the complications attending regional economic integration. The latter has been treated by its supporters as a straightforward process following the imperatives of economics. The various conflicts examined here, however, demonstrate the imperatives of politics to the extent that unresolved injustices of the past bleed into the present and compound what is an already complex set of national and continental relations. The legacies of slavery and the racial/ethnic, class, and gender hierarchies created and sustained over the centuries have produced inequalities that mean that regional economic integration affects those in the less secure and low-paid sectors of the three national economies in disproportionately negative ways. The resulting opposition to NAFTA by the Zapatistas and a wide range of civil society organizations in Mexico, for example, has been most forcefully expressed in the 2006 presidential election. Time will show whether the bitter aftertaste of an election widely regarded as fraudulent results in political instability, and whether it is a major setback or a moment of hope for the democratization process in Mexico.

Meanwhile, North American nation-states' presumption of territorial integrity and of their right to alienate lands and resources as they please are being seriously contested by Indigenous nations. In Canada, for example, persistent land and political rights issues are now coming before courts that have imposed on governments a duty to consult Indigenous nations over land use on their traditional territories. In addition, WTO and NAFTA tribunals have begun to recognize that Indigenous proprietary rights entitle them to a role in international trade regimes affecting their interests. Successful Indigenous sovereignty claims might well reduce states' capacities to enter into trade agreements covering national territories and/or make them vulnerable to NAFTA Chapter 11 compensation claims. Divided sovereignty regimes (between First Nations and nation-states) will certainly complicate the politics and economics of regional economic integration. Thus, the legacies of 500 years of history continue to shape contemporary North American domestic and continental politics, economies, and social relations in profound ways. Hopefully, it will not take another half millennium to resolve them.

Note

1   The Reverend Jesse Jackson charged that race was "at least a factor" in the slow response, and Ron Walters, a professor of government at the University of Maryland, stated that "Black people are mad because they feel the reason for the slow response is because those people are black and they didn't support George Bush" (CBS News, 3 September, 2005). See also, "Race an Issue in Katrina Response." Retrieved 3 September 2005 from <http://www.cbsnews.com/stories/2005/09/03/katrina/main814623.shtml>.

References

Abu-Laban, Y., and C. Gabriel. 2002. *Selling Diversity: Immigration, Multiculturalism, Employment Equity, and Globalization*. Peterborough, ON: Broadview Press.

Akomolafe, F. 1994. *On Slavery: The Retrospective History of Africa*. Hartford Web Publishing. <http://www.hartford-hwp.com/archives/30/013.html>.

Anderson, K. 2006. "What Went Wrong in Mexico: What the US Media Didn't Tell You." *The Humanist* (November–December): 14–17.

Anghie, A. 1996. "Francisco de Vitoria and the Colonial Origins of International Law." *Social and Legal Studies* 5, 3: 321–36.

Barndt, D. 1999. "Women Workers in the NAFTA Food Chain." In Mustafa Koc, Rod MacRae, Luc J.A. Mougeot, and Jennifer Welsh (eds.), *For Hunger-proof Cities: Sustainable Urban Food Systems*. Ottawa: International Development Research Centre. 162–66.

Benton-Banai, E. 1979. *The Mishomis Book: The Voice of the Ojibway*. St. Paul, MN: Indian Country Press.

Borah, W., and S.F. Cook. 1963. *The Aboriginal Population of Central Mexico on the Eve of the Conquest*. Berkeley: U of California P.

Brown, D.A. 1991. *Bury My Heart at Wounded Knee: An Indian History of the American West*. New York: Henry Holt.

CBS News. 2005. "Race an Issue in Katrina Response." 3 September. <http://www.cbsnews.com/stories/2005/09/03/katrina/main814623.shtml>.

Centre on Budget and Policy Priorities. 2003. "Number of Americans Without Health Insurance Rose in 2002." <http://www.cbpp.org>.

Chavez, L.F.V. 1995. "Privatization of Mexican Ejidos: The Implications of the New Article 27." *Berkeley McNair Journal* 3. <http://www.mcnair.berkeley.edu/95journal/LuisChavez.html.>

Churchill, W. 1997. "Deconstructing the Columbus Myth." In W. Churchill (ed.), *A Little Matter of Genocide: Holocaust and Denial in the Americas, 1492 to the Present*. San Francisco: City Lights Books.

———. 1999. "The Tragedy and the Travesty: The Subversion of Indigenous Sovereignty in North America." *Struggle for the Land*. Winnipeg: Arbeiter Ring. 37–90.

Clandestine Revolutionary Indigenous Committee. 2005. "Chiapas: Potentials and Limitations," l.6 (11 December). <http://www.peoplesmarch.com/archives/2005/nov-dec2k5/chiapas.htm>.

Collins, C., and J. Holland. 2006. "Evidence of Election Fraud Grows in México." *AlterNet* Vol. DOI. <http://www.globalpolicy.org/empire/media/2006/0802electionfraud.htm>.

Columbus, C., B. de las Casas, *et al.* 1989. *The Diario of Christopher Columbus's First Voyage to America, 1492–1493*. Norman, OK: U of Oklahoma P.

Cornelius, W.A., and D. Myhre (Eds.). 1998. *The Transformation of Rural Mexico: Reforming the Ejido Sector*. US-Mexico Contemporary Perspective Series. San Diego, CA: Center for US-Mexican Studies, University of California, San Diego.

Curry, B. 2006. "Bloc Plans to Prop Up Harper's Minority." *Globe and Mail*, 26 February.

de Ferranti, D., G. Perry, *et al.* 2003. *Inequality in Latin America and The Caribbean: Breaking with History?* Mexico City: World Bank Group.

DeFord, S. 1997. "How the Cradle of Liberty Became a Slave-Owning Nation." *Washington Post*, 10 December: H01.

de las Casas, Bartolomé. 1992. *The Devastation of the Indies: A Brief Account*. Original publication 1542. Intro. Bill M. Donovan. Trans. Herma Briffaul. New York: Johns Hopkins Press.

DehCho First Nations. 2006. "Alternatives North Report Supports DFN Position on Pipeline." <http://www.dehchofirstnations.com/documents/press/06_10_19_Alt_north_report_supports_dehcho.pdf>.

Donovan, B. 2001. "The Evolution and Present Status of Common Law Aboriginal Title in Canada: The Law's Crooked Path and the Hollow Promise of Delgamuukw." *University of British Columbia Law Review* 35: 43–90.

Eltis, D., F.D. Lewis, *et al.* 2004. *Slavery in the Development of the Americas*. Cambridge: Cambridge UP.

First Nations Drum. 2002. "Haida Launch Aboriginal Title Case in BC Supreme Court." April. <http://www.firstnationsdrum.com/Sum2002/TreatyHaidaBCCourt.htm>.

Forbes, J. 1988. *Black Africans and Native Americans*. Oxford: Basil Blackwell.

Foreign Affairs and International Trade Canada. 2006. "Canada's Trade and Industry Ministers and Ambassador to the US Welcome Long-Awaited Agreement to End the Canada-US Softwood Lumber Dispute." *News Release*, 27 April. <http://nouvelles.gc.ca/cfmx/view/en/index.jsp?articleid=210119&keyword=David+L.+Emerson&keyword=David+L.+Emerson&>.

Francis, A. 1995. "The Economics of the African Slave Trade." March. <http://dolphin.upenn.edu/~vision/vis/Mar-95/5284.html>.

Francis, Douglas R., Richard Jones, and Donald B. Smith. 2000. *Origins: Canadian History to Confederation.* Toronto: Harcourt.

Franklin, J.H. 1980. *From Slavery to Freedom: A History of Negro Americans.* New York: Knopf.

Gabriel, C., and L. Macdonald. 1996. "NAFTA and Economic Restructuring: Some Gender and Race Implications." In I. Bakker (ed.), *Rethinking Restructuring: Gender and Change in Canada.* Toronto: U of Toronto P. 165–86.

Gee, E.M., and S.G. Prus. 2000. "Income Inequality in Canada: A 'Racial Divide.'" In M.A. Kalbach and W.E. Kalbach (eds.), *Perspectives on Ethnicity in Canada: A Reader.* Toronto: Harcourt. 238–56.

Giddings, P. 1984. *When and Where I Enter: The Impact of Black Women on Race and Sex in America.* New York: W. Morrow.

Grand Council of the Crees (of Québec). 1995. *Sovereign Injustice: Forcible Inclusion of the James Bay Crees and Cree Territory into a Sovereign Québec.* Nemaska, QC: Grand Council of the Crees.

Gutiérrez, N. 1995. "Miscegenation as Nation-Building: Indian and Immigrant Women in Mexico." In D.K. Stasiulis and N. Yuval Davis (eds.), *Unsettling Settler Societies.* London: Sage. 161–87.

Harvey, N. 1998. *The Chiapas Rebellion: The Struggle for Land and Democracy.* Durham, NC: Duke UP.

Higginbotham, A.L.J. and B.K. Kopytoff. 1989. "Racial Purity and Interracial Sex in the Law of Colonial and Antebellum Virginia." *Georgia Law Journal* 77: 1967–2029.

Hildebrandt, W., S. Carter, *et al.* 1996. *The True Spirit and Original Intent of Treaty Seven.* Montreal and Kingston: McGill-Queen's UP.

Hofstadter, R. 1973. *The American Political Tradition and the Men Who Made It.* New York: Knopf.

Howlett, M., and M. Ramesh. 1992. *The Political Economy of Canada: An Introduction.* Toronto: McClelland and Stewart.

Janiewski, D. 1995. "Gendering, Racializing, and Classifying: Settler Colonization in the United States, 1590–1990." In D.K. Stasiulis and N. Yuval-Davis (eds.), *Unsettling Settler Societies: Articulations of Gender, Race, Ethnicity and Class.* London: Sage. 132–60.

Jhappan, R. (ed.). 2002. *Women's Legal Strategies in Canada.* Toronto: U of Toronto P.

Johnson, S. 1913. "Taxation No Tyranny: An Answer to the Resolutions and Address of the American Congress, 1775." *The Works of Samuel Johnson.* Troy, NY: Pafraets and Company.

Kamel, R., A. Hoffman, *et al.* 1999. *The Maquiladora Reader: Cross-border Organizing Since NAFTA.* Philadelphia, PA: Mexican-US Border Program, American Friends Service Committee.

Knowles, V. 1992. *Strangers at Our Gates: Canadian Immigration and Immigration Policy, 1540–1990.* Toronto: Dundurn.

Krauss, C. 2004. "Natives' Land Battles Bring a Shift in Canada Economy." *New York Times* 5 December.

Manuel, A. 2002. *Aboriginal Peoples v. Companies and Governments: Who are the Real Stewards of the Land and Forests? Growing International Understanding of Indigenous Proprietary Interests.* New York: Indigenous Peoples and Multilateral Trade Regimes: Navigating New Opportunities for Advocacy, New York University.

McFarlane, A. 1994. *The British in the Americas, 1480–1815.* London: Longman.

McIntyre, S., and S. Rodgers. 2006. *Diminishing Returns: Inequality and the Canadian Charter of Rights and Freedoms.* Toronto: Butterworths.

McKinnon, J. 2003. *The Black Population in the United States: March 2002.* Washington, DC: US Census Bureau.

Mexico Solidarity Network. 2006. "Zapatistismo." <http://msn@mexicosolidarity.org>.

Meyer, M.C., and W.L. Sherman. 1987. *The Course of Mexican History.* New York: Oxford UP.

Minges, P.N. 2004. *Black Indian Slave Narratives*. Winston-Salem, NC: John F. Blair.

Minister of Indian Affairs and Northern Development. 2003. *Resolving Aboriginal Claims: A Practical Guide to Canadian Experiences*. Ottawa: Indian Affairs and Northern Development, Minister of Public Works and Government Services Canada.

Mink, C.G. 1992. *Cahokia: City of the Sun*. Collinsville, IL: Cahokia Mounds Museum Society.

Mohawk Nation News. 1998. "Can Joe Norton's Band Council Assert Sovereignty for the Mohawk Nation in Kahnawake?" 18 June.

Nash, G.B. 1974. *Red, White and Black: The People of Early America*. Englewood Cliffs, NJ: Hall.

Otero, G. 1996. *Neoliberalism Revisited: Economic Restructuring and Mexico's Political Future*. Boulder, CO: Westview.

Palmer, C.A. 1976. *Slaves of the White God: Blacks in Mexico, 1570–1650*. Cambridge, MA: Harvard UP.

Porter, J.A. 1965. *The Vertical Mosaic: An Analysis of Social Class and Power in Canada*. Toronto: U of Toronto P.

Royal Commission on Aboriginal Peoples. 1996. *Report of the Royal Commission on Aboriginal Peoples* Vol. 2, Pt 2. Ottawa: Supply and Services.

Royal Commission on Bilingualism and Biculturalism, A.D. Dunton, *et al.* 1967. *Royal Commission on Bilingualism and Biculturalism*. Ottawa: Queen's Printer.

Spieldoch, A. 2004. "Beijing + 10 in Light of the North American Free Trade Agreement: How Have Women Fared?" Centre of Concern/US Gender Trade Network.

Stannard, D.E. 1992. *American Holocaust: Columbus and the Conquest of the New World*. New York: Oxford UP.

Stasiulis, D.K., and R. Jhappan. 1995. "The Fractious Politics of a Settler Society: Canada." In D.K. Stasiulis and N. Yuval-Davis (eds.), *Unsettling Settler Societies: Articulations of Gender, Race, Ethnicity, and Class*. London: Sage. 95–131.

Stillerman, J. 2003. "Transnational Activist Networks and the Emergence of Labour Internationalism in the NAFTA Countries." *Social Science History* 27,4: 577–601.

Taicho, Government of Canada. 2003. "Land Claims and Self-Government Agreement Among the Taicho and the Government of the Northwest Territories and the Government of Canada." Ottawa: Supply and Services.

Taillon, J. 2002. "Haida Nation Bids to Take Back its Land." *Windspeaker News*, April.

Thatcher, J.B. 1904. *Christopher Columbus*. New York: Putnam Sons.

Trigger, B. 1985. *Natives and Newcomers*. Montreal and Kingston: McGill-Queen's UP.

US Census Bureau. 2004. *Income Stable, Poverty Rate Increases, Percentage of Americans*. Washington, DC: US Census Bureau.

Van Kirk, S. 1980. *Many Tender Ties: Women in Fur Trade Society, 1670–1870*. Winnipeg: Watson and Dwyer.

Vitoria, F.D. 1557/1917. *De Indis et de ivre Belli Relectiones*. Washington, DC: The Carnegie Institute.

Weatherford, J. 1991. *Native Roots: How the Indians Enriched America*. New York: Fawcett Columbine.

Wherrett, J. 1996. "Aboriginal Peoples and the 1995 Quebec Referendum: A Survey of the Issues." Ottawa: Political and Social Affairs Division, Library of Parliament.

Wright, R. 1992. *Stolen Continents: The Americas through Indian Eyes Since 1492*. Boston, MA: Houghton Mifflin.

CHAPTER TWO

Nation-building and Regionalism in the US, Canada, and Mexico[1]

Claude Couture

Any comparative discussion of nation-building and sub-state regionalism (hereafter, regionalism) in countries of North America immediately triggers a discussion of so-called "American exceptionalism." In particular, the US is portrayed as distinct in its acceptance of values associated with "modernity" (especially liberalism, secularism, and cosmopolitanism) over those values associated with traditionalism (especially conservatism, religion, and particularism). This chapter highlights how this portrayal of "American exceptionalism" emerges in some of the key classical and even contemporary theoretical as well as historical treatments of nationalism.

By challenging traditional historiography, as well as by considering recent trends reflected in public opinion and elections, I will demonstrate that far from being unique, the US actually shares with Canada and Mexico similar internal divisions whereby peripheries (based on region and/or ethnicity) clash with a more powerful centre. The pattern that has emerged does not support the idea that the US is either wholly or uniquely modern. Rather, within all three countries there are communities reflecting both modern and traditional tendencies. Moreover, today, in the case of the US, the traditional and conservative tendencies are to be found at the "centre," further challenging the idea that that country at its central most powerful core is "modern."

To begin to highlight the significance of the understanding that is being suggested here, it is worth considering the literature on nationalism and how this literature treats nationalism expressed in the project of the modern nation-state versus the nationalism expressed by minorities within a nation-state. Curiously, what has emerged are two seemingly opposite paradigms of understanding nationalism with similar results: modernists and postmodernists, or social constructivists. For modernists (Smith 2000) such as Eric Hobsbawm (1990) or Ernst Gellner (1983), the nation is a creation of nationalism and therefore novel and recent. The "age" of nationalism started around 1830 with a "mass democratic and political nationalism" (Smith 2000: 28) of large nations, followed after 1870 by the divisive "ethnolinguistic and often right-wing nationalism of small nations" (Smith 2000: 29). After 1870 the "invented traditions" of smaller nations proliferated. From the modernist perspective, the nation is nothing but a wilfully created deception.

In apparent contradiction with the modernists (but, in fact, from a very similar result) the postmodernists and social constructionists treat the nation as a narrative or a "cultural artefact" (Smith 2000: 53). Once deconstructed, the narrative of any nation reveals its ethnic artefacts or constructed parts. Thus, according to authors such as Rogers Brubaker, the notion of a nation as a "real community" must be rejected (Brubaker 1996). These similarities in portrayals leave unchallenged a central feature of the modernist interpretation, namely, the relationship between nationalism and modernity. In the modernist tradition, authors such as Elie Kedourie (1960) and, again, Ernst Gellner (1994) suggest that nations could appear only when the conditions of "modernity" are in place and act as a "solvent" (Smith 2000: 29) to traditional societies. For Kedourie in particular, "nationalism" is an "unattainable dream of perfectibility" (Kedourie, as quoted in Smith 2000: 30). Similarly, for Gellner, nations are also novel and recent in the sense that they are essential in the production of an industrialist culture, one that is "specialist, literate and based on mass, standardized schooling" (Gellner, as quoted in Smith 2000: 30). However, the process of modernization, which is central in Gellner's theory, creates "winners" and "losers" among different ethnic communities sharing the same state, often creating a strategy on the part of the elites of the "loser" communities to oppose the process of modernization by a narrative based on "tradition."

Consequently, modernists view many of the "small" nations they describe as having a tendency to create a deeper and greater deception by justifying the fact that they are marginalized by the "centre" in the process of modernization as the result of their own affirmation of their attachment to what they perceive to be the main "traditional" characteristics of their nation. For example, in complex "nations" such as the US, Canada, and Mexico, regionally based expressions, especially by minorities, are viewed as expressions of "petty" nationalism against the powerful, modern, political, and economically dominant centre. What is "the centre" in each country? In the US, the centre, defined from a dominant political and economical point of view, was for a long time the East Coast. In Canada, the centre was the industrial and political heartland of Ontario (which is also geographically in the centre of the country). In Mexico, the centre was in the North. From this division of "centre" and "periphery," it has been assumed that the groups in the regions expressing "petty" nationalism or regionalism were also, by definition, opposed to modernity as expressed by the centre.

However, in what follows I will show something different about each country. In the case of the US, I argue that the politically dominant "centre" of the late twentieth and early twenty-first century is, in fact, an agglomeration of regions left out of the intensity of the process of modernization. In other words, contrary to the image contained by the idea of "American exceptionalism," where "the centre" (and force of modernity both domestic and international) is located in the large cities of the Atlantic and Pacific coasts, power over the political process has shifted to the political margins—the regions of the Midwest and South—whose political project opposes the erosion of "tradition." In Canada, Québec and First Nations nationalism always used extremely complex and modern ideas to situate their resistance to the very centre of the political process: Ontario and the federal government. The same could be said of Mexico, where the South—literally invading the centre of the

North—has often mobilized modern values. Put differently, the theories and predictions of modernists and nationalists are severely contradicted by the events in these three countries in the twenty-first century.

Why has this happened? The tensions expressed by certain regions of these countries, and the expression in some cases of a will to secede and thus possible fragmentation of the state (for example, Québec's opposition to Canada, Yucatan's to Mexico, or Puerto Rico's to the US) are actually part of a more universal tension around the very acceptance of political modernity. Within each of the three countries today there is a clear split between urban (modern) and regional (conservative) populations. This type of division, and the logjams which result, are clearly reflected in the national electoral results in each of the three countries since 2000. Thus, the pressure of specific regions have morphed into a larger clash over values within each country. To illustrate, each country, and its historiography, will be considered in turn.

The US Case

Until now, the theory of the "ideological fragment," associated with the work of Louis Hartz, has been vibrant in Canadian and American historiography (Grabb and Curtis 2004). In the 1950s, as a young political scientist, Professor Louis Hartz of Harvard University, argued in *The Liberal Tradition in America* (1955) that, as a result of historic migration patterns and the views held by migrants, the absence of feudalism was a basic factor that accounted for the pervasive and unique liberalism of the US political culture. According to Hartz, the absence of feudalism meant the absence of a static social order and, equally, the absence of a profound social passion to destroy that order. It deprived the US of both the traditions of reaction/conservatism and of true revolution. The American Revolution aimed only at national independence, not social change (Hartz 1955, 1964). Since 1783, political conflict in the US has been congealed in an atmosphere of consensus around "American exceptionalism" and individualism (Lipset 1990, 1996). "American exceptionalism" has also come to mean that the US itself is portrayed as the epicentre of modernity, while many other countries are deemed to be at the periphery and therefore not modern or not as modern as the US (Bouchard 2000; Greenfeld 1992, 2001).

However, with time, the significance of "individualism," associated with modernity, became contradictory in both the liberal and conservative traditions of the US. From the beginning, according to Gore Vidal (Hartz 1955; Lipset 1990; Vidal 2003), it was accepted that the US political tradition was essentially based on a liberal consensus. Even those Americans who rejected the liberal tradition—for example, the Communists of the 1930s and the McCarthyites of the 1950s—succeeded only by a relationship to liberalism, even as antagonists. For many authors (e.g., Lipset), the conflict between "liberalism" and "conservatism" never eroded the basis of the consensus over "American exceptionalism."

Nonetheless, the use of words like "liberalism" and "conservatism" pose a challenge today. After all, according to Hartz (1955, 1964) and other writers working in this tradition, like Seymour Martin Lipset (1963, 1968, 1990, 1996) or, arguably, Leah Greenfeld (1992, 2001), the absence of a feudal tradition had greatly affected the character of "conservatism" in the US. It had deprived the country of its European roots. Nevertheless, since the 1970s, a school of new conservatism has sought to rehabilitate the tradition of conservatism in the US, thus creating more apparent confusion. How does the conservative-liberal conflict resonate in terms of regional breakdowns and respective spaces of modernity and tradition? The brief overview below of three periods of US history elucidates the roads taken by American conservatism and liberalism and shows that, contrary to the theories of Hartz and Lipset, there was never, and still is no, consensus within US society about individualism and modernity. On the contrary, there has been, and remains, a deep division over the acceptance of modernity. A deeper consideration of different historical periods demonstrates this basic tension over the acceptance of modernity.

THE FIRST PERIOD: FROM THE REVOLUTION TO RECONSTRUCTION

In a nutshell, the modern sense of individualism had little significance until the end of the nineteenth century. "At the end of the eighteenth century, the autonomous modern individual, delighting in his or her uniqueness, had been at best tolerated rather than embraced by even the most progressive members of the American elite of that period.... The communal assumptions of the eighteenth century would thus long outlive that century in the norms of America's agrarian majority" (Shain 1994: 115). The individual could only be understood in the context of his or her local religious community. This attachment to the community, more than the modern conception of individualism, was the cornerstone of nationhood in the US.

During this period, territory gleaned militarily at the expense of the Indigenous peoples of the Midwest and Mexico made the West the key region in terms of its impact on the process of nation-building as based on violence and religious zeal (hardly "modern" values). From 1787, the year the Philadelphia Constitutional Convention drew up the first federal constitution, and 1791, the year the first ten amendments were passed, through the entire nineteenth century, constant tension between "individual rights" and "states rights" marked the political arena. But at the same time, the ultimate clash between modernity (individual rights) and tradition (states rights) was constantly delayed by the military expansion justified in the name of "Manifest Destiny" and the duty of the "Empire of Freedom" (Zinn 1980). That march by the Empire of Freedom and achievement of its territory was marked by several key events:

> » the Louisiana Purchase from the French in 1803, which doubled the size of the country since Louisiana at that time included a vast territory that exceeded the boundaries of today's state and included, for example, Missouri;
> » wars against Spain between 1810–19 in order to annex Florida;
> » the independence of Texas in 1836 and its integration in the Union in 1845;
> » the wars against Mexico between 1846 and 1853 and the annexation of territories from New Mexico to California, Oregon, and Washington State;
> » the purchase of Alaska from Russia in 1867;

» finally, the wars against the Indigenous peoples in the Midwest between 1865 and 1900 during the process of colonization. The federal state had already forced 14,000 Cherokees off their lands in 1838 (Zinn 1980). Although treaties with the Great Plains Nations signed in 1851 and 1868 granted sovereignty over their tribal lands, it did not prevent the complete occupation of their territories once gold was discovered after the Civil War. By the 1880s and 1890s, the remaining Indigenous Americans were confined to reservations. However, the discovery of uranium, coal, oil, natural gas, and other minerals in the late part of the nineteenth century, triggered the question of "rights" to the land on which the reservations were located. Since all of this was accomplished in the name of "modernization" and the modern destiny of the American people (Zinn 1980), the very real clash between modernity and tradition revealed around discourses of state rights and individual rights was muted.

Thus, while some argue that the US was isolationist, in fact, it devoted the entire nineteenth century to expanding its domestic frontiers. By 1894, it had turned into the world's top industrial power, and internal opposition to an expanded international presence weakened. The leadership of President Theodore Roosevelt in the White House established an entirely new phase with his tougher and more aggressive policy, appropriately called the "Big Stick." It resulted in the virtual annexation of Puerto Rico, intervention in Cuba through the Platt Amendment, and the active presence of the Marines, who landed in the Dominican Republic, Haiti, and Nicaragua in open support of American investments in those countries (Gran 1996).

THE SECOND PERIOD: FROM 1900 TO 1970

From 1870 to 1920, the population of the US went from 38 million to 106 million and the number of states from 37 to 48. Massive immigration coincided with an increase in industrial production: by the 1890s, the US surpassed Britain to become the most important industrialized power in the world. Both labour and suffragettes' movements were very active at the turn of the twentieth century, agitating to achieve the protection of workers and equal political rights for women (Zinn 1980).

With the rise of industrialization and urbanization after the Civil War, the process of redefining liberalism in terms of the social needs of the twentieth century was conducted by three presidents (Gran 1996): Theodore Roosevelt and his New Nationalism, Woodrow Wilson and his New Freedom, and Franklin D. Roosevelt with his New Deal. From these three leaders came important reforms, which led ultimately to the welfare state, which was based on the assumption that the national government had the responsibility to maintain high levels of employment, to regulate the methods of business competition, to supervise decent standards of life for labour, and finally to establish complex patterns of social security. Coming primarily from the pressure of the great cities—thus, from the two coasts and the Great Lakes region—this form of liberalism better acknowledged the needs of individuals who were removed further and further from traditional and religious communities who might support them in time of need (Zinn 1980).

However, the welfare state was not implemented without the fierce resistance of those still attached to the nineteenth century's form of conservative values based on local communities. This resistance fully expressed itself during the McCarthy years before finally conceding defeat, as President Eisenhower accepted as permanent most of the changes of the Roosevelt-Wilson-Roosevelt period. Still, prominent intellectuals of the period, like John Dewey and Thorstein Veblen, as well as leaders of the African American communities, Indigenous Americans, immigrant communities, and feminists considered the new leaders of that era as hopeless improvisers and opportunists only engaged in the futile patching of the old society (Gran 1996). Nevertheless, the changes made in this period, especially from 1900–52, were significant enough to be targeted for attack during the last twenty years.

THE THIRD PERIOD: FROM 1970 TO THE PRESENT

In their book *Regions Apart*, Edward Grabb and James Curtis (2004) question Lipset's theory of the Great Divide, which suggests that Canadians are more state-oriented and less liberal than Americans. Grabb and Curtis use survey evidence to show that those in the Northern US and English-speaking Canadians are actually deeply similar in terms of their ideological centrist stand on most issues. The two other regions they studied are the US South, which is clearly conservative, and Québec, which is clearly on the centre-left. In fact, the real divide in the US seems

Figure 2.1: Presidential Election in the US 2004

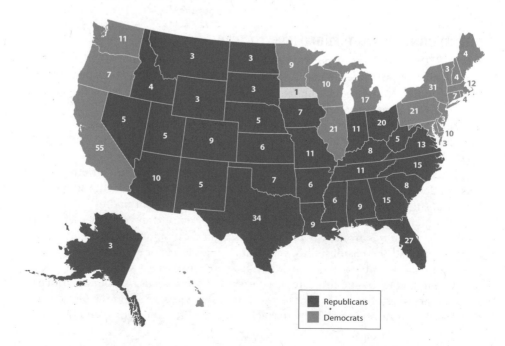

to be less between the North and South, but rather between the New England, West Coast, and Great Lakes regions against the rest, meaning the Southeast and the massive Midwest. As clearly indicated by the electoral results of 2000 and 2004 (see Figure 2.1) the US is divided 50–50, and that division corresponds to the aforementioned regional scheme (Micklethwait and Wooldridge 2004). This regional division will likely remain for the coming years, regardless of ebbs and flows in partisan control of the House and the Senate by Democrats and Republicans.

Thus, more than ever, the US is characterized by the absence of consensus: on one side, the "liberals" who try to salvage the vestiges of the Roosevelt-Wilson-Roosevelt period; on the other, a religious right fully committed to recreating the America of the nineteenth century characterized by the supremacy of local, religious, traditional communities against the perils of modern cities. More than anything else, this clash is threatening the cohesion of the nation.

This finding is notable given that the logical consequence of modernist theories of nationalism would have been that slowly and gradually modernity would erode the basis of conservatism and tradition in the US. However, on the contrary, today the dominant expression of nationalism in the US is the conservative movement led by George W. Bush, a movement that has many characteristics of the petty nationalism described by Hobsbawn and Gellner for the small nations or "losers" of the modernization process. Among these characteristics are:

> » fierce attachment to local communities and religion—for 60 per cent of Americans, religion is the most important dimension of their life;[2]
> » opposition to unions—today only 10 per cent of labour in the US is unionized (Grabb and Curtis 2004);
> » opposition to women's rights, such as through the strong opposition to abortion;
> » opposition to science—out of 35 countries surveyed in 2006 about the acceptance of the theory of evolution, the US was last with only 39 per cent of the people questioned accepting the principle of the theory (Miller, Scott, and Okamoto 2006).

Thus, in the case of the US, the political centre is now its geographical centre. This centre is expressing a deep commitment to a non-modern vision to the point of threatening the freedom of what it now its political margin, mostly the larger cities of the east and west coasts.

The Canadian Case

As we have seen, Hartz characterized the US as a pre-eminently liberal society. In Europe, he wrote, liberalism was a bourgeois political movement of opposition to the old feudal order, but in the US, where there had never been a feudal order, liberalism was associated with no particular class (Hartz 1955, 1964). Judged against this standard, Canada was often, but not always (McRae 1964) stigmatized as a more "conservative" place. A variety of historical factors were held to account for this difference.

First, at the economic level, according to the Hartz-Lipset model (Lipset 1990; the discussion below owes much to this source and to Hartz 1964), the coastal fisheries, farmlands, and coal and iron fields of the US were more accessible and more easily exploited than were Canada's resources. Canada's vastness, its less hospitable climate, and the remoteness of its valuable minerals made it necessary for large state-supported organizations to play a much bigger role in its economic life. In contrast, in the US more scope was left for the initiative of the lone frontiersman and the individual entrepreneur. In Canada, state-supported armies, police forces, ecclesiastical organizations, and corporate enterprises were needed to lay claim to the interior of the continent. As a result, the more pronounced Canadian tendency to respect authority, hierarchy, and the need for state control also involved a degree of opposition to the forces of liberal democracy.

Second was the pattern of migration. Historically, when the American Revolution took place, a substantial number of Americans who remained loyal to the Crown, fled to British North America. Hartz and Lipset viewed these Loyalists as the least liberal of Americans, people with Tory sympathies (although this portrayal may well be mythic). In any case, for Hartz and Lipset, the loyalist migration to the part of the continent that later became Canada firmly implanted a trace of conservatism in Canadian political culture and reinforced non-liberal tendencies. As for religion, the many Protestant sects that dominated religious life in the US were generally nonconformist and antiauthoritarian, stressing the individual's responsibility before God. Most Canadians, by contrast, were Roman Catholic or Anglican, and these hierarchical and relatively authoritarian churches inculcated a deep respect for authority that was at odds with the dominant religious ethos in the US.

Third and not least, the failure of the American Revolution to advance northward either in 1776 or during the War of 1812, as well as the crushing of the liberal-democratic rebellions in Upper and Lower Canada in 1837, further buttressed the forces of conservatism in British North America. Canada's core values were thus set by the middle of the nineteenth century: while the political culture of the US was purely liberal, that of Canada contained a significant admixture of Toryism (Hartz 1955). Lipset, as noted, came up with similar generalizations. Canada is, according to him, more elitist than the US in the sense that Canadians show more deference to authority and less opposition to class differences. Lipset views Canadians as less individualistic and entrepreneurial or achievement-oriented than Americans, accounting for why the welfare state (especially as measured in terms of access to universal health care) is better developed in Canada.

However, Grabb and Curtis in their recent surveys do not see any difference between the American North and English-speaking Canada and situate Québec more on the left and more individualistic: "we have found [...] that, in many ways, Quebec and the southern United States are really quite different from each other. These clear divergences, which we have already seen in such areas as religion, sexual morality, and criminal activity, are also apparent if we consider issues related to the role of the State" (Grabb and Curtis 2004: 174).

Although Grabb and Curtis have much to offer through their survey findings, their treatment of Québec raises some concerns. They explain Québec's exceptionalism as a deep reaction against the traditional, conservative Catholic culture that characterized the province before the 1960s. Suddenly, from being an anachronistic non-modern society until the Quiet Revolution, Québec became extremely individualistic and hostile to traditional forms of social solidarity like local communities, families, and religion. There seems to be a contradiction between the common explanation for Québec's nationalism, which is based on its economical backwardness fuelling attachment to tradition and culture and the sociological reality of twenty-first century Québec that even the literature using a "post-colonial" theoretical frame is unable to explain (Yuval-Davis and Stasiulis 1995; Sugars 2002). The Québec case is still key to understanding Canada, particularly when it comes to situating Canada and the US in reference to modernity. Also, since Québec has to be situated in a sphere of colonial dominance (as being in an unequal relationship to the English-speaking component of that sphere) it is important to "revisit" its case in light of the literature of the last three decades (Lamarre and Bourdon 1998).

Interestingly, the image of contemporary Québec in much historiography was first articulated in the work of the American sociologists of the 1930s associated with the Chicago School, who also influenced Québec sociologists of the mid-twentieth century (Couture and Denis 1994). These Québec sociologists, particularly Hubert Guindon, Jean-Charles Falardeau, and Marcel Rioux, put forward in their interpretations the image of the province as a fundamentally traditional society shoved by modernity into the twentieth century during the Quiet Revolution in the 1960s. The objective of these authors was to capture the elements of French-Canadian society from a synchronic angle at the moment of its dissolution due to the effects of industrialization and urbanization. The evolutionary schema of Québec society is the following (Couture 1992):

» during the period of New France, French Canada reproduced to a large degree the structures of pre-Revolutionary France, mainly centred on community, parish, and pre-capitalist mentality;

» following the Conquest, French Canadians, deprived of privileged contact with the English metropolis, turned to self-subsistence agriculture, which stressed a tendency to give priority to pre-Revolutionary, pre-capitalist values;

» after 1791 and the Constitutional Act, a French-Canadian nationalism emerged with responsible government as its main theme, but this vision came to an end with the failure of the patriotic movement of 1837–38;

» this failure precipitated the marginalization of French Canadians in the area of trade and reinforced the power of the dominant Catholic bureaucracy at the end of the 1860s, just a few years after Confederation in 1867;

» the Catholic bureaucracy emerged as responsible for the preservation of a conservative ideology centred on faith, tradition, agriculture, and anti-materialism just at the moment of the development of modern capitalism characterized by urbanization and, obviously, industrialization;

» upset by these phenomena, the dominant values of French-Canadian society were eroded little by little until they collapsed during the Quiet Revolution in the 1960s.

Since the 1980s, certain historians have rightly challenged this representation of Québec. Ronald Rudin (1997) used the word "revisionists" in the 1990s to capture this new work, which challenges the notion of a traditional and monolithic society before the Quiet Revolution. These historians suggest that there was no discrepancy between the popular classes and the elites in Québec before 1960, that liberalism was very well spread within the province, and that the French-Canadian bourgeoisie was prosperous and influential in Canada. They also insist that within Québec history there are numerous examples of the modern normalcy of the province, which in effect creates a new and different historical narrative (Roy 1988).

One of these examples is the question of migration and immigration. During the nineteenth century, large numbers of French Canadians moved to urban centres throughout North America. Despite the official but sometimes ambiguous opposition of the Church on the subject of migration, Quebecers left their rural homes as early as 1840 and moved to urban centres in New England or to cities in the province of Québec. From 1850 to 1930, the rate of the province's urban population grew steadily. In 1871, only 15 per cent lived in cities. Two decades later, the number had doubled until, by 1921, 52 per cent of the people were urban. This figure was above the Canadian average and comparable to that of Ontario. By 2001, Québec's urban population was 80 per cent, the second highest proportion in Canada, just behind Ontario with 83 per cent (Linteau *et al.* 1979). In other words, this was not a rural community oriented towards conservative values.

Québec was also, according to the historiography of the last three decades, a constant source of diversity. At the end of the eighteenth century, people of British origins made up 12.5 per cent of the total population. Several thousand of these people had come to Canada after the American Revolution (the Loyalists). During the nineteenth century, the source of immigration shifted to Britain, particularly Scotland and Ireland. During that century, 17 million people left Britain, 9 per cent of whom came to Canada. These included 53,463 Irish between 1825 and 1829; 185,953 between 1830 and 1834; and almost 200,000 during the Great Famine of 1845–49. About 20 per cent of these Irish immigrants settled in Québec. By the end of the nineteenth century, East European Jews and Italians replaced the predominantly Irish immigration (Linteau *et al.* 1979). The Jewish population in Québec grew from 1.5 per cent of the total population in 1901 to 5.7 per cent in 1941(Linteau *et al.* 1979). The Italian population was only 0.5 per cent in 1901 and 2.3 per cent in 1941. In 1996, the number of people claiming Italian origins totalled 4.2 per cent of the Québec population, while 2.6 per cent claimed Judaism as their religion. According to the 1996 census, the other important groups, each of them making up between 0.5 per cent and 1 per cent of the population, were Greek, Portuguese, Chinese, Haitian, Lebanese, and Southeast Asian. Since the Irish immigration of the 1830s and 1840s, Québec society has been demographically and culturally diverse (Roy 1988), a fact constantly overlooked in the older historical literature on Québec (Couture and Kermoal 2003).

Finally, as another example, the history of political parties in Québec reflects both the evolution of the identity of Quebecers and, as in all societies, contradictions in that identity. From 1867 to 1897 the Conservative Party dominated provincial politics, ruling for all but five of those years, 1878–79 and 1887–91. The power of the Conservative Party symbolized the alliance between the Church and business, as well as a commitment to a socially conservative society led by private enterprise. Wilfrid Laurier's victory at the federal level in 1896 propelled the provincial Liberals to power a year later. They remained in power for half a century, except between 1936 and 1939, until 1944. The Liberals maintained the alliance between the Church and private enterprise. The Church was given a free hand in social affairs and education while the political and economical spheres were left to politicians and business people (Couture and Cardin 1996).

The domination of the Liberals was interrupted in 1936 when Maurice Duplessis and the Union Nationale party defeated them. That party resulted from the 1935 merger of the provincial Conservative Party and a group of young Liberal dissidents active during the Great Depression. The name of the group was l'Action Libérale Nationale (ALN) and among its aims was nationalization of the private hydroelectricity companies. Once in power, however, the leader of the former provincial Conservative Party, Maurice Duplessis, who became leader of the Union Nationale coalition in 1936, did not implement any of the reforms proposed by the ALN, ruling the province the same way the Liberals had (Linteau *et al.* 1979).

It was the new leader of the provincial Liberal Party, Adélard Godbout, re-elected in 1939, who applied those reforms. The Godbout government was perhaps the most socially progressive provincial government of the twentieth century in Québec. Among its reforms were the right to vote for women at the provincial level, the formation of Hydro-Québec, and reforms in education. But World War II overshadowed its accomplishments when the federal government used its special wartime powers to intervene in provincial affairs. In 1944, the domination of the Liberal Party since 1897 came to an end. With only 35 per cent of the popular vote, Maurice Duplessis was re-elected and this time governed until 1959 (Couture and Cardin 1996).

The Duplessis government was characteristic of the early Cold War with its right-wing and vehemently anti-Communist slant. Opposition to this extremely conservative style of government in the 1950s prepared the field for the reforms of the 1960s. When a group of young liberals lead by Jean Lesage took power in 1960, it was the beginning of a new era and the period of reform known as the Quiet Revolution. The Church was replaced by the provincial state in social affairs, and the state intervened in the economy to promote the interests of French-speaking business. The emphasis on the provincial state corresponded with a change in the self-identification of many French Canadians in Québec as Quebecers first (Bouchard 2000). Nonetheless, the alliance of the Church and business, beginning from at least the second half of the nineteenth century, was, according to many recent authors, a typical contradiction of modernity (Couture 1998). To these observers, the changes of the 1960s, despite their magnitude, were not new but rather reflected a realignment of political and social forces in an already modern society, which is essentially what the revisionists argue.

Consequently, it seems that Québec, far from being at the margin of modernity, was in fact in its very centre, even before 1960.

Since 2000, it seems that the pressure that Québec applied to the Canadian federation after the Quiet Revolution has been replaced by a wider contradiction at the federal level between traditional and modern forces across the country, with tradition being expressed most clearly by Conservative Prime Minister Stephen Harper. The last two national elections have produced two minority governments, and all indicators at this point are that the next election will produce similar results (see Figure 2.2).

Figure 2.2: Provinces Where the Conservative Party Holds the Majority of Seats (2006 General Election)

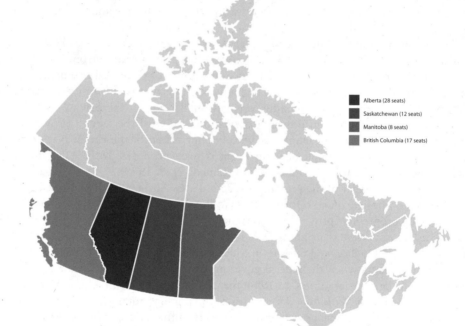

The case of the First Nations is similar to Québec in many ways. Recently, political scientist Tom Flanagan (2000) has suggested that the nationhood of the First Nations of Canada is pre-modern and unable to face the challenges of the post-modern world. However, the evidence contradicts this. For example, since the late nineteenth century, First Nations in Canada have systematically taken the legal path to defend their claim to property, beginning with the *St. Catharines Milling and Lumber CO. v. R.* in Ontario in 1888 (involving the Ojibway Nation) and continuing through out the twentieth century with the *Calder Case* in 1973, *Guérin c. la Reine* (1984), *Côté c. La Reine* (1993), *Queen v. Sparrow* (1990), and the *Delgamuukw Case* (1997), among others (Engelstad and Bird 1992). In each case, Indigenous peoples were able to defend their claims to property rights by using such documents of the colonialist society as the Royal Proclamation of 1763. In each step of their resistance, they used the principles of the dominant society in their favour to expose some of the contradictions of the colonizers. Today, it is not surprising that Indigenous communities, although still critical of all political parties, particularly reject the conservative movement in Canada.

Having that in mind, a quick look at the electoral map of the general election of 2006 shows that Canada, as in the case of the US, is clearly divided into regions of conservatism and regions of centre-left ideologies. On the horizontal line, there is a clear demarcation between the East, leaning to the centre-left (including Québec's separatist federal party, the Bloc Québécois) and the West, clearly more conservative, particularly in Alberta and in rural British Columbia. The North—the Yukon, Northwest Territories, and Nunavut—also leans to the centre-left. There are differences within these larger regions, however, particularly in the horizontal perspective, between cities, which vote for the centre-left (except in Alberta), and rural or small towns, who are clearly voting on the right. Once again, in this context, Québec is key for the right or the left to win a national majority. However, the Bloc Québécois refuses to ally itself with any of the other federal parties, even though in the past 15 years it has defended a centre-left agenda in Ottawa and so should logically ally itself with the social democratic New Democratic Party. Thus, the possibility of a long series of minority governments is a strong possibility.

As for the contrast between Canada and the US, as Grabb and Curtis (2004) have pointed out, it is difficult to see any "American exceptionalism" when both the US and Canada are deeply divided between centre-left and conservative ideological regions. The idea that there is a centre of modernity does not pass the test of a comparative analysis with Mexico either.

The Mexican Case

After the failure of the rebellions led by two priests, Hidalgo y Costilla in 1810–11, and Morelos in 1813–15, Mexico finally proclaimed its independence in 1821 under the leadership of Augustin de Iturbide who became emperor in 1822. However, as soon as March 1823, Iturbide had to face a rebellion led by Santa Anna and abdicated. Mexico became a republic in December 1823 with a Constitution similar to the constitution of the US in 1824. Between 1824 and 1871, although the period was dominated by the authoritarian presence of Santa Anna, Mexico had 52 different presidents and one Austrian emperor, Maximilian of Habsburg, from 1864 to 1867. It was also occupied by France from 1862 to 1867. A few years before that occupation, as a result of the war against the US between 1846 and 1848, Mexico had to renounce to its sovereignty on the territories of Texas, New-Mexico and southern California. Thus, the first period of arguably modern development in Mexico began in 1867 when Benito Juárez returned to Mexico City from exile in the US and Emperor Maximilian was executed. It took a liberal form under Juarez, who died in 1872, but also paradoxically under the authoritarian regime of Porfirio Diaz until the Revolution of the 1910s and again after the Revolution in 1934. It was during that last year that a state socialist regime led by Lazáro Cárdenas tried to implement a certain form of corporatism. However in 1940, the date of Avila Carnacho's accession to the presidency, liberalism reappeared and has dominated Mexico to the present day (Gran 1996).

In 1867, Mexico was, like Canada, a land with rich agricultural and mineral possibilities but with limited infrastructure and capital. As in Canada, and other countries like India, the leading sector of modern capitalism in Mexico was the rapid growth of the railroad system (Bethell 1991), which facilitated the development of an export-oriented economy and the formation of an industrial working class (proletariat). In 1876 there were only 666 kilometres of rail; by 1910 this had increased to 20,000 kilometres (Gran 1996: 162). With the spread of the railroad system came a revolution in the communications sector through telegraphy. All these changes benefited mostly the North. The South—the southern states and Central Highlands—constituted a distinct region, geographically, socio-economically, and demographically; it was poorer and more rural and had larger numbers of Indigenous peoples.

Barry Carr (1983), an Australian historian, has suggested that Mexico and Italy can be compared, although he did not develop this thesis substantially. As in Italy, the values held by people of the Mexican North stand in sharp contrast to those of the South. The North is more secular and the Catholic Church is weaker there; there are less concentrations of Indigenous peoples in the North; and capitalist farming has not resulted in debt *peonage* as in the South. Also in the North both wages and the level of foreign investment are higher. The North has a developed border industry that even competes with US capitalism and was for a while more politicized over the question of imperialism than the South. The South, like the south of Italy, is the place where cheap labour is produced and eventually exported through migration to the North (Bethell 1991).

Other differences between the two regions include the density of population, which is higher in the South as is the rate of infant mortality, while by contrast the levels of literacy, houses with running water, and the existence of usable roads are higher in the North (Gran 1996: 159). Over the twentieth century, the major statistical shift has been the percentage of the total population residing in the South, including both the peninsula and the Central Highlands, compared to the North. Until 1945, the South had more than one-half of the population, but with the intensification of internal migration after the war, this had slipped to 49.3 per cent in 1960 (Gran 1996: 159). The trend for more to live in the North has continued until today.

Another important difference is in the development of capitalism, which fostered the social structure in the North but destroyed it in the South, thereby creating the context for outward migration to the urban slums of the North or to the US. The agents of this capitalist development—the local landlord class in the case of the major southern cities such as Puebla and Mérida—have wilfully plotted this destruction (Gran 1996: 159). The Indigenous peoples were literally driven off their lands, and their social structure and way of life collapsed.

Although there are similarities between Mexico and Italy, there are also differences as pointed out by Peter Gran (1996). The hegemonic classes in Mexico are weaker overall, while the South, although without a doubt oppressed by the North, is a great deal stronger politically than the Italian South was or even is. This phenomenon has resulted in the formation of regions that are continuously resisting "Southernization," such as Morelos, the home of the famous peasant revolutionary Emiliano Zapata at the turn of the twentieth century, and of the even more southern state of Chiapas today.

People in Chiapas felt that the government had ignored their poor and largely agricultural area since the Constitution of 1917. One of their main complaints was that many Indigenous farmers were still required to pay rent to absentee landlords, even though, since the 1920s, the Mexican government had been promising them ownership of the land they had farmed and lived on for generations. Article 27 of the 1917 Constitution guaranteed Indigenous peoples the right to a communal land or "ejido." When Mexico restructured its economy after the 1982 financial crisis, the state privatized its holdings, and land reform became less of a priority, although it had been completed in most of the country, except in Chiapas. The Mexican government under President Carlos Salinas de Gortari decided to repeal the constitutional guarantee of communally owned ejidos for rural communities. By the time NAFTA came into effect, the Indigenous peoples of Chiapas felt increasingly betrayed (Rekacewiz 1997).

That dissatisfaction led to the rise of the Zapatista Army of National Liberation (Zapatistas, or *Ejército Zapatista de Liberación Nacional*), which began an armed rebellion against the Mexican federal government on 1 January 1994 as both a response to the negative implications NAFTA had for the Indigenous population, especially in southern Mexico, and the non-resolution of the "ejidos" claims in Chiapas. The group was named after the legendary revolutionary leader Emiliano Zapata who fought during the Mexican Revolution in the 1910s. Zapata became legendary[3] throughout Latin America for defending the rights of the poor agricultural sector of Mexico. Peacefully protesting in the beginning, the Zapatistas claimed they were forced to use arms to guarantee Indigenous right to ejidos. After the seizure of San Cristóbal de las Casas in Chiapas, the Mexican army surrounded the Zapatistas in their rural strongholds and seemed to have encouraged attacks by armed paramilitaries funded by local landowners. There were several massacres, most notably in 1997 in Acteal, where members from Indigenous communities, mainly women and children, were killed, even after a National Peace Accord had been signed (Lemoine 1998). Most importantly, the fight of the Zapatistas was embraced around the world as a just cause against abuses by landlords and corrupt governments (Lemoine 1998). While modernist authors would want to portray it as a "backward" movement resisting modernization, this is clearly inaccurate.

In Mexican historiography, liberal and Marxist authors saw the Mexican Revolution (1912–17) as the event that emancipated the country, brought education and suffrage, and thereby developed a new modern country. However, in their view, the Revolution was weakened by the strength of traditional feudal and conservative interests. For them, "not only the Revolution but the liberal Madero dynasty and the Marxist Cárdenas period that followed were symbolic of the crisis of Mexican Catholicism, a crisis that the Mexican people overcame through their bravery during the Cistero Revolt in the 1920s and 1930s" (Gran 1996: 161). However, after the 1950s, different interpretations were introduced, creating in Mexico a "revisionist" historiography similar to that found in Québec (Gran 1996: 161). Some of these revisionists authors—like Carlos Pereyra, Enrique Florescano, Alejandra Moreno Toscano, and Pablo Gonzalez Casanova—have expressed a more radical leftist point of view (Pereyra *et al.* 1980), while others, like Edmondo O'Gorman and the writer Octavio Paz, present a more centrist one. However, both have expressed a fascination for interpreting the South and its impact.

Since 1876, the revisionists argue, Mexico's political dominant centre was a triangle composed mainly of the Federal District of Mexico City (which is, indeed, geographically in the centre of the country), the State of Mexico, and Veracruz and Monterrey. However, in the twentieth century, Mexico City became an increasingly contested region because of migration. While in some countries migration was multi-directional, in Mexico much of the southern migration moved only toward the north in the direction of Mexico City or to the US (or the former northern part of the Mexican country before the Conquest by the Americans). As Mexico City absorbed a larger southern rural population, it became more "southern," perhaps to the point that it has become a southern city (Gran 1996). Internal migration thus had a very interesting political consequence: the potential unification of workers and peasants. The ruling class since the Revolution may remain in power, but it appears to be losing control of its national capital. The results of the last presidential election in Mexico seem to confirm this theory.

On 6 July 2006 the Federal Electoral Institute announced the final vote count in the 2006 presidential election, resulting in a narrow margin of 0.58 percentage points of victory for Felipe Calderón Hinojosa of the National Action Party (PAN). Calderón's victory was confirmed by the Federal courts on 5 September 2006, and he has been declared President-elect of Mexico (Ramonet 2006). However, López Obrador and his Party of the Democratic Revolution (PRD) reported irregularities in over 30 per cent of the country's polling stations. After the unsuccessful judicial appeal of the election results, street protests continued for months. The competition was fierce: PAN was determined to hold on to the presidency for a second period; the Institutional Revolutionary Party (PRI) was equally keen to regain the office it lost in the 2000 election for the first time in 71 years; and PRD, now in coalition with Convergence and the Labor Party and led by the charismatic López Obrador, believed it had a good chance to win (Ramonet 2006). The final vote recount of the top two candidates showed Calderón with 35.89 per cent and 15,000,284 votes; López Obrador with 35.31 per cent and 14,756,350 votes, a difference of only 243,934 votes, or 0.58 per cent; and Madrazo Pintado of the PRI with 22.3 per cent of the votes (Ramonet 2006). More importantly in the context of this chapter is the fact that the electoral map reveals a deep division between the South, eager for social reforms, and the North, now conservative, while the capital, Mexico City, is now the centre of the centre-left movement initiated by the South (Ramonet 2006).

Figure 2.3: General Election in Mexico 2006

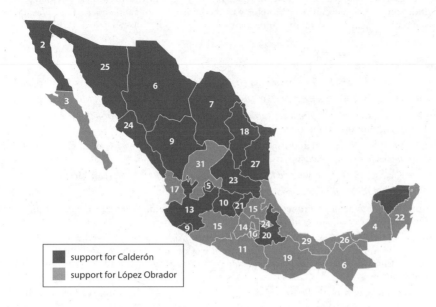

support for Calderón
support for López Obrador

Conclusion

For decades, the social sciences have been dominated by modernization theories, based on an ethicized representation of the location of modernity, with a specific Anglo-American centre and the rest of the world at the periphery. Additionally, many explanations of nationalism deny the existence of the nation and decry the possibility of national claims—particularly from smaller nations—as being "modern." At the core of these theories was and is still the idea of the US as the centre of modernity; thus, the idea of "American exceptionalism" has occupied the centre stage of the global modern world of today. But things are not so simple. The political centre of the US today is not clearly modern, nor does it reject tradition. Moreover, when compared to Canada and Mexico, there is nothing exceptional in the regional and ideological logjams in the US of today since both Canada and Mexico seem to be engaged in a similar pattern of confrontation between specific regions engaged in a conservative agenda and other regions engaged in social reforms.

Notes

1   I would like to thank my colleagues Yasmeen Abu-Laban and Donald Ipperciel for their precious help and insights.

2   "Among Wealthy Nations, US stands alone in its embrace of religion," The Pew Research Center for the People and the State, 19 December 2002. <http://people-press.org/.> See also: "Religion in Canada," Statistics Canada, Cat. #93-319.

3   Morelos was named after José María Morelos, one of the heroes of Mexico's War of Independence. Anenecuilco in Morelos was the hometown of Emiliano Zapata. The state was the centre of Zapata's revolutionary activity.

References

Bethell, Leslie (Ed.). 1991. *The Cambridge History of Latin America*. New York: Cambridge UP.

Bouchard, Gérard. 2000. *Genèse des nations et cultures du nouveau monde*. Montréal: Boréal.

Brubaker, Rogers. 1996. *Nationalism Reframed: Nationhood and the National Question in the New Europe*. Cambridge: Cambridge UP.

Carr, Barry. 1983. "Marxism and Anarchism in the Formation of the Mexican Communist Party." *Hispanic American Review* 63,2: 277–305.

Couture, Claude. 1992. *Le mythe de la modernisation du Québec*. Montréal: Méridien.

——. 1998. *Paddling with the Current*. Edmonton: U of Alberta P.

Couture, Claude, and Jean-François Cardin. 1996. *Histoire du Canada : Espace et différences*. Québec: Presses de l'Université Laval.

Couture, Claude, and Claude Denis. 1994. "La captation du couple tradition-modernité par la sociographie québécoise." In Terry Goldie, Carmen Lambert, and Rowland Lorimer (eds.), *Canada: Theoretical Discourse/Discours théorique*. Montréal: Association d'études canadiennes.

Couture, Claude, and Nathalie Kermoal. 2003. "The Multiple Affiliations of Quebec." In Janine Brodie and Linda Trimble (eds.), *Reinventing Canada: Politics of the 21st Century*. Toronto: Prentice Hall. 31–42.

Engelstad, Diane, and John Bird (Eds.). 1992. *Nation to Nation: Aboriginal Sovereignty and the Future of Canada*. Toronto: Anansi.

Flanagan, Tom. 2000. *First Nations, Second Thoughts*. Montreal and Kingston: McGill-Queen's UP.

Gellner, Ernst. 1983. *Nation and Nationalism*. Oxford: Blackwell.

——. 1994. *Encounters with Nationalism*. Oxford: Blackwell.

Grabb, Edward, and James Curtis. 2004. *Regions Apart: The Four Societies of Canada and the United States*. Toronto: Oxford UP.

Gran, Peter. 1996. *Beyond Eurocentrism: A New View of Modern World History*. Syracuse, NY: Syracuse UP.

Greenfeld, Liah. 1992. *Nationalism: Five Roads to Modernity*. Cambridge, MA: Harvard UP.

——. 2001. *The Spirit of Capitalism*. Cambridge, MA: Harvard UP.

Hartz, Louis. 1955. *The Liberal Tradition in America*. New York: Harcourt Brace and World.

——. 1964. *The Founding of New Societies*. New York: Harcourt Brace and World.

Hobsbawm, Eric. 1990. *Nation and Nationalisms since 1870*. Cambridge: Cambridge UP.

Kedourie, Elie. 1960. *Nationalism*. London: Hutchison.

Lamarre, Jean, and Yves Bourdon. 1998. *Le Québec, société nord-américaine*. Laval: Beauchemin.

Lemoine, Maurice. 1998. "Mexico's New Guerrilla." *Le monde diplomatique* (November).

Linteau, Paul-André, *et al.* 1979. *Histoire du Québec contemporain*. Montréal: Boréal.

Lipset, Seymour Martin. 1963. *The First New Nation*. New York: Basic Books.

——. 1968. *Revolution and Counterrevolution*. New York: Basic Books.

——. 1990. *Continental Divide: The Values and Institutions of the United States and Canada*. New York: Routledge.

——. 1996. *American Exceptionalism: A Double-Edged Sword*. New York: Norton.

McRae, Kenneth. 1964. "The Structure of Canadian History." In Louis Hartz (ed.), *The Founding of New Societies*. New York: Harcourt Brace and World.

Micklethwait, John, and Adrian Wooldridge. 2004. *The Right Nation: Conservative Power in America*. New York: Penguin.

Miller, Jon D., Eugenie C. Scott, and Shinji Okamoto. 2006. "Science Communication: Public Acceptance of Evolution." *Science* 313 (11 August): 765–66.

Pereyra, Carlos, *et al*. 1980. *Historia para que?* Mexico City: Sigle Veintiuno.

Ramonet, Ignacio. 2006. "The Great Mexican Election Theft." *Le monde diplomatique* (August).

Rekacewiz, Philippe. 1997. "Indians and Guerillas in Chiapas." *Le monde diplomatique* (January).

Roy, Fernande. 1988. *Progrès, Harmonie, Liberté : Le libéralisme des milieux d'affaires francophones à Montréal au tournant du siècle*. Montréal: Boréal.

Rudin, Ronald. 1997. *Making History in 20th Century Québec*. Montreal and Kingston: McGill-Queen's UP.

Shain, Barry. 1994. *The Myth of American Individualism*. Princeton, NJ: Princeton UP.

Smith, Anthony D. 2000. *The Nation in History*. Hanover, NH: UP of New England.

Sugars, Cynthia. 2002. "National Posts: Theorizing Canadian Postcolonialism." *International Journal of Canadian Studies* 25: 15–41.

Vidal, Gore. 2003. *Inventing a Nation*. New Haven, CT: Yale UP.

Yuval-Davis, Nira, and Daiva Stasiulis. 1995. *Unsettling Settler Societies: Articulations of Gender, Race Ethnicity and Class*. London: Sage.

Zinn, Howard. 1980. *A People's History of the US*. New York: Harper.

CHAPTER THREE

The Roots of North American Economic Development

Teresa Gutiérrez-Haces

In recent years, a considerable number of essays, articles, and books have been written about the idea of North America, largely due to the 1994 NAFTA. In fact, the economic, political, and social environment that resulted from NAFTA has curbed the traditional tendency to focus on bilateral relations between the US and its neighbours to the north and south. This chapter contributes a novel analysis of the different configuration of socio-economic relations by examining the dynamics of the economic development between Mexico and Canada, particularly as they were affected by the US long before either the CUFTA or NAFTA negotiations began.

In the early years of the twenty-first century, there has been increasing talk of the creation of a North American community (Pastor 2002; see also Chapter 20, this volume) and the possibility of creating a customs union (Diario Oficial de la Federación 2004). In this context, an understanding of the economic development of Mexico and Canada becomes especially relevant. During the NAFTA negotiations, officials from each of the three countries conducted the negotiation process according to their understanding of the economic development of their counterparts. Obviously, within this process Mexico and Canada knew quite a lot about their US partner, as the dominant economic force in the region, while at the same time they ignored several important aspects of their own situations. Although the subject of economic asymmetries was officially ignored at the request of the Mexican negotiating group, it was always present and greatly affected the course the negotiations would follow. Paradoxically, the Mexican team asserted its claim to equal dealings supported by its recent entry to the Organization for Economic Cooperation and Development (OECD) in 1994, as if, by magic, such membership had been able to erase the fact that relations among the three countries were and will continue to be structurally asymmetrical. As a result, no compensation mechanisms were established to address the imbalance of power and resources among the three states.

The purpose of this chapter is to analyze the origins of the asymmetries in the economic development of Mexico and Canada, rooting them in the presence of three hegemonic powers—Spain, Britain, and the US—as the actors that have most directly shaped the contemporary character of the state in these countries. My main argument is that the imperialist/capitalist system has permanently created a considerable number of inequalities that have moulded the character of the economic development of these countries and have determined the relations between the US and its two peripheries.[1]

I will begin by examining North America from the colonial period, when the interests, needs, and imperialist rivalries between competing European powers shaped the economic development of the continent. Largely exploited as resource hinterlands to serve metropolitan needs for raw materials, the colonies were deliberately underdeveloped by their mother countries. Nevertheless, it was the products of "the New World" that fuelled the Industrial Revolution in Britain and then the rest of Europe. The historical record shows that the economies of the lands that became Mexico, the US, and Canada were intricately interrelated from very early on, as territories changed hands in border squabbles and as their exclusive trade with their mother countries gave way to intra-regional commerce. The second part of the chapter examines Mexico's and Canada's mostly unsuccessful post-independence attempts (up to the 1940s) to rebalance the power asymmetries by negotiating trade reciprocity with their more powerful neighbour. Finally, I examine the role of tariffs and foreign investment in the creation of branch-plant economies in Canada and Mexico, as well as the debates around trade reciprocity that were to resurface with CUFTA and NAFTA in the 1980s and 1990s. My purpose is to counter the perception that NAFTA marks some kind of new relationship by illustrating the long history of interdependence of the three economies from the colonial period to the present.

The Colonial Period

The trajectory of Canada's economic development, like that of the US and Mexico, was to a large extent shaped by the evolution of the capitalist system in Europe, particularly as it was associated with three cores—first France and Britain and then the US. These latter two powers or core-countries have historically represented the epitome of capitalist power. The accident of geographical proximity provided Canada as well as Mexico with a privileged position beside the US. Mexico itself cannot be fully understood unless we consider that its economic development has been permanently conditioned by its relationship with its northern neighbour. Unlike Canada, which has reckoned with both Britain and the US as its dominant historical referents, as of the second half of the nineteenth century, Mexico has had a single conceptual referent to explain its own periphery: the US. The presence of Spain as the main link during the armed conquest and the colonial period was unquestionably predominant in Mexico from 1521 to 1810. However, this link was practically liquidated as a result of the independence movement, which turned New Spain into the Mexican Empire from 1821 to 1823 and thereafter an independent state.

The reluctance of a great number of inhabitants of the 13 colonies (US) and the British colonies (Canada) in North America to break free of the British Empire in the eighteenth and nineteenth centuries respectively (Nevins *et al.* 1994: 69; Robertson 1967: 149) is crucial to an understanding of the beginnings of the economic development of the territories that became the US and Canada. In contrast, Mexico not only broke free of Spain but also turned it into the subject of a "black legend" that influenced both its historiography and popular imagination.[2] This issue is especially relevant because, as in the US and Canada, there were specific sectors—known as *criollos*—who, despite Mexico's independence from the Spanish monarchy, advocated the retention of certain monarchical colonial institutions on condition that the commercial policies of the metropolis were modified (Stein 1977: 166). Whereas the US was careful to establish in the Constitution that "the President of the US was not the King of England," on two occasions after accomplishing its independence, Mexico established a monarchic government.[3] In view of the experiences of its neighbours, it is quite significant that the founders of the Canadian federation decided not only to stay under the political protection of the British Empire but also to propose that the name of the new Confederation (1867) would be the Kingdom of Canada, a proposal that was immediately rejected by the British Crown, which feared this would antagonize the US (Brown 1994).

The research on this period has rarely attached great importance to the fact that in all the colonies established in North American territory there were influential social groups who believed that the cancellation of the political and economic link with the European metropolis would be disastrous. Thus, even when their independence had been accomplished, they insisted on keeping many colonial institutions (Lipset 1990). Of the three countries, Canada was perhaps the most affected by this phenomenon, as some 80,000–100,000 British royalists (many of them government officials, landowners, wholesale merchants, Anglicans, and Quakers) fled the American Revolution by migrating north towards the remaining British colonies that would later become Canada. These "United Empire Loyalists" had the opportunity to perpetuate their political and economic ideas in a sort of greenhouse,[4] whereas in Mexico groups with similar ideas stayed active within the newly independent nation and became a counter-revolutionary element that deeply affected the future political development of the country.

In the early days of Mexican independence, the presence of the British Empire was even more important than that of the US. The first trade agreement signed by Mexico with a European nation was with the British government in 1825. During the stage of the first economic modernization of the country, at the time of the Porfirista Dictatorship (1876–80 and 1884–1911), Britain managed to exert a determining influence on the country through commerce, direct investment (especially in mining), and loans. Its economic strength suffered a major setback first with the Mexican Revolution (1910) and then with the Mexican state's expropriation of the oil companies, mines, and railways, as well as land reform in 1934. As the British economic presence weakened, that of the US grew accordingly, and by the end of World War II the latter's dominance had been consolidated.

Since that time, Mexico has vacillated between attempts to exit the North American orbit and to improve its position within it. Canada has found itself in a similar situation, but its approach to its position in the US orbit has undoubtedly been less defensive compared to that of Mexico.

GROWING UNDER THE SHADOW OF MERCANTILISM

Both Mexico and Canada based their economic growth on trade and commerce, particularly on exports of raw materials and base products. The "staples theory" developed by Harold Innis (1956) in Canada offers interesting clues for the analysis of the origins of the economic development of Mexico. Beginning with the Fur Trade, Britain's main economic interest in the colonies that became Canada from the seventeenth to the nineteenth centuries, Innis argued that the imperial or metropolitan state's demand for staples (raw materials) from its colonial peripheries (or hinterlands) warped their economic development. Instead of diversifying and industrializing their economies, the hinterlands were ensnared in the "staples trap" (Innis 1956; Drache 1995; Pomfret 1989; Howlett and Ramesh 1992; Drache and Clement 1985). Left in a dependent, export-based resource economy, minus the value added and employment opportunities to be gained from manufactured products, they were vulnerable to international commodity prices determined by the centre.

Although Canada and Mexico entered the world economy as resource-exporting colonial countries, Mexico was connected to overseas trade much earlier than Canada as Spanish colonization was accomplished a century before the great transformations that would be brought about by the expanding British Empire, Protestantism, and, above all, the Industrial Revolution (Vázquez and Meyer 1982). For Mexico, in the first stage of mercantilism (1500 to 1800), the highest economic values were attached to precious metals. In 1521, as Hernán Cortés was carrying out the conquest of Mexico, his famous phrase—"I came for gold, not to till the land like a farmer"—was a clear premonition of the Spanish enterprise in America. The conquerors' project of finding unimaginable mineral wealth in the search for *El Dorado* determined the character of economic development of Mexico.

The economic development of Canada also took place under mercantilism, but at a later stage and through the exports of second value goods such as furs, fish, and timber. Like the Spaniards, initially, the Europeans who moored at the coasts of the territories that were to become Canada were looking for deposits of gold and silver. Thus, the first incursions into Terra Nova in 1534 were doubtless disappointing for Jacques Cartier (Brown 1994: 21). In comparison to the precious metals found in New Spain, the staples available for exploitation in Canada were of lesser monetary value. Soon after 1534, Georges Etienne Cartier, facing the future territory of Canada, said: "this land should not be called Terra Nova, being made of stones and awful coarse rocks ... Moreover, I am inclined to believe that this is the land God gave Cain" (quoted in Ray 1994: 21). Nevertheless, such staples as there were played a crucial role in the economic development of the imperial centre as they provided some of the key materials that fueled the Industrial Revolution and a growing population. With the advance of the capitalist process, it became evident that other kinds of metals (such as iron, steel, copper, and aluminium) were essential for the fabrication of innumerable capital and durable goods. With the invention of steam engines, the mechanization of agriculture, the use of refrigerated transport, and the manufacturing of wire fences for cattle, the demand for other types of metal allowed other countries to join the international trade. The imperial centre's disappointment with the shortage of certain minerals in Canada underwent a radical change in 1858 with the discovery of gold in the Fraser River on the West coast and later on with the discovery of oilfields in Alberta and the production of nickel in Sudbury and aluminium in Québec and Ontario.

Practically every European government encouraged the process of conquering and colonizing the Americas, principally for economic and expansionist reasons, notwith-

standing the religious rationales offered (Christianizing and "saving" the "savages").
The central feature of mercantilism was the accumulation of metals that were used
to buy ships, weapons, soldiers, consumer, and sumptuary goods. If gold and silver
could not be directly obtained, they would be acquired by trading other goods such
as furs, textiles, timber, and multiple working tools. As the years went by, this form
of commerce was substituted by a more violent exchange carried out at gun-point as
state-sanctioned smuggling and piracy turned into a parallel practice of commerce to
obtain the merchandise other colonies produced.

Among the colonies of the Americas and the West Indies, there was an intense
commercial exchange in which, paradoxically, "the jewel of the Spanish Crown,"
New Spain, depended on the commerce that in Europe was mainly controlled by
the British. Such was the case of the products from the British colonies in North
America. Due to this circumstance, the Spanish colonies as well as the British ones
contributed to an often positive balance of payments that offered the raw materials
that were not found in the metropolis. In return, the colonies received all sorts of
processed goods.

Silver production in New Spain exemplified the new power Spain enjoyed. The
Mexican coin known as *Ocho Reales* or *Real de a Ocho*, was the first universal coin
that circulated around the world (López Rosado 1971: 293–94; Rosenzweig 1965:
791). Its origin dates back to 1497 when the Catholic monarchs of Spain, Isabel and
Fernando (1474–1504), issued the decree to regulate coining; the *Real de a Ocho*
was set up as a monetary unit. This coin was known in English as the *Spanish milled
dollar* or *pillar dollar* and circulated not only in Spanish territory but also throughout the rest of the European possessions, mainly those of Britain, Germany, Holland,
and Italy. For over three centuries, the *Real de a Ocho* was the principal export
product extracted from Mexican soil. Its radius of action covered North America, the
Antilles, Philippines, China, Japan, Indochina, India, and Malaysia. Britain, France,
and the US used it for their commercial transactions, especially with the Orient. So
large was the economic impact of silver on the development of New Spain and later
on Mexico that, of the coins circulating until the nineteenth century, 96.75 per cent
were made of silver, only 3.22 per cent were made of gold, and 0.03 per cent of copper (Bátiz 1976: 14). In fact, during the first half of the twentieth century, Mexico
contributed 57.5 per cent to the world production of silver (Willem 1959: 194).

Table 3.1: Production and Coinage of Silver in Mexico

PERIOD	SILVER COINED	PRODUCTION IN KILOS	WORLD PRODUCTION (%)
16th Century	166,000,000	2,812,000	13.12
17th Century	373,350,463	9,583,000	25.61
18th Century	1,225,327,353	32,488,000	56.96
19th Century	1,724,965,643	58,178,869	36.93
Total	3,489,643,459	103,061,869	37.70

Source: Fomento Cultural Banamex, A.C.; Academia Mexicana de Estudios Numismáticos; Sociedad
Numismática de México.

ECONOMIC DEVELOPMENT AND INDIGENOUS COMMUNITIES IN MEXICO

The colonial period in Mexico was a process of constant economic development that combined mercantilist commercial and production practices with pre-capitalist exploitation practices usually linked to the "inferior" social strata, especially the Indigenous communities. The Spanish colonial system aimed at obtaining the largest possible amount of metal for the least expenditure of metropolitan resources. This was only possible because the loot of the conquest included not only silver but also people and lands. The presence of large Indigenous villages that, due to their organization prior to the conquest, rendered them most useful to the colonial economy, was crucial for the success of the Spanish colonial enterprise (Halperin Donghi 2000: 19).

Despite the murder of hundreds of thousands of Indigenous peoples by the Spanish (Stannard 1992), they were not exterminated in Mexico as was very nearly the case for many Indigenous nations in the US. Neither were they the suppliers and mediators of the Fur Trade as occurred in Canada. The survivors were conquered, Christianized, and assimilated within a racially mixed society in which various Indigenous institutions persisted together with Spanish ones. The greatness and splendour of the Indigenous organization faced by the Spanish required a real war of conquest followed by a complex process of pacification that led to the cross-breeding of two civilizations.

The Spanish were racially mixed with the Indigenous peoples in the same way both mixed with African slaves and some Asians. The fusion of all these groups was "common coin" in Novo Hispanic customs. The white *Criollos* born in New Spain and who belonged to the richest sectors did not openly take part in this mix, so they were easily identifiable, and it was they who would be the promoters of the revolutionary and national independence ideas in the colony. Nevertheless, interracial blending, together with a policy of equal acknowledgement of all individuals from the Catholic Church and the Spanish Crown, eased the way for the subsequent Mexican liberalism in the nineteenth century and for the laws of Independent Mexico to establish an equal legal basis for all the inhabitants of the state.

Unfortunately for the Indigenous nations, this formal legal equality meant that there would be no recognition of their land, political, and cultural rights. Legal reforms liquidated their claims to specific rights as communities, and they were rendered effectively defenceless. Indeed, it is ironic that the liberal reform implemented by the only president of Indigenous origin, the Zapoteca Benito Juárez (1858, 1861–62, 1867–72), effected a series of measures that excluded Indigenous communities from the social structure of Mexico. This policy continued the disentitlement and disempowerment of the Indigenous populations that had begun in the colonial period, especially at the hands of the Spanish conquerors and their heirs—the *Encomenderos*—who were each granted a group of Indigenous labourers under their "patronage" to work the agricultural lands. So, paradoxically, while the Indigenous heritage of Mexico came to be romanticized and invoked to reject the demonized *conquistadores*, their treatment within both the colonial ecclesiastic structure of New Spain and later Mexico was characterized by oppression and gross injustice.

Meanwhile, compared to the US, whose economy was built upon the labour of enslaved Africans (especially in the southern states organized around single-crop plantation production), New Spain used relatively little African slave labour. Africans were deployed when the Indigenous population decreased drastically in the seventeenth century. However, they were emancipated half a century before the US Civil War resulted in the formal abolition of slavery in that country. In Mexico, slavery was more easily abolished, partly because slaves were neither the base nor the engine of the economy and partly because miscegenation (cross-racial mixing) was so widespread that it was difficult to distinguish people of African origin as a discrete group (Vázquez and Meyer 1982: 17). In fact, the abolition of slavery was a recurring theme for the independence movement; it was first proclaimed by Miguel Hidalgo in 1810 and again in 1829 by José María Morelos, who decided to put an end to all racial distinctions (Cockcroft 2001: 73, 84).

Table 3.2: Ethnic Composition of the Americas in 1920 (000)

	INDIGENOUS	MESTIZO	BLACK AND MULATTO	WHITE	TOTAL
Mexico	3,570	1,777	10	1,230	6,587
Brazil	500		2,500	1,507	4,507
Caribbean			2,366	554	2,920
Other	4,000	1,800	400	1,491	7,691
Total Latin America	8,070	3,577	5,276	4,776	21,705
United States	325		1,772	7,884	9,981
Canada	75			741	816
Total Americas	8,470	3, 577	7,048	13,407	32,502

Source: The World Economy: Historical Statistics, 2003: 115, OECD.

Table 3.3: Ethnic Population and GNP of Canada, 1700–1870

	POPULATION (000)			GDP (MILLION 1990 INTERNATIONAL $)			PER CAPITA GDP (INTERNATIONAL $)		
	EUROPEAN	INDIGENOUS	TOTAL	EUROPEAN	INDIGENOUS	TOTAL	EUROPEAN	INDIGENOUS	AVERAGE
1700	15	185	200	12	74	86	800	400	430
1820	741	75	816	708	30	738	955	400	904
1830	1,101	68	1,169	1,142	27	1,164	1,038	400	1,000
1840	1,637	61	1,697	1,948	24	1,972	1,191	400	1,162
1850	2,430	55	2,485	3,282	22	3,304	1,351	400	1,330
1860	3,319	50	3,369	4,867	20	4,887	1,466	400	1,451
1870	3,736	45	3,781	6,389	18	6,407	1,710	400	1,695

Source: The World Economy: Historical Statistics, 2003: 76, OECD.

Table 3.4: Ethnic Population and GNP of the US, 1700–1870

	POPULATION (000)			GDP (MILLION 1990 INTERNATIONAL $)			PER CAPITA GDP (INTERNATIONAL $)		
	EUROPEAN & AFRICAN	INDIGENOUS	TOTAL	EUROPEAN & AFRICAN	INDIGENOUS	TOTAL	EUROPEAN & AFRICAN	INDIGENOUS	AVERAGE
1700	250	750	1,000	227	300	527	909	400	527
1820	9,656	325	9,981	12,418	130	12,548	1,286	400	1,257
1830	12,951	289	13,240	18,103	116	18,219	1,398	400	1,376
1840	17,187	257	17,444	27,591	103	27,694	1,605	400	1,588
1850	23,352	228	23,580	42,492	91	42,583	1,820	400	1,806
1860	31,636	203	31,839	69,265	81	69,346	2,189	400	2,178
1870	40,061	180	40,241	98,302	72	98,374	2,454	400	2,445

Source: The World Economy: Historical Statistics, 2003: 71, OECD.

MINING IN MEXICO

By 1700, the Spanish colonizers had established a network of mining centres connected to powerful agricultural regions that in their turn were joined to urban centres that supplied food, raw materials, and durable consumer and capital goods. The colonial commercial system was organized to export gold and silver bullion to Spain, which then used it to purchase goods made in Europe or that came from the British, Dutch, Portuguese, and French colonies that were also sold in Europe. The golden age of Spain was, above all, a time of conquest and war to defend Spanish hegemony against the greed of the other European monarchies, especially the British. Paradoxically, as we saw above, the golden age was a time of silver, not of gold (Stein 1977: 30).

For the first 200 years, the colonial mining sector was designed to maintain Spain's metropolitan economy and international position. The mining centres demanded a lot of Indigenous manpower that was concentrated not far from the mines. Indigenous workers were periodically relieved and returned to their villages "half dead." New manpower was recruited through menacing threats, and the Indigenous population was drastically reduced due to the illnesses brought about by their contact with Europeans (such as smallpox and venereal diseases), their uprooting from their families and places of origin, and working conditions in the mines.

Mining created a powerful home market, and the production of wool and cotton textiles compared favourably against the imports from Europe. The Spanish, like the British and Portuguese, not only sacked the natural and human resources of the colonies but also established an iron policy to stop local production and organization. Innovation was overseen, controlled, and often suppressed when it meant disloyal competitiveness for the metropolitan commerce; the production of olives and olive oil, vineyards and wine production, and the cultivation of silk-worms were banned. Thus, the imperial centre was able to guarantee the economic underdevelopment of the colonies, keeping them subservient to its needs. The mining boom between 1545 and 1610 was a typical example of private enterprise whereby the miners, traders, and colonial state collaborated to share the benefits of a system based on the exploitation of the Indigenous people. In spite of the wealth of the colonies, during the eighteenth and nineteenth centuries, Spain was not able fully to make the transition from a feudal to a capitalist system. Within Europe, Spain in fact became an underdeveloped, semi-peripheral economy (Aguirre 2003: 46).

Despite all of the above, the precious metals found in New Spain totalled nearly half the amount of those that flowed into Europe throughout the sixteenth and seventeenth centuries. These metals brought about a high inflation rate but unquestionably pushed forward the capitalist development process in the Old World and therefore its main achievement: the Industrial Revolution (Jiménez Codinach 1991: 206). Silver as well as other valuable commodities were transported to the port of Seville to adjust the payment scale with French, Dutch, British, and Italian merchants. Mexican mining production paid for up to 90 per cent of the imports consumed in Spain and its colonies. This was the price the Crown paid for failing to create a local commercial bourgeoisie and for not developing colonial production of items such as iron, steel, paper, textiles, and other goods that had to be imported (Stein 1977: 31–34).

According to Angel Palerm (1979: 93–97) and Jiménez Codinach (1991: 205–06), silver played an important role in the whole of Novo Hispanic economic life, particularly in the development of local agriculture, home and overseas transportation systems, and the textile industry. Its triple destiny as a precious metal, commercial product, and money made it highly sought after by all the European powers. Yet, although mining wealth was paramount, agricultural production was also critical, since it both fed the local population and produced a surplus for export. To traditional Indigenous foods such as corn and beans, new crops were added, such as sugar cane, potato, vanilla, cocoa, and tomato, which, together with some animal products such as cochineal (red colouring) and vegetal products such as the dyeing stick of Campeche (indigo blue), sweetened and seasoned European cuisine and dyed in crimson and blue European tapestries and textiles.

At the end of the eighteenth century, Spain was heading towards a great fall. It had to defend its merchant ships in the Atlantic routes, although it was practically impossible to close its colonies' borders to products manufactured by the flourishing British industry. Its mining wealth and, with it, its economic power were not enough to meet the growing demand for imports. At the same time, the political, military, and economic organization of the American colonies had surpassed the limits of what Spain could hold and control. The formalization of large supervision and defence structures, the safeguarding of the fleet of escorted galleons, the payment of a heavy colonial bureaucracy, and the speculation of money lenders and merchants, together with an uncontrolled economic penetration by the other European powers, overwhelmed Spain the way the barbarians had besieged the gates of Rome.

THE DILEMMA: GROWING AND TRADING WITHIN OR WITHOUT THE METROPOLIS

Halfway through the eighteenth century, the Industrial Revolution in Britain altered the fragile political and economic equilibrium that prevailed on the Old Continent. The British Empire was ready to break into the territory that the rest of Europe acknowledged as the real and potential source of precious metals and raw materials, including gold and silver ingots, as well as a vast consumer market. The British economy had intertwined with those of Spain and Portugal as well as with its own colonies. Through smuggling in the Caribbean, the British obtained dyeing sticks from Campeche (Stein 1977: 11).Textiles, first woollen and then cotton, were taken to Africa in exchange for slaves and were used at the port of Cadiz to purchase silver to buy the raw materials Britain needed to forward the Industrial Revolution.

In 1783, through the Treaty of Paris, Britain acknowledged the independence of the US. Nonetheless, their political and economic relations were not tarnished but, in fact, became steadily closer, even though the US declared war in 1812 in a failed attempt to free Upper Canada from the British yoke. From 1846 onwards, the British Empire adopted free trade with the US and Mexico, as well as with its colonies in North America.

In contrast, the newly independent Mexicans faced the virtual loss of their principal market in a politically hostile environment. It was several years before Spain acknowledged the independence of its American colonies, and it nurtured hopes of a re-conquest, stationing ships in front of the Port of Veracruz. This dream was shattered, however, by the "Monroe Doctrine," the US declaration that it would not tolerate further European intervention or colonization in what it now considered its exclusive sphere of influence, the American continent. This declaration cut dead the expansionist dreams of certain European governments. It also caused Mexico to lose hope of recovering its metropolitan market and thus drove it into the US sphere.

The colonial heritage and external conditions before, during, and after the independence of Latin America created conflicts of interest that remained unsolved for decades after 1824 and erupted into internal wars between factions struggling to control government. Although a great part of the colonial elite wanted to remain loyal to Spain, they also wanted the right to negotiate directly with Europe and the US. However, Spain's intransigence left armed insurrection as the only option. In addition, while the production of sugar, fuel, coffee, hides, and salty meat increased, the Spanish merchant navy was blocked by the omnipresent British warships, and the colonies lacked sufficient means of transportation for their products. The Spanish, meanwhile, denied provisions and manufactured goods to the colonies; they could now only be obtained through massive smuggling operations, with British and US ships marauding close to their shores.

Similarly, in 1776, a considerable number of colonists in what was to become the US were unwilling to break ties with Britain, seeking instead to change the economic and trade rules that prevailed. They were unsuccessful, and the Americans declared independence from Britain anyway. However, the US Civil War of 1861–65 demonstrated that independence from the metropolis had not solved the political, economic, and regional differences within the new nation.

Of the three countries that make up North America, Canada was the only one able to maintain the links with its metropolis, though Britain had adopted free trade in 1846 and had signed a free trade agreement with France in 1860. The maintenance of links came at a high political cost, however; Canada did not become a fully independent republic but remained a Dominion within the British Empire. The latter clearly saw Canada as a handy substitute for the commercial functions the US had performed during its colonial period, though resentment of Britain's policies had triggered important protests and rebellions such as the one headed by Louis Joseph Papineau in 1837.

Annexation or Commercial Reciprocity in Canada

The future of British North America was the central point in every political debate in the colonies after the loss of the advantages of the Imperial Trading System in 1846, which was followed by economic depression in the US and the relative lack of demand for Canadian products. Anxious to remedy the situation, colonists considered a range of measures, including commercial reciprocity, annexation, the adoption of their own tariff policy, or joining the free trade that was beginning to be exercised by Britain.

In 1846, the Free Trade Association was established in Montreal, and a newspaper, *The Canadian Economist*, was founded and soon became one of the most influential promoters of free trade. Three years later, an annexation movement developed in Montreal, with support from the British American League of Upper Canada, and openly proposed the territorial linkage of Lower Canada and the US (Cross 1971: 9–22). Most of the support for annexation came from entrepreneurs who had been affected by the setback suffered by British preferences, mainly those in the timber business. This movement was mirrored in Mexico, first with the separation of Texas from Mexico (1836) and later its annexation to the US (1845), followed by the unsuccessful movement for the annexation of Yucatan to the US (1836) and the war between the latter and Mexico (1846–48). The fact that in the same period there was space for annexation ideas in Mexico as well as in the British colonies reflects, among other things, the increased attractiveness of the US market for its neighbours and the linkages that were being interwoven among the business communities of the three countries. The expansionism of the US brought about the urgent need to people its newly acquired territories; the construction of cities in the US. Mid-west resulted in an insatiable demand for timber, cereals, food supplies, and new means of communication (Cross 1971: 12).

The annexation movement was relatively short-lived, however, especially after the economic recovery in the US and the repeal of the Navigation Acts that, as of 1850, opened the navigation of the St. Lawrence River to any ship, thus lowering the freight costs of Canadian merchandise. Soon the idea of commercial reciprocity—the mutual reduction of customs taxes applied on products from other countries—reappeared. Indeed, for 65 years (1846–1911), reciprocity was the main objective of the international economic policy of Canada.

The idea of commercial reciprocity originated in Upper Canada. However, it arose in a politically difficult moment as the southern US states feared that the British colonies might support the cause of the northern states in the conflict that led to the US Civil War. In short, commercial reciprocity was looked upon as the anteroom of annexation (Masters 1932: 4; Tucker 1936: 110–11). Nevertheless, negotiations for commercial reciprocity between Washington and Britain began in 1847, though no agreement was signed until 1854.

Between Two Economic Orbits: England and the US

In the mid-nineteenth century, the US was able to increase its commercial power as the independence movements of the various Spanish colonies on the American continent led to the opening of a considerable number of markets and consumers, bearers of a great diversity of products. US economic expansionism involved a commercial penetration strategy that included British possessions as well as the Spanish ones. US ships carried sugar from Cuba to Europe, timber and dyes from Central America, and silk and spices from the Orient, as well as the European manufactures re-exported to the Americas, mainly from Britain. As a result, Britain became the main supplier of the merchandise the US in turn re-exported. Little by little, Mexico became such an important buyer of these re-exported goods that between 1820 and 1836 it bought two-fifths of them. Every purchase was paid for in silver (Jiménez Codinach 1991: 197–99).

Relations between England and the US were not always harmonious. After 1797 the new nation observed with mistrust the movements of the mother country in the Caribbean and South America, especially after the invasion of Buenos Aires and Montevideo in 1806–07. In turn, the British worried about the strength of US trade in zones it formerly controlled. The US's neutrality in the wars between the European powers had allowed it to sail at ease and carry on trade where Britain, France, and Spain could not. What exasperated the British most was that the Americans had become powerful shipbuilders who would soon be able to rival Britain's naval power (Jiménez Codinach 1991: 201).

In view of the economic growth and territorial expansion of the US, Mexico and Canada opted for the negotiation of commercial agreements, both to allow them to set the limits of their independence regarding the great powers and, at the same time, to guarantee their economic development, even if it meant the loss of their economic autonomy.

TRADE AGREEMENTS

As noted above, Britain's Enabling Act of 1846 removed all colonial preferences and warned all British colonies to unite under a customs union. Despite this pressure, the establishing of a free trade zone among the colonies was boycotted, and the colonists put pressure on Britain to negotiate a preferential trade agreement with the US (Pomfret 1989: 69–73). In fact, New Brunswick, Prince Edward Island, and Nova Scotia had already granted free trade treatment to a list of US goods as long as this was reciprocated. By 1852, the US wanted to include in the preferential trade negotiations free access to the Atlantic waters of the colonies, a move that would diminish the competitiveness of the fisheries in Nova Scotia, New Brunswick, and Prince Edward Island. In view of this possibility, the option of a reciprocity agreement that would include all these colonies became more significant (Norrie and Owram 1996: 181).

Articles 1 and 2 of the Reciprocity Agreement of 1854 offered reciprocal access, with a few exceptions, to the fisheries of the Atlantic coasts of British North America and of the US north of the 36th parallel. However, certain varieties such as salmon were excluded from reciprocity, as was fishing in rivers. Article 3 established a wide variety of free reciprocal imports that covered about 90 per cent of the trade established between the colonies and the US (Masters 1932: 7).

It is quite remarkable that these colonies, politically detached from one another but individually joined to Britain, were able to secure a commercial Reciprocity Agreement with an independent nation. This partly explains why the Canadian provinces have historically shown considerable independence in the handling of international trade policy, often ignoring the interests of the other provinces and the federal government. The achievement of such an agreement, together with railway construction after 1850, show that the existence of a national state, autonomous and independent from the mother country, is not a *sine qua non* condition to negotiate trade agreements with independent entities (Gutiérrez-Haces 2002: 23–24).

The 1854 Commercial Reciprocity Agreement remained in force for only ten years, cancelled by the US at the close of its Civil War. However, it had been mutually beneficial for both sides: the colonies got preferential entry for their natural products into the US market, while the US got free access to the territorial waters of the colonies and to the San Lorenzo River (Cross 1971: 14). When the Agreement was cancelled, the colonists thought that their unification as a single political entity would probably appeal to the economic interests of the US, yet they were afraid of US expansionism. Thus, they decided to remain under the protection of Britain as a Dominion. With this, they prolonged their subordination until 1931 when the Statute of Westminster bloodlessly freed them (and other white settler colonies) from the metropolis.

The future Canadians, displaying enormous pragmatism, ignored the US expansionist drive. Yet, for the first 12 years of the Dominion of Canada (1867–79), every government that headed it reaffirmed the search for a new agreement with its southern neighbour. The constant failure of these initiatives reinforced the position of those economic sectors interested in setting up protectionist trading practices through what would later be known as the National Policy (1879). They argued that the home market should be reserved to Dominion producers, which required building up tariff barriers high enough to discourage foreign competitiveness in order to consolidate a national manufacturing sector. Paradoxically, Prime Minister John A. Macdonald also hoped to attract the attention of the US and negotiate a new preferential entry agreement for Canadian products bound for the US market (Gutiérrez-Haces 2002: 25–26).

The National Policy was a mixed blessing: while producers substantially improved their production volumes, they quickly reached the limits of the home market. As a result, the demand for secure foreign markets arose again. At the same time, a number of US enterprises settled their subsidiaries on Canadian soil, attracted by the prospect of controlling Canadian manufacturing as well as other economic sectors, including natural resources, and the near-control of the internal market (Pomfret 1989: 140–42; Norrie and Owram 1996: 264, 424). And so it was that the Canadian economy was practically co-opted by US capital, which now enjoyed a captive market of producers and consumers, and the possibility of a new reciprocity agreement fast fell away.

Bartering or Negotiating: The Acknowledgment of Mexican Independence and Commercial Reciprocity

In spite of the evident anarchy that prevailed over the post-independence period, Mexico turned into the economic space in which the sorest rivalries between Britain and the US were played out. The British were active in South and Central American countries as well as in the Caribbean, but halfway through the nineteenth century, they turned their attention to the former Spanish and Portuguese colonies as destinations for British manufactures and investment, especially in mining, commerce, railways, and textiles (Meyer 1991: 15). This interest was a net benefit for Mexico, a country that had been politically isolated and devastated by the War of Independence, and for Britain, which needed various sites to place its surplus of capital and manufactures. In the mid-1820s, 624 British companies were created to operate abroad, of which 46 were to start working in Latin America. British investments in Mexico were focused on buying securities and exploiting natural resources, mainly precious metals (Rippy 1931: 17). Thus, Britain became the first European nation to fill the void left by the Spanish Crown, focusing on the trading, financial, and transport networks of countries such as Mexico, and garnering good profits from Latin America without having to assume political responsibility for them as in its remaining colonies in North America (Meyer 1991: 16).

In 1822, an envoy from the British government arrived in Mexico to explore the commercial possibilities offered by the Mexican economy. The British knew, from good sources, that the Spanish were also looking for an agreement with Mexico that would give Spain the monopoly over Mexican trade to "the exclusion of any other nation," even though Spain had not officially acknowledged Mexican independence (Bosch García 1946a). England also wanted to hasten the trade negotiations, knowing that the US government had decided to acknowledge the independence of Hispano America *de facto* (Bosch García 1946b).

The Mexican President, G. Victoria, ceded a 15 to 25 per cent decrease on import taxes on British goods and offered every commercial advantage within his power. The practically non-existent means of transportation in Mexico meant that the British could transport Mexican goods on British ships and build up railways by means of loans. Britain acknowledged Mexican independence from Spain and offered the inclusion of the clause of "most favoured nation" in a trade agreement.

After a long process of negotiation, the agreement was ratified in July 1827. Britain became Mexico's main supplier and priority customer for Mexican exports. In 1824, the total value of Mexican imports rose to 12.1 million pesos, of which British products accounted for 7.4 million pesos (61 per cent). By 1845, imports from Britain had risen to 14.4 million pesos, with only 2.8 million pesos' worth from France and 2.5 million pesos from the US. This data shows that during this period Britain was the main supplier of manufactured goods in Mexico, although its economic presence was even more pronounced in indirect investments. The "London Debt," for example, included two big loans to the Mexican government between 1824 and 1825, which together amounted to £5,281,400 sterling in 1831. This amount rose to £14,014,277 in 1848 as a result of redemption and accumulated interest. In 1867, £3,593,684 more were added due to the claim of British citizens for alleged damages during the expansionist war of the US against Mexico (1846–48) (Nicolau D'Olwer 1974: 976, 1005, 1011, 1029; Ceceña 1973: 30–39).

Up to 1825, the bonds between Mexico and the US were relatively informal. In 1822 the Emperor Agustin de Iturbide had sent an ambassador to Washington to negotiate a 10 million peso loan and to "find out about the real intentions of the US regarding the Northern border of Mexico and its expansion plans" (Bosch García 1946b: 333). Mexico was suspicious of a trade agreement with the US because the profound asymmetry between the merchant fleets of the two states would impose additional costs on Mexican foreign trade and because Washington seemed to consider itself the capital, not just of the US, but of Latin America (Bosch García 1946b: 331; Manning 1916). In truth, the US considered it had certain rights regarding Mexico, both as a neighbour and because it had been the first country to acknowledge Mexican independence. Consequently, it firmly believed that Mexico should not grant any trade and navigation advantages to European countries—especially Britain—that had not already been granted to the US (Bosch García 1986).

While Mexico opened the door to US expansionism because it was looking for financial resources to prop up its virtually bankrupt economy, the US was more interested in the delimitation of the ground border between the two countries, especially the layout of the best road for commerce and for their colonists settled on Mexican territory. Although talks began in 1825, the "Friendship, Trade, and Navigation Agreement between Mexico and the United States of the North" was not ratified by the US Congress until 1832. In that agreement, at the insistence of the US, both countries agreed not to grant any special privileges to other nations, and borders would be determined in a separate formal agreement. More importantly, it was stipulated that the contents would be revised after six years. Soon after its implementation, Texas was separated from Mexico (1836), thus fulfilling one of the secret assignments of the US delegate, J.R. Poinsett. Twelve years later, when the agreement reached its expiration date, two events soured US-Mexican relations: the Republic of Texas was annexed to the US (1846), and the US declared war on Mexico (Zea Prado 1982; Ibarra 1989).

Reciprocity versus Continentalization

Both tariffs and foreign investment have played a determining role in the economic development of Mexico and Canada. The first trade agreements between these countries and the US in 1831 and 1854 were both negotiated and signed when neither Mexico nor Canada were fully independent nations. The trade agreements served more than economic purposes. They reflected the important changes and events that occurred throughout the nineteenth century: the consolidation of international trade in the new capitalist mode, the boom of territorial expansionism, and the clash between those countries that reserved to themselves the right to intrude in international policy and in the fight against liberal and nationalistic movements. Neither Mexico nor Canada could avoid these forces. The historical circumstances surrounding these agreements expose the difficulties they faced in attempting to achieve relative economic autonomy.

The demarcation of continental borders, navigation regulations, and the circumscription of trading routes were the most crucial points that the British and US negotiators imposed on the Mexican government. Mexico saw in these agreements a means of putting pressure on Spain, which had still not officially accepted that it had lost its American possessions. The agreements also meant the promise of the long sought-after modernization, with all the ingredients Mexico needed to grow: railways, roads, industrialization, markets, and investment—in all, everything that would grant Mexico access to true economic development.[5] The Mexican government also aimed at stopping the territorial and political dismemberment of the country due to the reluctance of regional governments to accept centralist rule.

In contrast to what happened in Mexico, where the negotiation of these agreements looked more like the certification of economic and territorial distribution than a trade arrangement between autonomous nations, in the future Canada, the agreement of 1854 aimed at giving the colonies preferential access to the US market and that of its neighbours and the mother country, thanks to the imperial preference. In this sense, the colonies represented a commercial bridge between Britain and the US. Although the US negotiators considered the 1854 agreement as a framework for negotiations with Mexico, there were important differences in the final contents of the US-Mexico deal, as shown in Table 3.5.

Both agreements had a limited existence. The US did not try to extend the agreement with the Canadian colonies further than the established time limit; it was considered unnecessary, as the US would have access to almost all Canadian raw materials anyway. In the Mexican case, the real US interests beyond customs tariffs had not been met in the agreement, so it was decided that with no treaty whatsoever, they would take over what they really wanted—Mexican territory.

Table 3.5: Differences Between the Elgin-Marcy and the Forsyth-Montes and McLane-Ocampo Agreements

CANADA (1854)	MEXICO (1857 & 1859)
Reciprocal Access Liberalization of 28 products including: raw materials and products of agricultural and animal origin.	Customs tariff reduction in exchange for loan. Liberalization of more products than those stipulated in the British Agreement. It included: certain manufactured goods and agricultural produce.
Exemptions: manufactured goods, salmon and fishing at river mouths. The Agreement did not apply to the Atlantic coast south of the 36th parallel. Crustacean fishing was forbidden in all the North American shores. Fishing on the coasts of the British Pacific was not allowed. It included all the territory of the British colonies in North America.	Exemptions: cotton goods, especially brown sheeting and sugar (alone in the Agreement of 1857). It did not include port trading in the coasts of the Gulf of Mexico. It only included trade in the border zone of Northern Mexico with US.
Validity: ten years. Previous level of trading exchange between the two countries: low.	No termination date was set. The negotiated products represented 90 per cent of the bilateral trade.

Source: Based on the information provided by Norrie and Owram 1996: 180–85; Pomfret 1989: 73, 75–76; Riguzzi 2003: 70–72; Masters 1932: 7).

However short-lived these two trade agreements were, their lasting legacy was the establishment of a relation of profound economic dependency of Canada and Mexico on the US market and investment. After the abrogation of the agreements, Canada and Mexico searched for different ways to re-establish trade reciprocity with the US. Mexico negotiated five other agreements with the US between 1857 and 1911, though none survived the political gauntlet to achieve ratification. Canada, meanwhile, tried to negotiate a new trade agreement with the US on at least three occasions between 1866 and 1874. The failure of these attempts was an excellent argument for certain sectors of the Dominion who pushed Prime Minister Macdonald (1867–73 and 1878–91) to change the rules of the game that prevailed in relations with their neighbour. Four strategies aimed at creating a bulwark against the US: the political and commercial unification of the Canadian territory by means of an east-west railway system; a settlement policy to create and connect Western provinces with those of the East; the implementation of a national tariff policy (Laux and Molot 1988: 44); and the adoption of a strategy of import-substitution industrialization (Williams 1987: 15–40).

As neither the Dominion nor the US was prepared to totally relinquish bilateral trade, this policy did nothing but stimulate the one already put into effect by the US, so for a long period, the relationship was characterized by protectionism with concessions, bargaining, and mutual reprisals. Despite the permanence of the National Policy, both Liberal and Conservative Canadian federal governments established a double strategy, seeking a resumption of trading reciprocity with the US while at the same time cultivating their trading relationship with Britain. The British, in turn, continued with their free exchange policy started in the 1840s in spite of increasing protectionism, until they rejuvenated an imperial preferences system after World War I that once again favoured trading relations with their Dominions and colonies. By this time, however, the damage had already been done and the Dominion of Canada had practically fallen into the arms of the US (Hart 1998: 13).

Although the National Policy did not prompt a more favourable response from the US government, private investors seized it as the long-awaited opportunity to take over certain economic sectors in Canada, especially natural resources. The prospects of producing *in situ*, relying on a captive consumer market, and profiting from a favourable tariff system were important incentives for US capital to migrate to Canada. By the beginning of the twentieth century, a great number of Canadian companies were under foreign control. Little by little, US subsidiaries took over important segments of the chemical, electrical, and automotive industries (Laux and Molot 1988: 46). Thus, the US presence grew in step with the protectionist industrialization process.

By the time the US government showed it was genuinely interested in carrying out a simultaneous strategy with Mexico and Canada—known as dollar diplomacy—political and economic conditions had changed. Although foreign investments had always been well received in Canada, as noted above, broader trade policy had been the cause of several conflicts with the US, leading to the Confederation of the Colonies in 1867, the formulation of the National Policy in 1879, and eventually, to the fall of the Liberal government of Sir Wilfrid Laurier (1896–1911).

In January 1910, Laurier had managed to negotiate a reciprocity agreement with US President Taft, establishing free trade for primary agricultural products and for natural resources and products derived from them. There was also a tariff reduction on a number of manufactured goods, mainly farming tools and machinery. The US Congress speedily approved the agreement in July 1911, despite the fact that the business community in Canada as well as the financial and manufacturing sectors of Toronto and Montreal had publicly rejected it. Led by the Anti-Reciprocity League in Montreal and the Canadian National League in Toronto, the major rallying cry of the anti-reciprocity Canadians was "No truck nor trade with the Yankees" (Gutiérrez-Haces 2003: 27–30; Twomey 1993: 44). Indeed, so strong were the protests that the Governor General, Lord Grey, commented that "the feeling in Montreal and Toronto against the Agreement could hardly be stronger if the US troops had already invaded our territory" (quoted in Stevens 1970: 2).

Laurier's Liberals argued that reciprocity would enhance the market for natural resources and the transport system, and allow people to profit from the closest trading channels, on the north-south rather than the east-west axis (Dafoe 1911; Laurier 1911: 4751–71). Anti-reciprocity arguments were legion in the endless parliamentary debates about the agreement. Reciprocity, it was argued, would destroy the Canadian economy since it would encourage and deepen the north-south interchange between the two countries at the expense of those between the Canadian regions that had been achieved with the construction of the railways (Foster 1911: 3327, 3336–42, 3530–63); threaten the interests of transporters and producers who would be forced to compete at length with the imports from the US (Sifton 1911: 4385–4409); hasten the disappearance of local industries; lead to separation from Britain as it would sooner or later destroy the British preferences the Dominion enjoyed (Hawkes 1911); and, ultimately, promote the economic absorption of Canada by the US. Such arguments were reinforced by the revelation of a letter written by President Taft himself in which he asserted that "the amount of Canadian products we would take would produce a current of business between Western Canada and the US that would make Canada only an adjunct of the United States" (quoted in Stevens 1970: 3).

Laurier's rejection of a petition from parliamentarians to modify the contents of the agreement ultimately led to the downfall of both the Liberal government and the agreement. The election of 1911 centred on two antagonistic positions—nationalism versus continentalism. These positions were not novel but had co-existed for some time within the government, the political parties, and the population in general. However, the news that the Liberal government had negotiated a trade reciprocity agreement that had already been approved by the US Senate was interpreted as an act of high treason.

The fall of Laurier and the Liberals did not settle the issue of trade and economic relations between Canada and the US, however. Canada's economy at the time was driven by a mix of local entrepreneurs and US investors, who were happy to be producing for a captive market thanks to the protection offered by the National Policy. By 1914, US subsidiaries had managed to consolidate the manufacturing sector and dominate the natural resource sectors as well. Canada had more companies controlled by US capital than any other country. Approximately 40 per cent of this investment was found in the production of staples industries: minerals, newspaper, and fuel (which required sophisticated technology for its extraction and processing). In contrast, Canadian capital was concentrated in the more traditional labour-intensive industries such as footwear, textiles, clothing, furniture, iron, and steel (Laux and Molot 1988: 46).

The political debate surrounding the reciprocity agreement of 1911 in Canada was not alien to Mexico. Mexico also tried to negotiate two agreements with the US during the long period of dictatorship of General Porfirio Díaz (1876–80 and 1884–1911), the most important of which was concluded between 1909 and 1911. That agreement is particularly relevant because it was not in the end rejected by the US, as was customary, but by the Mexican government.

The negotiating process of both agreements raised an interesting debate in Mexico, similar to that seen in Canada. While this was going on, the Mexican government assumed a very proactive political position, supported by a buoyant economic situation thanks to the massive presence of foreign investments, which were not only from the US. In the end, the Mexican government rejected the customs union proposal as it would mean eliminating, or at least reducing, the tariffs that had been placed on foreign trade, a major source of government revenue. Moreover, it would put at risk the industrialization of the country, deepen its dependency on the US, and ultimately threaten its autonomy (Riguzzi 2003: 136). The position of the Mexican government is particularly interesting as it would echo its responses to future continental proposals, such as one during World War II that would have joined the economic development of Mexico and Canada to the US war effort and the 1947 proposal to create an international trading organization aiming at grouping all the countries under free trade (Gutiérrez-Haces 2002: 40–43).

Just as the National Policy in Canada had led US entrepreneurs to relocate to Canadian regions to produce products they used to export to Canada (thus lowering costs and monopolizing the market), the imposition of US tariffs led to the creation of a branch-plant economy in Mexico. The latter was perhaps inevitable after 1890, when the US Congress created the McKinley Tariff, a protectionist tool that led to the establishment of important US subsidiaries in Mexico. The high tariff imposed on Mexican minerals induced companies that had relied on their importation to move part or the whole of the production process to Mexico. Thus, processing and smelting plants linked to the Guggenheim, Kansas City Smelting and Refining, and the Omaha Grant corporations were set up in Mexico (Gutiérrez-Haces 2003: 6–9; Riguzzi 2003: 142). The establishment of these smelting plants was a major victory for Mexico, and the economic life of the zones that welcomed them vastly improved. But even more important was that for the first time a US protectionist measure had benefited Mexicans, thanks to location decisions taken by non-governmental actors. US entrepreneurs showed more shrewdness than their government officials, stuck as they were on the idea of protectionism at any price, which, however, resulted in private sector strategies to avoid its effects. The process was accelerated in the 1950s when the strategy of industrialization by import substitution caused the massive entrance of US subsidiaries into other sectors of the Mexican economy. At that moment, what had been true in Canada since 1879 was affirmed in Mexico: direct foreign investment was a lever for economic development, and as such, it should not face any restriction whatsoever.

Table 3.6: Foreign Investment in Mexico, 1911 (percentages for investment category)

CATEGORY	US	BRITAIN	FRANCE	GERMANY	HOLLAND	OTHERS	TOTAL	RANKING AS PERCENTAGE OF THE TOTAL INVESTMENT
Public debt	11.8	16.6	65.8	—	5.2	—	100	14.6
Banks	20.4	10.8	60.2	7.2	1.7	—	100	4.8
Railroads	47.3	35.5	10.3	1.7	2.0	3.2	100	33.2
Public utilities	5.5	89.1	4.2	—	1.3		100	6.9
Mining and metallurgy	61.1	14.3	22	—	—	2.7	100	24.1
Real estate	41.8	46.9	8.2	3.1	—	—	100	5.7
Industry	16.0	8.4	55.0	20.6	—	—	100	3.8
Trade	7.4		65.6	—	—	27.0	100	3.5
Petroleum	38.5	54.8	6.7	—	—	—	100	3.0
Total domestic as percentage of the total foreign investment	38.0	29.1	26.7	1.9	1.6	2.7	100	100

Source: Villegas 1974: Table 65, 115; and Hansen 1971: 25.

Table 3.7: Foreign Capital in Mexico, Mining and Metallurgy, 1910–11

	COMPANIES	CAPITAL (MILLIONS OF PESOS)	%
Total of the sector	31	281	100.0
US capital	17	229	81.0
British capital	10	42	14.5
French capital	2	5	2.0
Sum of the 3 countries	28	276	97.5

Source: Ceceña 1973: 55.

Porfirio Díaz, sly and cunning as he was, welcomed direct foreign investment no matter the national origin, repeatedly arguing that his modernization project for Mexico neither could nor should dispense with it. The presence of Canadian entrepreneurs during the Porfiriato was crucial for the construction of modern infrastructure in Mexico City and other important cities throughout the country. A contemporary of the governments of Macdonald and Laurier, Díaz admired the style that incarnated, in his opinion, the best of the British, French, and American. He was aware of the changes wrought by the unification project of Canadian Confederation and the way in which the National Policy and the railways had attracted foreign investment. If the Mexican president voluntarily put off the ratification of a customs union agreement that had been negotiated with the US government since 1909, it was because the country had all the investment it required.

President Díaz, like Canadian prime ministers, also applied certain protectionist measures, though not as extensive as the National Policy, designed to safeguard

Table 3.8: Direct Foreign Investments in Mexico, Value of the Investments for Countries (thousands of dollars)

COUNTRIES	1952	1953	1954	1955	1956	1957
Total	728,571	789,487	834,332	919,247	1,060,440	1,200,070
US	551,421	576,822	588,278	653,854	831,086	940,529
Canada	103,247	115,873	128,278	135,093	143,134	161,984
Sweden	35,621	41,249	49,636	60,840	10,649	12,045
England	27,712	32,744	36,460	39,222	45,415	51,391
Others	10,570	22,799	31,680	30,238	30,156	34,121

Source: Informe del Banco de Mexico 1958: 90.

Table 3.9: Direct Foreign Investments in Mexico, Value of the Investments for Activities (thousands of dollars)

ACTIVITIES	1952	1953	1954	1955	1956	1957
Total	728,571	789,487	834,332	919,247	1,060,440	1,200,070
Agriculture and Ranching	5,650	6,447	6,108	17,708	19,170	20,175
Mining	160,225	164,548	162,960	171,012	189,067	211,191
Petroleum	6,480	13,756	17,630	16,468	16,919	18,402
Industry Manufacturer	225,465	258,094	278,345	314,958	363,074	413,274
Construction	10,782	10,997	10,495	11,286	13,332	16,157
Electricity, Gas	160,381	173,377	189,192	203,838	212,665	230,755
Trade	116,099	117,010	116,168	118,535	179,846	218,290
Transport and Communications	40,137	39,766	47,937	59,205	58,877	63,532
Other[1]	3,352	5,492	5,497	6,237	7,490	8,294

1. Hotels, industry film, publicity, and propaganda, etc.
Source: Informe del Banco de México 1958: 90.

incipient Mexican industrialization. He bet that the railways, although built with foreign loans and concessions, would bring about the unification of the country and would ruin the regional leaders who had done nothing but initiate wars and separatism. He was a firm believer of progress coming in through foreign trade and enthusiastically assumed the role of supplier of raw materials and base products that the capitalist system assigned to the Mexican economy. His administration introduced the first modernization of Mexico, extending a friendly hand towards foreign capital and smothering with the other a population that was still largely Indigenous and rural (Gutiérrez-Haces 2003: 11–32; Nicolau D'Olwer 1974: 1017–18; 1087–90).

Table 3.10: Direct Foreign Investment in Mexico for Sectors, 1910–11

| | TOTAL | | FOREIGN CAPITAL | | |
ACTIVITIES	COMPANIES	CAPITAL (MILLIONS OF PESOS)	COMPANIES	CAPITAL (MILLIONS OF PESOS)	%
Railroads	10	665	8 (1)	183 (229)	27.5
Banks	52	286.4	28 (2)	219 (4)	76.5
Mining	31	281	29 (1)	276 (1)	98.2
Industry	32	109	25 (1)	92 (2)	84.3
Electricity	14	109	13 (1)	95 (2)	87.0
Petroleum	3	97	3	97	100.0
Agriculture	16	69	14 (1)	66 (1)	95.7
Other*	170	1,650.4	130 (9)	1,042 (239)	63.2 (14.5)
				1,281	77.7

*Includes: Trade, telegraphs, and telephones.
Source: Ceceña 1973: 54.

Conclusion

This chapter has analyzed the historical roots of the economic development and political relations of the three countries that make up North America from the colonial period to the 1940s and beyond. It has shown that although asymmetries of power were always present, the economic development of these countries has been intimately interconnected. The historical relationship between the constituent parts of North America is of a unique and exceptional character, incorporating a centre-hegemonic country, the US, and its two closest peripheries, Mexico and Canada.

This chapter has also demonstrated that, contrary (perhaps) to public opinion, the continental trade reciprocity project did not suddenly appear between 1990 and 1994 with NAFTA; it originated in 1910 when the US government proposed, based on "the special relations derived from the territorial nearness," two trade agreements with Mexico and Canada that marked a clear attempt to create a North American market dominated by the US. From that date onwards, the proposal reappeared at various points under different diplomatic formulae, mostly framed in terms of the bilateral rather than trilateral agendas of these countries (Hanningan 1980: 14).

In view of this history, it is clear that bilateral approaches to the economic development of and relations between these countries are inadequate. It is both more accurate and more illuminating to apply a comparative method that considers the historical experiences of Mexico, Canada, and the US as a single rather than a disintegrated process. Although most of the pre-NAFTA trade negotiations analyzed here were either short-lived or never reached fruition in their own time, they nevertheless generated a series of consequences and have greatly influenced the economic development of these countries as well as relations between them. NAFTA did not signify the writing of a new book, but merely the opening of a fresh chapter in a long history of ongoing relationships in which the idea of free trade has ebbed and flowed, as indeed it may do again in the years to come.

Notes

1   My analysis follows the approach of Immanuel Wallerstein (1984) to the history of capitalism and more specifically to the internal organization or configuration of the capitalist world-system itself, which is organized in a hierarchical, polarized, and unequal structure that subdivides this world-system into a small central area, a certain semi-peripheral area, and a vast peripheral area. This differentiated location of the countries within the world-system is simultaneously changeable and stable, allowing a given country to modify its specific status in the system over time, without fundamentally altering the overall structure of the system itself (Wallerstein 1984, 1998a, 1998b; Aguirre 2003: 5–46).

2   The anti-Spanish feeling in Mexico came about as a result of the Independence movement (1810). For decades, the word *gachupín* was used as a pejorative expression to refer to a person of Hispanic origins. It took Spain several years to acknowledge Mexico's independence. Although practically no Spanish-born *peninsulars* remained in Mexico after the war, the Creoles (*criollos*), being the children of the *peninsulars* born in Mexico, and having held the merchant and mining power, also faced the distrust of the Indigenous and half-caste population, especially when they became the dominant class. In the decades of 1930 and 1940, a nationalist movement arose that was defined by its anti-Spanish ideology and by the exaltation at all costs of everything that would be a reminder of the Indigenous past. This feeling continued until the end of the 1930s, when the government of General Lázaro Cárdenas partly changed the official attitude towards the Spanish by welcoming as refugees the Republicans of the Spanish Civil War and breaking diplomatic relations with the government of General Francisco Franco. Despite this, the people remained hostile towards everything related to the mother country.

3   The first is known as the First Empire under the government of Agustin de Iturbide, who ruled between 1822 and 1823 as Emperor of Mexico. The second occurred some years later, thanks to a political agreement between the conservatives and Napoleon III to establish a monarchic government under Maximilian of Austria (1864–67), though he ended his reign before a Mexican firing squad.

4   Seymour Martin Lipset (1990: 19) affirms: "The North Americans do not know it but the Canadians cannot forget that two countries arose from the North American Revolution, not just one. The United States is the country of the Revolution and Canada that of the counter-revolution."

5   From 1810 until 1876, Mexico suffered economic stagnation as the War for Independence practically destroyed the mining industry, exhausted agriculture, and caused a massive flight of capital. Moreover, the 11-year armed conflict disrupted the life of the country and left a balance of over one million dead. The Mexican political system was practically beheaded during the first 50 years of independence—more than 50 governments with 30 different presidents came and went. Besides the internal fights, there were two wars against France and one against the US, not to mention the foreign troops that were often stationed on Mexican shores, threatening to invade the country. In 1820, there were only three roads in Mexico that could be considered real highways; in 1860 the country accounted for only 24 kilometres of railways fit for use. In 1867, 95 per cent of customs revenues that constituted over four-fifths of total government revenue

were mortgaged to pay off the foreign debt. A precarious transport system, political instability, and high taxes conspired against the Mexican producer, who had to put up with higher costs than those imposed on his European and North American competitors (Hansen 1971: 19–21).

References

Aguirre Rojas, Carlos. 2003. *Immanuel Wallerstein: Critica del Sistema-Mundo Capitalista*. Mexico: Era.

Banco de México. 1958. *Informe Anual*. Mexico: Banco de México.

Batiz, Jose Antonio. 1976. *El Real de a Ocho Primera Moneda Universal*. Mexico: Fomento Cultural Banamex.

Bosch García, Carlos. 1946a. "El Primer Tratado Comercial Anglo-Mexicano: Intereses Económicos y Políticos." *El Trimestre Económico* 13,51: 495–532.

——. 1946b. "Discusiones Previas al Primer Tratado de Comercio entre México y Estados Unidos: 1822–1838." *El Trimestre Económico* 13, 50: 329–45.

——. 1986. *Problemas Diplomáticos del México Independiente*. Mexico: Universidad Nacional Autónoma de México.

Brown, Craig. 1994. *Historia Ilustrada de Canada*. Mexico: Fondo de Cultura Económica.

Ceceña, Jose Luis. 1973. *México en la Orbita Imperial*. Mexico: El Caballito Ediciones.

Cockcroft, James. 2001. *La Esperanza de Mexico*. Mexico: Siglo XXI.

Cross, Michael. 1971. *Free Trade, Annexation, and Reciprocity 1846–1854*. Toronto: Holt, Rinehart and Winston.

Diario Oficial de la Federación. 2004. Canales Clariond, Fernando de Jesús, Secretario de Economía, "Aviso mediante el cual se solicitan comentarios respecto a una posible armonización de los aranceles de nación más favorecida entre México, los Estados Unidos y Canadá y una posible liberalización de las Reglas de Origen del Tratado de Libre Comercio de América del Norte." Mexico.

Drache, Daniel (Ed.). 1995. *Staples, Markets, and Cultural Change: Harold A. Innis*. Montreal and Kingston: McGill-Queen's UP.

Drache, Daniel, and Wallace Clement. 1985. *A Practical Guide to Canadian Political Economy*. Toronto: James Lorimer.

Dafoe, J. 1911. *J.W. Dafoe Papers*, Sidney Fisher to John Dafoe, 10 March 1911. Public Archives of Canada.

Foster, George. 1911. *House of Commons, Debates, 1910–1911* (9 February 1911): 3327, 3336–42; (14 February 1911): 3530–63. Ottawa: Canada.

Gutiérrez-Haces, Teresa. 2002. *Procesos de Integración Economica en México y Canada, Una Perspectiva Historica Comparada*. Mexico: Miguel Ángel Porrúa.

——. 2003. *A Deep Mexico: Periphery or Semi-periphery*. Paper presented to Globalism and its Challengers Symposium. Bergen University, Norway, 15 October.

Halperin Donghi, Tulio. 2000. *Historia Contemporánea de América Latina*. Madrid: Alianza Editorial.

Hanningan, Robert. 1980. "Reciprocity 1911: Continentalism and American Realpolitik." Toronto: *Diplomatic History* 4: 1–10.

Hansen, Roger D. 1971. *La Política del Desarrollo Mexicano*. Mexico: Siglo XXI Editores.

Hart, Michael. 1998. *Fifty Years of Canadian Tradecraft: Canada and the GATT 1947–1997*. Ottawa: Carleton UP.

Hawkes, Arthur. 1929. "Sir Clifford Sifton and the Reciprocity Election of 1911." *The Manitoba Free Press*, 21 September.

Hawkes, Arthur. 1911, "An Appeal to the British-Born," *Campaign of 1911 Against Reciprocity*. Toronto: Canadian National League.

Howlett, Michael, and M. Ramesh. 1992. *The Political Economy of Canada: An Introduction*. Toronto: McClelland and Stewart.

Ibarra, Araceli. 1989. *El comercio exterior de México: Ruptura y Continuidad, 1821–1862*. Mexico: Fondo de Cultura Económica.

Informe del Banco de Mexico. 1958.

Innis, Harold A. 1956. *The Fur Trade in Canada: An Introduction to Canadian Economic History*. Toronto: U of Toronto P.

Jiménez Codinach, Guadalupe. 1991. *La Gran Bretaña y la Independencia de México 1808–1821*. Mexico: Fondo de Cultura Económica.

Laurier, Wilfrid. 1911. *House of Commons, Debates, 1910–1911* (7 March): 4751–71. Ottawa: Canada.

Laux, Jeanne, and Maureen Molot. 1988. *State Capitalism: Public Enterprise in Canada*. Ithaca: Cornell UP.

Lipset, Seymour Martin. 1990. *Continental Divides: The Values and Institutions of the United States and Canada*. New York: Routledge, Chapman and Hall.

López Rosado, Diego. 1971. *Historia y Pensamiento Económico de México: Comercio Interior y Exterior, Sistema Monetario y del Crédito*. México: Instituto de Investigaciones Económicas.

Manning, William. 1916. *Diplomatic Correspondence of the United States, Inter-American Affairs, 1831–1860*. Washington, DC: Carnegie Endowment for International Peace.

Masters, Donald. 1932. *La Réciprocité 1846–1911*. Ottawa: Société Historique du Canada.

Meyer, Lorenzo. 1991. *Su Majestad Británica Contra la Revolución Mexicana, 1900–1950. El Fin del Imperio Informal*. Mexico: El Colegio de México.

Nevins, Allan, Henry Commanger, and Jeffrey Morris. 1994. *Breve Historia de los Estados Unidos*. Mexico: Fondo de Cultura Económica.

Nicolau d'Olwer, Luis. 1974. "Las Inversiones Extranjeras." In Cosio Villegas (ed.), *Historia Moderna de México: El Porfiriato*. Mexico: Hermes. 973–1211.

Norrie, Kenneth, and Douglas Owram. 1996. *A History of the Canadian Economy*. Toronto: Harcourt Brace.

Palerm, Angel. 1979. "Sobre la Formación del Sistema Colonial. Apuntes para una Discusión." In E. Florescano (ed.), *Ensayos Sobre el Desarrollo Economico de México y America Latina, 1500–1975*. Mexico: Fondo de Cultura Económica. 29–36.

Pastor, Robert. 2002. *Toward a North American Community*. Washington, DC: Institute for International Economics.

Pomfret, Richard. 1989. *The Economic Development of Canada*. Scarborough, ON: Nelson Canada.

Ray, Arthur. 1994. "El Encuentro de Dos Mundos." In C. Brown (ed.), *Historia Ilustrada de Canada*. Mexico: Fondo de Cultura Económica. 21–114.

Riguzzi, Paolo. 2003. *Reciprocidad Imposible? La Política de Comercio entre Mexico y Estados Unidos, 1857–1938*. Mexico: El Colegio Mexiquense.

Rippy, Fred. 1931. *The United States and Mexico*. New York: F.S. Crofts and Company.

Robertson, Ross M. 1967. *Historia de la Economía Norteamericana*. 2 vols. Buenos Aires: Bibliográfica Argentina.

Rosenzweig, Fernando. 1965. "Moneda y Bancos." In Cosío Villegas (ed.), *Historia Moderna de México. El Porfiriato*. México: El Colegio de México. 789–885.

Sifton, Clifford. 1911. *House of Commons, Debates, 1910–1911* (28 February): 4385–4409. Ottawa: Canada.

Stannard, David E. 1992. *American Holocaust: Columbus and the Conquest of the New World*. New York: Oxford UP.

Stein, Stanley B. 1977. *La Herencia Colonial de América Latina*. Mexico: Siglo XXI.

Stevens, Paul. 1970. *The 1911 General Election: A Study in Canadian Politics*. Toronto: Copp Clark.

Tucker, Gilbert. 1936. *The Canadian Commercial Revolution 1845–1851*. New Haven, CT: Harvard UP.

Twomey, Michael. 1993. *Las Corporaciones Multinacionales y el Tratado de Libre Comercio de America del Norte*. Mexico: Fondo de Cultura Económica.

Vázquez, Josefina, and Lorenzo Meyer. 1982. *México Frente a Estados Unidos: Un Ensayo Histórico 1776–1980*. Mexico: El Colegio de Mexico.

Villegas, Cosío Daniel (Ed.). 1974. *Historia Moderna de México: El Porfiriato. : La Vida Económica*. Mexico: Hermes. 635–1297.

Wallerstein, Immanuel. 1984. *El Mercantilismo y la Consolidación de la Economía-Mundo Europea, 1600–1750*. Madrid: Siglo XXI.

——. 1998a. *La Segunda Era de Gran Expansionismo de la Economia-Mundo Capitalista, 1730–1850*. Mexico: Siglo XXI.

——. 1998b. *El Capitalismo Historico*. Mexico: Siglo XXI.

Willem, John M. 1959. *The US Trade Dollar*. New York: Whitman.

Williams, Glen. 1987. *Not for Export: Toward a Political Economy of Canada's Arrested Industrialization*. Updated ed. Toronto: McClelland and Stewart.

Zea Prado, Irene. 1982. *Gestión Diplomática de Anthony Butler en México. 1829–1836*. Mexico: Secretaría de Relaciones Exteriores.

PART TWO
Redefining Institutional Relations:
Continents, States, and Federalism

Although Canada, the US, and Mexico have entered a process of economic integration, they are governed by different institutions. The purposes of this section are threefold: first, to compare the North American integration process to the similar trend that emerged in Europe with the creation of the EU; second, to describe the political institutional settings of each country, to explain how national political institutions work, and to assess the extent to which they have been affected by or affect the North American integration process; and third, to analyze the impacts of economic integration on the capacity of subnational states to develop autonomous policies and their ability to remain important centres of power within and among the three federations.

Stephen Clarkson and Roopa Rangaswami, in Chapter 4, "The Governance of North America: NAFTA's Complex Institutional Structure," examine the institutionalization of the vast array of trans-border interactions involving people, goods, services, energy, information, and natural resources that flow between and across the three states. The authors identify three levels of institutionalization involving interactions between particular groups of actors: the macro level (governments, legislatures, and bureaucracies); the meso level (corporations and non-governmental organizations); and the micro level (individuals). They note the relatively weak macro-level institutional structures for implementation and dispute settlement created by NAFTA, a situation that tends to work in favour of the hegemon, the US, as demonstrated in a series of examples of disputes under NAFTA's Chapter 11. On the other hand, a range of informal civil society groups has been vigorously organizing around problems arising from NAFTA's labour and environmental side agreements, especially regarding the enforcement of labour standards and water and air issues. Through case studies of the automobile, textile, steel, and energy sectors, as well as stock exchanges, Clarkson and Rangaswami demonstrate the successes of market-led institutions in effecting deregulation, most of which has, again, favoured US corporate interests, often through the "harmonization" or assimilation of Canadian and Mexican regulations and practices to those of the US. Finally, after noting the asymmetrical relations regarding defence policies driven by the US's security fears, the authors conclude that the interactions of the macro-, meso-, and micro-level institutions "generate a continental governance that is interest-based, asymmetrical,

US-driven, and largely invisible" and that, taken together, are unlikely to be capable of constraining the actions of the hegemon.

In Chapter 5, "Birth of a Union: Lessons for North America from the European Union," Vincent Della Sala considers whether the 27-member EU can offer any lessons for North American policy and community. He traces the genesis and evolution of the European integration process since World War II, from the modest "coal and steel community" designed (in part) to incorporate Germany and make war a costly option in the future, to the current economic and monetary union developed through landmark agreements such as the 1957 Treaty of Rome, the 1986 Single European Act, and the 1991 Maastricht Treaty. Della Sala briefly outlines and explains the powers and functions of the key institutional structures of the EU: the European Commission, the unelected executive whose very existence has raised questions about democratic accountability and transparency; the elected but limited European Parliament; the European Council, which provides intergovernmental representation; and the European Court of Justice, whose decisions trump national courts and laws when they conflict with EU legislation. Apart from concerns about democracy, accountability, and national sovereignty, the institutions of the EU have triggered debates about identity and belonging to "social Europe," especially around issues such as immigration and the welfare state. In the author's view, the EU experience of multi-level governance might be of use to North America if designed on the "condominium" model or sectoral basis whereby specific institutions govern areas of overlapping policy such as the environment, security, and macroeconomic policy. However, Della Sala remains sceptical about the willingness of US political elites to defer to supranational institutions to set common policy or to resolve conflicts (note the US's continual disregard of five NAFTA tribunal/WTO decisions in Canada's favour in the softwood lumber dispute), unless manifestly in their national interest. Thus, any North American integration beyond the economic is bound to encounter serious challenges, especially in the areas of community building and democratic legitimacy in the context of a serious asymmetry of power.

The four following chapters examine the current political institutional structures of the three countries with a view to analyzing the extent to which they have been affected or have themselves affected North American integration in particular or globalization in general.

The themes of democracy and representation, group accommodation, and legitimacy undergird Samuel A. Bottomley's analysis of the effects of globalization and NAFTA on Canadian political institutions in Chapter 6, "Globalization and the Democratic Deficit: Challenging Times for Canada's Political Institutions." The author points out that Canada's political institutions have always been influenced by external forces, to wit, the virtual replication of the Westminster system of the imperial mother country, modified by a US-style (but more decentralized) version of federalism. However, the concentration of power in the federal executive has led to perceptions of a "democratic deficit" in Canada, as evidenced by falling voter turnout rates and calls from many quarters for reform of the ineffectual House of Commons, the unelected Senate, and the single-member plurality electoral system. The democratic deficit has been intensified over the last two decades as the flexibility of the Canadian system has permitted significant expansions of the already formidable powers of the prime minister (especially in foreign policy) as well as the role of the courts since the 1982 Constitution Act. The latter are scheduled to play an increasingly important role in adjudicating trade-related disputes under NAFTA and other international agreements, although given the few cases decided to date it is not yet clear whether such agreements have to be consistent with the Canadian Charter of Rights and Freedoms, or whether the courts can or will be willing to overrule NAFTA tribunal decisions.

As US political institutions (especially federalism) have had a significant effect on the design of their counterparts in both Canada and Mexico, Ross Burkhart assesses the ability of US federal institutions to maintain their integrity in this era of globalization and evaluates their strengths and weaknesses in Chapter 7, "Political Institutions in the United States." Burkhart argues that federalism, Congress, the presidency, the judicial system, and the bureaucracy have more shaped than been shaped by globalization. However, he notes that NAFTA may lead to a net decrease in the powers of US political institutions, notwithstanding the increased concentration of powers in the presidency post-9/11 and a rise in the power of certain arms of the bureaucracy, such as the Department of Homeland Security. Yet US institutions may ultimately be weakened by such forces as WTO and NAFTA dispute resolution mechanisms and tribunals (which can impose decisions and displace the courts as arbiters of the law regardless of domestic law and democratic preferences) and by corporate challenges to state laws or decisions under NAFTA's Chapter 11. Nevertheless, Burkhart concludes, in the absence of EU-style supranational political institutions, those that presently configure the US political system will probably survive more or less intact for some time to come.

Chapter 8, "Political Institutions in Mexico," by José Crespo, N. Borrego, and Ana Luz Ruelas, analyzes the legacy of an earlier form of globalization—colonialism—on the operation and functioning of Mexican political institutions. Specifically, the authors argue that although from the nineteenth century Mexico adopted a presidential system modeled on that of the US, the political and cultural legacy of the Spanish conquest (and the three-century viceroyalty period) was authoritarianism superimposed over sharp ethnic and class inequalities. As a result, the actual workings of the institutions associated with Mexico's presidential republic operate less than optimally from the standpoint of democracy. As one prominent instance, the authors highlight how in "unified governments" (when the president comes from the same party that holds the majority in Congress) there is the danger of the president emerging as a virtual dictator. Conversely, in "divided governments" (when the party holding the majority in Congress differs from that of the president) there is a danger that the president may seek to dissolve Congress illegally in order to avoid paralysis and exercise power.

Crespo, Borrego, and Ruelas trace contemporary examples that reflect the ongoing quest for a stable democratic regime in post-revolutionary Mexico. During much of the twentieth century, Mexico, while formally a multiparty system, was in actuality dominated by the Institutional Revolutionary Party (PRI) as well as by strong presidents. The PRI's defeat in the 2000 election, and the emergence of Vicente Fox from the National Action Party (PAN) as president, was thus a major change of power and reflected the emergence of a more competitive multiparty system in practice. This change, along with attempted reforms in the judiciary to consolidate the rule of law and new forms of transnational organizing in the NAFTA countries among popular groups (e.g., those relating to women, labour, and the environment) speak to the ongoing quest for democracy. Nonetheless, the 2006 presidential election has raised to the fore issues of democracy and legitimacy because the declared victory of Felipe Calderón (PAN) over Andrés M. López Obrador is marred by suspicions of electoral fraud on the part of the Mexican government.

François Rocher and Gordon DiGiacomo take on the vicissitudes of federalism in Chapter 9, "National Institutions in North America: US, Canadian, and Mexican Federalism." Although similar in some respects, the three systems differ in very important ways, especially in the fiscal powers allocated to central and provincial/state governments and in the degree of autonomy of the latter from the former. The authors review the different trajectories federalism took historically in each country, outlining the major factors that explain how, for instance, Canada became the least and Mexico the most centralized of the three. They assess the extent to which federalism has been affected by globalization in general and NAFTA in particular, suggesting that although international trade agreements have the potential to be a centralizing force, they have "not had the transformative effect on [the three] federal systems that many predicted." The effects on Mexican federalism have been indirect, through the rejuvenation of the competitive party system rather than by a redistribution of powers; in Canada, Ottawa's constitutional power over international trade was supplemented by its commitment to "collaborative federalism" to secure provincial agreement on invasions of their jurisdictions; and the US had already centralized economic regulation in Washington since the Great Depression, and besides, they argue, "globalization does not stand in fundamental contradiction, culturally or intellectually, to the American federal arrangement."

CHAPTER FOUR

The Governance of North America
NAFTA's Complex Institutional Structure[1]

Stephen Clarkson and Roopa Rangaswami

Introduction

At first glance, North America hardly seems to exist as a political entity. Unlike the more deeply institutionalized EU, it has no juridical standing in the global system of states with the capacity to sign treaties with other international players. Still, the term "North America" now designates considerably more than a triad of contiguous countries to the north of Guatemala.

NAFTA's implementation in 1994 by Mexico, Canada, and the US did much to make visible what had been developing over many decades: a continental reality that was somewhat more than the sum of its three states. While it remains true that the overwhelming majority of politically salient institutions on this vast territory operate within its three countries' national boundaries, it is also obvious that their frontiers are far from impermeable. Indeed the people, goods, services, energy, information, and natural resources which are constantly moving to and fro across the Canada-US and Mexico-US frontiers and even directly between Canada and Mexico create a multitude of transboundary relations requiring political supervision and regulation. It is these interactions whose variegated institutionalization we propose to discuss.

Were we, in exploring to what extent one can validly talk about the "governance" of North America, to set the conceptual bar very high, we could easily find the continent remarkable for having generated no institutions beyond the quite feeble bodies established by NAFTA. For this chapter, we lower the bar by starting from the premise that every relationship—at whatever level of society, whether formal or informal, permanent or occasional—can be understood as structured behaviour. The degree to which a given example of structured behaviour has been institutionalized[2] is a question for empirical research, and our objective in these pages is to show the enormous variety that characterizes the institutionalization of transnational relationships in North America. To do this it will help to distinguish between three levels of institutionalization, from most to least formal.

At the *macro* level, governmental structures operate as formal, often constitutionally established institutions such as legislatures and bureaucracies. When one Mexican state's environmental official interacts with a US state regulator across the binational border, this can be considered a transnational relationship. Even if it does not include a parallel Canadian component, this kind of intergovernmental interaction constitutes one element in North America's institutional structure.

At the *meso* level, NGOs in civil society and corporations in the marketplace generally have more self-directed than political mandates. When their interactions are institutionalized in the form of subsidiaries operating in another North American country, or of NGO alliances coordinating activities across one or both national borders, we are dealing with another, but more informal element of North America's institutional reality.

On the whole, relations at the *micro* level of daily human exchanges are institutionalized within, but not between states through public policies such as laws establishing the conditions for marriage. But when an Ontario Supreme Court ruling in favour of gay marriage is cited by the Massachusetts Supreme Court (Supreme Judicial Court of Massachusetts 2003) to justify a similar position, the subtle, if formally uninstitutionalized, fabric of North America's legal community becomes momentarily visible.

Starting with NAFTA (the one agreement that juridically, if incompletely, structured the three countries' economic relations) as a broad framework of continental governance, we will review the informal parallel institutions generated from civil society; survey leading examples of market-led institutions; and, finally, analyze the formal institutions created by the three federal governments to provide security against both state and non-state enemies. We will conclude with an assessment of the impact of formal versus informal institutions and their important linkages with the larger issue of continental governance.

This chapter takes issue with the notion that North America suffers from an institutional void (Clarkson 2000: 228–66). We ask not whether, but what types of institutions structure the myriad transborder relations of individuals, groups, corporations, and governments with the clear understanding that these structures are as likely to be informal as formal, as likely to be occasional as regular, and as likely to be changeable as fixed. Informal institutions have emerged as the salient force in a nascent continental governance, overshadowing in their impact the more formalized institutions, bodies, and working groups provided for in NAFTA. Without making any claim to completeness, our hope is that these probes of the North American reality will give readers a more nuanced understanding of the complex governance that lurks beneath the surface of North America's apparent institutional deficit.

NAFTA's Institutions for Economic Governance

As the official manifestation of continental economic integration, NAFTA was distinguished by each partner's extreme reluctance to institutionalize a continuing relationship. Understandably, the global hegemon had little interest in tying its hands with institutions that might concede some decision-making parity to its two geographical neighbours. For equal but opposite reasons, Canada had long resisted becoming involved in a more formal continental institution. Even when it negotiated CUFTA in 1988, Ottawa's main aim was to avoid institutional entanglements while putting limits on the harassment that the US government could impose on Canadian exporters by its unilateral acts of protectionism.

After President Vicente Fox's election in 2000, Mexico was to become the most articulate advocate of EU-type institutions that would presumably constrain the independent policy-making of the US. However, during the NAFTA negotiations in the early 1990s, his predecessor, President Salinas de Gortari, accepted CUFTA's weak-institution model as the organizational premise for his trade negotiations. Having had to comply with the prescriptions of the IMF and World Bank in the wake of its severe financial crisis in the early 1980s, Mexico felt it had been on the receiving end of enough US-directed multilateral institutions' dictates.

The lowest common denominator of the three states' differing motivations for signing up for continental economic integration was a formal institutional structure of almost laughable vacuity. The NAFTA Free Trade Commission (FTC) has neither address nor office, since it consists of little more than the sporadic meetings of the member-countries' trade ministers. Equally lacking in organizational infrastructure are the 30-odd committees and working groups established by the agreement's various chapters to oversee their provisions' implementation. In one case (tariff reduction), the working group did its job by accelerating the process and subsequently becoming dormant. In another instance (financial services), the periodic meetings of the three countries' delegated civil servants provided a means for the Mexicans to be kept informed of their neighbours' latest banking regulations, while the US and Canadian participants considered the committee's meeting a mere formality. NAFTA's implementation under the supervision of these working groups was meant to reduce the asymmetry inherent in the continent's power relations while simultaneously de-politicizing the manner in which conflicts were resolved between member governments. Since the three countries often had conflicting objectives, mid-level civil servants were severely circumscribed in their ability to carry out the working groups' apolitical mandate (Clarkson *et al.* 2005).

NAFTA'S JUDICIAL INSTITUTIONS

Even though NAFTA was carefully designed to maintain maximum national autonomy by preventing any strong institutions from developing, it nevertheless established a number of procedures for settling conflicts that might arise from differing interpretations of its multitudinous clauses. It would be too much to claim that the dispute settlement mechanisms provided in Chapters 20, 19, and 11—along with the conflict resolution processes contained in the environmental and labour side agreements—constitute a formal legal structure for the continent. Nevertheless, some of these adjudication mechanisms are NAFTA's most substantial institutional components.

The binational panels provided for under Chapter 20 to deal with general disputes arising from NAFTA's various provisions have turned out to be ineffective mainly because their rulings are not binding. Furthermore, certain Chapter 20 disputes have not been resolved satisfactorily without negotiation and court rulings, essentially nullifying the goal of institutionalizing a system of neutral arbitration. This is most clearly illustrated by the trucking dispute between the US and Mexico. In June 2004, after nearly ten years of meetings and diplomacy, the US Supreme Court overturned a prior ruling which essentially blocked the entry of Mexican trucks. The Chapter 20 panel's initial ruling that Washington was at fault and its recommendation that the US moratorium on Mexican trucks be lifted played a virtually negligible role in the issue's resolution. As a result of this kind of experience, the three states have resorted less and less to Chapter 20 in resolving their differences since it provides no genuinely depoliticized alternative to the US-dominated politics that had previously characterized bilateral relations in North America.

Chapter 19 panel rulings are binding in principle but ineffectual in practice when the periphery is confronting the hegemon on a major issue involving entrenched US interests. Designed to guard against the unfair application of countervail (CVD) and anti-dumping (AD) duties, Chapter 19 has had very different effects in each member country. The participation of US legal professionals in the panels' deliberations has caused Canada to become more accommodating to US interpretations of standards used in AD and CVD determinations. In Mexico, NAFTA required the creation of a completely new system of applying trade remedy legislation. In contrast to its civil law system, the Mexican government adopted new common-law judicial procedures to ensure uniformity in the application of trade remedy legislation continentally.

With the hegemon, the Chapter 19 story has been different. The US has complied with Chapter 19 panel decisions in cases of limited policy importance where complying with remands does not face strong resistance from domestic lobby groups. But disciplining the US's behaviour on issues of major policy importance is another matter. The long-drawn-out softwood lumber dispute between Canada and the US illustrates Chapter 19's institutional weakness: the US has repeatedly violated the spirit of its continental obligations when faced with a key national lobby. Compliance with panel decisions is easy when the economic stakes are low, but when faced with a politically volatile domestic interest, the US can be expected to disregard the NAFTA process.

The softwood lumber case highlights NAFTA's legal asymmetry: Chapters 19 and 20 are not able to constrain or determine the behaviour of the hegemon, which, for its part, can use these panels to enforce NAFTA rules in its periphery. But if Chapters 19 and 20 are weak as institutions of continental governance, Chapter 11 is remarkably strong.

Chapter 11's procedure for enabling NAFTA investors to get international tribunals to examine their claims against domestic governments' measures is significant because the resulting arbitration is binding. Since it operates according to the norms of international commercial law, Chapter 11 actually withdraws adjudication of disputes over government policies from the realm of national jurisdiction. This can be seen most clearly in two major Chapter 11 cases: the arbitration launched by Ethyl Corporation (against a ban on the cross-border trade of a gasoline additive thought to be a neuro-toxin) and S.D. Myers (against Ottawa's regulation disallowing the export of highly toxic PCBs) resulted in the invalidation of these legislative or administrative measures. Apart from its effect on the countries' sovereignty, Chapter 11's deference to corporate claims of expropriation has serious consequences for environmental regulation over which it has cast a chill.

EPISTEMIC COMMUNITIES

In conjunction with these formalized legal procedures, another continental institution is emerging in the shape of an informal community of the trade lawyers, retired judges, and trade-law scholars who staff these dispute settlement panels. As the body of arbitration and jurisprudence grows, panels are looking more seriously at one another's decisions and precedents, lending more consistency and continuity to the ad hoc panel process. This unstructured community is growing in importance, lending weight to proposals for a formal NAFTA trade court or appellate body to strengthen the continent's existing dispute settlement system.

Having reviewed NAFTA's judicial institution, we will now turn to the parallel institutions generated from civil society.

Institutions for Civil Society

Beyond its legal framework, NAFTA created two deliberately circumscribed commissions to give merely symbolic recognition to US environmentalists' and trade unionists' concerns about the implications of NAFTA's facilitation of growing continental trade and investment flows. The perception of these institutions' weakness has in turn fostered informal networks of civil society groups that are becoming significant in addressing various continental social issues. At the same time, less formal transborder institutions have been put in place in response to grass roots concerns about the availability, quality, or quantity of such necessities as water and air. This section will address these less visible manifestations of continental governance.

WATER

Intergovernmental cooperation on environmental matters along the borders has long pre-dated NAFTA. Agreements on how to manage, control, and remediate polluted lakes and rivers along and across their national borders were deemed necessary by all three governments as population growth and industrialization created competing interests for the use of the continent's water resources. Canada-US water governance dates back to the 1909 Boundary Waters Treaty, which established the International Joint Commission (IJC). This genuinely binational body, in which both partners have equal representation, has had its mandate extended from a quantitative oversight—supervising the flows, diversions, and water levels of rivers and lakes crossing the international boundary—to include such qualitative concerns as the toxification of the Great Lakes. The IJC is a formal transnational institution with substantial responsibilities, although the federal, state, provincial, and municipal governments in the border zones determine through their budget allocations and statutory regulations the actual fate of Canada-US water issues.

The management of water resources and pollution control along the Mexico-US border presents few parallels with the Canada-US situation. Formal US-Mexico cooperation began with the 1944 Treaty Relating to the Utilization of Waters of the Colorado and Tijuana Rivers and of the Rio Grande. Sixty years of industrialization and rapid demographic growth in the border area have put intense pressure on water supply and strained the region's limited sewage infrastructure. The emission of the new *maquiladoras*' hazardous waste into rivers shared with the US border states remains a contentious issue between the two countries. These problems are far more acute than those along the 49th parallel, and transborder water management remains both under-institutionalized and underfunded. With infrastructure quality at virtually third-world levels and water demand far exceeding supply, binational conflict has tended to trump transborder cooperation. While formal institutions have done little to address the problems of water management, cross-border citizen groups and local governments are becoming more vocal about border-region needs and are demanding solutions.

AIR

However essential for human health the quality of air may be, the transport of airborne toxins, which can travel long distances, is nearly impossible to regulate in a territory divided by jurisdictional boundaries. Government regulation of air quality issues in North America has traditionally been a mixture of domestic standards (whether federal, state, or provincial), bilateral agreements such as the air quality accord between the US and Canada, and multilateral protocols. Due to differing governmental standards, the multiple sources of pollution (from personal vehicles to large industries), and the difficulty in making polluters accountable for their transboundary impacts, conflict has characterized Canada-US relations concerning the management of air quality, because the hegemon is the larger source of pollution and its northern neighbour a net importer of noxious airborne chemicals.

Following intense pressure by Ottawa, the two countries signed air quality agreements in the early 1980s, but US commitments to reduce its acid rain production actually resulted from internal political struggles within that country during which the eastern states managed to impose some controls on the coal-burning electricity-generating states of the Ohio River Valley.

The impact of power asymmetries is apparent in this domain as well. When a Mexican coal-burning smelter threatened to pollute Texas, intergovernmental pressures were brought to bear more speedily and effectively than when the US was the exporter of acid rain. In effect, the institutionalized nature of air quality management in North America is an ad hoc system of intergovernmental relations in which the weaker peripheries deal separately with their dominant partner to obtain what concessions are compatible with its domestic political struggles.

Though there is no formal trilateral governmental regulation of air quality in North America, informal scientific networks and environmental NGOs working on the issue of transboundary air pollution are emerging. Informal institutions are also developing, thanks to the growing ability of communities affected by air pollution from foreign sources to confront polluters or governments in other jurisdictions, through lawsuits and/or bilateral agreements.

More apparently consequential was the creation of NAFTA's North American Commission for Environmental Cooperation (NACEC) to connect the environment institutionally with trade issues at the continental level. While it was heralded as an innovation, its mandate was constrained from the outset by governments seeking to avoid further continental commitments. As a result, the political importance of the NACEC has been the support it has offered to networks of NGOs and other informal transnational bodies, particularly helping Mexican environmentalists to gain legitimacy and to increase their effectiveness within their own polity. In sum, informal institutions have proved more important in generating environmental governance in North America, with formal institutions playing a weak supporting role.

LABOUR

Parallel with US environmentalists' fears that NAFTA would foster ecological disasters from uncontrolled *maquiladora* production along the Mexican border, US trade unions' concerns about job losses and a "race to the bottom" resulting from free trade led to the creation of the North American Commission on Labour Cooperation (NACLC) with a mandate to defend labour rights continentally. The NACLC does not create new continental labour norms; however, it does stipulate the enforcement of domestic labour standards in member states.

In practice, the NACLC's 11 labour rights were only as significant as their means of enforcement, and none of the eight standards prescribing trade union rights was enforceable through dispute settlement. Only three technical labour standards—protection for youth or children, health and safety, and minimum wages—were theoretically enforceable, but the dispute procedures were designed to make it virtually impossible for an NGO to win a case. Not only did the NACLC fail to make its members enforce their labour standards, it did not even prevent member governments from lowering their statutory protections for workers, as happened in Ontario under Premier Mike Harris in the late 1990s and in Mexico under President Fox after 2000.

There was an unexpected consequence of the NACLC's ineffectiveness as an instrument for trade unions trying to support workers' rights: some labour-union solidarity was fostered across the two national boundaries as workers' organizations learned to cooperate in their struggles for improved working conditions (Macdonald 2003: 29–52). In this respect, the NACLC and the NACEC inadvertently generated a modest, informal, and spasmodic institutionalization at the grass roots.

Market-led Institutions

The extraordinary feature of the North American marketplace is the extent to which its many sectors have increased their cross-border integration without the three states' establishing formal institutions to manage these economic relationships. Institutions have emerged, to be sure, but in response to specific problems and, generally, at the meso rather than the macro level.

Even when the three business communities mobilized their forces to direct their governments' trade negotiators, the business-government relationships in each country were institutionalized for that purpose alone. When the national borders again experienced a crisis following 9/11, various business coalitions were put in place and intense business-government negotiations ensued without any corporatist structures being left in place (Clarkson and Banda 2007).

AUTOMOBILES

Exceptional in this regard is the automobile industry which, in the Canadian case, was structured by a formal agreement negotiated between the Canadian and US governments, the Big Four companies' head offices, and their Canadian subsidiaries. The Auto Pact of 1965 established the parameters for the Canadian car-assembly sector until its provisions were dismantled under "free trade." NAFTA's rules of origin, which only specified how much North American—as opposed to Canadian—content was required in every car assembled, deprived the Canadian governments of the legal clout that the Auto Pact had once provided them to persuade the automobile transnational corporations (TNCs) to locate their activities north of the border. With the Auto Pact's remaining protections dismantled following a ruling by the WTO in 2000, the institutional framework established for Canada's industry disintegrated. As a result, the continental auto market is structured by the TNCs themselves in response to their continental and global competitive conjuncture.

TEXTILES

The same corporate-driven economic integration and the use of NAFTA's rules created a more regionally based thinking in the textile industry, which has been invisibly structured through free trade. NAFTA's rules of origin effectively protected the major US textile corporations while providing limited but specific access to the US market for Canadian and Mexican companies. Canada and the US became each other's largest export markets, while Mexican exports soared at the expense of Caribbean producers. Post-NAFTA, Mexico became the base of operations for North American firms seeking to reduce costs in intensive labour production.

An informal continental institution in the textile market emerged, as NAFTA created additional opportunities for North American textile manufacturers to take advantage of advanced Canadian and US technology to produce basic textile goods at relatively low labour cost in Mexico and ship them back to domestic markets quickly. While larger US or Canadian manufacturers invested directly in Mexico, some mid-sized firms entered joint ventures as a means of capitalizing on Mexico's competitive advantage in labour without the outlay required to set up their own factories. The size of the US industry and greater mutual textile trade between the superpower and its northern neighbour, coupled with Canada's focus on its own domestic industry, promoted the consolidation of a US-centred textile industry with strong peripheries, Mexico becoming a hub of out-sourcing for Canadian and US firms in the wake of growing global competition.

STEEL

NAFTA's failure to create genuine free trade by eliminating the application of AD and CVD to member states' exports had different structuring effects in the steel sector. This was noticeable in the Canadian industry, whose exports to the US continued to be victimized by that country's trade harassment measures. As an avoidance strategy, new investments by Canadian steel manufacturers were made principally in the US, where they became active members in the main lobby organization, the American Iron and Steel Institute. With a Canadian presiding over the industry's labour union, the United Steelworkers of America, the Canadian sector is becoming an integral part of what was formerly its US competitor. The resulting Americanization of the Canadian steel sector has created a more US-weighted continental industry in which Mexican and Canadian firms participate from newly located niches in the US.

ENERGY

Energy demonstrates another set of institutions, the characteristics of each fuel generating a different balance between market autonomy and state intervention. The oil sector has been mainly competitive in and between the US and Canada. Although the industry is now largely self-regulated, it still operates within the framework created by globally established prices; by CUFTA's prohibition of Canadian government interventionism; and by each country's tax policies, resource-management programs, policies, standards, and subsidies. While directed by government policy, the Canadian oil industry has integrated fully with its US counterpart on a regional basis under the aegis of US controlled corporate capital. The distribution of natural gas being a natural monopoly in which a single firm supplies the energy to all consumers, government policy has typically been more interventionist.

In Mexico, both oil and gas are protected under Article 27 of its Constitution as a public good. This constitutionally entrenched nationalization has restrained the integration that would otherwise have resulted from the high US demand for ever-increasing supplies of fuel. The two sectors are almost entirely owned and controlled by the state corporation, Pemex, which is the country's largest single exporter. With the government draining Pemex profits into its general revenue fund, the Mexican petroleum sector cannot modernize or expand through reinvestment.

Electricity has its roots as a public utility in all three NAFTA countries because of the high capital costs originally required for its generation and the natural monopoly created by single provider distribution. Directed in the US by the efforts of the Federal Energy Regulatory Commission (FERC) to create competition in generation and distribution, the forces of privatization are creating an increasingly deregulated private sector, with the different states linked by electricity trading through networks and grids. Ontario, Québec, and British Columbia's hydro-based public utilities have sold power to the US for a few decades, but by imposing reciprocity conditions on foreign entities wanting to sell in the US market, FERC requires Canadian provinces exporting electricity to adopt the same deregulatory policies as it imposes in the US. Although not sanctioned by NAFTA, FERC is forcing deregulation in those provinces, where corporate interests have supported the privatization cause. FERC's informal reciprocity dictates have more influence on provincial hydro policies than do NAFTA's less stringent national treatment provisions.

Protected from privatization and foreign ownership by Article 27 of its Constitution, Mexico's electricity market is dominated by the Comisión Federal de Electricidad. Limited binational integration exists in some US-Mexico border areas where electricity flows in both directions, but pressures for change come largely from the critical discrepancy between projections of rapid increases in demand and the system's incapacity to expand production and distribution.

NAFTA's energy provisions on continental integration and the current efforts at cooperation by the three governments in the North America Energy Working Group (NAEWG) are minor in effect but point to possible growth in intergovernmental activity, especially given Mexico's participation in this group. However, FERC has proven the more effective force dominating the continental political agenda in the energy sector.

STOCK EXCHANGES

The three countries' separate stock exchanges demonstrate a more market-driven institutionalization. For over a century prior to NAFTA, the US capital market dominated those of its northern and southern neighbours even in its early unregulated form. Institutionalization in this sector can be seen in the extent to which corporations in the two peripheries seek to list their shares in the US stock exchanges, and US TNCs raise capital in the markets where their branch plants operate.

Continuing continentalization can be seen when the reach of US exchanges causes Canadian and Mexican exchanges to harmonize their regulations with US standards. Much more autonomous in its formal sovereignty, the Mexican stock exchange has suffered from an even higher incidence of Mexican corporations raising capital in the US market. Increasing cross-listing of US-based TNCs in Canadian stock exchanges and Canadian-based corporations in the US market threaten to make the Canadian sector follow Mexico's steps, becoming a mere territorial extension of the US exchange.

However, formal institutions exist to mute the intensity of this integrative trajectory. The two peripheries' own stock exchanges are trying to bolster themselves in the face of US dominance. Efforts are being made in Canada to replace the provinces' separate regulatory regimes with a single exchange for the domestic market. In Mexico, where the government both manages and controls the market, hesitant steps are being taken to sustain a domestic capital market within a globalized system. This ineffectual response in the periphery to the continental leader is mirrored in the accountancy profession following the collapse of Anderson, when US reforms were adopted by Canadian and Mexican accounting firms.

State-generated Security Institutions

Security in North America has been institutionally skewed for most of the twentieth century, with Canada integrating actively in US military institutions and Mexico maintaining a committed non-alignment. The Cold War marked an important watershed in consolidating Canada's military dependence on its southern neighbour. During these four decades, when Washington's highest priority was security from the Soviet Union's nuclear threat, Canada's military stance was best described by the principle of "defence against help." This meant that, if Ottawa did not provide what the US considered adequate land, sea, and air forces to defend Canadian territory against enemy attack, the Pentagon would act unilaterally and with minimal consideration given to Canada's sovereignty. The chief expression of the resulting military integration was the North American Air Defence Organization (NORAD), in which the Royal Canadian Air Force operated as an integral part of the US Strategic Air Command. The extent to which the Pentagon determined Canadian military policy was illustrated in 1983 when, despite Prime Minister Trudeau's desire to suffocate the arms race, he found himself obliged to allow the US to test over Canadian territory the next generation of its long-range weaponry, the Cruise missile.

Since the outbreak of the Bush administration's war on terrorism, military security for the continent has been reconfigured by the Pentagon's Northern Command (NORTHCOM) with which the Canadian Army and Navy were pressed to cooperate. While NORAD is a formal institution, there exists almost no decision-making parity at the operational level. Strategic decisions are essentially made by US political authorities who allow minimal Canadian participation. Canada has continued to deepen its defence integration with the US due to its long history of military cooperation, pressure from its domestic defence establishment, a dependent and vulnerable economy, and constant US government pressure.

The US-Mexican defence relationship has seen few similar initiatives at integration. With minimal military cooperation in the past, a constitution strictly forbidding the movement of troops abroad, national resistance to integrative initiatives, and resistance from Mexican military leaders, Mexico seems unlikely to become an active partner with NORTHCOM and has adopted a stance of delaying and stalling. Little has developed in the domain of informal security institutions.

To the extent that security against terrorism is a non-military issue, Mexico has been drawn into closer integration with Washington's new policy paradigm which declares that its Mexican border must be as impenetrable to hostile agents and their weaponry as its northern border, which has been tightened by the numerous measures defined in the Canada-US 30-point Smart Border Plan of December 2001. US-Mexico security cooperation derives from the struggle against narcotraffic and the resulting transborder cooperation between adjacent municipalities and states. The elaboration of a parallel, 22-point Smart Border plan in early 2002 heralded a new level of intergovernmental coordination on the continent in which the two peripheries responded to Washington's requirements that its security be as absolute as humanly and technologically possible. In all these cases, security responses since 9/11 have bolstered intergovernmental institutionalization in the continent.

Conclusion

Reflecting on these various types of formal and informal institutions in North America, it is evident that the institutions established by NAFTA in the judicial, environment, labour, and market sectors have proven to be of minimal relevance in governing the continent, either because their functions have been deliberately circumscribed by the three member governments, or because the reality of the continent's power asymmetries has restricted their effectiveness. The weakness of formal institutions means that continental governance is less universal and more interest-based, utterly lacking in uniformity or coherence.

NAFTA's uneven dispute settlement processes have proven ineffectual in governing economic relations between Canada, Mexico, and the US, but Chapter 11's provisions for binding arbitration have significant potential for regulatory chill.

With one exception, little formal governance has been established to deal with continental market activities. Energy provisions in NAFTA and the NAEWG take second place to the directives of FERC and the larger forces of market deregulation. In the North American financial markets, there is a struggle between informal pressures attempting to advance integration and those institutions trying to resist it. The forces of capital integration are currently dominant, resulting in the further interpenetration of Canadian and Mexican stock exchanges by US capital.

The exception to the continuing insignificance of the continent's formal institutions is the Security and Prosperity Partnership of North America that was set up by the three national leaders in March 2005 and the North American Competitiveness Council (NACC) that was added one year later. To start with, the SPP amounted to little more than some 300 very specific, trade-related measures aimed to counteract the border barriers resulting from US-driven security concerns. What the NACC has added is a periodic meeting of ten top business executives from each country with the three countries' ministers or secretaries of foreign affairs, security, and trade. This institutionalized access privileging big business in the three states' federal executives and bypassing the three legislatures' democratic processes is an extraordinary innovation suggesting that the neoconservative paradigm still remains dominant. NACC may prove to be the embryo of a new corporate-led continental governance having a powerful impact in the shorter term on trilateral regulatory harmonization and sparking further continental integration in the longer term.

When looking at environmental and labour issues, cross-border coalitions of experts are developing, but not to the point that they challenge domestic governments. As institutions such as the IJC decline in importance in managing border issues, NGOs, human rights groups, and other members of civil society have created informal institutions and networks in response to NAFTA's incapacity to address important issues.

The interaction of institutions at the macro and meso levels generates a continental governance that is interest-based, asymmetrical, US-driven, and largely invisible. The contradictory impacts of these institutions result in struggles in the periphery between those pressing for still deeper integration and those seeking greater autonomy from the US. It is unlikely, however, that the creation of these informal institutions will successfully address the persistent power imbalances on the continent or constrain the actions of its hegemon.

Notes

1   We would like to acknowledge the assistance of Kate Fischer, Emily Tan, Christiane Buie, Nick Brandon, Ben Hutchinson, Nital Jethalal, and Ben Hyman, as well as the financial support of the Dean of the Faculty of Arts and Science at the University of Toronto which made possible a research trip to Washington, DC in March 2004 by the authors and these students. This research has also been supported by the Social Sciences and Humanities Research Council of Canada.

The text draws on two previously published works, Stephen Clarkson, *Uncle Sam and Us: Globalization, Neoconservatism, and the Canadian State* (University of Toronto Press and Woodrow Wilson Press, 2002), chapter 4; and Stephen Clarkson and Roopa Rangaswami, "Canada and Continental Integration under NAFTA," in James Bickerton and Alain Gagnon (eds.), *Canadian Politics*, 4th ed. (Broadview Press, 2004): 389–401.

2   Peter Hall (1986) defines institutions as the formal rules, compliance procedures, and standard operating practices that structure the relationship between individuals in various units of the polity and economy. Consequently, they have a more formal status than cultural norms. Since institutions may derive from conventions and customs, they do not necessarily form formal structures. Throughout this chapter, our emphasis will be on the relational character of various institutions; that is to say, on the way in which they structure the interactions of individuals, groups, or corporations.

References

Clarkson, Stephen. 2000. "Do Deficits Imply Surpluses? Towards a Democratic Audit of North America." In Michael Greven and Louis Pauly (eds.), *Democracy Beyond National Borders*. New York: Rowman and Littlefield and Toronto: U of Toronto P. 228–66.

Clarkson, Stephen, and Maria Banda. 2007. "Paradigm Shift or Paradigm Twist? The Impact of the Bush Doctrine on Canada." In Ricardo Grinspun (ed.), *The Slippery Slope: Canada, Free Trade, and Deep Integration in North America*. Montreal and Kingston: McGill-Queen's UP.

Clarkson, Stephen, and Sarah Davidson Ladly, Megan Merwart, and Carleton Thorne. 2005. "The Primitive Realities of Continental Governance in North America." In Edgar Grande and Louis W. Pauly (eds.), *Reconstituting Political Authority: Complex Sovereignty and the Foundations of Global Governance*. Toronto: U of Toronto P.

Hall, Peter. 1986. *Governing the Economy: The Politics of State Intervention in Britain and France*. Cambridge: Polity Press.

Macdonald, Ian. 2003. "NAFTA and the Emergence of Continental Labor Cooperation." *The American Review of Canadian Studies* (Summer): 29–52.

Supreme Judicial Court of Massachusetts. 2003. *Hillary Goodridge & Others [FN1] vs. Department of Public Health & Another.* [FN2] Docket No. SJC-08860. March 4–November 18.

CHAPTER FIVE

Birth of a Union
Lessons for North America from the European Union

Vincent Della Sala

There are few examples that North Americans may call upon to understand the process of continental integration that can match the EU. In the space of less than half a century, states and societies that had gone to war with each other repeatedly, leading to at least two major conflicts in the twentieth century, have forged a polity that has no parallel. Europeans not only share a currency and freedom of movement that is almost as easy as crossing state or provincial borders but also an emerging foreign policy, a defence component, and possibly in the near future a formal constitution. In January 2007, its membership expanded from 15 to 27 members, ranging from Ireland in the west to Bulgaria in the east, Finland in the north to Malta in the Mediterranean. Clearly, the EU is the most developed form of continental integration among member states that we can find today; as such, it has become a laboratory for scholars and observers of regional integration. But does it offer any lessons for the emerging North American polity and community?

In the following, I will identify some of the main steps in the European integration process as well as its most important institutional and societal features. There are many factors that make the European example unique, but this does not mean that there may not be useful lessons to be drawn from it. It illustrates the fact that important decisions that shape our lives are taking place in new sites, are taking on forms different from those based on the national state, and are forcing us to explore new models to map them out. The EU provides us with lessons and experiences that may help us to make sense of how politics beyond the boundaries of the state may take shape. I argue that rather than think about what kind of state-like structure we may be heading towards in North America, the case of the EU may provide us with different scenarios to consider. However, whatever path is pursued, it must address the fundamental question of how to govern increasingly complex relationships in ways that are compatible with democratic and legitimate governance.

Historical Context

Locating the historical locus of European integration can be a difficult affair that could take us back to the Renaissance or even ancient Rome. For present purposes, I will focus on attempts in the immediate aftermath of World War II (Gilbert 2003) when the task of reconstruction and the desire to avoid major conflicts on the continent led political and social actors to seek closer forms of cooperation. Plans for European integration considered not only the experiences that had led to war in the past 100 years but also to the emerging tension in Europe as the Cold War began to take shape at the end of the 1940s. Right from the start there were two camps that, although sharing a desire for closer ties between European states and societies, held different visions of the future European construction. The first group, which has been called that of the idealists, federalists, or supranationalists, aimed to create a new continental political union that superseded the national state. Their vision, despite the horrors unleashed by nationalism in the middle of the century, was premature in the late 1940s and 1950s. The second group, which might be called intergovernmentalist, looked to a looser form of integration between national states pursuing primarily limited economic objectives.

While the first steps towards integration may have had the intergovernmental imprint, they contained seeds that would eventually lead to integration that went well beyond the economy. The Schuman Plan, drafted by the French official Jean Monnet, was introduced in May 1950 by the French Foreign Minister, Robert Schuman. It called for the creation of a European "coal and steel community" in which the borders for these essential industrial materials would disappear. This seemingly technical measure had a precise political objective: to bring Germany into the European fold and begin a process of interdependence that would make war a costly option in the future. The European Coal and Steel Community (ECSC) was created in 1951 with six member states: France, Germany, Italy, Belgium, the Netherlands, and Luxembourg. The momentum for integration did not stop there, and there was an immediate push to create new "communities." An attempt to create a defence community was first proposed by the French but rejected by their Senate in 1954.

The turning point came with the Treaty of Rome in 1957. The members of the ECSC agreed that they would set up a common market as the central feature of the European Economic Community (EEC). The Treaty sought to create the conditions for the free movement of goods, services, people, and capital within the EEC. This meant not only the removal of tariffs and duties but also rules to regulate competition and state aid. However, the Treaty had more than just an economic objective; it also aimed to create an "ever closer union" which those looking for deeper forms of integration took to mean the eventual creation of a political union.

The early days of the EEC were characterized by a concern with creating the common market; that is, the focus was on removing tariffs between member states and developing a common commercial policy with the rest of the world. It began to "deepen" integration by developing common policies in areas such as agriculture. It readily achieved these objectives, and the integration process turned to widening in the early 1970s as the original six became nine with the accession of Denmark, Ireland, and Britain in 1973. This growth continued in 1981 with the entry of Greece and in 1986 with Spain and Portugal. Although membership by the mid-1980s had expanded to 12, the process of deepening integration had been frustrated by the economic stagnation and oil shocks of the 1970s. Member states sought their own solutions to stimulate economic growth, and the EEC could not seem to go beyond the original blueprint of the common market. Tariffs and duties may have been removed, but economic borders remained intact in the form of barriers to trade and to the movement of capital and people. The future of the EEC seemed uncertain. It had achieved its original objectives for some time and it had expanded to include new members, but there was little consensus on the future.

The Single European Act (SEA), signed in 1986 and taking effect in 1987, renewed the process of integration. SEA set out an ambitious plan to create a single market by the end of 1992; its aim was to remove all economic borders between all member states. It involved changes to over 300 areas of policy that ranged from transportation to standards for electrical appliances. This was facilitated by the widespread use of "mutual recognition" rather than harmonization of policies; that is, member states agreed that they did not necessarily have to agree on common standards or rules on many issues but would simply agree to recognize those of their partners as applicable within their own borders. There would be no need, then, for long, arduous negotiations to find a single policy position that was shared by all 12 members. In addition, as we will see below, the SEA introduced institutional changes that helped revive the integration process.

The move to create the single market, the end of the Cold War, and the collapse of the Berlin Wall helped fuel the view that Europe was experiencing an exceptional moment at the end of the 1980s and early 1990s. It was seized by European leaders in December 1991 with the Treaty on European Union (TEU), which was agreed upon at Maastricht. The Treaty introduced a number of institutional changes, including a name change to "European Union." It was constructed on three "pillars": 1) the economic pillar based on the Economic Communities, 2) the Common Foreign and Security Policy (CFSP), and 3) Justice and Home Affairs. Clearly, the central feature of the Maastricht Treaty was economic and monetary union (EMU), an ambitious plan to create a single currency within less than a decade (Dyson and Featherstone 1999). Member states that wanted to be part of the single currency had to meet the Treaty's "convergence criteria" that set targets for monetary policy and public finances. Public sector deficits that exceeded 3 per cent of GDP disqualified member states from entry into the euro, as the single currency would be called, as would public debt levels above 60 per cent of GDP. The single currency came into effect in 1999, and notes and coins appeared on 1 January 2002. Member states maintained their commitment to having their economies continue to converge even after the euro came online with the 1999 Growth and Stability Pact, which sought to keep public finances under control. The Pact and the single currency meant that the basic elements of macroeconomic policy—monetary and fiscal policy—were now being decided at the European level and no longer by national states.

The creation of the single market and currency meant that the objective of creating a borderless economy in the European space was nearly complete. The integration process has also proceeded along political lines since the Maastricht Treaty. By 2001, there was a serious discussion that the political future of Europe needed to be secured with a formal constitution. This was partly motivated by the expected enlargement with ten new members, mostly from the former Communist states in central and eastern Europe. The EU expanded from 12 to 15 members in 1995 with the entry of Austria, Finland, and Sweden. Institutions and structures that were essentially built for six members were felt to be inadequate to deal with the expected 27 after January 2007. A constitution was also seen as a way to formalize the mechanisms for a European foreign policy. At the summit of European leaders in Laeken in Belgium in 2001, it was agreed that a convention would meet to draft a constitutional treaty that would revamp European institutions to address the needs of the larger EU as well as questions about making it more democratic. The convention produced a draft constitution that would have created both a formal foreign policy mechanism as well as a form of presidency. The draft was not accepted by European leaders, but the pressure for constructing a political basis for the EU will not abate. The EU is now involved in almost every aspect of the lives of citizens. The Stability Pact shapes the decisions member states can take in their domestic policy choices, and the policy areas that have a direct role for the EU continue to increase (Featherstone and Radaelli 2003). The EU now looks to what political definition it will give to the original objective of creating "an ever closer union."

Union Institutions

The EU represents a form of institutional and policy "thickness" in governing beyond the state; that is, it has developed a range of structures and policies that have the capacity to penetrate deeply into political, economic, and social life. This contrasts to what may be called the institutional and policy "thinness" in North America, where the fledgling NAFTA structures have yet to affect outcomes as directly and expansively as they have in Europe. Clearly, the EU's institutions have developed over time and often in a haphazard way rather than by design. However, they can still shed some light on what shape North American structures may or should take.

THE EUROPEAN COMMISSION

It is useful to begin with what is perhaps the most unique structure within the EU; it is also the one that is hardest to describe using some of the traditional concepts employed when discussing structures of government. The European Commission is, in many ways, the executive of the EU. It is charged with the implementation of most EU policies and safeguarding the treaties. However, as an administrative structure, it is a fairly "light" institution as it does not have any frontline public servants, nor does it deliver very many services directly. Contrary to the popular myth of a Brussels bureaucracy, the Commission employs only 20,000 civil servants, 5,000 of whom are translators or scientific researchers. This is an exceptionally small number for the governing of a polity consisting of 27 members, which maintains diplomatic representations throughout the world and is responsible for administering a wide range of policies that affect over 450 million Europeans. The Commission as public administration, then, is not very present in the life of its citizens. It relies heavily on the authorities of member states in the implementation of European directives and regulations.

The Commission's importance goes well beyond its relatively small size as an administrative structure of governance. The focus of most attention on the Commission is the College of Commissioners, which may be seen as a sort of political executive. It has one representative from each of the member states; these representatives are responsible not only for implementation of a few policies but also the initiation of new ones. All European legislation must be initiated, at least formally, by the Commission, so that its role is more than just that of a passive structure administering decisions taken elsewhere. It has taken a key function in shaping the nature and scope of European integration. The most evident example was the Commission under Jacques Delors in the mid-1980s and early 1990s that played an instrumental role in the creation of the single market and the single currency.

There is some debate as to whether the commissioners are simply agents of the member states or whether they do have space for autonomy and to provide policy leadership for the EU. While the commissioners are appointed by the national governments and the decisions taken by member states may affect the Commission's agenda, they are seen as having to perform supranational roles. They take an oath to uphold the treaties, and each new Commission must be approved by the European Parliament, where the influence of national governments might be the least pronounced among EU institutions. Moreover, the Commission is able to develop links with important interest groups, non-governmental organizations, and subnational levels of government that can provide it with a basis for policy expertise and autonomy. Whatever its role has been in assuming policy and political leadership, the Commission has assumed an extremely important political role as the symbol of European integration. The President of the Commission is not the head of a European government and at best is a first among equals. However, he or she does represent the EU at international summits such as the G8 meetings and does conduct bilateral discussions with national states throughout the world.

The importance of the Commission in providing a degree of institutional "thickness" to the EU may not be so much *how* it decides (that is, its relative degree of autonomy) but in *what* it decides. There are certain areas in which the treaties give the Commission a great deal of power. This is clearly the case with competition policy that allows the Commission to decide on a range of activities, such as member state subsidies to industry and mergers between firms. In recent years, this power has been used even at the risk of drawing the ire of member states, as was the case with Commission action against Germany for aid to Volkswagen. In this instance, the EU prohibited the German government from providing subsidies to the car manufacturer to help upgrade plants in the former East Germany. It was deemed to go counter to EU law on state aid to industry and to harm competition. The decision was upheld in 2003 by the European Court of Justice. The Commission has also taken on rival economic powers, as illustrated by the ruling against the merger between General Electric and Honeywell, which drew criticism from the US. But the Commission's contribution to institutional "thickness" is not limited to competition questions. For instance, the very fact that it must initiate legislation makes it a focal point for interest groups in almost every area covered by policy-making in industrialized societies.

The roles of the Commission, then, vary from simple guarantor of the treaties to watchdog of the single market to symbol of a grand project for a political union. It has assumed these roles in a piecemeal fashion, partly as a result of the actions of incumbents, partly as a result of space provided by the treaties.

There is nothing like the Commission in NAFTA. There are functional bodies that assume responsibility for implementation of parts of the agreement, and indirectly, may promote further integration. However, neither NAFTA nor the political will of its member states provides these bodies with the opportunity to assume the policy and political leadership roles of the Commission in Europe. It is not likely that North American political leaders would accept such a commission, but some important lessons may be drawn nonetheless. First, regional integration takes on a decidedly different character and path when there is a structure dedicated to pursuing its objectives. Once these institutions are put in place, regardless of original intentions, they may be used for further integration by different political and social forces. The fact that NAFTA does not have an institution like the European Commission suggests that the stimulus and impetus for a closer form of integration needs to be found elsewhere and that regional integration will not take on the comprehensive nature that it has in Europe.

Second, the Commission experience suggests that the NAFTA approach of not having an all-embracing administrative structure but rather sector-specific agencies might be a useful way to approach issues and problems that may arise from the opening up of borders. The multiplicity of roles assumed by the Commission, and the vast area of policies that it has to cover, has led to criticism that the EU might be better served by a series of bodies that deal with specific issues such as the single market or external trade. This might allow the EU to disengage those areas of policy that might be more politically sensitive to member state interests, such as migration or internal security, from those in which there is space for a more European approach, such as competition policy.

Third, even with the best of intentions, any administrative structure whose most visible officials are appointed and not subject to direct political control, either by national governments or the wider public, will raise questions about democratic accountability, transparency, and responsibility. Many of the accusations levied against the Commission's lack of democratic legitimacy, such as claims that it does not pay attention to national interests or broader public opinion, may be unfounded. Governing complex societies will involve an administrative branch that will rely on technical expertise and will operate far from the visible political arena of representative assemblies. However, allowing institutions that are not accountable to democratically elected structures to make important decisions and initiate policy, even after extensive consultation with a wide range of actors, will raise questions about democratic legitimacy. Regional integration, in whatever form that it takes, will always be seen as a political process and not simply a technical exercise that will provide the most efficient means of solving common problems. It is simply not enough to say that administrative structures such as a Commission do not engage with fundamental questions when citizens begin to see that many of the important decisions that affect their lives go through these institutions. North America, like the EU, will have to find a way to make the structures it creates transparent and accountable.

THE EUROPEAN PARLIAMENT

The one institution that most North Americans recognize the most easily is the European Parliament (EP), which contains many of the features found in legislatures in national states. Its members, who are elected directly every five years, represent constituencies that are defined geographically and sit with political groups that represent familiar families of political parties. It holds parliamentary debates in the assembly, and it has parliamentary committees based on similar policy areas to those found in a national legislature. Granted, it has its peculiarities—its members must regularly travel to sit in the assembly in Strasbourg despite having state-of-the-art facilities in Brussels (this to satisfy a French demand to house at least one EU institution).

When we begin to look more closely at the EP, we find that, while it has many of the trappings of a regular parliament, it may not fulfill many of the traditional roles assigned to it. The most basic function of a legislature is to be a law-making body. In this respect, the EP faces a number of challenges to pass the grade. It is not the final deliberative body in the EU decision-making structure. In fact, its deliberative role is limited in ways that even legislatures in executive-dominated systems, such as the one in Canada, do not experience.

The EP's role in decision-making has evolved substantially since the late 1980s. Until 1987, the EP could only count upon the treaty guarantee of consultation before final decisions were taken by the Council (see the next section for a description of this body). That year, the changes introduced by the SEA, known as the cooperation procedure, gave the EP a right to a second reading for most legislation dealing with the completion of the single market and subject to a qualified vote in the Council. The EP was given the power to propose amendments to legislation presented to it that had been approved by the Council or reject it altogether; the amended legislation would then go back to the Commission and the Council. The legislation could still be approved in its original form if the Council provided unanimous support. Under this procedure, the EP could shape policy outcomes when the member states were divided on issues. The EP's law-making capacity was enhanced by the Maastricht Treaty (1992), which introduced the co-decision procedure. In the new framework, when the EP assumes a position on second reading different than the one adopted by the Council, a Conciliation Committee is struck to find an agreed-upon text. Clearly, the EP is still only an indirect law-making body, but its influence has been growing.

The EP's ability to provide oversight of the EU, and more particularly the Commission, is rather limited. The Treaty of Amsterdam (1997) has given it power to approve a new president and commission, and it retains the power to dismiss an entire commission. However, as it cannot target individual commissioners, it has difficulty in developing conventions and practices of ministerial responsibility. It can ask questions of the Commission and of the Council, but the oversight and scrutiny powers have yet to develop to the same level as one might find in conventional legislatures.

It is with respect to the function of providing democratic legitimacy that we might draw some lessons from the EP. It is a unique institution in that no other supranational organization has a representative assembly that has developed structures and processes that can have such an impact on policy decisions. The co-decision-making procedure provides a concrete way for directly elected representatives to affect decisions made by the EU. However, despite what seem to be extensive powers, there are still questions about whether the EP can provide the EU with democratic legitimation. Moreover, there are questions as to whether it connects European citizens to the EU institutions and the decisions that affect their lives. Clearly, direct elections and indirect decision-making powers are not enough to legitimate the decision-making process of a supranational polity. It may be the case that the EP is slowly building up its credibility as an effective decision-making institution and that eventually the co-decision-making procedure will allow it to be seen as an effective centre of power within the EU. However, it also may be the case that legislatures work best in tandem with a clearly identified executive that they can scrutinize, censure, and dismiss.

THE COUNCIL

The Council is perhaps the central point in the EU institutional architecture, but in some ways, it is the most amorphous of all the institutions. It is, in effect, a number of different structures. The most visible is the European Council, which refers to the summit meetings of the heads of government. These normally take place twice a year but may be convened in extraordinary circumstances. They receive the most attention, and some have become symbols of important turning points in the history of European integration. However, the more concrete work of the Council takes place in two other structures: the Council of Ministers and the Committee of Permanent Representation (COREPER). The Council of Ministers takes on at least 20 different forms as it brings together a representative of each member state responsible for a specific policy area. For instance, the EcoFin refers to the Council of Ministers that brings together the finance or economic ministers from the member states on a regular basis to deliberate on European economic policy matters. The COREPER is composed of the officials, some at the ambassador level, who are assigned to the member states' permanent delegation in Brussels. They coordinate the work that will be deliberated upon in the various Councils of Ministers.

The Council is a hybrid structure not simply because it grafts together a number of different bodies. It also aims to bring together the interests of 27 member states and mould them into a European position. The conventional view is that the Council represents the intergovernmental side of the EU. It is here where national interests are presented and protected. Although this is largely the case, it needs to be qualified somewhat. Many decisions—for instance, almost all questions related to the single market—in the EU are now subject to qualified majority voting (QMV) so that a structure such as the Council will not guarantee the protection of national interest on its own; the push is to extend this to areas such as foreign and security policy. A member state could find itself in the minority in the Council if a matter were to come to a vote. The Council, through its various bodies, is engaged in a complex set of discussions and deliberations that involves the Commission, the EP, member states, and national and European interest groups and governments at different levels. Clearly, national interests are at the heart of these discussions but what emerges is a European policy that reflects not a single interest but a hybrid of different national and European interests.

Canadians can look to their own federal-provincial relations for parallels to the Council of Ministers. Meetings between the prime minister and provincial and territorial premiers are similar to the European Council, while the deliberation on policies takes place largely at the ministerial level and between officials of the two levels of government. While a Council-like structure might seem familiar to Canadians, it also may be difficult to see it implemented in a North American polity. The difficult balance that is maintained in the Council within the EU is facilitated by the presence of a number of cross-cutting interests and powers. There is not one single hegemonic power that might feel it has the most to lose by pooling its national interests. The larger EU members—namely, Germany, France, Britain, Italy, and to a certain extent Spain—have a number of competing or contrasting interests in different areas that prevents them from establishing rules that will penalize some of the smaller EU member states. In North America, a Council would be useful to establish regular and structured meetings between political leaders and important officials. It would provide an opportunity for Canadian interests to be expressed and possibly protected. However, it is unlikely that a voting scheme could be devised that would allow the interests of the smaller partners to trump that of the largest—the US—in devising a North American position. This is not to say that all decisions in North America would be US decisions; however, the presence of such a hegemonic power will mean that intergovernmental bodies in North America will probably not develop the same level of institutional depth and expansiveness that they have within the EU.

THE EUROPEAN COURT OF JUSTICE

On the surface, the European Court of Justice (ECJ) looks very much like the constitutional or supreme court that one finds in any national system, especially a federation. It interprets whether national, subnational, and EU legislation respects the treaties in much the same way as a constitutional court interprets the basic law of any nation. What is distinct with the ECJ, and European law in general, is that it trumps national courts and national law when they are in conflict with EU legislation. The ECJ is the most visible expression of the extent to which the EU has developed as a polity, with its own legislation that interacts with citizens and governments on a number of levels. One of the paradoxes of the ECJ is that, despite its capacity to interpret European law over and above national law, thereby touching upon national sovereignty in a very direct way, it has not been a source of contention. Moreover, its rulings have been seen as important elements in fostering greater and deeper levels of integration.

The ECJ and European law provide important lessons for North America. First, they point to the ways in which integration may take place in a number of important arenas that are far from the public eye, including courts. This may allow for a less polarized discussion about the extent to which treaties are respected, but it may not make it easier to have the polity gain widespread acceptance. Second, the success of European law has been based partly on a willingness of all the parties involved to accept it as a binding authority, and, in some cases, for it to set the pace of integration. The experience with the dispute settlement mechanism of CUFTA, and then within NAFTA, might suggest that the North American partners are not ready to show the same level of acceptance of third-party resolution mechanisms.

INSTITUTIONS, POLICIES, AND INTEGRATION

The development of European institutions that are extensive and "thick" reflects, and contributes to, the development of a wide range of policy areas. In contrast to North America, where the emphasis has been on liberalizing trade, with some mention of the environment and labour standards, there are few areas within the member states of the EU that have not become "Europeanized." There has been a steady spread of the policy areas covered by the EU, with integration more intense and deeper in such areas as macroeconomic policy and less so in others such as social policy. While there may be arguments that this is the result of some sort of inevitable policy spillover or "creep," it also has been facilitated by the political commitment to create "an ever closer" union that has been at the heart of the European project. At different points in time, the integration project has pushed ahead not because the path was set by previous decisions but because political decisions were taken by a constellation of forces for a wide and sometimes contradictory range of reasons.

Social Europe

The rapid push to further integration that characterized the period after the SEA raised questions about whether or not the EU could be a polity based simply on policy or performance legitimacy. A debate emerged about whether or not it required that citizens of the member states also see themselves as members of, and belonging to, this broader entity called the EU. The discussion about "social Europe" has taken on many different dimensions; for present purposes, I will focus on discussions about identity and belonging and about the European social model (ESM).

Constructing a political union might, in some ways, be easier than creating a political community. The union is about finding the right set of institutions and architecture that has the capacity and legal right to make decisions that will govern large parts of people's lives. As we saw above, the path has not always been an easy one, but Europe has put in place the institutions and structures that define a political union. The discussion is less clear about the political community because it ventures into issues such as whether or not the EU requires a sense of belonging by those who are governed by it, on what basis will belonging be determined, and who will define what is Europe and by what criteria. Clearly, constructing a political union and a community are not unrelated. The steady progress in creating institutions and policies has given Europeans reason and reference points that might make them feel part of a community. However, as the EU has widened and deepened, so has the debate about political community.

One argument is that the EU does not need a "demos"; that is, the EU's evolution is not like that of the nation-state, which was based on a strong sense of identity and belonging rooted in some social or group characteristic or loyalty (Weiler 1999). The EU is a new form of political construction that reflects a new basis of politics that is much more fluid and without a central reference point. In this form of social organization, individuals can feel that they belong to many different types of political communities, some of which may require a stronger sense of belonging (such as the "nation") while others may simply be matters of convenience or the most effective way to solve policy problems or preferences (from the local to the continental level). In this interpretation, while the EU has developed a very articulated discourse about European citizenship, this refers to something that pulls less at the heart-strings and more at the practical considerations of how best to manage issues and problems in an interdependent world that does not recognize national borders so easily. This vision of belonging to a political community might resonate very clearly for a discussion of NAFTA.

However, the discussion of this looser form of belonging has been challenged by the growing importance of the EU in the lives of the citizens of its member states. So long as European integration was primarily about issues that, while affecting many aspects of public policy, seemed distant and not directly related to the daily lives of citizens, it was possible to take an almost apolitical view of the project. Once the European Community became the European Union and began to enter into areas such as monetary and even foreign policy, then it would be expected that individuals might ask in whose name all this was being carried out. For instance, the convergence criteria were cited by almost every member state government as the reason why public spending had to be brought under control in the 1990s. It is natural that citizens would ask why their health service or their pensions were being affected because of the EU. It is no coincidence, therefore, that in the last decade or so, the EU has spared no effort in an attempt to create a sense of belonging to Europe that goes beyond simple policy expediency with a discourse about shared values, cultural experiences, and even history.

There is, of course, always the danger when trying to construct a political community that it will slip into defining who does not belong, especially when identifying points in common might be problematic, as is the case in the EU. Europe's push to create a political union occurred at the same time as the continent experienced widespread movement of people. The collapse of the Communist regimes in the east and the consequences of economic globalization in Asia and Africa led to large-scale migration towards Western Europe in the 1990s. As internal borders were disappearing within Europe, there was a heightened interest in finding common ways to define its external borders. Immigration policy remains primarily a national responsibility, but the last decade has seen many steps towards a common policy on visas, the granting of political asylum, and patrolling borders. It also has led to a discussion about what immigration has meant for a European identity. In the constitutional convention, there was a push from some countries, such as Italy, Spain and Poland, to include a reference to Europe's "Judeo-Christian" roots. The attempt failed, but it did reveal that there is anything but consensus on what it means to be a European. This is clearly the case with enlargement. The criteria set in the early 1990s emphasized political, economic, and administrative features but was vague on the geographic boundaries of Europe. There have been calls to expand membership to include Israel and Russia. On the other hand, Turkey, which is geographically closer than some of the current members and whose historical engagement with Europe is unquestioned, continues to wait to enter.

An important part of the creation of a sense of belonging in Europe has centred on the debate about the shared values based on the European social model (ESM) (Habermas 2001). European states have taken very different approaches to regulating social life, yet in the 1990s a discussion emerged about a distinct European approach to social policy, the welfare state, and balancing market and social forces. It is not my purpose here to examine whether such a model actually exists. What is important for this discussion is that reference to such a model was seen as a necessary element in the integration process. It is no coincidence that discussion about ESM became a central feature of discussion about European governance at roughly the same time as the economic liberalization projects of the single market and currency were becoming the basis of policy-making within member states. What had previously been an area of almost exclusive national jurisdiction and therefore diversity—that is, social policy—came to be seen as an area that provided a thread that bound all Europeans (Grahl and Teague 1997). There was an attempt, in the wake of the SEA, to make Europe more than just an economic project. It was in the idea of a particular basis of organizing social life that supposedly made Europe distinct and could provide a form, not only of what has been described as policy legitimacy, but regime and polity legitimacy as well. There is nothing unique in looking to social policy as the means to generate a sense of belonging and attachment to a polity; for instance, Canada's public health care system is an important source of national identity, especially as a point of comparison to the omnipresent neighbour to the south. However, what might be different about the ESM is that the discussion of the model seems to grow in intensity in relation to the increasing pressures on its preservation and transformations that may be calling its very nature into question. It is open to question whether this notion of a shared "social model" might be the basis for a discourse of a political community in North America, especially as any leveling is likely to be down to the US standard rather than up to the Canadian one.

Europeanization and Globalization

The discussion about the possible tension between the European social model and economic integration leads us to the question about the relationship between Europeanization and globalization. Europeanization has emerged as an attempt to understand an evolving process in which decisions to govern the European space are made. This takes place in a number of different sites and at a number of different levels. Its focus may be on the ways in which the EU has become Europeanized just as much as it can be on how national states adapt to a changing relationship between different levels of government and with non-state actors (Borzel and Risse 2000). Arguments about "Europeanization" have begun to emerge to refer to, among other things, the ways in which the dynamics of the new polity shape national politics, allowing for various elements of what have been identified as part of the "European" model of governing to adapt in a period of globalization.

There is no easy assessment of whether European integration is a means by which to resist or temper the pressures that come from an increasingly interdependent global economy. On the one hand, the economic model that was at the heart of the single market and currency was based on economic liberalization and tended to limit state intervention in the economy. It has led to policy processes that have made competition rather than social solidarity and minimizing collective risk the central target of policy-making. On the other hand, European integration might also serve as a way to avoid regulatory competition between states that ratchets downwards standards and protection. For instance, in areas such as the environment and anti-discrimination, some member states have been forced to adopt stricter rules and standards because of European commitments. However, the centrality of economic integration has tended to overshadow the ways in which Europeanization might allow national states to offset the effects of globalization.

Mapping Regional Integration

European integration has drawn a great deal of interest from scholars and practition-ers alike who have tried to find ways to understand the process over the last 50 years. The result is a broad set of approaches and models that make different assumptions and imply different forces at work. The lack of consensus reflects the challenge to the ways we have understood governing that arise from regional integration, especially in the EU. They might provide us with useful ways in which to understand continen-tal integration in North America.

NEO-FUNCTIONALISM AND INTERGOVERNMENTALISM

This is the classic debate in the literature on European integration. Neo-functional-ism grew out of the postwar thinking of functionalism, which argued that governing should be based on international functional agencies. The aim was to make govern-ing a "technical" exercise left to functional experts and interests rather than to the political sphere of government. Neo-functionalism accepted some of these basic premises in that it rejected the primacy of the state as an international actor or, at least, argued that interest groups and functional interests could play an important role in fostering governing beyond borders. It introduced the notion of "spillover," applied in two particular ways. The first is functional spillover—the argument that in complex societies and economies, integration in one specific area, such as coal and steel, is likely to lead to pressures for integration in other areas. The second, political spillover, follows from the first in that as integration spreads into more areas of the economy, national political leaders increasingly look to supranational solutions to govern relations that have now spilled across borders. Neo-functionalist arguments were popular in the 1950s and 1960s, and they were once again the focus of atten-tion in light of the creation of the single market and the single currency in the 1980s and 1990s.

Intergovernmentalism is often seen as simply another way in which the national state pursues and protects its interests. It does not give primary importance either to supranational institutions or to non-state actors. The construction of the EU was the result of choices that reflected the interests of national actors and not supranational institutions; the outcomes took into account the relative bargaining positions of the member states rather than some ideal of constructing a European position or policy. One could point to many recent examples where national interests remain at the heart of European integration. For instance, the provisions for a common foreign policy are still cast primarily in terms of the intergovernmental structures and pro-cedures of the EU rather than by the supranational Commission or the EP. On the other hand, intergovernmentalism has no way of accounting for the vast range of important policy areas—such as macroeconomic policy or external trade—where it is difficult to define and defend strictly national interests.

The conventional models might have something to offer to an understanding of integration in North America. The neo-functionalist argument may shed some light on, for example, the claim that has been made about the growing link between trade and security. The need to maintain as open as possible a border for trade means interests with respect to external borders begin to converge more and more. This point is brought home not only by national political leaders but by economic actors who have a vested interest in keeping the border open for trade. The problem with neo-functionalism is that while one can see functional spillover in North America, it is not likely that there will be a corresponding political spillover. The asymmetry in the relationship between the three countries means that US political elites are not likely to look to supranational institutions or structures to resolve issues that result from functional spillover. Moreover, the probable reluctance of US political leaders to accept supranational institutions in general would create limits on the extent to which political spillover might take place. At the same time, many Canadians and Mexicans would be wary of supranational North American institutions if they did not account for the asymmetries that exist between Canada, Mexico, and the US. This would suggest that intergovernmental solutions would be an alternative. However, intergovernmentalism will always find Canada and Mexico dealing with a hegemonic power that might have less incentive to negotiate or compromise its national interests with a junior partner.

MULTI-LEVEL GOVERNANCE AND FEDERALISM

The seemingly endless debate between supranationalism and intergovernmentalism in the EU has led some to look for other ways to understand integration. Multi-level governance and federalism offer two very different alternatives. The first wants to think about governing without the state, while the second assumes that regional integration may be understood as a form of evolving federalism. Both emphasize the complex nature of governing with multiple levels of government and the ways in which that creates multiple sites for decision-making, as well as many different sets and forms of non-state actors. Multi-level governance has tried to look at the sorts of policy and issue networks that are being formed throughout Europe to solve specific policy questions. It is useful in that it forces us to think about the ways in which various levels of government, from the local to the supranational, interact with non-state actors to address shared concerns. It would seem that it might be helpful to think about issues shared by different parts of North American society. For instance, one can think of how Canadians and Americans address trans-border environmental questions. However, one of the limitations of the multi-level governance argument is that it is relatively silent on questions of political power. Given what has been said about how North American integration is conditioned by the asymmetries of power, any approach that does not address this problem—the fears it may raise in Canada and Mexico, the indifference or reluctance it may cause in the US—will be of limited use.

Although they can shed great insight into relations between different levels of government and different parts of civil society, federalism arguments also face constraints. First, federalism implies that the regional polity has, at its core, many of the essential characteristics that we have associated with the national state, namely, a sovereign body and symmetry between political authority and territory. There may be many features of the EU that look like a federation: a division of powers between levels of government, a constitutional court, and an emerging constitution. However, the complex web of relationships that are at its core do not fit into any neat scheme for a federation or a confederation. Moreover, federalism also implies a deep sense of belonging on the part of citizens to territorial units at many different levels. The

EU has made many efforts to create this sense of being "European," but it is a long way from achieving the levels that one might find even in the most decentralized federations. On both these counts—implying a sovereign core and a sense of belonging—federalism does not work any better as a model for North American integration. There may be many ways in which a North American "community" may be forming, but it is unlikely to create the sense of belonging generated in a federation. Again, the asymmetries of power will cause many Canadians and Mexicans to worry about a loss of distinctiveness and identity in a North American federation.

CONSORTIUM AND CONDOMINIUM

European integration has spawned a number of other ways to think about regional integration, many of them hybrids of those listed above. Philippe Schmitter (1996) has presented two possible scenarios that may be particularly useful for our discussion of North America. He accepts that the symmetry between what he calls functional and territorial representation that characterized the national state is breaking down. The political authorities that had governed distinct political communities for most of the modern period may no longer have the capacity to make authoritative decisions on matters that govern the lives of citizens. He speculates on what kind of polity may emerge in Europe once we no longer assume that there may be differences between citizens' sense of belonging on a territorial basis and the authorities that have the capacity to make decisions that govern their lives. He talks of federation and confederation as possible scenarios in the European future; however, it is his discussion of consortium and condominium that might offer some promise for thinking about a North American future.

The two models present different ways in which functional and territorial representation may evolve. In the consortium model, there is a fixed number of national states with clear identities that cooperate on a range of variable and overlapping functional tasks, in much the same way as we have with a group of business firms that come together. There is no fundamental change to the basis of territorial representation, and citizens continue to identify with their national states. However, the latter no longer have the capacity to govern a range of functional tasks so they create a series of administrative bodies to address them. We can think of a number of existing structures that fit this description in North America. For instance, the Great Lakes Commission might be seen as a consortium between Canada and the US to manage a policy question that cannot be governed by a single state on its own.

The consortium does imply a ceding of exclusive authority in specific areas but does not impinge upon more politically sensitive questions about territorial representation. It does not call for new structures that require a new way to think about territorial representation. One can imagine a future that gives a more formal role to the many regional bodies that already exist across the North American borders. However, one limit that the consortium model may face is that it may be a transitional stage. As was the case with functionalism, complex economies and societies make it difficult to contain issues to narrow policy areas. One can foresee the need to develop formal structures that go beyond the policy areas of the consortium and that begin to raise questions about the basis of territorial representation.

The condominium model requires a greater leap into unexplored terrain. It assumes not only that variable functional bodies but also territory would no longer be thought of as having a single centre. For instance, in the case of the EU, there are three member states (Sweden, Denmark, and Britain) that are not part of the single currency. Within the North American condominium, there would be many different units that are autonomous of each other but that would share in some of the common concerns of the entire structure. One could imagine how membership in each of the units would vary and could be overlapping. For instance, a North American Environmental Community might be imagined that does not include all parts of the territory but only those units that share a common concern and ways to address it. We could imagine a Social Charter for North America, again with those units that share a similar concern with providing certain levels of social programs and services coming together to create structures to pursue their objectives. The condominium would not require that all the units belong to each of these communities; in other words, there would not be just one North America but many. In some ways, it could resemble forms of asymmetrical federalism where constituent units could decide to come together on some issues—say, for instance social policy—and decide to choose other constituent units for another policy.

Challenges to Integration

Economic integration in Europe has been an ideal mechanism for building union by stealth. It has, operating under the radar, put in place mechanisms and structures that have led to a need for continent-wide rules, institutions, and decision-making processes (Egan 2001). The construction of a European economy was kept largely separate from difficult political decisions about what kind of political authority would govern the European space and about what priority would be given to collective objectives such as redistribution of resources. The challenges faced by any attempt at regional integration beyond the boundaries of the state are evident in the discussion of institutions and models that come from the European experience. These may be divided into the related areas of community building and democratic legitimacy. Integration in North America, if it continues to evolve, will run up against elements of each of these two sets of questions.

The discussion of a consortium and a condominium points out that there may be ways to have integration that either ignores questions of belonging to a new community or imagines many political communities within a regional body. The European project has been made easier because there has not been an asymmetry of power as we have in North America that can generate fears about a loss of one sense of community. As we have seen in our discussion, many of the institutional structures adopted by the EU may be problematic for North America because they could touch upon questions about the loss of sovereignty and identity. The condominium model seems to offer a way to address some Canadian fears of being engulfed in a North American structure dominated by the hegemonic power to the south. However, multiple and overlapping functional and territorial communities may not necessarily be the basis on which to create a sense of belonging to something that is truly North

American. The experience of the EU suggests that venturing into politically sensitive areas requires a stronger sense of belonging.

The EU has been a tremendous success in terms of developing an extensive and sophisticated institutional architecture to govern a wide range of policies. It also has made some progress with respect to creating a sense of belonging to "Europe" and being "European." Perhaps its greatest challenge is to gain acceptance as a legitimate democratic polity. The paradox is that models such as multi-level governance and condominium might be appropriate ways in which to govern complex societies where there is no clear identifiable centre. However, this makes it difficult for citizens to have certainty about where decisions that affect their lives are being taken—and by whom. While the new scenarios may be more flexible, the European experience suggests that they create a greater distance between institutions and citizens. Moreover, it also may increase dissatisfaction and frustration with existing institutions to which citizens still look primarily but which no longer have the capacity to respond to their demands.

The success of any North American project will depend on the extent to which citizens feel that it is both representative and responsive to their needs. It is unlikely that the institutional "thickness" that has characterized the EU can address some of the specific challenges of integration in North America. However, some of the European institutional architecture might be used to construct a North American condominium. If citizens can begin to construct different North American communities that address their specific concerns, from the environment to security to macroeconomic policy, they may be able to see that there is room for many different forms of governing in the structure. Moreover, it might be able to address the challenge of responding to the demands of a clear hegemonic power while leaving room for concerns about loss of sovereignty and identity in Canada and Mexico.

References

Borzel, Tanja, and Thomas Risse. 2000. "When Europe Hits Home: Europeanization and Domestic Change." *European Integration online Papers* 4,15. <http://eiop.or.at/eiop/texte/2000-015a.htm>: 1–24.

Dyson, Kenneth H.F., and Kevin Featherstone. 1999. *The Road to Maastricht: Negotiating Economic and Monetary Union*. New York: Oxford UP.

Egan, Michelle. 2001. *Constructing a European Market*. Oxford: Oxford UP.

Featherstone, Kevin, and Claudio Radaelli (Eds.). 2003. *The Politics of Europeanization*. Oxford: Oxford UP.

Gilbert, Mark. 2003. *Surpassing Realism: The Politics of European Integration since 1945*. Lanham, MD: Rowman and Littlefield.

Grahl, John, and Paul Teague. 1997. "Is the European Social Model Fragmenting?" *New Political Economy* 2,3 (November): 405–27.

Habermas, Jürgen. 2001. "Why Europe Needs a Constitution." *New Left Review* 11 (September-October): 5–26.

Schmitter, Philippe. 1996. "Imagining the Future of the Euro-Polity with the Help of New Concepts." In Gary Marks, Fritz Scharpf, *et al.*, *Governance in the European Union*. London: Sage.

Weiler, J.H.H. 1999. *The Constitution of Europe*. New York: Cambridge UP.

CHAPTER SIX

Globalization and the Democratic Deficit
Challenging Times for Canada's Political Institutions

Samuel A. Bottomley

For many countries, the increased political and economic integration associated with globalization is seen as a relatively new phenomenon. Canada, however, has always been heavily influenced by forces beyond its borders. This is especially true of Canada's political institutions which, although they may have developed distinctly Canadian characteristics, have their origins elsewhere. When Canada's current governmental structure was established, it was as a Dominion of the British Empire with direct political control residing in London. As such, the authors of Canada's 1867 constitutional document faithfully modeled the new colony's political institutions after those of the mother country.

The American experience has also significantly informed the development of Canadian political institutions. Both federalism, which was a direct import from the US, and the 1982 Canadian Charter of Rights and Freedoms (the Charter), which was largely inspired by US-style constitutionalism, are core components of Canadian government. Due to Canada's geographic, economic, and cultural proximity to the US, the latter's political experience has long influenced debates regarding the operation and reform of Canadian political institutions. The ties between Canada and the US are so longstanding that NAFTA and the prospect of further North American integration have had only a minimal impact on Canadian political institutions thus far. As they have demonstrated a remarkable degree of flexibility, it is unlikely that significant formal institutional change will be necessary to deal with Canada's changing relationship with the rest of North America and the world. In particular, Canada's ability to adapt to changing international circumstances is and will continue to be aided by the concentration of power inherent in the Westminster system of government, which allows the prime minister and cabinet to act quickly and decisively in the area of foreign relations and trade.

Canada's political institutions differ fundamentally from those of its NAFTA partners. The most obvious difference is that they have never been swept away by revolution. As a result, many are built on foundations that are older than the country itself. With some notable exceptions, the underlying theme of institutional change in Canada has been continuation and gradual organic evolution. Until recently, the fundamental structure of most Canadian political institutions went relatively unchallenged. At present, however, Canadians appear to be in an unprecedented mood for institutional change. Many, including former Prime Minister Paul Martin (defeated in the January 2006 federal election), have argued that institutional reforms are necessary to correct the so-called "democratic deficit" many have observed in Canadian politics (Office of the Prime Minister 2005). To deal with this problem, Prime Minister Martin appointed the first Minister Responsible for Democratic Reform to his cabinet in December 2003. Of course, Martin is not alone in his desire for change; calls for the reform of longstanding institutions, including the electoral system, Parliament, the power of the prime minister, the selection of judges, and others, appear to be growing in intensity. The election of Stephen Harper's Conservative government in January 2006 has kept the issue of institutional reform on the agenda. Harper has long supported reforms such the creation of an elected Senate and fixed election dates as well as reducing the power of political parties. In 2007, institutional reform continued to be listed as the top priority for the prime minister. In fact, the Harper government has vowed to "[c]ontinue to reform our political institutions and the political process to make them more accountable and more democratic" (Office of the Prime Minister 2007a).

Behind the drive for reform is the increasing perception that many of Canada's core institutions are outdated and unable properly to represent the diverse characteristics of contemporary Canadian society. A significant drop in voter turnout over recent elections (Elections Canada 2005a),[1] as well as polls indicating that a substantial portion of Canadians have lost some faith in their political system, are often cited as signs of growing malaise with Canadian political institutions (Environics-CBC 2005).[2] Although reform is on the agenda, there is no guarantee that any significant transformation is underway. This may change, however, with the election of the Conservative Party—a recent amalgamation of the Reform Party and the Progressive Conservative Party—in January 2006. The Reform Party in particular, with its chief support base in western Canada, made federal institutional reform a linchpin of its platform for over a decade, and the issue was a live one in the 2006 federal election. Political institutions display a significant amount of inertia, however, and are inherently resilient to alteration. Canada's political institutions may prove to be too entrenched and too beneficial to those in power to change dramatically. Despite the resistance to formal change, there is no doubt that existing institutions are adapting and evolving as they take on new roles in a changing environment, including those resulting from globalization and economic integration.

This chapter examines the historical evolution and current operation of Canada's major political institutions and considers the contemporary challenges each faces. The Constitution, the electoral system, and all three branches of government, as well as the bureaucracy, are explored within the context of Canada's changing position within the North American continent and the rest of the world. Clearly, globalization and increased continental integration has had a different impact on different Canadian political institutions. For example, both the prime minister and the Canadian judiciary have seen their domestic importance grow because of Canada's increasing interconnectedness with other jurisdictions. On the other hand, institutions such as Parliament are perceived as being too slow to deal effectively with rapidly changing relationships and demands placed on Canada, a perception that has hurt the image of the institution. In addition, improvements in communication technology and increased international linkages have exposed potential reformers of Canada's institutions to the experience of political institutions elsewhere and have provided models for change. Some groups trying to reform Canada's political institutions are even part of larger international movements working toward specific institutional reforms worldwide (Fair Vote 2005). Yet, despite the pressure for reform, Canada's political institutions have demonstrated remarkable flexibility in the past and should be able to adapt to the challenges posed by growing continental integration.

The Canadian Constitution

Canada's Constitution distinguishes it from its North American neighbours. Unlike the US and Mexico, Canada's Constitution was not the product of a revolutionary government seeking to throw out the old constitutional order. On the contrary, Canada became independent from Britain very gradually and without a struggle. The process of becoming a completely sovereign country took place over such a long period of time that the precise year or even decade in which Canada became independent is unclear (Heard 1990: 1). Because Canada inherited a British-style constitution, and because of the manner in which Canada gained its independence from Britain, the Canadian Constitution is generally organic in nature, is not ideologically coherent, and is heavily reliant on convention.

Like the British Constitution, the Canadian Constitution cannot be found in one definitive text and is often described as having two distinct parts: formal and informal. The formal constitution consists of written parts listed in s.52 as well as in the schedule of the Constitution Act, 1982. These include the Constitution Act, 1867 (formerly known as the British North America Act) and various amendments to that Act, as well as key British statutes and orders-in-council. Certain important federal statutes, such as the Alberta Act and the Saskatchewan Act (which created those provinces), are also listed as part of the Constitution. The most significant amendment to the formal Canadian Constitution took place in 1982 with the addition of an amending formula, entrenched civil liberties in the form of the Charter, and the first constitutional recognition of the rights of the Aboriginal peoples of Canada.

The informal constitution includes historical documents,[3] certain British statutes, as well as Canadian federal and provincial statutes that are seen as representing important principles in Canadian government.[4] The rules of Parliament and the provincial legislatures should also be rightly considered to be part of the informal constitution as should key judicial decisions regarding its interpretation (Monahan 2002: 4–10). The Canadian Constitution, however, also contains many important unwritten elements in the form of conventions. These have been described as the "rules of constitutional behaviour which are considered to be binding by and upon those who operate the Constitution" (Marshall and Moodie 1968: 26). Constitutional conventions fill in the gaps left in the written text and include some of the most important constitutional principles and practices in Canadian politics.

While all constitutions make use of conventions to some degree, the Canadian Constitution relies very heavily on them. For example, that Canada employs a Westminster parliamentary system is not found in the written text but flows from convention. The principle of responsible government, a central premise of Canada's parliamentary system which requires that the government can only continue so long as it is supported by Parliament, is based on convention only. In addition, a literal reading of the Constitution would give the impression that the monarch is absolute in power. In reality, the Canadian monarchy is constitutional and is almost completely constrained by convention. Perhaps the best example is provided by the office of the prime minister (PM). Although the PM is unquestionably the most powerful figure in Canadian politics, the powers and even the existence of that office are not discussed in the Constitution. At times, the heavy reliance on conventions may create some political uncertainty when there is debate regarding their precise nature. However, it also allows a substantial degree of flexibility and permits the Constitution to evolve without formal amendment.

One defining organizational principle of the Canadian Constitution is its federal division of powers. Federalism is so central to Canada's political system that the creation of the country would have been a political impossibility without it. Canada was only established in 1867 because four British colonies (Ontario, Québec, Nova Scotia, and New Brunswick) agreed to be "federally united" under a constitution "similar in Principle to that of the United Kingdom." In fact, the Canadian Constitution was the first attempt to combine a British Westminster system with US federalism, indicating that its authors were looking south of the border for inspiration when seeking to alter the original British institutional framework.

The adoption of US-style federalism was a necessary condition of the 1867 Confederation agreement. Québec and, to a lesser extent, the two Maritime provinces were unwilling to join a new centralized political entity where they would be unable to protect their own distinctiveness. Federalism was an obvious solution to this problem. The creation of provincial governments would allow local interests and identities to be expressed and protected, while still being part of a much larger political community. Federalism was also seen as crucial for French-speakers in Québec; although they would be a national minority, as a provincial majority they could use the powers of provincial government to protect their interests as well as their culture.

Federalism also demonstrates the flexibility of the Canadian Constitution. Originally, Canada was designed to be a highly centralized federation. In fact, because the Constitution gave the federal government the power to disallow provincial legislation, early Canadian federalism has been described as only "quasi-federal." The powers of the central government were intended to be so strong that Canada's first PM, John A. Macdonald, even predicted that the provinces would be "nothing more than glorified municipalities" (Rocher and Smith 1995: 57). Macdonald's prediction could not have been more incorrect. Since 1867, Canada has evolved into one of the most decentralized federations in the world. This trend was facilitated by a variety of factors, including the growth of a provincial rights movement, judicial interpretation of the division of powers in the Constitution, the increased ability of the provinces to raise money, the disuse of federal controls over the provinces, and the unexpected growth in importance of provincial powers. Most importantly, a highly centralized federation was not a good fit for such a large, diverse society like Canada (Cairns 1971: 319–20). This is particularly true in the case of Québec where provincial elites, representing a linguistic minority, were committed to protecting and expanding provincial powers. It is important to note that although the nature of Canadian federalism has been altered fundamentally since 1867, very few formal constitutional changes were necessary to support this decentralizing trend, further demonstrating the flexibility of Canadian political institutions.

The relationship between the federal and provincial levels has undoubtedly been, and will continue to be, affected by the forces of globalization. International trade agreements have had a substantial impact on the workings of Canadian federalism (McBride 2003: 252–53). For example, while Ottawa has the sole authority to sign international treaties such as NAFTA, much of the substance of those agreements falls under provincial jurisdiction. As a result, substantial federal-provincial consultation often takes place before international agreements are signed to ensure that Ottawa can meet its international obligations. One obvious influence of globalization is that the federal government enters into trade agreements that may limit the scope of action for provincial government. For example, in the past, the federal government agreed to terms under GATT/WTO (General Agreement on Trade and Tariffs/World Trade Organization) removing barriers to liquor sales, a policy area completely under provincial jurisdiction (Skogstad 2002: 162). NAFTA may also have indirect effects on provincial policy (McBride 2003: 260). Recently, the government of New Brunswick abandoned its plan to implement a public automobile insurance scheme for the province because of threats from insurance companies that this amounted to governmental expropriation and they would litigate for compensation under NAFTA (Bourque and Barlow 2005). Some critics even fear that NAFTA will encourage the privatization of provincial health care systems (Epps and Flood 2002: 747). As a result, two opposing views have been put forward regarding the impact of free trade on federalism: either NAFTA will have a centralizing impact on the Canadian federation as provinces are forced to conform to the standards of the agreement, or it will have a decentralizing impact on provincial economic policy because the provinces will develop differing strategies to deal with their individual economic circumstances arising from the agreement (Courchene 2004: 24).

Federalism and related questions of identity have long been the source of much constitutional debate and jurisdictional squabbling in Canada. In contrast with the US Constitution, which is seen as a unifying symbol for that country, the Canadian Constitution has been the source of longstanding tension for Canadians with different visions of federalism and the character of the country (Russell 2004). Originally, the need to embark on constitutional change was driven by the desire for Canada to take control of its Constitution from Britain. However, during the 1960s, patriation of the Constitution was increasingly discussed as part of a package of fundamental reforms. By considering sweeping institutional changes, Canada departed from its tradition of gradual, organic change and constitutional pragmatism. Suddenly, the Constitution, which until the late 1960s had only been the concern of political and legal elites, was at the centre of a prolonged and heated debate regarding the very essence of Canada. During this era of "mega constitutional" politics, the very legitimacy of the Constitution and, therefore, the country was called into question (Russell 2004: 72). Issues and demands that had previously been dealt with at the political level were elevated to the constitutional level. This was complicated by resurgent Québec nationalism which demanded constitutional recognition of that province as having a special place in the Canadian federation. For over 30 years,

Canadians debated the fundamental nature of Canada and attempted to define the essence of the country in the Constitution.

On 29 March 1982, the Canada Act was passed by the British Parliament, giving Canada the ability to amend its own Constitution, and on 17 April 1982, an unprecedented package of constitutional amendments was added to the Constitution Act of 1867. This added a complicated amending formula to the Canadian Constitution, recognized Aboriginal rights, and, most importantly, included for the first time an entrenched bill of rights. While the Charter was authored in Canada and was a response to domestic demands and experiences, its adoption was also inspired by international events. As Alan Cairns has noted, after World War II, an entrenched "Bill of Rights became an almost essential attribute of contemporary statehood" (1992a: 29). There are those who have suggested that the Charter, with its privileging of individual over collective rights, has had a significant Americanizing influence on Canadian society. In fact, S.M. Lipset argues that the Charter "probably goes further toward taking the country in an American direction than any other enacted structural change, including the Canada-US Free Trade Agreement" (1990: 116).

The Charter enshrined constitutional rights for individual citizens for the first time in Canadian history. Although most of these rights already existed in Canadian law, entrenching them in the Constitution changed the very nature of Canadian politics and the relationship between the state and the citizenry (Russell 1983: 43–44). With the Charter, Canadian courts were empowered to strike down any law or governmental action that conflicted with Charter rights. While the exact impact of the Charter has been debated, there is no doubt that it has had a profound impact on Canadian politics at many levels (MacIvor 2006: preface). At the highest level, it has been argued that it has made Canadian citizenship richer and more participatory, primarily because it has drastically increased the number of constitutional players (Cairns 1992b: 74). Not surprisingly, this has complicated constitutional politics significantly. After the passage of the Charter, Canadians are no longer willing to leave constitution-making to politicians, and those groups specifically listed in the Charter (i.e., race, national or ethnic origin, colour, religion, sex, age, or mental or physical disability) demand greater consultation on constitutional matters.

From a public policy perspective, the Charter ended parliamentary supremacy and replaced it with constitutional supremacy. Canadians, as well as groups and corporations, can now by-pass Parliament and pursue their political strategies through litigation. Consequently, the Charter has had a profound impact on most areas of public policy, including some of the most controversial matters in Canadian politics. Issues such as abortion, gay marriage, tobacco advertising, pornography, rights of the accused, and countless others have been shaped by Charter jurisprudence. Not surprisingly, politicians have adapted to the new institutional environment established by the Charter and have avoided dealing with many heated issues by deferring them to the court.

The Charter, and the rest of the 1982 constitutional package, was intended to end Canada's ongoing constitutional debate. However, because the 1982 amendments were passed despite the objections of Québec, they only added fuel to the constitutional fire. From the mid-1980s to the early 1990s, Canadian politics was dominated by negotiations associated with two successive constitutional packages. The goal of the first of these, the Meech Lake Accord, was to address the constitutional concerns of Québec. It failed in June 1990 after it did not get the approval of the legislatures of Manitoba and Newfoundland. It was also opposed by many Canadians who did not agree with the constitutional recognition of Québec as a distinct society or with the process of constitutional reform which only included the 11 first ministers. In the wake of the failure of the Meech Lake Accord, the Charlottetown Accord was presented to Canadians. This package of constitutional amendments called for significant institutional change and incorporated the demands of a diverse range of constitutional interests. Despite widespread public consultation, the Charlottetown Accord was rejected in Canada's only national referendum on the Constitution on 26 October 1992. Charlottetown was the last of the large scale proposals for constitutional reform. By the turn of the new millennium, Canada gradually returned to "constitutional normalcy" (Russell 2004: 228).

Canada's Electoral System

Until very recently, any discussion of the Canadian electoral system would have been a straightforward account of the single-member plurality (SMP) system that has remained fundamentally unchanged throughout Canada's history. Suggestions for reform surfaced occasionally, but contemplating changes to the electoral system was largely an exercise reserved for academics. However, in the last decade, support for electoral reform has increased dramatically. Organizations such as Fair Vote Canada, which is dedicated entirely to the issue of electoral reform, have raised the profile of the issue through their constant lobbying for an overhaul of the system (Fair Vote Canada 2005). Additionally, in 2004, the Law Commission of Canada recommended that the Canadian government alter Canada's electoral system to guarantee more proportionality between seats won and votes cast (Law Commission of Canada 2004). Other factors supporting the call for electoral reform included a number of unusual provincial elections, the outcome of which seemed to defy the wishes of the voters.[5] Also, the federal elections of 1993, 1997, and 2000 produced results that left many feeling alienated from a system that consistently produced a Liberal majority government despite that fact that the Liberals did not come close to winning a majority of the vote in any of those elections.

Canada's current electoral system divides the country into 308 electoral districts, each represented by a single member of Parliament (MP) in the House of Commons. Unlike the US Congress, this number is not fixed and is revised after every ten-year census with new seats added to account for Canada's growing population (Elections Canada 2005a).[6] Determining the number of seats is more complicated than it appears. Canada's population is not divided into constituencies evenly across the country. Instead, each province is assigned a number of MPs by a somewhat complicated formula. Provinces are protected from losing MPs after redistribution because of two provisions. The first of these is known as the "grandfather clause" and guarantees that no province can lose seats below the number it had in 1976. In addition, the "senatorial clause" specifies that a province must have at least as many MPs as it does senators. The addition of MPs due to these two clauses results in substantial distortion in the size of provincial representation and the number of voters in each electoral riding. As a result, every province, other than Ontario, Alberta, and British Columbia, is overrepresented in Parliament. For example, the average population per riding in Ontario is 107,642 whereas federal constituencies in Prince Edward Island average only 33,824 people (Elections Canada 2005b).

Perhaps the most substantial complaint against Canada's electoral system is that it does an exceptionally poor job of accurately translating votes into parliamentary seats. As a result, electoral outcomes do not accurately represent the voting behaviour of Canadians. This is largely because of the presence of more than two competitive parties at the federal level, which generally lowers the threshold of votes needed to win a plurality in many ridings. Although SMP is also used in the US, it is much more representative of the wishes of the voters primarily because there are only two competitive parties, thus avoiding much of the vote-splitting that takes place in Canadian federal elections.

The distortions produced by the electoral system can be observed at two levels. First, the electoral system is criticized as being unrepresentative and even undemocratic at the local level because the candidate who wins the riding often does not receive a majority of the vote. In many cases, the candidate may win with a very small plurality. Results from the 2004 election in the British Columbia riding of Newton-North Delta demonstrate the problem that results when more than two parties are competitive in any given riding. In that constituency, the Conservative candidate was elected with less than a third (32.8 per cent) of the votes cast. The Liberal candidate was supported by 31.5 per cent of the electorate, and the New Democratic Party (NDP) candidate came a close third with 29.2 per cent. Two other candidates combined for 6.4 per cent of the total vote (Parliament of Canada 2005). While most ridings do not produce this kind of result, it is by no means an anomalous example; similar results are produced in numerous ridings in each and every election (Parliament of Canada 2005). In situations like the one presented above, more than two-thirds of the voters in that riding did not support the winning candidate, yet that candidate is the sole representative of the riding in Parliament, leaving those voting for other parties and candidates feeling alienated. The alienation can be magnified if the election was fought over a specific contentious issue, and support of one side of the issue was divided among two parties. If the majority opinion is divided between two or more candidates, the result can be that the minority opinion is the one that is represented in Parliament. Vote splitting, therefore, can as much be the determining factor of who gets elected as the ballots cast by the voters.

The distortions caused by SMP at the constituency level are magnified significantly when viewed from a national perspective. The best example of this is demonstrated by the three federal elections in Canadian history since 1921 that actually resulted in the party that came second in terms of the popular vote actually winning the election.[7] Only twice since 1921 has any party at the federal level received more than 50 per cent of the vote, yet there have been 16 majority governments since that time.[8] This means that 14 elections since 1921 have produced "artificial" parliamentary majorities. While some argue that this produces stronger, more effective government, critics claim that it is undemocratic. When artificial majorities are created, it means that more people voted against the government than for it, and a minority of the electoral minority actually won control of Parliament and, therefore, the government. Table 6.1 demonstrates how significant the distortions between votes and seats at the nation level can be.

Table 6.1: Disparities Between Seats and Votes in Three Federal Elections[1]

| | 1997 ELECTION | | | 2000 ELECTION | | | 2006 ELECTION | |
PARTY	% OF VOTE	% OF SEATS	PARTY	% OF VOTE	% OF SEATS	PARTY	% OF VOTE	% OF SEATS
Liberal	38.4	51.5	Liberal	40.8	57.1	Con.***	36.3	40.3
Reform	19.4	19.9	Alliance	25.5	21.9	Liberal	30.2	33.4
PC*	18.8	6.6	PC	12.2	4.0	NDP	17.5	9.4
NDP	11.0	7.0	BQ	10.7	12.6	BQ	10.4	16.6
BQ**	10.7	14.6	NDP	8.5	4.3	Green	4.5	0

* Progressive Conservative Party
** Bloc Québécois
*** Conservative Party of Canada (merger of Alliance Party and the PCs)
1. The election of 2004 is not included in this chart. The results of that election were (vote %/seat %): Liberals: 36.7/43.8; Conservatives: 29.6/32.1; NDP: 15.7/6.2; BQ: 12.4/17.5.

Of all of Canada's political institutions, the electoral system appears to be the one most likely facing the prospect of formal change. While it seems unlikely that there will be reform at the federal level, some provinces are genuinely moving toward reform. Adopting a clearly US measure, British Columbia and Ontario have moved to fixed election dates, removing the longstanding governmental advantage of being able to determine the timing of the next election.[9] Other more substantial reforms have also been acted on. On 17 May 2005, a referendum on adopting a single transferable vote (STV) system in British Columbia failed to meet the required threshold of 60 per cent, but got the support of 57.7 per cent of voters, a result which will only fuel the electoral reform movement in that province and throughout the country (Elections BC 2005). On 28 November 2005 Prince Edward Island voted in a plebiscite on electoral reform. The initiative failed convincingly with 64 per cent of the provincial electorate rejecting the move to a mixed-member plurality system (Elections PEI 2006). With New Brunswick, Ontario, and Québec also musing about electoral reform, the issue will continue to be on the agenda for the foreseeable future.

The Executive

Canada also differs significantly from its NAFTA partners in the organizational structure of its executive branch. Unlike the US and Mexican systems, the Canadian system has a dual executive, with the Queen as the head of state and the PM as head of government. The Queen and her Canadian representative at the federal level, the Governor General, constitute the formal or ceremonial executive, and the PM and cabinet represent the political executive. As Canada's monarchy is constitutional, it does not play an active role in politics. Today, the Governor General must act on the advice of the PM and only in the rarest of constitutional crises exercises any discretion.

Effective executive power in Canada is held by the PM and cabinet. The PM is by far the most important player in Canadian politics. Donald J. Savoie points out that "Canadian prime ministers ... particularly when they have a majority government in Parliament, have in their hands all the important levers of power" (1999: 72). While the PM has always been a central figure in Canadian politics, over recent decades the role has become increasingly powerful in relation to other federal institutions, particularly Parliament and the cabinet. The PM's power has grown so extensively that many have characterized the Canadian government as prime ministerial government. Indeed, some have gone so far as to describe the PM as a "closet autocrat" (Wallace 1998: 16) or a "friendly dictator" (Simpson 2001).

The powers of the PM are indeed vast. The PM alone determines who will sit in the cabinet and which portfolio each minister will have. In addition, the PM can shuffle the cabinet at any time, remove ministers from the cabinet or demand their resignation, and even create new departments and abolish others. Contrary to the US, where the president's selections for the cabinet must be ratified, the PM faces no such legislative oversight. Because ministers obtain and retain their portfolios at the PM's pleasure, the cabinet cannot provide a significant check on the PM, as any difficult minister can be easily removed. Furthermore, the size, structure, and agenda of the cabinet is controlled by the PM. The cabinet is not a democratic institution; decisions are not taken by votes but when the PM decides that a consensus has been reached, ensuring that the PM's view on any given issue will prevail.

Like the cabinet, Parliament is another institution dominated by the PM, especially when the government controls a majority in the House of Commons. Because of the fusion of the executive and legislative branches under the Westminster parliamentary system, the PM and cabinet must, by convention, sit in the House of Commons. The PM is expected to attend Question Period regularly and is the main focus of attention for both the opposition and the media. Therefore, unlike the US president, who is unable to participate directly in the activities of the legislature, the PM is able to shape the legislative agenda and, using his or her majority, ensure that his or her policies become law. While it is logistically impossible for the PM to take control of all policy decisions made by the Canadian government, the PM can guide those policies he or she chooses through any stage of the legislative process. The ability of the PM simultaneously to exercise both executive and legislative authority makes him or her a uniquely powerful player in Canadian politics.

The PM is able to dominate Parliament because of the strict party discipline imposed on MPs. As Docherty notes, "[p]arty discipline and cabinet solidarity are hallmarks of the Canadian legislative system" (1997: 139). The PM, as government party leader, effectively controls the votes of all the members of the government caucus in most instances. Since party policy is determined by, or at least approved by the PM, he or she can thus assure that his or her policy preferences are pushed through the House. The fact that the PM is also the party leader helps to keep backbench MPs in line; the PM has the power to expel renegade MPs from caucus or even from the party. There are many sanctions the PM can use to ensure that government MPs toe the party line, even refusing to sign the nomination papers for MPs who have embarrassed or caused difficulty for the government. Doing so means that they are unable to run under the party banner in the next election, which may very well end their political career.

The media can also be a source of power for the PM. Coverage of Canadian politics is largely focused on party leaders (Savoie 2005: 21). While voters technically cast ballots for their own representative in Parliament, it is understood that the election is really about the popularity of the party leader and his or her platform. MPs, therefore, recognize that, to a substantial degree, they owe their election to the popularity of the PM and the party platform. This increases the legitimacy of the PM and discourages MPs from challenging him or her.

The PM also derives a significant amount of power from the nature of the leadership selection process. The PM is the only political figure at the federal level who possesses a national constituency. Every PM is elected with a majority vote by the general membership of his or her political party and then is indirectly selected by the Canadian electorate in a general election. This process effectively gives the PM double democratic legitimacy, a status no other federal politician possesses. Individual MPs are only chosen by their local party organization and the voters in their constituencies. Cabinet ministers are ordinary MPs who have been appointed to their position by the PM. Given that the PM is chosen by the general membership of the party and the national electorate, backbench MPs and cabinet ministers do not have the legitimacy to challenge a sitting PM. This explains, in part, why there have been few caucus or cabinet revolts in recent Canadian history. While outright caucus coups are unlikely to occur in the Canadian system, a PM who has become a liability to the party may face intense pressure to step down if he or she has lost support of government members (White 2005: 73–74).

Like the US and Mexican presidents, the PM also possesses the power to make many governmental appointments: senators, deputy ministers, heads of Crown corporations, members of certain federal boards and commissions, federal judges including Supreme Court justices, the lieutenant governors of the provinces, and the Governor General. The PM even has the ability to appoint diplomats and other international representatives. While some appointments, such as those to the Supreme Court, have to meet certain established criteria, the PM has a free hand to fill many of his appointments, and many are made in the name of patronage and doled out to loyal supporters. The power of appointment effectively means that, apart from the House of Commons, whose members are elected, the PM effectively appoints the personnel of the other major federal political, judicial, and bureaucratic institutions. This power is another tool the PM uses to keep his caucus and party members in line by rewarding those who have followed the party's wishes.

The PM's unique ability to conduct foreign affairs is another source of power. The PM possesses the authority to negotiate treaties and enter international agreements on his or her own initiative without the necessity of consulting cabinet or Parliament. The signing of any international agreement does not change Canadian law, however, and usually requires enabling legislation to be passed by Parliament to conform to the treaty. However, if the PM controls a majority government in the House of Commons, the passage of the supporting legislation is usually not in doubt, as was the case with NAFTA. The 1988 Canada-US Free Trade Agreement (CUFTA) is an exception to this example. In that instance, the Liberal-dominated Senate forced PC Prime Minister Brian Mulroney to call an election before they would agree to pass the necessary supporting legislation for the agreement. The enabling legislation for CUFTA became law on 31 December 1988, only after Mulroney's government was re-elected (Campbell and Pal 1991: 213, 216).

Savoie points out that "the globalization of the world economy means that many more issues, or files, will fall into the prime minister's in-basket" (1999: 651). As previously stated, much of the PM's international activity is conducted without consultation with the party, the caucus, or even the cabinet. The power of the PM to act independently in international affairs is demonstrated by the fact that Prime Minister Chrétien negotiated NAFTA before he had even appointed his cabinet (Savoie 1999: 651–52). As decisions need to be made more quickly to deal with changing international events and circumstances, the PM will only continue to grow in influence in the area of foreign affairs.

Although the PM is very powerful in relation to other political institutions, he or she does face significant checks. The media and public opinion clearly constrain his or her options. The Constitution, especially federalism and the Charter, establish significant areas of jurisdiction where the PM has only limited influence. The PM can also be hampered by the financial situation of the government or when the government does not command a majority in the House of Commons, as was the case after the 2004 election. In that instance, Prime Minister Martin was forced to alter the budget significantly to gain the support of the NDP and ensure the continuation of his government. Prime Minister Harper's minority Conservative government will also have to moderate its policies or it will run the risk of being defeated in Parliament by the opposition parties.

After the PM, the cabinet represents the rest of the political executive in Canada. Cabinet ministers are responsible for the administration of their respective departments and, in theory, are responsible to Parliament for the action of the officials under them. Because of the principle of responsible government, the cabinet must speak with a single voice, as it would be impossible to hold the government to account if it were divided. Consequently, cabinet ministers who disagree with governmental policy must either keep silent about their objections or resign. Beyond administrative duties, the cabinet is also a representative body. By convention, the cabinet should reflect the regional diversity of the country. Generally, every province should be represented in the cabinet, as should certain regions and cities. This focus on geographic representation has generally led to overrepresentation of cabinet ministers from certain areas of the country, especially Québec, in an effort to secure political support from that province. The fact that more than half of the cabinet ministers are routinely from Ontario and Québec means that the cabinet is not effective at representing regions other than central Canada.

Although secondary to geographic representation, cabinet appointments have also attempted to reflect the social diversity Canada, with only limited success. In the years following Confederation in 1867, it was politically important that both Protestants and Catholics be present at the cabinet table. In recent decades, there has been an attempt to expand this type of representation to include more cabinet positions for women and ethno-cultural and religious minorities. However, because the main principle of representation remains rooted in geography, women and minorities have been consistently underrepresented in the cabinet. For example, Paul Martin's first cabinet had 39 members, only nine of whom were women (23 per cent). In February 2006, Stephen Harper's first cabinet had only six women ministers out of 27 in total (22 per cent). In 2007, Harper increased the size of his cabinet to 32 members, with only seven women ministers (22 per cent). Harper was also criticized for having only one visible minority member in his first cabinet (3.7 per cent). This representational aspect can significantly constrain the PM in choosing ministers and means that, in many cases, representation, not merit, is the first criterion for the appointment (White 2005: 162). Another consequence of the cabinet functioning as a representative body is that the federal cabinet contains more members than are administratively necessary to ensure that as many segments of Canadian society are represented (White 2005: 30).

Parliament

The Canadian Parliament is the symbolic centre of political life in Canada. However, the role of Parliament in Canadian politics has changed significantly over recent decades, because of the expansion of the powers of the PM and the increased importance of the courts under the Charter. Globalization and the prevalence of trade agreements have also marginalized Parliament to some extent, as the House of Commons has little impact on the conduct of foreign relations, which is dominated by the PM. Furthermore, liberalizing trade agreements has limited the ability of Parliament to develop comprehensive economic policy, especially those policies that favour state intervention or increased regulation.

While parliamentary reform has been discussed for decades, Parliament has come under increasing scrutiny in recent years. In fact, reform of Parliament was made a "top priority" in 2004 by former Prime Minister Martin in his quest to address and correct the "democratic deficit" (Office of the Prime Minister 2005). It is also very high on the agenda of the new Conservative government. Furthermore, Docherty notes that "legislatures at the provincial and national levels seem to be wallowing in new lows of public approval ratings" (2005: 3). Despite the perception that Parliament is in need of substantial reform, it is important to point out that the terms "crisis" or "decline" are often overused. C.E.S. Franks, a leading parliamentary scholar, once noted that, "Parliament is more in need of understanding than of change" (1987: 261). It may be the case that Parliament is in transition as it adapts to changing international circumstances.

THE HOUSE OF COMMONS
Although the Canadian Parliament is bicameral, the House of Commons is the centre of legislative activity. The House is where the government (the PM and cabinet) is held to account for its policies, actions, and inactions by the opposition. Parliamentary politics in Canada are dominated by parties and defined by party competition. The dynamic of the House of Commons is entirely adversarial, and

every aspect of parliamentary activity is structured by partisanship. Party politics are very much ingrained in the institutional culture of Parliament.

Unlike the US, where parties exercise little control over their elected members, Canadian political parties can almost dictate the behaviour of their MPs, allowing them very little discretion, especially during parliamentary votes. While there is slightly more flexibility on the opposition side of the House, MPs almost always vote in blocs according to their party affiliation: government MPs are expected to support the government, and opposition MPs are expected to oppose the government. An MP's failure to obey the party can result in serious consequences; renegade MPs can be removed from committees, suspended from the parliamentary caucus, and even expelled from the party. Furthermore, defying the party almost certainly rules out any possibility of a future promotion to cabinet or retiring to an appointment in the Senate. Given the relatively few safe seats that exist at the federal level, and the low success rate of independent MPs in federal elections, crossing the party can be a risky proposition. MPs also realize that they were elected more because of their party affiliation, their leader, and the party platform than on their own personal strengths.

Party discipline in Canada flows largely from the confidence convention associated with responsible government: the government of the day is only permitted to continue in power if it has the continued support of a majority of MPs. Losing the confidence of Parliament results in the defeat of the government and an election call. Such a defeat occurred on 28 November 2005 when Parliament voted 171 to 133 in support of a non-confidence motion, thus ending the Liberal minority government and precipitating an election. However, a government losing the confidence of the House of Commons is a relatively rare occurrence. Before 2005, the last time this happened was in 1979, when the Clark PC government was defeated on a budgetary matter. While maintaining the confidence of Parliament is a cornerstone of Westminster democracy, successive PMs have interpreted the notion of confidence very broadly to keep their members in line. If most votes in Parliament are declared to be confidence motions by the government, MPs from the government side of the House are obligated to support them, regardless of their own convictions or the views of their constituents.

There is really no reason why so many measures in the Canadian Parliament should be considered confidence measures; losing a single vote on an ordinary piece of legislation does not necessarily mean that the government has lost the confidence of the House. Moreover, such a rigid interpretation of the confidence convention is relatively new. In the past, governments used to lose the occasional vote in the House of Commons but demonstrated that they still had the confidence of the House by passing other legislation or by winning a confidence motion. For example, although both Prime Ministers Pearson and Trudeau lost more than one parliamentary vote during their tenure, their governments continued after demonstrating that they had enough support in Parliament to govern (Docherty 1997: 142). One problem with this confidence convention is that it is not always clear how to define exactly when the government has lost confidence in the House of Commons. For example, on 10 May 2005, the House passed a motion of non-confidence. The Liberal government, however, refused to acknowledge that it had lost the confidence of the House because the motion was procedural in nature. The following week the Liberals were able to pass the budget (by the narrowest of margins) and, thus, confirmed that they still had the support of the House.

There is a healthy debate regarding the impact of party discipline on Canadian politics. Those who see it as positive point out that a substantial degree of party discipline is required under the principle of responsible government. Party discipline, even in most minority parliaments, produces a remarkable degree of stability and predictability in Canadian politics: once the parties have announced how they will vote on any matter, it is usually clear how that vote will go. Unlike in the US Congress, where observers must calculate how individual legislators will vote to predict what the outcome will be, in Canada each party essentially gets the same number of votes as it has attending members in the House. This also ensures that MPs are not unduly influenced or lobbied by outside interests since they must follow the party line.

Others see party discipline in Canada as a negative attribute of Canada's Parliament and a significant contributor to voter alienation. Since MPs are beholden to the party, many have argued that they are not adequately able to represent their constituents or their own points of view. The limited discretion is often very frustrating to backbench MPs. This fact is noted by Atkinson and Docherty who argue that "... once MPs arrive in Ottawa, the Westminster model assigns them a rather prosaic task. If they sit on the government side of the House, their job is to express confidence in their leadership by voting for government-sponsored measures; if they are opposition members they are expected to oppose those measures, at least if directed to do so by the opposition party leadership" (Atkinson and Docherty 2000: 10). One MP, disappointed with his lack of input into the system, echoed this sentiment with a football metaphor: "I went [to Ottawa] to play halfback or defensive lineman, instead they gave me a pair of pom-poms and sent me to the cheering section" (Brown 1994). Because ordinary MPs play only a minimal role in the policy-making process, many backbenchers turn to constituency work, which is perceived as a more rewarding part of the job (Docherty 1997: 192–93). Loosening party discipline is not only seen as a way of providing MPs with more rewarding duties, but as a way of checking the power of the PM. If MPs had more freedom, the PM could not automatically count on their vote and would therefore be more accountable to the caucus.

Attempts to break party discipline have been the subject of much discussion. The most noteworthy of his attempts to reduce the influence of party discipline was the adoption of the three-line whip by the Liberal Party in 2004. The three-line whip has long been part of British parliamentary practice and, in theory, is able to simultaneously reduce party discipline substantially while still maintaining the core principle of responsible government. Under this system, votes are categorized into three different levels of importance:

> a three-line vote will be for votes of confidence and for a limited number of matters of fundamental importance to the government. Government members will be expected to support the government. Two-line votes are free votes on which the government will take a position and recommend a preferred outcome to its caucus. Ministers are bound to support the

government's position on a Two-line vote, as are Parliamentary Secretaries
of Ministers affected by it, but Private Members are free to vote as they
wish. On One-line free votes, all government MPs, including Ministers,
will be free to vote as they see fit. (Office of the Prime Minister 2005)

Those in favour of this system believe that MPs will be able to better represent the
views of their constituents and exercise more of their own discretion. However, as
the whip system is an informal practice and the ranking of the bills is determined by
the party, deciding how important any given bill is would still be out of the control
of individual MPs.

These reforms have not had much of an impact on parliamentary practice and
the voting behaviour of MPs. This can be attributed primarily to the results of the
2004 election which left the Liberal government with only a tenuous minority in
Parliament. With the threat of the government falling on any given vote, there was
no room at all for any dissent in the party ranks. In the end, the three-line whip
system was abandoned by the government. The few MPs who disagreed with the
government were forced to leave the party and sit as independents. Likewise, during his first year in power, Prime Minister Harper tightened party discipline to an
unprecedented level to ensure that the Conservative caucus remained cohesive in a
tenuous minority situation.

Some have suggested that the problem lies with the principle of responsible government itself and have therefore suggested Canada move to a system that does not
require such strict party discipline. One way this could be achieved is through direct
democracy. The use of referendums, recall, initiative, and Senate reform are seen
as ways of reducing the power of parliamentary parties to control their members.
Electoral reform is also often presented as an indirect way of reforming Parliament;
a more proportional electoral system would make majority governments much
less likely and, as a corollary, reduce the PM's control over the legislative branch
substantially.

THE SENATE

Canada's upper house, the Senate, is a strange institution that cannot be explained
by its current role in the Canadian political system. According to the Constitution,
the Senate is a very powerful institution. In practice, however, it plays only a minor
role in Canadian politics because it lacks democratic legitimacy; all of its members
are appointed by the Governor General on the advice of the PM.[10] However, with
only two exceptions, the power of the Senate is constitutionally equal to that of the
House of Commons. Because of the principle that only the people can tax themselves, money bills may not be introduced into the Senate (Monahan 2002: 86). The
Senate, however, must approve all bills passed by the House of Commons (including
money bills) before they can become law. The only other restriction placed on the
Senate is found in the Constitution Act, 1982, which removed its absolute veto over
constitutional reform. The Senate now only possesses a 180-day delaying power over
most constitutional amendments.

The Senate was originally designed as a check on the impulses of the lower house.
Suspicious that the expansion of the franchise would allow the masses to control

the House of Commons, the drafters of the 1867 Constitution envisaged the Senate as a conservative body which would protect the interests of property.[11] It was also intended to be a representative body as each senator is appointed from a specific province (Ajzenstat 2003: 14). The Senate, however, has not been an effective voice for the provinces in Ottawa because senators are unelected, unaccountable, and appointed by the federal PM.

As a fully appointed chamber, the Senate has long been criticized as a retirement home for government party loyalists and as a prime patronage plum for the PM to dole out to his cronies (Hoy 1999: preface). Recent PMs have attempted to rehabilitate the image of the Senate by occasionally appointing senators who are prominent members of the community in addition to those appointed on a patronage basis.

The most popular model for Senate reform over the last 20 years has been the "Triple-E Senate" modeled after the US Senate: Elected, Effective, and with Equal representation for each province. Reforming the Senate in such a manner is seen as a method of checking the power of the PM and increasing provincial voices in Ottawa. The NDP and other critics have long called for the abolition of the Senate, leaving the House of Commons to function as a unicameral legislature. In the 2006 election campaign, the Conservatives indicated their support for an elected Senate either through an official constitutional amendment or informally by the PM "appointing" senators that have been elected by provincial voters. The election of senators would have serious implications for the operation of the Canadian Parliament. Not only would the Senate possess the legitimacy it currently lacks to challenge governmental policy, it could provide a serious check on the PM and lead to political deadlock between the two houses of Parliament. The issue of Senate reform remains a central plank in the Conservative government's agenda of increased accountability for Canadian political institutions.

The Canadian Judiciary

The relationship of the Canadian judiciary to other political institutions has changed dramatically within the last quarter century. The adoption of the Charter increased the importance of Canadian courts exponentially. Prior to the Charter, the courts did not have the power or the public profile that they have today. Until 1982, the Canadian constitutional order supported the notion of the supremacy of Parliament. Consequently, the only judicial review permitted in Canada came from the court's role as the adjudicator of federalism. However, the adoption of the Charter ended the principle of legislative supremacy and moved it to constitutional supremacy.

The Canadian courts are currently adapting to a new role resulting from Canada's signing of NAFTA. Canadian judges are now making rulings under NAFTA that have set important precedents for interpreting both the trade agreement and decisions made by NAFTA tribunals. One of the most significant NAFTA decisions made by Canadian courts to date is that of *S.D. Myers v. Canada* (International Trade Canada 2005a). That case began in November 2000 when the NAFTA tribunal awarded S.D. Myers (an American waste disposal company dealing in PCBs) $8 million in compensation after the company complained that it was discriminated against by the Canadian government under Chapter 11. The Canadian government appealed the decision to the Federal Court of Canada, which dismissed it in January 2004 and ordered that compensation plus interest must be paid (Jack 2005).

Canadian courts have also taken on the new role of adjudicating disputes that arise under NAFTA even if those cases do not involve Canadian companies or public policy. The best example of such a case is *Karpa v. Mexico*. In *Karpa*, the NAFTA tribunal ruled that the government of Mexico had discriminated against Marvin Roy Feldman Karpa (a US citizen) under article 1103 because it would not issue him rebates for export taxes on cigarettes (International Trade Canada 2005b). As the tribunal's decision was made at an Ottawa locale, the case fell under the jurisdiction of the Ontario Superior Court, which ruled in favour of Karpa and upheld the ruling of the NAFTA tribunal (Ontario Court of Appeal 2005a). The case was then appealed to the Ontario Court of Appeal (OCA), which also ruled that Karpa's business practices had been unfairly discriminated against under NAFTA. Perhaps more importantly, the OCA ruled that under both Ontario and federal law Canadian courts should generally be deferential to NAFTA tribunal rulings (Ontario Court of Appeal 2005a).

Canadian courts have recently dealt with the constitutionality of NAFTA's investor protection provision found in Chapter 11. In March 2001, the Council of Canadians, the Canadian Union of Postal Workers, and the Charter Committee on Poverty Issues launched legal action arguing that Chapter 11 violated the terms of the Charter (International Trade Canada 2006).[12] According to the complainants, the terms of NAFTA violate those rights in the Charter that protect fundamental justice, equality, and fairness (Ontario Court of Appeal 2005b). Critics maintain that secretive NAFTA tribunals currently operate illegally outside of the framework of Canadian law. From their perspective, this situation is unconstitutional because the Canadian Constitution is the supreme law of the land, and all decision-making bodies must therefore conform to constitutional provisions, including the Charter. As a corollary, NAFTA and the Canadian laws supporting it are unconstitutional. The litigants opposed to Chapter 11 also argued that the federal government's treaty-making power does not permit it to make treaties that override constitutional provisions such as the rule of law, democracy, and constitutionalism. The case was heard by the Ontario Superior Court in January 2005 and was dismissed on all counts in July of that year. The constitutionality of NAFTA was upheld in November 2006 by the OCA (Council of Canadians 2006). It is only a matter of time before the Supreme Court will have to deal with the issue. These cases have resulted in substantial controversy, and the continued interpretation of NAFTA, and how it relates to the Charter and other Canadian political institutions will be contentious for some time.

Because of the increased role Canadian courts now play in the shaping of Canadian public policy, particularly in their role of interpreting the Charter, they are under heavy academic scrutiny. Some argue that the courts have become too powerful and have overstepped their traditional bounds by interfering in the policy-making process (Knopff and Morton 2000). The selection of judges, especially at the Supreme Court, has also been criticized. Currently, the PM alone has the power to appoint federal judges, including Supreme Court justices, but regularly consults experts and seeks out recommendations. With the increased importance of judges, some believe that PMs are now appointing judges based on ideological preferences to ensure a certain interpretation of the Constitution. For a long time many have been critical of the appointment process because it is too secretive and does not allow for public scrutiny. Suggestions for reform of the process include parliamentary ratification of judicial appointment as well as greater provincial involvement, both of which may further politicize the judiciary. In fact, less than a month after coming into power, the Conservative government announced that a new, more open process would be used to appoint new justices to the Supreme Court of Canada (Office of the Prime Minister 2007b). Shortly after, in February 2006, history was made when Marshall Rothstein, the PM's nominee to fill a vacancy on the Supreme Court, appeared before an *ad hoc* parliamentary committee and answered questions from MPs. While this was a move toward more transparency in the selection process of Supreme Court justices, the PM retains control over the process.

The Canadian Bureaucracy

Like all modern democracies, Canada has a complex organizational bureaucracy that carries out the work of government. Originally, the Canadian bureaucracy was staffed according to the spoils system (Simpson 1988). However, by the early 1900s, the merit system was adopted, and patronage gradually ended in the civil service. Today, the Canadian public service is staffed almost entirely by professional, permanent, and non-partisan employees. Unlike the US, with its high number of partisan staff, after a general election in Canada, the personnel in the public service remain the same, regardless of the electoral outcome. Only the partisan support staff of ministers and the PM are replaced when there is a change in government or cabinet.

Very early on in the history of the federal civil service there were concerns about representation within it. Given that Canada is a country with deep social divisions, the issue of representation remains important today. The most significant issue in terms of representation is bilingualism in the federal bureaucracy, which has been a substantial source of tension over the years. In Canada's early days, the operational language of the bureaucracy was generally English, and most civil servants came from Ontario. When Canada moved to the merit principle, "merit" included competence in the English language as well as other characteristics that mirrored the existing bureaucracy (Dyck 2004: 542). The result of systemic discrimination against francophones meant that there were few opportunities for French-speaking bureaucrats, and they generally occupied lower ranks within the bureaucracy. This began to change in 1969 with the passage of the Official Languages Act, which sought to make the federal public service bilingual. This policy has been a substantial success as the number of positions available for francophones has increased dramatically and at all levels. In 2004, 39 per cent of federal civil service positions were listed as bilingual, with an additional 5 per cent designated as "French essential" (Public Service Human Resources Management Agency of Canada 2005a).

Other issues of representation have been significant at the federal level; concerns that women, Aboriginal peoples, visible minority Canadians and the disabled were not adequately represented, especially at the higher ranks of the bureaucracy, were acknowledged with the Employment Equity Act, 1986. That Act, which applied both to the government and large private sector companies under federal regulation, mandated for preferential appointments of these enumerated groups to ameliorate discrimination of the past. In the 2003–04 fiscal year, the Public Service Human Resources Management Agency (PSHRMA) reported that 53 per cent of federal civil servants were women. However, only one in three executive positions were held by women. In addition, 4 per cent of civil service positions were staffed by Aboriginal peoples, 8 per cent were filled by visible minorities, and 6 per cent were held by persons with disabilities (Public Service Human Resources Management Agency of Canada 2005b). According to the PSHRMA, women, Aboriginal peoples, and persons with disabilities are "well represented" in the civil service. Visible minorities, however, were below the PSHRMA's goal of 10.4 per cent (Public Service Human Resources Management Agency of Canada 2005b).

Another increasingly contentious issue in Canadian politics is the proper relationship between elected officials and the public service and to what degree there is enough democratic control of the bureaucracy. Canada inherited the British principle whereby each ministry, department, and agency of government is responsible to Parliament through a minister of the Crown. In theory, the minister is accountable for every action taken by his or her department. In the past it was often the case that a minister would resign even if he or she had no knowledge of, or involvement in, the error or inappropriate activity that occurred in the department. Over recent years, however, ministers are no longer automatically accepting responsibility for events with which they were not directly involved, arguing that their departments are too complex for them realistically to monitor every single activity. The debacle in Human Resources Development Canada, as well as the recent sponsorship scandal, have also demonstrated the unwillingness of politicians to resign or accept responsibility for what happens in their departments.[13] This changing relationship between ministers and their departments will have a substantial impact on Parliament's ability to check the activity of the bureaucracy and will raise many core issues about democratic control of the civil service.

Conclusion

There can be no doubt that the forces of globalization and increased continental integration are transforming many Canadian political institutions. Much of this change, however, has not required any formal institutional change. Unless increased economic integration is accompanied by political integration, significant changes to Canada's political institutions will not be necessary because they possess a remarkable degree of flexibility and adaptability.

The impact of these international forces has not been felt equally across all of Canada's political institutions. The PM, for example, has gained power at the expense of other Canadian institutions, not only for domestic reasons, but also because of the PM's ability to conduct foreign affairs. Because of the concentration of power inherent to the Westminster system, the PM is able to make international commitments and can do so quickly and with very few institutional checks or impediments.

This allows for some stability in the conduct of Canadian trade and foreign policy. If international agreements are signed by Canada, a strong PM is able to ensure that they are implemented and enforced. Consequently, so long as the PM is supportive, then Canada should face few barriers to more substantial integration. However, the opposite is also true; if Canadians elect a PM who opposes closer ties with Canada's NAFTA partners, it could be a substantial barrier to further continental integration.

Like the PM, the Canadian judiciary has also been empowered by NAFTA as it plays an increasing role in arbitrating trade disputes. This will be an increasingly important duty of the courts. On the other hand, the cabinet and Parliament are institutions that, at this point, have generally suffered because of globalization and declined in relative power compared with the PM. In an age of rapid communication and executive decision-making, Parliament, which is by definition slow and deliberative, appears to many Canadians to be unable to keep pace with the changing world. The shortcomings of Parliament are undoubtedly overstated. However, there is a perception held by many, including the government, that it is an institution in crisis and in serious need of reform. Only time will tell how Canadian political institutions adapt to their new surroundings in a changing economic and political order.

Notes

1   Turnout in federal elections has dropped steadily in recent years. The 1988 election had a turnout rate of 75.3 per cent followed by the election of 1993 (70.9 per cent), 1997 (67 per cent), 2000 (64.1 per cent) and 2004 (60.9 per cent) (Elections Canada 2006). The 2006 election had a voter turnout of 64.9 per cent.

2   This poll found that there was low trust in government. When asked, what the "most important issue facing the country" was, poor government/poor leadership got the second highest number of responses with 12 per cent, only after health care. The poll also demonstrated that there was substantial support for institutional reform, such as moving to fixed election dates.

3   For example, the Royal Proclamation of 7 October 1763.

4   A clear example of a British statute that is considered of constitutional significance would be the Statute of Westminster (1931). Important federal statutes that some argue have constitutional status include acts such as the Parliament of Canada Act, Canada Elections Act, and the Citizenship Act among others.

5   For example, in the 1998 Québec provincial election, the Parti Québécois (PQ) won a majority in the Québec National Assembly with only 42.7 per cent of the vote. The Liberals received a larger percentage (43.7) but won 27 fewer seats.

6   The size of the House of Commons has grown dramatically over the years. In 1867 there were only 181 MPs. By 1917 the number had grew to 235. In 1965 there were 265, and today there are 308.

7   This occurred in 1957, 1962, and 1979.

8   In 1940, the Liberals received 52 per cent of the vote. In 1953, the Progressive Conservatives (PCs) won 54 per cent of the vote. The 1949 Liberals and the 1984 PCs each won 50 per cent of the vote (Thorburn and Whitehorn 2001: 486–87).

9   The new federal Conservative government has also indicated its preference for fixed election dates.

10 By convention, the Governor General has no discretion regarding the appointment of senators and must follow the advice of the PM. Senators hold their position until they reach the age of 75.

11 For example, according to the Constitution, senators are required to be over 30 years of age, and a "Senator's Real and Personal Property shall be together worth Four thousand Dollars over and above his Debts and Liabilities." In 1867, this would have been a substantial barrier that would have precluded the vast majority of Canadians from holding a Senate seat.

12 *The Council of Canadians and al. v. Canada* (A.G).

13 In 2000 it was revealed that, according to an internal audit, Human Resources Development Canada (HRDC) had lost track of $1 billion worth of employment creation grants. This resulted in numerous police investigations and political scandal as the audit found that HRDC money was used for questionable purposes in the ridings of Liberal cabinet ministers, including that of Prime Minister Jean Chrétien. The sponsorship scandal surfaced in 2002 when the Auditor-General of Canada discovered that a fund set up to increase the presence of Canada in Québec after the 1995 referendum on Québec sovereignty had not followed proper rules and that millions of dollars were misspent. Over $100 million was spent by the government on Liberal-friendly communication firms for fees and commissions; some of this money was, in turn, donated to the Liberal Party, leading to obvious charges of corruption. The sponsorship scandal was a key issue in the elections of 2004 and 2006 and has become synonymous with corruption in government.

References

Ajzenstat, Janet. 2003. "Bicameralism and Canada's Founders." In Serge Joyal (ed.), *Protecting Canadian Democracy: The Senate You Never Knew*. Montreal and Kingston: McGill-Queen's UP.

Atkinson, Michael M., and David C. Docherty. 2000. *Parliament and Political Success in Canada*. Toronto: Nelson.

Bourque, Deborah, and Maude Barlow. 2005. "So Remind Us Again Why Canada Had to Sign NAFTA?" *Globe and Mail*, 9 January. <http://www.theglobeandmail.com/servlet/story/RTGAM.20050901.wcomment0901/BNStory/National/>.

Brown, Bert. 1994. "Parliamentary Discipline: An Informal Survey of Opinion." *Canadian Parliamentary Review* 17,2. <http://www.parl.gc.ca/Infoparl/english/issue.htm?param=149&art=1002>.

Cairns, Alan C. 1971. "The Judicial Committee and Its Critics." *Canadian Journal of Political Science* 4: 301–45.

———. 1992a. "International Influence on the Charter." In *The Charter versus Federalism*. Montreal and Kingston: McGill-Queen's UP.

———. 1992b. "The Charter and the Constitution Act, 1982." In *The Charter versus Federalism*. Montreal and Kingston: McGill-Queen's UP.

Campbell, Robert M., and Leslie A. Pal. 1991. *The Real Worlds of Canadian Politics: Cases in Process and Policy*. Peterborough, ON: Broadview Press.

Council of Canadians. 2006. "Court Upholds Corporate Rights Under NAFTA." 1 December. <http://www.canadians.org/trade/issues/NAFTA/decision_Nov30_2006.html>.

Courchene, Thomas J. 2004. "Pan Canadian Provincialism: The New Federalism and the Old Constitution." *Policy Options*, November, IRPP. <http://www.irpp.org/po/archive/nov04/courchene.pdf>.

Docherty, David C. 1997. *Mr. Smith Goes to Ottawa: Life in the House of Commons*. Vancouver: U of British Columbia P.

———. 2005. *Legislatures*. Vancouver: U of British Columbia P.

Dyck, Rand. 2004. *Canadian Politics: Critical Approaches*. Toronto: Nelson.

Elections BC. 2005. "Final Referendum Results." <http://www.elections.bc.ca/elections/ge2005/finalrefresults.htm>.

Elections Canada. 2005a. "Representation in the House of Commons."<http://www.elections.ca/scripts/fedrep/federal_e/RED/representation_e.htm>.

——. 2005b. "Representation Formula: Detailed Calculations for the 2001 Census." <http://www.elections.ca/scripts/fedrep/federal_e/repform_e.htm>.

——. 2006. "Voter Turnout at Federal Elections and Referendums, 1867–2004." <http://www.elections.ca/content.asp?section=pas&document=turnout&lang=e&textonly=false>.

Elections PEI. 2006. "Plebiscite on Mixed Member Proportional Representation System: Official Results." <http://www.electionspei.ca/plebiscites/pr/results/index.php>.

Environics-CBC. 2005. "A Matter of Trust." Poll released on 31 May, cited on 1 June. <http://erg.environics.net/news/default.asp?aID=581>.

Epps, Tracey, and Colleen M. Flood. 2002. "Have We Traded Away the Opportunity for Innovative Health Care Reform? The Implications of the NAFTA for Medicare." *McGill Law Journal* 47. 747–90.

Fair Vote. 2005. <http://www.fairvote.org/index.php>.

Fair Vote Canada. 2005. <http://www.fairvotecanada.org/fvc.php/>.

Franks, C.E.S. 1987. *The Parliament of Canada.* Toronto: U of Toronto P.

Government of New Brunswick, Commission on Legislative Democracy. 2006. "Final Report and Recommendations, March 31." <http://www.gnb.ca/0100/index-e.asp>.

Heard, Andrew S. 1990. "Canadian Independence." <http://www.sfu.ca/~aheard/324/Independence.html>.

Hoy, Clair. 1999. *Nice Work: The Continuing Scandal of Canada's Senate.* Toronto: McClelland and Stewart.

International Trade Canada. 2005a. "Dispute Settlement." <http://www.dfait-maeci.gc.ca/tna-nac/SDM-en.asp>.

——. 2005b. "Dispute Settlement." <http://www.dfait-maeci.gc.ca/tna-nac/mexico-en.asp>.

——. 2006. "Dispute Settlement." <http://www.dfait-maeci.gc.ca/tna-nac/cupw-en.asp>.

Jack, Ian. 2005. "Court Upholds NAFTA Tribunal in Ruling over Ottawa's PCB Move: $8-Million Judgment." *National Post*, 15 January.

Knopff, Rainer, and F.L. Morton. 2000. *The Charter Revolution and the Court Party.* Peterborough, ON: Broadview.

Law Commission of Canada. 2004. *Voting Counts: Electoral Reform for Canada.* Ottawa: The Queen's Printer for Canada.

Lipset, Seymour Martin. 1990. *Continental Divide: The Values and Institutions of the United States and Canada.* New York: Routledge.

MacIvor, Heather. 2006. *Canadian Politics and Charter Era.* Toronto: Thompson Nelson.

Marshall, Geoffrey, and Graeme Moodie. 1968. *Some Problems of the Constitution.* London: Hutchinson and Co.

McBride, Stephen. 2003. "Quiet Constitutionalism in Canada: The International Political Economy of Domestic Institutional Change." *Canadian Journal of Political Science* 36,2 (June). 252–73.

Milner, Henry. 2004. *Steps Toward Making Every Vote Count.* Peterborough, ON: Broadview Press.

Monahan, Patrick. 2002. *Constitutional Law.* 2nd ed. Toronto: Irwin Law.

Office of the Prime Minister. 2005. "Democratic Reform." Cited on 1 June. <http://pm.gc.ca/eng/dem_reform.asp>.

——. 2007a. "Priorities." 10 March. <http://www.pm.gc.ca/eng/feature.asp?featureId=5>.

——. 2007b. "Prime Minister Harper Announces Nominee for Supreme Court Appointment." 23 February 2006. <http://www.pm.gc.ca/eng/media.asp?category=1&id=1030>.

Ontario Court of Appeal. 2005a. *The United Mexican States v. Marvin Roy Feldman Karpa.* Docket C41169, 11 January. <http://www.investmentclaims.com/decisions/Feldman-Mexico-OntarioCourtofAppeal-11Jan2005.pdf>.

——. 2005b. Factum: *The Council of Canadians et al. v. Canada* (A.G). Court file case no. C43995. <http://www.dfait-maeci.gc.ca/tna-nac/documents/factum-of-appeal.pdf>.

Parliament of Canada. 2005. "History of Federal Ridings Since 1867." <http://www.parl. gc.ca/information/about/process/house/hfer/hfer.asp?Language=E&Search=G&Source= AboutParl_Process>.

Public Service Human Resources Management Agency of Canada. 2005a. "Annual Report on Official Languages: Table 2." <http://www.hrma-agrh.gc.ca/reports-rapports/ arol-ralo2_e.asp#Table%201>.

——. 2005b. "Employment Equity in the Federal Civil Service 2003–04: Presidents Message." <http:// www.hrma-agrh.gc.ca/reports-rapports/ee-04-1_e.asp>.

Rocher, François, and Miriam Smith. 1995. "Four Dimensions of the Canadian Constitutional Debate." In François Rocher and Miriam Smith (eds.), *New Trends in Canadian Federalism*. Peterborough, ON: Broadview Press.

Russell, Peter H. 1983. "The Political Purposes of the Canadian Charter of Rights and Freedoms." *Canadian Bar Review* 61: 30–54.

——. 2004. *Constitutional Odyssey: Can Canadians Become a Sovereign People?* Toronto: U of Toronto P.

Savoie. Donald J. 1999. "The Rise of Court Government." *Canadian Journal of Political Science* 32,4 (December): 635–64.

——. 2005. "The Federal Government: Revisiting Court Government in Canada." In Luc Bernier *et al.* (eds.), *Executive Styles in Canada*. Vancouver: U of British Columbia P.

Simpson, Jeffery. 1988. *Spoils of Power: The Politics of Patronage*. Toronto: Collins.

——. 2001. *The Friendly Dictatorship*. Toronto: McClelland and Stewart.

Skogstad, Grace. 2002. "International Trade Policy and Canadian Federalism: A Constructive Tension." In Herman Bakvis and Grace Skogstad (eds.), *Canadian Federalism: Performance, Effectiveness, and Legitimacy*. Toronto: Oxford UP.

Thorburn, Hugh, and Alan Whitehorn. 2001. *Party Politics in Canada*. Toronto: Prentice-Hall.

Wallace, Bruce. 1998. "For the Love of Power: Is Jean Chrétien a Closet Autocrat?" *McLean's*, 19 October.

White, Graham. 2005. *Cabinets and First Ministers*. Vancouver: U of British Columbia P.

CHAPTER SEVEN

Political Institutions in the United States

Ross E. Burkhart

N orth Americans are living in an era of regional economic integration, thanks to accords such as NAFTA. The economic results of this integration are dramatic. Trade between the NAFTA partners (Canada, Mexico, and the US) has reached $1.7 billion dollars a day. Canada is the US's largest trading partner, and Mexico is the US's second largest trading partner. Canada's exports to Mexico and the US have increased in value by 104 per cent during the NAFTA era (Office of the United States Trade Representative 2004).

NAFTA is more than a decade old, and will quite possibly expand beyond its three-country membership into either a Central American free trading zone or, more ambitiously, into a Free Trade Area of the Americas (FTAA). Despite these deepening economic ties, which are emblematic of the globalization era, and the rules that will bind their interactions, countries will retain their sovereignty and domestic institutions. It is thus important to understand the institutions of each of the current NAFTA members, for at least two reasons: (1) assessing their ability to maintain their integrity in this regional economic integration era and (2) comparing their strengths and weaknesses.

The political institutions of the US cannot be discussed without reference to the federal-state relationship. This chapter begins with a section on federalism and then introduces the major political institutions at the federal level in the US: Congress, the presidency, the courts, and the bureaucracy. It discusses their constitutional powers and illustrates how these powers work in practice, noting how these institutions have changed during the current era of globalization which spans from the early 1970s onward (Steger 2003: 35). The working definition of globalization employed in this chapter is that "globalization is characterized by an increasing global scope for technological advances, international regimes, and trade flows" (Burkhart 2002: 34). Globalization thus encompasses a diverse set of behaviours that include the integration of financial markets, the creation of international institutions to solve problems common to nation-states, and the flow of capital trade and human beings via emigration. (This chapter will not discuss the cultural aspects of globalization.) The overall theme is delineating the powers of the US political institutions and the extent to which they have been shaped by globalization (which I contend is but a rather small amount, given the US's prominence in the North American economy) or how they have shaped globalization (which I contend is a rather large amount).

Political institutions in the US, as in any other nation-state, provide both a framework for making decisions on political matters and a means by which the prevailing political culture adapts to changing times. The institutions discussed in this chapter are either direct creations of the US Constitution or, as in the case of the bureaucracy, emanate from the delineation of these institutions in the Constitution. Thus, their place within the US political scene is permanent, and their influence on political discourse and decision-making is undeniable.

Despite the fact that the word "institution" connotes an imposing edifice, resistant to change, political institutions adjust to the times and the demands of the public. Sometimes the adjustments result from a democratic policy process, sometimes not. Given the focus of this book on North American politics and the impact that globalization has had on it, I will pay special attention to the changes wrought by globalization to US political institutions. While I have suggested that the US has had more influence on globalization than it has been influenced by it, there are some exceptions to that rule that are quite important in current political discourse, such as the 2001 USA Patriot Act (H.R. 3162) and the 1993 NAFTA (Public Law 103–192). The USA Patriot Act gives greater power to law enforcement to interdict suspected terrorists, whether they are in the US or in other countries. Law enforcement can acquire information and skirt privacy laws in the process. NAFTA creates a regional free trade zone that attempts to consolidate the power of two G-7 countries on an increasingly competitive global trading stage.

While it is common to think of the framework aspect of institutions in that laws are made via a process that incorporates elected representatives within legislative, executive, and judicial bodies, the cultural side of institutions is relatively neglected. Institutions can be defined as "the beliefs, customs, laws, rules and norms that guide the behaviour of individuals and groups within society" (Cornwall and Cornwall 2001: 69). Therefore, the institutional culture of Congress, or of the Supreme Court, or of the bureaucracy that envelops the Department of Defense or Department of State, must also be examined in order more fully to understand the influence of institutions on American political life.

The framers of the US Constitution—Alexander Hamilton, Benjamin Franklin, Thomas Jefferson, and James Madison—gave institutional prominence to the Congress. They envisioned that the weighty decisions of the republic would be made principally by the people's chamber. While events have largely disproved this republican vision, given Congress's prominence in the Constitution, it is appropriate that Congress be examined first because it is a fulcrum for political change.

The institution of the US presidency is particularly relevant in that it has acquired a tremendous amount of power in the post-World War II period. US historian Arthur Schlesinger's observation that the Nixon administration's drift toward an "Imperial Presidency," complete with palace guard uniforms that President Nixon asked the White House security detail to don (a request later rescinded following considerable public criticism), is prescient and prophetic regarding the acquisition of power by future presidential administrations. The powers acquired by the Bush administration in the wake of the events of 9/11, such as those contained in the US Patriot Act, arguably tipped the balance of institutional power away from the legislative branch and further toward the executive branch in the early years of the twenty-first century.

Following analysis of the executive branch, the chapter concludes with an examination of the courts and the bureaucracy, pointing out the impact that globalization has had on each, especially in threatening their legitimacy and weakening their impact on US domestic politics and their influence on US foreign policy.

Federalism

Fundamentally, we must note that the guideposts that demarcate institutional development in the US originate with the federalist nature of the Constitution. The US sought a mechanism by which to mitigate the centralizing power of the unitary parliamentary monarchy that characterizes British governance (Rocher 2000). Throughout the colonial era, the states increasingly chafed under the hand of the monarchy and developed a distaste for centralized power.

There was also a practical side to the US Constitution, which speaks to the ability of the US to bring about institutional evolution. The framers wished to avoid the problems caused by the confederation of states and the national government that arose during the Articles of Confederation, which were passed in 1777 as an alternative to the British parliamentary monarchy and were fundamentally opposite to the British system in that the federal government derived its powers from the subunits, the states. Hence, "the national government in a confederacy is weaker than the sum of its parts" (O'Connor and Sabato 2004: 42). While the Articles allowed the federal government to raise a military and to defend the country, the states retained full sovereignty and had to be unanimous in agreeing to the passage of any matter, with each state having a single vote in the Continental Congress, regardless of the size of its population. The Articles failed to provide a central administration for the country, leaving a great deal of power to the states. The federal government could not tax, coin money, or regulate commerce. In general, it could not conduct any activity that was reserved to the states. All this resulted in a politically weakened country, where uprisings such as Shays' Rebellion[1] painted a picture of economic doom (an alarming rise in bankruptcies left citizens vulnerable to the chaotic commercial rules of the individual states) and societal lawlessness. The new federalist framework as drafted during the Constitutional Convention of 1789 in Philadelphia would provide a key balance between unitary and confederal versions of government and thus save the Union.

While federalist theory could be gleaned from the theoretical writings of Montesquieu, among others, and the creations of Aboriginal peoples such as the Iroquois and Huron confederacies (see Barreiro 1988), it was left to the young country to attempt to put theories of separate branches of governmental power into existence. The risks of federalism would be assumed by the new republic, but it was not a reckless endeavour. The considerable spread of the new US states up and down the East Coast ensured that geographic distance would be a factor in the governance of the country. Given the history of the former colonial governments, some power would have to be "reserved" by the federal government to the states. The colonial legislatures effectively combated the power of the London-appointed colonial governors through the appropriations process as they wilfully failed to provide funds for activities they did not favour (Covington and Burkhart 1994). Through such concessions as the "3/5ths Compromise" that counted African-Americans as 3/5 of a person for the purposes of enumeration and taxation, and the "Great Compromise" that created the bicameral Congress with the enumeration-based House of Representatives and the state-based Senate, the framers recognized the powers of the states in the maintenance of the Union and their serious role as players in this drama.

The framers gave the states significant powers through Article 1 of the Constitution. "The Constitution mentions state governments at least fifty times. States are guaranteed territorial integrity, the power to maintain a state militia ... and authority both to ratify amendments to the Constitution and call a new constitutional convention" (Light 1999: 84). These powers are substantial ones, though they certainly do not overwhelm the powers that the federal government possesses. The history of federalism is, in fact, one during which the states and national government have traded off periods of first one and then the other being dominant. For instance, federalism was at question during the Civil War. Which vision of the US would prevail, that of "states' rights" as put forth by the southern states of the Confederacy or that of the supremacy of the federal government as believed by the Union of the northern states? Ultimately, the northern vision prevailed. Federal supremacy was clarified during the presidency of Franklin D. Roosevelt (1933–45), as Congress created an alphabet soup of agencies at his behest. The mandate of these agencies, including the Civilian Conservation Corps and the Tennessee Valley Authority, was to create more opportunities for gainful employment that was sorely lacking during the Great Depression. The federal government thus assumed an enhanced responsibility for the economic welfare of the citizenry, and it has retained that responsibility even through significant conservative eras such as the "Reagan Revolution" of the 1980s and the current Bush administration. Trade agreements such as NAFTA consequently have as a key impetus within the US this understanding of federal concern over the state of the economy.

Thus, federalism shapes the governing role of the central government in Washington vis-à-vis the role of the 50 states and seven territories. In what follows, the influence of Washington on the states will be addressed, though it should also be noted that the "New Federalism" literature envisions a much greater responsibility for the states in the implementation of public policy (Ferejohn 1997). An example of New Federalism is the reliance on states to change their disbursement of welfare services by virtue of the 1996 welfare reform law that reduced the number of welfare claimants through tougher state regulations.

Federalism has changed with the times and may be directly affected by the economic integration resulting from globalization. Has this integration, which has appreciably sped up in the 1980s and 1990s, changed the nature of federalism in the US? According to Kincaid, the evidence of such a change is lacking:

> To date, globalization has had no impact on the constitutional design or basic institutional structure of the federal system of the United States of America, nor has it significantly altered domestic intergovernmental relations. Instead, American federalism can be said to have had an impact, though indirectly, on the world insofar as the United States has driven

globalization more than it has been driven by globalization. (Kincaid 2003: 37)

While new regional trade institutions such as NAFTA provide a challenge to extant decision-making procedures within the US federal system, they have in a sense already been taken into account by the relevant political institutions. Globalization has proceeded in waves. Indeed, the US itself was a product of an earlier wave of globalization, the era of European imperialism that began with Columbus's "discovery" of "Hispaniola" (now known as Haiti and the Dominican Republic) in 1492. The first modern wave of globalization occurred from the late nineteenth century to the beginning of World War I (Waltz 1999); subsequent waves followed World War II, the neo-liberalist era, and the post-9/11 period. The Great Depression of the 1930s "induced a significant centralization of economic regulation in Washington, DC, which produced new federal laws and institutions equipped to cope with later globalization while, nevertheless, preserving substantial political and economic autonomy for the constituent states ... which the states wish to protect against new global institutions such as the World Trade Organization [WTO]" (Kincaid 2003: 39). Thus, the US federal system, since its inception, has been highly adaptable.

Congress

The framers deliberately spread institutional power at the federal level, and this is reflected in the specificity of the different Articles of the Constitution, especially the enumerated powers of the Congress in Article I, section 8, which range from taxation and regulation of commerce, to patent protection, to raising a military. The "elastic clause" that allows Congress the ability "[t]o make all Laws which shall be necessary and proper for carrying into Execution the foregoing Powers" gives it regulatory flexibility. (In contrast, the institutional powers of the president are much more vaguely defined.)

The US Congress as a whole remains the most popular institution in US politics, because at least one half of it, the House of Representatives, has been directly elected by the eligible voting public since 1789. House members are elected from congressional districts, one member per district. There are 435 members of the House; due to the Supreme Court's decision in *Baker v. Carr* (1962) that mandated that each voter have an equal vote in House elections, all congressional districts have roughly 500,000 in population. The other half of Congress, the US Senate, was indirectly selected by state legislatures until the passage of the Seventeenth Amendment to the Constitution in 1913 allowed for their direct election by the eligible voting public. Their allocation remained the same despite the passage of the amendment: two senators per state, regardless of state population size, to yield a 100-member Senate.

Congress is fundamentally autonomous from the executive branch and the president. This separation of powers principle was created to provide a system of checks and balances on political power at the federal level. Only members of Congress can submit legislation, and all revenue bills originate in the House of Representatives. This law-making arrangement is profoundly different from the parliamentary system, in which the executive is fused with the legislature. "It is perhaps unsurprising that political observers in parliamentary countries [such as Canada] would jump so quickly to the conclusion that the switch in party control of Congress would disable the President" (Whittington and Carpenter 2003: 495). In fact, partisan control of Congress is hardly a guarantee that the institutions will work well together. President Clinton, a Democrat, needed Republican votes in the House of Representatives in order to pass the legislation enabling NAFTA to take effect. The stubborn refusal to vote in favour of NAFTA on the part of 156 Democratic members of the House can be traced to several factors: the presence within their home districts of industries that had been battered in the 1980s by cheaper imports, the relatively high level of unionization present in many of these districts, and the perception that free trade would be of greater benefit to large corporations who could take advantage of market share to benefit at the expense of the "Mom-and-Pop" small business. This unease over the impact of continental free trade was directly reflected in the slender 34-vote majority that President Clinton mustered in support of NAFTA, a vote that revealed a cleavage within the Democratic Party on a major globalization issue. Only 102 of the 258 Democrats voted in favour of NAFTA, while only 43 of the 175 Republicans voted against it.

The president lacks not only the power to introduce legislation but also to compel its passage. The president can veto legislation, although in this activity presidents have remarkably slowed since the zenith of 372 vetoes by Franklin D. Roosevelt and Harry S. Truman. For instance, as of March 2007, President George W. Bush has vetoed one piece of legislation, the Stem Cell Research Enhancement Act of 2005 (H.R. 810), which would have allowed the federal government to fund research using stem cells from destroyed embryos. The reasons for the decreased use of the veto include the reluctance of presidents to lose their accumulated "political capital" on the complex legislative process and the reaction by congressional leaders to threats of presidential vetoes. The threat tactic worked especially well for President Clinton in the mid-1990s. Speaker Newt Gingrich claimed a congressional mandate to enact the principles in the "Contract with America" on which the Republican Party successfully contested the 1994 congressional elections, winning a majority of seats in the House for the first time since 1954. One of the principles in the Contract was to substantially reduce the size of government. President Clinton opposed this principle and chose to allow the shut-down of government with a veto threat and placing the blame on the House leadership.

Congress's development as an institution includes norms of conduct that have evolved through the centuries. These include deference to seniority (senior members of Congress being assigned to the most prestigious committees where legislation is honed), inviting members of the minority party to draft amendments and have votes on them, and bipartisan cooperation in the introduction of legislation (especially on the floor of the US Senate). "[I]t is not far from the truth to say that Congress in session is Congress on public exhibition, whilst Congress in its committee-rooms is Congress at work," said Woodrow Wilson in his 1885 classic book *Congressional Government* (Wilson 1956: 69), and to make committee work run smoothly, norms such as these are essential.

The committee structure has taken shape in the context of a two-party system. For various reasons, third parties have failed to break through and achieve substantial representation in Congress. The development of the party system in the US is oriented around the plurality election rules for congressional districts. When substantial third parties have arisen—for instance, the Populist Party of the late nineteenth century and the Socialist Party of the early twentieth century—the major political parties have successfully co-opted the principles of those parties, rendering them ineffective as an electoral force. There are ideological reasons as well why the US has not formed a successful third political party, especially on the political left. Generally speaking, the US electorate is middle-of-the-road across the country, with only a few substantial pockets of one-party dominance. For instance, Idaho has not voted in the majority for a Democratic presidential candidate since 1964. The support for a left-wing political party is even more diffuse across the country, not reaching a majority in any congressional district save one (the state of Vermont) in the past 50 years.

However, despite the stability of the two-party system in the US, these institutional norms of congressional operation are disappearing. Congress has become more partisan from the 1970s onward, first because of the climate of mistrust that has prevailed in the political culture of Washington, fueled by the presidential scandals of:

» Watergate (President Nixon's knowledge of a 1972 burglary of the Democratic Party headquarters and subsequent cover-up of the crime),

» Iran-Contra (President Reagan's policy decision, against federal law, to supply weapons to the right-wing *contra* rebels in Nicaragua in the mid-1980s via monetary transfers from Iranian sources),

» Monica Lewinsky (President Clinton's lies about an affair he had with a White House intern in the mid-1990s led to his impeachment, making him only the second president to be impeached), and

» "Iraq's weapons of mass destruction" (President George W. Bush's admission that his main reason for invading Iraq—that Saddam Hussein possessed weapons of mass destruction and could use them within a 45-minute time period to attack a foe—was wrong and based on bad intelligence data).

These scandals have eroded the public's belief in their president's word. Presidential weakness has been exploitable by the opposition congressional party in order to bolster its power.

Secondly, the perceived importance of victory and defeat on legislation for majority and minority parties has increased. A recent example is the November 2003 passage of the prescription drug benefit under the Medicare program for senior citizens. The vote in the House chamber was, upon the initial end of the time limit for voting, a close defeat for the majority Republican party, which had introduced the bill. The House Republican leadership proceeded to keep the voting stations open for another three hours, in the hopes that the leadership could change the minds of a small number of "fence-sitters" to vote for the bill. Among those persuaded was Representative Butch Otter of Idaho, who said that "I do not want to vote for this bill" but was persuaded of its merits by the leadership to change his mind. He switched his vote. Thus, by bending the procedural rules of the House to its advantage, the Republican party managed to achieve the reversal of the initial vote.

This procedural manoeuvre is just one indicator that, with the changing times, the institution of Congress has also changed its ways; and while change is always unsettling, it could be for the worse. Long-time observers of Congress fear that its institutional procedures, created through two centuries of custom and common sense, are degrading. The *National Journal*, a respected Capitol Hill publication, recently identified no less than a dozen institutional changes in Congress's ways of doing business:

> » the abolition of the norm of seniority that establishes who committee chairs will be;
> » the use of continuing resolutions to maintain current governmental operations without consideration of the funding streams for these operations;
> » senators placing "holds" on legislation with greater frequency, causing legislative bottlenecks as bills are not reported on the Senate floor for debate;
> » the lack of genuine debate within the Senate on issues of the day;
> » lack of inclusion of the minority party in conference committees that reconcile differing versions of the same bill passed by both the House and Senate;
> » the consistent failure to pass budgetary appropriations out of the House and Senate appropriation committees in a timely manner as dictated by budgetary law;
> » the failure to pass appropriations that match the authorization for programs that are passed by the authorizing committees, with the consequence that programs are terminally under-funded;
> » the centralization of power in the hands of partisan political leaders. (Cohen, Victor, and Baumann 2004: 86–87)

These are strong indictments of the Congress as an institution designed originally to conduct the "people's business" as the only directly elected representatives of the people. Unlike in parliamentary systems of government, in which Members of Parliament are expected to vote the party line on pending legislation, individual Congress members by default are allowed "free votes" on legislation and need not feel compelled to vote as the party wishes. Yet, the current congressional leadership is the most centralized in over 100 years, and the institutional floundering we have seen has come about through the choice of that leadership, which has eroded the legislative independence that members of Congress have traditionally enjoyed. The threat to the power of a Congress that has lost its independent voice within the federal government structure is unmistakable and derives from a changing institutional culture. "Welcoming congressional docility," Kaiser suggests, "the Bush administration has made a conscious political decision to reassert executive-branch prerogatives" (Kaiser 2004: 22).

Presidency

The US president is elected indirectly by the people through the Electoral College mechanism, which allocates "electoral votes" among the 50 states and the District of Columbia, based on the total number of US House seats per state/district, plus two for the two US senators allocated for each state (except for the District of Columbia, which is allocated two Senate seats even though it does not elect senators). Thus, for each presidential election there are 538 electoral votes, for which the US public technically votes, even though few citizens ever actually have a chance to meet the electors in the Electoral College for their state. At the conclusion of the election, the electors then, by convention, pledge their electoral votes to the candidate who received the most votes in the state in each presidential election. There are two exceptions to this allocation. First, two states, Maine and Nebraska, allocate electoral votes based on the presidential vote-share in the congressional districts. Thus, they can cast electoral votes for both candidates. There have also been "faithless electors" who have cast their electoral votes for someone other than their party's presidential candidate. The most recent instance of this occurred in 1988 when a West Virginia elector cast her electoral college vote for the Democratic Party's vice-presidential candidate, Senator Lloyd Bentsen of Texas, instead of presidential candidate, Governor Michael Dukakis of Massachusetts. In what appears to be a case of an "accidentally faithless elector," an unknown Minnesota elector in 2004 cast a vote for the Democratic vice-presidential candidate, Senator John Edwards of North Carolina, instead of the presidential candidate, Senator John Kerry of Massachusetts. Thus, in a key manner, the electoral vote is not a mere national formality, but rather a pitched state-to-state battle.

US presidents have accumulated much power over time, through creative uses of executive branch privileges. There are established constitutional powers of the president that have not been challenged effectively by the other branches of government, though they are under watchful eyes. Though declaring war is the prerogative of the Congress, the president is the "Commander in Chief" and has always been recognized as such. When military officers threaten insubordination, such as General Douglas MacArthur during the Korean War in the 1950s, they have not succeeded in remaining in their posts.[2]

The institutional power of the president to conduct war has not gone unchallenged by Congress, especially in the post-Vietnam War era when military decision-making by presidents was called into question. After the North Vietnamese navy fired upon two US destroyers in 1964, prompting President Johnson, a Democrat, to have a Democratic Party-dominated Congress pass the Gulf of Tonkin Resolution authorizing the president to take action in Vietnam, the Congress essentially ceded decisions about the conduct of foreign policy to the executive branch. Not only was Johnson's conduct of the Vietnam War (mobilization of a half-million troops at its peak in 1968) called into question, but also President Nixon's promise of "peace with honor" was severely compromised by his secret bombing of Cambodia in May 1970 and the continuance of military engagement of the North Vietnamese forces until 1973 and the signing of the Treaty of Paris. Over-riding President Nixon's veto, Congress in 1973 passed the War Powers Act (Public Law 93-148, 93rd Congress, HJ Res. 542), which was intended to give it some significant oversight powers in military campaigns in exchange for allowing the president greater latitude in inserting military forces into battle. The president is required, under law, to report to Congress the rationale for the engagement of force within 48 hours, its constitutionality, and the president's best estimate of the duration and severity of the engagement.

However, no president has ever recognized the constitutionality of the War Powers Act (Jillson 1999: 343). Post-World War II presidents especially have claimed that the spectre of nuclear war and its potential immediacy force them to have more flexible decision-making powers than were originally written into the Constitution, when war mobilization took a much longer period of time (though the build-up to the first Persian Gulf War in 1991 involved a six-month mobilization of troops in the Middle East, mainly in Saudi Arabia and the Indian Ocean and Persian Gulf). The War Powers Act has proven to be ineffective in Congress's ongoing institutional debate with the executive branch. In fact, Congress's role in the prosecution of war has become that of a bystander, with the last serious debate regarding the US involvement in military conflict taking place prior to the first Persian Gulf War against Iraq in January 1991, under President George Bush, Senior. The debate on the floor of the Senate was particularly thoughtful on that occasion, eventually leading to a vote in support of the war. In contrast, the congressional debate in October 2002 leading up to the second Persian Gulf War against Iraq was focused on a narrower matter, that of giving the president authorization to conduct military operations if the United Nations Security Council did the same. The Security Council did not authorize a military response to events in Iraq, and the Bush administration lacked both congressional and international support for the war it began in March 2003.

While the institutional support for war-making powers has been controversial, other aspects of presidential power vis-à-vis foreign policy have proven to be contentious as well. Presidents are authorized to appoint ambassadors and make treaties "with the advice and consent of the Senate" (Article II, Section 2 of the US Constitution). In both of these activities presidents and Congress have not always enjoyed an easy relationship. Rougher moments tend to come when Capitol Hill and the White House are controlled by different political parties, though this is not a uniform rule. For instance, the Senate refused to ratify the Strategic Arms Limitation Treaty II (or SALT II) in 1979; in a sense, it was encouraged in its refusal by the "Carter Doctrine," advanced by President Jimmy Carter, that the US should be willing to use military force if necessary to defend shipping lanes for oil pumped from countries in the Persian Gulf region (Kegley and Wittkopf 2004: 118). While Carter did ask for the passage of SALT II, which would have limited the extent to which missiles carrying nuclear warheads could have MIRVs (Multiple Independently Targeted Re-entry Vehicles) placed on them, he was unable to convince enough senators that passing the treaty was a sound course of action at that stage of the Cold War. Carter's plea for passage fell on deaf ears in part due to the invasion of

Afghanistan by the Soviet Union at this time, as well as lack of public knowledge about the treaty, which meant that no large constituency was advocating its passage (Russett, Starr, and Kinsella 2004: 158).

The Senate has also had its moments of conflict with the president regarding ambassadorial appointments. The Senate must pass the nominee by a majority of votes. Presidential ambassadorial appointments are of two kinds: 1) skilled foreign service officers who have a working knowledge of the country in which they are serving the US (generally in difficult places in the world, such as sub-Saharan Africa); and 2) friends of the president who have, through campaign contributions or significant campaign work, been selected for higher profile slots in wealthier countries in Europe or the Caribbean. The less controversial nominees are of the first variety, as the Senate defers to the State Department's recommendation for these tricky posts. The second, however, can cause problems. The recent gridlock over the nomination of James Hormel is a case in point. Hormel was nominated in October 1997 by President Clinton to be ambassador to Luxembourg, but his nomination met with opposition by two senators, James Imhofe of Oklahoma and Tim Hutchinson of Arkansas, because Hormel was gay. President Clinton eventually resorted to a recess appointment of Hormel in June 1999. Recess appointments take place sparingly because they appear to short-circuit the Senate confirmation process, yet they are allowed under the Constitution. The president could appoint trade representatives via recess appointment; however, such appointments would likely ruin the comity that exists between the White House and Capitol Hill, especially regarding trade policy.

Courts

The basic structure of the US court system, the rulings on legal principle that come from it, and its sheer size, will ensure that the courts receive their fair share of institutional attention and action. Undergraduate political science curricula throughout the US higher education system include courses on public law, such as constitutional law, civil liberties, and the philosophy of law. Public law is inherently political.

The US court structure, as defined by the Constitution, allows it to have a significant role in the policy-making process but always in a reactive fashion, in that the courts can only rule on what comes before them. For instance, the Supreme Court can choose which cases to hear but can do so only from among cases that are submitted to it for consideration. In other words, it cannot seek out its own docket. Only those who petition the Supreme Court for a *writ of certiorari* (or to have the facts of the case put before it) will succeed in having their case heard. The Supreme Court has some original jurisdiction powers, but the vast majority of its cases are appellate reviews of "lower court" decisions. The Supreme Court can make advisory opinions but rarely does so.

The phrase "The Supreme Court follows th' election returns," popularized in the mid-twentieth-century comic strip "Li'l Abner," seems apt, notwithstanding its decisive role in the 2000 presidential elections when it stopped the recounting of Florida ballots (thus favouring a deeply contested version of the election returns) and, through this action, brought about the declaration of Governor George W. Bush of Texas as president. One of the remarks made by Supreme Court Justice Sandra Day O'Connor, in fact, had a significant political impact on the recount of the Florida ballots: "Well, why isn't the standard [for the counting of votes] the one that voters are instructed to follow, for goodness sakes? I mean, it couldn't be clearer" (Danner 2001: 48). This standard was echoed by the Republican Party in Florida during the recount and was opposed by a more liberal standard of ascertaining the intention of the voter that was favoured by the Democrats. The example indicates that the high court justices have a great deal of political influence in their public pronouncements, whether they necessarily intend to do so or not. This quality of the Supreme Court, and of the federal court system in general, brings it institutional notice.

Article III of the US Constitution only addresses details about the Supreme Court and directs Congress to create additional "inferior" courts as needed. Thus, Congress, through its ability to reshape the jurisdiction of federal courts, and the executive branch, which is given the task of nominating judges to the bench, will both have substantial institutional impact on the composition and behaviour of the judiciary. Moreover, there is little constitutional detail about the composition of the Supreme Court. For example, the number of Supreme Court justices is established by Congress, which in 1869 settled on nine after a period when the number of justices was increased and decreased for political ideological reasons (Gitelson, Dudley, and Dubnick 1998: 384).

The executive branch is not immune either from temptations to reshape the Supreme Court. The most famous instance of this was in 1937, when President Franklin D. Roosevelt attempted to "pack" the Supreme Court with an extra justice for each one who was above 70 years of age. Roosevelt's reasoning was that younger justices would be more sympathetic to his economic plans that he believed would help end the Great Depression and thus would reverse previous Court rulings on the constitutionality of such "New Deal" programs as the National Industrial Recovery Act (Patterson 1990: 39). In all, Roosevelt proposed that there be 15 justices. Congress did not pass this court-packing plan. Yet, Roosevelt won the larger conflict with the Court when it began to rule that his economic plans were constitutional, overturning 30 years of insistence that businesses had "rights" like citizens did and that federal government agencies had no right to interfere with the corporation's right to private property. (An example of a case in this vein was *Lochner v. New York*, 1905). Such developments can be important in the NAFTA era. Sovereignty of business is under debate. The Metalclad case suggests that significant US corporations will file cases under the NAFTA statutes and expect redress of their grievances, possibly emboldened by the legally exalted place that business enjoys in US politics.[3]

Another important feature of the courts is the scope of the US justice system. The Supreme Court, Courts of Appeal, and District Courts at the federal level, as well as the vast state and local court systems, comprise in total more than 18,000 criminal and civil courts (Gitelson, Dudley, and Dubnick 1998: 380). This allows citizens to exercise legal action at any number of levels. The US is perceived as being a very litigious society in comparison to other industrialized democracies such as Japan, and the extensive use of the legal system by Americans seems to bear that perception out.

Globalization challenges the US court system as the supreme arbiter of the law. The WTO's Dispute Settlement Mechanism procedure can enforce international trade agreements by resolving country-to-country disputes. The US forced the EU to open its markets for bananas at the conclusion of the "Banana War" (1993–2001), during which the EU faced 100 per cent duties on luxury items if it would not eliminate quotas for bananas from former colonies in the Caribbean or West Africa. The WTO has recently ruled against the US on a series of tax breaks that the US gives to "Foreign Sales Corporations" in violation of international trade rules against such favouritism. In this case, the US Congress is faced with the unappealing prospect of having to change its laws to suit international law (Miller 2004). The extent to which national courts can override international law is questionable. Perhaps it is only through mechanisms for redress such as the Chapter 11 expropriation provision in NAFTA that national actors can make legitimate claims that international law infringes upon national sovereignty.

Bureaucracy

Bureaucracy is defined as "a hierarchical organization in which offices have specific missions and employees are assigned specific responsibilities based on merit, knowledge, and experience" (Jillson 1999: 361). The organization takes the form of the administrative apparatus of the 15 Cabinet agencies and roughly 60 independent agencies, ranging from the African Development Foundation to the Bureau of Land Management (especially important in managing federal lands in the western US) from the Interstate Commerce Commission to the US Postal Service. The federal bureaucracy employs nearly 3 million people (the largest being the newest cabinet-level Department of Homeland Security, created in the wake of the events of 9/11, with approximately 180,000 employees) and is given the explicit task of policy implementation and the implicit task of policy formation. Technically, bureaucrats are supposed to follow rules that they set out, guided by the parameters of federal law, executive orders, and Supreme Court decisions. The rules create procedures that are meant to bring about a sense of fairness for all in terms of equal access to the law. But bureaucratic discretion is also utilized, which conceptually means that bureaucrats can make rules that abide by the spirit of federal law. The US is also unusual in that the top echelon in the bureaucracy can be changed by the president. Most countries do not see such a wholesale house-cleaning of the cabinet, and consequently of high-level bureaucrats, such as that performed by President Bush after the 2004 elections when nine of 15 cabinet secretaries were asked to resign.

While the term "bureaucrat" is almost pejorative in the minds of Americans, forming the image of a faceless rule-enforcer who stifles individual freedom in the process of enforcing the rules, in actuality the bureaucracy seeks to both "look like America" in its diverse makeup and acquire input and comment from the public in its rule-making. Affirmative action procedures dictate that groups historically discriminated against—African-Americans, Asian-Americans, and American Indians—must be given special consideration in hiring. These rules come from such acts as the federal Civil Rights Act of 1964 (Public Law 88-352, 88th Congress, H.R. 7152), which, among other provisions, forced employers under federal contract to end discriminatory hiring practices; and the Equal Employment Opportunity Act of 1972 (20 USC Sec. 1703), which made state and local governments conform to the hiring procedures of federal contract employers and expanded the Civil Rights Act to include prohibitions of discrimination on the basis of age, disability, gender, national origin, pregnancy, race, and religion.

The Equal Employment Opportunity Commission (EEOC) is the regulatory arm of the Equal Employment Opportunity Act and entertains roughly 80,000 charges of discrimination brought by plaintiffs. Additionally, the EEOC can file lawsuits against employers. In the fiscal year 2003, for which the latest statistics are available, the EEOC filed 393 lawsuits, of which there were 378 resolutions amounting to monetary benefits of $148.7 million.[4] The results of this vigilant attitude are that of 1.81 million executive branch non-Postal Service employees on 30 September 2002, 44.6 per cent were female and 30.8 per cent were ethnic and racial minorities: 16.9 per cent African American, 6.9 per cent Latino, 4.8 per cent Asian American, 2.2 per cent American Indian.[5] Given that, according to the US Census, the US female population is 50.9 per cent and the white population is 69 per cent, the executive branch bureaucracy is beginning to look more like the US, though African Americans are overrepresented and females and Latinos remain numerically underrepresented. A guiding principle behind affirmative action is that a bureaucracy that "looks like America" will be more accepted by Americans.

Support for affirmative action is controversial, however. There are several cleavages: partisanship, gender, income, and race. According to the 2000 National Election Study from the University of Michigan, overall about twice as many Democrats as Republicans favour affirmative action, and nearly twice as many Republicans as Democrats oppose it. Independent partisan identifiers in the survey are almost perfectly split on whether to support it or not: 37.2 per cent in favour, 36.7 per cent opposed. About 40 per cent of surveyed females overall support and 32 per cent oppose affirmative action. This same "40–30 split" takes place with annual income earners below $15,000 as opposed to those earning annually equal to or above $35,000. Roughly 40 per cent of the lower income earners surveyed support the policy, as opposed to approximately 30 per cent of the higher income earners. Finally, by a two-to-one margin (62.3 per cent to 30.7 per cent), people of colour support affirmative action as opposed to whites.

Aside from the institutional composition of the bureaucracy, its independent constitutional foundation is more in doubt than it is for the Congress, presidency, and Supreme Court. Neither the word "bureaucracy" nor the federal bureaucratic framework is mentioned in the Constitution. Given this lacuna, the three established branches make claims on bureaucratic oversight. The result is that agencies ask conflicting masters for help with completing their tasks. For instance, the Bureau of Land Management (BLM), in order to fight fires on federal lands, will often have to call upon "Hot Shots" firefighters who are employees of the US Forest Service, which is housed in the Department of Agriculture. Indeed, during an active fire season, US military personnel will also pitch in to fight fires. The National Weather Service, housed in the Department of Commerce, will provide "fire weather" forecasts. The Federal Emergency Management Agency will assist in evacuations of burnt-out areas

(Gitelson, Dudley, and Dubnick 1998: 350–51). The Bush administration, through its reorganization of 22 agencies into the Department of Homeland Security, seeks in the long term to circumvent the cross-branch battles for bureaucratic supremacy, but this will very much be a long-term task.

The bureaucracy continues to grow as a result of the growth in government. The main growth in employees has taken place at the level of the states, though globalization throughout the twentieth century has forced the federal government to be more active and the size of the bureaucracy has increased accordingly.[6] For instance, the number of federal agencies in 1933, with the election of activist President Roosevelt, was nearly twice the number of agencies at the beginning of the century (Gitelson, Dudley, and Dubnick 1998: 356). There has not been an appreciable cutback in the size of government since the 1930s. World War II, the continued heavy defence spending of the Cold War and the Vietnam War, and the expansion of the social welfare state that resulted from the Great Society programs of President Lyndon Johnson in the 1960s, all contributed heavily to the maintenance of a large federal government presence. The share of government consumption as a percentage of the total GDP thus is approximately 14 per cent; see Figure 7.1 (OECD 2004).

Figure 7.1: US Federal Government Consumption as Percentage of GDP, Q3 2001–Q3 2003

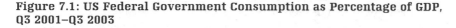

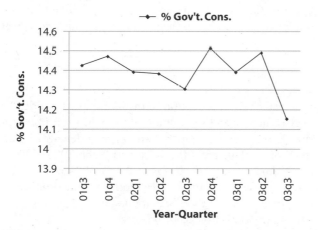

Source: OECD

The bureaucracy is not powerless in this minuet of competing interests. It has information and expertise at its disposal in completing its tasks. Max Weber, one of the most important theorists of bureaucracy, wrote that:

> [T]he pure interest of the bureaucracy in power ... is efficacious far beyond those areas where purely functional interests make for secrecy.... Bureaucracy naturally welcomes a poorly informed and hence a powerless parliament—at least insofar as ignorance somehow agrees with the bureaucracy's interests. (Gerth and Mills 1946, quoted in Henry 1986: 15)

Lower and mid-level bureaucrats wield enormous discretion in the US political system because of their permanence or security of tenure as opposed to the comings-and-goings of elected officials. (This permanence they share with judges on the federal benches.) Their level of expertise will give them advantages in power struggles within the federal government. For instance, the scientific expertise of career meteorologists will make others defer to their judgements about the upcoming fire season in the western US. If firefighting tasks on federal lands remain in the purview of the federal government, then it will need to maintain the National Weather Service's capacity to forecast the probability of fires. Bureaucracies thus maintain their privileged position within US politics.

Politically, observers of the federal legislative process have long noted the presence of "iron triangles"—relevant congressional committees, bureaucratic administrative agencies, and interest groups—dominating the legislative process in specific policy areas such as defence spending. However, this model of policy-making neglects the diffuse nature of interest groups in the US on other issues, and "issue networks" can form around issues with myriad constituencies such as health care. Interest groups advocating for patients, physicians, and insurance firms clash and thus do not form "a third corner of the iron triangle" (Light 1999: 642). Potentially, a bureaucracy as large as the Department of Homeland Security could find itself part of a security issue network of policy-making. As the USA Patriot Act and its provisions of secretive surveillance (a direct effect of the global "war on terrorism") demand bureaucratic compliance in order to implement the law, so the power of bureaucracies grows.

Conclusion

This chapter has given the reader an introduction to the interplay of political institutions of the US federal government and the impact of globalization upon them. If "the practices and politics associated with globalization are undeniably inflected, if not driven, by the interests of nation-states" (Schirato and Webb 2003: 130), then it is valuable to study national institutional evolution to gain insight into this process. My main conclusion is that as the forces of globalization grow, institutional power shifts, even in hegemonic powers such as the US. Nation-states are both shapers and shaped by globalization, and the US is no exception.

The study of US political institutions proves this point. NAFTA will force the US to confront the issue of regional trade, possibly superseding what were heretofore considered to be national-level powers, as corporations can pursue Chapter 11 claims against governments. Regarding international trade, the WTO tribunals can rule against government policy, such as the November 2004 WTO tribunal decision to uphold Antigua's claim that the US domestic law prohibiting offshore gambling violates US international legal obligations under the General Agreement on Tariffs and Services (GATS) that effectively promote gambling. An apparent consequence of this decision is that "if an activity is loosely regulated in some parts of a country, then strict prohibitions in other parts of the country cannot be justified when they are barriers to trade" (Gould 2004: 2). The branches of the US government will continue to be pressured by globalization forces.

Yet, some actions are unlikely to take place in the face of regional integration pressures. For instance, the creation of a North American single currency, such as the Euro, is a very remote possibility, because "the representation of US commercial interests in the twelve districts of the US Federal Reserve system is irreconcilable with the public mandate of the Bank of Canada ... and, for that matter, the *Banco de México*" (Huelsemeyer 2004: 21). Moreover, "despite the influence of market forces and the activism of local and regional governments and international organizations, national states may remain in control of their borders." This is due to there being no "comprehensive supra-national institutions similar to those of the EU" (Brunet-Jailly 2004: 6, 7). US political institutions within the paradigm of North American regional integration thus remain relevant and, for now, are here to stay.

Notes

1   Shays' Rebellion occurred in 1786 and pitted farmers against the State of Massachusetts legislature when it passed a law that required all debts to be paid in cash to the cash-strapped state treasury. The Massachusetts Supreme Court ruled that the farmers' mortgages could not be foreclosed based on the law.

2   MacArthur was famously recalled from duty during the Korean War by President Truman in 1951 after his repeated attempts to suborn the president's commander-in-chief role through "field commander orders" such as bombing the Yalu River bridges in November 1950 in direct violation of the president's policy not to widen the war; see Johnson 2004.

3   The Metalclad case involved the Metalclad corporation in the US, which claimed it illegally lost its right to operate a toxic waste facility in Mexico that it purchased in 1991. See Chapter 11, this volume.

4   See <http://www.eeoc.gov/stats/litigation.html>.

5   *Federal Civilian Workforce Statistics: Demographic Profile of the Federal Workforce since September 2002*, <http://www.opm.gov/feddata/demograp/02demo.pdf>.

6   This is especially true in the globalization of international financial matters, with governments exerting their power to purchase securities in order to affect international currency flows. Larger economies tend to be more influential in this arena.

References

Barreiro, Jose (Ed.). 1988. *Indian Roots of American Democracy*. Ithaca, NY: Cornell American Indian Program.

Brunet-Jailly, Emmanuel. 2004. "Comparing Local Cross-Border Relations Under the EU and NAFTA." *Canadian-American Public Policy* 58.

Burkhart, Ross E. 2002. "Globalization, Regimes, and Development." In Steve Chan and James R. Scarritt (eds.), *Coping with Globalization*. London: Frank Cass.

Cohen, Richard E., Kirk Victor, and David Baumann. 2004. "The State of Congress." *National Journal*, 10 January.

Cornwall, John, and Wendy Cornwall. 2001. *Capitalist Development in the Twentieth Century: An Evolutionary-Keynesian Analysis*. Cambridge: Cambridge UP.

Covington, Cary R., and Ross E. Burkhart. 1994. "Executive-Legislative Relations." In Joel H. Silbey (ed.), *Encyclopedia of the American Legislative System*. New York: Scribner's.

Danner, Mark. 2001. "The Road to Illegitimacy." *The New York Review of Books* 22 (February): 48–51.

Ferejohn, John, *et al.* (Eds.). 1997. *The New Federalism: Can the States Be Trusted?* Stanford, CA: Hoover Institution Press.

Gerth, H.H., and C. Wright Mills (Trans. and Eds.). 1946. *From Max Weber: Essays in Sociology.* New York: Oxford UP.

Gitelson, Alan R., Robert L. Dudley, and Melvin J. Dubnick. 1998. *American Government.* 5th ed. Boston, MA: Houghton Mifflin Company.

Gould, Ellen. 2004. "The GATS US-Gambling Decision: A Wakeup Call for WTO Members." *Canadian Centre for Policy Alternatives Briefing Paper: Trade and Investment Series* 5,4.

Henry, Nicholas L. 1986. *Public Administration and Public Affairs.* 3rd ed. Englewood Cliffs, NJ: Prentice-Hall.

Huelsemeyer, Axel. 2004. "Toward Deeper North American Integration: A Customs Union?" *Canadian-American Public Policy* 59.

Jillson, Calvin C. 1999. *American Government.* New York: Thomson Learning.

Johnson, Rick L. 2004. "Harry Truman's Decision to Fire Douglas MacArthur Came After Months of Insubordination." *Military History* 21, 74–77.

Kaiser, Robert G. 2004. "That Giant Hissing Sound: What You Hear is Congress Giving Up Its Clout." *The Washington Post National Weekly Edition*, 22–28 March.

Kegley, Charles W., Jr., and Eugene R. Wittkopf. 2004. *World Politics: Trend and Transformation.* 9th ed. New York: Thomson Learning.

Kincaid, John. 2003. "Globalization and Federalism in the United States: Continuity in Adaptation." In Harvey Lazar, Hamish Telford, and Ronald L. Watts (eds.), *The Impact of Global and Regional Integration on Federal Systems: A Comparative Analysis.* Montreal and Kingston: McGill-Queen's UP.

Light, Paul C. 1999. *A Delicate Balance: An Introduction to American Government.* 2nd ed. New York: St. Martin's/Worth.

Miller, Scott. 2004. "US Firms Face EU Trade Sanctions." *The Wall Street Journal*, 26 February.

O'Connor, Karen, and Larry J. Sabato. 2004. *American Government: Continuity and Change.* Alternate 2004 Edition. New York: Pearson Longman.

Office of the United States Trade Representative. 2004. "NAFTA: A Decade of Success." <http://www.ustr.gov/Document_Library/Fact_Sheets/2004/NAFTA_A_Decade_of_Success.html>. Accessed on 19 February 2007.

Organization for Economic Development and Cooperation. 2004. *OECD Economic Outlook.* Paris: OECD.

Patterson, Thomas E. 1990. *The American Democracy.* New York: McGraw-Hill.

Rocher, François. 2000. "Dividing the Spoils: American and Canadian Federalism." In David M. Thomas (ed.), *Canada and the United States: Differences that Count.* 2nd ed. Peterborough, ON: Broadview Press.

Russett, Bruce, Harvey Starr, and David Kinsella. 2004. *World Politics: The Menu for Choice.* 7th ed. New York: Wadsworth Publishing.

Schirato, Tony, and Jen Webb. 2003. *Understanding Globalization.* London: Sage.

Steger, Madfred B. 2003. *Globalization: A Very Short Introduction.* New York: Oxford UP.

Waltz, Kenneth. 1999. "Globalization and Governance." *PS: Political Science and Politics* 32,4: 693–700.

Whittington, Keith E., and Daniel P. Carpenter. 2003. "Executive Power in American Institutional Development." *Perspectives on Politics* 1: 495–513.

Wilson, Woodrow. 1956. *Congressional Government: A Study in American Politics.* New York: Meridian Books.

CHAPTER EIGHT

Political Institutions in Mexico

José A. Crespo, Norma Borrego, and Ana Luz Ruelas[1]

The Mexican political regime is, like most in Latin America, a presidential republic, which from the beginning of its independent life in the early nineteenth century was modeled on the US's peculiar political system, which at that time seemed to be the only real democracy. In Europe, the French Revolution's radical democratic experiment had caused a period of anarchy and instability, followed by a "revolutionary empire" led by Napoleon (and, in practice, not very democratic at that), finally returning to the reinstatement of the monarchy under Louis XVIII, brother to the overthrown—and guillotined—Louis XVII. In Britain, even though the 1648 and 1688 revolutions had set the foundations for modern parliamentary democracy and constitutional monarchy, by the nineteenth century there were few democratic features; although Parliament wielded the greater part of royal power, such power was scarcely representative (until 1832, only 6 per cent of the population had a right to vote due to their properties). Moreover, the very idea of monarchy as a form of government made this system appear less than democratic. For Latin American liberals, democracy could only be conceived as a republican system with near-universal voting (although indirect for some time). It is evident that in that period only the US system was anywhere closest to the democratic ideals designed during the French Revolution. Hence, after some monarchical attempts in some countries (in Mexico from 1822 to 1824 and later from 1864 to 1867, and in Brazil up until 1870), the new countries leaned towards a US-style presidential republic.

This is not to say that political and cultural conditions, products of a peculiar colonization very different to that in the US, were always the best suited to sustain that type of democracy. The opposite is true; the political and cultural legacy produced by the long *Virreinato*, the viceroyalty period, which itself was a product of the Spanish conquest, has placed and continues to place numerous obstacles to the adequate performance of institutions conceived as republican and democratic. The *Virreinato*, which lasted approximately three centuries in the entire subcontinent, assumed a regime that was

» authoritarian—decisions flowed from the apex to the base;
» patrimonialist—social property was considered the King's private property and delegated to viceroys and other functionaries;

» classist and racist—the rigid class society was based on ethnic origin, nearly impervious between strata;
» exploitative—the system was designed to exploit the social bases in favour of elites located at the cusp of the social pyramid; and
» monopolist—economic activity was restricted to a few who obtained exclusive concessions from the king or viceroy for the exploitation of the subcontinent's great natural riches.

The result was a highly authoritarian society with powerful economic restrictions on development and a quite unjust distribution of income; in other words, the opposite of a democratic and enlightened society. This viceroyal legacy, despite being treated differently in each of the countries where it emerged as a consequence of struggles for independence, is still present to some degree to the point of obstructing political, social, and economic development in Latin America.

Mexico is no exception. We must consider this weighty legacy in order to understand the enormous difficulties encountered in the installation of a stable and efficient democratic political regime, an enterprise which, after repeated failures throughout history, has gained new life in the past few years.

The Presidential System

After a brief attempt at monarchy at the beginning of independence, Mexican liberals came to power and adopted, through the 1824 Constitution, a US-style presidential system. The head of the executive branch (also head of the government) is elected differently from the legislative body, in contrast to the parliamentary systems that prevail in Europe and Canada where the head of government is a member of Parliament and also head of the party or majority coalition that forms the government. The US conceived the presidential regime as a somewhat hasty adaptation to the monarchy against which it had fought for independence. The founding fathers had no notion of a clear separation between the head of government emerging from Congress or Parliament and a head of state with limited and almost exclusively formal powers, similar to kings in constitutional monarchies or presidents in parliamentary republics. They did not have the parliamentary model at hand to adapt it to a republican situation, which the French had in 1875, nearly 100 years after the US Constitution was written.

Although emerging Latin American republics adopted the US system, the political experiment has not entirely functioned. This was clearly detected by Alexis de Tocqueville in the nineteenth century, when he compared US institutions to Mexican ones:

> The inhabitants of Mexico ... worked from and almost wholly copied the constitution of the anglo-americans, their neighbours. But in transporting the letter of the law, they could not transpose at the same time the spirit which enlivens them. It was seen how the gears of their double government got in each other's way unceasingly ... Currently Mexico is

> still dragged unceasingly from anarchy to military despotism, and from military despotism to anarchy. (de Tocqueville 1994: 159)

It is worth noting that since the executive and legislative branches are elected independently under this presidential system, there are two basic options for government configuration. First is "unified government": the party that holds the presidency also holds an absolute (50 per cent plus one) majority in Congress. Second is "divided government," when the president's party does not hold that majority, meaning the opposition can jointly gain absolute majority and thus hinder or block initiatives sent by the executive. In the US both government configurations have occurred, though neither has resulted in an excessive concentration of power in the president's hands or into a situation of paralysis and blockade in government and legislative tasks. This is due to the peculiarities of that country's historical evolution, as well as the relatively lax character of the political parties and the short ideological distance (left to right) between the two dominant parties.

But such favourable conditions for the functioning of the presidential system are rarely, if ever, found in Latin American countries. Thus, when "unified" governments have existed, the president wields enough power to subdue the legislative branch and become a virtual dictator. He is no longer subject to real institutional controls and lacks accountability, which is essential in democracy; therefore, he is able to abuse power with complete impunity. On the other hand, when governments have been "divided," the president is too weak; he does not have the necessary support in Congress to propel his government agenda successfully. The parties that control Congress, being different and antagonistic to the party that holds the presidency, have great ideological differences with the governing party, because prevailing distances between "left and right" in Latin America are much greater than those between Democrats and Republicans in the US. In this way, democratic balance, which demands a head of government who is strong enough to further his government agenda but not strong enough to abuse power with impunity, is harder to reach and sustain. This is a consequence of the authoritarian and centralizing legacy of the viceroyalty, outlined above. As historian Will Fowler points out regarding the Mexican regime:

> What is interesting to note is the tension or dialectic which emerges from Guadalupe Victoria's rise to the presidency in 1824 until Ernesto Zedillo completed his term in 2000, to wit, the Mexican people's paradoxical need for a strong president and a strong congress at the same time. In other words, it would seem that Mexicans want to avoid the arrival to power of overbearing leaders yet they rebel against those presidents who, because they heed Congress's orders, are labeled as weak. (Fowler 2004: 14)

In effect, in a presidential system that operates under conditions different from those that prevail in the US, the risk is precisely that in "unified" governments the president tends to amass so much power that he is able to disregard institutional controls and govern almost as a dictator; under a "divided" government, the president's weakness is such that he is either paralyzed or is tempted to dissolve Congress illegally (since under presidentialism he has no legal power to do so, unlike a prime minister in a parliamentary system), which leads to virtual dictatorship. Alternatively, faced with enough tension between the executive and legislative branches, the latter might decide to remove the president and replace him with another, although it also has no legal power to do so. Needless to say, in either of these extreme situations, the country is placed not only outside the constitutional framework but frequently at the brink of a coup or civil war. In other words, a "divided" government in the Latin American context tends to generate instability that can lead to either a dictatorship (covert or open) or periods of unrest and anarchy. In contrast, parliamentary systems possess an institutional design in which executive-legislative conflicts are less likely, since, by definition, there are always unified governments. In cases where conflict does happen, there are effective mechanisms of resolution without having to leave the constitutional framework and the censure vote or dissolution of Parliament; thus, there is minimum risk of instability.

BRIEF HISTORICAL OVERVIEW OF PRESIDENTIALISM IN MEXICO

Without going into great detail, it can be said that throughout its independent life Mexico has suffered endemically from the excesses and crises we pointed out above. During the nineteenth century Mexican political life witnessed a double conflict: first, between attempts by conservatives to impose either monarchy or dictatorship as a form of government and liberals who held to the model of presidential democracy inspired by the US system; and second, between the executive and legislative branches when a formal democracy prevailed and the president faced a divided government, which occurred most of the time. The result was over 50 years of permanent agitation and disorder from 1821, when independence was achieved, until 1876, when a virtual dictatorship began that lasted for over 30 years. Samuel Huntington explains:

> The Latin American experience ... is almost exactly the opposite of the American one. After its independence, the United States conserved essentially the same political institutions it had before, and which adapted quite well to their society. When Latin American countries reached independence, they inherited and maintained a social structure which was essentially feudal. They tried to superimpose republican institutions on it ... which made no sense in a feudal society. Those first efforts to attain republicanism left Latin America with weak governments, which until the twentieth century lacked the necessary authority and power to modernize society. (Huntington 1972: 128)

In 1867 republicans led by Benito Juarez—the greatest Mexican hero—managed to expel the French troops who supported the Emperor Maximiliano of Hapsburg who had been made Emperor of Mexico three years earlier by Napoleon III. Juarez initially invoked the Constitution of 1857, a liberal-democratic constitution of great political significance. However, since it granted Congress great power over the executive branch, President Juarez decided to override the constitutional norm, becoming a near-dictator, albeit a civil one, surrounded by republican forms. After his death, and after a brief interregnum, another great dictator ascended to the presidency by way of a coup. Although a military man, the new president, Porfirio Diaz, nevertheless maintained democratic forms and rituals. Both Juarez and Diaz were able to centralize all power in their hands and, without formally disbanding the other powers (legislative and judicial), subordinated and domesticated them. Thus, in those years the president was so strong that he was never subject to any institutional control or accountability.

During Diaz's 30 years in power as absolute president, the lack of political mobility and effective democratic controls amid considerable social inequality (despite economic growth) provoked the Mexican Revolution of 1910. Diaz left the country, and his seat was occupied by the first leader of the revolution, Francisco I. Madero who, in truly democratic spirit, held himself accountable to the Constitution. The result was a very weak presidentialism; lacking a clear majority in Congress, Madero faced a divided government. This allowed another military coup, which precipitated another revolutionary uprising.

Once the country was essentially pacified (towards 1929), and with the revolutionaries' clear victory, a new political regime gradually arose. The 1917 Constitution had granted the president new powers to face his differences with Congress, but the underlying problem was still unresolved. Even after the revolution the political conditions that derived from it allowed the formation of a strong presidentialism which, like Juarez's and, above all, Diaz's, was gradually able to subordinate the legislature and courts, as well as the governors of the different states within the Republic.

This outcome can be explained as the effect of the revolution itself. It cleared the way for a genuine monopoly of power in the hands of the revolutionaries, who had the option of creating either a party dictatorship (as in the Soviet Union, China, or Cuba) or a formally democratic system in which formidable powers (beyond those specifically granted by the Constitution) would be held by a president. The new regime's form was a presidential democracy, but power was gradually concentrated almost absolutely in the institution of the president. The major difference between this post-revolutionary presidentialism and that of Juarez and Diaz was that after the revolution the principle of presidential non-re-election was established and consolidated, whereas the nineteenth-century presidents could be re-elected indefinitely (Juarez was president from 1858 until his death in 1872; Diaz was president from 1876 until 1910, when Madero's revolution forced him to leave the country). Since no president could be re-elected even if he wished it, the result was political mobility and, consequently, a lasting stability. The principle is still current to this day, in contrast to the US, where a president may be re-elected for one additional term, and several Latin American countries. It is a peculiarity of the Mexican presidential regime. Nevertheless, in exchange for that limitation, the president could, until a short time ago, decide who would succeed him in office. He could choose from among his collaborators (typically members of his cabinet) who would first become the ruling party's candidate and then automatically the next president by virtue of another defining trait of the post-revolutionary regime: the hegemonic party system.

THE PARTY SYSTEM

Just as in other modern social revolutions (Russia, China), in Mexico the revolutionaries wound up owning the political landscape. A genuine monopoly of power enabled them to put into practice their social and economic program without hindrance. Such a monopoly is usually wielded effectively only through a twentieth-century mechanism: the mass political party, which manages to concentrate power and, at the same time, encompasses most politically organized groups. This powerful political apparatus has an authoritarian nature, which guarantees stability over several decades. In Mexico, the role was played by the Institutional Revolutionary Party (PRI), founded in 1929 (under a different name). Thus, the two key pieces in the Mexican post-revolutionary regime were an exceedingly strong president, able to subdue the legislative and judicial branches (and the presumably federated state governors), and the political party, PRI, which was an instrument of political and electoral control in service to the current president.

The PRI, however, was never the only party as in other countries that endured a social revolution, nor was it socialist or communist in ideology. It maintained the monopoly of power, but, forced to sustain a formally democratic scheme, it had to legally acknowledge the existence of other parties, which were able to present their own candidates and gradually win real spaces of power. In other words, the party system in Mexico was formally plural, but in practice it was a monopoly devoid of real competition, since the ruling party possessed every element to guarantee its continuity in power, winning formally contested elections whose results in favour of the official candidates were foregone. The very fact that the PRI was not the only party gave the Mexican political regime some very particular traits, not found in such authoritarianism systems as military dictatorships (very frequent in the rest of Latin America) or one-party states (as in the Soviet Union, China, or Taiwan). In order to maintain the democratic legitimacy that would allow it to continue in power, the PRI was forced, over time, to share growing segments of power to its opposing parties; otherwise, they would disappear from the political scene either from electoral death or by choice. If that happened, the PRI would then indeed be the only party, unveiled, which would lead to the loss of the minimum of democratic legitimacy.

Given this situation, the best course for the PRI was to gradually open the electoral and party systems, to make elections more competitive, and to share power with the opposition without consequently losing the real monopoly of power, at least as long as politically possible. In this manner, opposition victories of a few congressional seats were acknowledged, as well as some municipal presidencies (1946), some state capitals (1958), and a few senators and the executive in some states (1989). Meanwhile, the presidency and the majority in Congress were preserved by the PRI through multiple frauds and diverse electoral artifices, which devalued the citizens' belief in the ballot boxes. But increasing pressure from opposing parties, strengthened by an ever-growing number of citizen votes, and diverse recurrent economic crises in 1976, 1982, and 1988 forced PRI governments to cede more and more power, until in 1997, through a genuinely democratic electoral reform, it went from predominant to simply the governing party, under conditions more similar to those of true democracies. The PRI not only lost the absolute majority in the lower house, causing a divided government for the first time in decades, and control of the capital's government, which had been in its hands for seven decades, but most importantly, it also gave up controlling the electoral authorities, as it had done until then. All of this, together with a decreasing electoral trend, opened the door to the PRI's defeat in the presidential elections in 2000 (Crespo 1998). The National Action Party (PAN) candidate, Vicente Fox, fulfilled years of effort by attaining the presidency, constituting the first peaceable change of power in Mexican history since its independence in 1821.

From that time onward, Mexico fully entered into a multiparty and truly competitive system. The president automatically lost the special (non-constitutional) powers the office had enjoyed until then; there was enough institutional counterweight in the legislative branch; the judicial branch acquired a new autonomy; and the media enjoyed more freedom than ever before. The peculiar unwritten rule that the current president may designate his successor was lost, first, through the power change itself, and, second, because President Fox was unable to get his favourite pre-candidate (his minister of the interior) nominated to be presidential candidate for his own party. It was the party's militants and not the president who chose the representative in the next presidential election (2006).

However, although the presidency and the party system under Fox was more democratic, the government was divided. Not only did his government lack an absolute majority (50 per cent plus one) in the legislative houses, it did not even have a relative majority, which remained in PRI hands, This produced, as in other countries with presidentialist regimes, a legislative paralysis, as the opposing majority in the legislative branch systematically blocked a great deal of the government's agenda, either because it disagreed with it or in order to prevent the governing party from reaping the accolades deriving from legal reforms and modifications.

The Legislative Branch in Mexico

Mexico's first Constitution in 1824 created an indirect representative system that is the basis for the modern Mexican state and that is still present in the current Constitution of 1917 (Carpizo 2003: 157). One of its fundamental principles is the notion of separation of powers. Article 6 stated that the supreme power of the federation is to be divided into three branches: legislative, executive, and judicial (Carpizo 2003: 271). In accordance with Article 50, a General Congress (El Congreso de la Union) is in charge of the legislative branch, which is divided into two chambers, deputies and senators, who can discharge their duties jointly or separately.

ATTRIBUTIONS OF THE GENERAL CONGRESS

Congress provides order to the main economic, political, and social relations of the country, including matters of property, budget, energy, treaties, and foreign relations (Carpizo 2003: 277–78). The chambers function by periods known as *ordinary*. The first one starts on 1 September each year and ends normally on 15 December that same year; the second starts on 15 March and ends on 30 April the same year. There are also *extraordinary periods*, in accordance with article 78 of the Constitution, and those are called whenever time runs out in the ordinary period and there are still important matters pending for Congress or one chamber in particular to consider.

In accordance with Article 70, every resolution by Congress is either a law or a decree[2] with federal jurisdiction. This makes Congress's decisions the main platform for public policy elaboration. Article 73 explains some of the decisions that Congress can make:

>» admit new states into the federal union;
>» determine the contributions or taxes needed to cover the budget;
>» define the criteria for the executive branch to request loans on behalf of the country, in accordance with the capacity for repayment;
>» declare war based upon information provided by the executive; and
>» issue laws on matters of nationality, the legal status of foreigners, and immigration, among others.

Congress is empowered also to grant licence or accept the resignation of the president and to appoint the citizen who would replace him as interim or provisional president.

ATTRIBUTIONS OF THE CHAMBER OF DEPUTIES

Elections for the Chamber of Deputies have a mixed system, which combines uninominal (or first-past-the-post) districts with proportional representation. The Chamber of Deputies consists of 500 members elected for a period of three years, in accordance with Articles 52 and 53. Of those, 300 are elected by the principle of first-past-the-post and are known as *majority representatives*. The other 200 are elected by *proportional representation*, with the territory of the republic divided into five regions. Political parties present lists for each region and are granted a number of seats proportional to the total voting obtained in the election.

In accordance with Article 74, the Chamber of Deputies is exclusively in charge of:

>» publishing the President Elect Declaration issued by the Electoral Tribunal of the federal judicial branch;
>» examining, discussing, and approving annually the federation's revenue law and the budget;
>» deciding when it is possible to indict public servants who commit a crime that abuses the privileges of their position;
>» revising public accounts to ascertain how and on what the budget for the previous year was expended; and
>» other items reserved by the Constitution.

ATTRIBUTIONS OF THE CHAMBER OF SENATORS

Basically, the Senate fulfills three specific functions: legislation; supervision of the actions of high ranking officers and particularly of the executive branch; and representation of the political interest of the nation as a whole, as well as of the state in which they were elected (Raigosa Sotelo 2003; Carpizo 2003: 158). The Chamber of Senators is composed of 128 members elected for a period of six years, according to Article 56. Sixty-four (two per state plus two for the Federal District) are elected by simple *majority*; 32 are assigned to the first minority, in other words to the political party that gets the second largest number of votes in the elections; and another 32 are elected in accordance with the principle of *proportional representation*, from the lists presented by each political party and in relation to the total vote obtained.

Article 76 provides that the Senate is exclusively in charge of:

» analyzing the foreign policy developed by the executive branch;
» approving all international treaties and diplomatic conventions signed by the executive;
» authorizing the sending of troops abroad, as well as the transit of foreign troops through Mexican territory;
» sitting as a jury in cases of political trials against public servants accused of violations of public trust;
» appointing Supreme Court ministers from among the proposals presented by the president; and
» other items specifically reserved by the Constitution.

THE PERMANENT COMMISSION

Because Congress functions primarily in two ordinary periods, its duties are discharged during recess by a Permanent Commission. This is composed of 37 members (19 deputies and 18 senators), named by their respective chambers just before the end of each ordinary period.

According to Article 79 of the Constitution, the duties of the Permanent Commission, among others, are:

» to preside over the swearing in of the president;
» to receive the initiatives of law and other proposals addressed to Congress, and to direct them to the proper commission for analysis;
» to work out an agreement with the executive branch in order to call for an extraordinary session of Congress or of one chamber;
» to grant or deny ratification of the appointment of the Attorney General;
» to grant leave of absence to the president for a period of up to 30 days.

THE LEGISLATIVE PROCESS IN MEXICO

The legislative process is a series of steps that the chambers must follow in order to create a law, to reform one, or to issue a decree subject to the approval of Congress. Those steps are:

1. *Presentation of an initiative.* Article 71 provides that initiatives can be presented by the president, deputies, senators, and state legislatures. Initiatives by deputies and senators must be presented first in their own chamber.
2. *Discussion and approval.* For the discussion and approval of laws and decrees that are not exclusive of a certain chamber, they will be labeled as coming from a Chamber of Origin and to a Chamber of Revision; the first is the chamber that receives the initiative. Either chamber can be of origin or revision, but there are a few cases in which only the deputies can receive an initiative.
3. *Sanction.* The sanction is the executive's right to veto or make observations on an initiative. The president cannot veto resolutions in which Congress or the chambers act as electoral organ or jury, or when the Chamber of Deputies decrees that it is acceptable to indict a high ranking officer of the federation for official crimes. The decree by the Permanent Commission calling an extraordinary period of sessions cannot be vetoed either. An initiative that has been vetoed has to return to Congress for a new discussion, and in order to bypass the veto it has to be approved by two-thirds of the members of both chambers. Without that majority, the president can paralyze certain functions of Congress (Article 72).
4. *Publication and entry into effect.* Once a law has been sanctioned, it must be published in the Official Gazette of the federation and in some cases also in state gazettes. Publication includes information about the moment the law or decree will come into effect.

HISTORIC RELATIONS BETWEEN EXECUTIVE AND LEGISLATIVE BRANCHES

According to Aguilar Camín (1996: 15–17), the new Mexican state that began its integration after the social revolution begat a political and social pact that protected for the first time the collective rights of citizens to work, health, and education, as well as patrimonial rights of the nation. That historic pact supposed that the responsibility for the direction of the country's political, economic, and social life was in the hands of a new breed of politicians.

The foundation of the National Revolutionary Party (PNR) in March 1929 allowed the integration of all the different revolutionary factions into one political organism. This assured commitment to the revolutionary principle of non-re-election, as well as the continuity of government programs (Córdova 1978: 174).

The Cardenas period (1934–40) was instrumental in the construction and consolidation of Mexico's political institutions. In 1938, Cardenas launched a new political party, the Party of the Mexican Revolution (PRM), to replace PNR. This assured the leadership of that president within this party, beginning a presidential regime (Meyer 2000: 1323) in which the executive branch, represented by the powerful president, became the predominant force and centre of all public life in the country (Carpizo 2003: 336–38).

According to Espinoza-Toledo (2003: 3), Congress has known two major stages in its relationship with the executive branch since that time. In the first, up to 1997, Congress was no more than a resonance box for the president. This does not mean Congress was unimportant but that it was an instrument of the prevalent presidential domination, and therefore uninterested in exercising the numerous attributions given to Congress by the Constitution. The great majority of legislators belonged to the ruling party, so they knew that opposing the president could mean the end of their political careers (Carpizo 2003: 339). Therefore, deputies, senators, local congresses, governors, and even judges followed the party line, which is to say the president's (Lerdo de Tejada 2004: 30–31).

The second stage began in 1997 when a plural Congress was elected. This led to the revision of all internal government rules in both chambers (Espinoza-Toledo 2003: 3). A new system started its profile that year, upon the possibility of PRI losing its majority in the Chamber of Deputies, and it deepened in 2000 when PAN won the presidency, to be consolidated in July 2003, when no party was able to win an absolute majority in Congress and the presidency at the same time, as had happened before (Lerdo de Tejada 2004: 13). In the current relationship between the president and the legislature, consensus among branches is necessary in order to achieve the reforms sought by the executive. This reciprocity is a new element in the Mexican political system, which is noticeable in the president's discourse, particularly when he complains that legislators "have not given him the necessary instruments to direct the country" (Garduño and Méndez 2004). Decisions do not depend on the will of one person now but rather on the participation of the diverse actors of the political arena.

LOBBYING IN MEXICO

The federal elections of 1997 initiated a new correlation of forces, since it became necessary to obtain the support of opposition parties in order to get reforms approved. Before 1997, to speak of "lobbying" in Mexico meant negotiating all demands and interests with the president or his secretaries, since approval came from the executive only. Now, since the 57th Legislature (1997–2000), it is possible to speak of true lobbying in Mexico. The term refers appropriately to the possibility of influencing the decision-making process in collective bodies. According to Tejada y Godina, lobbying means a process of negotiation in public decisions, which is available to citizens as well as enterprises (Lerdo de Tejada 2004: 7–9).

The Mexican Judicial Branch

The judicial branch in Mexico reveals an endemic weakness that places it at a disadvantage with respect to the other branches. This fact has brought about some harmful consequences, such as the weakening of the rule of law and loss of credibility in the organs that dispense justice.

INTEGRATION AND FUNCTIONS

The judicial branch was introduced to Mexican institutional life in 1824[3] after the country had gained independence. Its functions are the meting out of justice by resolving controversies or by legal actions resulting from the application or observance of federal law and protecting the civil rights of the citizenry. It has two jurisdictions: federal and local. The former governs the entire country; the latter governs each of the 31 federative entities and the Federal District. In Mexico, as opposed to the systems in Canada and the US, justice is not dispensed through oral trials and juries but through written trials.

The federal judicial branch is in charge of two fundamental jurisdictions: constitutional and ordinary. The first consists of the knowledge and resolution of conflicts arising from the violation of the federal Constitution by dispositions contained in laws as well as in actions by federal or local authorities. In other words, the judicial branch is responsible for maintaining national juridical order by protecting the Constitution's supremacy. The second, ordinary jurisdiction, consists of the obligation of federal judicial organs to know and resolve conflicts arising from the application of federal laws (Gamas Torruco 2001: 959).

STRUCTURE AND FUNCTIONS OF THE FEDERAL JUDICIAL BRANCH[4]

In order to exercise the functions we have mentioned, the judicial branch's structure integrates the Supreme Court of Justice of the Nation (SCJN), collegiate and unitarian circuit courts, district courts, the Council for the Federal Judicature, and the Electoral Tribunal.

THE SUPREME COURT OF JUSTICE OF THE NATION

The SCJN is the highest court; it consists of 11 ministers (or judges) and functions either as a whole or by committee and resolves constitutional controversies, disputes between the federation and federative entities, and unconstitutional actions.[5] The president of the SCJN is elected internally every four years. Judges are referred to as ministers and are appointed to 15-year terms by the president of the Republic from a list of proposals he submits to the Senate whenever a minister retires or his term expires.

Two committees in the SCJN consist of five ministers, with one of them presiding. The president of each is in office for two years. The first committee attends to penal and civil matters, while the second addresses administrative and labour issues. They are concerned with writs that challenge the constitutionality of laws, appeals against resolutions of federal court, and challenges to its own jurisprudence.

Matters that have come to the attention of the SCJN in recent years are related to the country's problems and derive essentially from the process of political plurality which began in the late 1980s. Some examples are legal recourses filed against the Indian Rights and Culture Law (September 2001),[6] against the establishment of time zones,[7] against fiscal law,[8] and conflicts between the president and Congress,[9] to name a few.

One of the bastions of Mexican justice is the writ of *amparo*, which is the main legal recourse that citizens possess to protect themselves against actions by any public authority from any branch of government. It has been the fundamental institution of justice in the constitutional system since its inception in 1847.

UPPER CIRCUIT COURTS AND LOWER DISTRICT COURTS

Upper circuit courts, or tribunals, are either collegiate or unitary. Each collegiate tribunal is composed of three magistrates, one presiding for a one-year term. Magistrates sit for six-year terms. These tribunals hear direct *amparo* writs, revision of indirect *amparo* writs, and other materially legislative acts. Each unitary tribunal consists of one magistrate, who serves for a six year term. It hears writs of indirect *amparo* against actions by another unitary tribunal.

Lower district courts have one judge for a six-year term and hear writs of indirect *amparo*. Collegiate and unitary circuit tribunals, as well as lower district courts, may specialize in different matters such as penal, civil, merchant, administrative, and labour law.

THE FEDERAL JUDICATURE COUNCIL (FJC)

The FJC was created by a constitutional reform in December 1994. In June 1999, several articles in the Constitution were reformed in order to determine the juridical nature of the FJC, that is, to recognize it as an organ of the federal judicial branch, with technical autonomy.[10] Its principal function is to administer, oversee, and maintain discipline in the federal judicial branch, except the SCJN; in matters involving the Electoral Tribunal, a special judicature committee must be formed. The FJC deals with judicial careers; it appoints and removes magistrates and judges and determines the number, circuit division, territorial competence, and specialization of collegiate and unitary tribunals and circuit courts. It is composed of seven members: the president of the Supreme Court, three counselors selected from magistrates, two more appointed by the Senate, and one appointed by the President of the Republic.

THE ELECTORAL TRIBUNAL

The most recently created legal institution, the Electoral Tribunal receives suits in electoral acts and resolutions from the electoral authority that violate constitutional norms. It functions with one Superior Committee and five regional ones.

JUDICIAL SYSTEM REFORMS

In recent years there have been important reforms in the judicial system, both federal and local. These have been clearly insufficient, so that the system's endemic weakness in general persists. The most relevant are those that deal with the operation and integration of the SCJN.

The first reform was launched on 1 January 1995; it was the most important modification to the judicial branch's institutional framework in the past 70 years since the reform by President Alvaro Obregon in 1928.[11] Its purposes were to reorganize the local organs of justice, achieve better efficiency in the administration of justice, improve the quality and performance of jurisdictional function, and undertake actions to raise the independence of the heads of the organs of justice. According to Samuel del Villar,[12] the reform was insufficient and has been widely criticized because incoherence, contradiction, insecurity, and centralism continue to prevail, along with archaic techniques and procedures, artificial and exponential workload expansion, and hindrances to the judges' capacity to do their duty.

The reform of 1995, following the declaration of NAFTA a year earlier, cleared the way for the evolution of the SCJN as a constitutional tribunal, returned it to its original integration of 11 instead of 26 ministers, and established its competence to resolve actions of unconstitutionality in order to control governmental acts. Furthermore, it integrated the federal Electoral Tribunal into the federal judicial branch and restricted its subordination to the president by granting the Senate power to appoint ministers from a list presented by the executive. The reforms established the Federal Judicature Council and granted it first administrative and disciplinary competence over the judicial branch. Later, in 1999, it was granted the capacity to appoint, ascribe, and remove magistrates and judges.

The 1995–2000 National Development Plan acknowledged the importance of the reform for the consolidation of rule of law. It alludes to the lack of certainty and the need to avoid lags and delays as well as the margins of discretion, negligence, and bad faith in the administration of justice. Despite these aims, less than ten years later the Plan's inefficacy and the fact that long-standing problems cannot be solved by reforms on paper were patent. Social and political conflicts arising from the application of laws remain. To illustrate the most recent changes to the Constitution and its scant effect on the efficacy of judicial organs, we may observe that the text of the Constitution referring to the judicial branch (14 articles) was modified on 44 occasions during the terms of three recent presidents—Miguel de la Madrid, 1982–88; Carlos Salinas, 1988–94; and Ernesto Zedillo, 1994–2000—and yet its effects on the administration of justice are frankly disappointing.

Recently, on 22 August 2003, the Supreme Court announced a National Survey for an Integral and Coherent Reform of the Justice Administration System of the Mexican State,[13] which took place in 2004. The core of this initiative is the assumption that judicial reforms have so far failed. Items subject for consultation show the grave state of the justice system: budget autonomy and independence of the judiciary; the incorporation to the judiciary of specialized tribunals dealing with such matters as labour, agrarian, and administrative issues; implementation of oral procedures, mandatory bar incorporation for all lawyers, the Mexican state and international justice, criminal justice and human rights, international treaties, hierarchy of norms in internal law, and alternative means for conflict-solving procedures.

PUBLIC OPINION

Increasingly, public opinion has been demanding better quality in justice administration. Several public personalities and authorities have insistently chastised the SCJN, trying to push for a more direct involvement in the solution of the most important national problems: Indigenous rights, abortion, excessive power in the executive branch, past crimes, etc. The SCJN is now seen as a valid interlocutor, one which must be pressed so that it opens up and participates more in solving the roughest national conflicts. The Chief of Government of Mexico City, Andrés Manuel López Obrador, who confronted the judiciary and requested the creation of a special Commission at the SCJN to address the problem of multi-millionaire compensation for some urban lots (known as the San Juan Spot), called the judicial system "corrupt, deprived of credibility, and detached from justice" (*El Universal* online: 24 Octuber). This type of confrontation was not even thought of before 2000, the SCJN being considered at the time as an isolated organ, incapable of taking decisions independently of the president and a small group of powerful officers.

The dispensation of justice has been highly criticized recently. The demand for profound reforms has come from all kinds of experts, from members of the judiciary themselves (ministers and magistrates of the SCJN and other federal courts, as well as judges from the states) to the United Nation's Commissioners on Justice Administration and Human Rights, the World Bank, OCDE, and even the President of the Republic. Perhaps the most devastating report, which clarifies the state of justice dispensation in the country, referring specifically to criminal justice in the last ten years, came from the United Nation's International Experts Commission dealing with the case of the murdered women of Ciudad Juarez, Chihuahua, at the northern border. It reports systemic failures and states that those crimes are provoked by "the lack of proper infrastructure and rampant corruption in the administration of justice.... Judicial Officers act discretionally and Justice is overtaken by the criminal elements" (Gil Olmos 2003). In a nutshell, they conclude that the Mexican judicial system is collapsing and that the dysfunctions evident in the Juarez case are not exclusive—they are part of the faults of the procedural system prevalent throughout the country.

This situation is the result of decades of neglect. Writer Carlos Monsivais, referring to the role of judges for decades, has qualified what has traditionally happened at the tribunals as a "grotesque process," particularly trials that took place during the 1970s against left-wing politicians that led to a veritable "juridical and ethical dissolution of the Judiciary" (Monsivais 2004). Renowned Mexican historian Lorenzo Meyer makes reference to the serious mistrust prevalent in the country regarding the application of the law as "one of the great deficits of contemporary Mexico." That lack of confidence of the average citizen in the rule of law and justice dispensation, he remarks, "leads to generalized corruption and total inefficiency in bureaucratic structures. Both phenomena are a serious obstacle for the proper functioning of civil society, as well as politics and the economy" (Meyer 2003).

THE JUDICIAL BRANCH UNDER SCRUTINY

Surveys of the population's perception of the judicial system and justice administration provide some relief and hope that, in the short term, other steps can be taken in order to build up an ideal judicial Branch. The poll taken by the Juridical Research Institute of the National Autonomous University in September 2003 is notable in that it revealed that there at least 65 per cent of Mexicans mistrust justice dispensation. The reason for this lack of confidence, according to the research, is the perception that the law is applied in a discretionary way, granting privileges to those that wield economic or political power. Other data from the National Public Safety

System reveal that the lack of credibility of the authorities derives mainly from the limited number of crimes that are actually punished, since out of every 100 crimes committed, only 20 are denounced and just five are punished. This crisis, it is reiterated, is due to corruption, low salaries, and low investigation capacity, plus daily workloads that overflow the institutional capacity to attend to crimes.

Conclusion

Since NAFTA encouraged the liberalization of commerce and investment, created mechanisms to protect intellectual property, establish dispute settlement mechanisms and oversee labour and environmental norms, certain political perceptions have emerged that consider cooperation a strategic condition for efficiency, competitiveness, and the welfare of the three nations. This fact has been acknowledged through a joint statement by the presidents of the US and Mexico and the prime minister of Canada, which establishes that "Our security and prosperity are dependent and complementary" (Council on Foreign Relations/COMEXI/CCCE 2005).

Although the degree of regional integration is smaller and less equal compared to the European Union (O'Brien 1995; Imtiaz 2006) due to the asymmetry of the economies, regionalization produces incentives that push each country's behaviour towards convergence. Economists use the term "convergence" to evaluate advances in the process of dismantling economic barriers. Nonetheless, for authors such as Weintraub (1988), convergence does not refer solely to economic matters and state practices. He suggests for the first time the concept of a "North American Community" to refer to the integration process between the US and Canada at the time of the signing of the free trade agreement in 1988. As a consequence of that process and despite the fact that NAFTA avoided the creation of supranational institutions, its implementation inevitably affects other areas.

Theorists of the European experience developed the concept of "spillover" in economic integration processes (O'Brien 1995; Imtiaz 2006). It included only economic matters first but then assumed that the economic dynamic would sooner or later draw the governments involved together to deal with the challenge of increasing political and social integration. The result of the spillover effect is the emergence of a North American political community, and although this was not the original aim of the governments, an informal common arena has been formed, impelled by the economic agenda impelled since the 1980s. Likewise, the border between domestic and foreign affairs is blurring, as the domestic affairs of each country are of increasing interest to its commercial associates.

Twelve years after the onset of NAFTA, 80 per cent of Canadian and Mexican commerce occurs with the US, and 30 per cent of US commerce occurs with Mexico and Canada. Nevertheless, one of the main challenges the region faces in the immediate future is finding a common vision on priority issues like energy and security. The pending agenda in regional security involves terrorism, drug trafficking, organized crime, and immigration.

CIVIL SOCIETY TRENDS

NAFTA has encouraged new political alliances between groups such as labour, women, and the environment and has forced them to join forces and get organized on a transnational basis (O'Brien 1995: 723). Although it is true that the participation of social groups in Mexico is not as lively or institutionalized as it is in the US and Canada, civil organizations do mobilize more and the integration dynamic encourages the tendency towards debate and solution proposals for diverse problems in a joint manner.

DEVELOPMENTS IN THE MEXICAN POLITICAL SYSTEM

Despite certain imminent trends of convergence, there are also areas that forestall advances towards a more equal and inclusive integration process; one such area is linked to the unequal growth in the interior of Mexican regions.

The northern Mexican states have grown at a rate ten times greater than those in the centre and south, which increases inequality and encourages immigration, corruption, poverty (in rural and urban zones), and violence. These trends represent severe risks to the stability and security of the entire region (Council on Foreign Relations/ COMEXI/CCCE 2005: 3–5). In addition, Mexico has not built the institutional framework that would allow it to face these new situations; discussion regarding a new arrangement between the federation and state governments is still pending.

Also present is the threat of legislative paralysis deriving from more competitive electoral processes and changes in the composition of the two chambers of Congress. These facts have moved many analysts to state the necessity of introducing reforms to make re-election of representatives and senators possible, in order to make the legislative process more accountable and efficient. Rule of law is the weakest part of the legal system, and Mexico needs to implement effective enforcement mechanisms. Besides, democratic transition is stuck at state level, as PRI still governs in 17 states. Other paramount concerns are how much more liberalization is possible and which public sectors or industry are next on the deregulation agenda in Mexico (Imtiaz 2006: 169).

Another matter of great relevance for Mexico and its commercial partners will be the improvement of dispute settlement mechanisms between trade, natural resources, and agricultural products. Even though there are studies over the past 20 years that have shown a convergence of values, with at least 34 per cent of Mexicans considering themselves "North American" and two-thirds supporting the development of a North American Security Strategy (Pastor 2006: 218), there are still powerful sovereignty preferences prevailing over oil and natural resources in Mexico, as well as a vision towards achieving a comprehensive agreement on immigration with the US.

The 2006 Mexican presidential election involved an unexpected eventuality that usually appears in all democracies: a close result between first and second place. The flagman of the right-oriented party, the PAN (National Action Party), Felipe Calderón, barely won with 233,000 votes more than his rival, just 0.6 per cent of total votes. The election was perceived to be rife with irregularities, errors, and inequities. Although such problems can and have occurred in other advanced democracies, in Mexico they undermined the citizens' faith in the ballot box. The official election loser, the leftist party candidate Andrés M. López Obrador, opposed the results, and he and his followers do not recognize the decision of the Electoral Tribunal confirming Calderón's victory. They justified their attitude by appealing to diverse federal government attitudes of hostility and interference with the election. For instance, President Fox tried to disqualify Obrador as a candidate as early as 2005 and later thwarted his probable triumph during the 2006 campaign. That fact, accompanied by several legal inconsistencies in the vote's official count and mistakes by the electoral authorities, generated the suspicion there was indeed an electoral fraud operation led by the Mexican government. As a consequence, in spite of at least one decade's effort by the IFE (Federal Electoral Institute), nearly half the Mexican citizenry believes in the existence of an electoral fraud, thus putting Calderón's triumph in doubt.

The result of the last election is a conflictive and polarized political environment, institutional weakness, and a lack of legitimacy for the new Mexican federal government that should be in office until 2012.

Notes

1   We would like express our gratitude to our students in the Canadian and American Studies Graduate Program, Enrique Hubbard (in translation) and Miguel A. Niebla (in research).

2   Arteaga Nava quotes Manuel Herrera y Lasso, who argued that we should understand that "law" is "... a general and abstract norm, general because it is applied indistinctively to any one falling within the hypothesis included in it, and it is abstract because, issued as an archetype of an ideal order; it has no notion of its own reach." In relation to a decree, he maintained "... it is a particular and concrete norm because its contents resolve a unique case, or it limits its scope to a specific authority or person" (Arteaga Nava 2001: 173).

3   Its creators modeled it on the US Judiciary Act of 1789, thereby adopting the terminology to designate the three component levels of the federal judicature: Supreme Court of Justice, upper circuit tribunals, and lower circuit courts (Gamas Torruco 2001: 941).

4   This section is based upon the texts of Elisur Arteaga Nava (2001: chapter 7); José Gamas Torruco (2001: chapter 22); and the chapter on Mexican constitutional law in Cesar Carlos Garza García (1997: 153–58).

5   Likewise, it effects revisions of *amparo* against laws and direct *amparo*, the sovereignty *amparo*, accusations of thesis contradiction in committees, and petition of jurisprudence modifications.

6   On 3 September 2001, 248 controversies were submitted by 247 Oaxacan municipal presidents and the Tlaxcala state government, to impugn the law which came into effect on 14 August 2001 (*El Universal*, 4 September 2001).

7   On 5 March 2001, the Head of Government in the Federal District, Andrés Manuel López Obrador, submitted a constitutional controversy before the SCJN against President Fox's decree regarding time zones (*El Universal*, 1 May 2001).

8   On 4 March 1999, then Head of Government for the Federal District, Cuauhtémoc Cárdenas, submitted a constitutional controversy against the Fiscal Coordination Law, which denied the federal district access to funds from the municipal aid fund (*El Universal*, 28 December 2000). Before that, in 1998, he had presented another controversy over a similar matter.

9   To declare the unconstitutionality of the Federal Superior Audit over interest payments to the Savings Protection Bank Fund (Fobaproa), which depends on the Lower House.

10   See <http://www.cjf.gob.mx/organizacion/antecedentes.asp>.

11 The Constitution was changed in chapter IV regarding this branch, as well as the Organic Law of the Federal Judicial Power, and the Regulatory Law for Constitutional Article 105 was approved.

12 For a more detailed opinion and critique of the performance of national tribunals and the judicial reform itself, see the seven-article series published by Samuel I. del Villar in the newspaper *La Jornada*, under the following titles: "Crisis y reforma judicial/I" (26 January 2004), "Reformas judiciales inexistentes/II" (27 January 2004), "¿Reforma judicial o hacendaria?/III" (28 January 2004), "Objetivos de la reforma judicial/IV" (29 January 2004), "Inferioridad de la Constitución/V" (30 January 2004), "Centralismo judicial/VI" (31 January 2004), and "Irresponsabilidad judicial/VII" (1 February 2004).

13 See <http://www.scjn.gob.mx>.

References

Aguilar Camín, H. 1996. *Después del milagro*. Mexico: Cal y Arena Editions.

Arteaga Nava, E. 2001. *Derecho constitucional*. Mexico: Oxford UP.

Carpizo, Jorge. 2003. *Estudios constitucionales*. Mexico: Porrúa Editors.

Córdova, Arnaldo. 1978. *La formación del poder político en México*. Serie Popular 15, 6th ed. Mexico: ERA Editors.

Council on Foreign Relations/COMEXI/CCCE. 2005. "Building a North American Community." Council of Foreign Relations (Report No. 53) <http://www.cfr.org/publication/ 8102/>.

Crespo, José A. 1998. *¿Tiene futuro el PRI? Entre la supervivencia democrática y la desintegración total*. Mexico: Grijalbo Editors.

de Tocqueville, A. 1994. *La democracia en América*. 7th ed. Mexico: Fondo de Cultura Económica.

Espinoza-Toledo, Ricardo. 2003. *La oposición parlamentaria en México*. Paper presented at the 14th International Congress of the Latin American Studies Association, Dallas, Texas.

Fowler, Will. 2004. "Introducción; El presidencialismo en México." In Will Fowler (ed.), *Presidentes Mexicanos*. Tomo I. Mexico: Instituto Nacional de Estudios Históricos de la Revolución Mexicana.

Gamas Torruco, José. 2001. *Derecho Constitucional Mexicano*. Mexico: Porrua.

Garduño, R., and E. Méndez. 2004. "La relación con el Legislativo, ruta hacia el distanciamiento insalvable." *La Jornada*, 30 November.

Garza García, C. 1997. *Derecho Constitucional Mexicano*. México: McGraw-Hill.

Gil Olmos, José. 2003. "La ONU ataca." *Proceso* (Weekly Review), 7 December: 6–8.

Huntington, Samuel. 1972. *El orden político en las sociedades en cambio*. Buenos Aires: Paidós.

Hussain, Imtiaz. 2006. "Elections, Political Integration, and North America: Exploring the Unknown," *North America Today: Outstanding Issues* 1,1 (January–June). Mexico: CISAN/CNAS.

Lerdo de Tejada, S., 2004. *El Lobbying en México*. Mexico: Porrúa.

Meyer, Lorenzo. 2000. *Historia general de México 2. La institucionalización del Nuevo régimen*. Mexico: El Colegio de México.

——. 2003. "¿Qué hacer?" [What to do?]. *Reforma*, 28 January.

Monsivais, Carlos. 2004. "García Ponce en el 68." *Noroeste Newspaper*, 18 January. <http://www.noroeste.com.mx>.

O'Brien, Robert. 1995. "North American Integration and International Relations Theory." *Canadian Journal of Political Sciences* 28,4 (December): 693–724.

Pastor, Robert A. 2006. "A North American Community." *North America Today: Outstanding Issues* 1,1 (January–June). Mexico: CISAN/CNAS.

Raigosa Sotelo, L. 2003. *Las funciones legislativas y no legislativas del Senado*. Mexico: Senado de la República/ITAM/Porrúa.

El Universal Online, AMLO cuestiona al poder judicial (AMLO call Judicial Power into question), 24 October, 2003. <http://www.eluniversal.com.mx/noticias.html>.

Weintraub, Sidney. 1988. *Mexican Trade Policy and the North American Community*. Vol. 10,14. Washington, DC: Center for Strategic and International Studies.

CHAPTER NINE

National Institutions in North America
US, Canadian, and Mexican Federalism

François Rocher and Gordon DiGiacomo

Canada, the US, and Mexico (officially, the United Mexican States) have federal political systems characterized by a distribution of powers between a central government and subnational or regional governments, called provinces in Canada and states in the US and Mexico. Thomas J. Anton defines federalism as:

> ... a system of rules for the division of public responsibilities among a number of autonomous governmental agencies. These rules define the scope of authority available to the autonomous agencies—which can do what—and they provide a framework to govern relationships between and among agencies. The agencies remain autonomous in that they levy their own taxes and select their own officials, but they are also linked together by rules that govern common actions. (Anton 1989: 3)

In federal systems, neither the central government nor the constituent governments can unilaterally change the division of powers as set out in the constitution. Such a provision exists to safeguard the autonomy of governments. To make that autonomy meaningful, federal constitutions try to ensure that governments have access to the necessary resources, fiscal and otherwise.

The Canadian, US, and Mexican federal systems share a number of similarities. However, they differ markedly in terms of the powers, especially fiscal powers, allocated to the central and provincial/state governments. In Canada, the degree of fiscal and political autonomy enjoyed by the provincial governments is considerable. The US states, while without the range of financial resources that the Canadian provinces possess, nevertheless have much more autonomy vis-à-vis the central government than do Mexican states.

Some data illustrate the point. In the mid-1990s, federal expenditures as a percentage of all government expenditures (after transfers) came to 61.2 per cent in the US and 40.6 per cent in Canada (Watts 2002: 466). In Mexico in 1996, the federal government was responsible for 75 per cent of total expenditures (Mizrahi 2002: 200). Even this figure understates the degree of fiscal centralization in Mexico, since in Mexico the most important taxes are collected by the federal government. As a result, in 2003, an average of 94 per cent of all Mexican states' revenues came from the federal government in the form of transfers (Gutiérrez González 2005: 227). Though centralism is slowly diminishing in Mexico, the constitutional division of powers strongly favours the federal government.

The goal of this chapter is to present some of the similarities and differences among these three federal states. It does so by looking briefly at the context within which the constitutions were drafted, by highlighting some of the constitutional provisions and the major developments in the evolution of their constitutional law, and by reviewing the trajectories that federalism took in the three countries. Generally, what one finds in each country is a state of tension between the central government and the constituent governments arising from the ongoing debate about where the balance of power should rest. Before concluding, the chapter discusses the impact of globalization generally and NAFTA specifically on the federal arrangement in the three countries.

Three Federal Constitutions

Historical developments explain the adoption of federal regimes by Canada, Mexico, and the US. It is worthwhile to consider the intentions and circumstances that marked the drafting of the three states' constitutions, for the political conditions which led to the writing of these constitutions inform us about the relationships that were to be established between the central and constituent governments.

The US was the first country to adopt federalism as a means of governance, although nowhere in its Constitution is the word "federal" mentioned. Well before 1781, the majority of states were in a position to carry out important political and social reforms allowing for the reorganization of their own political institutions. Virtually from the moment of the signing of the Declaration of Independence in 1776, almost all adopted new constitutions that replaced colonial charters.

The creation of a constitution for the new country required two attempts. The first was the Articles of Confederation of 1781. Based on a confederal model, the Articles limited the central government to a few specified responsibilities (for example war and foreign affairs), but gave it no authority over the states or over the citizens of the states. It could not tax or conscript citizens, nor could it subject them to its laws. It could not regulate trade, prevent trade wars between the states, establish common external tariffs, or create a common currency (Orban 1992: 48–53). As G. Alan Tarr notes (2005: 383), the result was that "the states could, and did, disregard mandates and requests for funding by the confederal government." In addition, the actions of Congress required the unanimous approval of the states. The demise of the confederal experiment came in 1788 when the current US Constitution replaced the Articles of Confederation.

The second constitution was adopted to address the problems resulting from sectionalism and interstate rivalry and "majority tyranny in the states." It therefore delegated to the federal government such powers as the power to establish uniform rules of bankruptcy, to make currency, to regulate commerce among the states, and to borrow money. It also prohibited the states from taking certain actions including making currency or imposing duties on imports or exports. According to Tarr, the constitutional drafters:

> believed that the federal government could be entrusted with enhanced powers because, with its checks and balances, it was better constructed than the state governments and thus less likely to tyrannize. In addition, as Madison argues, majority faction (tyranny) tends to flourish in small, homogeneous political societies, in which a single group might dominate. In contrast, the federal government, encompassing an extended commercial republic with a multiplicity of groups, would be less susceptible to the formation of majority factions. (Tarr 2005: 385)

It should be noted that the US Constitution did not explicitly establish the basic principles of federalism, for the division of powers was not exhaustive. According to Anton (1989: 8), "the most important reason for the persistence of federalism as a political issue in the United States is that spheres of autonomous action lack precise definition." That is to say, the powers of the states are poorly defined insofar as residual powers are concerned. The consequence of this imprecision is that the demarcation of powers belonging respectively to the central government and the states is difficult to establish. Nevertheless, it can be said that it is the states that control local governments, as well as health and welfare—notably public assistance, unemployment insurance, and family allowances—even though the central government largely administers social security. The states also have responsibility to administer the police and justice, transportation, communications, and many areas related to the protection of the environment.

Among the key constitutional provisions intended to protect the autonomy of the states is the Tenth Amendment. Adopted in 1791, it specifies that the powers not delegated to the central government are reserved to the states. However, the framers of the US Constitution also inserted other provisions that have been responsible, to a substantial degree, for the immense expansion of national government power. For instance, under the supremacy clause, Article VI, state laws may be declared unconstitutional if they conflict with federal laws. Also, a clause in section 8 of Article I empowers Congress to make all laws it deems necessary and appropriate to execute the listed powers, reserving the other areas for the states.

The US Constitution explicitly recognizes the sovereignty of American Indian tribes. "The drafters of the Constitution, in express wording in the commerce clause, recognized Indian nations as something distinct from the United States" (Wilkins and Lomawaima 2001: 5). Numerous judgments from federal and state courts have confirmed that the US Constitution does not apply to Indian tribes. As a result, according to Tarr, "They devise their own constitutions, elect their own leaders, and exercise significant governing authority" (Tarr 2005: 388). However, the three branches of the US government, as well as many states, have often acted in ways inconsistent with the sovereign nation status of American Indian tribes. Indeed, Deloria and Wilkins contend that in recent years the US Supreme Court has adopted a "much narrower view of tribal sovereignty," enabling Congress to "wield extraordinary power over tribes while at the same time legitimizing state efforts to exercise an increased amount of jurisdictional authority over tribes and their resources" (Deloria and Wilkins 1999: 80).

Canadian federalism dates back to the Constitution of 1867, the British North America Act, now called the Constitution Act, 1867. While conceptualized in Canada, the Act was a British law until 1982. That year, the Canadian Constitution was patriated; that is, at the request of Canada, the British Parliament passed a law that included a package of amendments (which were formulated in Canada) to the Canadian Constitution and that stated that, henceforth, no law enacted by the British Parliament would extend to Canada as part of Canadian law.

Unlike the US Constitution, the Canadian Constitution is comprised of several documents. The most important are the Constitution Act, 1867, which, among other things, sets out the powers of the governments in Canada, and the Constitution Act, 1982, which is comprised of the Canadian Charter of Rights and Freedoms and constitutional amending mechanisms.

As was the case with US federalism, Canadian federalism was the result of a compromise between those wishing to establish a unitary state and those wishing to preserve the autonomy of the constituent units of the new state. The new political structure sought to meet the economic and political needs of the dominant economic groups as much in the colonies as in the imperial metropolis. In economic terms, the creation of the new state was perceived as an instrument to consolidate public finances and to allow the investments necessary for the integrated economic development of the British colonies in North America, notably with respect to the creation of railways to link the country east to west.

One of the motivations that propelled the country's founders was fear of US expansionism. Some of the actions of the US government after the Civil War—for example, ending trade reciprocity—were, to Canadian political leaders, indicators of annexationist intentions (Knopf and Sayers 2005: 107). A united country in the northern half of the continent would, they believed, deter this tendency.

Many political leaders, including Sir John A. Macdonald, the first prime minister, wanted Canada to adopt a unitary political system. Other important political actors did not share his views and considered the provinces to be important political communities which should be guaranteed as much political autonomy as possible. To secure Québec's agreement and that of the Maritime provinces, Macdonald accepted the federal arrangement for Canada. Still, the intention of the country's founders was to create a strong central government to which the provinces would be subordinate, and the resulting Constitution, signed by representatives from Ontario, Québec, New Brunswick, and Nova Scotia, clearly reflects that intent.

Canada thus became a state for pragmatic reasons, adopting the federal form on the grounds that it was necessary to come to terms with diverse regional, national, and economic entities. The political and institutional choices that guided the founders of the federation were inspired at once by tradition and the US experience. The Constitution borrowed the parliamentary system from Britain, and the federal system, borrowed from the Americans, was adapted to accommodate the cultural differences in Canada.

It should be noted here that the cultural characteristics that were accommodated by Confederation were those of the French and English, not those of the First

Nations, whose pre-existing legal rights to their territories and to self-government had been recognized in the Royal Proclamation, 1763. This document laid out certain principles to govern relations between Britain and its colonies and Aboriginal peoples. According to Raymond Samuels, the document "presents the First Nations in terms of allies, rather than as British subjects" (2003: 135). Among other things, the Proclamation established the right of First Nations peoples to use and occupy "Crown" lands, and it created reserve lands on which no white settlement was allowed unless they were legally acquired by the Crown through purchase or treaty with First Nations. The Proclamation also prohibited British subjects from purchasing or taking possession of any land reserved for First Nations without the permission of the Crown, and it ordered all those who "either wilfully or inadvertently seated themselves" on First Nations land that was not ceded to or purchased by the crown "forthwith to remove themselves" from such land (Samuels 2003: 141). Notwithstanding the Royal Proclamation's recognition of Aboriginal peoples' legal right to their lands, the question of their concurrence with the creation of Canada appears not to have even arisen in the minds of Canada's founders. As Radha Jhappan observes, "Their consent was either merely assumed or considered irrelevant" (1995: 158).

Keenly aware of the Civil War that raged in the US during the years of constitutional discussion, the designers of the emerging federation wanted to better demarcate the powers granted to the central and subnational governments. They also thought that a strong central government was necessary to prevent the kind of tragedy that was occurring in their neighbour to the south. They agreed on a division of responsibilities between the central government and the provinces that was compatible with the goals of the time, namely military defence, the integrated development of British North America, and the maintenance of harmony between English and French-speaking citizens (Smiley 1987: chap. 4). What resulted was a federalism much more centralized, at least on paper if not in practice, than the federalism designed in the US.

While the framers of Canada's Constitution gave substantial powers to the provincial governments, in the form of a list in section 92 of the Constitution Act, 1867, that includes jurisdiction over social policy, health policy and natural resources policy, they also gave a number of powers to the federal government to ensure its dominance. Those powers include the following (Reesor 1992: 80–82):

» the almost unlimited power to levy both direct and indirect taxes;
» the power of the federal Parliament to spend as it sees fit, even in areas of provincial jurisdiction, provided that provincial compliance with a federal spending program remains voluntary;
» the power of Parliament to legislate for the "peace, order and good government" of Canada (the residual power), though this power has been severely circumscribed by the courts;
» the power to declare certain "works" coming under provincial jurisdiction to be for the general advantage of Canada and, therefore, to be regulated by federal law; the uranium mining

industry is an example of an industry declared to be for the general advantage of Canada; and

» the powers of reservation and disallowance, which essentially enable the federal government to strike down provincial legislation; these powers have fallen into disuse.

Generally, it can be said that the federal structure is more clearly delineated in the Canadian Constitution than in its US counterpart, and the powers of the federal and component governments are more clearly identified. As will become evident later, the practice of federalism has led the two countries to follow rather divergent trajectories.

Of our three countries, Mexico has the youngest constitution, dating back to 1917. It declares that "It is the will of the Mexican people to organize themselves into a federal, democratic, representative Republic." The 103 million people of the country live in 31 states and a Federal District (Mexico City). Federalism in Mexico actually originated with the 1824 Constitution. However, fear of national disintegration impelled the drafters of this document to provide for a strong executive (Mizrahi 2002: 194). It was an understandable fear: in 1836, the state of Texas declared its independence from Mexico.

The 1917 Constitution was the outcome of the Mexican Revolution which erupted first in the periphery in reaction to the repressive regime of Porfirio Diaz. While the framers of this constitution clearly set out to establish a federal system, they also gave the executive substantial powers, as did the drafters of the 1824 Constitution, suggesting that Mexicans have long harboured an ambivalent attitude about the capacity of federalism to keep the country together.

The history of centralism in Mexico is a long one. Indeed, Victoria Rodríguez suggests that it originated in the pre-Hispanic period when "The Aztec center maintained firm control over the country's other regions." After the Conquest, the Spanish did introduce federal principles but "within the confines of centralism." Rodríguez concludes that, while decentralist trends emerged with the Spanish rule over Mexico, "the tradition of central control imposed on Mexico during the colonial period is of critical importance because it provided the basic framework for the future organization and functioning of the political system as a federation" (Rodríguez 1998: 236).

As with the US Constitution but unlike the Canadian one, Mexico's Constitution assigns the residual power to the states. However, several amendments over the years have resulted in a shifting of a number of formerly state powers to the federal government. In addition, "virtually all articles in the constitution contain restrictions that limit the power of the states" (Mizrahi 2002: 197). Again like the US Constitution but unlike the Canadian, the Mexican Constitution provides for the representation of the constituent governments in the central government through an elected Senate. It is comprised of 128 members, with each state electing the same number of senators. However, 32 of the senators are elected through proportional representation on a nation-wide basis, thus attenuating the influence of the states to some extent.

Two provisions of the constitution in particular have ensured the supremacy of the federal government. One is Article 97, which gives the federal government the authority to bring into its jurisdiction matters that are within the states' competence. The other is Article 133, which states that the "Constitution, the laws of the Congress of the Union that emanate therefrom, and all treaties" made in accordance with the Constitution "shall be the supreme law of the whole Union." Juan Marcos Gutiérrez González explains that this article requires state courts to comply with the Constitution and with international treaties and federal laws "regardless of any contradictory provisions that might exist in the constitutions or laws of the states." He explains further that:

> ... the Supreme Court of Justice recently ruled that Mexico's federalist system functions according to a hierarchy of law. The highest level of authority resides in the federal constitution, followed by international treaties approved by a majority of the Senate, and then by the ordinary laws enacted by the Congress of the Union. (Gutiérrez González 2005: 217)

It should also be noted that centralization in Mexican government is facilitated by the extraordinary powers given to the president. For example, Article 89 allows the president to declare the powers of a state government null and void, while Article 76 allows the president to remove a governor and replace him/her with a provisional one (if the Senate approves).

The political hegemony of the Partido Revolucionario Institucional (PRI) has been another factor contributing to Mexico's highly centralized federalism: "From its founding in 1929 until 1989, the PRI controlled the presidency, the Congress of the Union, the 31 state governments, the Federal District, and most of the nation's 2,448 municipal governments" (Rodríguez 1998: 211). The president, as the head of the PRI, decided who could run for governor and could and did punish governors for a variety of "offenses." Because of the absence of political alternatives, because of the fiscal dependence of the state governments on the central government, and because of Article 76, a state governor was not likely to challenge federal authority. The problem was compounded, as we shall see, by the weakness of the Mexican judiciary.

Countering the centralist emphasis somewhat is Mexico's constitutional recognition of municipalities. Unlike the Canadian, US, and numerous other constitutions, Mexico's gives municipalities not only constitutional status but also certain exclusive powers and a guarantee of federal and state fiscal transfers, "as well as broad spending autonomy" (Rodríguez 1998: 214–15).

All of the governments can levy taxes. However, the major revenue sources are collected by the federal government which, by law, must share the revenues with the state and municipal governments. Together, the state and municipal governments receive about a quarter of the revenues subject to sharing, and they have full authority to expend those funds as they see fit. But not all revenues are subject to sharing; 60 per cent of the federal government's total revenues are to be distributed to the state and municipal governments. As a result of the Fiscal Coordination Act of 1980, the state and municipal governments also have access to federal grants-in-aid. They are larger than the revenue shares but they come with conditions attached, and they can be reduced or cancelled altogether by the Congress of the Union. The Constitution provides that the federal government must share with the states and municipalities a portion of what it collects from the special taxes that it levies on some of its exclusive sources of revenue, such as electrical energy, tobacco products and gasoline (Rodríguez 1998: 226–28). Finally, the state and municipal governments are eligible for subsidy programs the details of which are set out in intergovernmental agreements.

Alberto Díaz-Cayeros points out that the extraordinary fiscal dependency of the state and municipal governments was tolerated when all of the governors and leading politicians at the subnational levels belonged to the same political party "and depended for their career advancement and electoral success on the federal government." But once multiparty competition took hold, the fiscal arrangement was no longer acceptable, "which explains the increased demand for devolution of authority to states and municipalities witnessed in the last decade" (Díaz-Cayeros 2004b: 309).

Experiencing Federalism

THE ROLE OF THE COURTS

It would be useful to introduce this discussion of the actual experience of federalism of the three countries with a note on the differential effects of court decisions on the constitutional evolution of Mexico, the US, and Canada.

In Mexico, the weakness of the judicial system has contributed to the growth of the highly centralized federalism. That is to say, the dominance of the courts by the executive branch, a process that began in the 1920s and 1930s when successive presidents undertook to curb the Supreme Court's capacity for independent action, has enabled the enlargement of federal power to proceed virtually unchecked.

The fact that many Supreme Court members were PRI members as well also contributed to the deferential stance of the Court. It has been calculated that, between 1933 and 1995, 47 per cent of the members of the Supreme Court held a political position prior to appointment. The implications for Mexican federalism were noted by Kenneth Holland: "When intergovernmental conflicts nevertheless do arise and reach the courts, the Supreme Court, staffed with members of the PRI appointed by the PRI president and confirmed by the PRI Senate, tends to rule in favor of federal power and the president's preferences" (Holland 1993: 722). This, of course, assumes that state political leaders felt empowered enough to challenge the constitutionality of federal laws in the first place. But, in the case of Mexico, this assumption, until recently, could not have been made because of the dominance of the PRI throughout the country, because of the fiscal dependence of the state governments, and because of the power of the president to replace state governors.

In 1994, President Zedillo enacted reforms to Mexico's judicial system that expanded the scope of judicial review and enhanced the capacity of the Supreme Court to address constitutional issues. As a result of these reforms and of the emergence of opposition political parties, Mexico's highest court may, in the future, have a much greater impact on Mexican federalism than it had in the past.

In contrast to the situation in Mexico, court judgments have had a profound impact on Canadian federalism. As noted earlier, the framers of the Canadian federation set out to create a federal system with a dominant central government. However, the handiwork of the founders was almost totally undone by the judgments of a foreign entity, Britain's Judicial Committee of the Privy Council (JCPC). The JCPC is a committee of the British House of Lords that served as an appellate court for the nations of the British Commonwealth (and still does for some countries). While Canada has had a Supreme Court since 1875, it did not become the final court of appeal until 1949. During its time as Canada's last court of appeal, the JCPC consistently favoured the provinces. Peter Russell points out that "[b]etween 1880 and 1896 the Judicial Committee decided eighteen cases involving twenty issues relating to the division of powers. Fifteen of these issues (75 per cent) it decided in favour of the provinces" (1993: 42). The tilt of the JCPC continued throughout its time as Canada's final appellate court. The central government's residual power, its trade and commerce power, and its treaty power were among those that were severely circumscribed by the JCPC.

Since 1949, Supreme Court judgments have restored some of the strength of the federal government. For instance, it is generally agreed that the Supreme Court's decision in *R. v. Crown Zellerbach Canada Ltd.*, [1988] 1 S.C.R. 401 strengthened the federal residual power, and its decision in *General Motors of Canada Ltd. v. City National Leasing*, [1989] 1 S.C.R. 641 enlarged the federal trade and commerce power. Because of the nature of the constitutional division of powers, one effect of these two decisions has likely been to expand the federal government's treaty implementation power. Nevertheless, a reading of the Court's judgments would show that it remains exquisitely attuned to the sensitivities of those who support a strong central government and those who favour greater provincial autonomy.

In the US, "[t]he paramount feature of American constitutional history has been the expansion of the power of the federal government." The process has been aided by "the Supreme Court's broad interpretation of the powers granted to Congress and by constitutional amendments" (Tarr 2005: 389). The expansion of federal power has been accompanied by a diminution of state power, even though the Tenth Amendment gives the residual power to the states.

The first judicial interpretations of the US Constitution, under the leadership of Chief Justice John Marshall (1801–35), confirmed the predominance of the central government over the states. The Court opposed state actions and supported federal action, citing the need to unify the country. Subsequent interpretations of the Constitution favoured the states. Indeed, right up to the mid-1930s, the Supreme Court consistently upheld the jurisdiction of the states. As Holland notes, "the Tenth Amendment became analogous to the First Amendment, and was read by the Court as saying: 'Congress shall make no law destroying powers that states exercised before ratification of the Constitution'" (Holland 1993: 89).

From the mid-1930s until the 1990s, the US Supreme Court was a strong supporter of federal power. In case after case, it upheld federal jurisdiction. We get some idea as to how far the Court was willing to go in support of federal power by noting Justice Blackmun's comment in *Garcia v. San Antonio Metropolitan Transit Authority*, 469 US 528 (1985) in which the justices upheld a federal labour law on the basis of the Constitution's interstate commerce clause. Writing for the five-member majority, Justice Blackmun declared that the country's founders:

> ... chose to rely on a federal system in which restraints on federal power
> over the states inhered principally in the workings of the National
> Government itself, rather than in discrete limitations upon the objects
> of federal authority. State sovereignty interests, then, are more properly
> protected by procedural safeguards inherent in the structure of the fed-
> eral system than by judicially created limitations on federal powers. (See
> Ostrom 1991: 100)

In other words, the restraints on federal power are embedded in the structure of the
federal government itself, that is, the Senate. For John Kincaid, "[t]his case epitomizes
coercive federalism...." (1996: 43).

Since the mid-1990s, the Supreme Court has tilted somewhat in favour of state
autonomy. For instance, in one decision, it placed limits on congressional use of the
interstate commerce clause to regulate non-economic activities (Tarr 2005: 405).
Still, there is a deep reluctance in the US to curtail national power.

THE AMERICAN FEDERALISM EXPERIENCE SINCE WORLD WAR II

The economic crisis of the 1930s and World War II led the central government to
mobilize considerable resources for the restoration of economic growth and the
attainment of full employment. The increase in US state intervention after the war
was achieved through cooperative agreements between Washington and subordinate
governments. Broad goals were articulated by the central government, while the
implementation of programs was undertaken by the states in exchange for grants.
The central government adopted a series of laws allowing it to regulate numerous
fields (transportation, environmental protection, workplace safety, health, education,
energy, etc.) which were traditionally reserved for the states.

In this context, it is not surprising that grants to state and local governments
increased more rapidly than any other element of the national budget. In fact,
national grants constitute the greatest source of revenue for the states and municipalities, surpassing even sales and property taxes. Numerous programs have become
intergovernmental, meaning in a way that a reduced number of them can be operated solely by either the federal government or the state governments. According to
Anton:

> Washington increasingly has acted as a banker for state and local govern-
> ments operating national programs; national government employment has
> been essentially stable for two decades, while state and local personnel
> have tripled in number. The confluence of the social empowerment state
> with the component state has led to a practical, if not theoretical, division
> of responsibilities. (Anton 1989: 44)

In this way, US federalism came to be characterized by substantial centralization
of decision-making with the state governments confined to the implementation of
central government initiatives.

Compared to the federal government in Canada, the federal government in the US
imposes more stringent conditions on its grants to the states, which is an indicator

of centralization. Hence, there is less recourse to block grants than formula grants, allowing the federal government to reach a specific clientele in sectors like education, employment, or transportation, or to project grants based on the principle of competition among bidders for the realization of broad goals. The federal government was able to strengthen these mechanisms of intervention by setting indirect conditions when grants are bestowed, which do not necessarily have any direct relation with the goals of financial aid awarded to governments (cross-cutting). Washington also uses the technique of cross-over sanctions to impose financial sanctions if the recipient government of grants does not respect the established demands.

The US does not have a system of equalization payments. This does not mean that there are no federal resources being transferred to states, but rather that the transfer payments do not have the objective of equalizing the states' capacity to offer public services. It has been demonstrated that it is the states with well-organized administrations which are able to negotiate with the central government that receive federal largesse. But in a system of equalization payments, it is the states that have a greater proportion of the poor, the elderly, youth, or other disadvantaged groups which receive proportionately the most transfer payments. In the US case, the states with a fiscal capacity have little influence upon the central government.

Nevertheless, the redistribution of resources towards local authorities remains an important aspect for these administrations. Amounts transferred to local authorities represent approximately 20 per cent of their resources and "although it is only between 10% and 15% of federal outlays it could therefore have a significant role in leveling the fiscal capacities of states; and if it does not, then that is for reasons as much ideological as pragmatic" (Théret 1999: 503). In ideological terms, the dominant idea is that the market will ensure an equitable redistribution of economic conditions across the federation. Thus, equalization payments are perceived as disincentives for local economies to be administered efficiently (Peterson 1995: 24).

Apart from these political ideals, we must consider pragmatic political factors. The political system in the US is structured in such a way as to give a monopoly on decision-making to a conservative coalition for whom the ideal of free market economy contradicts any initiatives towards social reforms that attempt to limit market forces. For these reasons, unconditional transfers to states (which are not to be confused with equalization payments) are only secondary. In 1991, these payments represented only 14.5 per cent of the total federal transfers (Théret 1999: 504). Moreover, the conditional transfers are targeted over a time period. They may double over a short period of time, confirming that these transfers are discretionary and that they are not the result of a compromise relying on federal principles but rather are at the discretion of Congress. Once again, it is noteworthy that the discretionary nature of the centralization that characterizes US federalism results in the better organized states receiving the most federal funding. According to Théret, "the difference in destination of federal transfers to rich and poor states actually contributes to the growth of economic inequalities between regions, since it favours the development of already developed regions and tends to keep poor states in a poverty trap" (Théret 1999: 505).

As a result of the fiscal dominance of the federal government, the control it exerts on the state and local governments, the diversity of economic and social conditions in each state, the configuration of political institutions that allows regional interests to be represented within central institutions, and the absence of party discipline that in effect liberates politicians from partisan constraints, US federalism has a high degree of centralization. State and local governments, while important in the distribution of services, are not significant players.

Attempts at decentralization under the Republican administrations of Richard Nixon and Ronald Reagan, labeled the "New Federalism," sought more to relieve the central administration of the budgetary weight of the programs it financed than to better respect the principles of federalism (Conlan 1988; Williamson 1990). The hallmark of Nixon's New Federalism was general revenue-sharing. Unlike block grants, which were federal grants to states intended for specific purposes, general revenue-sharing funds were transferred with very few strings attached and were not limited to a specific program. However, although much of the decision-making over the expenditure of funds was transferred to the states, "the federal government retained control over the allocation of funds, and even though it was formula driven, these formulas were also dictated by the center" (Ward and Rodríguez 1999: 48).

While Nixon's New Federalism sought to establish a federal system better suited to contemporary challenges, Reagan's was guided by his desire to reduce the role of the federal state or, at least, the social side of the federal state. Greater state autonomy was a secondary objective. As a result, President Reagan, "while rhetorically advocating states' rights, signed more federal laws preempting state powers than had any previous president" (Tarr 2005: 391).

In the 1990s, the evolution of US federalism was influenced by the deficit reduction goals set by the central government. Although President Clinton promised to invest in infrastructure programs as well as health services, he quickly came to understand that the importance of the deficit reduction goals left little room for new federal initiatives. At a conference in 1993 on intergovernmental relations, state representatives displayed their frustration towards the federal system, especially concerning the lack of communication and trust between the levels of government. Moreover, "conference participants complained that fragmented and restrictive federal programs impeded their ability to solve problems rationally and cohesively. Their solution: national policy focused on ends rather than means. They claim that such a reorientation would better tap the innovation inherent in a federal structure" (Bowman and Pagano 1994: 1). The Clinton administration adopted an approach under which the central government would establish national objectives while offering states sufficient flexibility for the implementation of policies. The federal government also offered lump sum transfers to state governments.

Clinton's approach faced stiff opposition in Congress where it was feared that a devolution of powers towards the states would translate into a "race to the bottom" for health and social programs targeting disadvantaged individuals. In the end, the devolution of powers that was to result from the lump sum transfers did not take place, for Washington retained its power to prescribe state political actions or to limit certain state activities. Hence,

> these recent developments suggest how hard it is for federalism to reform itself. Federal policymakers have to exercise national power in order

to devolve it to the states. In the process, the temptation to hang onto national power presents itself. The net result is what Posner calls "opportunistic federalism" where, depending on your political ideology, certain federal mandates are acceptable. (Schram and Weissert 1997: 3)

The reticence of federal politicians to renovate US federalism in support of greater state autonomy has persisted, regardless of the political party represented in the White House. Indeed,

> Presidents have tended to encourage centralized solutions for perceived problems—for example, President George W. Bush's initiatives with regard to elementary and secondary education and tort reform—and Congress has responded to interest-group pressure by federalizing a variety of ordinary state-law crimes, such as drug possession and violence against women. Whether this federal reach can be restrained will be important in determining the future course of American federalism. (Tarr 2005: 405)

David B. Walker has described the American system as "permissive federalism." The expression "pretty well captures the systemic dilemma of states and localities because it underscores the basic constitutional, political, representational, and political ascendancy of the national government, its institutions and its processes" (Walker 1991: 118). US federalism, it would appear, is always open to certain forms of decentralization and to the initiatives of the states and local bodies but at the discretion of or with the permission of national authorities. The phrase "permissive federalism" reflects the centralist tendency of US federalism and the "nation-centred system."

THE EXPERIENCE OF CANADIAN FEDERALISM SINCE WORLD WAR II

As in the US, the Great Depression, World War II and the postwar reconstruction effort produced a more centralized federalism in Canada. The "watertight compartments" approach was abandoned in favour of cooperative federalism, manifested in particular by intergovernmental accords on tax collection and shared-cost programming. The need for constitutional reform was apparent but governments were unable to come to agreement on its nature. Thus, only two significant constitutional amendments were adopted in that time period; a 1940 amendment gave the federal government jurisdiction over unemployment insurance and a 1951 amendment made old age pensions a concurrent responsibility.

The increase in the number of shared-cost programs made the division of powers between the federal and provincial governments less clear. By stipulating numerous and detailed conditions to federal grants, Ottawa was able to exercise greater control over the nature and range of provincial activities. Hence, Canadian federalism was altered less by resorting to constitutional changes than by reaching agreements of a fiscal or administrative nature. Provinces were responsible for the implementation of numerous social programs financed on a shared-cost basis. In 1957, the federal government started an equalization program, based on the revenues of representative provinces, which sought to compensate provinces whose income per capita was inferior to the average. With the exception of many Québec politicians and observers, this period was considered to be the golden age of Canadian federalism because of the great flexibility it demonstrated.

From the end of the 1950s to the mid 1970s, the rapid growth in provincial government activities, associated with the dynamic of province-building, helped make federal-provincial relations more complex (Simeon and Robinson 1990). In Québec, the "Quiet Revolution" brought the province into the modern era, reinforcing the autonomist ambitions of many Québec politicians. In Alberta, a more regionalist vision was being promoted. Unlike the US Senate, Canada's appointed Senate does not represent subnational interests in a meaningful way. Thus, it is provincial governments that have become the spokespersons and defenders of the specific needs of provincial communities. What has therefore emerged is "executive federalism," a much-criticized process that brings together leaders of the federal and provincial governments or their senior officials to fashion policy for the country.

In the mid-1960s, the deficiencies of the Canadian Constitution emerged as a major problem for Canada. The opening of this dossier resulted from pressures from the Québec government, which wanted to revise the division of powers in order to increase its manoeuvrability in economic, social, and cultural affairs. There was disagreement in Québec regarding how far the province should go. Some preferred outright secession. Others wanted Québec to remain within Canada but with vastly increased powers. Still others supported the federal government's vision of constitutional reform. The latter's main elements were patriation of the Constitution, the adoption of an amending formula, and a constitutionally entrenched Charter of Rights and Freedoms; once these measures were adopted, discussions could then begin on the division of powers. The conflict came to a head in the 1980 Québec referendum which asked the population for a mandate to negotiate a new constitutional arrangement called sovereignty-association. The vision that decisively prevailed in this popular consultation was that put forward by the federal government.

Having won the referendum, the Liberal federal government under Pierre Trudeau proceeded to implement its constitutional vision. Despite important concessions to provincial autonomy, and despite the concurrence of nine provinces, it was unable to secure the agreement of the government of Québec, although the overwhelming majority of federal members of Parliament from that province supported the reforms.

In the late 1980s and the early 1990s, the Progressive Conservative federal government of Brian Mulroney and the provincial premiers endeavoured to come to an agreement that would result in Québec's formal signing of the constitution. Their efforts were rejected by public opinion, although by and large the elites in the country supported the proposals, principally because of concerns about the "distinct society" status accorded Québec, concerns about the diminution of federal powers, and anger about the process. The Charlottetown Constitutional Accord, which had the support of major Aboriginal organizations in addition to the federal and provincial governments, was rejected in a referendum in most of the provinces, including Québec, and by most Aboriginal voters.

The failure of the two constitutional reform efforts, the Charlottetown Accord and its predecessor, the Meech Lake Accord, effectively put an end to constitutional discussions. There were two particularly noteworthy effects of the constitutional battles of the period between 1987 and 1995. First, the failure of the Meech Lake Accord to obtain ratification infuriated many Quebecers. And they expressed their anger in October 1995 when the secessionist government of Québec held a second referendum on sovereignty-association. This time, the secessionists lost by only a fraction of a percentage point. Secondly, the content of the Meech Lake Accord and the secretive and exclusionary process by which it was negotiated infuriated Canadians outside of Québec. It became acceptable to discuss how Québec secession would be negotiated (Young 1998). The divisibility of Canada, as well as the divisibility of Québec, became acceptable topics of conversation. It could also be said that Canadians outside of Québec began to re-think, in clearer terms, what they had to accept to keep the country together.

The narrow defeat of the secessionist option forced the federal government to review its national unity strategy (Cameron 1999). It opted to bring forth a reference case to the Supreme Court, asking it whether a unilateral declaration of independence by Québec, as proposed by secessionists in the case of failed negotiations on renewed partnership, would be legal. At the end of August 1998, the Supreme Court answered negatively but qualified its answer by adding that, if the population of Québec indicated in a clear question that it no longer wanted to be part of Canada, Canada was constitutionally obligated to negotiate in good faith the terms of secession. The rift between Québec and the rest of Canada was made wider when the federal government made it clear in November 1999 that it would not negotiate the terms of secession if it judged that the question asked in a referendum was not clear or if the secessionists only won by an absolute majority of the votes (50 per cent plus one). In doing so, the federal government introduced the principle of a qualified majority. This led some political observers to charge that the federal government plays by one set of rules when it is confident of victory but changes them when it fears that the rules will not play in its favour next time around (Rocher 2004). Others suggest that the federal actions were long overdue, that they were the legitimate responses of a national government determined to keep the country together on its terms, and that in other countries secession is expressly forbidden in their constitutions (Dion 1999).

Although federal and provincial politicians had little appetite for discussions on the Constitution after the 1992 referendum on the Charlottetown Accord, they did negotiate a number of significant intergovernmental agreements on various policy issues. For example, in 1996, in response to a long-standing Québec demand, the federal government agreed to withdraw from the field of labour market training. It thus negotiated bilateral agreements with each province and territory, including Québec, that set out the details of the transfer of responsibility. In 1999, the federal and provincial governments, except that of Québec, negotiated a Social Union Framework Agreement. A key feature of this Agreement is the stipulation that forbids the federal government from creating a new social policy initiative unless it has the support of a majority of the provinces. The stipulation has been criticized by many provincial autonomy advocates because it allows the federal government to proceed with an initiative without the consent of Québec and Ontario which, between them, have 60 per cent of the Canadian population (Gagnon and Segal 2000). On the other hand, the Agreement represents the first time that the federal government has agreed in writing to a limitation on its spending power.

Other important federal-provincial-territorial agreements include the Agreement on Internal Trade, the health care accords, the bilateral child care agreements, and the Canada-Wide Accord on Environmental Harmonization.

It bears noting that, in its relations with the provinces, the federal government generally adheres to the equality of the provinces vision. That is to say, what it offers one province, it offers to all. Thus, it shies away from according Québec special status. It also bears noting that the federal government has accepted a confederal arrangement in some policy areas. For instance, labour market training policy in this country is fashioned to a considerable degree by the Forum of Labour Market Ministers. Similarly, the Canada-Wide Accord on Environmental Harmonization is managed by the Canadian Council of Ministers of the Environment. And health care policy has a new confederal Health Council of Canada. For some, what these and other confederal arrangements represent is federal acknowledgement of the federal nature of the Canadian political regime. For others, the emerging confederalism is an unwelcome development since it suggests the continuing erosion of federal authority.

THE MEXICAN EXPERIENCE OF FEDERALISM

The outstanding feature of Mexican federalism, that is, its highly centralized nature, remained in place, virtually unchallenged and unquestioned, for over 70 years. According to Victoria Rodríguez, "[t]he postrevolutionary centralization of power crystallized during the presidency of Lázaro Cárdenas (1934–1940), and by the end of his administration the authoritarian features of the state had been firmly established" (1997: 19). For decades afterwards, Mexico's governing elites focused on the goals of political stability and economic growth. Unlike Canadian political leaders who, from the founding of the country, have been preoccupied with federal-provincial relations, those in Mexico concentrated on implementing a certain model of development that, in effect, subordinated "democracy and socioeconomic justice to a sterile stability" (Levy, Bruhn, and Zebadúa 2001: 6). They showed little interest in crafting a more innovative or more balanced federal arrangement or, for that matter, a more vibrant democracy.

However, in the early 1980s, the notion of a more decentralized federation began to enter Mexican political discourse. Yemile Mizrahi suggests that the reason for this development was essentially economic: "once the economy started to decelerate during the 1970s, centralization began to be perceived as a problem and a major obstacle to equitable and sustainable development.... With a slowing economy, the federal government became overloaded with many responsibilities and functions it could not meet" (2002: 199). Rodríguez agrees, but she also cites the political impacts of excessive centralism, namely, growing resentment toward the centre and intensifying political alienation.

The administration of President Miguel de la Madrid (1982–88) was the first to make a serious effort to increase the autonomy of the state and local governments. His Municipal Reform of 1984 is described by Ward and Rodríguez as "the first major attempt at weaning municipalities from their traditional dependence on state and federal control and largesse" (1999: 54). He also began the process of transfer-ring responsibility for health and education to the states.

President de la Madrid was followed in office by Carlos Salinas de Gortari (1988–94). He furthered the decentralization of education initiated by de la Madrid. According to Rodríguez, "Salinas transferred to the state governments both respon-sibility *and* money for education and granted them full autonomy for spending these funds" (1997: 83; emphasis in original). With respect to the transfer of health serv-ices, many states were reticent about accepting responsibility without an assurance that the necessary resources would also be transferred. Thus, during the Salinas administration, there were no additions to the 14 states that accepted responsibility for health under de la Madrid.

Despite these initiatives, under Salinas, the movement toward greater politi-cal decentralization (through the enhancement of state government autonomy, as opposed to administrative decentralization) advanced only minimally. Rodríguez sums up his administration as follows:

> The Salinas administration ... presents something of a paradox. On the
> one hand, we saw measures leading to decentralization, municipal auton-
> omy, greater pluralism, and the targeting of resources directly to marginal-
> ized rural and urban areas.... On the other hand, there is also considerable
> evidence that on balance his administration generated more centralism.
> In fiscal terms, the federation strengthened its control over revenues and
> showed no willingness to increase the amounts transferred to the states
> and municipalities. (Rodríguez 1997: 59)

Rodríguez also points out that while he was president Salinas removed half of the country's governors from office for one reason or another.

Salinas was succeeded in office by Ernesto Zedillo (1994–2000). More committed than his predecessors to political devolution, Zedillo launched a new initiative, which he called "New Federalism." Its five goals were to increase revenue-sharing alloca-tions to the states; expand the opportunities for the states to raise revenue; increase the percentage of funds, intended for local social development projects, controlled by state governments; strengthen the municipalities' administrative capacity; and clarify the administrative functions of the federal, state, and municipal governments.

Generally, it can be said that President Zedillo made substantial progress in turn-ing Mexico into a more balanced federal state. The state and municipal govern-ments received increased responsibilities as well as increased resources to fulfill those responsibilities. The decentralization of education to the states was completed during his administration and in 1996 he signed agreements with all of the states for the complete decentralization of health care (Rodríguez 1997: 149).

Zedillo had less success addressing an issue that emerged during tenure. In January 1994, the Zapatista rebellion erupted in Chiapas, the country's most impoverished state and the state with the second highest proportion of Indigenous people. The uprising exposed Mexico's breathtaking regional inequality as well as the histori-cal repression of Mexico's Indigenous population. Two years after the uprising, the Mexican federal government and the Zapatista Army of National Liberation signed the Accords on Indigenous Rights and Culture in the city of San Andrés Larráinzar. The Accords, endorsed by the multiparty congressional Commission on Concordance and Pacification (COCOPA), provided for the:

> recognition of indigenous peoples as social and historical subjects. The implications of this recognition are profound because it involves modifying the Mexican constitution to recognize not only individual citizens but also indigenous peoples. Autonomy for Indian peoples further implies the real transfer of faculties, functions, and jurisdictions that currently fall to government agencies. These include political representation within the community and the municipality, autonomy of the local justice system, control over administrative affairs, and control over land and natural resources.
>
> [Furthermore] Internal political representation would allow indigenous peoples to bypass the realm of regular electoral participation and the political party system and name their own community and municipal authorities.... Political representation at the state and national levels would be assured through the creation of new electoral districts and special mechanisms to facilitate indigenous participation in elections as voters and as candidates. (Navarro and Carlsen 2004: 449)

Clearly, the implementation of the Accords would have meant greater autonomy for Mexico's Indigenous peoples, and that would inevitably have meant a devolution of some federal, state, and municipal powers to their communities. Although the Constitution was amended to recognize Mexico's "pluricultural composition," and although there has been some activity at the state level to recognize Indigenous peoples' rights, little of substance has been done to meet the autonomy demands of the Indigenous population. The reason, according to a Zedillo administration official, is that the initiative "divides the country by positing territorial autonomy and special privileges for indigenous persons, which threatens national sovereignty over subsoil resources and involves establishing a fourth level of government" (Navarro and Carlsen 2004: 452). Obviously, the Mexican federal arrangement has not readily accommodated Indigenous peoples' self-government aspirations. In this, it is not unlike those of its two North American partners.

In their assessment of federalism in Mexico, Ward and Rodríguez suggest that Mexico is moving toward a coordinate model of federalism, that is, a model in which the central and state governments have sufficient powers to act relatively independently of each other. They also note that the growth of a political opposition is facilitating the development of an authentic federalism.

> While the dependence of municipal government continues to be ever present, especially in smaller and poorer municipalities, there appears to be an increasingly autonomous relationship between state governments and the federal government. This is particularly true of states governed by the opposition. As the number of states governed by parties other than the PRI continues to grow, and as PRI governors themselves increasingly

insist on being somewhat more autonomous and detached from both the president and the party than in the past, we expect the coordinate model to develop more fully throughout the country. (Ward and Rodríguez 1999: 50–51)

It is of some significance that Zedillo's successor, Vicente Fox, had been a state governor and is a member not of the PRI but of the Partido Acción National (PAN, National Action Party).

Mexican federalism remains highly centralized and the movement toward coordinate federalism will not be uneventful. One difficulty is that the historical lopsidedness of Mexican federalism has left many of the subnational governments in a politically and administratively underdeveloped condition, unprepared to assume additional policy-making responsibilities. While some areas have a vigorous civil society and political parties with growing strength that can hold a state government accountable, others are still governed in an authoritarian fashion. Such uneven democratic development could exacerbate Mexico's deep socioeconomic inequalities and place added pressure on the central government to intervene (Levy, Bruhn, and Zebadúa 2001: 107, 275).

NAFTA's Impact on Federalism

At a conference held in 2000, participants from several countries with federal systems discussed the impact of globalization and regional integration on federal systems. One of the main conclusions that emerged from the conference is that globalization and regionalization have *not* caused transformations in the federal arrangements in the countries discussed. In their analysis of the conference deliberations, Lazar, Telford, and Watts concluded that:

> federal and federal-like systems have been highly stable in spite of the huge growth of global and regional influences on their polities, economies, and societies. In particular, there is little evidence of external pressures forcing major changes to basic institutional features of the countries studied.... [T]here is evidence of some degree of adjustment in institutional structures and arrangements as a precondition to effectively dealing with global and regional economic forces. But on the whole these changes have been modest.
>
> ... Federal structures are normally found in societies that include substantial diversity. A question of primordial interest here is whether the federal bargain that underpins each of these societies is being undermined or at least significantly affected by the forces of global and regional integration. We found no support for this idea. To date at least, the forces of global and regional integration have not eroded the political stability that is required to sustain the federal systems we have examined. (Lazar, Telford, and Watts 2003: 31–32)

In other words, "the basic political equilibrium" in the federal systems has held, despite free trade agreements like NAFTA. Among the federal systems where the equilibrium has held are those of the US and Canada. Can the same be said of Mexican federalism?

MEXICO

The short answer is, yes, the same can generally be said of Mexico. However, some explanation is in order.

As noted earlier, there is a hierarchy of laws in Mexico, with the Constitution being the supreme law of the land. As an international treaty, NAFTA takes precedence over ordinary legislation enacted by the legislatures. "This hierarchy gives a treaty greater standing than both the domestic laws of the federation and the laws of the states" (Gutiérrez González 2005: 217). Ordinary legislation, referred to as secondary legislation in Mexico, that emanates from either the federal or state governments must conform to the requirements of a treaty. Have the state governments been negatively affected by NAFTA? Gutiérrez González declares that they have not: "... NAFTA has not been a factor in creating or eliminating the powers of the subnational governments because trade matters are under federal jurisdiction" (Gutiérrez Gonzalez 2005: 229).

However, NAFTA may have been partly and indirectly responsible for the strengthening of the states and, therefore, for the rejuvenation of federalism in Mexico. Carla Huerta and Alonso Lujambio, in their 1994 analysis of the impact of NAFTA on Mexican federalism, insist that the imbalance in federal-state relations had little to do with the "centralization of the distribution of fiscal resources." Rather, "... it has a strictly political character: the most important variable which explains the precariousness of post-revolutionary Mexican federalism is the hegemonic, rather than competitive, party system." In other words, they say, it has been the PRI's monopoly on power that has stifled Mexican federalism:

> as long as governors cannot be re-elected and owe their mandate not to their constituencies through competitive elections, but to the central power, and as long as they consider the president their political boss—who is simultaneously the leader of the hegemonic party—federalism will never reach its full potential, no matter how many administrative duties, policies, and resources are decentralized. (Huerta and Lujambio 1994: 65)

However, Huerta and Lujambio predicted that, because of NAFTA, the continuing use of fraudulent practices by the PRI would become increasingly difficult. They "will be viewed very poorly by Canada and the US...." As a result, space would open up for the emergence of vigorous opposition parties within the states, which would, in turn, "strengthen the political dynamics of Mexican federalism" (Gutiérrez Gonzalez 2005: 66).

The data suggest that Huerta and Lujambio predicted well. While the PRI lost only three gubernatorial elections before 1993, it lost the governorships in 11 states between 1993 and 1999 and was able to win more than 50 per cent of the popular vote in only four states (Díaz-Cayeros 2004a: 222). In the 1996–98 period, one in every three Mexicans lived under non-PRI governors (Ochoa-Reza 2004: 285). While it is true that the political contestation within the states began before NAFTA, it is arguable that it gained momentum after the signing of the treaty. And while the growth of strong opposition parties may not have been the only factor to account for the re-activation of Mexican federalism, it seems logical and reasonable to conclude that it was an important factor. And although Mexican federalism remains somewhat out-of-balance, the impulse toward centralism appears to be waning.

In sum, then, the minimal impact of NAFTA on Mexican federalism occurred indirectly, that is, through the contribution it made to the rejuvenation of the competitive party system.

CANADA

Scholarly assessments of the impact of NAFTA on Canadian federalism are mixed. On the one hand, there are those who suggest it has had a centralizing impact. They point out that the NAFTA implementation legislation asserts "the right of Parliament to enact legislation to implement any provision of the Agreement" (Clarkson 2002: 80). They also note that NAFTA's requirement that the federal government take "all necessary measures" to ensure subnational compliance with NAFTA's obligations gives Ottawa an enforcement role.

Ian Robinson, while acknowledging that Ottawa "lost more regulatory and redistributive capacity than provincial governments did," nevertheless insists that "we have seen a centralization of the power to determine the basic parameters within which economic policy is made ..." (2003: 224). In Robinson's view, the centralization results from the federal government's capacity to impose obligations on the provinces through trade and other international agreements. However, that capacity is limited, as evidenced by the fact that the North American Agreement on Labour Cooperation (NAALC), a NAFTA side agreement that deals with an issue falling largely under provincial jurisdiction, has been implemented in only a handful of Canadian jurisdictions, with Ontario, the country's most populous province and its economic powerhouse, being one of those choosing not to implement it.

In addition, as Grace Skogstad argues in her analysis of international trade policy-making, the provinces had considerable input into the shaping of NAFTA.

> Both NAFTA and the WTO agreement intruded into provincial jurisdiction to a far greater extent than the FTA. Accordingly, Ottawa obtained provinces' agreement for provisions that affected their jurisdiction. It also excluded from the terms of the agreement matters on which provincial consensus and consent were not forthcoming. (Skogstad 2002: 164)

Thus, Ottawa was able to conclude and implement NAFTA not only because it has the constitutional power to do so but also because it secured provincial agreement on those NAFTA sections that deal with issues falling under provincial jurisdiction.

So closely do Ottawa and the provinces collaborate on international trade matters that, in Skogstad's estimation, "the current pattern of intergovernmental relations in international trade constitutes a partnership of *de facto* concurrent jurisdiction"

(Skogstad 2002: 164). In other words, Ottawa has not used international trade agreements to invade provincial jurisdiction.

Richard Simeon contends that globalization and regionalization have had "surprisingly little" impact on Canadian federalism. The changes that have occurred—some devolution of responsibilities to the provinces and an emphasis on intergovernmental agreement rather than unilateral federal action—have come about as a result of domestic factors: "Global pressures lurk well in the background" (Simeon 2003: 162).

Perhaps the main conclusion to be drawn from the above is that international trade agreements have the *potential* to be a centralizing force. Perhaps, too, the possibility of unilateral federal action has given Ottawa some leverage over the provinces and convinced them to coalesce behind federal leadership. In any event, the federal government in Canada has chosen not to proceed unilaterally on international trade issues but, rather, to practice collaborative federalism by bringing the provinces into the policy process.

THE US

In 1994, Mark Tushnet pessimistically wrote: "NAFTA confirms the nearly complete dissolution of federalism as a significant feature of US constitutionalism" (Tushnet 1994: 60). He made this prediction because the US Supreme Court has consistently supported assertions of federal power, and because multinational corporations have become more important political actors than state governors. As a result, just as the nationalizing of the US economy led to the centralization of governing authority, so too will the globalizing of the US economy (Tushnet 1994: 62).

Has Tushnet's prediction come to pass? Not quite. While conceding that there has been considerable centralization of the federal system during the late twentieth century, John Kincaid concludes from an analysis of the impact of globalization on US federalism that, in fact, "... globalization has not yet altered the federal system or eroded state powers within the federal system in significant ways" (Kincaid 2003: 78). He identifies a number of hypotheses to explain why globalization and regionalization have not greatly affected American federalism. One is that the huge US economy "can absorb global economic shocks more easily than most nations and shield the federal system from excessive global turbulence" (Kincaid 2003: 38). Most US states have larger economies and larger government budgets than the majority of the world's nation-states (Kincaid 2003: 59). Thus, globalization, as manifested by the WTO or NAFTA, is not felt as profoundly in the US as it is in other countries.

Moreover, Kincaid makes the important point that American values are "consistent with the values commonly associated with globalization" (Kincaid 2003: 41). Largely fostered by the US, globalization does not stand in fundamental contradiction, culturally or intellectually, to the US federal arrangement. Indeed, the vast majority of state governors urged Congress to ratify both NAFTA and the WTO agreement, and many states have themselves become global players, seeking out foreign investment and promoting exports.

Another hypothesis advanced by Kincaid is that, throughout the twentieth century, the US "had substantially prepared its federal system for today's globalization...." For example:

The Great Depression induced a significant centralization of economic regulation in Washington, DC, which produced new federal laws and institutions equipped to cope with later globalization, while, nevertheless, preserving substantial economic and political autonomy for the constituent states ... (Kincaid 2003: 39, 40)

Thus, substantial alterations to the system were not necessary.

One concern that has emerged among the states is the expansion of the federal pre-emption power, which allows federal law to displace state law. Congress recently empowered the president to pre-empt state laws where they conflict with WTO rules. According to Kincaid, it is not yet clear how far the president "will be able to carry this unprecedented pre-emption power" (Kincaid 2003: 75).

Though globalization has not seriously affected American federalism, new institutions have been developed within the federal government to ensure state and local input into federal international trade policy-making. The US State Department, the Commerce Department, and the Office of the US Trade Representative all have mechanisms to receive the input of state and local governments.

Conclusion

What the foregoing tells us is that federalism emerged in the three countries under very different circumstances but for essentially the same reason—that is, to enable the constituent units to reap the benefits of unity while accommodating their diverse aspirations. It is also clear that the evolution of constitutional law has proceeded along very divergent paths. In the US, it produced a highly centralized federalism; in Canada, the opposite. In Mexico, the political subordination of the judicial branch meant that the courts were unable to serve as a check on the magnification of federal power.

Tracing the three countries' experience of federalism leads us to draw some conclusions about federalism in those countries. In the US, the consensus supports a powerful central government. In Mexico, the consensus supports increased decentralization, although the obstacles preventing rapid movement in this direction are formidable. In Canada, the people tend to accept the need for government intervention in society and the economy but they have yet to decide how much of that intervention should be by the federal government and how much should come from their provincial government. For all three countries, globalization in the form of NAFTA has not had the transformative effect on their federal systems that many predicted.

References

Anton, Thomas J. 1989. *American Federalism and Public Policy: How the System Works*. Philadelphia, PA: Temple UP.

Bowman, Ann O'M., and Michael A. Pagano. 1994. "The State of American Federalism, 1993–1994." *Publius: The Journal of Federalism* 24 (Summer): 1–21.

Cameron, David. 1999. *The Referendum Papers: Essays on Secession and National Unity*. Toronto: U of Toronto P.

Clarkson, Stephen. 2002. *Uncle Sam and Us: Globalization, Neoconservatism, and the Canadian State*. Toronto: U of Toronto P; Washington, DC: Woodrow Wilson Center Press.

Conlan, Timothy. 1988. *New Federalism: Intergovernmental Reform from Nixon to Reagan*. Washington, DC: The Brookings Institution.

Deloria, Vine, and David E. Wilkins. 1999. *Tribes, Treaties, and Constitutional Tribulations*. Austin, TX: U of Texas P.

Díaz-Cayeros, Alberto. 2004a. "Decentralization, Democratization, and Federalism." In Kevin J. Middlebrook, (ed.), *Dilemmas of Political Change in Mexico*. London, Institute of Latin American Studies. 198–234.

———. 2004b. "Do Federal Institutions Matter? Rules and Political Practices in Regional Resource Allocation in Mexico." In Edward L. Gibson (ed.), *Federalism and Democracy in Latin America*. Baltimore, MD: Johns Hopkins UP. 297–322.

Dion, Stéphane. 1999. *Straight Talk: Speeches and Writings on Canadian Unity*. Montreal and Kingston: McGill-Queen's UP.

Gagnon, Alain-G., and Hugh Segal. 2000. *The Canadian Social Union without Quebec*. Montreal: Institute for Research on Public Policy.

Gutiérrez González, Juan Marcos. 2005. "United Mexican States." In John Kincaid and G. Alan Tarr (eds.), *Constitutional Origins, Structure, and Change in Federal Countries*. Montreal and Kingston: McGill-Queen's UP. 208–38.

Holland, Kenneth M. 1993. "Federalism in a North American Context: The Contribution of the Supreme Courts of Canada, the United States and Mexico." In Marian C. McKenna (ed.), *The Canadian and American Constitutions in Comparative Perspective*. Calgary: U of Calgary P. 87–106.

Huerta, Carla, and Alonso Lujambio. 1994. "NAFTA: Recent Constitutional Amendments, Sovereignty Today, and the Future of Federalism in Mexico." *Constitutional Forum* 5,3/4 (Spring-Summer): 63–67.

Jhappan, Radha. 1995. "The Federal-Provincial Power-Grid and Aboriginal Self-Government." In F. Rocher and M. Smith (eds.), *New Trends in Canadian Federalism*. 1st ed. Peterborough, ON: Broadview Press: 155–84.

Kincaid, John. 1996. "From Dual to Coercive Federalism in American Intergovernmental Relations." In Jong S. Jun and Deil S. Wright (eds.), *Globalization and Decentralization: Institutional Contexts, Policy Issues, and Intergovernmental Relations in Japan and the United States*. Washington, DC: Georgetown UP. 29–47.

———. 2003. "Globalization and Federalism in the United States: Continuity in Adaptation." In H. Lazar, H. Telford, and R. Watts (eds.), *The Impact of Global and Regional Integration on Federal Systems: A Comparative Analysis*. Montreal and Kingston, McGill-Queen's UP. 37–85.

Knopf, Rainer, and Anthony Sayers. 2005. "Canada." In John Kincaid and G. Alan Tarr (eds.), *Constitutional Origins, Structure, and Change in Federal Countries*. Montreal and Kingston: McGill-Queen's UP. 103–42.

Lazar, H., H. Telford, and R. Watts. 2003. "Divergent Trajectories: The Impact of Global and Regional Integration on Federal Systems." In H. Lazar, H. Telford, and R. Watts (eds.), *The Impact of Global and Regional Integration on Federal Systems: A Comparative Analysis*. Montreal and Kingston: McGill-Queen's UP. 1–34.

Levy, Daniel, Kathleen Bruhn, and Emilio Zebadúa. 2001. *Mexico: The Struggle for Democratic Development*. Berkeley, CA: U of California P.

Mizrahi, Yemile. 2002. "Mexico." In Ann L. Griffiths (ed.), *Handbook of Federal Countries, 2002*. Montreal and Kingston: McGill-Queen's UP. 192–207.

Navarro, Luis Hernández, and Laura Carlsen. 2004. "Indigenous Rights : The Battle for Constitutional Reform in Mexico." In Keith J. Middlebrook (ed.), *Dilemmas of Political Change in Mexico*. London: Institute of Latin American Studies. 440–65.

Ochoa-Reza, Enrique. 2004. "Multiple Arenas of Struggle: Federalism and Mexico's Transition to Democracy." In Edward L. Gibson (ed.), *Federalism and Democracy in Latin America*. Baltimore, MD: Johns Hopkins UP. 255–96.

Orban, Edmond. 1992. *Le fédéralisme? Super État fédéral? Associations d'états souverains?* Montréal: Hurtubise HMH.

Ostrom, Vincent. 1991. *The Meaning of American Federalism*. San Francisco, CA: ICS Press.

Peterson, P.E. 1995. *The Price of Federalism*. Washington, DC: Brookings Institution.

Reesor, Bayard. 1992. *The Canadian Constitution in Historical Perspective*. Scarborough, ON: Prentice-Hall Canada.

Robinson, Ian. 2003. "Neo-Liberal Trade Policy and Canadian Federalism." In François Rocher and Miriam Smith (eds.), *New Trends in Canadian Federalism*. 2nd ed. Peterborough, ON: Broadview Press. 197–242.

Rocher, François. 2004. "Questioning Constitutional Democracy in Canada: From the Canadian Supreme Court Reference on Quebec Secession to the Clarity Act." In Alain-G. Gagnon, Montserat Guibernau, and François Rocher (eds.), *The Conditions of Diversity in Multinational Democracy*. Montreal: Institute for Research on Public Policy. 207–37.

Rodríguez, Victoria. 1997. *Decentralization in Mexico*. Boulder, CO: Westview Press.

——. 1998. "Recasting Federalism in Mexico." *Publius: The Journal of Federalism* 28,1 (Winter): 235–54.

Russell, Peter. 1993. *Constitutional Odyssey*. 2nd ed. Toronto: U of Toronto P.

Samuels II, Raymond. 2003. *Canadian Constitutional Development Since 1535: Part I*. Ottawa, ON: The Agora Cosmopolitan.

Schram, Sanford, and Carol S. Weissert. 1997. "The State of American Federalism, 1996–1997." *Publius: The Journal of Federalism* 27,2 (Spring): 1–31.

Simeon, Richard. 2003. "Important? Yes. Transformative? No. North American Integration and Canadian Federalism." In H. Lazar, H. Telford, and R. Watts (eds.), *The Impact of Global and Regional Integration on Federal Systems: A Comparative Analysis*. Montreal and Kingston: McGill-Queen's UP. 125–71.

Simeon, Richard, and Ian Robinson. 1990. *State, Society and the Development of Canadian Federalism*. Toronto: U of Toronto P.

Skogstad, Grace. 2002. "International Trade Policy and Canadian Federalism: A Constructive Tension?" In H. Bakvis and G. Skogstad (eds.), *Canadian Federalism: Performance, Effectiveness, and Legitimacy*. Don Mills, ON: Oxford UP. 159–77.

Smiley, Donald V. 1987. "The Two Themes of Canadian Federalism." In R.S. Blair and J.T. McLeod (eds.), *The Canadian Political Tradition: Basic Readings*. Toronto: Methuen. 62–78.

Tarr, G. Alan. 2005. "United States of America." In John Kincaid and G. Alan Tarr (eds.), *Constitutional Origins, Structure, and Change in Federal Countries*. Montreal and Kingston: McGill-Queen's UP. 381–408.

Théret, Bruno. 1999. "Regionalism and Federalism: A Comparative Analysis of the Regulation of Economic Tensions Between Regions by Canadian and American Federal Intergovernmental Transfer Programmes." *International Journal of Urban and Regional Research* 23,3 (September): 479–512.

Tushnet, Mark. 1994. "NAFTA and Federalism in the United States." *Constitutional Forum* 5,3/4 (Spring-Summer): 60–62.

Walker, David B. 1991. "American Federalism from Johnson to Bush." *Publius: The Journal of Federalism* 21 (Winter): 105–19.

Ward, Peter, and Victoria Rodríguez. 1999. *New Federalism and State Government in Mexico*. Austin, TX: Lyndon B. Johnson School of Public Affairs, University of Texas at Austin.

Watts, Ronald. 2002. "The Distribution of Powers, Responsibilities, and Resources in Federations." In Ann L. Griffiths (ed.), *Handbook of Federal Countries, 2002*. Montreal and Kingston: McGill-Queen's UP. 448–71.

Wilkins, David E., and K. Tsianina Lomawaima. 2001. *Uneven Ground: American Indian Sovereignty and Federal Law*. Norman, OK: U of Oklahoma P.

Williamson, Richard S. 1990. *Reagan's Federalism: His Efforts to Decentralize Government*. Lanham, MD: UP of America.

Young, Robert. 1998. *The Secession of Quebec and the Future of Canada*. Montreal and Kingston: McGill-Queen's UP.

PART THREE
Redefining Economic and Social Relations:
Public Policies and Human Rights After NAFTA

Since the end of World War II, human rights has emerged as a key principle at the international level. The discourse of human rights has served to establish a means by which political claims can occur both from within or from outside the limits of a single nation-state. In addition, political claims and processes can also be shaped by regional integration. From the founding of the European Coal and Steel Community to today's EU, there has been a growing Europeanization of policy-making, albeit unevenly across such distinct areas as agricultural policy and foreign and security policy. Similarly, since the signing of the NAFTA in 1993 (and its coming into force in 1994) there has been a regionalization of policy in North America, though it has been quite uneven across different policy sectors. Each chapter in this section examines a key area of policy in order to address: first, the extent to which substantive policy content has evolved since NAFTA; second, whether (and if so, how) the social and state actors involved in the policy-making process have changed; and third, the implications of such changes for both human rights and for understanding North America.

As noted above, all three North American states are vulnerable to claims that they have not secured their territorial integrity in ways consistent with international law, their own constitutions, or the principles of natural justice. Julián Castro-Rea and Isabel Altamirano-Jiménez take up such themes in Chapter 10, "North American First Peoples: Self-Determination or Economic Development?," focusing on the late twentieth-century resurgence of Indigenous peoples who mobilized around demands for land and compensation for past (and current) injustices. They explore the common problems and interests of Indigenous peoples in the three states in light of the different state policies that nonetheless shared the similar aims of eliminating, dispossessing, or assimilating them. They briefly summarize the specific trajectories of British, French, and Spanish colonization and the mobilization of military, institutional, and political power to deny Indigenous nations' self-determination and to exploit their territories and resources. They outline both the processes of reclamation of Indigenous rights via "pan-Indian" and nationalist movements and the appeal to international laws, institutions, and instruments to assert a prior and coexisting sovereignty and the right to self-determination for Indigenous peoples. They also analyze key moments in movement organization and government policy responses in each state, noting the influence of Reaganomics of the early 1980s, which stressed self-sufficiency based on economic development and the private sector. Although the discussion demonstrates the very significant differences in form between constitutional and legal enactments in the three NAFTA states since the 1970s, in the most recent laws dealing with Indigenous peoples in each state, whatever recognition of self-determination there may be does not include territorial rights. Indeed, self-government is understood as a devolution of management of government-designed programs on municipal-style local government models. Indigenous peoples, Castro-Réa and Altamirano-Jiménez argue, are presented with a zero-sum choice between self-government or economic development, with the risk of attaining neither.

The rights of Indigenous peoples may be understood as human rights claimable by virtue of one's membership in a community, a theme explored in Chapter 11, "Default Convergence? Human Rights and Fundamental Freedoms in North America." Here David Schneiderman illuminates broad human rights issues by focusing on a specific case of corporate/property rights versus community rights. Schneiderman addresses the underlying assumption of the universality of human rights, an assumption belied by diverse expressions in different national contexts. He describes the three national regimes for the protection of human rights and freedoms in light of their mixed human rights records. Although these regimes differ, however, he argues that there seems to be a "default convergency" in the area of property rights as a result of NAFTA, specifically along US lines. NAFTA has created a constitution-like system of property rights protections, illustrated by way of the Metalclad case in which a US company claimed damages against a Mexican local government's refusal to permit a hazardous waste facility to be built in the city of Guadalcazar. The new model rules of NAFTA's Chapter 11 amount to a bill of rights for investors, Schneiderman argues, as Metalclad's success meant overruling local governments' constitutional right to protect public health and the environment. Property rights, in other words, have trumped human rights. Other agreements similarly show how regional transnational standards are encroaching upon national rights regimes, though the author hastens to point out that these are not inevitable and are indeed resistible.

The triumph of property rights over democratic politics is also a central theme in Chapter 12, "Under Pressure: The Impasses of North American Labour Movements," in which Gregory Albo and Dan Crow point out the critical role trade unions have historically played in advancing democracy and social justice in capitalist societies by mobilizing the collective power of wage-labourers to offset the structural advantages of the owners of capital and by advocating universal participation in politics, extension of civil rights, and universalization of social programs. However, the promotion of free markets and property rights under neo-liberalism, and especially since NAFTA, has raised new challenges for social justice and democracy in North America. The new production regime, the shifting international division of labour, leaner and meaner labour laws, and retrenched social policies have each strained unions' ability to protect the interests of workers and to forge international solidarity.

Albo and Crow outline some of the common pressures confronting the North American labour movements and their responses to those pressures. Their key purpose is to consider the prospects and potential strategies available to such movements to break the organizational impasse in which they currently find themselves. They discuss the different approaches the national labour movements of the three NAFTA countries have taken to fighting neo-liberalism and labour market pressures on workers and unions: the compromising "partnerships" and concession bargaining with employers forced upon Canadian unions; the "business unionism" of US unions that has limited their capacity to resist neo-liberalism and compounded the aggressive and state-sanctioned tactics employers have used to prevent unionization; and the corporatist arrangements with the state and business in Mexico that have resulted in unions that have often coerced rather than represented their members. The labour movements in each state, still bound by national industrial relations regimes and obliged to negotiate locally, had differentiated responses to continental free trade in accordance with their perceived interests. Their internal fragmentation renders international solidarity an elusive goal. Albo and Crow conclude that what is needed is more rank-and-file participation in democratically structured national and local unions if new political projects are to be sustained.

The prospects for deepening democratic participation seem rather glum, however, given trends in social policy. In Chapter 13, "Ragged Cruelty?: Social Policy Transformations in North America," Lois Harder and Marcus Taylor track reforms in each of the three North American states that "deepened the existing trend of pushing citizens towards an increased reliance on the market, rather than the state, as a source of social provision." Globalization and neo-liberal ideology have produced changes in economic structures, the nature of work, and the nuclear family, changes exacerbated in the post-NAFTA period. Decentralization and privatization have been the key strategies in Canada and the US (where income support policies are especially imbued with race politics), while Mexico has retreated from its earlier constitutional commitment to providing collective security for all individuals to programs targeting the rural poor. However, after analyzing income support programs in the three states, the authors conclude that neo-liberal promises of a generalized improvement in the standard of living have not materialized. Instead, incomes have become increasingly polarized, poverty rates have increased (as have the number of "working poor"), and "decentralization of responsibility for social programs and the use of targeting in delivering benefits have contributed to highly fragmented citizenship regimes in all three countries."

In Chapter 14, "Ten Years After: Continental Free Trade and Environmental Policy in North America," Luc Juillet assesses the effects of NAFTA on environmental policies and governance, particularly in light of environmentalists' pre-NAFTA concerns about the potential for downward harmonization of standards, relocation of polluting industries to the country with the least onerous environmental laws (namely, Mexico), and constraints on governments in the setting of their own environmental standards. After noting the significant influence the US environmental movement was able to exert on the NAFTA provisions and the side-agreement, followed by the virtual derailment of the movement by the US government's "parallel track" proposal, Juillet examines a decade of environmental policy under NAFTA. His analysis of institutions such as the Commission for Environmental Cooperation (CEC) reveals a lack of coordination between environmental and trade policies, leading him to conclude that fears of a "regulatory chill" are somewhat substantiated by NAFTA's investment protection provisions as corporations have successfully used an expanded definition of "regulatory takings" and claims of discrimination to wrest compensation from governments, especially in Canada and Mexico. However, Juillet argues that quite apart from downward harmonization, industry relocation, and regulatory chill, more insidious environmental threats from trade liberalization may come from less high-profile factors such as the shift in production of crops and concentration in large-scale, export-oriented farms; increasing pressure on groundwater; and more contamination from agro-chemicals, population displacement, deforestation, and loss of biodiversity. Although the environmental side-deal and the CEC have contributed modestly to increased environmental cooperation between the three states, Juillet argues, in the end, "they do not seem to have provided an effective safeguard against the environmental challenges that have emerged under continental free trade."

CHAPTER TEN

North American First Peoples
Self-Determination or Economic Development?

Julián Castro-Rea and Isabel Altamirano-Jiménez

Among the most significant political issues of the late twentieth century world-wide was the resurgence of Indigenous peoples as political actors, asserting their right to self-determination. In North America, the most immediate manifestation of this resurgence was Indigenous mobilization around demands for land and compensation for past injustices. Perhaps less obvious but more crucial, issues related to the politics of recognition of Indigenous rights were also raised within the context of a critique of the nature of colonial and post-colonial national states.

In Mexico, Canada, and the US, Indigenous peoples have been historically displaced from the political decision-making process and the benefits of economic development. By benefiting from economic development we mean full participation in the creation and expansion of a domestic market and the improvement of their living conditions. More recently, governments in the three countries have practised assimilation policies intended to incorporate these peoples into the mainstream economy by appealing to a discourse that stresses development opportunities for Indigenous peoples while undermining their aspirations to self-government. As part of this process, the governments of these countries have endeavoured to facilitate the exploitation of Indigenous territories and natural resources, even if Indigenous communities object and do not benefit from this model of development.

Since the 1960s, the first peoples of North America have renewed their struggle to defend their identities, territories, and resources, and their right to self-determination. The goal of this chapter is to explore the common problems and interests among these peoples in the three countries, with a focus on contemporary issues. We will show that commonalities among Canada, Mexico, and the US are by no means limited to issues of trade and investment. Based on a comparative approach, we will identify the similarities and differences of contexts in which Indigenous claims emerge and the government policies that have been designed to deal with them. Our central argument is that the deepening of the globalization process, the creation of frameworks for economic integration, and the expansion of the global market have had an impact on the ways in which governments are dealing with Indigenous demands. Government policies, in this context, are aimed at making self-determination equivalent to economic development, an approach that could be considered a new expression of policies aimed at assimilation. As far as such policies are concerned, it does not matter whether Indigenous peoples maintain their cultural difference as long as they partake in the mainstream economy.

In the following sections we will first provide a brief characterization of colonial relations between European settlers and Indigenous peoples in order to outline the historical and legal differences among the three countries. Secondly, we will explore the resurgence of Indigenous peoples as political actors since the late 1960s. Thirdly, we will discuss government policies formulated to deal with their demands, by focusing on the most recent comprehensive policies aimed at Indigenous peoples in North America: the Indian Self-Determination and Education Assistance Act (1975) in the United States, the First Nations Governance Act (2003) in Canada, and the Indigenous Law (2001) in Mexico. Finally, we will compare these policies to show that, beyond differences in form, they are similar in purpose.

Indigenous Peoples, Tribal Peoples, and First Nations

The notion of North America as a specific, interconnected region was not born with NAFTA. Even before Europeans landed in the continent, many Indigenous peoples shared the notion of Turtle Island, a vast territory roughly encompassing contemporary US, Canada, and Mexico. Rather than east-west, the continent had a particular south-north logic of economic and cultural exchanges among different Indigenous civilizations. With the colonization of the territories by several European powers, the interconnectedness of the North American region was gradually hidden, and a new east-west logic was imposed internally in each newly created colonial state.

From this historical context, relationships between the colonizers and Indigenous peoples have evolved in different directions and have created different concepts for the naming of North America's original inhabitants. The terms "Aboriginal peoples," "Indigenous peoples," "Native Americans," and "First Nations" are variously employed to designate the descendants of pre-European peoples as a whole, and each term has a specific legal connotation. Yet, all the peoples identified with these generic names are in fact nations contained within sovereign states, and as such they have over time claimed their right to self-determination. According to Monserrat Guibernau (1999), being stateless nations, Indigenous peoples share a number of common attributes: they are conscious that they comprise a distinctive social entity that has named itself; they share a culture that includes a common ancestry and a common myth of origin; they are attached to a specific homeland; their shared remembrance of some historical events often involves memories of a time when the community enjoyed its own independent institutions; and they have the will and the right to decide upon their common political future. Within each section below, we will use the legal category most common with that country.

In order to understand the contemporary struggle of Indigenous peoples of North America for self-determination, it is important to identify historical and legal differences among the three countries within the continent.

THE US

The history of Native Americans or Tribal peoples in the US has been extensively addressed in the literature.[1] It is not our purpose to redo that account but to provide some background information in order to understand the main changes experienced by Native Americans in their relationship to the US federal government. Treaty relations before the War of Independence in 1776 featured relations between autonomous entities, whose status was later governed by a paradigm of domestication. This refers to a process whereby governments manipulate and use institutionally or politically biased mechanisms or arguments to either reframe, limit, or extinguish the conditions under which pre-national state treaties and treaty rights can be recognized (Schulte-Tenckhoff 1998).

Before Europeans crossed the Atlantic Ocean in the late fifteenth century, more than 300 nations lived in the western hemisphere. They were self-sufficient and autonomous political entities with developed functions of government, including leadership, decision-making, implementation of law, and binding rules for group members. They were fully organized peoples, each with their own distinct culture, language, traditions, and territory. Once Europeans decided to colonize the territories, however, Indigenous peoples were no longer the only players controlling the continent (Dupuis 2002: 41).

The British Empire's interests in North America were framed in a context of ferocious competition with France and Spain, the latter being the first European power that had firmly established colonies in the New World. It has been common to emphasize treaty relations as a distinctive element of British imperial policy. Nevertheless, other European colonial powers also pursued treaties with Tribal peoples in their competition with rival European empires. France, for instance, also made extensive use of treaty-making whenever its colonial interests were at stake, though such treaties generally acknowledge military alliances rather than cede lands and governing authority to the French (Delâge 1991). Whereas Spain did not enter into treaties in Mexico, it did so with some Native groups such as the Choctaws of Nueva Vizcaya in what is now the southwestern US and also with the Mapuches in what is now Chile (Parry 1969). The British established treaties with Native peoples mainly to ensure their alliance in territorial competition with other colonial powers. Additionally, the British sought to acquire lands from these peoples and guarantee commerce with them.

The treaties between the British and Native tribes resembled negotiations between sovereign governments. Indeed, even after the settler revolt that resulted in independence from Britain in 1776, British policy was more or less continued. Between 1778 and 1781, 370 treaties with Native groups were ratified by the US Senate, basically because the US federal government feared wars with them would jeopardize its claim of sovereignty over a territory under British and Spanish influence. However, once the territory was secure, the tribes that inhabited it lost the ability to make alliances and became vulnerable to non-Native pressure for land.

The new state's federal government assumed Tribal affairs as its responsibility. While Congress was given the power to regulate commerce with Native peoples, the president, with the consent of the Senate, was authorized to make treaties with them. Under the guise of protecting Tribal peoples from settlers, the federal government implemented a policy of isolating Native nations from each other as well from non-Natives. However, growing settlers' pressure altered the previous dynamic of nation-to-nation treaty relations, which was replaced by forced relocations, war, and a relationship framed under the biases of the paradigm of domestication.

After 40 years of "Indian wars" (as recorded by the federal government) and forced removals of virtually all tribes from the eastern half of the continent under the Indian Removal Act of 1830, most nations were forced into taking treaty after being overwhelmed militarily and by the influx of settlers. In negotiating treaties, the federal government implemented the institutional bias by using its political power and its institutional capacity to abrogate unilaterally some aspects of treaty rights, while extending state sovereignty over Native lands. Under the institutional bias, treaties were used to force Tribal peoples to cede large extensions of land for European settlement in exchange for recognized Indian sovereignty over a limited territory or reservation, where the US government would guarantee protection from settlers' intrusion. As Schulte-Tenckhoff (1998: 253) argues, the fundamental ambiguity of US policy towards Tribal peoples resides in the fact that being treated as "domestic dependent nations" they are at the same time sovereign and wards of the US government, that is, they are under a "trust relationship." "Trust relationship" is a legal term rather than a specific relationship between two parties formally characterized by respect and good faith. The term came from a court decision (*Cherokee nation v. Georgia*) in which Chief Justice Marshall found in 1831 that "Indians" have a "quasi-sovereignty" status to freely engage in treaties yet are incapable of taking care of themselves.

By 1871 the US government had abandoned treaty-making as a policy altogether. It then made use of the political bias—that is, the articulation of political arguments—to deny the validity of earlier treaties and to break treaty promises by claiming either that Tribal rights never existed or that, if they had, they had been extinguished (Schulte-Tenckhoff 1998). The end of the treaty-making process exacerbated land conflict between Native peoples and new settlers. Until the 1920s, Tribal nations and immigrants competed for land through violent means, including war, massacres, and legal tools such as the 1887 General Allotment Act.

Under the General Allotment Act, the president acquired the capacity to allot Tribal lands in a designated acreage to individuals and to hold such land in trust for them for 25 years, until Native people showed they were capable of dealing with their own affairs. If they were able to do so to the satisfaction of non-Native authorities, this land became fee simple; that is, it became subject to a form of unfettered individual ownership whereby the land is viewed as property that is freely alienable or hereditary. Under this legislation, those who received allotments became US citizens, subject to criminal and civil law. In other words, this act promoted the extinction of residual Native sovereignty and weakened communal ownership and organization. Deloria (1984: 115) has argued that when a Tribal territory was dissected and transformed into "private property" and jurisdiction over it was transferred to the states, Tribal government lost its authority over its subjects.

Moreover, although the idea of domestic dependent nations hinges on the idea of residual sovereignty, the Department of the Interior worked to move non-Natives onto Native lands. Since the General Allotment Act, it has successfully transferred large proportions of reserved Tribal lands for the exclusive use of non-Natives. Around 0.3 per cent of the US non-Native population own land or live on Tribal reservations (Centre for World Indigenous Studies 1988: 3). The rationale behind this strategy was to undermine Native American communities and governments by creating conflicting interests and jurisdictions or by disempowering them with the creation of new boundaries.

The concept of disempowering by boundaries refers to a strategy intended to fragment Native communities. The strategy separates Tribal self-government from territory, thus transforming the identity of Native peoples or nations into just any other minority without territorial attachment.[2] Further, the presence of non-Natives within Native territory actually reduces the size of reservations and opens the "annexed land" to state government control. State governments have increasingly responded to these concerns by arguing that where non-Natives reside inside reservations, the authority of state governments can apply and will be extended (Centre for World Indigenous Studies 1988: 4). This has created an overlap of government jurisdictions, where state laws are added to the more than 5,000 federal laws presently regulating every aspect of life and affairs within reservations (Churchill 1999: 341).

Despite all efforts made during the nineteenth and early twentieth century to erase Tribal identities, they have continued to survive. After the release of the Meriam Report in 1928 criticizing the activity of the Bureau of Indian Affairs, the Roosevelt government appointed John Collier as Commissioner of that bureau. Collier not only believed in traditional societies, he even romanticized them; he promoted the Indian Reorganization Act 1934, with the supposed aim of encouraging Tribal self-government (Franks 2000: 230). However, this legislation did very little to strengthen Tribal governance. On the contrary, it focused on Tribal economic development within the mainstream economic model. In fact, its purpose was to bring Native Americans closer to the mainstream lifestyle.

Despite this attempt, poverty among Native Americans has since remained the highest among population categories in the US. Although figures vary among reservations, poverty indicators demonstrate that reservation-based Native Americans lag behind the general population. Overall, 50.7 per cent of Native Americans residing on reservations and trust lands were below poverty level at the beginning of the 1990s. Rates for reservation dwellers ranged from 49.4 per cent to 66.6 per cent. One-fifth of Native houses on reservations and trust lands lacked plumbing facilities (US Bureau of the Census 2000).

In the early 1950s, US Tribal policy shifted again, with the re-application of the political bias of the paradigm of domestication. The solution was known as the Termination Policy and was aimed at ending the trust relationship existing between the federal government and tribes by transferring all responsibilities to state governments and by extinguishing individual "Indian" and Tribal status without the consent of the affected. As a result of this policy, around 109 tribes were terminated and lost their land base and all authority over Tribal affairs (Wilkinson and Biggs 1977).

Importantly, US shifts in policy influenced Mexico's *indigenismo* or Indigenous policy and to a lesser extent Aboriginal policy in Canada (Kehoe 1981: 535). The main difference is that whereas neither the US nor Mexico abandoned their position that Native peoples are subordinated to the national state and to its government policies, Canada to some extent did.

THE CANADIAN EXPERIENCE

Like the First Nations elsewhere on the continent, the original inhabitants of the territories now known as Canada constituted fully sovereign nations. French and British policies towards Aboriginal peoples practiced in North America were greatly influenced by the colonial competition between the two imperial powers along with Spain.[3]

Aboriginal peoples had strong bargaining power at least until the eighteenth century. Relations between them and Europeans were initially complex and diverse, though basically consensual and mutually advantageous. However, policy towards Aboriginal peoples featured several contradictory elements. Perhaps the document that best represents these contradictions is the Royal Proclamation of 1763. Under this document, which became law just after France was defeated and New France was ceded to the British Crown, Aboriginal peoples were recognized as autonomous political entities capable of signing treaties with the Crown, but at the same time, they were subordinated to it (Frideres and Gadacz 2001: 15–16). Aboriginal lands could not be taken without the consent of the nations involved, but they could be ceded to the Crown through treaties, a constitutional requirement that survives to this day.

Before the Royal Proclamation, the British had signed several treaties for peace and military cooperation with First Nations populations, aimed at neutralizing both French and Spanish contenders in trade and settlement privileges. However, after the Royal Proclamation, relations between Aboriginal peoples and white settlers were redefined by domination. Land and trade became a priority over peace and military cooperation. The Royal Proclamation became the tool to sign treaties to acquire increasingly more First Nations lands (Armitage 1998). By the time of Confederation in 1867, most of the "Indian" policy was already defined by domination. This trend was confirmed with the Confederation settlement, in which the federal government assumed control over "Indians and lands reserved for the Indians" under section 91(24) of the British North American Act (today referred to as Constitution Act, 1867). As in the US, in Canada the institutional bias, inherent in the paradigm of domestication, was also used by the government to abrogate or reframe unilaterally some aspects of treaty rights and to extend state sovereignty over Aboriginal lands.

One of the earliest creations of the new Canadian government was the Department of Management of the Indians and Ordinance Lands, predecessor of the Department of Indian Affairs and Northern Development. In the 1870s, the reserve system was created and the Indian Act was passed in 1876 to "manage" Indian affairs by increasing the federal government's control over reserves and land sales. The Canadian government was thus making use of the institutional bias to frame Aboriginal treaty rights within Confederation; that is, it used its political power and its institutional capacity to abrogate unilaterally some aspects of treaty rights, while extending state sovereignty over Aboriginal land.

In the late 1800s, the imperial colonizing enterprise entered a new stage in Aboriginal policy, one in which various Christian churches would be a key actor: implementing residential schooling. Residential schools were institutions where

Aboriginal children from different nations were gathered and taught the English or French languages, religion, basic schooling, and crafts. Parents were coerced to send their children from an early age, so they lost influence over their development. Residential schools were institutions of cultural genocide that disappeared only in the 1960s. The role of churches in implementing assimilation policies on behalf of the Canadian state has left a negative legacy with which Aboriginal communities are still struggling. In addition, modifications made to the Indian Act at the end of the 1800s created a new legal definition of "Indian" to control even further their lands and properties, which were vested in the hands of government commissioners. Ironically, Aboriginal peoples did not acquire full political rights until the 1960s (Hueglin 2000: 190).

Although assimilation policies were implemented through residential schools and enfranchisement, unlike the US and Mexico in Canada the political bias of the domestication paradigm—outright extinction of Aboriginal and treaty rights—was never implemented. Treaties are not only still valid but have been constitutionally enshrined in the 1982 Constitution Act, Section 35(1), which recognizes and affirms "the existing Aboriginal treaty rights of the Aboriginal peoples of Canada." As such, they constitute a key issue in defining present and future relations with Aboriginal peoples, as we will see later in this chapter. Also in the 1982 Constitution Act the term "Aboriginal" was recognized as a term that collectively describes First Nations, Inuit, and Métis, the three different legal categories of the first peoples of Canada. The First Nations are culturally diverse peoples living all over the country; some of them signed treaties and some never did. Inuit are the people living in the Circumpolar North, and the Métis are the descendants of the mixing of white settlers and First Nations people.

These three categories have different political goals and expectations, and most of them were subjected to assimilation policies. Although assimilation policies were crucial in Canada, economic integration policies such as the ones implemented in the US did not have a strong impact. This is due partly to Canada's huge land mass and its frontier condition and partly to the strong involvement of the churches in Aboriginal programs, which prolonged colonial nineteenth century policies and attitudes for a longer period of time (Kehoe 1981: 536).

Paradoxically, this contrasting situation ended up in a similar outcome: the impoverishment of Aboriginal peoples. Even today these people continue to rank first Canada-wide in terms of unemployment, lack of education and poor health indicators. An unemployment rate of 60 to 80 per cent among Inuit people is common. Life expectancy is consistently lower among Aboriginal peoples than the non-Aboriginal Canadian population. About three-quarters of Aboriginal housing is inadequate and fails to meet basic Canadian standards of safety and decent living (Statistics Canada 1995; Royal Commission on Aboriginal Peoples 1996). Therefore, even though reached through different paths, the situation of Aboriginal peoples in both the US and Canada is painfully similar in terms of dire living conditions.

THE MEXICAN EXPERIENCE

When the Spaniards arrived in the territory now known as Mexico, they found a variety of Indigenous peoples. Some were independent kingdoms, others were subjugated peoples, and some were highly organized empires such as the Aztecs. Spanish colonization meant for Indigenous peoples a process of conquest, colonization, illness, and enslavement that dramatically shrank their numbers from 25 million to under 2 million (Borah and Cook 1963). Unlike the British and French, when Spain extended its sovereignty over what is now Mexico at the beginning of the sixteenth century, it did not need Indigenous peoples as allies in fighting other empires. Therefore, for most of the sixteenth century Spain was relatively free to secure its dominion overseas and to exploit Indigenous labour force.[4]

After having conquered and pacified most of the central territories, the Spanish Crown passed a specific legislation named *Leyes de Indias*, which led to the creation of the so-called *República de Indios* in 1532. The *República de Indios* was a distinct public regime applicable to Indigenous peoples and separated from the colonizers' *República de Españoles*. The purpose of this legislation was to institutionalize the method of indirect rule by creating self-governing peasant communities of Indigenous peoples that were widely dispersed, in order to generate taxes and tributes for the Spanish Crown (Barthas 1997: 5). As a result of such legislation, Indigenous communities were left alone as centres of social, cultural, and economic reproduction (Florescano 1998: 186). Indigenous communities' land titles included water, forestry, and several kinds of land for communal and individual use. Perhaps the most important aspect of the *Leyes de Indias* was the creation of a separate tribunal, the *Juzgado General de Indios*, whose stated goal was to insulate Indigenous peoples and Indigenous title from Spanish settlers' interference so the Spanish Crown could directly deal with and control Indigenous issues (Borah 1985: 90).

As John Tutino (1990: 41) has pointed out, this special legislation produced unexpected consequences. Indigenous peoples obtained local political independence and different types of land for their collective use and social reproduction. These lands were protected by colonial legislation from non-Indigenous disturbance and invasion. This way, without treaties and in response to pragmatic situations, Indigenous communities were recognized as collective entities during the Colonial period. The governments of those communities were elected through traditional mechanisms and had a variety of functions such as taxation, regulation of lands, organization of communal and religious celebrations, and representation outside their communities. While these communities enjoyed a broad autonomy to reproduce themselves socially, culturally, politically, and economically, they were subjected to colonial legislation and had to pay tributes to the Spanish Crown.

Consistent with a doctrine that holds that Indigenous rights only exist to the extent that the state declares them to exist, with the Mexican Independence in 1810 the "Indian" status was abolished because under the new liberal rationale it belonged to the colonial and conservative past. The newly independent country was a regionally and culturally diverse state, which was in conflict with the liberal nation-building project that required a single common national identity. The chosen national identity synthesized the cultural mix between Spaniards and Indigenous peoples into a common *mestizo* identity.

The extinction of "Indian" status also affected Indigenous peoples' land title. The aim was to promote individual property as a way to make them ordinary citizens without communal property and the special status they enjoyed under the old regime.

However, what this legislation really provoked was the seizure of lands belonging to Indigenous communities and the creation of *latifundios* or large individual land holdings. As a result, the nineteenth century witnessed important Indigenous revolts for the defence of their lands and natural resources such as water sources, forests, and rivers (Reyna 1990). In order to defend their land title and political autonomy, Indigenous peoples resorted to different strategies such as alliances with local strongmen and the Conservative Party, mobilized opposition or even engaged in open confrontation aimed at dividing the political elite on Indigenous issues (Tutino 2000: 131).

Indigenous uprisings against policies that stripped them of their land continued until they merged with the Mexican Revolution in 1910. As a consequence, Indigenous demands were incorporated into the Mexican Constitution of 1917, which under Article 27 recognized communal land and *ejidos*. The latter were land grants from the state to communities. Although *ejido* plots may be farmed and inherited by individuals, they were not owned by the grantees, and they could neither be sold, bought, nor left idle.

The consolidation of the post-revolutionary state, from 1917 to 1934, relied on a populist regime that worked through what has been called "corporatist citizenship," a model of authoritarian political integration based on popular mobilization loyal to the political regime (Harvey 2001). Interestingly, the emergence of *indigenismo* or Indigenous assimilation policies, under the government of Lázaro Cárdenas (1934–40), coincided with the policy prompted by the Reorganization Act in the US. *Indigenismo* in Mexico was a revision of institutional structures aimed at expanding citizenship through economic reforms within Indigenous communities. In these years, a great deal of effort was put into integrating Indigenous peoples into a modern, *mestizo*, Spanish-speaking society. Despite these efforts, however, Indigenous peoples remained at the bottom in terms of socio-economic conditions with gross discrepancies in income, health care, and education between them and mainstream society. For instance, 95.4 per cent of the Indigenous communities are highly marginalized; the child mortality rate among Indigenous people is higher than among *mestizo* people; and 46.08 per cent of the Indigenous population live in extreme poverty. Overall 38 per cent of Indigenous housing units lack running water and 76.3 per cent lack sewage systems (Serrano Carreto *et al.* 2002: 47).

Reclaiming Indigenous Rights

As we have seen, government policies have been aimed at diminishing and extinguishing both Indigenous peoples' control over their territories and self-government. For generations, Indigenous peoples have struggled to oppose these policies and to preserve their integrity as differentiated peoples. The 1970s constitute a landmark in the emergence of North America's Indigenous peoples as political actors, who demanded the recognition of their collective identity as nations.

There is a number of elements that, when combined, created contexts favourable to the emergence of a pan-Indian movement in North America. By the 1960s, decolonization movements had created numerous new states around the world. The 1970s were years of major global changes; the scope and pace of international integration as well as linkages among nations began to increase. A renewed pressure for energy and petroleum, mining, and hydroelectric resources was sparking interest in Indigenous territories (Saladin d'Anglure and Morin 1992: 14). Liberal movements and struggles for the expansion of citizen rights, such as the Black Power movement in the US, favoured an explosion of rights consciousness (Cairns 1995: 148).

The United Nations and other international organizations also contributed to the emergence of a new discourse on Indigenous rights. For example, the Organization of American States (OAS) and the United Nations Education Science and Culture Organization (UNESCO) recommended that states promote the revival of Indigenous cultures. Also, a then recently published study on Indigenous peoples' situation from the International Labour Organization (ILO) made public the exclusion of Indigenous peoples and their status as internal colonies in most countries. The study and its impact prompted the adoption of ILO's Covenant 107 (later on ratified as Covenant 169) and Recommendation 104 for the protection and integration of Indigenous and Tribal populations—the first international legal instruments to protect the rights of people whose way of life was threatened by dominating cultures.

Although with differences of degree, in the three countries of North America we can observe the political evolution of a new generation of Aboriginal leaders committed to making use of both national and international strategies to repudiate and counteract government policies. As Taiaiake Alfred (2000) has posited, two of the most relevant strategies toward that end have been the assertion of a prior and coexisting sovereignty, particularly in Canada and the US, and the assertion of the right to self-determination for Indigenous peoples as stated in international legal tools such as Covenant 169, as happens in Mexico. As a consequence of Indigenous organizations' pressure for the recognition of their rights, both at the domestic and international levels, the federal governments have had to respond. However, there has been a wide gap between what is demanded and what governments are willing to concede.

Alfred (2000) has argued that in considering the question of Indigenous peoples' rights within state borders, national states have taken several positions: first, the classic strategy of denial of Indigenous rights; second, a theoretical acceptance of Indigenous rights along with the claim that they have been historically extinguished; and third, the legal doctrine that transforms Indigenous rights from their autonomous nature to contingent rights, existing under the frame of colonial law. All three strategies, we may add, are variations of what we have called earlier in this article a political bias against Indigenous peoples. The first strategy has been applied in both Mexico and the US and to a lesser extent in Canada. The second one has been used in Canada and the US. The third has been used in all three states.

In response, in the US, where there is a limited form of recognized Tribal sovereignty, resistance has focused on the material aspect of such rights and on repudiating assimilation. In Canada, Aboriginal peoples have mobilized for the constitutional recognition of Aboriginal and treaty rights and against assimilation policies. Finally, in Mexico Indian movements have mobilized for the constitutional recognition of Indigenous peoples and for political autonomy.

THE US GOVERNMENT AND THE NATIVE AMERICAN MOVEMENT

In the US, the Native American movement emerged in the context of the civil rights movement of the 1960s. At that time, Native Americans were facing the consequences of the Termination Policy of 1954, by means of which the trust relationship they had with the federal government was abolished. By the late 1960s, several representatives of different tribes came together to discuss the problems their people were facing such as police aggression, open discrimination, unemployment, and broken treaties. Out of these meetings came the American Indian Movement (AIM), committed to fight for immediate Tribal needs but also to pursue Tribal sovereignty and the control of Native education.

The most articulated claims in this struggle came from a young generation of educated urban Natives, who were proud of their heritage and unwilling to accept white paternalism as previous generations had. Instead, they advanced a discourse around the concept of internal colonialism to demand self-determination. From this perspective, Tribal reservations were seen as internal colonies that were exploited by the dominant group. As, during the 1960s, colonies from the "Third World" were pursuing decolonization, Tribal peoples, considering themselves part of the "Fourth World," were fighting for self-determination. The term "Fourth World" first entered the vocabulary in the 1960s. The growth of the urban Native American population contributed to the emergence of the Red Power movement and to a process of "retraditionalization" of communities and individuals who moved back from cities to reservations (Josephy *et al.* 1999: 7). This activism in the US, where as we have discussed there is an arbitrary and limited recognition of Tribal sovereignty, has since focused on defending and expanding the political and economic implications of this right. In this sense, the struggle in the US can be understood as material as well as philosophical.

As a result of Native American activism, formal assimilation policies were withdrawn, and the Supreme Court and the federal government became gradually more willing to recognize Tribal rights. Nonetheless, self-determination and sovereignty, as concepts that entail a universe of political goals, remain a battlefield between the government and Native Americans.

During the 1970s, the US government's attention was drawn from one Native protest to another, from the temporary seizure of vacated penitentiary facilities in Alcatraz to the occupation of federal buildings and national parks, to the siege of Wounded Knee, which was met with police mobilization and the use of military force (Smith and Warrior 1996).

As a response, federal policy started to shift towards the notion of self-determination and the strategy of funding Native organizations as a method of defusing their resentment. Within this policy, self-determination was driven by an emphasis on economic development, which reveals competing visions of the concept. From the Native American leaders' perspective, self-determination had three core components: preservation of treaty rights, consultation on policy changes, and economic self-sufficiency. To policy-makers involved with the "war on poverty" during the 1960s, self-determination simply meant greater Native control over funds and the delivery of government programs (Riggs 2000).

Although these initiatives were no doubt useful to Native communities, they indicate how the administrations of Presidents John F. Kennedy and Lyndon Johnson were concerned with Native Americans more as impoverished minorities than as domestic nations. During President Richard Nixon's administration, a more comprehensive policy for self-determination was developed. The Indian Self-determination and Education Act of 1975 defined a set of measures to place greater control in tribal hands. Although it has been argued that Nixon's intention was to break federal paternalism while emphasizing the trust relationship between the tribes and the federal government, the legislation passed to meet this goal failed to do so since it put constraints on Native decisions (Cook 1994). Theoretically, the trust relationship was to strengthen Tribal institutions as well as position them to play a more relevant role in Native American development. In practice, however, the "trust" became an avenue for federal control and complete subjugation of Native peoples in the decision-making process (Jaimes 1988; Barsh 1994).

On the bright side, this legislation can also be considered a small step forward for Native people in the US, for the following reasons. According to the Indian Self-determination and Education Act, tribes may enter into "self-determination contracts" with the Secretary of the Interior and the Secretary of Health and Human Services to administer programs or service delivery that otherwise would have been managed by the federal government (Coverage Issues under the Indian Self-determination Act 2004). The Act, from this perspective, creates the legal means through which tribes can assume greater control over government programs without fearing termination. However, federal bureaucracies still had a heavy authority in determining the feasibility of such contracts (Coverage Issues under the Indian Self-determination Act 2004). In addition, although the Act provided financial resources and control for Tribal education programs, the emphasis is put on services and development, as in this legislation there is no land base included to support Tribal self-sufficiency. Native lands are held in trust by the federal government, and any project to develop these lands must be approved by that government.

Therefore, even though the 1975 Act provides a framework for Native American policies, they have changed over the years. Perhaps the most disturbing trend regarding the executive's interest in "Indian" policy emerged in the 1980s, during the presidency of Ronald Reagan, with the application of neo-liberal policies to these issues. Reagan's philosophy that the responsibility to act and administer the resources should belong to the government closest to the people also applied to Native Americans. He intended to include tribes under his domestic policy of "New Federalism," which basically reduced Tribal governments to local entities comparable to townships, except for the fact they enjoyed somewhat greater financial control over social and economic programs. The key element in this policy was to promote self-sufficiency based on economic development and the private sector. Because it was acknowledged that tribes have limited opportunities to invest in their own economies because they often do not have the resources to promote their communities' development, they were encouraged to attract private investment (cited in Josephy *et al.* 1999: 126). It is a different story regarding Tribal lands containing energy resources. In those cases, the federal government directly promotes exploitation of energy resources by attracting private funding for economic development ventures on reservation lands.

Similarly, the Tribal Self-Determination Act (1987) and the Tribal Self-Governance Act (1988) have both encouraged activities appealing to private enterprises and local initiatives. While these policies have channelled more government funding, there is a continued paternalistic assumption that Native Americans still need policies orienting the direction of their governance (Barsh 1994).

So far, we can discern several common elements in the governmental response to claims for self-determination that are important to underline. The first is the use of the strategy of disempowering by borders, which is expressed in the separation of self-government from its territorial base. Secondly, self-government is considered to be exclusively a devolution of management of government-designed programs. Thirdly, there is an emphasis on fighting poverty through the promotion of development, based largely on private investment for the exploitation of natural resources. Fourthly, the government has the final say on self-government initiatives. Finally, in the government-to-government relationship, Tribal governments are reduced to the township level. From this perspective, Tribal governments are considered entities able to contract loans and carry out administrative functions rather than autonomous political bodies able to define their own policies and with land and a resource base to promote economic development according to their own needs.

As Diane Duffy and Jerry Stubben (1998: 53) have argued, the general focus on economic development without taking into account identity and culture have exacerbated the cycle of poverty among most Native Americans. Besides, even though there is a strong emphasis on development, the financial resources to promote investment are lacking within reservations, since there are countless barriers that tribes have to face simply to make ends meet. Therefore, they must rely on non-Native private investment, which further puts their difference at risk.

THE ABORIGINAL MOVEMENT AND CANADA'S RESPONSE

In 1969, the newly elected government of Prime Minister Pierre Elliott Trudeau published a "statement on Indian policy," commonly known as the White Paper, whose primary goal was to extinguish Aboriginal status. This proposal attempted to revoke the Indian Act and fragment First Nations territories into individual property, to delegate responsibility of enfranchised Aboriginal people to provincial governments, and to eliminate the Department of Indian Affairs and Northern Development (DIAND) (Frideres 1993: 321). This policy was based on what Alfred (2000) calls the classic strategy of denial of Aboriginal rights, which in this article we have labeled political bias. In addition, the White Paper was based on a strong adherence to the liberal principle of equality and individual rights (Abele et al. 1999: 259). Clearly, this principle could not adequately address Aboriginal issues, since decades of domination and exclusion from citizenship for Aboriginal peoples had left an imprint on these communities and on their sense of alienation vis-à-vis the Canadian political community.

The White Paper was put forward against the backdrop of the emergence of Aboriginal organizations in most provinces throughout the 1960s. They denounced racism, expressed their sense of alienation, agitated for changes to Aboriginal government policies, and claimed the right to speak for their own peoples. This Aboriginal movement was mainly based on ethnicity, race, nationalism, and, to a lesser extent, on class consciousness (Adams 1995: 89). Numerous organizations coalesced in their opposition to the White Paper, creating one of the most important pan-Canadian cooperative efforts among Aboriginal people, which was aimed at stopping this initiative. According to Harold Cardinal (1999: 12), opposition to this proposal and the convergence of young charismatic chiefs helped to set up the National Indian Brotherhood (now known as the Assembly of First Nations) with the purpose of defending Aboriginal interests and restraining the government from negotiating with individual First Nations.

Aboriginal leaders articulated a set of political issues not only to defeat the White Paper but to end the government's tutelage and recover their capacities to govern themselves. From their perspective, Aboriginal people have collective rights and special needs; borrowing the words from the 1966 Hawthorne Report, they could be considered "citizens plus" (Kulchysky 1995: 62). According to this leadership, sovereignty was an attribute given to them by the Creator rather than by human beings. In other words, sovereignty is an inherent right that exists by itself and is not dependent on any government's recognition.

The Canadian government withdrew the White Paper in the face of the strong opposition and unprecedented mobilization it had provoked, especially because AIM was having some influence on its Canadian counterpart. As happened in the US, the Canadian government then deployed the classic co-optation strategy of channelling financial assistance to Aboriginal organizations in order to appease their resentment. This move was an attempt to shape their political strategies and to boycott AIM's interference and potential transnationalization of what the government preferred to keep as a domestic issue. The Canadian government strategy was successful in making Aboriginal organizations seek solutions in conjunction with the government rather than against it, although they continue to pursue goals of autonomy that the government would prefer not to promote (Kehoe 1981: 539).

Also around this period, Aboriginal peoples challenged the Canadian government on other fronts, through institutions such as the Supreme Court. In the *Calder* case in 1973 (named after the Aboriginal lawyer of the Nisga'a nation who brought forward the legal challenge), the Supreme Court determined that Aboriginal peoples possessed collective rights that survived the general legislation that the Canadian state had enacted since the contact period. This case is particularly interesting because it changed the legal landscape from denying Aboriginal title to a theoretical acceptance of Aboriginal rights. Although technically the Nisga'a people lost their bid to secure legal recognition of their title, the case set a precedent for Aboriginal peoples who never signed treaties when claiming territorial rights.

As Augie Fleras (1999: 111) has shown, Aboriginal peoples in Canada have insisted on the following demands as a minimum for atonement and reform of their relations with the Canadian state: a new nation-to-nation relationship; repossession by Aboriginal peoples of land and natural resources, unless clearly ceded in the past by treaty or conquest; recognition of the fact that legitimacy of settlements rests on Aboriginal people's consent rather than in state authority; and recognition of Aboriginal people as sovereign for the purposes of entitlement and engagement.

Since the 1970s, the government and Aboriginal peoples have focused on how to renew their relationship in order to enhance their autonomy. Simultaneously, Aboriginal organizations pushed for the entrenchment of their inherent rights in the Canadian Constitution. In other words, the struggle has focused on the philosophical revision of Aboriginal status as nations; however, its success has not been clear. During the process of constitutional patriation in the early 1980s, Aboriginal leaders lobbied the British Parliament to make sure the Constitution Act itself and the proposed Charter of Rights and Freedoms would not erode or ignore their collective rights. As it turned out, the Canadian government recognized and affirmed Aboriginal and treaty rights under sections 25 and 35 of the Constitution Act, 1982.

The claim for self-government became a very politicized issue for Aboriginal people, who took advantage of another proposed amendment to the Canadian Constitution, the 1992 Charlottetown Accord, by pushing for the explicit constitutional recognition of self-government. As Mary Ellen Turpel (1993: 121) has argued, the participation of Aboriginal representatives in the Charlottetown discussion set a precedent for contemporary struggles. It successfully asserted their right to sit at the constitutional table when matters such as inherent rights to self-government, treaty rights, the status and rights of Aboriginal peoples, and Aboriginal consent to constitutional amending formula changes are involved.

Yet, the Charlottetown Accord was rejected in a national referendum and thus was never ratified. It is difficult to explain this failure in terms of any particular proposal, as the package included a wide array of issues raging from Senate reform to the recognition of Québec as a distinct society, issues that reactivated much negative sentiment among various sectors of the population. With regard to its Aboriginal contents, there were a number of spoilers: the exclusion of different organizations—especially the Native Women's Association of Canada—from the discussion, the hostility to collective rights within the framework of a Canadian liberal mindset, and fear among Aboriginal peoples that a third order of government would mean putting an end to the nation-to-nation relationship established with treaties (Turpel 1993: 132). Although the very extensive set of proposed constitutional amendments on Aboriginal issues contained in the Charlottetown resolutions showed that their struggle had reached a philosophical stage that forced the state to recognize their inherent sovereignty, it also shows the differences among the three categories of Aboriginal peoples and their political interests.

After failing constitutionally to define Aboriginal inherent rights, the Canadian government shifted strategy and focused on negotiating agreements with individual Aboriginal Nations and promoting an Aboriginal economic development agenda. In August 1995, the government of Prime Minister Jean Chrétien set forth a policy statement on Aboriginal self-government, which has basically been oriented to separate self-government from territorial claims (Abele *et al.* 1999: 277). According to that new policy, negotiation of individual treaties is based on the identification of priorities and particular interests rather than on the recognition of Aboriginal rights. In so doing, the federal government has focused on the delegation of responsibilities and social services to Aboriginal governments. For some scholars, what the government calls devolution is simply transferring governmental administrative responsibilities to Aboriginal communities (Frideres 1998: 192).

Furthermore, the scope of each of these modern treaties is determined, to a large extent, by the political ability of individual First Nation leaders to negotiate important financial compensations for their people and to secure their participation in the co-management agreements on natural resources. Paul Rynard (2000) observes that negotiation of new agreements such as the Nisga'a Agreement in 1998 has enshrined the idea of "welcome in, but check your rights at the door." That is to say, First Nations are required to surrender their inherent right to self-government in order to receive the financial support needed to alleviate their dire economic situation. Menno Boldt (1998) contends that this policy is not oriented toward the development of Aboriginal nationhood but rather toward the creation of new forms of governmental dependency and constraint. In a similar vein, other authors argue that the government's strategy has been to create certainty and opportunities for private investors to exploit natural resources within Aboriginal territories. However, this strategy does not necessarily promote self-sufficiency as most Aboriginal communities do not benefit from economic development (Ratner *et al.* 2003; Altamirano-Jiménez 2004).

Although the initial rationale of the 1995 policy was to move away from the constitutional wrangling that had characterized Canada in previous years, this rationale continued with the 1998 Canada Aboriginal Action Plan, Ottawa's response to the 1996 Royal Commission Report on Aboriginal Peoples, which was created in August 1991 to look into the conditions of life of the Aboriginal peoples of Canada and to recommend ways to solve their problems and fulfill their aspirations. After over five years of work, it presented its report, which consists of 3,536 pages and 400 specific recommendations. As Cairns (2000: 116–20) points out, the Royal Commission Report provides the most rigorous Aboriginal perspective ever in several fields such as historical analysis of pre-contact time, Aboriginal voices, past injustices, constitutional recommendations, and a radical approach to self-determination. However, the Canadian government's response was a public apology for the past injustices to which Aboriginal peoples were subjected and a promise to find ways to replace the old Indian Act.

In looking for alternatives to renew its relationship with Aboriginal peoples, DIAND approached the US Department of the Interior to hold a round of talks on Aboriginal issues. The main objective of these talks has been to promote in Canada an Aboriginal policy similar to the one implemented by the US government during the past 25 years, especially regarding economic development. In order for Canada to follow the US development strategy, the US Department of the Interior affirmed that Ottawa should eliminate some legal constraints (US Department of the Interior 2002). This measure would perhaps mean the full application of the political bias that was implemented in the US over one century ago, by means of which treaty relations ended. Ironically, Canada has been more successful in implementing Aboriginal development programs than the US, and social expenditure on this matter is much lower in the US than in Canada, as shown by James Frideres (1998).

The controversial First Nations Governance Act (FNGA) tabled in 2002 emerged in the context of these talks. It was aimed at replacing the Indian Act with the implementation of an intergovernmental cooperative approach that would deal with urgent social and economic priorities while working toward some form of municipal Aboriginal self-government. While this document would have provided the framework for the adoption of liberal democratic principles and accountability for First Nations, it also would have legalized their "band status" instead of recognizing them as sovereign First Nations. Moreover, land issues were completely sidestepped, since the act would have enshrined another piece of legislation, the Land Management Act. While the Land Management Act, passed in 1999, applied only to signatory First Nations, the FNGA would have automatically applied to all First Nations.

The FNGA's main stated objective was to improve the conditions of life of First Nations through economic development. To that end, the document creates a new framework for Aboriginal peoples to enter into contracts and borrow money in order to promote development projects. Also under this act, Aboriginal traditional lands can be expropriated by the federal government if required for reasons of "national interests" in exchange for other lands and adequate compensation (Indian and Northern Affairs Canada 1999). Basically, then, by isolating self-government from territorial rights, the strategy of disempowering by boundaries re-emerged.

However, the FNGA faced strong Aboriginal opposition. Hence, when Prime Minister Paul Martin came to power in December 2003, he withdrew the bill. The perspective on development and limited self-government continues, nonetheless, to be the cornerstone of Aboriginal policy in Ottawa. The strategy of disempowering by boundaries will still apply whenever Aboriginal peoples enter into modern treaties.

According to Steven Globerman (2001: 141), one of the main arguments behind the promotion of First Nations' modern treaty settlements is the reduction of uncertainty about how resources on Crown lands can be used, since uncertainty prevents private investments from flowing. Another consideration behind this policy is the emphasis on corporate/Aboriginal relations, because Aboriginal peoples claim at least 20 per cent of Canada's landmass. This situation poses potential problems for developing or exploiting natural resources, pipeline utilities, etc. (Frideres 1998: 178).

To sum up, in contemporary Canada the actions taken by federal and provincial governments with regard to the Aboriginal population are characterized by: first, cutting budgets allotted for Aboriginal peoples; second, delegating services to Aboriginal communities under the argument that the inherent right to self-government is met through service delivery; third, promoting an economic development approach that relies on the separation between self-government and a land base; and fourth, promoting corporate/Aboriginal relations to respond to the pressure of the global market and business environment. This is particularly clear in First Nations lands with strategic natural resources such as oil and gas.

THE INDIGENOUS MOVEMENT IN MEXICO

The 1970s is also a landmark in the development of Indigenous struggles in Mexico. Nonetheless, Indigenous peoples in this country were less vocal than their counterparts in the US and Canada partly because, despite the prevalent ideology of a homogenous *mestizo* national culture, assimilation policies in Mexico did not mean the total loss of Indigenous heritage (Kehoe 1981: 539) and partly because the Indigenous movement was somewhat fragmented. According to Consuelo Sánchez (1999: 85), during the 1970s Indigenous organizations in Mexico were divided among those that emphasized Indigenous identity and Indigenous rights; those that underlined their class position; and those that stressed Indigenous identity but, at the same time, tried to articulate their struggle with other social sectors such as peasants.

As happened in Canada and the US, Indigenous intellectuals also played an important role in revitalizing Indigenous culture and identity in Mexico. However, the revival of Indigenous identity in Mexico was belated for a number of reasons. These include the fact that Indigenous peoples had an outlet for active political participation under both pro-government and independent peasant umbrella organizations. In addition, an educated Indigenous elite was early incorporated into the government bureaucracy, in agencies such as the National Indigenous Institute (INI), which participated—although marginally—in implementing *indigenismo* or policies aimed at integrating Indigenous peoples into the mainstream society. The identification of Indigenous struggles with other social sectors such as peasants' organizations, which historically have focused on land issues, also played a role. Not least, the existence of Article 27 of the Constitution protected and recognized Indigenous communal lands and resources, a major difference from the situation in the US and Canada. Therefore, although an incipient Indigenous revival appeared in the 1970s, the movement fully entered the national political arena, with a defined discourse of collective identity, only with the uprising of the Zapatista Army in January 1994.

The Zapatista uprising in Chiapas responded to a series of legal changes that severely affected Indigenous lands. The government of President Carlos Salinas de Gortari took several steps oriented toward adjusting national laws to the implementation of economic structural reforms and international agreements such as NAFTA. Salinas came to power in 1988 with the promise to "modernize" Mexico. For his government, this meant integrating the countryside and its resources into the global market. In addition, the government wanted to introduce neo-liberal reforms under the guise of eliminating bureaucratic paternalism. By these means, a new relationship between the state and Indigenous people was established. Yet, Indigenous organizations quickly came to see this new relationship as based on the purely symbolic recognition of cultural Indigenous rights while the real agenda was to transform Indigenous land tenure radically.

In preparation for NAFTA, a comprehensive neo-liberal agenda was implemented. Measures included privatization of state-owned corporations, trade liberalization, and restructured government budgets and agencies, along with social programs to alleviate the impacts of these reforms. With regard to the countryside, the expression of such neo-liberal policies was the modification of Article 27. As mentioned earlier, after the Mexican Revolution this article protected communal land ownership or *ejido* from being sold and bought and gave a special status to communal authorities. Article 27 was reformed in 1992 to force this land into private property and abolish communal tenure. In contrast, the right of landless peasants to request a piece of land to make a living, an important component of the original revolutionary claims enshrined in Article 27, was simply abolished (Harvey 1999: 187).

In addition to the reform of Article 27, an Agrarian Law was also approved to give *ejidatarios* (*ejido* tenants) legal rights to sell, rent, or use as collateral for loans individual plots and communal lands. Under this law, private companies were allowed to purchase land up to 25 times the size permitted to individual shareholders. The reform also allowed new forms of association between private investors and *ejidatarios*.

Article 27 was not the only constitutional article modified. Article 4 was also reformed to recognize the multicultural nature of the Mexican nation and to legally define Indigenous peoples. At the same time, the government ratified the ILO's Covenant 169, which defines the status of "peoples" for Indigenous populations and their collective rights, including self-determination. However, neither the modification of Article 4 nor the ratification of Covenant 169 went beyond a symbolic recognition, since Indigenous collective rights were not legally protected. Indeed, reforms of Article 27 and Article 4 were contradictory and at the end were oriented to separate self-government from land. As the US and Canadian governments have done before, in Mexico the strategy of "disempowering by boundaries" was also implemented. It is in this context that the Indigenous rebellion in Chiapas emerged.

In broad terms, the Zapatistas demanded respect by the Mexican state and its agencies for Indigenous cultures and traditions; constitutional recognition of their cultural, political, and judicial autonomy; the right to full education for all Indigenous people; the end to racism and discrimination against Indigenous peoples; Indigenous peoples' right to live with dignity; the right to trustworthy information through a radio station managed and guided by Indigenous peoples; and, last but not least, financial and social support to Indigenous women (Frente Zapatista de Liberación Nacional 1996). In contrast to the experience in the US and Canada, the Indigenous movement in Mexico enjoyed the wide support of other sectors of the civil society due to the fact that the Indigenous population is not as segregated from the mainstream society as it is in the other two North American countries. Thanks to this support, the Mexican government felt compelled to start a national dialogue with the Zapatistas and other Indigenous organizations. The Indigenous movement thus intersected with other social movements in Mexico.

It took two years of negotiations between the rebels and the federal government before the San Andrés Accords were reached in February 1996. The accords were subsequently translated into a bill by the congressional committee *Comisión de Concordia y Pacificación* (Commission for Agreement and Peace, COCOPA). This committee played an important role in the negotiation process. In November 1996, COCOPA presented its bill to the Zapatistas and to the federal government. It was accepted by the Zapatistas but rejected by the federal government, who did not want to fulfil its commitment and argued that the COCOPA bill did not reflect the original accords.

When President Fox came to power in December 2000, he promised to solve the Chiapas conflict by implementing social policies to fight poverty and create opportunities to access loans for the promotion of small enterprises. The Zapatista rebels, though, did not agree with this approach. In an attempt to send a strong message to the new government about their resolve to defend the San Andrés Accords, a large delegation of Zapatista militants marched from Chiapas to Mexico City in March 2001. Step by step, they were able to overcome opposition from the government and other political forces; the mobilization culminated when a masked Zapatista female delegate addressed the full Congress to defend the COCOPA bill.

However, on 25 April 2001, that same Congress passed an Indigenous Law that had little to do with the original COCOPA initiative. In order to be approved, laws that have constitutional implications such as this one must be ratified by two-thirds of the Congress and the majority of state legislatures.[5] The law was eventually passed, even though it was not ratified by the governments of Oaxaca, Guerrero, and Chiapas, the three states with the largest Indigenous populations (Román 2001). This new law recognizes limited Indigenous communitarian self-government to rule internal affairs but denies the collective right of Indigenous peoples to own and have access to land and natural resources. Furthermore, it only gives them the right to be consulted whenever a development project is implemented in their territories. Therefore, despite the armed movement and continued Indigenous protest, the 2001 Indigenous Law kept in place the separation between Indigenous self-government and its territorial base (Higgins 2001).

Indigenous peoples demand political autonomy in order to have more control over their social, economic, and political future, but the Mexican government insists on economic development alone. As stated in the Indigenous Law: "It is important to support productive activities, sustainable development of communities through actions oriented to increase their incomes, private and public investment" (México 2001). Perhaps the best example of this strategy is the Puebla Panamá Plan put forward by Fox's government with the support of international financial institutions, whose goal is to promote private investment in southern Mexico and Central America.[6] Under this model of development, Indigenous peoples will be offered low-paid jobs in assembly plants. The current Mexican government is thus promoting a form of development based on a *maquiladora* (assembly plant) model to allegedly solve Indigenous political claims. Andrés Aubry (2002) has pointed out how, in Chiapas, the *finca* or *hacienda*[7] is already being substituted by new *maquiladoras* promoted by the Puebla Panamá Plan, whose main characteristic is its ability for steady relocation if cheaper labour is found elsewhere in the world or labour problems arise.

Conclusion

As we have seen, there are significant legal and historical differences between the US, Canada, and Mexico in the way in which they have dealt with Indigenous peoples, such as the treaty-making policy in Canada and the US that was absent in Mexico. Nonetheless, an important commonality in the three countries is how governments have attempted to assimilate these populations into the mainstream economy, dominant politics, and culture.

During the 1970s, in the three North American countries a new Indigenous leadership emerged, articulating a political discourse based on Indigenous identity and rights. Some differences were still noticeable. In both Canada and the US Indigenous peoples mobilized to oppose policies designed to extinguish "Indian" status, something that had already happened in Mexico when it achieved independence in the early nineteenth century. While Mexico broke with colonial legislation, the US and Canada kept a common law tradition that has been used by Indigenous movements to attempt to make valid notions of prior sovereign existence, treaty obligations, and Indian self-government.

The US, however, differs substantially from Canada because it terminated treaty rights while Canada continues to recognize them. On the other hand, although in Mexico the elimination of "Indian" status happened earlier, Indigenous communities' struggle managed to bring into the 1917 Constitution the protection of Indigenous lands and forms of communitarian political organization. These legal protections, however, were later modified in the context of NAFTA implementation.

Indigenous demands are similar in the three countries: the right to self-government, self-determination, and political autonomy. Together, these demands also imply a land base. The two main strategies Indigenous movements have used in the three countries are nonetheless contrasting: the assertion of a prior and coexisting sovereignty, particularly in Canada and the US, and the assertion of the right to self-determination for Indigenous peoples in international law in Mexico. In Canada and Mexico Indigenous movements have focused on the constitutional status of First Nations or peoples. In the US, in contrast, the Native American movement has centred on defending and expanding the economic and political implications of a limited legally recognized Tribal sovereignty.

Government responses to Indigenous demands in the three states bear also several similarities in the way in which they have framed Indigenous rights and development. On the one hand, in each country there is a nominal recognition of Indigenous peoples as collective identities. In the US this recognition takes the form of acceptance of limited Native sovereignty, in Canada of acknowledgement of Aboriginal rights and treaties, and in Mexico recognition of Indigenous peoples as the original inhabitants in that country. The existence of this nominal recognition, however, is not necessarily coherent with governmental policies, characterized by their stress in separating the right to self-government from land claims. From a nominal recognition perspective, Indigenous governments are accepted as local authorities and given certain functions to rule their internal affairs, but acknowledgement of their unfettered ownership and sovereignty over a land base or territory to promote their social, cultural, and economic reproduction as quasi-national entities is still missing. In the most recent laws dealing with Indigenous peoples in the three countries—the US Indian Education Assistance Act, Canada's First Nations Governance Act, and Mexico's Indigenous Law—the recognition of self-government does not include territorial rights. In addition, Indigenous government is reduced to a simple local level of government, not very different from non-Indigenous local administrations. Indigenous land management is defined in terms of development. The strategy pursued by all three federal governments is based on opening these lands to private investment and development. By separating self-government from its territorial base, the federal governments strengthen their control over what is left of Indigenous lands, legitimizing this policy with the need to eliminate uncertainty for private investment.

Certainly, there are deep differences in terms of the financial support for Indigenous peoples present in each country. In Canada, this financial support is higher than in the US, while in Mexico it is limited to programs to fight poverty and to alleviate some of the negative consequences of NAFTA on agriculture. From this perspective, Indigenous peoples are considered vulnerable populations that, nonetheless, must partake in the global economy in order to reverse their marginal conditions of life. In all three countries Indigenous peoples rank first in marginalization, unemployment, and lack of education, so government responses focus on economic development as if it were the ultimate solution to these problems. Nonetheless, this type of economic development is mainly intended to open Indigenous lands to the market rather than to provide Indigenous peoples with the means for their social reproduction.

In other words, Indigenous peoples in North America presently face an excruciating dilemma: if they want to improve their living conditions, they will be supported by the state but pressured to enter the market; if they want to preserve their sovereignty, they will face governmental indifference and reluctance, if not open hostility and cannot count on economic support. In short, they are forced to choose between self-determination and market-oriented development and always risk ending up with neither.

Notes

1   For a comprehensive review of US relations with tribal peoples see Williams 1990, Cohen 1982, Deloria and Lytle 1983, Churchill 2002, and Zinn 1980, among others.

2   The concept of disempowering by boundaries can be originally found in Booth *et al.* 1997. A reviewed definition of this concept is found in Altamirano-Jiménez 2004.

3   For a comprehensive account on the relations between Aboriginal peoples in Canada, see Dupuis 2002, Riendeau 2000, Green and Dickason 1993, among others.

4   General historical overviews of the history of Indigenous peoples in Mexico include León Portilla 2003, Florescano 1998, Guerra and Annino 2003, and Todorov 1999, among others.

5   According to constitutional Article 135.

6   An overview and critique of this plan is found at <http://www.rmalc.org.mx/ppp/index.php>.

7   *Finca* or *hacienda* is a form of rural production that combined illegally large extensions of land with overexploited labour. Workers were bound to the land through ongoing debt with the landlord. Despite the unconstitutional status of the *finca*, it survived after the Mexican revolution.

References

Abele, Frances, *et al.* 1999. "Negotiating Canada: Changes in Aboriginal Policy over the Last Thirty Years." In Leslie Pal (ed.), *How Ottawa Spends 1999–2000.* Toronto: Oxford.

Adams, Howard. 1995. *A Tortured People.* Vancouver: Theytus Books. 251–92.

Alfred, Taiaiake. 2000. "From Sovereignty to Freedom: Toward an Indigenous Political Discourse." In P. Deloria and N. Salisbury (eds.), *Blackwell Companion to Native American History.* Oxford: Blackwell. 460–74.

Altamirano-Jiménez, Isabel. 2004. "North American First Peoples: Slipping Up into Market Citizenship?" *Citizenship Studies* 8,4: 349–65.

Armitage, Andrew. 1998. *Comparing the Policy of Aboriginal Assimilation: Australia, Canada, and New Zealand.* Vancouver: U of British Columbia P.

Aubry, Andrés. 2002. "Chiapas: de República bananera a República maquiladora." *La Jornada,* 6 January: 10.

Barsh, R. 1994. "Indian Policy at the Beginning of the 1990s: The Trivialization of Struggle." In Lyman Legters and Fremont Lyden (eds.), *American Indian Policy*. Westport, CT: Greenwood Press. 55–70.

Barthas, Brigitte. 1997. "La comunidad indigena como organizacion, el caso de la Huasteca." Paper presented at the Latin America Studies Association Annual Conference, Guadalajara, Mexico, 17–19 April.

Boldt, Menno. 1998. *Surviving as Indians: The Challenge of Self-Government*. Toronto: U of Toronto P.

Booth, D. *et al*. 1997. *Popular Participation: Democratization in Rural Bolivia*. Stockholm: Stockholm UP.

Borah, Woodrow. 1985. *El Juzgado general de Indias en la Nueva España*. Mexico City: Fondo de Cultura Económica.

Borah, Woodrow, and Sherburne Cook. 1963. *The Aboriginal Population of Central Mexico on the Eve of the Spanish Conquest*. Berkeley, CA: U of California P.

Cairns, Alan. 1995. *Reconfigurations: Canadian Citizenship and Constitutional Change*. Toronto: McClelland and Stewart.

———. 2000. *Citizens Plus: Aboriginal Peoples and the Canadian State*. Vancouver: U of British Columbia P.

Cardinal, Harold. 1999. *The Unjust Society*. Seattle, WA: U of Washington P.

Centre for World Indigenous Studies. 1988. "Competing Sovereignties in North America, the Right Wing and the anti-Indian Movement." Preliminary Findings of the Right-wing Extremism and Anti-Indian Network Project, January. <http://www.cwis.org/fwdp/Americas/rwain.txt>.

Churchill, Ward. 2002. *Struggle for the Land*. Winnipeg: Arbeiter Ring.

Cohen, F.S. 1982. *Handbook of Federal Indian Law*. Washington, DC: Hcin.

Cook, Samuel. 1994. "What is Indian Self-Determination?" *Red Ink* 3,1 (May). <http://faculty.smu. edu/twalker/samrcook.htm>.

Coverage Issues under the Indian Self-determination Act. 2004. <http://www.usdoj.gov/olc/isdafin. htm>.

Delâge, Denys. 1991. *Le pays renversé: Européens et Amérindiens en Amérique du Nord-Est, 1600–1664*. Montreal: Boréal.

Deloria, Vine Jr. 1984. "'Congress and its Wisdom': the Course of Indian Legislation." In Sandra L. Cadwalader and Vine Deloria, Jr. (eds.), *The Aggressions of Civilization: Federal Indian Policy since the 1880s*. Philadelphia, PA: Temple UP. 297–306.

Deloria, Vine Jr., and R.M. Lytle. 1983. *American Indians, American Justice*. Austin, TX: U of Texas P.

Duffy, Diane, and Jerry Stubben. 1998. "An Assessment of Native American Economic Development: Putting Culture and Sovereignty Back in the Models." *Studies in Comparative International Development* 32,4 (Winter): 52–78.

Dupuis, Renée. 2002. *Justice for Canada's Aboriginal Peoples*. Toronto: James Lorimer.

Fleras, Augie. 1999. "The Politics of Jurisdiction: Pathway or Predicament." In David Long and Olive Patricia Dickason (eds.), *Visions of the Heart: Aboriginal Issues*. Scarborough, ON: Nelson. 107–42.

Florescano, Enrique. 1998. *Etnia, Estado y nación*. Mexico City: Aguilar.

Franks, C.E.S. 2000. "Indian Policy: Canada and the United States Compared." In Curtis Cook and Juan Lindau D. (eds.), *Aboriginal Rights and Self-Government*. Montreal and Kingston: McGill-Queen's UP. 221–63.

Frente Zapatista de Liberación Nacional. 1996. *Acuerdos sobre Derechos Indígenas*. Mexico City: Ediciones del Frente Zapatista de Liberación Nacional.

Frideres, James. 1993. *Native Peoples in Canada*. Scarborough: Prentice Hall.

——. 1998. "Indigenous Peoples of Canada and the United States of America: Entering the 21st Century." In Leen d'Haenens (ed.), *Images of Canadianness: Vision of Canada's Politics, Culture, Economics*. Ottawa: U of Ottawa P. 167–96.

Frideres, James, and René Gadacz. 2001. *Aboriginal Peoples in Canada: Contemporary Conflicts*. Scarborough, ON: Prentice Hall.

Globerman, Steven. 2001. "Investment and Capital Productivity." In Roslyn Kunin (ed.), *Prospering Together: The Economic Impact of the Aboriginal Title Settlements in BC*. Vancouver: The Laurier Institution. 139–68.

Green, L.C., and Olive P. Dickason. 1993. *Law of Nations and the New World*. Edmonton: U of Alberta P.

Guerra, François-Xavier, and Antonio Annino. 2003. *Inventando la nación*. Mexico City: Fondo de Cultura Económica.

Guibernau, Monserrat. 1999. *Nations without State: Political Communities in a Global Age*. London: Polity Press.

Harvey, Neil. 1999. *The Chiapas Rebellion: The Struggle for Land and Democracy*. Durham, NC: Duke UP.

——. 2001. "Globalization and Resistance in Post-Cold War Mexico: Difference, Citizenship, and Biodiversity Conflict in Chiapas." *Third World Quarterly* 22,6: 1045–61.

Higgins, Nicholas P. 2001. "Mexico's Stalled Peace Process: Prospects and Challenges." *International Affairs* 77,4 (October): 885–903.

Hueglin, Thomas O. 2000. "Federalismo constitucional y federalismo por tratado en Canadá." In Consuelo Márquez Padilla and Julián Castro Rea (eds.), *El nuevo federalismo en América del Norte*. Mexico City: UNAM. 175–216.

Indian and Northern Affairs Canada. 1999. *Land Management Act*. <http:www.fafnlm.com/LAB. NSF/vSysAboutDoc./English>.

Jaimes, M.A. 1988. "Federal Indian Identification Policy: A Usurpation of Indigenous Sovereignty in North America." *Policy Studies Journal* 16: 778–98.

Josephy, Alvin M. Jr., *et al.* (1999). "Introduction." In Alvin M. Josephy Jr., *et al.*, *Red Power: The American Indians' Fight for Freedom*. Lincoln, NB: U of Nebraska P. 1–9.

Kehoe, Alice B. 1981. *North American Indians: A Comprehensive Account*. Upper Saddle River, NJ: Prentice Hall.

Kulchysky, Peter. 1995. "Aboriginal Peoples and Hegemony in Canada." *Journal of Canadian Studies* 30,1 (June): 60–68.

León Portilla, Miguel. 2003. *Pueblos indígenas de México: Autonomía y diferencia cultural* 1. Mexico City: UNAM-El Colegio Nacional.

México. 2001. *Ley Indígena*. <http://www.cddhcu.gob.mx/servddd>.

Parry, C. (Ed.). 1969. *The Consolidated Treaty Series* 49. New York: Oceana Publications.

Ratner, R.S., *et al.* 2003. "Wealth of Nations: Aboriginal Treaty Making in the Era of Globalization." In John Torpey (ed.), *Politics and Past*. Lanham, MD: Rowman and Littlefield.

Reyna, Leticia. 1990. *Revueltas indígenas en el siglo XIX*. Mexico City: Siglo XXI.

Riggs, Christopher K. 2000. "American Indians, Economic Development and Self-Determination in the 1960s." *Pacific Historical Review* 69,3: 431–63.

Riendeau, Roger E. 2000. *A Brief History of Canada*. New York: Facts on File.

Román, José Antonio. 2001. "La ley indígena amenaza la paz: Samuel Ruiz." *La Jornada*, 1 July. <http://www.jornada.unam.mx/2001/jul01/010702/017n1pol.html>.

Royal Commission on Aboriginal Peoples. 1996. *Final Report*. <http://www.Indigenous.bc.ca/rcap. html>.

Rynard, Paul. 2000. "Welcome In, But Check Your Rights at the Door: The James Bay and Nisga'a Agreements in Canada." *Canadian Journal of Political Science* 33,2: 211–43.

Saladin d'Anglure, Bernard, and Françoise Morin. 1992. "The Inuit People, Between Particularism and Internationalism: An Overview of their Rights and Powers in 1992." *Inuit Studies* 16,1–2: 13–19.

Sánchez, Consuelo. 1999. *Los pueblos indígenas: del indigenismo a la autonomía*. Mexico City: Siglo XXI.

Schulte-Tenckhoff, Isabelle. 1998. "Reassessing the Paradigm of Domestication: The Problematic of Indigenous Treaties." *Review of Constitutional Studies* 4,2: 239–89.

Serrano Carreto, Enrique, *et al.* 2002. *Indicadores socioeconómicos de los pueblos indígenas de México*. Mexico City: INI-PNUD-CONAPO.

Smith, Paul Chaat, and Robert A. Warrior. 1996. *Like a Hurricane: The Indian Movement from Alcatraz to Wounded Knee*. New York: New Press.

Statistics Canada. 1995. *A Profile of Canada's Aboriginal Peoples*. Ottawa: Statistics Canada.

Todorov, Tzevetan. 1999. *The American Conquest. The Question of the Other*. Norman, OK: U of Oklahoma P.

Turpel, Mary Ellen. 1993. "The Charlottetown Discord and Aboriginal Peoples' Struggle for Fundamental Political Change." In Kenneth McRoberts and Patrick Monahan (eds.), *The Charlottetown Accord, the Referendum, and the Future of Canada*. Toronto: U of Toronto P. 117–31.

Tutino, John. 1990. *De la insurrección a la revolución en México*. Mexico City: Era.

——. 2000. "Comunidad, independencia y nación: las participaciones populares en las historias de México, Guatemala y Perú." In Leticia Reina (ed.), *Los retos de la etnicidad en los Estados-nación del siglo XXI*. Mexico City: CIESAS-INI-Miguel Angel Porrúa. 125–52.

US Bureau of the Census. 2000. *Census of Population and Housing*. Washington, DC: Government Printing Office.

US Department of the Interior. 2002. *Canada/US Bilateral Talks on Indigenous Peoples Issues Yield Spirit of Cooperation*. Press Release, 13 May. <http.www.doi.gov/ncw/o20513.html>.

Wilkinson, Charles F., and Erick R. Biggs. 1977. "The Evolution of the Termination Policy." *American Indian Law Review* 5: 139–84.

Williams, R.A. Jr. 1990. *The Discourses of Conquest*. Oxford: Oxford UP.

Zinn, Howard. 1980. *A People's History of the United States*. New York: HarperCollins.

CHAPTER ELEVEN

Default Convergence?
Human Rights and Fundamental Freedoms in North America[1]

David Schneiderman

National constitutional regimes for the protection of human rights and fundamental freedoms are paradoxical things (Brown 1995: 97–98). Rights and freedoms are meant to transcend the particular and aspire to the universal, yet most often they are articulated in very specific ways within national legal systems. This is the case for the each of the three countries of North America.

When we speak of the universality of human rights, we make claims about rights and freedoms that transcend specific political cultures and national contexts. All individuals, we might say, are the bearers of certain inalienable rights (Habermas 1998: 122). These usually are understood as rights claimable against political actors—so-called negative liberties—such as freedom of speech or the right to be free from discrimination on the grounds of race or sex. Other rights claimable against the state are characterized as collective or group rights. These are rights usually exercised by a group of people collectively, whether they are the right to use a particular language, to perform traditional cultural practices, or to collectively own property. There also are social rights to basic human needs—positive obligations to provide food, shelter, and clothing, for instance—that are viewed as necessary corollaries to traditional human rights. Human rights and freedoms are abridged by non-state actors, whether they are employers denying the right to freedom of association in the workplace or private police firms exercising their authority in an arbitrary or discriminatory way, and so private actors may be subject to the disciplines of human rights. Claims about the universality of rights facilitate the critique of state and non-state action by individuals and social movements around the globe.

Constitutional orders have attempted to give voice to some or all of these rights claims. This has resulted in different formulations of rights as different states define and balance rights claims differently. As there is no single transcendent understanding of how to realize universal human rights and freedoms—operating, as they do, at the level of the "ahistorical, acultural and acontextual" (Brown 1995: 97)—this variety comes as little surprise (Baxi 2006). The 1948 Universal Declaration of Human Rights, for instance, is so "open textured" (Hart 1994: 128) as to invite conflicting interpretations about the rights it declares to be universal. How does one reconcile, for instance, the Universal Declaration's "right to life" with rights to "liberty" and "privacy" in the context of a woman's freedom to choose whether to carry a foetus to term (Cook and Dickens 2003)?[2] The articulation of particular rights and freedoms will, then, reflect particular national experiences; they are after all, expressions of local trajectories that are path-dependent. Rights and freedoms, in this way, are caught up in the bind between universality and particularity (Balibar 1991: 54).

Were rights and freedoms converging around a single model for their realization and protection, the paradox would be avoided. From this angle, if we were to observe North American continental convergence toward a single model for the protection of rights and freedoms, this may be viewed as a good thing insofar as it would result in a shared set of values and enforcement mechanisms beyond the scale of the nation-state. This moves us further along the path toward the realization of universality of rights. It may also be viewed as favourable to the extent that it results in more efficient markets; individuals and business firms are better equipped to navigate across time and space where uniform standards are in place. From another angle, however, convergence may herald the supremacy of particularistic expressions of rights and freedoms with spurious claims to universality (Bourdieu 2000; Nedelsky 2000; Kennedy 1997; Santos 1995). If we accept that there is no single prefabricated path by which to realize the full human potential of individuals and the communities of which they form a part, such convergence short-circuits the possibility of expressing rights and freedoms in diverse and even better ways.

Take the right to private property, for instance. It has been said that this is a right that facilitates the fulfillment of every other right (Ely 1998). This connection between property and freedom was shared in the eighteenth-century revolutions in the US and in France (Arendt 1963: 180) and has resulted in the inclusion of some form of property right in many constitutions in the world (Daintith 2004; Van der Walt 1999). Yet property is the quintessential contestable concept (Radin 1993: 139)—it is the terrain over which debates concerning the relationship between politics and markets, between public interest and private rights, often will be fought. Property rights, it is often claimed, are negative rights to be free from state interference in the use and disposition of property. Yet these "rights," on the other hand, have always been subject to numerous qualifications that make them more conventional than other human rights. Indeed, the capacity of states to perform certain key functions, including the redistribution of wealth, turns on its ability continually to trump this right (Underkuffler 2003). In this case, it is a right with so many qualifications built into it, it cannot be defined "once and for all, [as] a kind of immutable concept" (Durkheim 1957: 215).

Property rights, then, will be treated differently within different national legal systems and this is so in the three constitutional systems of North America. In the US the right to property is considered a central organizing feature of the Constitution. In Canada, there is no constitutional right to property; rather, it is assumed that private property rights will be secured and respected by government. In Mexico, property is a constitutionally protected right that is expected to serve certain social functions, not merely the interests of individual property owners. These particularistic expressions of property rights may be converging toward a single standard of protection as a result of the investment chapter of NAFTA. Though it is still early to say, one of the effects of NAFTA on the region may be to move the three party states to converge around a single standard of protection, one that is reflective of the hegemonic US constitutional experience. This result is not entirely a foregone conclusion, though the scales appear to be tilted decidedly in that direction. The countries of North America may be leaning in the direction of "default convergence," a situation where hypothetical alternatives "are not perceived to exist" and so the outcome is "default (policy) convergence" or "default liberalism" (Hay 2000: 520). If so, this may be a good opportunity to begin a discussion about rights and freedoms that attends to pluralism and difference (Santos 1995: 352) and to the possibility that "diverse and local experiences and conceptions of emancipation" may be lost in the process (Kennedy 2004: 18).

In the first part of this chapter, each of the three constitutional regimes for the protection of rights and freedoms is described. The object here is to highlight some of the key distinctions and similarities between them with a particular focus on property rights. This is not to say that North America's human rights record otherwise is unblemished. On the contrary, each of the North American states have been guilty of some notorious human rights abuses in the past (consider the dispossession of Aboriginal peoples in all three countries or the detention of Japanese Canadians and Japanese Americans in World War II) and even in the present day (for instance, the killing of human rights defenders in Mexico; the torture of detainees at Abu Ghraib prison in Iraq by the US military; and the mistreatment, resulting in at least one death, of Aboriginal persons in Canadian police custody). Their mixed human rights records, though not the main focus of discussion in this chapter, provide a backdrop for the discussion of each country's constitutional regime.

In the second part of the chapter, NAFTA's legal architecture for the protection of foreign investment is analyzed to show how it is a constitution-like system of rights protections that mimics, yet goes further than, the regime for the protection of property rights in the US. By way of illustration, the third part of the chapter reviews the first successful NAFTA investor-rights case against Mexico, that of Metalclad Corporation of Newport Beach, California versus the United Mexican States. Metalclad claimed millions of dollars in damages for the taking of its investment interest—a hazardous waste facility site in the town of Guadalcazar—by the Mexican government. By contrasting the viability of Metalclad's claim under Mexican domestic law with its success under NAFTA, we can identify the contours of a new constitution-like regime for the protection of foreign investors to which all North American states will be bound far into the future.[3] This is a version of rights protection, however, that can be traced back to classical liberal understandings of rights associated with the US constitutional experience.[4]

North America's National Legal Systems

THE US

The constitutional experience of the US has cast a long shadow over constitutional experiences elsewhere, including those states in closest proximity to it. Though it was the spectacle of the French revolution that "set the world on fire" (Arendt 1963: 49), the US construction of constitutional rights is both an exemplar and a cautionary tale for many states in the world today (Choudhry 2004; Scheppele 2003). The framing of the 1787 US Constitution was intended to solve problems associated with the loose confederation forged out of the War of Independence. These problems included a weak national authority and strong states issuing currency and laws relieving debt obligations owed out-of-state (Madison 1999). Though it contemplated a new "energetic" national government, the new Constitution structured a bicameral federal government of limited and enumerated authority, held in further check by a separation of powers between the executive, legislative, and judicial branches of government. The framers were of the view that this constitutional structure was sufficiently protective of rights and freedoms that no further enumeration of them was necessary. A government so fragmented was in no need of further restraints, it was argued. Moreover, an enumeration of rights would "contain exceptions to powers not granted." Why, Alexander Hamilton continued, "should it be said that liberty of the press shall not be restrained, when no power is given [to the federal government] by which restrictions may be imposed?" (Hamilton *et al.* 1961: 513–14).

Various state governments, nevertheless, would not agree to ratification of the new arrangement without a Bill of Rights, which were appended to the US Constitution in its first ten amendments. These addressed only federal government action. Congress, for instance, could not abridge the freedom of speech, nor establish any religion (the First Amendment), nor take property for public use without the provision of "just compensation" (the Fifth Amendment). A handful of provisions that addressed the authority of states concerned mostly economic subjects that would impede enterprise within the new national economic unit. The Constitution, for instance, prohibited states from "impairing the obligation of contracts" (Article I, section 10, clause 1). The states otherwise were considered the repository of the people's rights (Diamond 1992: 102); as the Tenth Amendment put it, powers not delegated to the federal government "are reserved to the States respectively, or to the people." With the threat of southern secession and the bloody civil war that followed, the Constitution finally spoke to the distrust of state authority as well. The ensuing amendments to the Constitution abolished slavery (the Thirteenth Amendment), extended the franchise to freed slaves (the Fifteenth Amendment), and required states not to deny the equal protection of the laws or to deprive any person of "life, liberty, or property, without due process of law" (the Fourteenth Amendment).

The question of whether these amendments were intended to secure only freedom for the former slaves or for society-at-large was resolved in favour of the freedom of business firms. In the period known as the Lochner Era, running roughly from the 1880s to the 1930s, the US Supreme Court struck down all varieties of regulatory interventions into the marketplace. These interventions were characterized as "special" or "class" legislation; any disruption of the balance of class forces in US society was considered beyond the state or federal government's constitutional capacity (Gillman 1993: 67). At the same time, the "race question" continued to preoccupy the US constitutionally. Though the framers of the Fourteenth Amendment may only have anticipated formal equality under the law and no public intermixing of races, in *Brown v. Board of Education* (1954) the US Supreme Court eschewed the idea of the framers' intent guiding constitutional interpretation and ordered the desegregation of all public schools in the US. This precipitated immediate disobedience in the South and continuing resistance in many other parts of the country toward the idea of equality rights beyond the requirement of a colour-blind legal regime (Patterson

2001). If *Brown* signaled the conquest of legal equality, the continuing social inequality of the races exposes the limits of any model of rights and freedoms. Nevertheless, just as Thomas Jefferson insisted and as some justices of the US Supreme Court currently maintain (*Printz* 1997: 921), the US constitutional experience remains an important exemplar for the North American region and for the world.

Although it relaxed the scrutiny of social and economic legislation under the Fourteenth Amendment after the new deal crisis in 1937, the Supreme Court nevertheless continued to police legislative action that, in the famous words of Justice Oliver Wendell Holmes, "goes too far" (*Pennsylvania Coal* 1922). Legislatures, it has been said, must avoid "extreme forms of regulation" (Tushnet 2003: 65). According to this understanding of rights and freedoms, those modes of regulation that are considered deviations from some imagined norm are inherently suspect (Kennedy 2004: 176–77; Tarullo 1987). While courts will permit governments to regulate property for environmental purposes, for instance, they will discourage them "from being [as] aggressive about regulation as they might otherwise be" (Tushnet 2003: 61). This is most evident in the US Supreme Court's "regulatory takings" jurisprudence—cases concerning the regulation of property through land use, municipal, or environmental regulation—that give rise to some limitation on rights requiring the provision of just compensation. Though the doctrine is in much disarray, the Supreme Court will vindicate the interests of property claimants in all cases where there has been a physical invasion of private property or where regulation deprives land of all economically beneficial use (Been and Beauvais 2003: 60–61). In all other instances, it will undertake an ad hoc factual inquiry weighing, among other things, the "economic impact" of the regulation and the extent to which it interferes with "distinct investment-backed expectations" (*Penn Central* 1978: 124). Successful takings claims are hard to make, but property rights will be shielded when regulations "go too far." It is in the US, then, that courts have come closest to recognizing "a property right to an unchanging world" (Horwitz 1992: 151).

CANADA

The Canadian Constitution of 1867 was understood as representing a mixture of British parliamentary practice and US federalism. Power was divided between federal and provincial governments with a tilt decidedly in favour of the federal government in ways the US model did not. Divided authority, importantly, would accommodate the maintenance of a French-speaking majority in Québec by granting key jurisdiction in the area of "property and civil rights" to the provinces. Subject to the supervisory authority of the imperial Parliament sitting in Britain, each level of government had complete authority within its respective spheres of jurisdiction (*Hodge* 1883). As was said in Britain, so it could be said in Canada that, together, government could "make or unmake any law" (Dicey 1908) for there was no enumerated bill of rights to hamper legislative authority as in the US.

It was not until after World War II that provinces—first Ontario and then Saskatchewan—introduced human rights instruments prohibiting discriminatory treatment at the hands of government and private actors in the marketplace, for instance, when hiring employees or renting residential premises (Tarnopolsky 1975: 67). In 1959, the Canadian Parliament enacted the Canadian Bill of Rights, which prohibited discrimination and guaranteed certain fundamental liberties including freedom of speech, the rights of the criminal accused, and even a right to property. There were several flaws to this scheme, however. Like its provincial counterparts, this was an ordinary legislative enactment binding only upon the federal government (MacLennan 2003). Moreover, the judiciary interpreted the Canadian Bill of Rights as narrowly as possible; it was merely declaratory of existing rights—it did not create new rights and freedoms. This narrow construction prompted the observation that this was a "frozen" bill of rights. Even the property rights provision, an interest with which the Canadian judiciary would have been familiar, was read as being merely declaratory of the common law rule, discussed below, that governments could take property without compensation if they made their intention plain (*Authorson* 2003).

With the entrenchment of the Canadian Charter of Rights and Freedoms in 1982, rights and freedoms finally were granted recognition in constitutional text. The Charter guaranteed a number of fundamental freedoms, such as freedom of expression and religion (section 2); democratic rights (section 3); mobility rights (section 6); the right not to be deprived of life, liberty, and security of the person except in accordance with the "principles of fundamental justice" (section 7); and equality rights (section 15). The Charter also included several group-based collective rights. Thus, national minority language rights were addressed in provisions concerning official language (section 16) and minority education rights (section 23). The 1982 Constitution also included a section recognizing and affirming "existing Aboriginal and treaty rights" (section 35); not since the Royal Proclamation of 1763 had the Crown recognized Aboriginal rights in this way (see also Chapter 10 in this volume). The Canadian judiciary was much more responsive to this newly entrenched constitutional text and proceeded to test a variety of government actions against its strictures. Meanwhile, provincial and federal human rights codes complemented the Charter by continuing to prohibit discrimination in the private sector. Nevertheless, the Charter was marred at its inception by one significant fact, namely, the unanimous opposition of the Québec National Assembly to the new Constitution. This was not opposition to the guarantees of human rights and freedoms but to the manner in which the Constitution was imposed over the objections of provincial representatives from Canada's only province with a French-speaking majority (Schneiderman 1998).

Though 1982 heralded an entrenched-rights regime, Canadians were already familiar with the idea of rights and freedoms. This had to do not only with the proliferation of US cultural products within Canada but also with shared origins (with the exception of the province of Québec) in the Anglo-American tradition of the common law. These shared roots prompted some to liken the unwritten part of Canada's constitution to the written constitutional limitations in the US. "We," the constitutional historian W.P.M. Kennedy wrote of Canadians, "profess to find most emphatically in the common law what you profess to find in your constitution" (Kennedy 1932: 17). The idea of property rights, for instance, was a familiar notion in the Canadian legal system. As under the British common law from which Canadians derived their principles of property law, statutes interfering with private property rights were to be strictly construed. Any doubts or ambiguities found in statutory language were be construed against the legislature and in favour of property owners (Schneiderman 1996). This common law presumption gave expression to the supposition that legislatures were not inclined to confiscate property without making their intentions plainly manifest (*Manitoba Fisheries* 1978). The important distinction between this common law rule of statutory interpretation and the US constitutional rule, however, is that the Canadian rule may be overridden by legislators when their intentions are made clear and plain. In Canada, then, there is no constitutional requirement that property taken by the state be for a public purpose or that it be accompanied by the provision of just compensation (Lajoie 1971: 104).

There is one exception to this rule, and that is the constitutional requirement of compensation in the case of the taking of Aboriginal title. In *Delgamuukw* (1997), the Supreme Court of Canada recognized that where Aboriginal title has been infringed, "fair compensation will ordinarily be required" (1997, para. 165). This is the reverse of the constitutional position in the US where, paradoxically, courts have supported government claims that the taking of Aboriginal title does not give rise to the constitutional duty of compensation under the Fifth or Fourteenth Amendments (*Tee-Hit-Ton* 1955).

Having, for the most part, not bracketed economic subjects in ways Americans had done under their constitutional scheme (Forbath 1991; Lazare 1998: 32), economic alternatives could be the subject of national and subnational political debate in Canada. This institutional analysis helps to explain, alongside other explanations based on differences in political culture (Horowitz 1966), the wider spectrum of political alternatives available in Canada than in the US. It also helps to explain why Canadian political leaders, when they adopted a constitutional Charter in 1982, chose not to include property rights or what might be called "pure" economic rights—those protecting contracts or freedom of enterprise. It also is the case that Canadian political leaders chose not to entrench social rights, such as a right to food, shelter, or health care (Bakan and Schneiderman 1992). Instead, economic interests would receive protection indirectly, via provisions guaranteeing freedom of expression or liberty and security of the person (Bauman 1997). Nevertheless, every jurisdiction in Canada provides some procedure by which property owners will be compensated for the taking of real property. There is usually no compensation under statute, however, for "regulatory takings," that is, limitations of use or reduction in the value of property through regulation which, in the US, can give rise to a constitutional requirement of compensation. Only "confiscation" (Bauman 1994: 574) which amounts practically to an "acquisition" (*Mariner Real Estate* 1999) will give rise to the statutory requirement of compensation.

THE UNITED MEXICAN STATES

The Mexican Constitution of 1917 was born out of a different type of revolution than that of the US. Rather than consolidating only the power of political and economic elites, the Mexican Constitution also assuaged the demands of a peasant agrarian movement mobilized in the Revolution of 1910. In its first 29 articles, the 1917 Constitution guarantees individual rights associated with liberty, equality, due process rights, property rights, and social rights (Chapter 1). The framers of the Constitution understood these rights as not only declaratory of existing rights but as imposing a positive obligation on the state to make these rights available to all persons within Mexico (Carpizo 1969: 185–87). Notions of equality and liberty already had made an appearance in the 1857 Constitution (González 1999: 104–06), though they were omitted from the 1824 Constitution because the power to limit rights was reserved to the states (Fix-Zamudio and Fix-Fierro 1996: 80) in an argument reminiscent of US debates in 1787. There is little doubt that the framers were influenced by ideas expressed in the US Declaration of Independence and the US Constitution (Carpizo 1969: 188). The Mexican Constitution prohibits slavery and race discrimination (Article 1), guarantees a right to possess arms but only within one's domicile (Article 10), and provides for freedoms of the press (Article 7) and religion (Article 24). The guarantees of property and social rights, however, distinguish the Mexican frame of rights and liberties from its North American counterparts. The Constitution guarantees a right to education (Article 3) and labour rights (Article 123) and expressly recognizes the ability of the state to intervene in order to steer the national economy (Articles 25–28). It is Article 27, the clause that establishes property rights and the manner in which natural resources can be exploited, that deserves special mention for the purposes of this chapter.

Property is considered part of the national patrimony. Original ownership of land and water belongs to the state, while private property is expected to serve "social functions." Property can be expropriated "for a public purpose and with compensation." The state also "has at all times the right to impose on private property the modalities so required by the public interest, and to regulate the manner in which the natural resources are to be exploited for the common social benefit" (Article 27, paras. 1–3). The idea that property serves a social function derives from the work of French sociologist Auguste Comte (1851) and legal theorist Léon Duguit (1918). The authority of the state was justified by the function it performs, and according to Duguit, that function was to provide for certain social needs. Private property, too, was justifiable to the extent that it served and was limited by this social mission (Duguit 1918: 13, 295).

Article 27 also restricts ownership of property to Mexican nationals, unless foreign nationals agree to "consider themselves Mexican citizens" and "do not seek the protection of their government in relation to the acquired property." Should a foreign national seek the aid of the home state in any dispute with Mexico, the consequences are harsh: they "forfeit the acquired property" (Article 27, para. 9; Sandriño 1994: 286). The treatment of foreign nationals along these lines usually is traceable back to the work of Argentinian jurist Carlos Calvo (1887). Precipitated by the dismal Latin American experience with interventionist international capital, Calvo argued that the countries of Latin America were entitled to the same degree of respect for their internal sovereignty as were the United States of America and the countries of Europe (1887: 266). Among Calvo's precepts was the proposition that states should be free, within reason, from interference in the conduct of their domestic policy. From this, he could argue that foreign nationals could not lay claim to greater protection in their disputes with sovereign states than the citizens of these same countries (Garcia-Mora 1950). Foreign nationals who chose to establish themselves within the territorial confines of the host state—through direct investment, for instance—were entitled to no greater protection from state action than were those nationals residing within the acting state (Shea 1955: 19). These precepts came to be reflected in the Mexican

Constitution's "Calvo clause," which prohibits foreign investors from seeking the protection of their home state in any dispute with the Mexican host state.

Beginning with small-scale expropriations of land after 1917 to the full-scale expropriation of the petroleum industry in 1938 (US Congress 1963: 10–12), Article 27 provided the constitutional basis for a "strong interventionist state" (Hamilton 1982: 63). It was this constitutional ideology that precipitated the stand-off between Mexican President Cárdenas and US Secretary of State Cordell Hull over whether the standards of international law mandated the payment of compensation in the event of expropriation (Mexico 1938). Article 27 also generated the constitutional basis for communally held lands or *ejidos*. Though the 1917 Constitution largely ignored the demands of dispossessed Indigenous peoples in Mexico (Vargas 1994: 42), Article 27 recognized the "legal personality" of collectively organized communities to hold communal lands for agricultural or commercial purposes (para. 7). This gave rise to a body of agrarian law that entitles Mexican nationals, and Indigenous peoples in particular, to obtain land from the government in the form of *ejidos* (Vargas 1994: 47; Fernández 1965: 160–61).

Throughout much of the twentieth century, despite a constitutional framework of both individual and social rights, political power largely was unchecked by constitutional constraints. With the ascendance of President Salinas (1988–94), the commencement of negotiations toward NAFTA precipitated a series of constitutional, legislative, and administrative reforms (Clarkson and Palacios 2000). Human rights abuses by federal and state police, attracting national and international attention, moved the Salinas administration to begin to address human rights violations (Lutz *et al*. 1991), creating the National Human Rights Commission by presidential decree in 1990. The Commission attained constitutional status in 1992 (Article 102[b]) and further independence by constitutional amendments in 1999.

NAFTA precipitated other reforms, both statutory and constitutional. NAFTA's investor rights (discussed in the next section), impose a variety of disciplinary measures on party states, including stringent compensation standards in the event of an expropriation that are enforceable before international trade tribunals. These provisions appear incongruent with the Calvo Clause and other aspects of Mexico's "social" state. In order to avert legal uncertainty, the government of President Salinas issued a number of informal constitutional edicts in order to neutralize the full effect of Article 27 and to assuage US and Canadian concerns. Salinas guaranteed that NAFTA would not be subject to constitutional attack (Erfani 1995: 177; Daly 1994: 1189) and reassured investors by enacting a "Law Regarding the Making of Treaties" that empowered the state to negotiate international treaties with enforceable dispute settlement mechanisms (Cánovas 1992: 391). The Mexican House of Representatives, in addition, declared that submission of disputes to international tribunals "is not, in any manner, an invocation of diplomatic protection by a foreign government" and, thereby, in contravention of the Calvo Clause (Cánovas 1992: 391).

Numerous constitutional amendments were undertaken in the run-up to NAFTA (Ayllón 1999: 331; Huerta and Lujambio 1994: 64), and though the Calvo Clause was not directly altered, other key parts of Article 27 were amended. These amendments, in part, provoked the Zapatista National Liberation Army (EZLN) to armed rebellion in the state of Chiapas on New Year's Day 1994, the same day NAFTA entered into force. Article 27, as we have seen, is the constitutional foundation for property rights, both public and private. President Salinas radically altered Article 27 in 1992, claiming chronic "underusage" of collective lands while welcoming the introduction of high-volume agricultural exports to the US and Canada (Smith 1992: 20). The communal property provisions of Article 27 were amended to permit individual property holding, to relax limits on the numbers of acres that could be held, and to grant legal capacity to *ejidatarios* to enter into commercial or industrial ventures with third parties (Vargas 1994: 21). It is no coincidence, then, that the Zapatistas insisted that the Article 27 amendments be repealed and that the "right to land ... once again be part of our constitution" (Vargas 1994: 75).

The New Model Rules of NAFTA's Investment Chapter

In previous work (Schneiderman 2000, 2004) I have argued, as have others (Clarkson 2003; McBride 2003), that NAFTA's investment chapter (Chapter 11) constitutes a regime for the protection of rights familiar to national constitutional systems. Tantamount to a bill of rights for investors, the investment chapter entitles investors to sue state parties for damages before international trade tribunals for violation of the investment protections contained in NAFTA. Similar disciplines can be found in over 2,500 bilateral investment treaties entered into by countries from every corner of the globe. It is no exaggeration to say that a worldwide web of investor rights is now in place.

Many of the obligations undertaken in NAFTA's investment chapter are organized around the idea of "non-discrimination" (Jackson 1997). States may not distinguish, for the purposes of legal regulation, between domestic and foreign investors. Other rules mandate not just equality of treatment but place substantive limits on state control. NAFTA's takings rule, for instance, prohibits measures that "directly or indirectly" expropriate or nationalize investment interests and measures "tantamount to" expropriation. The rule has been described by one commentator as the "single most important goal" of the US bilateral investment treaty program (Vandevelde 1992, 1998). The object is not merely to prohibit outright takings of property by the state but to combat "regulatory" expropriations—measures that have such impact on an investment interest that they are equivalent to a taking (Vandevelde 1992: 121). This rule is intended to catch regulatory changes that, in the famous words of Justice Oliver Wendell Holmes, "go too far" (*Pennsylvania Coal* 1922). The underlying premise is that governments cannot be trusted to intervene in markets; rather, they should be expected to perform only minimal regulatory functions.

The objective of US foreign trade policy, according to Vandevelde, was to develop a body of state practice establishing the highest standards in regard to expropriations that would rise to the level of international law (1992: 25). It should not be controversial to say that the rule is informed by the US constitutional experience under the Fifth and Fourteenth Amendments (Wild 1939: 10). Attempts at this kind of "transference" of local rules to the global plane have not been uncommon (Sornorajah 1994: 294; Santos 1995). The NAFTA rule goes substantially further, however, as it includes within the scope of protected investments not just real property interests (as in the US) but almost every kind of economic interest, including ownership of shares, stocks and bonds, rights under contract, and intellectual property rights. It does not merely replicate the local rule, then, but is intended to go somewhat further. As Rittich notes in a similar context, "the most important effect may be to discredit local deviations and alternatives, including pre-existing institutional systems and structures." The real object may be to "cabin the available responses to social and economic dilemmas and place constraints on alternative ways of organizing economic and social life" (Rittich 2002: 96).

The NAFTA prohibition on takings grants exceptional rights to foreign investors. Should an investment have been subjected to expropriation and measures "tantamount to" expropriation, NAFTA entitles investors to sue before international trade tribunals. The awards of these arbitration panels are then enforceable within the domestic courts of the offending state party. The prohibition is unique, in that the usual means of enforcement of international law obligations is via states, not via private enforcement (Sands 2005: 117ff; Roth 1949: 62).

Given the variety of measures that may be caught by NAFTA's takings rule, it comes as little surprise that business firms have invoked the prohibition (or its earlier version in the Canada-US Free Trade Agreement) to challenge market regulations that impair a variety of investment interests. I have traced a number of these claims in earlier work (Schneiderman 1996, 2000), including, for instance, a challenge by large US tobacco manufacturers against Canada for threats to mandate the "plain packaging" of cigarettes by Parliament. A small number of trade panel decisions under NAFTA's Chapter 11 have been rendered to date. Some guidance has been provided by panel rulings, and I turn to one such ruling in the next section.

If in the contemporary world, the outright taking of title by the state is less likely to occur than in the past—via programs for the nationalization of private industry, for instance, though they are being contemplated by governments in Bolivia and Venezuela—takings problems will arise in a wide variety of unanticipated scenarios. Consider circumstances where a foreign investor establishes an investment, perhaps with encouragement of the host state. What is the liability of the host state when the established investment gives rise to vociferous local opposition? More specifically, what is the relationship between local rules governing the conduct of foreign investors and NAFTA's rules for the protection of foreign investment? In order to explore these questions, it is useful to examine the first case in which investor rights were invoked successfully by a foreign investor against Mexico: the Metalclad case.

The Metalclad Case[5]

One of the few NAFTA investor-rights cases to have made it through the arbitration process, including subsequent review of that decision by a Canadian court in British Columbia, is *Metalclad v. The United Mexican States* (2000). The Metalclad Corporation of Newport Beach, California purchased in 1993, via its US and Mexican subsidiaries, the Mexican company COTERIN. COTERIN owned and previously operated a waste management and landfill site in the town of Guadalcazar in the Mexican state of San Luis Potosi. COTERIN's operation of the site had raised serious concern for each level of government. The company had improperly stored hazardous waste and failed to contain leakage into local water supplies. Citizens blockaded the road leading to the plant in September 1991, demanding immediate inspection of the facility (Wheat 1995). Federal investigation led to the immediate closing of the plant by order of the Mexican government. Metalclad was intent on redeveloping COTERIN's hazardous waste management facility site, but when the company announced it was taking over operations, nearby *ejidos* mobilized in opposition.

With the encouragement of representatives of the Mexican federal government, Metalclad rehabilitated the Guadalcazar site (United Mexican States 2001). Metalclad, the company claimed, was assured by federal authorities that all necessary permits were in place and that local permission was not required. However, as the company had not applied for the requisite municipal permit, the town of Guadalcazar ordered a halt to construction in October 1994. Metalclad considered challenging the shut-down order but, instead, applied for the permit in November and promptly resumed construction (United Mexican States 2001: 21). Without the consent of the proper authorities, the hazardous waste site opened ten months later, though Guadalcazar had denied Metalclad's construction permit. The municipality cited earlier denials to COTERIN in 1991 and 1992 for similar permits and also took notice of the "unanimous support for the Council's decision to deny the Construction permit as was evidenced in the public session held by this Council" (Azuela 2004: 29–30). The following year, and only three days before the expiry of his term in 1996, the state governor issued an ecological decree declaring the hazardous waste facility site part of a natural area for the protection of rare cactus. Metalclad claimed that these municipal and state actions effectively put a halt to their proposed multi-million dollar operation.

The municipality refused to reconsider its decision, and so Metalclad proceeded to challenge the decision in Mexican federal court under the *judicio de amparo*, a legal remedy, influenced by the US practice of judicial review, available in federal courts to enforce the Mexican Constitution (Karst and Rosenn 1975: 127). The federal court denied Metalclad's application as the company had failed to exhaust all available remedies—the company had not made application to the State of San Luis Potosi Administrative Tribunal, a legal prerequisite under *amparo* law (Article 73, section XV). Metalclad appealed this denial of *amparo* to the Supreme Court of Justice of Mexico. The municipality also commenced its own *amparo* application action against the federal Ministry of the Environment and Natural Resources. Guadalcazar claimed that the federal agency involved had no authority to enter into agreements with Metalclad without the requisite local permits. An interim order was granted, and Metalclad's operation suspended, but the municipality ultimately lost on the merits, and the order was denied. A decision never was rendered in Metalclad's application, as the company abandoned domestic legal proceedings in October 1996 in favour of a NAFTA Chapter 11 suit. The company alleged violations of the takings rule and of other related provisions in NAFTA, including a denial of the minimum standard of treatment required under international law. The arbitration panel agreed with the company on both counts and awarded the investor US$16.6 million in damages.

The panel, headed by Cambridge University scholar Eli Lauterpacht, found that the Mexican federal government was accountable for the acts of its subnational governments (*Metalclad* 2000: para. 73). Of great concern to the panel was the absence of clear standards that would be applied by the municipality when deciding whether to issue a construction permit. There "should be no room for doubt and uncertainty" in regard to legal requirements, the panel ruled. Once "authorities of the central government of any Party ... become aware of any scope for misunderstanding or confusion in this connection, it is their duty to ensure that the correct position is promptly determined and clearly stated so that investors can proceed with all appropriate expedition in the confident belief that they are acting in accordance with all relevant laws" (*Metalclad* 2000: para. 76). Ultimately, it was the responsibility of the federal government—the level of government that had signed the NAFTA treaty—to ensure that subnational governments had clear and transparent rules in this regard. This lack of transparency, predictability, and procedural fairness (Metalclad was given no notice of the town council meeting where the construction permit was denied) amounted to a denial of "treatment in accordance with international law, including fair and equitable treatment" (*Metalclad* 2000: para. 100). Among the problems with this part of the ruling is the fact that the panel read into Chapter 11's requirements obligations that arise in other parts of NAFTA (namely, the transparency obligations that arise in Chapter 18). This part of the ruling was subsequently overturned by a Canadian court on appeal (*United Mexican States* 2001). This is because NAFTA entitles states to seek review of NAFTA panel rulings, and, as Vancouver was the site of the Metalclad arbitration, the state of Mexico applied to a British Columbia Court to review its decision.

The arbitration panel also discussed the expropriations claim. By "permitting or tolerating" the "unfair and inequitable treatment" already identified, Mexico was held to have "participated and acquiesced" in the denial of Metalclad's rights. In this way, Mexico had "taken a measure tantamount to expropriation" (*Metalclad* 2000: para. 104). The panel added that the issuance of the governor's ecological decree alone would have amounted to an expropriation requiring compensation (*Metalclad* 2000: para. 111). It also explained what amounts to a taking under NAFTA. The rule caught not only the outright seizures of property by the host state—this was the most obvious case—but also "covert or incidental interference with the use of property which has the effect of depriving the owner, in whole or in significant part, of the use or reasonably-to-be-expected economic benefit of property even if not necessarily to the obvious benefit of the host State" (*Metalclad* 2000: para. 103). Non-discriminatory exercises of regulatory power could give rise to compensation under NAFTA when the regulation wholly or significantly deprives investors of reasonably expected returns on that investment. This version of NAFTA's takings rule strikingly resembles criteria taken into account by US courts when determining whether a measure gives rise to the requirement of compensation under the US Constitution (*Penn Central* 1978: 124; Been and Beauvais 2003: 62).

Yet the panel made little mention of the troubles that gave rise to the local populace's opposition to Metalclad's reopening of the COTERIN operation. The local opposition expressed by nearby *ejidos* was entirely foreseeable given the hazardous way in which COTERIN previously had managed the waste site. Metalclad was pressed to move its waste facility to an alternative site when a new state governor took office in 1993 (before NAFTA entered into force), but the company held steadfast (Tamayo 2001: 76). Nor would the panel accept that Metalclad was aware that municipal permits were required for this type of operation (Tamayo 2001: 77). COTERIN previously had been denied municipal construction permits, and these denials were in the hands of Metalclad personnel (Posadas 2000), though this was denied by the company (*Metalclad* 2000: para. 52). The panel would not admit, then, that local *ejido* resistance to the operation of the facility on public health grounds and the requirement of a municipal construction permit in order to proceed were reasonable investor expectations.

Even more surprising is the manner in which the panel dismissed Mexico's rejoinder that there was no denial of the minimum standard of treatment required by international law. Mexico claimed that the municipality was acting within its constitutional authority when it refused to issue a construction permit. This was denied by Metalclad's expert on Mexican law (a 1994 law graduate of the University of Arizona who was pursuing a master of laws degree in Monterrey, Mexico) (*Metalclad* 2000: para. 81; United Mexican States 2001: 138). The panel mysteriously preferred the company's interpretation. Referring to a federal law that grants power to authorize hazardous waste sites to the federal government, the panel was of the view that federal authority "was controlling and [that] the authority of the municipality only extended to appropriate construction considerations." In other words, Guadalcazar had no constitutional authority to refuse a permit other than for reasons having to do with the "physical construction or defects in that site" (*Metalclad* 2000: para. 86). The municipality had no constitutional authority, the panel held, even to take into account environmental concerns in the issuance of a municipal construction permit. Whatever the procedural irregularities that gave rise to Metalclad's claim, it is remarkable that the panel, sitting as if it were a constitutional court, felt that it could arrive at definitive conclusions regarding the constitutional authority of Mexican municipal governments precisely opposite to those claimed by the state party itself.[6] The Constitution clearly authorizes municipalities to issue construction permits and to "control and supervise the use of land within their own territories" (Article 115, sec. V).[7] Moreover, state governments have constitutional authority to establish municipalities and to delegate the exercise of municipal power (United Mexican States 2001: paras. 415–17). State law authorized the municipality to take into account environmental impacts in the issuance of municipal construction permits (United Mexican States 2001: 135–36).

Would the claim have fared as well under Mexican law? Metalclad had wagered, probably correctly, that Mexican law would not entitle the company to compensation for sunk costs and lost profits and so abandoned the Mexican legal proceedings. It is not certain that Metalclad's legal proceedings would have resulted entirely in failure, however. Some legal commentators are of the view that the municipality's decision not to grant the construction permit "was lacking in the most basic legal requirement" expected of any legal decree, including the constitutional rights to a hearing (Article 14)[8] and to legal reasons (Article 16),[9] which are expected to accompany every decree or decision issued by a competent authority. According to the federal environmental prosecutor at the relevant time, "under no circumstances" would the municipality's decision have passed constitutional muster (Azuela 2004: 30).[10] If Metalclad had pursued a remedy before the state courts of San Luis Potosi or in federal courts under *amparo* proceedings, the municipality may have been ordered to institute fairer proceedings and to issue more compelling reasons. Neither of these remedies would have ensured large amounts of compensation be paid to Metalclad.

What about the company's claim of expropriation? It is unlikely that it would have succeeded in securing compensation for the loss of its investment. The refusal to issue a construction permit by a municipality in Mexico probably does not amount to an expropriation requiring the provision of compensation under Mexican law (Perezcano 2002: 216). With regard to the ecological decree issued by the state governor nine months after the municipality's decision, the answer perhaps is less clear. It should be borne in mind, however, that Metalclad proceeded with construction when it was aware that municipal permits had been required in the past and in the face of a shutdown order issued by the municipality in October 1994 for failure to make application. If there were an expropriation, damages presumably would be limited to those legitimately suffered prior to remediation and construction of the site. Property rights, as we have seen, are secured by Article 27 of the Constitution, which provides that expropriations can only be done for (1) a public purpose and (2) with compensation. The public purpose requirement would be satisfied if one of the objectives of the *Ley de Expropiacion* of 1936 are met, and these purposes include preserving "public peace," and "conserving" or "preventing the destruction of natural resources."

Article 27 also lays out the method of determining compensation owed, which "will be determined by the value that the property has under the records of the fiscal and/or revenue authorities." There is no role for judicial oversight of this process except for the valuation of "renovations or additions made to the property after the determination of the fiscal value of the property" (Article 27, para. 9, sec. VI). Mexican law originally called for compensation less than that required under NAFTA (NAFTA calls for full market value in funds fully transferable and immediately realizable). In order to accommodate the accession of Mexico to NAFTA's strict compensation requirements, the method of valuation as reflected in the *Ley de Expropiacion* was modified by the Mexican Congress in 1993. Compensation for expropriation would now be determined "according to the market value of the expropriated property, and in no case can the compensation paid be lower than the fiscal value that appears on the records of the fiscal and/or revenue authorities" (Article 10). Representative Alfonso Rivera Domínguez acknowledged during debate in the House of Representatives that the amendment probably would prevent future abuses by public authorities. But this amendment was precipitated by NAFTA's strictures, and, in this way, "Mexican negotiators were consciously negotiating against a textual provision of Mexican law and therefore they were compromising *ex ante* the amendment we have before us today without informing the Mexican people ..." (Mexico 1993). As Grinspun and Kreklewich have noted, the neo-liberal restructuring associated with NAFTA is largely elite-driven and undemocratic; it is a "conditioning framework" intended to restrict policy choices at the local level that "would not otherwise meet with general support" (Grinspun and Kreklewich 1994: 35, 36). Though Representative Domínguez expressed a similar concern, the amendment passed in the Mexican Congress.

It is interesting to note that, even under US constitutional law, it is unlikely that Metalclad would have succeeded in its takings suit. Courts there are loathe to award damages where developers have undertaken construction without the requisite building permits, even where considerable sums of money have been expended. According to Been and Beauvais, "US Courts are wary of claims that property has been taken if the property at issue was developed either without the required approvals or in reliance upon erroneous approvals by government agencies" (2003: 78). Nor would the governor's ecological decree necessarily have resulted in compensation. It is not clear that the decree satisfied the categorical rule of denying all economically beneficial use—it is not clear, in other words, that the site could not be put to other economically valuable uses (Been and Beauvais 2003: 63, fn. 153).

The implications of the panel's ruling are mitigated somewhat by an appeal of that ruling launched by Mexico and heard by the Canadian court. Justice Tysoe reversed only that part of the panel's ruling that imposed transparency obligations under the minimum standard of treatment and expropriations rule (United Mexican States 2001: paras. 72, 79). The panel's findings regarding the capacity of Mexican local governments to consider environmental impacts were rendered immaterial. The state parties to NAFTA made the same point as Justice Tysoe in an "interpretive note" issued two months after the court's ruling (NAFTA Free Trade Commission 2001). Justice Tysoe confirmed the panel ruling, however, in so far as the panel found a compensable taking by reason of the governor's ecological decree (United Mexican States 2001: para. 100). The panel's very broad interpretation of the takings rule—including "incidental interference" that has the effect of depriving owners of a "significant part" of the "use or reasonably-to-be-expected economic benefit of property"—was shielded from judicial review, however, as this was a "question of law" beyond the purview of a reviewing court. Justice Tysoe warned, though, that the panel's interpretation was sufficiently broad "to include legitimate rezoning of property by a municipality or other rezoning authority" (United Mexican States 2001: para. 99). Mexico subsequently delivered a cheque in the amount of US$15.6 million to Metalclad (*New York Times* 2001b). In the result, Mexico's version of property rights, bounded by conceptions of the social function of property and the public interest, were overtaken by the narrower and individualistic version reflected in NAFTA's takings rule. The health of local residents, given expression through both the constitutional rule and the machinery of local self-government, were trumped by the economic imperatives of continental integration.

Conclusion

The object of this chapter has been, first, to explore some of the differences and similarities in the regimes for the protection of rights and freedoms in the three national constitutional systems of North America. In the US, one finds one of the most property-protective constitutional systems in the world. In Canada, by contrast, private property rights usually are respected by government though not the subject of superordinate constitutional protection; only the collective property rights of Aboriginal peoples in Canada attract constitutional scrutiny. Lastly, in Mexico property rights are recognized in the Constitution and are cabined by public interest requirements. The collective property rights of Indigenous peoples in Mexico were also protected until the constitutional amendments precipitated by NAFTA. The second object has been to look for indicators of regional convergence within and across these systems. For these purposes, I contrasted the treatment of property rights in these countries with the rights accorded to foreign investors under NAFTA. Indications are that the three states are converging toward a single standard for the treatment of investment interests covered by NAFTA and that the standard toward which all are pointing resembles, in most ways, the US constitutional system. This is a system premised on a distrust of government and structured so as to grant enforceable legal entitlements to powerful economic actors. The regional rule, however, extends beyond the kinds of interests usually protected by US constitutional law, namely, those holding interests in real property. Instead, contractual expectations, shareholder interests, and all varieties of economic interests are protected by NAFTA's foreign investment chapter.

This convergence toward a single set of standards for the protection of property and economic rights is not only occurring within North America. By virtue of the web of regional and bilateral investment treaties (BITs), national states all over the world are committed to upholding similar constitution-like standards for the protection and promotion of foreign investment. It is the case, however, that the states of North America are on the front line of this movement. The Metalclad decision reveals precisely how new regional/transnational standards are encroaching on national rights regimes and usurping previously agreed-upon national commitments. Nor is it likely that these protections will remain available only to foreign investors. Proponents of this movement admit that there is no reason why such rules "cannot protect domestic as well as foreign investors." Vandervelde goes on, "This would ensure genuine investment neutrality and create a host state constituency, in support of an enduring liberal investment regime" (Vandevelde 1998: 639). Limiting the regulatory capacity of states via constitutional rights is freely acknowledged as the end game.

This convergent tendency is not the inevitable outcome of the regionalization of investor rights, however. One could imagine alternative outcomes; after all, there are three constitutional systems capable of vying for supremacy. Moreover, there are conflicting national constitutional commitments—commitments, as in Mexico, to social rights—that rub against this trend. National constitutional courts in each of the countries will be duty-bound to uphold these commitments when they conflict with regional obligations arising under NAFTA or under other commitments demanded by institutions promoting economic globalization. Consider, for instance, the series of decisions issued by the Hungarian Constitutional Court in 1995 that declared various parts of an IMF-imposed austerity program inconsistent with the Hungarian constitution. The Court shielded cuts to a variety of social benefits such as health insurance, pensions, maternity benefits, and child support (Scheppele 2004: 1945). Other courts may find it difficult, however, to resist these kinds of pressures (Schneiderman 2002; Kelsey 1999).

The problem is the presence of a strong and universalistic discourse of property rights, foundational to one of the oldest constitutional regimes in the world, and marketed by the most powerful economic and military actor in the contemporary world. Along such a path, human rights and fundamental freedoms become tools of emancipation for only the small, economically advantaged strata of society. The challenge is to devise paths that both are more inclusive and more faithful to the idea of the human dignity and equal worth of all persons across the region as well as globally.

Notes

1   I would like to thank Rodrigo Garcia Galindo for excellent research assistance and for translation of key documents. I also am pleased to acknowledge the support of the Social Sciences and Humanities Research Council.

2   This is not to say that there is no specific jurisprudence emerging out of the UN system. The Human Rights Committee, for instance, operating under the International Covenant on Civil and Political Rights (enshrining rights under the Universal Declaration of Human Rights of 1948) is developing concrete formulations of rights intended to bind states across the UN system. See Heinski and Scheinin 2003.

3   I do not take up here the inter-American system for the protection of human rights operating under the auspices of the Organization of American States (OAS). Due to its infancy and its limited resources, it is too early to state the extent to which it will develop into a binding human rights system for the hemisphere. See Harris 1998.

4   For a discussion of classical liberal legal thought, see Horwitz 1992.

5   Part of this chapter is drawn from Schneiderman 2004.

6   Consider that these sorts of panels are composed usually of international trade lawyers chosen from a very short list of qualified personnel, namely, those who value and promote the logic of investment rules disciplines (Sornarajah 2000).

7   Article 15, section V(f), more particularly, provides: "The Municipalities, in accordance with the Federal and State laws, are authorized to ... f) grant construction licenses and permits."

8   Article 14 provides: "No law can be applied retroactively in prejudice of any person." "No one can be deprived of life, freedom, of its property, possessions or rights, without being afforded a trial before a previously established court, in which all the formalities of the due process of law are complied with, and in accordance with laws issued before the matter at bar."

9   Article 16 provides: "No one can be disturbed in its person, family, domicile, documents or possession, without a written decree of a competent authority, who establishes the legal cause and motive of the procedure."

10 Elizarrarás takes note of the municipality's "regrettable negligence and legal inexperience," which were key factors leading to the arbitration panel's rejection of the municipality's authority (Elizarrarás 2001: 556).

References

Arendt, Hannah. 1963. *On Revolution*. New York: The Viking Press.

Azuela, Antonio. 2004. "Con olor a NAFTA. El caso Metalclad y la nueva geografía del Derecho Mexicano." Paper prepared for the International Congress "Culturas y Sistemas Jurídicos Comparados." Legal Research Institute, Universidad Nacional Autónoma de México, Mexico City, January.

Bakan, Joel, and David Schneiderman (Eds.). 1992. *Social Justice and the Constitution: Perspectives on a Social Union for Canada*. Ottawa: Carleton UP.

Balibar, Etienne. 1991. "Racism and Nationalism." In Etienne Balibar and Immanuel Wallerstein (eds.), *Race, Nation, Class*. London: Verso. 37–67.

Bauman, R.J., 1994. "Exotic Expropriations: Government Action and Compensation." *The Advocate* 52: 561–79.

Bauman, Richard. 1997. "Business, Economic Rights, and the Charter." In David Schneiderman and Kate Sutherland (eds.), *Charting the Consequences: The Impact of Charter Rights on Canadian Law and Politics*. Toronto: U of Toronto P.

Baxi, Upendra. 2006. *The Future of Human Rights*. 2nd ed. New Delhi: Oxford UP.

Been, Vicki, and Joel C. Beauvais. 2003. "The Global Fifth Amendment: NAFTA's Investment Protections and the Misguided Quest for an International Regulatory Takings Doctrine." *New York University Law Review* 78: 30–143.

Bourdieu, Pierre. 2000. *Pascalian Meditations*. Trans. R. Nice. Stanford: Stanford UP.

Brown, Wendy. 1995. *States of Injury: Power and Freedom in Late Modernity*. Princeton, NJ: Princeton UP.

Calvo, Charles. 1887. *Le droit international théorique et pratique*. 4th ed. Paris: Guillaumin.

Cánovas, Antonio Garza. 1992. "Introductory Note." *International Legal Materials* 31: 390.

Carpizo, Jorge. 1969. *La Constitución Mexicana de 1917*. Mexico City: Universidad Nacional Autónoma de México.

Choudhry, Sujit. 2004. "The Lochner Era and Comparative Constitutionalism." *International Journal of Constitutional Law* 2: 1–55.

Clarkson, Stephen. 2003. *Uncle Sam and US: Globalization, Neoconservatism, and the Canadian State*. Toronto: U of Toronto P.

Clarkson, Stephen, and Olga Palacios. 2000. "Reform From Without and Reform From Within: NAFTA and the WTO's Role in Transforming Mexico's Economic System." In Joseph S. Tulchin and Andrew D. Selee (eds.), *Mexico at the Millennium*. Boulder, CO: Lynne Rienner Publishers.

Comte, M. Auguste. 1851. *Cours de politique positive*. Vol. 1. Paris: L. Mathias.

Cook, Rebecca, and Bernard Dickens. 2003. "Human Rights Dynamics of Abortion Law Reform." *Human Rights Quarterly* 25,1: 1–59.

Daintith, Terence. 2004. "The Constitutional Protection of Economic Rights." *International Journal of Constitutional Law* 2: 56–90.

Daly, Justine. 1994. "Has Mexico Crossed the Border on State Responsibility for Economic Injury to Aliens? Foreign Investment and the Calvo Clause in Mexico After NAFTA." *St. Mary's Law Journal* 25: 1147–93.

Diamond, Martin. 1992. "What the Framers Meant by Federalism." In Martin Diamond (ed.), *As Far as Republican Principles Will Admit*. Washington, DC: The AEI Press. 93–107.

Dicey, A.V. 1908. *Introduction to the Study of the Law of the Constitution*. 7th ed. London: Macmillan.

Duguit, Léon. 1918. *Manuel de droit constitutionnel*. 3rd ed. Paris: Ancienne Librairie Fontemoing.

Durkheim, Emile. 1957. *Professional Ethics and Civic Morals*. London and New York: Routledge.

Elizarrarás, Miguel A. Velázquez. 2001. "La controversia en materia de inversiones entre Metalclad Corporation y los Estados Unidos Mexicanos, a la luz del capitulo XI del Tratado de Libre Comercio de América del Norte." *Anuario Mexicano de Derecho Internacional* 1: 543–56.

Ely, Richard T. (1998). *The Guardian of Every Other Right: A Constitutional History of Property Rights*. New York: Oxford UP.

Erfani, Julie A. 1995. *The Paradox of the Mexican State: Rereading Sovereignty from Independence to NAFTA*. Boulder, CO: Lynne Reinner Publishers.

Fernández, Ramón y Fernández. 1965. "The Mexican Agrarian Reform: Backgrounds, Accomplishments, and Problems." In T. Lynne Smith (ed.), *Agrarian Reform in Latin America*. New York: Alfred A. Knopf.

Fix Zamudio, Héctor, and Héctor Fix Fierro. 1996. *El Consejo de la Judicatura*. Mexico: Universidad Nacional Autónoma de México.

Forbath, William E. 1991. *Law and the Shaping of the American Labor Movement*. Cambridge, MA: Harvard UP.

Garcia-Mora, Manuel R. 1950. "The Calvo Clause in Latin American Constitutions and International Law." *Marquette Law Review* 33: 205–19.

Gillman, Howard. 1993. *The Constitution Besieged: The Rise and Decline of Lochner Era Police Powers Jurisprudence*. Durham, NC: Duke UP.

González, María del Refugio. 1999. "Las transiciones jurídicas en México del siglo XIX a la revolución." In María del Refugio González and Sergio López Ayllón (eds.), *Trasiciones y diseños institucionales*. Mexico: Universidad Nacional Autónoma de México. 85–134.

Grinspun, Ricardo, and Robert Kreklewich. 1994. "Consolidating Neoliberal Reforms: 'Free Trade' as a Conditioning Framework." *Studies in Political Economy* 43: 33–61.

Habermas, Jurgen. 1998. *Between Facts and Norms: Contributions to a Discourse Theory of Law and Democracy*. Trans. William Rehg. Cambridge, MA: The MIT Press.

Hamilton, Alexander, James Madison, and John Jay. 1961. *The Federalist Papers*. Ed. C. Rossiter. New York: New American Library.

Hamilton, Nora. 1982. *The Limits of State Autonomy: Post-Revolutionary Mexico*. Princeton, NJ: Princeton UP.

Harris, David. 1998. "Regional Protection of Human Rights: The Inter-American Achievement." In D. Harris and S. Livingstone (eds.), *The Inter-American System of Human Rights*. Oxford: Clarendon Press.

Hart, H.L.A. 1994. *The Concept of Law*. 2nd ed. Oxford: Oxford UP.

Hay, Colin. 2000. "Contemporary Capitalism, Globalization, Regionalization, and the Persistence of National Variation." *Review of International Studies* 26: 509–31.

Heinski, Raija, and Martin Scheinin (Eds.). 2003. *Leading Cases of the Human Rights Committee*. Turku, Finland: Institute for Human Rights.

Horowitz, G. 1966. "Conservatism, Liberalism, and Socialism in Canada: An Interpretation." *Canadian Journal of Economics and Political Science* 32: 141–71.

Horwitz, Morton J. 1992. *The Transformation of American Law, 1870–1960: The Crisis of Legal Orthodoxy*. New York: Oxford UP.

Huerta, Carla, and Alonso Lujambio. 1994. "NAFTA: Recent Constitutional Amendments, Sovereignty Today, and the Future of Federalism in Mexico." *Constitutional Forum* 5: 63–67.

Jackson, John H. 1997. *The World Trading System: Law and Policy of International Economic Relations*. 2nd ed. Cambridge: The MIT Press.

Karst, Kenneth, and Keith S. Rosenn (Eds.). 1975. *Law and Development in Latin America*. Berkeley, CA: U of California P.

Kelsey, Jane. 1999. "Global Economic Policy-Making: A New Constitutionalism?" *Otago Law Review* 9,3: 535–55.

Kennedy, David. 2004. *The Dark Side of Virtue: Reassessing International Humanitarianism*. Princeton, NJ: Princeton UP.

Kennedy, Duncan. 1997. *A Critique of Adjudication: Fin de Siècle*. Cambridge, MA: Harvard UP.

Kennedy, William P.M. 1932. *Some Aspects of the Theories and Workings of Constitutional Law*. London: The Macmillan Company.

Lajoie, Andrée. 1971. *Expropriation et fédéralisme au Canada*. Montreal: Les Presses de l'Université de Montréal.

Lazare, Daniel. 1998. "America the Undemocratic." *New Left Review* 232 (November-December): 3–40.

López-Ayllón, Sergio. 2000. "Globalización' y transición del Estado nacional." In María del Refugio González and Sergio López Ayllón (eds.), *Trasiciones y diseños institucionales*. Mexico: Universidad Nacional Autónoma de México. 301–42.

Lutz, Ellen, Clifford Rohde, Peter D. Bell, and Ivan Arellanes. 1991. *Unceasing Abuses: Human Rights in Mexico One Year After the Introduction of Reforms*. New York: Americas Watch.

MacLennan, Christopher. 2003. *Toward the Charter: Canadians and the Demand for a Bill of Rights, 1929–1960*. Montreal and Kingston: McGill-Queen's UP.

Madison, James. 1999 [1787]. "Vices of the Political System of the United States." In J.N. Rakove (ed.), *James Madison, Writings*. New York: Library of America.

McBride, Stephen. 2003. "Quiet Constitutionalism in Canada: The International Political Economy of Domestic Institutional Change." *Canadian Journal of Political Science* 36: 251–73.

Mexico. 1938. "Mexico-United States: Expropriation by Mexico of Agrarian Properties Owned by American Citizens." *American Journal of International Law* 32: 181–207.

Mexico, House of Representatives. 1993. *Report of the Legislative Process Attached to the Decree of Publication of the Law of Expropriation*. Official Federal Gazette, 10 December, published 22 December.

NAFTA Free Trade Commission. 2001. "Notes of Interpretation of Certain Chapter 11 Provisions" (31 July), *World Trade and Arbitration Materials* 13: 139–40.

Nedelsky, Jennifer. 2000. "Communities of Judgment and Human Rights." *Theoretical Inquiries in Law* 1: 245–82.

New York Times. 2001. "Eye on Investors, Mexico Pays U.S. Company (29 October).

Patterson, James T. 2001. *Brown v. Board of Education: A Civil Rights Milestone and its Troubled Legacy*. New York: Oxford UP.

Perezcano, Hugo. 2002. "Roundtable Discussion on Domestic Challenges if Multilateral Investment Treaties are Interpreted to Expand the Compensation Requirements for Regulatory Expropriations Beyond a Signatory State's Domestic Law." *New York University Environmental Law Journal* 11: 208–63.

Posadas, Alejandro. 2000. "*Metalclad Corporation v. The United Mexican States*: Background Information Relevant to Presentation by Prof. Alejandro Posadas, Counsel for Mexico." <http://www.law.duke.edu/curriculum/courseHomepages/fall2000/555_01/PosadasNotes.pdf>.

Radin, Margaret Jane. 1993. *Reinterpreting Property*. Chicago, IL: Chicago UP.

Rittich, Kerry. 2002. *Recharacterizing Restructuring: Law, Distribution, and Gender in Market Reform*. The Hague: Kluwer Law International.

Roth, Andreas H. 1949. *The Minimum Standard of International Law Applied to Aliens*. Leiden: A.W. Sijthoff's Uitgeversmaatschappij N.V.

Sandrino, Gloria. 1994. "The NAFTA Investment Chapter and Foreign Direct Investment in Mexico: A Third World Perspective." *Vanderbilt Journal of Transnational Law* 27: 259–327.

Sands, Philippe. 2005. *Lawless World: America and Breaking of Global Rules*. London: Allen Lane.

Santos, Boaventura de Sousa. 1995. *Toward a New Common Sense: Law, Science, and Politics in the Paradigmatic Transition*. New York: Routledge.

Scheppele, Kim Lane. 2003. "Aspirational and Aversive Constitutionalism: The Case for Studying Cross-Constitutional Influence Through Negative Models." *International Journal of Constitutional Law*: 296–324.

———. 2004. "A Realpolitik Defense of Social Rights." *Texas Law Review* 82: 1921–61.

Schneiderman, David. 1996. "NAFTA's Takings Rule: American Constitutionalism Comes to Canada." *University of Toronto Law Journal* 46: 499–537.

———. 1998. "Human Rights, Fundamental Differences? Multiple Charters in a Partnership Frame." In Roger Gibbins and Guy LaForest (eds.), *Beyond the Impasse*. Montreal: Institute for Research and Public Policy.

———. 2000. "Investment Rules and the New Constitutionalism," *Law & Social Inquiry* 25: 757–87.

———. 2002. "Exchanging Constitutions: Constitutional Bricolage in Canada." *Osgoode Hall Law Journal* 40: 401–24.

———. 2004. "Taking Investments Too Far: Expropriations in the Semi-Periphery." In M. Griffin-Cohen and S. Clarkson (eds.), *Governance on the Edge: Semi-Peripheral States and the Challenge of Globalization*. London: Zed Books. 218–38.

Shea, Donald R. 1955. *The Calvo Clause: A Problem of Inter-American and International Law and Diplomacy*. Minneapolis: U of Minnesota P.

Smith, Welsley R. 1992. "Salinas Prepares Mexican Agriculture for Free Trade." *Mexico Trade & Law Reporter* 2,10: 7–8.

Sornarajah, M. 1994. *The International Law on Foreign Investment*. Cambridge: Cambridge UP.

——. 2000. *The Settlement of Foreign Investment Disputes*. The Hague: Kluwer Law International.

Tamayo, Arturo Boja. 2001. "The New Federalism in Mexico and Foreign Economic Policy: An Alternative Two-Level Game Analysis of the Metalclad Case," *Latin American Politics and Society* 43: 67–90.

Tarnopolsky, Walter Surma. 1975. *The Canadian Bill of Rights*. 2nd ed. Toronto: McClelland and Stewart.

Tarullo, Daniel K. 1987. "Beyond Normalcy in the Regulation of International Trade." *Harvard Law Review* 100: 547–628.

Tushnet, Mark. 2003. *The New Constitutional Order*. Princeton, NJ: Princeton UP.

US Congress. 1963. *Expropriation of American-Owned Property by Foreign Governments in the Twentieth Century*. Washington, DC: US Government Printing Office.

Underkuffler, Laura S. 2003. *The Idea of Property: Its Meaning and Power*. Oxford: Oxford UP.

United Mexican States. 2001. "Petitioners Outline of Argument," filed 5 February 2001 in *United Mexican States* v. *Metalclad Corporation* in the Supreme Court of British Columbia, No. L002904, Vancouver Registry. <http://www.vancouver.indymedia.PDF>.

Van der Walt, A.J. 1999. *Constitutional Property Clauses*. Dordrecht: Kluwer International Law.

Vandevelde, Keneth J. 1992. *United States Investment Treaties: Policy and Practice*. Deventer: Kluwer.

——. 1998. "The Political Economy of a Bilateral Investment Treaty." *American Journal of International Law* 92: 621–41.

Vargas, Jorge A. 1994. "NAFTA, the Chiapas Rebellion, and the Emergence of Mexican Ethnic Law," *California Western International Law Journal* 25: 1–79.

Wheat, Andrew. 1995. "Toxic Shock in a Mexican Village," *Multinational Monitor* (October) 16(10). <http://www.essential.org/monitor/hyper/mm1095.07.html>.

Wild, Jr. Payson S. 1939. "International Law and Mexican Oil." *The Quarterly Journal of Inter-American Relations* 1: 5–21.

CASES

Authorson v. Canada (Attorney General) [2003] Supreme Court Reports.

Brown v. Board of Education of Topeka, 347 U.S. 483 (1954).

Delgamuukw v. British Columbia [1997] 3 Supreme Court Reports 1010.

Hodge v. The Queen (1883) Appeal Cases 117 (JCPC).

Manitoba Fisheries Ltd. v. The Queen (1978) 88 Dominion Law Reports (3d) 462 (SCC).

Mariner Real Estate Ltd. v. Nova Scotia (Attorney General) [1999] 68 LCR 1 (NSCA).

Metalclad Corporation and the United Mexican States. 2000. [2001] World Trade and Arbitration Materials 13: 47–80.

Penn Central Transportation Co. v. New York City, 438 U.S. 104 (1978).

Pennsylvania Coal v. Mahon, 438 U.S. 393 at 1569 (1922).

Printz v. United States, 521 U.S. 898 (1997).

Tee-Hit-Ton Indians v. United States, 348 U.S. 272 (1955).

United Mexican States v. Metalclad, 2001 BCSC 664 (BCSC).

CHAPTER TWELVE

Under Pressure
The Impasses of North American Labour Movements

Gregory Albo and Dan Crow

Trade unions have been perhaps the most effective organization for the advancement of democracy and social justice in capitalist societies. Certainly, they have been the most important means by which those who have only their labour-power to sell to earn their livelihoods partially equalize the structural advantages that the owners of capital assets have in bargaining over wages and the distribution of value-added (i.e., the new production of goods and services) at workplaces. Unions have been integral, as well, to advancing democracy through their persistent advocacy of universal participation in politics, extension of civil rights (such as freedoms of association, assembly, and dissent), and universalization of social programs to improve equality of opportunity for all. Each of these advances for social justice was opposed historically—and continues to be opposed in varying degrees—by the business classes. The steady consolidation of neo-liberalism since the 1980s has presented new challenges for social justice and democracy in North America, both in general and in the particular form of NAFTA. Neo-liberalism has advanced free markets and corporate property rights at the expense of even modest attempts to secure a more democratic determination of economic priorities to meet social needs. The current impasses of the North American labour movements need to be seen in this context.

While the formation of NAFTA in 1994 encouraged new relationships among unions in North America, it also brought a new set of pressures to the labour movements of Canada, the US, and Mexico. Indeed, it has posed several central challenges for North American workers. First, at the point of production, workers have been challenged by the new production regime and international division of labour of flexible manufacturing systems in a more integrated world market. This has been a continental challenge for all the North American union movements, as collective bargaining capacities and organizational levels have all around suffered decline. Second, at the level of the state, workers confront a neo-liberal policy regime of "punitive austerity," which has characterized North American politics since the "Volcker shock" of sky-high interest rates in 1981 and the Mexican peso crisis of the early 1980s. And, third, at the level of the continental North American market, the internationalization of capital has posed new obstacles to internal national development to meet social needs, thus compromising the further development of international solidarity in support of workplace demands.

In the first section of this chapter, the nature of labour movements in capitalist societies and the challenges facing North American labour movements today will be placed in conceptual context. The second section will elaborate on some of the common pressures confronting North American labour movements. These pressures have met with distinct responses by national movements in the three countries, and these are discussed in the third section. Finally, the chapter concludes with a consideration of the prospects for and potential strategies available to North American labour movements. We argue that neo-liberalism and free trade have brought severe pressures on North American labour; that the national labour movements have each reached an organizational impasse; and that new organizing and collective struggle by unions within each state will be needed as a pre-condition for the international solidarity between workers that is necessary today.

Workers, Unions, and Politics

Unions are highly complex organizations. They organize workers in capitalist societies as market actors, as components of wider collective organizations for the production of goods and services, and as agents of a social class pursuing democracy and social justice. There is large variation within states as well as between them as to how unions are organized, their class capacities, and their societal roles. The union movements of North America are no exception, and it is important to locate them organizationally before turning to the common pressures of neo-liberalism and economic integration and the divergent strategies they have adopted in response.

Unions come properly into view only when we understand how capitalism organizes production and how individual capitalists continually restructure industry as a consequence of competitive imperatives to expand productive capacity in an effort to maintain profitability (Kelley 1988; Regini 1992). Workers individually sell their labour-power for a wage to enable them to buy their means of existence. Capitalists and other employers attempt to deploy the labour-time purchased in spatially specific labour processes in order to produce new value embodied in goods and services or to produce services that facilitate the circulation of commodities and social integration into capitalist markets. Unions thus emerge at the point of production, and their organizational capacity in the first instance is wholly dependent upon the power they exercise there.

Labour processes exist, however, in the wider scale of labour markets with different skill levels, working conditions, and labour reserves of unemployed all factoring into the negotiations between workers and employers over wages and hours of work. Thus, unions become inextricably linked to the community politics that structure local labour market conditions. The distribution of labour processes across the world forms an international division of labour, which creates some of the distinct characteristics of national labour movements. But it is the vast differences in the labour markets and social relations of each country that are crucial to the conditions of workers, for example, in Mexican auto plants, where wages and working conditions are lower than in Canada and the US even though the technology employed might be quite similar. It is specific social relations that produce and deploy technology (always as a historical political project), and unions are crucial social actors shaping this process.

Labour markets are, in turn, embedded and legitimated in the even wider processes of state formation. Nation-states provide a common currency, legal structure, and social institutions, and remain the central location of power and class formation. For unions, states present the legal framework in which they must conduct themselves, develop the social policies through which the conflicting interests of workers and employers over employment security versus labour market flexibility are struggled over, and establish the key institutional matrix in which social classes contest political power. The US, for example, forms its industrial relations system in the highly legalistic and restrictive national Taft-Hartley Act of 1947, which followed the more favourable Wagner Act of 1935. The Taft-Hartley Act gives US unions legal certification to represent specific groups of workers in particular workplaces but highly restricts forms of collective action at and beyond individual workplaces. Canada adopted a similar certification process through the Industrial Relations and Disputes Act of 1948. In Canada, however, the provinces are the central locales of industrial relations legislation, and since they widely vary, unions have preserved a far greater scope for collective action at workplaces, especially in the public sector compared to US unions, and in sectoral bargaining (Swartz 1993: 388–89). In contrast, Mexican unions were incorporated into the Mexican state system after the revolution through a corporatist type of labour relations system in which unions were given legal status as the voice of a specific "producer" group. The 1931 Federal Labour Law in particular made union leaders effectively part of the state bureaucracy, leaving union workplace representation, initiative, and capacity severely truncated (Middlebrook 1995). It is impossible, therefore, to speak of a singular North American labour movement without accounting for these distinct national union histories, struggles, and legal and political contexts (Albo 2005).

This still leaves the terrain of the world market, where unions need to form some organizational capacity as well. The processes of capital accumulation always occur in an encompassing world market enforcing competitive imperatives on each firm and state to cut costs and innovate, thereby continually transforming conditions of work. The world market also forms new interdependencies as place-specific labour processes and markets become linked through the increased circulation of commodities and labour. For example, in the late nineteenth-century phase of industrialization, even while they were each forming their modern territorial states, Canada, the US, and Mexico were more interlinked, whereas in the postwar period, they all adopted more nationalist policies in which trade unions played a larger role as part of national "social accords" that framed wage and industrial policies. The trade integration of NAFTA and the global processes of the internationalization of capital have posed a new context of competition and interdependencies for the labour movements of North America to address. In the auto industry, for example, labour processes in all three countries are directly intertwined through international production networks linking the circulation of parts and production volumes of individual plants (Moody 1997).

This complex organizational terrain—of local, national, and international scales of social structures and organizational action—has made for enormous variety in the form of unions (Jackson 2004). In the simplest sense unions can be defined as combinations of workers pursuing wage improvements and better working conditions through collective bargaining and political actions. Workers are organized into unions on the basis of both their craft (such as carpenters or nurses) and sector of employment (such as steel or retail), and these are still the predominant forms of organization in North America. The shift from manufacturing to service sector work has, however, altered any strict functional relation between occupation and sector and union. Most industrial unions have, for good and ill, become general unions, with a steel union like the United Steelworkers of America (USWA) just as likely to be representing employees in the service sector today in both Canada and the US. Mexican unions are less heterogeneous in this sense, but they are also more complex in their relation to the enormous informal sector and peasant organizations.

Trade unions are also organized into centrals (or national federations) that attempt to organize workers and their varied unions into a political force capable of reinforcing local and sectoral struggles and forging a common political program. In Canada, for example, the Canadian Labour Congress (CLC) has organized the majority of unions under its umbrella since 1956. But there also other smaller trade union groupings outside of the CLC; for instance, Québec has its own centrals in the form of the Québec Federation of Labour and the Confederation of National Trade Unions, reflecting the linguistic and national differences internal to Canada. In the US, the American Federation of Labour-Congress of Industrial Organizations (AFL-CIO) was consolidated in 1955 and gathers virtually all US unions together.

Mexico, however, has a quite distinct array of union structures. The *Partido Revolucionario Institucional* (PRI) long dominated the Mexican state in a form of one-party rule, and its associated unions were largely gathered in the largest Mexican union federation, the *Confederacion de Trabajadores de Mexico* (CTM) and in the *Congreso del Trabajo* (CT), along with a few smaller federations organizing peasants. These centrals have been declining in strength from the 1980s on, and since 1997 the *Union Nacional de Trabajadores* (UNT) has also contested for the terrain of official trade unionism and traditional corporatist bargaining, while also providing some space for union memberships to push for democratization. Other new centrals, such as the *Frente Autentico del Trabajo* (FAT), have pushed for even further democratization of Mexican unions and a more aggressive stance for "class independence" and linking unions with class struggles. These competing federations in Mexico are coupled with an enormous number of local unions of various sorts—estimated at over 30,000—with all manner of operations, from managing protection-type contracts insulating employers from legitimate unions to ones negotiated by democratic but isolated class struggle unions (Donnelly, LaBotz, and Geffert 1999).

The organizational matrix of national labour movements only begins to tell us how workers are organized as a class and their class capacities to structure collective bargaining outcomes and struggle over state policies. There are several types of union organizations.

1. The division of workers into separate workplaces may result in "sectionalism" in a union as it focuses narrowly on its own workers' wages and job security. Such a focus on economic inter-

ests is often termed *business unionism* for its concern only with servicing members.

2. A variant of this type of unionism is a *"social partnership"* whereby a union also works closely with the employer in shaping bargaining demands that ensure firm-level competitiveness.

3. *Corporatist unionism* adopts these same concerns but integrates them into formal institutions of tripartite negotiations with employers' associations and the state.

4. In contrast, *social movement unionism* is oriented to building the capacities of union members to challenge hierarchical relations in the workplace beyond just wage bargaining. Social movement unions attempt to organize the "working class as a whole" in the struggle for democratization and social justice.

These political divisions are central to situating the past and present politics of North American unions (Robinson 1994; Madrid 2003).

As a result of the militant opposition of US business, including the extensive use of private violence against union organization to this day, unions in the US have been pushed to embrace a narrow business unionism and have never overcome workers' disorganization in the face of repeated employers' offences. Reliance on the business-oriented Democratic Party for political representation has provided little relief and, indeed, has reinforced the union focus on maintaining local workplace representation. In Mexico, corporatist unionism has often made it difficult to distinguish union positions from the policies of the Mexican state and the PRI. This provided union leadership historically with some access to the Mexican state but often at the cost of limited rights with respect to strike action, mandated and open collective bargaining, and freedom for political activities. In contrast, unions in Canada have been linked to social democratic parties and ideology, and this has provided some space for social unionism there. However, there have also been parallels with US practices of marginalizing radical union currents, and seldom have Canadian unions moved beyond the goal of more managed forms of welfare capitalism.

These types of divisions in the political strategies of unions also appear as divisions over international union solidarity in the world market (Waterman 2001). The concern of business unionism, for example, with firm-level competitiveness and economic interests may push unions in the direction of policies of chauvinism toward workers in other countries. In contrast, social movement unionism often encourages union development internationally and provides material solidarity with workers engaged in critical struggles. North American unions have had an ambiguous and often sordid record with respect to internationalism. Dominated by business and corporatist unionism, their field of political action has been dominated by local concerns, seldom even extending to national agendas for coordinating industrial action. The AFL-CIO has, moreover, often been deeply protectionist of US jobs, while at the same time backing US government policy of compelling states to integrate into the world market and blocking alternative models of development. The legacy of an authoritarian state and corporatism has made Mexican unions often more of an instrument of Mexican state policy than of worker internationalism. Canadian unions have been, in this context, more open to strategies of solidarity but with minimal organizational energies and strategic focus, particularly at the federation level. Internationalism in Canadian unions has also had a central paradox: the many international unions in Canada have often been drawn into the conservative international agendas of the AFL-CIO, while the more nationally based Canadian unions have become, the more they have attempted to establish a serious international orientation. Union strategies to build a more unified North American labour movement to parallel the economic integration project of NAFTA have thus had a fledgling foundation on which to build.

Common Pressures: Neo-liberalism and North American Workers

National industrial relations systems are, according to the theoretical points above, always politically specific and contingent institutional arrangements for accommodating and containing structural conflicts between social classes over wages and control of the work process. Even if the competitive pressures of the world market are general, they are always particular in how they impact on specific workplaces and how national institutions, companies, and labour movements respond. Three common pressures—economic slowdown, neo-liberal labour market policies, and the internationalization of capital on North American labour movements under NAFTA—need to be briefly highlighted.

THE POSTWAR ECONOMIC SLOWDOWN

The "long slowdown" since the 1980s has intensified competitive imperatives and economic integration. It followed the postwar boom, which favoured more inward development strategies that also strengthened the bargaining power of unions and conditions for workers. Rapid growth, mass production industrial systems, and expansionary welfare policies all contributed to high labour demand and union formation as unemployment fears lessened. But as economic instability struck in the 1970s, a long phase of industrial rationalization began. Slower growth increased international competition across the world market. This generated, especially in North America, labour-saving plant shutdowns and a massive shift in industry from its concentration in the northeast of the US and central Canada to the southern US and, in part, northern Mexico. Workers in unionized manufacturing jobs that were supposedly secure now faced unemployment and wage pressures. In the public sector, government cutbacks—which hit all three North American countries with the high interest rate and peso crisis of the early 1980s—also impacted public sector employees (Albo 1990). Partly as a result of these trends and partly as a result of tendencies in capitalist development as a whole, private service sector jobs grew enormously. These were often forms of contingent work in jobs of questionable quality: involuntary part-time work in private services in Canada and the US and informal sector work in Mexico. In these new areas of employment, there was little or no coverage by unions (Campbell *et al.* 1999).

It was these trends that began a process of social polarization that has character-ized the neo-liberal period of trade integration and liberalized markets that began in the mid-80s and has continued to this day. It is, indeed, difficult to disentangle the push for free trade and international capital mobility that begin in this period from the "employers' offensive" at the workplace. Both were destined to restore profit-ability and facilitate industrial restructuring. The flexible manufacturing systems that have followed mass production, for example, have been implemented in the form of "lean production" where work intensity and increased work-hours have been important aspects of technological changes to squeeze more surplus labour out of workers while trimming wage costs. Workers across North America have consistently taken a smaller share of the value they add at work while employers have increased their share. Hence, although growth rates in the second half of the 1990s picked up (with a mild recession taking hold in 2000), various government reports suggest that unemployment rates in North America are likely to remain higher than they were in the 1970s and 1980s, contingent and informal sector work is likely to continue to grow, and the wage compression and wage inequalities that have grown since the 1970s are unlikely to see a reversal (OECD 2004: 11, 48–49, 129; Commission for Labor Cooperation 2003: 6). While these economic trends all suggest the need for unions to defend workers, the period of neo-liberalism has hardly been the most propitious for union organization.

NEO-LIBERAL LABOUR MARKET POLICIES

A second pressure on unions has come from neo-liberal policies for restructuring the labour market. This has been the notion of introducing "flexibility" into the labour market to overcome the "rigidities" of past labour policies introduced when unions were stronger. Previous labour policies provided a degree of "security" for workers against loss of income—workers' compensation, unemployment insurance, univer-sal health care, welfare, and so on. The neo-liberal strategy has been to limit access, eliminate programs, and cut benefit levels in the name of wage and job flexibility (these policies may be more accurately described as cheapening labour). Other post-war policies were to provide "employment" security against loss of work—job crea-tion policies for full employment and training and adjustment programs for laid-off workers. Neo-liberal labour market polices have also cast high employment polices aside under the unfounded belief that only the private sector and not the government can create jobs (although we plainly know that teachers, nurses, police, and parks supervisors all have jobs). This has in fact meant a huge increase in service sector jobs, some in high-technology work and producer services, but the largest number in retail and "servant" occupations (Economic Council of Canada 1990).

Neo-liberal market policies of flexibility also have attempted to limit unions by imposing restrictions on organizing and bargaining activity to the favour and ben-efit of employers. The various anti-union legal restrictions of the last 20 years have led to fewer organized workers and more coercive and unequal work relations. In Mexico, such labour reforms have been coupled with the mass privatizations of state enterprises and the spread of the *maquiladora* sector where labour regulations are minimal, radically altering the context for union organizing and bargaining. Right-to-work laws, which prevent unions from forming a union shop with a compulsory dues check-off formula (what is labeled the Rand Formula in Canada), is one of the strongest policy measures the US uses to impose labour market flexibility. A vast number of US businesses have moved to the US south where these laws prevail. The National Labour Relations Board in the US has also moved systematically in the direction of heeding employers' efforts to delay and block union recognition (Fantasia and Voss 2004: 125). Legal restrictions on union organizing have also been part of Canadian industrial relations with neo-liberalism, coupled with extensive use of back-to-work legislation compelling union contract settlements on terms favourable to employers (Panitch and Swartz 2003).

THE INTERNATIONALIZATION OF CAPITAL

A third pressure on unions is the internationalization of capital. Straightforwardly, increased capital mobility provides leverage for employers relative to the immobility of workers (the provisions for labour mobility in NAFTA apply to professionals in comparison to the free movement of labour in the European Union). NAFTA has reinforced the liberalization of capital movements in a number of ways. Most directly, the creation of a free trade zone and limiting of the use of tariffs provide a single market for employers, and investor protection measures through NAFTA encourage capital mobility. These make it difficult for governments to roll back liberalization measures and adopt policies that might encourage industrial intervention or social welfare. Indirectly, increased capital mobility strengthens employer bargaining capacity and opposition to unionization by threat of capital flight, particularly as the increasing market competition compels employers to drive down unit labour costs (Robinson 1994: 664–65).

Such global labour arbitrage of playing one group of workers off against another is given added feasibility by the fact that world trade and private sector production is dominated by transnational corporations (TNCs), with their integrated production networks being a key element of regional integration. The dominant TNCs are in the US. The auto industry, for example, increased the number of parts, engine, and leading assembly plants in Mexico in the wake of NAFTA to export these back to the US and Canada, particularly taking advantage of Mexican labour costs that could be up to one-tenth that of workers north of the border. Telecommunications production has seen even more radical shifting of production to Mexico, while continuing to concentrate research and development in Canada and the US (Moody 1997: 70–71, 77). Thus, NAFTA encouraged a significant shift of some 2 million less skilled jobs to Mexico, particularly in the *maquiladoras* at the northern border, with manufacturing employment in both the US and Canada declined as a share of employment (Roman and Velasco 2002). But Mexico's low wage strategy in NAFTA has in turn faced pressures from a shift of US and Asian factories from Mexico to China. And countries like Honduras have also gained trade access to the US market and expanded their export-zone *maquiladora* operations in low wage, low value-added production. International competition and capital mobility, whether within trade zones such as NAFTA or at the world market level, are a crucial pressure that union strategies today cannot avoid confronting.

Divergent Responses: North American Unions in Crisis

Despite processes of regional integration, states remain the principal location of political power and continue to be the guarantors of the legal frameworks that enable capitalist production (Panitch 2001: 374–75). When organized into unions, working classes develop capacities primarily to contest power locally at the point of production and at the levels of the nation-state (and the various subnational scales of state institutions). Any discussion of the power of unions and workers must begin, it was argued above, with their ability to struggle successfully within the confines of their domestic states. Given different historical developments, organizational capacities, and political circumstances, the national labour movements and central labour federations of Canada, the US, and Mexico have taken divergent approaches to fighting neo-liberalism and labour market pressures on workers and unions. Moreover, given the divisions within each movement, individual affiliate unions of the central federations of each state have varied in their responses to state and economic restructuring. As will be shown from an examination of each country, this has implications for the attempts unions have made to coordinate activities across national borders, which remain, at best, fledgling.

CANADA

In many respects, Canadian unions have been the most successful of the three movements in resisting the pressures to de-unionize that have come with neo-liberalism and free trade. Nonetheless, state policies to create flexible labour markets, labour law reforms that are intended to make unionization more difficult, and employer strategies to shift production away from unionized shops have had a distinct impact on the Canadian labour movement. Union density (the proportion of the labour force organized into unions) has dropped from a high of 40 per cent in 1983 to a rate of 31 per cent in 2003 (Panitch and Swartz 2003: 245). This level of unionization is due to the high rate of public sector unionization at 72.5 per cent,[1] whereas private sector unionization has dropped to only 18 per cent. Union density in Canada has also been threatened by patterns of labour process "flexibilization" and new job creation. As manufacturing jobs have been relocated to other sites in the trade bloc, and jobs in unionized plants are outsourced to non-union shops, the union density in manufacturing has declined since the late 1980s. In 1988, the last year before the Canada-US Free Trade Agreement, density in manufacturing was 45.5 per cent; this figure had dropped to 32.4 per cent by 2002 (Jackson 2003: 10) The tendency for jobs to be created in service sectors of the economy that have traditionally been difficult to organize suggests that the trend towards de-unionization of the Canadian economy may well continue. In the absence of new organizing drives and labour law reforms that would facilitate organizing in the private service sector, the basic organizational capacity of unions to intervene in the labour market and to act as a central vehicle of forming and representing the interests of workers—both labour market actors and the social class—will continue to be strained.

All is not gloomy, however, for the Canadian labour movement. Relative to other OECD countries, there has been a strong resistance to pressures to decrease unionization rates. Whereas Canada saw an increase in absolute numbers of union members (though not enough to maintain density given increased numbers within the labour force), 13 OECD countries saw union membership decrease. Canada now ranks as having the eighth highest unionization rate of 19 OECD countries, with a higher rate than Germany, Australia, New Zealand, Britain, and the Netherlands (Ogmundson and Doyle 2002: 416). In an exceedingly bad context, these figures show that the Canadian labour movement is doing a relatively good job of maintaining potential strength in the face of global trends towards weakening unions, but it is not good enough to offset the common pressures of neo-liberalism. Retention of union membership might also be judged a success within the context of Canadian labour law reform that is intended to facilitate decertification of unions and to make it more difficult to organize new ones (Martinello 2000).

The ability to stem the tide of de-unionization has in large part been the result of increased organizing efforts. During periods of stable or slowly growing membership rates, continuing through the period of government and employer promotion of postwar mass manufacturing production, unions paid little attention to organizing new members, particularly in the service sector. As service sector employment has increased, alongside other forces of economic restructuring, unions in both the public and private sector have needed to refocus their energies into organizing. Even unions traditionally associated with the manufacturing sector, such as the Canadian Auto Workers (CAW) and the USWA, have begun to broaden their efforts in an attempt to organize workers in the service sector (Yates 2000: 31–32). But this has, in turn, caused its own set of problems: raiding other unions' memberships, organizing competition between unions, and the emergence of overlapping general unions across sectors with little coordination to aid bargaining capacity or anything in the way of a strategic direction for the union movement as a whole or in terms of sectors. Indeed, strategic inertia seems to rule the day in the absence of direction from the CLC on issues of jurisdiction and consolidation.

Another area in which Canadian unions have been more resilient than others is in their propensity to strike. In an era marked by concessions bargaining, where unions are pressured to give up previously won wages, benefits, and standards in working conditions, Canadian unions continued to exhibit strike rates higher than other advanced capitalist countries. This suggests that Canadian workers have been more willing to resist downward labour pressures than are other labour movements and that they engage in lengthy disputes to do so (Ogmundson and Doyle 2002: 422). Yet, in absolute terms, the Canadian strike rate shows a steady decline from a postwar high of 1,218 strikes in 1974 to 1,028 strikes in 1980, 579 strikes in 1990, and 379 in 2000—which represented a slight rebound from the mid 1990s (Panitch and Swartz 2003: 244). Again, Canadian labour's position appears to exhibit a strong resistance to restructuring only in a comparative perspective. The willingness to strike should also be understood in the context of the fact that Canadian governments at all levels regularly resort to ad hoc back-to-work legislation to end strikes in both the private and public sectors (Panitch and Swartz 2003). Governments of all stripes (even the social democratic New Democratic Party, which has been in government in various provinces) have made use of back-to-work legislation, often including contract settlements that benefit employers in the legislation itself. As such, the utility of strikes as a means of resisting downward labour market pressures has been significantly circumscribed.

The declining strike rate should also be understood in the context of unions' increasing tendency to enter into partnerships with employers as a defensive strategy. Partnerships include arrangements between unions and employers to manage corporate restructuring, work reorganization, and often even wage restraint. The trade-off for unions is that they gain both some negotiating power over the impacts of restructuring on their members and perhaps some job protection. Among the most dramatic of recent partnership arrangements was a 2003 agreement between the United Food and Commercial Workers (UFCW) and the Loblaws chain of grocery stores. The employer, feeling competitive pressures from the US-based Wal-mart chain, which was intending to break into the sale of groceries, requested that the union agree to re-open its collective agreement and accept wage rollbacks, particularly for part-time workers (whose wages were reduced to minimum wage, minus union dues), and agree that new stores (those intended to compete with Wal-mart in the sale of low-cost department store goods) would not fall under the collective agreement. Under pressure, the UFCW leadership agreed to the concessions behind closed doors and then brought the changes to rank-and-file members as a done deal.

Other unions, too, have agreed to partnerships in the face of employer pressure, often including threats to relocate jobs. Unions engaged in partnerships and concession bargaining include the USWA, the Hospital Employees Union in British Columbia, and the Communications, Energy and Paper Workers of Canada (CEP), to cite only the most prominent examples. Even the CAW, a union that split from the United Auto Workers (UAW) in 1985 as a protest against the US union's insistence on concession bargaining with General Motors (Gindin 1995), has engaged in some forms of partnerships. There appears to be an increasing frequency of labour-management cooperation in the automotive sector, usually springing from pacts between individual locals and plant managers, but often supported (both implicitly and explicitly) by the CAW leadership. Such patterns of cooperation, especially as exhibited by one of the most confident and conflictual unions, bodes ill for improving union political capacity in that it undermines the realization of independent class formation (Wells 1997: 169–70).[2]

Despite such defensive postures, Canadian unions have also begun to show new forms of resistance to neo-liberalism. Broadly speaking, these can be characterized as the development of social movement unionism, which includes increasing internal democracy within unions to allow for more rank-and-file participation, broader based bargaining to address issues beyond wages and benefits (and which benefit the wider community), and making concrete links between unions and other social movements such as environmentalists and anti-poverty groups (Moody 1997: 4–5; CAW/TCA 2003). Instances of social movement unionism include working with anti-globalization activists in organizing protests against the Free Trade Area of the Americas (FTAA) in Québec City in 2001. Perhaps the events that indicated the potential of such protests were the "Days of Action" from 1995–97 in Ontario, a series of one-day strikes across the province orchestrated as a broadly based protest against a Progressive Conservative government that pursued a hard right neo-liberal agenda (Munro 1997). Although the "Days of Action" did not result in a sustained movement, they did demonstrate that unions and other social movements could combine their strengths to pursue common goals.

The opposition of the Canadian labour movement to the FTAA is consistent with its rejection of NAFTA and free trade going back to the 1980s. It has opposed both the wage compression and the drive to competitiveness through the intensification of work that was predicted to result—and has been the case—of free trade and NAFTA (Peters 2002), as well as the anti-democratic and neo-liberal components of NAFTA restraining government intervention while enhancing private property rights. Concrete measures to sustain this opposition and to develop new forms of international union cooperation have, however, been more sporadic. Five major Canadian unions have developed international solidarity funds that are intended to foster greater linkages between unions of the north and south. However, because matching funds are provided by a federal state agency, the Canadian International Development Agency, they are limited in their ability to develop union linkages capable of creating autonomous labour political activity.

Individual unions have made movements toward building greater linkages, including the CAW's educational programs for Mexican workers and the CEP's links between its leadership and that of the Mexican Telephone Workers' Union. Some linkages have also been made between public sector unions in Canada, the US, and Mexico (Wells 1998). There has been a general lack of coordination, however, and there is a tendency for ties to take place primarily at the level of union leadership. Although some attempts have been made to develop international relationships and to take struggles to the continental level rather than leaving them within the confines of the nation-state, to date these have not diverted Canadian labour's political attentions away from issues of a more local nature. A major difficulty here, in any event, has been the organizational setbacks experienced by unions in the US and the disorganization of the US working classes.

THE US

The labour movement in the US entered the neo-liberal era of the 1980s substantially behind its Canadian counterpart. Although Canadian unions also exhibit some bureaucratic practices that create divisions between the wider interests of rank-and-file members and the leadership (and union staff), US unions have been much more likely to pursue practices of business unionism. As Nissen notes, business unionism is a practice wherein unions accept the values of business and provide "special services to members (a contract, contract enforcement) for a fee (dues). Generally, unions became *servicing bureaucracies*, and participation suffered" (Nissen 2003a: 331). The cozy relationship with employers coupled with a membership base alienated from the structures of the union have left US unions in a position ill-suited to resist neo-liberalism. In part, this is because of the bureaucratic practices of unions, which downplayed organizing the wider class of workers in general and instead focused on servicing existing members. It is also due to the legislative assault on unions in the US, including the Taft-Hartley Act of 1947, which limited the capacity of unions to organize; "right-to-work" legislation in many states; and President Reagan's controversial firing of striking air traffic controllers in 1981. Within such a restrictive legislative regime, and given signals from the National Labor Relations

Board (NLRB) that anti-union practices, ranging from hiring anti-union consultants to actually firing employees engaged in organizing, would be tolerated, employers in the US have become much more aggressive in their quest to prevent unionization (Nissen 2003a: 324).[3]

Thus, union density in the US has declined precipitously. Reaching a high point of 31.8 per cent in 1955, it declined to 13.5 per cent by 2001 and has since held steady at that level (Panitch and Swartz 2003: 245). Breaking this figure down, the weakness of US labour comes into clearer focus: public sector density remains at 37.4 per cent, while only 9 per cent of private sector employees are unionized (Levi 2003: 47). A further sign of the incapacity of unions in the US to resist downward labour market pressures is the low strike rate. In 1969 the number of strikes involving more than 1,000 workers was 412; this number had fallen to 298 by 1971. By 1999 the number of large-scale strikes was down to an astonishing level of just 17, although in 2000 it was up to 39, still reflecting a very significant decline from earlier periods (Levi 2003: 48). A labour movement exhibiting such a low union density, a tendency for rank-and-file members to feel alienated from the union, and a disinclination to use the strike weapon would appear to be in a weak position in its fight against downward pressures on wages and working conditions.

Yet, there are still signs of life in the labour movement in the US. Even though the number of strikes has decreased in recent years, there have been important examples of workers willing to strike against employer demands for concessions and efforts to rebuild. In 2002, the International Longshore and Warehouse Union, in the face of an employer lockout, maintained strong pickets to fight against concessions. In the end, it took a presidential injunction by President George W. Bush, the first in decades, to end the strike. But the willingness to fight was a healthy sign (Levi 2003: 50). Even more encouraging was the nationwide Teamsters' strike at UPS over job security in 1997; it was the first major victory for the movement in years and showed that the labour movement still has some capacity to fight against concession bargaining and competitive pressures. Although the infrequency of these strikes means that it is not possible to generalize this as a new trend towards greater union strength, they do signal a potential for renewed defence of union principles in the US.

Along with some movement towards renewed use of strikes by affiliate unions comes another optimistic sign. In 1995, the AFL-CIO union central underwent a dramatic leadership change. A new president, John Sweeney, and a slate of representatives running under the banner "New Voices," took over the leadership of the organization. They proposed that all unions put significantly more resources into organizing the unorganized and also placed emphasis on developing new organizing tactics, such as training rank-and-file members to take leading roles in new campaigns (Voss and Sherman 2000). The drive towards organizing had some success. The Service Employees International Union successfully organized 75,000 homecare workers in California in 1999, the largest single success for the labour movement since 1937. A renewed focus on organizing, however, has done nothing to rebuild union density levels, although it does seem to have stemmed further decline.

Long-standing practices of business unionism have meant that the primary response of US unions to concessionary bargaining has been to work in partnership with employers. Important examples of this trend include Union of Needletrades,

Industrial and Textile Employees partnerships at both Xerox and Levi Straus, the USWA with several steel manufacturing plants, and partnerships entered into by the Communications Workers of America at several telecommunications firms. One of the most significant partnership arrangements is that between the UAW and Saturn in Spring Hill, Tennessee, which includes "directed work teams, off-line problem-solving teams, labor-management committees, and the like. But all levels of staff and line management are filled with dual union and management personnel, making Saturn a co-management partnership example...." (Nissen 2003b: 137). In essence, this kind of partnership encourages unions to take on the role of managers, assisting in solving problems for employers, even if these solutions involve the unions policing their own members. Such partnerships are not without their contradictions though. In 1999, after rank-and-file mobilization for change, the existing executive of the local UAW was removed from office. The new executive was able then to negotiate a new contract that eliminated some of the terms of the partnership (Nissen 2003b: 137). Partnerships might very well be the dominant form of response for US unions, but just as a grassroots movement could take over the leadership of the AFL-CIO (whatever the subsequent limits of its period at the helm), so too this can happen at the local level. Such ad hoc responses are unlikely to lead to very much if left un-coordinated. That rank-and-file members still hold onto aspirations beyond co-management and are willing to challenge the existing leadership, however, are the forces on which all labour movements have been built.

These organizational weaknesses and divisions within the AFL-CIO remain a major obstacle to any aspirations for a revitalization of the North American labour movement as a whole. It has been reflected directly in the US labour movement's position on NAFTA. After largely ignoring the implications of the original Canada-US Free Trade Agreement, the AFL-CIO mounted an extensive campaign against NAFTA, and it has continued to oppose other free trade agreements. This has been as much, if not more, about defensive protection of vulnerable unionized jobs and sectors in the US as it is opposition to an alternative societal project for reorganizing work and industry. A sign of the AFL-CIO's continuing ambiguous and often conflicting responses to trade expansion can be seen in its condemnation of the creation of a Central American Free Trade Agreement, while simultaneously arguing for inclusion of protections of workers' rights in all future trade agreements. And even as it calls for inclusion of labour protections in new agreements, US labour condemns the North American Agreement on Labour Cooperation as an ineffective tool for the advancement of labour rights, particularly with regard to employer uses of unfair labour practices in Mexico (AFL-CIO 2003).

At the level of individual unions, however, there have been more consistent attempts to create internationally coordinated struggles. For example, the United Electrical, Radio and Machine Workers of America has consistently supported independent union organizing in Mexico and has developed long standing ties to the FAT (Moody 1995: 111). A good example of the weakness of US labour's internationalism can be seen in a traditional industry such as auto, where there is still no coordination between the UAW and the CAW. In fact, the dominant form of labour internationalism coming out of the US has been the promotion of business unionism, often undermining progressive regimes through the international bureau of the AFL-

CIO in "cold war" fashion. The most conservative unions in Canada, for example, have tended to be the national branches of US internationals.

MEXICO

Owing to its less developed economy and long history of authoritarian rule, the Mexican case is the most unique among the three states. Historically, the working class in Mexico has been enmeshed in corporatist structures of the state. This has resulted in a lack of union autonomy from the state and the PRI, the instrument of one-party domination within Mexico until recently (Rodriguez 1998: 71). The largest Mexican union federation, the *Confederacion de Trabajadores de Mexico* (CTM) along with the *Confederación Revolucionaria de Obreros y Campesinos* (CROC), *Confederación Regional Obrera Mexicana* (CROM), and the *Congreso del Trabajo* (CT), all official unions tied to the authoritarian corporatist arrangements, represent the majority of Mexican workers. Furthermore, these corporatist arrangements have resulted in unions that have acted as coercive agents against their members. Corrupt union bosses became *de facto* members of the state apparatus, and their privileged positions became dependent upon keeping militant workers in check. As a result, union densities were higher than in other comparable states but were nonetheless ineffectual at improving working conditions (Roman and Arregui 1998: 128). In 2000, overall union density in Mexico was only 15.7 per cent, down from a recent high in the 1980s of 25 per cent. Rates are highest in public administration, at 31.2 per cent, and density in services (including education and health care) is 23.8 per cent (Dumas 2003). With union leaders often in collaborative relationships with employers and the state, internal practices of democracy and independent action for unions were all but impossible.[4] In addition, state coercion was also prominent. Strike activity was traditionally very low as the state made the conditions for work stoppages illegal in most cases. In those cases where strikes did occur, direct physical coercion was regularly used (Cockcroft 1998: 160).

Wage distribution has never been beneficial for the working classes in Mexico, and it has been getting worse with the rise of neo-liberal state practices. IMF restructuring programs and the devaluation of the peso has undermined workers' real wages, throwing impoverished workers into a much worse state (Ramirez 1997: 126–27). In part because of devaluation of the peso, minimum wage earners in 1997 could purchase about 30 per cent of what they could in 1980. State policies of retrenchment, including privatization of pensions and other services, contributed to the devastation of living standards. While the top 10 per cent of income earners increased their wealth, there was a 600 per cent increase in incidence of malnutrition in Mexico City (Cockcroft 1998: 154–56). As a measure of working-class capacity, wage distribution demonstrates that workers in Mexico are in anything but a strong position.

The expansion of production in *maquiladora* zones along the Mexico-US border has done nothing to alleviate poverty, has resulted in adverse health and ecological conditions, and has made little room for new independent unions to organize. *Maquiladora* zones are intended to provide a low-wage labour market to attract foreign investment. Although job growth in these regions has been substantial (ten times its 1981 level while non-*maquiladora* employment in manufacturing was lower in 2000 than it was in 1981), unionization rates and standards of living have been dismal (Cypher 2001: 20; Wise, Salazar, and Carlsen 2003: 215). Frequently, before plants are even opened in the *maquiladoras*, the existing "official unions" will meet with employers to sign collective agreements that do little more than cover the basic provisions of the existing labour laws. Furthermore, these unions do little to support workers in grievances against employers. For example, *maquiladora* work has a tendency to cause significant health problems for employees, including exposure to toxic chemicals and repetitive strain disorder. Unions in these factories usually side with employers when grievances are brought forward, telling their members to return to work (Obrera 2003: 154–55). For these unions, stable collective bargaining helps maintain membership levels and thus a degree of legitimacy within the Mexican state. For Mexican capitalists, the presence of compliant unions guarantees that independent unions with a more aggressive project for protecting workers will have a much more difficult time trying to organize these workers.

Public sector employees have been just as affected. As part of its neo-liberal restructuring program, the Mexican state has taken a very active policy of privatizing state assets. It had traditionally taken a strong role in promoting economic development and thus acquired a large number of public corporations to facilitate this process, for example, in steel, telecommunications, mining, and oil. As part of restructuring programs prompted by the state by trade integration and structural adjustment policies from the international lending agencies and the US government, but also because of internal pressures from Mexican capitalists for divestment, hundreds of these corporations were sold off (Williams 2001: 91–92). In order to make such sale more attractive, unions were pressured to grant concessions in terms of wages and working conditions. Even in the face of resistance by public sector unions (and peasant rebellions in some of the regions of Mexico), privatization could not be stopped.

As with the other national union movements, there are some positive signs that Mexican workers are willing to organize to resist downward pressures on working conditions and standards of living. As the Mexican state engages in uneven processes of democratization, democratic pressures are not only affecting the state. There has also been a significant rise of independent unions in Mexico, most notably the FAT. Although the working class is still dominated by the official unions of the CTM/PRI era (Middlebrook 1995: 265–67), progress has been made in developing unions that are controlled by their members, free of state interference in internal workings, and willing to challenge employers openly. Space has been created for increased independent strike action, and there is more room for unions to develop independent political practice. Furthermore, unions are now more capable of building networks of solidarity, both domestically and internationally (Roman and Arregui 1998: 131–33). This leaves some room for optimism, but considering the historic practices of the state and capital in Mexico, as well as the declining standard of living, all optimism must be tempered with a realistic assessment of the weak position of the Mexican working class.

Indeed, it is precisely this weak position that has cast a long shadow over the attitude of the Mexican labour movement toward NAFTA. In almost a reverse position of US unions, the Mexican labour movement was partly in favour of NAFTA for potential job gains it envisioned from the reduction of trade barriers in sectors it saw as having a competitive advantage and in the hope of attracting new industries; and it was partly against free trade as it clearly extended the neo-liberal reordering of the Mexican state and the marginalization of whatever advantages the CTM had gained through its corporatist relationship with the PRI and the state. Unions representing workers in state-owned industries were the most likely of the official unions to oppose NAFTA insofar as the trade agreement was a further impetus to privatize these corporations. Over time, however, even these unions were pressured into working with the state in the process of privatization, as a means by which the unions could maintain at least some representation within the state. Of late there has been a division between the CTM (along with the CROC and CROM) and the independent unions over support for NAFTA. The former have been able to able to maintain the right to "represent" workers in the *maquiladoras* by signing deals with employers before workers have a chance to decide which union will represent them. The latter oppose free trade because of the downward pressures on living standards but still maintain linkages with some unions in Canada and the US in order to help build their capacities to organize and represent members. These international linkages, however much they have assisted the independent unions in surviving, have not yet given the FAT security. This state of organizational weakness and strategic disorientation is, indeed, why the Mexican labour movement still remains an uncertain actor and tentative ally in any attempt to reinvigorate the North American union movement.

Conclusion: North American Unions and International Solidarity

In the face of common pressures, the labour movements of North America have varied in their capacity to respond to neo-liberalism. The Canadian movement has exhibited some weakening and is now clearly in a defensive posture in the face of concessions, although it remains the strongest of the three. In the face of declining membership and pressures from both capital and the state, Canadian unions have taken tentative steps towards diversifying organizing strategies and building a broader based social movement. The success of these steps should not be overstated, but at the very least a project for change is on the table and is being advocated by some of the strongest unions in Canada (such as the CAW and Canadian Union of Public Employees). Beginning from a weaker position, the labour movement in the US has been more prone to accept concession bargaining and partnerships with employers. Yet, even there there have been advances, limited though they may be, in the direction of social movement unionism. "Jobs with Justice," "Justice for Janitors," and a range of city-based campaigns include efforts by unions like the Service Employees International Union to promote a living wage for workers in precarious employment positions (Nissen 2003b: 138–42). Even more than the Canadian case, however, the debate over social movement unionism has been very limited and has not gained widespread support in the broader labour movement. Mexican unions are in the most complex position. They have traditionally been tied to official corporatist structures in an authoritarian state and have played a role in limiting the independence of workers' struggles. State-based attempts to restructure to meet international obligations and to attract investment have consistently led to officially sanctioned anti-union strategies and economic policies that have undermined the living standards of Mexican workers. Given the weak position of independent unions in Mexico, and the severity of neo-liberal pressures, the best that can be hoped for is a continued movement towards independent unions that can develop the capacity to resist further downward labour market pressures.

Many union activists and academics have suggested that unions in Canada and the US could assist workers in Mexico in their bid for an independent and effective structure. The North American Agreement on Labour Cooperation (NAALC) was, in part, intended to do just this. Under pressure from the AFL-CIO, the Clinton administration pressed for inclusion of the labour side agreement in NAFTA in 1993 (Williams 1996). The agreement itself is intended to promote the enforcement of 11 core labour rights, "including freedom of association and the right to organize, free collective bargaining, prohibitions on child labor, and the right to safe and healthy work environments" (Singh 2002: 438). Through the agreement, National Administration Offices (NAOs) are established in each country to process any complaints made by individuals or organizations. If a claim is deemed to have sufficient merit, and if initial negotiations do not resolve the dispute, the NAO can send disputes to "conciliation" and "arbitration." To date, however, no dispute had gone this far (Singh 2002: 438). Although the AFL-CIO's promotion of the NAALC was alleged to have been designed to force Mexico to uphold the union protections guaranteed in its Constitution, and thus create conditions for a strong independent Mexican labour movement, the underlying reason was to protect jobs in the US. The NAALC is the only example of the creation of a supranational body that is intended to regulate labour, but its limited capacity to effectively sanction states that violate the agreement renders it almost meaningless. Moreover, the NAALC, despite its claim to promote labour cooperation, has no effective means by which to facilitate connections between the labour movements of North America. This leaves the three labour movements to focus political activities on their own national states and to pursue international linkages in the absence of any form of continental state apparatus actually enforcing freedom of association and other labour rights.

Proposals to create independent ties between labour movements can be classified as "international solidarity," union strategies to act internationally to counter an already internationalized capitalist class (Moody 1997). This could be a positive strategy, instituted by unions themselves, to create active links that provide mutual support in struggles. There are, however, limitations to proposals for international solidarity. Unions within each country remain internally fragmented. They have exhibited limited capacity to coordinate strategy *within* national borders—indeed, the union centrals in all three countries seem all but strategically incapacitated—let alone between different national union movements with distinct histories and established practices. It will also be necessary to develop greater rank-and-file participation in democratically structured national and local unions if new political projects are to be sustained (Gindin and Stanford 2003: 435–36). In the absence of direct member involvement, links between movements will simply be formalistic agreements without the capacity to be implemented fully. Finally, even though there has been movement towards the creation of a single North American market space, this has not translated into a unified political space or the differentiation of national economic developments and dilemmas. Unions still negotiate locally (itself a political act) and are bound by national state-based industrial relations regimes that regulate union activities. Without the deepening of democratic sovereignty within national states (which enables workers and citizens to exercise some policy capacity over the policy issues that most immediately affect them in their daily lives) and the reformation of working-class and union capacities at the local, sectoral, and national levels, international struggles, as imperative as they are to undertake, will be limited in their impact.

In the immediate future at least, international solidarity might assist unions in organizing at particular plants (as unions in one space lend organizing and financial resources to workers elsewhere), or might be able to act to try to prevent certain activities (for example, protests against neo-liberal trade deals or coordinated boycotts of employers engaging in abhorrent employment practices). But this strategy is not likely to put positive proposals on the political agenda. Such proposals, made at the level of the nation-state, could include attempts to control capital flows, thereby reducing the capacity of employers to use the threat of capital flight to wring concessions out of unions. Moreover, controls on capital mobility would enable states effectively to plan trade (and aid), targeting investment in areas that promote human welfare. Proposals could also include labour law reform. In all three countries, reforms might also revolve around changes that facilitate organizing in the service sector to boost union density or that include sectoral bargaining. Sectoral bargaining would allow workers in sectors characterized by small workplaces to negotiate en masse with employers, giving unions greater protection against competitive pressures. Because these proposals grate against the logic of neo-liberalism, they are not likely to be implemented any time soon. However, it is only through challenging the logic of neo-liberalism that union movements in North America can hope to carve out a space in which they are not continually forced onto the defensive.

Notes

1   As governments have downsized and contracted out, the number of government employees has been significantly reduced, even though density has been maintained as a percentage of those employed in the public sector. Over the past decade, the federal government has shed 19 per cent of its workforce, the provinces have shed 11 per cent, health and social service employment has been reduced by 7 per cent, and local government has lost 4 per cent of the workforce (Swimmer and Bartkiw 2003: 584).

2   Recent partnerships between the CAW and employers included provisions for job security given government support for the industry (for which both the union and the employer are to lobby).

3   Michael Wachter (2003) argues that another reason for increased employer hostility to unionization stems from increased competitive pressures.

4   Within the corporatist structures, the most significant resource of the CTM (the main official union central) was its ability to keep militant workers under control. This gave incentive to the CTM leaders to repress their members (Middlebrook 1995: 268).

References

AFL-CIO. 2003. "Report: NAFTA Fails Workers," 18 December. <http://www.aflcio.org>.

Albo, Gregory. 1990. "The New Realism and Canadian Workers." In James Bickerton and Alain Gagnon (eds.), *Canadian Politics*. Peterborough, ON: Broadview Press. 471–503.

——. 2005. "Contesting the 'New Capitalism.'" In D. Coates (ed.), *Varieties of Capitalism, Varieties of Approaches*. London: Palgrave. 63–82.

Campbell, Bruce, *et al.* 1999. *Pulling Apart: The Deterioration of Employment and Income in North America Under Free Trade*. Ottawa: CCPA.

CAW/TCA. 2003. "Union Resistance and Union Renewal." Seventh Constitutional Convention Toronto, 19–22 August.

Cockcroft, James. 1998. *Mexico's Hope: An Encounter with Politics and History*. New York: Monthly Review Press.

Commission for Labor Cooperation. 2003. *North American Labor Markets: Main Changes Since NAFTA*. Washington, DC: Commission for Labor Cooperation.

Cypher, James M. 2001. "Developing Disarticulation Within the Mexican Economy." *Latin American Perspectives* 28,3: 11–37.

Donnelly, Robert, Dan LaBotz, and Peter Geffert. 1999. "The Mexican Political-Economic Year in Review: Crisis Continues." *Mexican Labor News and Analysis*, 4: 1.

Dumas, Martin. 2003. "Recent Trends in Union Density in North America." Paper prepared for the Secretariat of the Commission for Labor Cooperation, August. <http://www.naalc.org>.

Economic Council of Canada. 1990. *Good Jobs, Bad Jobs: Employment in the Service Economy*. Ottawa: Supply and Services.

Fantasia, Rick, and Kim Voss. 2004. *Hard Work: Remaking the American Labor Movement.* Berkeley, CA: U of California P.

Gindin, Sam. 1995. *The Canadian Auto Workers: The Birth and Transformation of a Union.* Toronto: James Lorimer.

Gindin, Sam, and Jim Stanford. 2003. "Canadian Labour and the Political Economy of Transformation." In Wallace Clement and Leah Vosko (eds.), *Changing Canada: Political Economy as Transformation*. Montreal and Kingston: McGill-Queen's UP. 422–42.

Jackson, Andrew. 2003. "From Leaps of Faith to Hard Landings: Fifteen Years of 'Free Trade.'" Ottawa: Centre for Policy Alternatives, December.

——. 2004. "Economic and Social Impacts of Trade Unions." Canadian Labour Congress Working Paper, February. <http://www.clc-ctc.ca>.

Kelley, John. 1988. *Trade Unions and Socialist Politics*. London, Verso.

Levi, Margaret. 2003. "Organizing Power: The Prospects for an American Labor Movement." *Perspectives on Politics* 1,1. <http://www.apsanet.org>.

Madrid, Raul. 2003. "Labouring Against Neo-liberalism: Unions and Patterns of Reform in Latin America." *Journal of Latin American Studies* 35: 53–88.

Martinello, Felice. 2000. "Mr. Harris, Mr. Rae, and Union Activity in Ontario." *Canadian Public Policy* 26,1: 17–33.

Middlebrook, Kevin J. 1995. *The Paradox of Revolution: Labor, the State, and Authoritarianism in Mexico*. Baltimore, MD: The Johns Hopkins UP.

Moody, Kim. 1995. "NAFTA and the Corporate Redesign of North America." *Latin American Perspectives* 22,1: 95–116.

——. 1997. *Workers in a Lean World: Unions in the International Economy*. London: Verso.

Munro, Marcella. 1997. "Ontario's 'Days of Action' and Strategic Choices for the Left in Canada." *Studies in Political Economy* 53: 125–40.

Nissen, Bruce. 2003a. "The Recent Past and Near Future of Private Sector Unionism in the US: An Appraisal." *Journal of Labor Research* 24: 323–38.

——. 2003b. "Alternative Strategic Directions for the US Labor Movement: Recent Scholarship." *Labor Studies Journal* 28,1: 133–55.

Obrera, Pastoral Juvenil. 2003. "The Struggle for Justice in the Maquilladoras: The Experience of the Autotrim Workers." In Timothy A. Wise, Hilda Salazar, and Laura Carlsen (eds.), *Confronting Globalization: Economic Integration and Popular Resistance in Mexico*. Bloomfield CT: Kumarian Press. 173–94.

OECD. 2004. *Employment Outlook*. Paris: OECD.

Ogmundson, Richard, and Michael Doyle. 2002. "The Rise and Decline of Canadian Labour/1960 to 2000: Elites, Power, Ethnicity and Gender." *Canadian Journal of Sociology* 27,3: 413–54.

Panitch, Leo. 2001. "Reflections on Strategy for Labour." In Leo Panitch and Colin Leys (eds.), *The Socialist Register 2001: Working Classes, Global Realities*. London: Merlin. 367–92.

Panitch, Leo, and Donald Swartz. 2003. *From Consent to Coercion: The Assault on Trade Union Freedoms*. 3rd ed. Toronto: Garamond.

Peters, John. 2002. *A Fine Balance: Canadian Unions Confront Globalization*. Ottawa: Canadian Centre for Policy Alternatives.

Ramirez, Miguel. 1997. "Mexico." In L. Randall (ed.), *The Political Economy of Latin America in the Postwar Period*. Austin, TX: U of Texas P.

Regini, Marino (Ed.). 1992. *The Future of Labour Movements*. London: Sage. 111–48.

Robinson, Ian. 1994. "NAFTA, Social Unionism, and Labour Movement Power in Canada and the United States." *Relations Industrielles* 49,4: 657–93.

Rodriguez, Rogelio Hernandez. 1998. "The Partido Revolucionario Institucional." In Monica Serrano (ed.), *Governing Mexico: Political Parties and Elections*. London: Institute of Latin American Studies.

Roman, Richard, and Edur Velasco Arregui. 1998. "Worker Insurgency, Rural Revolt, and the Crisis of the Mexican Regime." In Ellen Meiksins Wood, Peter Meiksins, and Michael Yates (eds.), *Rising From the Ashes? Labour in the Age of "Global" Capitalism*. New York: Monthly Review Press. 127–41.

——. 2002. "Mexico in the Crucible: Workers, Continental Integration and Political Transition." *Labour, Capital and Society* 35,2: 318–41.

Singh, Parbudyal. 2002. "NAFTA and Labor: A Canadian Perspective." *Journal of Labor Research* 23,3: 433–46.

Swartz, Donald. 1993. "Capitalist Restructuring and the Canadian Labour Movement." In Jane Jenson and Rianne Mahon (eds.), *The Challenge of Restructuring: North American Labour Movements Respond*. Philadelphia, PA: Temple UP. 381–402.

Swimmer, Gene, and Tim Bartkiw. 2003. "The Future of Public Sector Collective Bargaining in Canada." *Journal of Labor Research* 24,4: 579–95.

Voss, Kim, and Rachel Sherman. 2000. "Breaking the Iron Law of Oligarchy: Union Revitalization in the America Labor Movement." *American Journal of Sociology* 106,2: 303–49.

Wachter, Michael. 2003. "Judging Unions' Future Using a Historical Perspective: The Public Policy Choice between Competition and Unionization." *Journal of Labor Research* 24,2: 339–57.

Waterman, Peter. 2001. *Globalization, Social Movements and the New Internationalisms*. New York: Continuum.

Wells, Don. 1997. "When Push Comes to Shove: Competitiveness, Job Insecurity, and Labour-Management Cooperation in Canada." *Economic and Industrial Democracy* 18,2: 167–200.

——. 1998. "Labour Solidarity Goes Global." *Canadian Dimension* 32,2 (March/April): 33–36.

Williams, Edward J. 1996. "Discord in US-Mexican Labor Relations and the North American Agreement on Labor Cooperation." January. The National Law Center for Inter American Free Trade. <http://www.natlaw.com>.

Williams, Mark Eric. 2001. "Learning the Limits of Power: Privatization and State-Labor Interactions in Mexico." *Latin American Politics and Society* 43,4: 91–126.

Wise, Timothy A., Hilda Salazar, and Laura Carlsen. 2003. "Lessons Learned: Civil Society Strategies in the Face of Economic Integration." In Timothy A. Wise, Hilda Salazar, and Laura Carlsen (eds.), *Confronting Globalization: Economic Integration and Popular Resistance in Mexico*. Bloomfield, CT: Kumarian Press. 213–34.

Yates, Charlotte. 2000. "Expanding Labour's Horizons: Union Organizing and Strategic Change in Canada." *Just Labour* 1: 31–40.

CHAPTER THIRTEEN

Ragged Cruelty?
Social Policy Transformations in North America[1]

Lois Harder and Marcus Taylor

The social policy regimes of Canada, the US, and Mexico have undergone profound changes since the 1994 implementation of NAFTA. Although NAFTA's provisions did not explicitly extend to the realm of social policy, and its proponents insisted that social programs were exempted from the agreement, its critics were quick to point out that the prevailing neo-liberal ideology that infused the agreement would have far-reaching consequences for the well-being of North Americans. Specifically, these critics pointed to NAFTA's requirement that signatories list government programs and services to be exempted from its trade and investment rules, thus creating a situation in which non-listed programs, especially new programs, would be subject to them (McBride 2001: 109–10). Canadians, in particular, worried that the listing requirement would effectively preclude any development of new national social programs, such as a national drug insurance plan, and would provide a back door through which private health care providers could take over Canada's public health system.

More than a decade after its passage, the impact of NAFTA on the social policy regimes of Canada, the US, and Mexico has been both more profound than its proponents envisioned and, with regard to the possibility of new programs, less restrictive than its critics had anticipated. Yet while new programs have been implemented—as examined below—their shape and objectives nonetheless reveal a shift in social policy thinking. This shift might be characterized as a move away from social programs providing protection from market failures (such as unemployment insurance) toward enhancing citizen attachment to labour markets (such as work for welfare or training programs). Such reform deepened the existing trend of pushing citizens towards an increased reliance on the market, rather than the state, as a source of social provision. The change in emphasis reflects responses to a series of social and economic transformations often described under the rubric of globalization, including both changes in economic structures and the nature of work and the transformation of the nuclear family (Esping-Andersen 1997: 6–7).

In an era in which firms have had to radically restructure their operations to remain profitable, employers have frequently sought to address competitive pressures by reducing wages and benefits and by encouraging states to increase the disciplinary effects of labour markets by limiting the capacity of workers to rely on state-provided income supports. By reducing access to unemployment insurance benefits, for example, workers are more likely to remain in unappealing jobs because they lack the resources to exit the workforce temporarily in the search for more rewarding employment. Pressure on governments to restrict benefits has come from business-led criticisms of public sector inefficiencies, of the tax burdens that result from social provision, and of the fiscal crises incurred by states, allegedly as a result of overly generous social spending.

Relatedly, economic restructuring in the era of globalization has brought about a decline in manufacturing in industrialized countries. The result has been a transformation in the nature of work. Today, workers are overwhelmingly employed in the service sector. While the latter encompasses some high-paying professional jobs, it also includes extremely low-paying restaurant, retail, and hospitality sector "McJobs" (Ritzer 2002). The contemporary model of employment is frequently low-paying and without benefits and may involve non-standard hours of work, limited-term contracts, and part-time work (Fudge and Vosko 2003: 183). Whereas the *maquiladora* phenomenon in Mexico—whereby firms have established assembly plants in Mexico to take advantage of cheaper labour—has stymied the loss of manufacturing jobs noted elsewhere, such employment provides lower wages and more precarious job security than previous industrial-sector jobs. Rather than providing good jobs and an expansion of the middle class, as neo-liberal reformers promised, economic liberalization and service sector growth has increased polarization and expanded the phenomenon of the "working poor" in all three NAFTA member countries (Kerstetter 2002; US Census Bureau 2001; Dussel Peters 2000). As detailed below, social policies in all three countries have also been transformed in a manner congruent with these changes in labour markets.

The need for social policy reform has also been propelled by the transformation of the nuclear family. Women have increasingly been drawn into paid work as wages have declined and a single income is less able to support a family. Liberalized divorce laws and increases in non-marital births have also transformed familial norms. The growth in the number of single-parent families has invoked considerable moral outrage, particularly among US conservatives, who revile the lack of male responsibility and the weak sexual mores of women that such a situation is claimed to represent. But even for those who reject such normative judgements, the decreased capacity of a single adult to support a family gives rise to concerns for families' economic security and general well-being.

Even before NAFTA, efforts to address this conflation of pressures became crystallized within a package of neo-liberal policies focused upon reductions in social spending, a decentralization of responsibility for service provision and funding, increased reliance on private sources of provision, and increased targeting of remaining public resources towards high-priority social groups. A number of inherent tensions can be highlighted within this policy prescription that has, in different manners and to varied degrees, been implemented in all three North American countries.

Decentralization was heralded as a way of making government more responsive to user demands and therefore minimizing wastage and corruption. As the World Bank (2000: 4) asserts, "localization nourishes responsive and efficient governance." Further, decentralization has been lauded as a means to support policy innovation. By encouraging new program initiatives at the local level, the commitment of resources can be limited and ideas can be tested with less risk (Devigne 1994: 99–100). At issue, however, is whether the decentralization of welfare provision has placed demands upon subnational and local government structures that enjoy neither the financial nor the administrative resources to effectively undertake such tasks. Moreover, there is no *a priori* justification for suggesting that regional governments will be less prone to corruption and abuse of power than national governments.

Privatization was presented as a manner of introducing market mechanisms to service provision that would maximize efficiency and individual freedom of choice through competition between providers while concurrently enabling the state to reduce its fiscal burden by offloading services to the private sector. Nevertheless, the essential presupposition of privatization is that efficiency, personal choice, and the provision of services can all be subordinated to profitability without compromising the perceived rationality of market-based service provision. In this way, privatization necessarily creates a strong articulation between the quantity and quality of services received and the ability of the individual household to pay for them, a situation that can exacerbate noted trends toward social polarization across North America.

Finally, the targeting of social expenditures is the reverse side of privatization and retrenchment. It offers a means to address the social needs of the poorest (or at least those deemed most "deserving" among the low-income population), even within a system that compels the majority of citizens personally to assume a growing share of the burden for their well-being. Targeting social benefits is thus claimed to improve efficiency, by ensuring that only those citizens "who really need them" can have access to benefits and programs. But targeted programs also carry the risk of pitting one group of citizens against another and of undermining a sense of common entitlement to citizenship as the product of shared life experiences. The result can be declining social cohesion, political cynicism, and decreased state legitimacy and authority.

In addition to the common trends in North American social policy reform, the specific histories and socio-political contexts of each country, as well as the effects of privatization and decentralization within specific national constitutional frameworks, ensure manifold national and subnational particularities. Our analysis will therefore proceed by considering the broad parameters of Canadian, US, and Mexican social policy transformation, with a specific focus on income support initiatives since NAFTA's implementation. Space limits these analyses to selective and cursory overviews, but we suggest that the identification of general trends supports our claims regarding the common atomizing effects on citizens of neo-liberal social reform strategies even as they are filtered through distinctive national contexts.

National Contexts

CANADA

In the North American context, Canada has a reputation as a bastion of progressive social policy-making. Indeed Canada's social policy regime and its system of universal health care provision in particular are regarded as a key constituent of the Canadian identity (Brodie 2002: 178). This (arguably fading) *national* attachment to a compassionate social policy regime is all the more remarkable in that the provinces have constitutional jurisdiction over social policy. Constitutional amendments shifted authority for old age pensions and unemployment insurance to the federal level (Rice and Prince 2000: 81), but other social programs, including health care, have resulted from federal-provincial negotiations in which the federal government has shouldered its way into the social policy domain through its spending power and its willingness to attach conditions (national standards) to these funds. The motivations for this federal interest in social policy are complex, but at a general level, the federal government's involvement can be ascribed to the need to articulate a common national identity in a country marked by a persistent sense of exclusion in the French-speaking province of Québec and by regional tensions in the west and the Atlantic provinces, as well as the link between the state's legitimacy and its role in securing the well-being of citizens.

Regardless of Canada's reputation within the North American context, the literature on comparative welfare states in industrialized countries locates both Canada and the US in the category of liberal or residual welfare states. In such states, citizens are required to meet the majority of their social needs through the market (Esping-Andersen 1990). Even in the 1970s, when the Canadian welfare state was in its heyday, social assistance programs, for example, were not particularly generous, with benefits pegged well below the poverty line. While social assistance did provide a last resort for people who had spent down their assets and had no other means of support, these programs expressed the expectation and normative judgement that paid work, or at least marriage to a paid worker, was the preferred means to secure well-being.

Other important state-provided social services, including Unemployment Insurance and the Canada Pension Plan/Québec Pension Plan (CPP/QPP) reinforced labour market participation as the foundation of citizen entitlement by limiting benefits to workers and, in the case of the CPP/QPP, their spouses. Less overt in their normative expectations, the contributory dimension of these programs, in which the employee and employer (and, for a time, the state) paid into the insurance program, gave claimants a sense of entitlement to these benefits. Other contributory schemes, such as the Registered Retirement Savings Program (RRSP), which encourages individual or spousal retirement savings, and, more recently, the Registered Education Savings Plan (RESP), which encourages parents to save for the post-secondary education of their children, are primarily accessed by more affluent Canadians. These programs encourage savings through privileged tax treatment in the case of the RRSP and additional state contributions in the case of RESPs.

The few universal social programs that were implemented in Canada included a family allowance, old age security, primary and secondary education, and health care. Currently, the only remaining universal programs are primary and secondary education and health care.

In the post-NAFTA era, compassion and social policy have become increasingly estranged. Canada's welfare state began its neo-liberal reformation in the late 1980s, but the most significant changes have occurred since the implementation of the Canada Health and Social Transfer (CHST) in 1996. The CHST represented the abandonment of the practice of 50–50 federal-provincial cost-sharing with federal conditions attached. Instead, the amount of money transferred to the provinces is unilaterally fixed by the federal government and, at least as it was initially proposed, decreases over time. Moreover, because the CHST is a fixed sum, the amount of money transferred to the provinces does not alter in accordance with fluctuations in the strength of the economy. When citizens face economic crisis due to market down-turns, the provinces have to bear the burden of increased demand for social services on their own (Prince 1999: 179).

Because the CHST comes in the form of a block grant and is transferred to the general revenues of the provinces, there is little oversight available to citizens or to the federal government regarding the programs in which the money is actually invested (Harder 2003: 182). It is generally accepted, however, that provinces have chosen to direct the decreasing federal dollars towards cash-hungry health care pro-grams. As a consequence, the federal government has effectively vacated the realm of social assistance (certainly for poor adults) leaving the financing of programs for Canada's most economically vulnerable citizens solely to the provinces (Battle and Torjman 1996: 57). The reduction in federal transfers has exacerbated fiscal pres-sures experienced by the provinces in their efforts to create tax regimes that will attract investment. Thus, social programs have become a common target of budget reductions with the predictable consequences of intensified income polarization and a reduced capacity of public transfers and social programs to offset the negative effects of low income (McKeen and Porter 2003: 121). But most significantly, the ability to speak of a national social policy regime in Canada has all but disappeared. Instead, citizens' entitlement to social provision depends on their province of residence, their incomes, and the level of family support on which they can rely.

Nonetheless, the story of post-NAFTA social policy developments in Canada is not a straightforward tale of reduced state involvement in providing for social well being. As struggles over the retention of a public health care system and the develop-ment of the National Child Benefit reveal, the state still has a key role to play. The juxtapositions of a safety net and a trampoline, or "a hand up rather than a hand out," can be seen to express the transformation from the postwar welfare state to the contemporary form of social provision.

INCOME SUPPORT

Canada's income support programs fall under three broad categories depending on their target constituency. Canadians over age 65 may receive the CPP/QPP, Old Age Security (OAS), and the Guaranteed Income Supplement. In addition, Canadians are encouraged to save for their old age through retirement savings plans and may also have access to private employer pensions. At least until recently, Canada's system of elderly benefits has been recognized as an unmitigated success in reducing poverty levels among people over 65 (Beauvais and Jenson 2001: 19). Nonetheless, the sys-tem has come under increasing strain and challenge. The formerly universal OAS has become a means-tested benefit. CPP/QPP benefits are forecast to fall for people who began contributing to the pension plan in 1997 as the result of a pension reform ini-tiative, and while Canada has resisted calls to replace its public pension system with mandated personal retirement savings plans, this idea has strong currency in some policy circles (Sayeed 2002: 1).

Unemployed Canadians may have access to the Employment Insurance program (EI), and people who are not entitled to EI and whose assets are sufficiently depleted have recourse to provincial social assistance programs. As well, low-income families with children are entitled to the National Child Benefit (NCB). The NCB is a complicated federal-provincial-territorial program largely designed to shore up the earnings of low-waged workers who have children.

Canada's unemployment insurance program (EI) underwent a significant transformation in 1996, resulting in a dramatic reduction in the number of Canadians eligible to receive benefits as well as a reduction in the value of those benefits. As part of this restructuring, the program was renamed *Employment* Insurance, providing a clear signal that the reforms were designed to strengthen the tie binding workers to their jobs. One result of these changes has been the development of a $45 billion surplus in the Employment Insurance fund, an amount equivalent to five times the fund's total annual payments (CLC 2003). Moreover the number of workers eligible for EI has dropped dramatically, from 83 per cent of unemployed Canadians in 1989 (Prince 1999) to 38 per cent in 2002 (CLC 2003). All workers are, nonetheless, obliged to contribute to the EI fund.

The 1996 reforms to unemployment insurance reflect an attempt to both reduce government expenditures and to ensure a more competitive labour market. The determination of benefit eligibility was shifted from weeks to hours, the work requirement increased, and benefits were limited to workers who had been laid-off. Hence, workers who are mistreated, harassed, or dissatisfied with their work have much less freedom to pursue alternatives or to hold their employers accountable. In the absence of income support for job-leavers, employers' power is substantially increased (Stanford 1996: 144). Additional changes to the program, including the reduction in benefits from 60 to 55 per cent of earnings and the reduction in the duration of benefits from 50 to 45 weeks also ensures that workers will be more willing to comply with the demands of their employers (Prince 1999: 181).

The logic and design of the National Child Benefit is particularly revealing of the post-NAFTA social policy era. Since eliminating the universal Family Allowance in 1992, Canada's federal government has been under growing pressure to recognize the costs that child-raising imposes on families (Lefebvre and Merrigan 2003: 9) and to fulfil a promise to address child poverty. Also, growing concerns were being expressed among anti-poverty activists and social policy think tanks about the lack of incentives for social assistance recipients to enter the paid labour market (Battle 1999: 43). Many provincial social assistance plans provided recipients with supplementary medical benefits and subsidies for school supplies and school transportation. These benefits were lost once benefit recipients joined the labour force. Another concern was the fact that the kind of work for which most social assistance recipients would be hired did not provide wages sufficient to meet the costs of labour force participation, including clothes, transportation, and child care. This combination of "perverse incentives" to remain on social assistance was termed the "welfare wall" (Battle 1999: 43).

Announced in 1998, the NCB represented a modest return of the federal government to the realm of income support.[2] The federal portion of the program provides a monthly payment, varying with the number and ages of the children, to all low-income families with children under 18. In fact, although the payment decreases as income increases, a portion of the NCB stretches sufficiently far up the income scale to reach 80 per cent of Canadian children (Boychuk 2001: 136). From the perspective of the federal government, it does not matter whether a person's income comes from paid work or from provincial social assistance/welfare programs: if a family's net income as reported on their tax return falls below $22,615 and they have children, they are entitled to the full benefit.[3] Despite the federal government's broadly inclusive claim, however, the program is explicitly designed to enable the provinces to reward wage earners over social assistance recipients.

Under the terms of the NCB, provincial governments may (and are, in fact, expected to) claw back part of the payment to families who are receiving social assistance. What is happening, in the minds of the policy designers at least, is that a portion of the provincial social assistance payment that went to children is now being paid by the federal government. Children are being shifted off the provincial welfare rolls and are, instead, receiving an allegedly non-stigmatized, guaranteed income from the federal government. And with the money that the provinces save from not having to support children in social assistance families, they are expected to develop new programs to assist low-income *working* families. Because the provinces can determine what these programs will be, they can tailor them to address the specific needs of the provincial labour market.

The federal government insists that families on social assistance are not supposed to be any worse off under the new policy—welfare families should experience the receipt of the NCB as revenue neutral. By contrast, low-income workers now receive additional money every month to augment their meagre wages and also have access to new provincial services. They are thus encouraged to remain in the labour market, even when they have to hold down low-paying, often extremely alienating, and highly exploitative jobs. People with low incomes are clearly being encouraged to "choose" labour force participation rather than resorting to social assistance. Regardless of federal claims that the NCB applies to *all* low-income families, they are also very clear that the program is designed to promote "attachment to the workforce resulting in fewer families having to rely on social assistance—by ensuring that families will always be better off as a result of finding work...." (Canada 1999: 1233).

Since the implementation of NAFTA, the link between social well-being and paid work has intensified in Canada. The federal government has increasingly vacated the social policy realm, shifting financial responsibility for social spending to the provinces and territories, and, in the process, heightening tensions in the federation. Only in the area of health care has federal interest been retained, though funding here is only just returning to pre-CHST levels (Boychuk 2004: 19). For individual Canadians, the social safety net of the post-NAFTA era is threadbare. Targeted programs ensure that the elderly poor and working poor can subsist, and an ongoing commitment to public health care ensures that the vast majority of citizens will get help when they are ill. For the majority of citizens, however, employee-benefit packages, savings and credit, and/or individual creativity have replaced the assurance of social protection.

UNITED STATES

Among industrialized nations, the US is designated a "welfare state laggard" (Myles 1997: 116). Highly reliant on the market to provide social goods, a situation that has intensified since the mid-1990s, many Americans have no assurance that public programs will assist them if they fall on hard times. Fourteen per cent of the US population (about 43 million people) are without health insurance (Lancet 2004: 179) and poor people, including poor children, have no guaranteed entitlement to income assistance. There are, however, some important exceptions to this stark scenario. Elderly people, in particular, are entitled to the relatively generous social programs of old age pensions (known as Social Security) and medicare. But also significant is the degree to which employer benefits figure in the US social policy landscape. Indeed, it might be argued that US governments have escaped pressure for greater social protections because the majority of the middle class has historically been able to rely on work-related benefits and, as a result, have not agitated for state provided programs (Orloff 2002: 101–02). With the increase in flexible work, however, employer-provided benefits are eroding (Esping-Andersen 1997: 8), and there is some evidence that pressure is mounting for new public programs. Nonetheless, as the Commission to Strengthen Social Security appointed by President George W. Bush in 2001 revealed, market-based solutions have certainly not been discredited.

The residualism of the US social policy regime is a product of that country's political institutions, the operation of federalism, and the ways in which both the politics of race and the dynamics of the US south have played out in these arenas. The arduous process of passing legislation in the US congressional system necessitates a constant state of negotiation across party lines and between the executive and legislative branches of government. As a result, the creation of directly funded social programs represents an impressive legislative accomplishment. In this context, US policy-makers have increasingly turned to indirect programs delivered through the tax system. Such programs may only appear as line items in omnibus budget bills and thus may avoid significant controversy and debate (Howard 1997: 70).

The relationship between the federal and state governments also contributes to the shape of the social policy regime in the US. Social programs have historically been considered a state responsibility, but the US Constitution does not exclude the federal government from this policy arena. In practice, the federal government largely funds social programs, while the states and local governments are responsible for their delivery (Rocher 2000: 270). This practice has emerged for two reasons. First, most states operate under balanced budget requirements, a situation that prevents them from using deficits to finance increased social program spending in periods of economic downturn (Blank 1997: 92). As a result, federal funding is important to maintaining social programs when they are needed most. Second, federal involvement in the social policy realm, particularly with the Great Society initiatives of the 1960s, resulted from a desire to curb the practice of excluding African Americans from benefits, a situation that was common in the US south (Myles 1997: 129; Blank 1997: 92).[4] In providing funding and attaching conditions to receipt of that funding, the US federal government was able to mandate racial equality for reluctant states and thus establish a more uniform condition of citizenship.

Since the era of President Ronald Reagan (1980–88), and particularly since the welfare reforms of the mid-1990s, social policy discretion has returned to the state level in an effort to reduce funding and, more recently, to encourage policy innovation (Rocher 2000: 273). With regard to the latter objective, states are able to attain waivers that allow them to receive federal funding but deviate from federal program guidelines.

As the prevailing global economic power, the US creates its own weather; it is, arguably, the key influence in establishing the economic framework that shapes the activities of markets and polities throughout the world, whether this is to concur with or resist US policy prescriptions. Certainly for Mexico and Canada, the US is synonymous with global economic forces. Because the US was an initiator of neo-liberal governance, decentralization, privatization, and targeting are sharply in evidence in recent US social policy reform initiatives.

INCOME SUPPORT

The primary income support programs in the US include Old Age, Survivors and Disability Insurance (OASDI)—generally known as Social Security—the Earned Income Tax Credit (EITC), Unemployment Insurance Benefits (UIB), Food Stamps, and Temporary Aid to Needy Families (TANF). We will limit our remarks to TANF, the EITC, and Social Security.

Although it is a relatively small program, reaching approximately 5 million people (of a total US population of 291 million) and costing approximately $18 billion annually, TANF is probably the most controversial and widely debated income support program in the US. Initiated in 1996 under the auspices of the Personal Responsibility and Work Opportunity Reconciliation Act, TANF transfers federal funds to states, which must agree to decrease their welfare rolls by compelling labour force participation. TANF enables states to experiment in developing programs that will increase labour force attachment, including providing child care, training, and transportation subsidies. But in addition to work expectations, TANF also requires states to reduce out-of-wedlock pregnancies and, under the administration of President George W. Bush, to promote marriage and responsible fatherhood (Congressional Research Service 2003).

TANF, like its predecessor Aid to Families with Dependent Children (AFDC), is directed almost exclusively at single mothers. Unlike AFDC, however, TANF does not represent an entitlement to income support for these families. Instead, benefit receipt is conditional upon participation in paid work or engagement in work-related activities. Recipients may only receive benefits for two years at a time and face a lifetime limit on benefit receipt of five years.

TANF reflects a sea change in thinking about women's roles in the home and in the workplace. As increasing numbers of women combine paid work and child-rearing, it has become increasingly difficult to justify state support for poor women to care for their children on a full-time basis (Orloff 2002: 105). But the adoption of TANF also reflects race politics in the US. The image of the single mother has shifted from a white widow to an unmarried or divorced African-American woman, a shift that has been expressed in the vitriolic language of "welfare queens" and moral outrage surrounding unwed mothers. In this context, then, support mounted to "end welfare as we know it" (Orloff 2002; Weaver 2000).

Since the implementation of the 1996 welfare reforms, the number of families receiving assistance has dropped dramatically (Tanner 2003: 62–63), but whether this was because of TANF or a dramatic upswing in the US economy is not clear.[5] This ambiguity results from the observation that poverty rates have tracked the economic cycle, begging the question as to the effectiveness of TANF in reducing poverty. Indeed, for many of TANF's critics, welfare reform was less about income support than reflective of a desire to punish and/or discourage single parenthood and shift the income dependency of single mothers from the state to the market or to a lawfully wedded husband.

In contrast to the profound distaste for welfare benefits exhibited by US policy-makers, there has been a great deal of support for the EITC, a program delivered through the tax system that provides a modest top-up to the earnings of low-wage workers and encourages them to address their social needs in the market, rather than relying on government services. Like Canada's National Child Benefit, the EITC is designed to offset the effects of neo-liberal globalism for those who suffer its effects most keenly; unlike the Canadian program, the EITC is not restricted to families with children, although childless families make up a very small portion of recipients and receive a much smaller benefit (Burman and Kobes 2003: 1769). Also, the EITC targets a growing portion of the US electorate as the middle class has shrunk and incomes have polarized (Howard 1997: 142; Skocpol 2000: 4–5). Howard cites the findings of pollster Stanley Greenberg who observed that the working poor were "frustrated about doing everything right in terms of work and family and still being unable to afford a house, child care or health insurance or to save for retirement" (Howard 1997: 142).

Over the 1990s, the EITC expanded three-fold and, in 2000, represented nearly the combined spending on TANF and Food Stamps, or $31.5 billion (Hotz and Scholz 2003: 141–42). In the effort to increase labour market attachment as part of the 1990s welfare reform initiatives, former President Bill Clinton's objective was to increase the EITC sufficiently that, in combination with a minimum wage job and food stamps, the net incomes of working poor families would rise above the poverty line (Hotz and Scholz 2003: 146). In fact, this objective was only achieved for families with fewer than three children and only after the minimum wage was increased to $4.75/hr in 1996 and $5.15 in 1997 (Hotz and Scholz 2003; US Department of Labor n.d.).

The role of the EITC in dampening wage demands should also be noted. As long as low-wage workers can rely on a subsidy from the government, they may be less inclined to demand higher wages from their employers. Hence, the EITC's benefits extend beyond the working poor to their employers, who are, in fact, enjoying a wage subsidy from the state. Indeed, the EITC might be read as an explicit endorsement of a low-wage economy.

The most generous US income support program and, indeed, the most successful in terms of reducing poverty levels, is the Old Age, Survivors and Disability Insurance program, commonly known as Social Security. Originally established as part of President Roosevelt's New Deal in 1935, Social Security has largely retained its original shape and intent, with a few actuarial adjustments, to the present day. Social Security is understood to be nearly universal, reaching 90 per cent of Americans over age 65 (Diamond and Orszag 2004: 15). The program is funded by a combined employer-employee payroll tax and, as such, is a work-related benefit. Spouses of workers are entitled to either 50 per cent of their partners' pensions or their own pension entitlements, whichever is greater (Diamond and Orszag 2004: 23). Social Security was not intended to be the sole source of income support in old age, but rather it was to be used in combination with private pensions and savings. However, as Diamond and Orszag observe (2004: 15), Social Security provides the only source of income for 20 per cent of beneficiaries over age 65. Like the Canadian OAS, the US system combines an employment-related pension with private employer pensions; individual retirement accounts (IRAs) that receive favourable tax treatment and are most frequently accessed by high income earners; and a modest, income-tested pension for the lowest income seniors (as well as people with disabilities), known as the Supplemental Security Income Program.

The enormous popularity of Social Security among Americans has not exempted it from reform initiatives and critique, despite the accepted wisdom that "politicians treat Social Security as the 'third rail' of US politics: 'Touch it and you die'" (Gramlich 2002: 68).[6] Nonetheless, in light of the impending retirement of the baby boomers, declining real wages, the stock market boom of the 1990s, an unwillingness to increase payroll taxes, and a growing distrust of government, both the Clinton and the G.W. Bush administrations ventured into these sacred waters. It should be noted that the pension fund has a 75 year forecasting requirement and hence that the demographics of the US population were well appreciated by the pension fund (Gramlich 2002: 69). As a result, the Social Security Trust Fund is currently in a period of substantial surplus, although it is anticipated that payments to retirees will outstrip payments to the fund as early as 2016 (Frank 2002: 31). It is in this context, that both the administration of Democratic President Bill Clinton and that of Republican President George W. Bush attempted to implement pension reform.

Arguably, the most controversial recommendation of the Clinton plan was to invest some of the Social Security Trust Fund's assets in stock index funds rather than government securities. Among the objections to this proposal were that, as a major institutional investor in the stock market, the government would have an inordinate and inappropriate influence over business (Gramlich 2002: 77). George W. Bush tackled the issue of pension reform by appointing the pro-privatization Commission to Strengthen Social Security. Ironically, the commission's preliminary recommendations were announced as US stock indices plunged and revelations of mishandled pension funds were exposing fraudulence in the corporate US (Frank 2002: 31). The commission's key recommendation was that the social security payroll tax be replaced by compulsory saving. Every worker would have her own account and would be responsible for investing her money as she saw fit.

The recommendation for personal retirement accounts has come under attack from critics who charge that such a move would subject the base level of retirement savings to the vagaries of the market and, hence, provide no guaranteed income security in old age (Diamond and Orszag 2004: 134). Also, the establishment of individual accounts and the administrative fees and commissions that would accompany them would represent an enormous transfer of wealth from workers to investment brokers (Frank 2002: 38). Rather than risk the retirement incomes of future workers, these critics charge, it would make more sense to address the stagnation in earnings, since higher wages would, in fact, result in larger contributions to the Social Security Trust Fund and thus ensure its ongoing viability (Frank 2002: 35). At present, no legislative action has been undertaken on these proposals, and, given the broad support for Social Security among voters, it seems unlikely that they would have much success. Still, given the Bush administration's enthusiasm for these initiatives, the sustainability of the current Social Security system is an open question.

MEXICO

Systems of welfare provision in Mexico historically have been far less extensive than in the other NAFTA countries. The national Constitution of 1917, created in the wake of the 1910–17 Mexican Revolution, provided a constitutional basis upon which workers and peasants could be granted social rights, although a substantial national welfare regime only emerged in 1943 (Mesa-Lago 1989: 144–45). Given the nature of the corporatist political system that was established in the post-revolution period, benefits were provided by the state to the most important politically mobilized worker and peasant groups in return for their political support. This led to what could be termed a "fragmented universalism" of welfare provision in which, despite a universalistic ethos, benefits were unevenly distributed between different social groups and often benefited principally the organized, urban, middle, and working classes (Duhau 1997). The large informal sector and much of the rural workforce were either left out or only partially included in social security systems, while health and education infrastructures tended to be more prevalent in urban areas. Nonetheless, health, education, and social security programs underwent noted expansions in the postwar period with, for example, illiteracy falling from 43.2 per cent of the population in 1950 to 16 per cent in 1980 (Muñoz Patraca 1999: 4).

Two key events marked dramatic changes in the Mexican political-economic landscape, with manifest implications for the existing social policy regime. In 1982 Mexico succumbed to a profound economic crisis and defaulted on its foreign debt. As a response to this crisis, the government adopted neo-liberal reforms sponsored by the IMF that imposed a new fiscal discipline upon the state and began to undermine many of the corporatist institutions through which resources had previously been channelled. Furthermore, in 1994–95, and despite receiving praise for its policies from the IMF and World Bank, Mexico was once again subsumed in a deep economic crisis. For the second time in a little over a decade, Mexican real wages fell significantly, and the incidence of poverty and social inequality rose in a sustained fashion. As such, the context in which the institutions and policies of social welfare were transformed was one of repeated economic, social, and political crisis.

With regard to social policies, the immediate effect of the 1982 crisis was a rapid retrenchment of state expenditure, with many programs suffering budget cuts in conditions of rampant inflation. Social expenditure in general was reduced in a precipitous manner following the 1982 crisis, therein unravelling many institutional forms of the tenuous post-revolution social compact. Subsequently, the three successive administrations of Carlos Salinas (1988–94), Ernesto Zedillo (1994–2000), and

Vicente Fox (2000–06) were involved in a more comprehensive project to reform Mexican social policies. On the one hand, health, education, and pension programs have been restructured under the hallmarks of decentralization and privatization, with an increasing emphasis placed on state, rather than federal, provision. On the other hand, relatively large-scale anti-poverty programs were introduced in order to stem the deleterious social consequences of economic crises while concomitantly providing new political tools for ensuring social stability and the disarticulation of opposition to adjustment policies.

In this manner, the direction that Mexican social policy has taken in the last 20 years has been a retreat from the constitutional commitment to providing collective security for all individuals, however partial this was in practice. In contrast, the 1980s and 1990s were characterized by a large-scale rationalization of social policy administration and expenditure alongside an attempted targeting of income benefits towards those most affected by the trends of neo-liberal economic restructuring. Initially, targeted anti-poverty programs were intended merely to act as compensatory packages for the "losers" of the economic adjustment process, with an important political legitimization function for the ruling Partido Revolucionario Institutional (PRI) regime. However, as poverty levels did not ameliorate over the course of the 1990s, and with a second bout of economic and social dislocation in 1994–95, a reformed approach to anti-poverty policy has emerged, as detailed below.

INCOME SUPPORT AND ANTI-POVERTY PROGRAMS

In Mexico, President Carlos Salinas initiated a systematic reform of social policy in 1989 following the quantitative retrenchments of the previous years. This was achieved primarily through the replacement of several disparate government agencies with SEDESOL, a new centralized secretariat to implement and manage social development policies, and the establishment of a flagship anti-poverty program called PRONASOL (National Solidarity Program). Both these initiatives were moments of what Salinas labelled as a new philosophy of "social liberalism" that claimed to buttress neo-liberal restructuring through the provision of a stronger social safety net. As a mark of Salinas's commitment to the new project, the resources involved in PRONASOL were substantial. By 1993, the annual budget had grown from an initial US$680 million to $2.5 billion, with the expenditure covered primarily by tax revenues, funds generated by the government's large-scale privatization program, and World Bank loans. Notably, alternative income support programs and basic food subsidies were largely shut down and their resources incorporated within the new program.

Whereas previous anti-poverty policies depended heavily upon universal subsidization of staple foods, PRONASOL introduced a system of credit funds for development projects alongside the targeted distribution of consumption subsidies in rural areas (PROCAMPO). The credit funds operated on the relatively innovative principle of participatory social development practices that involved communities in the design and implementation of local anti-poverty projects. Communities that wanted to receive PRONASOL funding were obliged to form a committee to plan and oversee a small- to medium-sized social development project, commonly infrastructural in nature. This format contributed to breaking up the notion of access to these infrastructural necessities as social rights and their reformulation as prizes to be gained in competition with other communities. In addition, communities were required to contribute toward total costs and provide labour for project implementation. Active participation in this manner was extolled on grounds of the increased efficiency of projects as well as the formation of social solidarity and cohesion. In contrast, however, resources were controlled in a highly centralized manner with the program run by SEDESOL in close conjunction with the president's office. In bypassing the traditional forms of resource disbursement and fostering the active participation of target communities, the initiative was suggested to represent a new form of state-society relations in Mexico, an attempt to engineer a stronger civil society in a top-down fashion. The civil society that Salinas envisaged, however, was one that would articulate its political support for, or at least acquiescence to, both the governing PRI and the neo-liberal project at large (Soederberg 2001).

Given the wide extent of poverty in Mexico and its exacerbation under the crisis and subsequent austerity and structural adjustment reforms introduced since 1982, PRONASOL had limited effectiveness in poverty reduction. Figures from the United Nations Economic Commission for Latin America and the Caribbean (ECLAC 2002) show a slight decrease from 39 to 36 per cent of households in a condition of poverty between 1989 and 1994, although the contribution of PRONASOL to this trend was not significant. Within selected communities, PRONASOL-funded projects played an important role in providing basic infrastructure such as the provision of a water supply, electricity, drainage systems, paving, and housing. Other projects also contributed to the formation of human capital, such as school and clinic construction. However, recipient communities were not necessarily the poorest, and, likewise, the majority of PRONASOL expenditure was not targeted on the poorest states but rather on the most politically sensitive ones (Dresser 1994). The eruption of the Zapatista rebellion in the state of Chiapas in 1994 and continued guerrilla struggles in other southern states, moreover, challenged the effectiveness of the PRONASOL and associated initiatives to ensure social cohesion in the countryside (Nash and Kovic 1996).

The change of administration in 1994 and the devastating Mexican Peso Crisis of 1994–95 led to a further retrenchment and reformulation of social policy, culminating in the replacement of PRONASOL with a new program that, in 1997, would become known as PROGRESA (Program for Education, Health, and Food). Institutionally, PROGRESA represented a break with previous programs by introducing a broad decentralization of responsibility and resources from federal to state levels. The program also reduced credit funds and accentuated the trend towards targeted subsidies. This targeting was achieved through extensive processes of social profiling to demarcate populations in extreme poverty. Once identified, households under the stipulated threshold received direct benefit transfers for a period of three years (renewable for a further three), including income subsidies, nutritional support, and provision of health and education, goods, and services. In return, households would assume certain responsibilities, such as the enrolment and attendance of children in schools and the maintenance of a regular schedule of health clinic visits. The program thus presented itself as a targeted intervention to build the human capital of the poorest sectors of society.

PROGRESA represents a clear reaction to the social devastation of the 1994–95 Peso Crisis. With poverty rates rising in a sustained fashion and real wages undergoing a second dramatic decrease, finding a more efficient manner of sustaining the social reproduction of the extreme poor was of paramount importance. The political repercussions of the 1994 Zapatista uprising added to this sense of urgency. PROGRESA did not suffer from the same levels of overt political manipulation as PRONASOL, although statistical studies do reveal a continued diversion of funds to politically important states (Rocha Menocal 2001).

The overall effectiveness of PROGRESA is still debated. Proponents assert that by 2000, recipient households numbered 2.3 million and, in the best-case scenario, received subsidies worth up to 25 per cent of their incomes. Critics suggest, however, that given the extent of the problem, the program was insignificant, as it provided adequate compensation to less than one-quarter of households in extreme poverty (Laurell 1999). In the late 1990s poverty levels did decrease, returning to just below the 1984 level of 34 per cent of households. Nevertheless, as with Canada's National Child Benefit and the welfare caseload reduction resulting from the Personal Responsibility Act in the US, it is difficult to determine the effectiveness of PROGRESA in isolation from the impact of economic growth in the late 1990s.

At a more technical level, serious questions have been raised concerning the methods used to identify the target population. Given the stipulation of school and health clinic attendance as prerequisites for participation, PROGRESA often overlooked communities where no, or limited, education or health services were available. In addition, the selection of recipient households was based on a screening process that first highlighted areas of dense poverty and then delineated the most impoverished households within these localities. Rural communities tended to benefit from this process, owing to higher and more compact incidences of poverty than are characteristic of urban centres in which income levels are more heterogeneous. Hence, urban neighbourhoods were largely bypassed by the initial PROGRESA screening process, despite 7 per cent of the urban population living in conditions of indigence in 1998 (ECLAC 2002). This is not to deny the deep entrenchment of poverty in rural Mexico; indeed, rural areas have been particularly hard hit by economic liberalization. Rather, it is to observe that PROGRESA's design effectively ignored the largest portion of Mexico's poor, since a majority of poor people live in urban areas.

Finally, OPORTUNIDADES (Opportunities) is the latest permutation of anti-poverty policy, established under the administration of Vicente Fox in 2001. Although the myriad of sub-projects supported broach some new areas, substantive changes in form and content are few, and the program does not differ greatly from the tenets established by the PROGRESA template. However, the potential for OPORTUNIDADES to act effectively as an anti-poverty program very much depends on the wider political economy trajectory in Mexico. Although OPORTUNIDADES, like PROGRESA, has been labeled as a program to build human capital, it is problematic to expect that providing the poorest sections of society with increased skills will automatically result in the genesis of suitable jobs. In this respect, the neo-liberal reforms of the last two decades have proved to be remarkably uneven in providing employment opportunities, as evidenced by increased levels of social polarization and the continuing expansion of the informal sector (cf. Damián 2002). With the economic slowdown across North America since 2001, the continuing flight of *maquiladora* industry from Mexico to China, and the uncertain economic prognosis for the upcoming years, this situation does not appear likely to change. As a result, OPORTUNIDADES will continue to function as a form of regulating poverty in Mexico while the population continues to wait for neo-liberal economic reforms to finally deliver on the promise of strong and sustained growth with mass job-creating potential.

Conclusion

Income supports provide rich ground for examining both the convergences and divergences in North American social policy since the implementation of NAFTA. In spite of the neo-liberal promise that the increasing marketization of social life would bring sustained growth and concurrent increases in human welfare, it has largely been unable to deliver on its promise of a generalized improvement in the standard of living. This failure, as we have argued, has had profound social and political implications. Incomes have become increasingly polarized in Canada, the US, and Mexico. Poverty rates have risen as income support programs have failed to adjust to new configurations in labour markets and family forms. And while increasing numbers of people are integrated into labour markets, employment income provides no guarantee of security from poverty. Efforts have been undertaken in all three North American states to address the precarious position of at least some of the poor. In Canada and the US, these efforts have been primarily directed at the "working" poor, in Mexico at the rural poor. But the efficacy of these initiatives is tempered by stricter criteria surrounding unemployment benefits in Canada, by the removal of an entitlement to poor relief in the US, and by the limited nature of Mexican anti-poverty programs.

In all three countries, perceived shortcomings in public programs have given rise to calls for increased private sector involvement in the social policy realm, whether in administering programs, in providing insurance against social risk, or as a site for the investment of pension and education savings. In addition, the decentralization of responsibility for social programs and the use of targeting in delivering benefits have contributed to highly fragmented citizenship regimes in all three countries. NAFTA, as one of the motive forces for these processes and the ideology that supports them, must bear some of the responsibility for these outcomes. Of course, NAFTA did not explicitly address social policy. Nonetheless, in liberalizing trade within North America, a set of neo-liberal policy prescriptions were employed in all three member countries that included social spending reductions, decentralization, privatization, and the targeting of programs to particular populations. Neo-liberalism, we argue, begat NAFTA. The social policy consequences of NAFTA were thus a product of this broader ideological framework.

It is important to underscore that the adoption of neo-liberal policy prescriptions has not led to the same policies or precisely the same outcomes in each NAFTA signatory. As this brief survey of selected national responses has demonstrated, social policy outcomes are not automatic responses to impersonal market forces but are shaped through conflicts in the political sphere within nationally specific political-economic conjunctures. To date, the outcome of these developments has fallen well short of providing security to North America's most vulnerable citizens. Indeed, the overall effect may well have been to increase the general insecurity of a majority of citizens. But in Canada, the US, and Mexico we also see a dawning realization of the political liabilities associated with neo-liberal policy prescriptions. It is to be hoped that future reforms will assess the well-being of citizens as paramount to markets.

Notes

1   The phrase "ragged cruelty" is derived from Thomas Frank's discussion of American proposals for Social Security reform in *Harper's Magazine*. The full quotation is: "Having rolled back welfare, having stopped every effort to win national health insurance, having taken massive steps toward eliminating affirmative action, the right now looks out at the world it has created and finds in the raggedness of its cruelty a mandate for abolishing the welfare state altogether" (2002).

2   It should be noted that Québec did not agree to the program, given its long-standing insistence that the federal government respect the constitutional jurisdiction of provinces over social policy. Nonetheless, Quebecers do receive the NCB, although with a made-in-Québec payment schedule (Beauvais and Jenson 2001: 20, 40). It should be noted that Alberta also employs its own payment schedule.

3   The value of the CCTB varies depending on the number and ages of the children. In 2003, the benefit for one child over seven was $2,719. Canada Revenue Agency, "Canada Child Tax Benefit (CCTB) payment amounts," 2003. <http://www.cra-arc.gc.ca/benefits/cctb_payments-e.html>.

4   The Great Society was a program of federal grants designed to support a range of social policy needs to improve the earnings opportunities of poor Americans. Programs included low-income housing, Head Start programs for children, and enhanced educational opportunities (Myles 1997: 121). The "Great Society" is generally understood as the high-water mark of the US welfare state and has subsequently been the target of conservative critics who oppose high levels of social spending and support state autonomy in social policy (Katz 2001: 84).

5   The steepness of the decline in welfare caseloads varies across the states, but the majority report at least a 50 per cent decline from 1996 to 2002, with some states, such as Idaho, reporting an 89 per cent decrease (Tanner 2003: 62).

6   Programs for the elderly, including Social Security and Medicare, have enjoyed considerable political support. Older Americans are both more likely to vote than non-seniors and they have established impressive lobbying organizations. The American Association of Retired Persons, for example, has a membership "totaling more than half of Americans aged fifty and over, [a] paid staff of 1700, [...] and a budget of $500 million a year ..." (Skocpol 2000: 81–82).

References

Battle, Ken. 1999. "The National Child Benefit: Best Thing Since Medicare or New Poor Law?" In D. Durst (ed.), *Canada's National Child Benefit: Phoenix or Fizzle?* Halifax: Fernwood.

Battle, Ken, and Sherri Torjman. 1996. "Desperately Seeking Substance: A Commentary on the Social Security Review." In Jane Pulkingham and Gordon Ternowetsky (eds.), *Remaking Canadian Social Policy: Social Security in the Late 1990s*. Halifax: Fernwood. 52–66.

Beauvais, Caroline, and Jane Jenson. 2001. *Two Policy Paradigms: Family Responsibility and Investing in Children*. Ottawa: Canadian Policy Research Networks. 38–60.

Blank, Rebecca. 1997. *It Takes a Nation: A New Agenda for Fighting Poverty*. New York: Russell Sage Foundation.

Boychuk, Gerard. 2001. "Aiming for the Middle: Challenges to Federal Income Maintenance Policy." In Leslie Pal (ed.), *How Ottawa Spends 2001–2002*. Toronto: Oxford UP.

——. 2004. "The Chrétien Non-Legacy: The Federal Role in Health Care Ten Years On ... 1993–2003." In Lois Harder and Steve Patten (eds.), *Review of Constitutional Studies: Special Issue on the Chrétien Legacy* 9,1/2: 221–40.

Brodie, Janine. 2002. "An Elusive Search for Community: Globalization and the Canadian National Identity." *Review of Constitutional Studies* 7,1/2: 155–78.

Burman, Leonard, and Deborah Kobes. 2003. "EITC Reaches More Eligible Families Than TANF, Food Stamps." *Tax Notes* (17 March): 1769.

Canada, Department of Finance. 1999. *Working Together Towards a National Child Benefit System*. Cited in Ken Battle, "Child Benefit Reform: A Case Study in Tax-Transfer Integration." *Canadian Tax Journal* 47: 1219–57.

Canadian Labour Congress (CLC). 2003. "Submission in response to Finance Canada's EI Premium Rate-Setting Mechanism Consultation." June. <http://www.fin.gc.ca/consultresp/eiratesResp_2e.html>.

Congressional Research Service. 2003. "Summary of H.R. 4737, The Personal Responsibility, Work, and Family Promotion Act of 2002." In G. Mink and R. Solinger (eds.), *Welfare: A Documentary History of US Policy and Politics*. New York: New York UP. 785–91.

Damián, Araceli. 2002. *Cargando el ajuste: los pobres y el mercado de trabajo en México*. Mexico City: Colegio de México.

Devigne, Robert. 1994. *Recasting Conservatism: Oakeshott, Strauss, and the Response to Postmodernism*. New Haven, CT: Yale UP.

Diamond, Peter, and Peter Orszag. 2004. *Saving Social Security: A Balanced Approach*. Washington, DC: Brookings Institution Press.

Dresser, Denise. 1994. "Bringing the Poor Back In—National Solidarity as a Strategy of Regime Legitimation." In Wayne Cornelius, Ann Craig, and Jonathan Fox (eds.), *Transforming State-Society Relations in Mexico: The National Solidarity Strategy*. San Diego, CA: U of California P. 143–66.

Duhau, Emilio. 1997. "Las políticas socials en América Latina: ?del universalismo fragmentado a la dualización?" *Revista Mexicana de Sociología* 2: 185–207.

Dussel Peters, Enrique. 2000. *Polarizing Mexico: The Impact of Liberalization Strategy*. Boulder, CO: Lynne Rienner Publishers.

ECLAC (United Nations Economic Commission for Latin America and the Caribbean). 2002. *Statistical Yearbook for Latin America and the Caribbean, 2002*. Santiago, Chile: ECLAC.

Esping-Andersen, Gøsta. 1990. *The Three Worlds of Welfare Capitalism*. Cambridge: Polity Press.

——. 1997. "After the Golden Age?" In G. Esping-Andersen (ed.), *Welfare States in Transition: National Adaptations in Global Economies*. London: Sage. 1–31.

Frank, Thomas. 2002. "The Trillion-Dollar Hustle: Hello Wall Street, Goodbye Social Security." *Harper's Magazine* 304 (January): 31–39.

Fudge, Judy, and Leah Vosko. 2003. "Gender Paradoxes and the Rise of Contingent Work: Towards a Transformative Political Economy of the Labour Market." In W. Clement and L. Vosko (eds.), *Changing Canada: Political Economy as Transformation*. Montreal and Kingston: McGill-Queen's UP. 183–209.

Gramlich, Edward. 2002. "Social Security Reform in the Twenty-First Century: The United States." *Journal of Aging and Social Policy* 14,1: 67–80.

Harder, Lois. 2003. "Whither the Social Citizen." In J. Brodie and L. Trimble (eds.), *Reinventing Canada: Politics of the 21st Century*. Toronto: Prentice Hall. 175–88.

Hotz, Joseph V., and John Karl Scholz. 2003. "The Earned Income Tax Credit." In Robert Moffitt (ed.), *Means-Tested Transfer Programs in the United States*. Chicago, IL: U of Chicago P. 141–98.

Howard, Christopher. 1997. *The Hidden Welfare State: Tax Expenditures and Social Policy in the United States*. Princeton, NJ: Princeton UP.

Katz, Michael B. 2001. *The Price of Citizenship: Redefining the American Welfare State*. New York: Henry Holt and Company.

Kerstetter, Steven. 2002. *Rags and Riches: Wealth Inequality in Canada*. Ottawa: Canadian Centre for Policy Alternatives. <http://www.policyalternatives.ca/publications/ragsandrichessummary.html>.

Lancet. 2004. "2004 US Election Campaign: Health at Home and Abroad." *Editorial*, 17 January: 179.

Laurell, Asa Cristina. 1999. "La reforma del estado y la política social en México." *Nueva Sociedad* 164: 146–58.

Lefebvre, Pierre, and Phillip Merrigan. 2003. "Assessing Family Policy in Canada: A New Deal for Families and Children." *Choices* 9,5 (June).

McBride, Stephen. 2001. *Paradigm Shift: Globalization and the Canadian State*. Halifax: Fernwood.

McKeen, Wendy, and Anne Porter. 2003. "Politics and Transformation: Welfare State Restructuring in Canada." In W. Clement and L. Vosko (eds.), *Changing Canada: Political Economy as Transformation*. Montreal and Kingston: McGill-Queen's UP. 109–34.

Mesa-Lago, Carmelo. 1989. *Ascent to Bankruptcy: Financing Social Security in Latin America*. Pittsburgh, PA: U of Pittsburgh P.

Muñoz Patraca, Víctor Manuel. 1999. "En busca de mayor justicia social: la descentralización de los servicios de salud y educación en México." *Revista Mexicana de Sociología* 4: 3–21.

Myles, John. 1997. "When Markets Fail: Social Welfare in Canada and the United States." In G. Esping-Andersen (ed.), *Welfare States in Transition: National Adaptations in Global Economies*. London: Sage. 116–40.

Nash, June, and Christine Kovic. 1996. "The Reconstitution of Hegemony. The Free Trade Act and the Transformation of Rural Mexico." In James Mittelman (ed.), *Globalization: Critical Reflections: International Political Economy Yearbook Vol. 9*. Boulder, CO: Lynne Rienner Publishers. 165–85.

Orloff, Ann. 2002. "Explaining US Welfare Reform: Power, Gender, Race, and the US Policy Legacy." *Critical Social Policy* 22,1: 96–118.

Prince, Michael. 1999. "From Health and Welfare to Stealth and Farewell: Federal Social Policy, 1980–2000." In Leslie Pal (ed.), *How Ottawa Spends 1999–2000*. Toronto: Oxford UP. 151–96.

Rice, James, and Michael Prince. 2000. *Changing Politics of Canadian Social Policy*. Toronto: U of Toronto P.

Ritzer, George. 2002. "McJobs: McDonaldization and Its Relationship to the Labor Process." In G. Ritzer (ed.), *McDonaldization: The Reader*. Thousand Oaks, CA: Pine Forge Press. 141–47.

Rocha Menocal, Alina. 2001. "Do Old Habits Die Hard? A Statistical Exploration of the Politicization of Progresa, Mexico's Latest Federal Poverty-Alleviation Program, under the Zedillo Administration." *Journal of Latin American Studies* 33,3: 513–38.

Rocher, François. 2000. "Dividing the Spoils: American and Canadian Federalism." In David Thomas (ed.), *Canada and the United States: Differences that Count*. 2nd ed. Peterborough, ON: Broadview Press. 262–83.

Sayeed, Adil. 2002. *The 1997 Canada Pension Plan Changes: Implications for Men and Women*. Ottawa: Status of Women Canada, August.

Skocpol, Theda. 2000. *The Missing Middle: Working Families and the Future of American Social Policy*. New York: W.W. Norton.

Soederberg, Susanne. 2001. "From Neoliberalism to Social Liberalism: Situating the National Solidarity Program Within Mexico's Passive Revolutions." *Latin American Perspectives* 28,3: 104–23.

Stanford, Jim. 1996. "Discipline, Insecurity and Productivity: The Economics Behind Labour Market Flexibility." In Jane Pulkingham and Gordon Ternowetsky (eds.), *Remaking Canadian Social Policy: Social Security in the Late 1990s.* Halifax: Fernwood. 130–50.

Tanner, Michael. 2003. *The Poverty of Welfare.* Washington, DC: Cato Institute.

US Census Bureau. 2001. *Historical Income Tables*, Table F-1. <http://www.census.gov/hhes/income/histinc/f01.html>.

US Department of Labor. n.d. "Fact Sheet #29: Fair Labour Standards Act Amendments of 1996." <http://www.dol.gov/esa/regs/compliance/whd/whdfs29.htm>.

Weaver, Kent. 2000. *Ending Welfare as We Know It.* Washington, DC: Brookings Institution.

World Bank. 2000. *World Development Report 1999/2000: Entering the 21st Century.* Oxford: Oxford UP.

CHAPTER FOURTEEN

Ten Years After

Continental Free Trade and Environmental Policy in North America

Luc Juillet

A t the time of its ratification in the early 1990s, environmental concerns loomed large in the debates about NAFTA. Opponents of the treaty commonly argued that the further removal of tariffs among Mexico, Canada, and the US would make it easier and more attractive for corporations to relocate their production activities to the country offering a less stringent and costly regulatory environment, presumably Mexico. It was feared that, as a result of these competitive pressures, the three countries would soon engage in an environmental "race to the bottom," lowering their environmental standards in a never-ending quest to attract or retain industry. Alternatively, if this race to the bottom did not occur, the more polluting industries would simply migrate to Mexico to take advantage of weaker environmental standards and enforcement, turning the country into a "haven" for the polluting industries of North America. Furthermore, the agreement's environmental opponents feared that the development of a more robust rules-based trading regime solely focused on expanding the free trade of goods and services, and firmly rooted in a neo-liberal mindset poorly attuned to ecological concerns, would place additional constraints on the ability of national states to address ecological and health concerns through more stringent environmental regulations. In sum, as it considered its ratification, most of the North American environmental movement believed that NAFTA, like the broader ideological project from which it derived, would prove detrimental to environmental protection.

In response to this critique, and the intense vocal lobbies that articulated it, especially in the US, the three countries took unprecedented steps to answer these environmental concerns. In this respect, the arrival of the Democrats at the White House in 1992 and, to a lesser extent, the election of a Liberal government in Canada in 1993 constituted important catalysts. In 1993, despite the fact that their predecessors had already declared NAFTA to be the most "environmentally friendly" trade agreement in history because of some of its environmental provisions, the Clinton administration led the three governments to take the additional step of negotiating an "environmental side-deal," the North American Agreement for Environmental Cooperation, to be ratified as a companion agreement to NAFTA. In an unprecedented effort to strengthen continental institutions for environmental governance, this agreement created a new ministerial-level trilateral Commission for Environmental Cooperation (CEC) to promote environmental protection on the continent as well as extraordinary supranational procedures meant to ensure that national governments properly enforced their own environmental laws. As a whole, the combination of the NAFTA's own environmental clauses and its innovative companion agreement allowed the three governments to answer their environmental critics with the promise that the new continental trade regime would not only avert a race to the bottom but could even usher in a new era of environmental cooperation in North America.

About ten years after the ratification of these agreements, what are we to make of the fears and hopes expressed in the NAFTA debate? What impact did NAFTA have on environmental politics and governance in North America? As I will argue in this chapter, the emerging picture of the two agreements' impact on environmental policies and politics is less straightforward and more equivocal than the ratification debate had anticipated. In particular, while the ratification debates had led to a focus on downward harmonization of standards and relocation of polluting industries, these concerns have now largely given way to concerns about the emergence of continental norms on foreign investment protection, which may be hindering national environmental policy-making. Meanwhile, although the environmental side-deal and the new trilateral commission have contributed modestly to increased environmental cooperation on the continent, they can hardly be seen as significant drivers of environmental policies and governance in the three countries, and their most innovative measures have fallen short of expectations.

NAFTA's Environmental Politics

While the interplay between free trade and environmental protection became a salient political issue around the same time on the global stage (see, for example, Bhagwati 2004: 135–61), the North American debate on the environmental consequences of NAFTA was unprecedented in its intensity and significance (Johnson and Beaulieu 1996: 25). For the first time, environmental issues came to the forefront of a high-stakes trade policy debate, and the future of a major trade agreement seemed to depend, in some significant measure, on how governments would address environmental preoccupations associated with trade liberalization. Taking advantage of political circumstances and procedural requirements (Audley 1997), environmentalists were able to play an important role in the politics of NAFTA, especially in the US where the debate marked the "coming of age of the American environmental movement in the politics of trade policy" (Vogel 2000: 85). In fact, while several Canadian and Mexican environmental groups also opposed the agreement and lobbied against its provisions (Johnson and Beaulieu 1996: 28–29), it is clearly the environmental movement and domestic politics in the US that had the most influence on the treaty's environmental provisions.

The US influence on NAFTA's environmental politics can be explained not only by the economic and political predominance of the US among the three trading partners, but also by the favourable domestic conditions enjoyed by US opponents. The US president's need to gain congressional support for the treaty's negotiation and ratification, combined with the volatile context of the 1992 presidential election, allowed US environmental groups to exert exceptional influence on trade policy

(Audley 1997; Johnson and Beaulieu 1996: 24). Exploiting latent fears about the implications of deeper economic integration with a less developed country, they raised serious doubts about the environmental consequences of NAFTA, doubts that were seized upon and echoed by other influential opponents of the agreement in the labour movement and in Congress. In alliance with some domestic producers and unions concerned about increased competition from Mexican industries and farmers, national organizations, such as the National Wildlife Federation, the World Wildlife Fund, and Friends of the Earth, mounted a lobbying campaign demanding significant modifications to the agreement. Among other things, they asked for assurances that the NAFTA text would guarantee the upward harmonization of environmental standards among the three countries, the possibility of trade sanctions against countries that did not properly enforce their own environmental laws, and a more transparent and environmentally sensitive dispute resolution process (Johnson and Beaulieu 1996: 28). Substantial remedial action on the Mexico-US border was also considered a priority.

In fact, in the advocacy campaign against the treaty, the representation of Mexico as an environmental laggard played a central role. In particular, the dreadful environmental condition of the US-Mexico border, itself the legacy of decades of industrial pollution, weak regulations, and lax law enforcement in the *maquiladoras*, served to illustrate the potentially disastrous effect of expanding Mexican-US trade. Although the Mexican government made significant progress in developing an environmental protection framework through the 1980s (Gallagher 2004: 63–65), it was nevertheless widely acknowledged that the Mexican environmental bureaucracy remained weak and that enforcement of environmental laws was deficient. As a result, environmentalists argued, competitive pressures would lead US corporations to move there in search of weaker environmental standards (and therefore lower compliance costs), worsening the Mexican environment and, by the same token, depriving Americans of jobs. Moreover, because of the interconnected nature of ecosystems, this migration of polluting industries would not only create additional, and intolerable, pressures on the Mexican environment, it would also affect the whole continent, for example, through the destruction of migratory species' habitat and the travel of air pollutants across the border. Furthermore, to attempt to counter these competitive pressures and avoid Mexico becoming a pollution haven for dirtier North American industries, Canada and the US would have to lower their own environmental standards. In this way, NAFTA would lead to a "race to the bottom" in environmental standards, affecting domestic environmental legislation in all three countries. As we will see, these related arguments about a "race to the bottom" in standards and Mexico turning into a haven for polluting industries had a deep impact on the outcome of NAFTA's environmental debate.

While these concerns were the dominant themes of the debate, environmentalists were also concerned about the constraining effect that NAFTA might have on the legal ability of governments to set their own environmental standards. In this regard, the landmark *Tuna-Dolphin* decision, issued by a GATT panel in August 1991, undoubtedly contributed to heightened concerns about the potential impacts of NAFTA on domestic environmental laws. The case, which was initiated by Mexico against the US, challenged a US marine wildlife protection law that banned the import of tuna caught with a certain type of commercial fishing net, which unintentionally killed a large number of dolphins. Ruling in favour of Mexico, the panel declared that the import ban was inconsistent with GATT rules because, in practice, it discriminated against foreign producers, including Mexican producers, on the basis of their methods of production, as opposed to expressing legitimate concerns about the characteristics of the product sold to consumers in the US. The *Tuna-Dolphin* controversy sparked a heated debate in international circles and alerted the environmental movement to the potential significance of trade agreements. In the context of the NAFTA debate, it represented a sort of "smoking gun" for environmentalists—a tangible example that trade laws could constrain the legislative authority of governments to protect the environment. In fact, conscious that it would fuel environmental opposition to NAFTA, the Mexican government never submitted the panel's ruling for its adoption by the GATT Council. But the political damage was done. With the *Tuna-Dolphin* example in the background, environmentalists argued that several sections of the NAFTA text might also impair the ability of Congress to adopt laws (with regard to the import of food grown with the use of pesticides, for example) necessary to protect the environment and the health of consumers (see, for example, Ritchie 1993: 211–16) and that Mexico would prove to be insensitive to environmental concerns (Audley 1997: 73).

Despite considerable public sympathy for the environmentalists' arguments, governments were not receptive to their demands at the outset, insisting that the trade agreement would not hinder environmental protection and that, in any case, Mexico had made considerable progress in protecting the environment since the early 1980s. However, in the spring of 1991, it became evident to the administration of President George Bush (senior) that alleviating environmental concerns would prove necessary in order to obtain a congressional fast-track authorization for trade negotiations. In May 1991, responding to the concerns of the congressional leadership, President Bush proposed to address environmental issues related to NAFTA through a "parallel track" (Audley 1997: 57). While a small group of environmentalists would be appointed to the public advisory committee on trade negotiations and the administration would seek some language ensuring the protection of the environment in the treaty itself, environmental issues would mostly be addressed through separate processes and initiatives. In particular, before it was submitted for approval, the government would conduct an environmental review of the agreement, and it would work with the Mexican government on resolving the environmental problems of the border area.

The Bush administration's "parallel track" proposal proved to be a pivotal event. Firstly, in strategic terms, it essentially split the US environmental movement in two and bolstered the government's position. While a majority of environmental organizations continued to oppose congressional authorization, a few, such as the National Wildlife Federation and the Environmental Defence Fund, shifted to a more conciliatory position, eventually actively supporting fast-track authorization. Then, under the Clinton administration, the same groups publicly supported the ratification of the negotiated agreement, arguing that the environmental provisions contained in the text, combined with an additional agreement on environmental cooperation and investments in environmental protection and remediation in Mexico, would adequately answer their concerns. Moreover, they argued that trade-induced economic growth could help alleviate poverty in Mexico, a reality contributing to environmental deterioration and a plague in its own right. In the end, the NAFTA debate proved so divisive for environmentalists that it probably represented the "nastiest internecine squabble in the movement's hundred-year history" (Dowie 1995: 187). But, more importantly for NAFTA's future, the division of the movement ultimately broke the back of the environmental opposition to the agreement, since the US government could always point to a few high-profile environmental organizations, mainly the National Wildlife Federation, that supported its position.

In addition to weakening environmental opposition, the decision to deal with environmental concerns as much as possible outside the trade negotiations profoundly affected the nature of the environmental initiatives that resulted from the NAFTA debate. Despite some unprecedented, if limited, provisions in the text itself, much of the effort deployed by governments remained outside the realm of trade policy. For example, in order to ease concerns about the environmental conditions at their border, the US and Mexican governments adopted an Integrated Border Environmental Plan (IBEP), which promised to spend billions of dollars in cleanups of contaminated sites, environmental infrastructure development, and improved enforcement of existing regulations. While a positive step, the IBEP also had the convenient effect of keeping environmental issues largely out of the real NAFTA negotiations. By stressing bilateral environmental cooperation and short-term increased spending on the border region, governments reduced pressures to incorporate environmental safeguards into the framework being negotiated for increased economic integration in North America. As it turns out, the additional investments in environmental infrastructures in the border area have also proven inadequate to handle the growth in industrial activity that followed the implementation of the trade agreement (OECD 1998).

The effect of the parallel track approach is even more visible in the adoption of a separate agreement on environmental cooperation, the North American Agreement on Environmental Cooperation (NAAEC), by the three countries in September 1993[1] (Johnson and Beaulieu 1996: 123). A few months before the presidential election of November 1992, environmental and labour concerns continued to mark the debate in the US on NAFTA. In response, the three countries announced the launch of a new round of negotiations that would focus solely on environmental issues and aim to create a new cabinet-level environmental council that would act as a trilateral forum for environmental cooperation. Himself unwilling to reopen the trade agreement (as many opponents were demanding) but confronted with the need to act on the environmental concerns raised during the presidential campaign, the Democratic candidate, Bill Clinton, welcomed the initiative to negotiate a separate agreement on environmental issues. In October, he declared publicly that he would not ratify NAFTA unless environmental and labour issues had been satisfactorily addressed in separate agreements (Audley 1997: 69–70).

To accommodate the needs of domestic politics in the US, the Canadian and Mexican governments, who were equally opposed to reopening the trade agreement, agreed to proceed with this separate negotiation over the course of 1993. In the case of Canada, the side-deal approach also eventually suited the purpose of the Chrétien government, which came to power in 1993 and faced a similar conundrum due to the Liberal Party's criticism of NAFTA during the national election campaign. However, the negotiations between the US and its trading partners were difficult. The Mexican government, in particular, argued in favour of a broader focus on trilateral environmental cooperation, as opposed to an agreement that would address more narrowly the environmental implications of trade (Johnson and Beaulieu 1996: 122–23). Both Canada and Mexico also resisted the US government's insistence on the inclusion of strong enforcement measures, including a binding dispute resolution process and the potential imposition of trade sanctions (Johnson and Beaulieu 1996: 212). In contrast, seeking to counter domestic environmental opposition, the US favoured a treaty that would provide some protection against its trading partners using lax enforcement of standards to obtain an undue competitive advantage, hurting their environment in the process.

After a year of negotiations, the outcome was the adoption of an innovative trilateral environmental treaty focused on furthering environmental cooperation in North America, notably through the establishment of the CEC. The CEC is headed by a council composed of a cabinet-level environmental official from each country and supported by a permanent secretariat located in Montreal. But the NAAEC attempts to go further than trilateral cooperation by including unprecedented provisions to ensure that NAFTA countries are accountable to their trading partners for the enforcement of their own domestic environmental laws. While it avoids setting any substantive standards of environmental protection, it commits each country to provide a "high level of environmental protection" (Article 3) and to "effectively enforce its environmental laws and regulations" (Article 5). While the exact obligations entailed by those commitments are uncertain (see, for example, the discussion in Johnson and Beaulieu 1996: 177–209), the agreement comprises unusually potent mechanisms of enforcement for an environmental treaty.[2] In this regard, two sets of provisions clearly stand out: a state-to-state binding dispute resolution process that can lead to trade sanctions and a mechanism allowing citizens to ask the CEC to investigate cases where a country allegedly fails to effectively enforce its environmental laws.

The first set of measures, contained in part five of the NAAEC, allows a government to file a complaint against another government for showing "a persistent pattern of failure of effective enforcement" of its environmental laws. If the complaint cannot be settled through political negotiations, the ministerial council heading the CEC, by a two-thirds vote, can strike a dispute resolution panel to investigate the matter and make recommendations for the settlement of the dispute. The government at fault must then prepare a remedial enforcement plan to implement the panel's recommendation. If it fails to submit or to implement the remedial plan, the panel can be reconvened to impose a fine, which can exceed US$20 million. Finally, if the country refuses to pay the fine, some of its trade benefits can be suspended under NAFTA[3] (Johnson and Beaulieu 1996: 211–23).

The second set of measures, specified by Articles 14 and 15 of the agreement, allows any citizen or organization to request the CEC to investigate a case of alleged failure by one of the governments to effectively enforce its environmental laws. Once a citizen's submission meets some basic criteria, the CEC will ask the government allegedly at fault to provide an answer to the allegations. If this answer is not considered satisfactory, the ministerial council, again by a two-thirds majority, can allow the secretariat to investigate and prepare a "factual record" on the issue. The factual record will then be made public, unless the ministerial council unanimously decides to veto its release. While these factual records do not comprise recommendations and do not entail binding corrective measures, the publication of a damning factual record would presumably alert public opinion and may pressure the faulty government into changing its enforcement practices. Alternatively, it could also lead one of the two other governments to bring the matter to the binding dispute resolution process already described (Johnson and Beaulieu 1996: 152–58).

In the end, the environmental politics of NAFTA resulted in a push for greater environmental cooperation in North America, but these efforts at greater cooperation were partly meant to avoid having to make difficult choices about how to reconcile trade and environmental imperatives through a more integrated legal and policy framework. The separate track approach that deeply affected the outcome of the debate contributed to the continued relative separation of trade and environmental policies. As a result, the procedures and norms inscribed in NAFTA hardly allow for a considered weighing of competing economic and environmental objectives. Environmental policies largely remain considered as measures to be assessed for their compatibility with dominant commercial and investment rules by panels with no or limited expertise or interest in environmental protection. Such an approach hardly seems consistent with the governments' purported commitment to sustainable development, which would require thinking about economic, social, and environmental considerations in an integrated manner (see Juillet 2001).

The environmental debate about NAFTA also underscores the importance of how domestic politics in the US shapes North American politics and governance. Domestic US interests deeply affected the nature of the debate, with its emphasis on the "race to the bottom" and the "pollution haven" scenarios, and the policy decisions that resulted from it. Despite the efforts deployed by environmentalists in both Mexico and Canada, the US environmental movement remains mostly responsible for the environmental provisions of the agreement. Without their influence on the congressional and presidential politics of US trade policy, it is doubtful that the environmental concerns about NAFTA would have had much impact on policy outcomes. Similarly, the concerns and the approach of the US government significantly influenced the decision to pursue a separate set of environmental negotiations, which ultimately established a new continental regime for environmental cooperation. In the end, both the environmental provisions of NAFTA and the new continental environmental institutions owe a lot to the particularities of US politics.

A Decade of Environmental Policy under the NAFTA

While hardly considered a major victory for them, there is no doubt that environmentalists had a noticeable impact on the outcome of the NAFTA debate. Under the pressure of the US government and, to a lesser extent, their own environmental critics, Canada and Mexico agreed to include some environmental guarantees in the agreement. Given the nature of the debates described in the previous section, it is not surprising that these guarantees essentially focused on preventing a downward spiral of environmental standards and ensuring proper enforcement.[4] In this section, I examine the main environmental provisions inscribed in the NAFTA text and consider their value in view of the developments of the last decade.

THE HARMONIZATION OF ENVIRONMENTAL STANDARDS

The first set of measures was meant to address concerns about the downward harmonization of environmental standards due to the regulatory constraints that NAFTA might place on its signatories. While encouraging governments to harmonize their technical and sanitary standards "to the greatest extent practicable," the agreement states that, if governments were to seek such harmonization, they should not do it by reducing their level of protection for human health and the environment.[5] Logically, these measures would, indirectly, lead countries toward upward harmonization since the country with the more stringent standards would be unable to lower them in the name of continental harmonization.

However, as the terms "to the greatest extent practicable" indicate, there is no obligation for the signatories to engage in such a process of (upward) harmonization. As a result, these provisions appear largely unenforceable and might have been meant mostly to provide guidance for future discussions about the harmonization of regulations (Johnson and Beaulieu 1996: 114–15). In any case, as some legal observers pointed out, the language used in the text does not prevent governments from lowering their environmental standards for purposes other than harmonization, such as business conditions, the state of scientific knowledge, or social preferences (Charnovitz 1994: 63). Furthermore, the environmental standards in place at the time of NAFTA's ratification could still be challenged for failing to comply with other obligations contracted under the trade agreement. As a result, it is clear that these measures do not necessarily constitute a guaranteed minimum level of protection, and they do not appear to create any enforceable obligation for upward harmonization.

Other environmental guarantees contained in NAFTA concern international standards. While NAFTA exhorts the parties to use them to guide their harmonization efforts, it also explicitly recognizes that governments can set norms that are more stringent than international standards.[6] At the request of US negotiators, NAFTA also clearly states that governments can establish the level of protection that they consider appropriate for their citizens (Steinberg 1997: 245).[7] However, in setting these standards, governments would have to show, if challenged, that they are necessary to achieve their stated purpose and that they do not constitute disguised barriers to trade. For sanitary standards, such a demonstration would entail explicit reliance on scientific evidence and risk assessment (Esty and Geradin 1997: 311–12). Moreover, the past application of general trade rules also suggests that governments would have to show that their norms were designed to be the least trade restrictive possible (Juillet 2001: 131–32). Ultimately, whether governments meet those criteria would be for a trade dispute resolution panel to decide, a forum where trade principles and objectives are understandably considered to be paramount and environmental expertise is not necessarily sought.[8] As a result, some observers feared that these caveats might in fact deter governments from raising their environmental standards above recognized international norms (Charnovitz 1994: 16–17). In particular, environmentalists feared that the emphasis on scientific evidence and risk assessment might deter governments from taking precautionary measures in cases of scientific uncertainty but potentially severe environmental and health damages.

A decade after the negotiations, these measures meant to protect higher environmental and health standards against trade challenges remain largely untested. In contrast to the fears expressed at the time, the trade-compatibility of environmental regulations has not been widely challenged since NAFTA came into force. As I will discuss in the next subsection, the clashes between NAFTA and environmental regulations have essentially concerned investment provisions, and they were dealt with through international arbitration processes. Even if they can have some environmental implications, the major trade disputes involving natural resources, such as the US-Canada dispute on softwood lumber, have been argued on other grounds and did not directly involve environmental laws. As a result, the effectiveness of the above-noted environmental guarantees in the context of an eventual trade dispute remains in doubt.

With regard to harmonization, there is also scant evidence of either a "race to the bottom" or a systematic trend in upward harmonization across the continent. CEC's efforts to induce the three countries to improve the compatibility of their standards in order to limit the potential environmental impact of a more integrated market (in areas such as the regulation of transborder hazardous waste shipments or environmental laboratories) have had little effect (Block 2003: 528). In fact, examining the record of the last ten years, Block notes that, despite engaging in trilateral discussions, there is a sense that "the United States is not likely to accommodate its neighbours by bringing its policies, laws, or standards closer to Canada or Mexico, irrespective of the environmental benefits that could accrue from such action" (2003: 519). To the extent that there is some evidence of upward harmonization, it essentially concerns Mexico and results from the assistance of the CEC in building the environmental policy capacity of that country as opposed to a more systematic continent-wide effort at harmonization. In this case, Mexico's creation of a chemicals division in its environmental department, as well as the recent regulation or ban of some toxic substances and the establishment of a public registry of industrial pollution modelled on the US and Canada, are usually quoted as the most compelling results.

In the coming years, the work of NAFTA's implementation committees and technical working groups might be more instructive of the real impact of harmonization efforts associated with continental integration. Some of these committees are examining the compatibility of technical standards affecting trade in sectors with important environmental implications, such as pesticides and automotive products. While it remains difficult at this stage to appreciate the environmental consequences that these efforts will have, early published studies do not permit much optimism. After looking at the work of the first three years, a study found that, with some exceptions, these technical bodies had had "a paucity of contact" with the CEC and that environmental concerns were not considered an integral part of their work (CEC 1997: 64–66). A review of the CEC's first ten years of operation concluded that these findings are still relevant today (TRAC 2004: 25). This lack of environmental consideration continues despite the fact that the CEC was explicitly mandated to work in collaboration with NAFTA's institutions to ensure that environmental issues were properly considered throughout the implementation of the agreement.[9] It also seems at odds with NAFTA's own preamble, which lists the promotion of sustainable development as one of its objectives.

Meanwhile, in an attitude that is reminiscent of the "separate track" approach that was espoused at the time of NAFTA's negotiation, the three governments have not much encouraged greater collaboration between trade and environmental institutions. A decade after the ratification of the agreements, despite overtures by the CEC, no joint meeting of environment and trade ministers has taken place (TRAC 2004: 25). There is also similar resistance or indifference at the level of technical working groups, which have largely ignored environmental concerns in their work. In fact, the Mexican government has argued that NAFTA committees must focus on securing greater market access for Mexican goods. In this perspective, environmental concerns should be addressed in so far as they are used by the US as a barrier to trade and rarely, if at all, out of concerns for the impact that the working groups' work might have on the environment (CEC 1997: 61). In another example of such resistance, the US government even had to be ordered by a US court in 1999 to "make a good faith effort to expedite the appointment of at least one properly qualified environmental representative" to two advisory committees to these technical bodies (Block 2003: 529). In the end, this lack of coordination between environmental and trade policies is likely to create a disservice for environmental protection and hinder progress toward a more environmentally sustainable form of development on the continent.

INVESTMENT PROTECTION AND THE DANGER OF "REGULATORY CHILL"

In addition to these measures on harmonization, NAFTA also includes some unprecedented provisions on investment policies. In a direct response to environmental concerns about a race to the bottom that would ensue because of the dynamics of competition, the chapter on foreign investment protection states that it is inappropriate for the trading partners to attempt to attract investments by waiving or derogating from environmental standards.[10] However, in the event that such behaviour is alleged, the agreement only states that the two countries involved "shall consult with a view to avoiding any such encouragement." There is no recourse to a binding dispute resolution mechanism (Charnovitz 1994: 62–63). Another important caveat is that the article seems to forbid states to grant *specific* waivers to *particular* firms in a bid to attract them, but it does not seem to preclude governments from engaging in a general weakening of standards for the purpose of improving their country's competitive position and, thereby, attract or retain firms more generally (Charnovitz 1994: 63; Esty and Geradin 1997: 315). Hence, its purview appears rather limited against the broad concerns raised by environmentalists.

As with provisions concerning harmonization, these measures against investment-related environmental derogations have rarely been invoked in the context of a trade dispute. Their apparent irrelevance is stunning when one considers that the last decade was marked by a series of investment-related disputes with significant environmental implications. In fact, in NAFTA's first ten years, at least ten disputes involving foreign corporations challenging environmental regulations have been submitted to its investor-state dispute resolution procedures (Godshall 2003: 272). However, while these disputes have galvanized the environmental movement's opposition to NAFTA, the nature of the cases, which mostly focused on allegations of discrimination in favour of domestic corporations, violations of minimum standards of treatment afforded to foreign investors, and "indirect expropriation" of foreign investments due to the adoption of new environmental rules, was unexpected, and, as a result, the investment-related environmental protections inscribed in the agreement have proven irrelevant.

These challenges against environmental laws find their source in the guarantees that NAFTA's Chapter 11 provides to foreign investors.[11] For example, foreign investors are ensured that they will be treated without discrimination compared to domestic firms in similar circumstances (Article 1102) and that their investments will be treated at least in accordance with minimum international standards (Article 1105). One of the most controversial provisions (Article 1110) also states that a party to the agreement may not, directly or indirectly, expropriate an investment made by a corporation from another party or take a measure that would be "tantamount to an expropriation" except when it is done for a public purpose and on a non-discriminatory basis. However, even in these legitimate cases, the expropriation must take place in accordance with due process of law, must ensure that investors are afforded minimum standards of treatment, and must provide adequate financial compensation (International Institute for Sustainable Development and World Wildlife Fund 2001: 25–36).

In addition to these guarantees, Chapter 11 also establishes an investor state dispute resolution mechanism founded on the rules of international arbitration. In contrast to traditional trade dispute resolution mechanisms (which can be accessed only by governments), the investment dispute resolution mechanism allows a corporation to bring a claim directly against a foreign government whose actions have allegedly expropriated its investments. The claim is then submitted to binding arbitration and decided by an ad hoc arbitration tribunal composed of three members selected by the parties involved in the dispute.[12] Moreover, because international arbitration is considered a private matter, there is no obligation for the arbitration tribunal to make its proceedings public or even to disclose its rulings (Poirier 2003: 864); a rather stunning situation for a binding legal procedure involving governments on significant matters of public policy.

Unexpectedly, in the last decade, it is those provisions on investment protection that have been mostly used to challenge environmental laws and policies. For example, exploiting the lack of clear definitions in the agreement (Beauvais 2002: 257–58), corporations have claimed that some environmental laws and regulations adopted by the three governments have had the effect of depriving them of the expected benefits of their investment, thereby representing "measures tantamount to expropriation." These claims often rely on an expansive interpretation of what constitutes a "regulatory taking," that is, an expropriation that does not occur as a result of an actual transfer of property to the state but as the (unintended) result of adopting regulations that deprive an owner of the use of her/his property (Beauvais 2002: 259). While "regulatory takings" is a recognized legal concept, the NAFTA text and arbitration tribunals have stretched its conventional application. In particular, the Chapter 11 provisions do not solely protect the property of investors but cover "investments" more broadly. For example, the tribunals have already stated that a reduction in a corporation's market access or market share could constitute investments that could be expropriated through regulatory takings, thereby requiring government compensation (Beauvais 2002: 280).

Environmentalists fear that this expansive reading of what constitutes "measures tantamount to expropriation," the secrecy and inaccessibility of the ad hoc tribunals' proceedings, and the capacity of corporations to directly challenge states with the expectation of financial return may combine to create a "regulatory chill" in North America, because governments will shirk from adopting new environmental regulations for fear of being challenged by foreign investors and having to pay substantial sums of money in compensation. These fears have not been alleviated by the fact that, in the cases seen to date, claimants have often asked for considerable financial compensation. The still pending *Methanex* case represents the largest claim to date: Methanex, a Canadian corporation, is claiming $970 million from the government of California to compensate for the loss of expected profits following the state's phase-out of a fuel additive considered to have health and environmental effects. Among the cases settled so far, the highest compensation award paid by a government was $16.7 million.

The first environmental case considered under the Chapter 11 provisions seemed to confirm the worst fears of environmentalists. In September 1996, the US-based Ethyl Corporation filed a claim for $250 million for lost sales and profits against the Canadian government. The claim concerned Canada's decision for reasons of environmental health to ban the importation of MMT, an octane-enhancing gasoline additive only produced by Ethyl and exported to the Canadian market. In 1998, before the case was decided on its merits by an arbitration tribunal, the Canadian government agreed to a settlement, withdrawing its law banning MMT and paying $13 million to the US company. While there might have been merit to the company's claim that Canada's behaviour had as much to do with protecting the interest of its Canadian competitors in the gasoline additive market as with environmental and health concerns, the case nevertheless seemed to be a "poster child" for the regulatory chill argument: a government had withdrawn an environmental law in the face of a NAFTA-based lawsuit by a foreign investor.

Since the voluntary settlement in the *Ethyl* case, a few cases involving environmental measures have actually been decided by arbitration tribunals. In contrast to the fears expressed by environmentalists, these decisions have not been very favourable to corporate arguments defending a very expansive definition of what would constitute a "regulatory expropriation." In the *S.D. Myers* case, the tribunal even explicitly warned against reading an unusually generous concept of regulatory expropriation into the NAFTA text (Beauvais 2002: 273–74). Even in the *Metalclad* case, the only one where an expropriation was found to have occurred under the terms of Chapter 11 (see Chapter 11, this volume), the ad hoc arbitration tribunal's expansive interpretation of regulatory expropriations was curtailed on appeal by a Canadian court. Ultimately, the Mexican government had to pay compensation to the company because it turned the territory on which the company operated its hazardous waste treatment facility into an ecological preserve, making the facility's operation impossible and thereby "indirectly expropriating" the company's investment (Godshall 2003: 281–84). As such, the ruling relies on a more limited and conventional conception of indirect expropriation.

While corporate claims of indirect expropriation may not have been as successful as environmentalists had feared, foreign investors also had some success challenging environmental policies for discrimination and inadequate standards of treatment. For example, in the *S.D. Myers* decision, the tribunal forced the Canadian government to pay an award of $6 million to a US company because it adopted a ban on the export of toxic polychlorinated biphenyls (PCBs) waste. The S.D. Myers Corporation had created a Canadian subsidiary to collect PCB waste, which it then planned to export for disposal to its parent company in the US. Despite Canadian claims that the ban was supported by the Basel Convention, an international treaty regulating the international trade in hazardous wastes, the tribunal found that the ban was essentially a discriminatory policy meant to protect the Canadian market for Canadian toxic waste disposal companies and, therefore, a violation of Chapter 11's national treatment provisions (Article 1102) (Godshall 2003: 274–75; Beauvais 2002: 274).

In some cases, foreign investors were also successful in claiming compensation for inadequate treatment by governments. For example, in the *Metalclad* case, the tribunal held that the Mexican municipality that had originally tried to stop the operation of the hazardous waste treatment facility by denying a building permit had unjustifiably based its decision on environmental concerns and public opinion, factors that were unrelated to the construction concerns that it was legally mandated to consider for such a permit. As a result, the tribunal held that, in its efforts to protect local water supplies, the municipality had denied Metalclad the minimum international standard of treatment that NAFTA guarantees to foreign investors (Article 1105) (Godshall 2003: 279–81). In addition to the finding of indirect expropriation (discussed above), this violation of minimum standards of treatment forced the Mexican federal government to pay the company $16.7 million in compensation.

As a whole, these early adverse findings or settlements under NAFTA's investment provisions have generated much concern and opposition by environmental and nationalist groups. Having granted unprecedented powers to foreign corporations to challenge domestic environmental laws, with the potential for substantial financial gains for doing so, Chapter 11 is now seen as one of the main threats to environmental protection resulting from the continental trade agreement. While future decisions will help clarify the true extent of this threat, even the three governments appear to have acknowledged that this emerging "jurisprudence" goes beyond what they themselves had anticipated during negotiations and that, as a result, it may create an undue burden for establishing legitimate environmental protections demanded by citizens. In an unusual step, on 31 July 2001, the three governments issued a joint statement to "clarify" their own interpretation of these investment provisions. In response to criticism of secrecy, the statement stipulates that Chapter 11 should not prevent governments from providing public access to documents submitted to, or published by, arbitration panels. Moreover, it affirms that, with respect to minimum standard of treatment due to foreign companies, NAFTA should not be interpreted to create obligations in excess of what is found in customary international law.[13] However, given that this statement does not modify the text of NAFTA and that the governments do not control the arbitration process, it is not clear what effect, if any, such a clarification could have on future dispute resolutions and on emerging continental legal norms.

TEN YEARS AFTER: A RACE TO THE BOTTOM OR A CHILL ON ENVIRONMENTAL REGULATION?

As we have seen, while clearly ground-breaking for a trade agreement, the environmental provisions written into the NAFTA text remain limited and their potential effectiveness in supporting higher environmental standards or preventing a race to the bottom can be questioned. However, and perhaps more importantly in assessing NAFTA's impact on environmental policy-making, they remain largely untested. Over a decade after their adoption, they appear to be largely irrelevant. The state-initiated legal challenges of environmental standards that they were meant to alleviate have not occurred. Instead, the debate has shifted to the emerging norms of investment protection and direct challenges of environmental laws and decisions by foreign corporations under international arbitration provisions. Vocal concerns about a race to the bottom in environmental standards have largely given way to fears of a chill over the adoption of new environmental regulations for fear of having to pay compensation to foreign investors.

In practice, however, the actual extent of the regulatory chill created by arbitration panel decisions is hard to ascertain. Notwithstanding the vivid illustration provided by the Canadian voluntary withdrawal of a parliamentary bill in the *Ethyl* case, the empirical confirmation of the regulatory chill argument would essentially require the assessment of what regulations *would have been* adopted by governments in the absence of the potential for Chapter 11 claims by foreign investors. This is a rather difficult task. Certainly, the decade that followed the adoption of NAFTA has not been one of complete inaction with regard to environmental policy-making in the three countries. In Canada, for instance, the federal government finally adopted long-awaited legislation to protect endangered species and the law controlling toxic substances has been strengthened, with several new regulations coming into force. Moreover, it would be difficult to attribute most policy setbacks to NAFTA. For example, in recent years, US environmental laws have certainly been under attack, but the influence of NAFTA on these events appears quite secondary to the domestic power of the business lobby, the anti-regulation agenda of a Republican-dominated Congress in the mid-1990s, and the ideological fervour of the Bush administration (see, for example, Kennedy 2004; Devine 2004; Kraft 2000: 31–33). Similarly, the Canadian record of the last decade also suggests the pre-eminence of domestic factors, such as federal-provincial relations or shifts in public opinion (Juillet 2005).

Similarly, despite the absence of a significant trend in standards' harmonization across the three jurisdictions, fears about Mexico becoming a haven for North America's most polluting industries have not been substantiated. In accordance with the results of research conducted in other countries (Jayadevappa and Chhatre 2000), one of the few studies on NAFTA's environmental impact on Mexico recently found that, with respect to air pollutants, industries facing higher marginal environmental abatement costs in the US (i.e., those that would lower their environmental compliance costs if they moved to Mexico) actually represented a declining share of the

Mexican economy in the years following the agreement's implementation (Gallagher 2004). In fact, with regard to air pollution, Gallagher did not find any evidence that Mexico is becoming a pollution haven or that there had been a large-scale migration of pollution-intensive industries to that country (Gallagher 2004: 25–33). The reason, he suggests, is that the costs of compliance with environmental standards remain a very small part of most firms' operational costs and that they would not justify the relocation of a firm's operations. Other factors, such as labour costs, qualification of available employees, and proximity to markets are typically more important in location decisions.

However, it is important to note that, despite the lack of evidence of a pollution haven scenario, Gallagher's study also confirmed that air quality in Mexico nevertheless deteriorated over the 1990s due to expanding levels of industrial production. In other words, notwithstanding its favourable compositional shift away from the dirtier industries, significant growth rates led the Mexican economy to generate an increasing volume of air pollutants. This finding illustrates an increasingly important dimension of the relationship between continental trade and environmental policies, especially in Mexico: domestic environmental policies may not have kept up with the environmental consequences of trade-induced industrial growth and restructuring. For example, in the case of air pollution, it is obvious that Mexican laws and enforcement have not been adequate in alleviating the environmental side-effects of industrial expansion. In fact, after having expanded them considerably in the years leading to NAFTA's ratification, the Mexican government has severely reduced the level of enforcement activities after 1994 (Gallagher 2004: 71–72).

Similar problems have been found in the agricultural sector. For example, Vaughan found that trade liberalization has contributed to a shift in the composition of the crops produced in some regions of Mexico as well as to the concentration of the agricultural sector in favour of large-scale, export-oriented farms. Depending on the crop and the region, the growth in the volume of production and the changes in farming techniques have created additional pressures on groundwater resources tapped for irrigation and resulted in higher levels of discharges in water-polluting agrochemicals (Vaughan 2003: 62–64). Moreover, while the production of some commercial crops has expanded, freer trade has also resulted in lower prices for some crop varieties that are economically crucial for some segments of Mexican society. As a result, in the southern part of Mexico, which is exceptionally rich in biological diversity, the increased poverty of subsistence farmers has generated more deforestation, and the concomitant loss of biodiversity, as families cut trees as a source of fuel and turn the land into arable areas to sustain their declining income (Vaughan 2003: 81). In the end, these increased environmental pressures induced by trade liberalization may prove a more serious challenge to adequate environmental protection than industry relocation or any legal challenge arising out of the NAFTA provisions.

NAFTA Politics and the Strengthening Continental Environmental Governance

In addition to the measures discussed above, the main environmental legacy of the NAFTA debate remains the adoption of the treaty on trilateral environmental cooperation, the NAAEC, and the associated creation of the CEC. As discussed in the first section of this chapter, the CEC's mandate extends well beyond trade-related matters and includes a whole range of environmental issues that may benefit from greater trilateral environmental cooperation, ranging from wildlife conservation to pollution prevention and sustainable development (Johnson and Beaulieu 1996: 140–45). While its secretariat operates on a relatively modest annual budget of US$9 million (TRAC 2004: 10), the CEC reports on environmental trends and emerging issues, coordinates the sharing of information and the development of the environmental policy capacity of the members states, conducts or funds research on priority issues, and has funded community-based environmental projects across the continent. Through its consultation processes, it has also provided a unique continental forum for the participation of citizens and NGOs in environmental debates. In this last regard, the openness of the CEC's work, and its constant engagement with the Mexican environmental department, might have contributed to democratize Mexico's environmental decision-making process somewhat and to raise awareness of ecological issues within Mexican civil society (Block 2003: 516).

Ten years after its creation, the CEC has had some influence on environmental policy debates through its research and information dissemination activities. For example, it has probably attracted the most public attention for publishing *Taking Stock*, a controversial annual report tracking industrial emissions on the continent that has received significant attention in the media (TRAC 2004: 16). As noted earlier, the CEC's work in assisting in the development of Mexico's policy capacity is also cited as a success. In addition, it has helped finance pollution prevention initiatives for small and medium-sized Mexican businesses (Block 2003: 516–17). Finally, the CEC has had some success in fostering the development of a more continental approach to tackling some environmental challenges, notably the management of chemicals and the conservation of some shared wildlife species (TRAC 2004: 15).

While these realizations are not negligible, they remain quite limited in view of the environmental challenges shared by the three countries. In fact, since its creation, the CEC has had difficulty establishing itself as an important forum for addressing continental environmental problems. In its ten-year review, a high-level committee recently felt the need to ask the three governments to "strengthen and renew" their commitment to the CEC "as their institution of choice for trilateral environmental cooperation" (TRAC 2004: 48). The review committee found that the work of the CEC's secretariat had been unfocused, that the secretariat and the ministerial council were often in conflict and distrusted each other, and that the secretariat's budget had suffered a 20 per cent reduction in real terms since 1994 (TRAC 2004: 19). Some of these difficulties are due to the fact that the secretariat has been pushing the boundaries of its autonomy under the NAAEC, while the three environmental ministers have been repeatedly attempting to limit the CEC's purview and the scope of its citizens' submission process.

Despite the potential value of the CEC as a forum for continental environmental cooperation, it is clearly the provisions on the enforcement of domestic environmental laws as well as those allowing citizens to request an investigation into ineffective domestic enforcement that attracted the most attention at the time of the NAAEC's negotiation. A decade after they came into force, the effectiveness of these mechanisms, and their impact on the environmental policies of the three countries, has been extremely limited. In the case of the binding dispute resolution process, it has never been used by the NAFTA governments. Even in the face of the decline in enforcement activities in Mexico after the ratification of NAFTA, these enforcement provisions have never been invoked by the US or Canada either. Furthermore, while the three governments have seemingly tacitly agreed not to use the process, the Mexican and Canadian governments would even favour its removal from the agreement (TRAC 2004: 37). In hindsight, all the emphasis placed by the US government on the need for sanction-backed enforcement at the time of negotiations appears to have served little purpose.

The citizens' submission process, which can trigger investigations into a party's alleged failure to effectively enforce its environmental laws, has also been plagued with difficulties. While there have not been as many submissions as expected, the CEC had nevertheless received 51 submissions by July 2005. Out of the 40 files closed by then, ten led to the publication of a factual record, almost all of them regarding Mexico (five cases) or Canada (four cases).[14] Since the agreement does not require any response or follow-up to the publication of a factual record, it is difficult to ascertain whether the process has a significant impact on environmental policy-making. There is at least anecdotal evidence that the public attention and criticism associated with factual records have led to some minor policy changes in Canada and Mexico (TRAC 2004: 46).

However, what is certain is that the citizens' submission process has been a significant source of conflict between the three NAFTA environmental ministers and the CEC's secretariat. Environmental ministers believe that the secretariat is abusing its autonomy by publicly adopting an adversarial stance toward its government members, and their officials have been somewhat distraught about the allegations of widespread ineffective enforcement that have been at the heart of some submissions. As a result, the CEC's ministerial council has limited the scope of factual records (for example, by telling the secretariat to circumscribe the scope of its investigations to specific cases and events as opposed to broader patterns of enforcement).[15] The governments have also proposed to tighten the criteria that citizens must meet to see their submission accepted by the secretariat, such as setting a higher burden of proof for submitters or requiring them to exhaust all other domestic remedies before making a submission to the CEC (TRAC 2004: 44–45). These decisions have been widely criticized by environmentalists and the CEC's own public advisory body. Overall, this controversy regarding the citizens' submission process has significantly contributed to the strained relations between the environmental ministers of the three countries and the CEC secretariat and, in the end, probably hindered the CEC's overall effectiveness by costing it support from its own member governments.

In sum, while the CEC has certainly contributed to increasing the level of environmental collaboration among the three national governments somewhat, it has not become a major driver of environmental policy on the continent. Moreover, its most innovative and forceful provisions have largely fallen short of the expectations generated through the NAFTA ratification debate.

Conclusion

More than a decade after their ratification, the environmental legacy of the NAFTA and its environmental side-deal remain ambiguous. As our examination of the ratification debates revealed, the inclusion of Mexico, considered an environmental laggard, in the trade agreement, as well as the dynamics of domestic US politics, profoundly shaped the continental environmental politics of NAFTA and influenced the nature of the unprecedented continental norms and institutions that were finally adopted by the three countries. However, in retrospect, these norms and institutions do not seem to have provided an effective safeguard against the environmental challenges that have emerged under continental free trade.

With regard to environmental protection standards, the more important concerns of the time, such as a downward spiral in levels of standards and the relocation of dirty industries, have proven to be overstated. At the same time, other issues that were not prevalent in the concerns of environmentalists, especially the consequences of investment protection provisions, are now occupying centre stage. Fears of races to the bottom have given way to concerns about regulatory chill. However, overall, there is little evidence at this point that NAFTA has had a major impact on the evolution of domestic environmental policies in the three countries.

With regard to institutions of continental governance, the creation of the CEC represents an important step forward in institutional development. There is some evidence that it has furthered continental environmental cooperation in modest ways and helped build environmental policy capacity in Mexico. However, these gains remain modest in view of the significant environmental challenges faced by North America, and the most innovative and forceful measures associated with the CEC, such as the binding dispute resolution process, have proven to be ineffective. The CEC itself has become an embattled organization, finding it difficult to navigate between the roles of effective forum of intergovernmental cooperation and strong advocate for environmental protection with a more direct relationship with citizens of the continent.

Nevertheless, despite this mixed record, deepening continental market integration will continue to be an important environmental policy issue in the coming decades. Forthcoming arbitration panel rulings based on Chapter 11 may still generate even more significant constraints or disincentives to the development of strong national environmental policies. As some industrial sectors move to further harmonize their regulatory standards to facilitate the exchange of goods, emerging continental norms may also have important implications for environmental protection. Moreover, as the realities of heightened continental competition force industries to restructure and change their modes of production, the changing demands placed on continental environmental resources, from water resources to our soil and air, may exacerbate our environmental problems and require new policy responses. In order to respond adequately to these trade-related challenges, a more resolute commitment to environmental protection and more extensive trilateral cooperation than we have seen in the last decade will be required.

Notes

1   Despite being characterized as a "package," NAFTA and its environmental side-deal are clearly separate entities. To the limited extent that they are related, the side-deal on environmental cooperation is subordinate to the trade agreement. Furthermore, withdrawal of one of the parties from the environmental side-deal would leave NAFTA intact (Johnson and Beaulieu 1996: 126–29).

2   In the following years, some other environmental treaties also included relatively stringent measures of enforcement, notably the Kyoto Protocol to the Framework Convention on Climate Change, signed in 1997. But, at the time of its signature, the NAAEC dispute resolution mechanism stood out even more significantly, and its provisions allowing for citizen submission are still quite innovative.

3   It should be noted that a special regime has been put in place for Canada under Annex 36A of the NAAEC. Under this special regime, Canada is exempted from all trade sanctions. As an alternative, the CEC has been granted special standing in Canadian courts and could obtain a court order to force the Canadian government to comply with the panel's findings (see Johnson and Beaulieu 1996: 225–28). Annex 41 also makes special provisions for cases involving Canadian provinces.

4   An important exception concerns some dispositions regarding multilateral environmental agreements (MEA). NAFTA states that a limited number of MEA with trade implications, such as those on the international trade of endangered species and hazardous waste, will be considered preponderant in the event of a conflict. At the time of its adoption, this measure made NAFTA a more environmentally sensitive trade agreement than the GATT, and it was lauded as a ground-breaking and progressive attempt to clarify the relationship between international trade and environmental regimes. However, given that the three governments must specify which environmental treaties will benefit from such consideration, conflicts with future agreements are not impossible, especially with relation to the control of trade in genetically modified organisms (e.g., the Carthagena Protocol on Biosafety). Moreover, even environmental measures adopted to implement the three treaties already given preponderance by NAFTA could be challenged if they are not deemed to be the least trade-restrictive measures available (Block 2003: 507).

5   See Articles 714 and 906 of NAFTA.

6   See Articles 713 and 905 of NAFTA.

7   See Articles 712 and 904 of NAFTA.

8   We should note, however, that NAFTA's dispute resolution process might improve over what prevailed under the GATT with regards to disputes involving environmental issues. Firstly, under NAFTA, the party challenging the regulation would have to prove that it violates the agreement, reversing the traditional burden of proof. Secondly, NAFTA stipulates that the parties to a dispute, and the panel itself, can convene a panel of scientific experts to assist in considering technical issues raised by the dispute (see Esty and Geradin 1997: 312).

9   See Article 10(6) of the NAAEC.

10 See Article 1114 of NAFTA. The ban on performance requirements on foreign investments also exempts environmental measures (always subject to the fact that such requirements are not found to be disguised protectionist measures or applied discriminatorily). See Article 1106(6).

11 It is interesting to note that the genesis of Chapter 11 on investments, much like the negotiation of the NAAEC, rests in concerns about Mexico's legal regime. However, in this case, it is the business community that showed concern about the trustworthiness of the Mexican state

as it feared that unpredictable and unreasonable government behaviour would threaten the viability of investments. Canadian and US authorities wanted to provide guarantees to their respective business sectors that investments into Mexico would be secure and that full benefits could be derived from greater continental integration. Similarly, in order to attract potential foreign investors, Mexico wanted to reassure them that its property regime would be sound and that it would ensure a stable business environment. In this context, traditional provisions of national treatment, which would seemingly have guaranteed foreign corporations a fair access to national expropriation and regulatory takings provisions of individual countries, were not seen as sufficient. The creation of a continental investment protection regime was deemed more likely to reassure Canadian and US investors that any eventual Mexican nationalization and regulatory takings would be properly compensated.

12 Each party chooses one member and the third is selected by agreement or, if an agreement is not possible, imposed by a designated international organization (see Beauvais 2002: 250).

13 The full text of the statement, entitled *Notes of Interpretation of Certain Chapter 11 Provisions*, is available on the following website: <http://www.dfait-maeci.gc.ca/tna-nac/NAFTA-Interpr-en.asp>.

14 Data on the number and status of citizens' submissions can be found on the CEC's website at <http://www.cec.org>.

15 Originally, Canada was at the forefront of these efforts to circumscribe the scope of the submission process, which were resisted by the US. However, after a US case was filed with the CEC, the Bush administration also proposed to narrow the scope of factual records (see Block 2003: 518).

References

Audley, John. 1997. *Green Politics and Global Trade: NAFTA and the Future of Environmental Politics*. Washington, DC: Georgetown UP.

Beauvais, Joel. 2002. "Regulatory Expropriation Under NAFTA: Emerging Principles and Lingering Doubts." *New York University Environmental Law Journal* 10: 245–96.

Bhagwati, Jagdish. 2004. *In Defense of Globalization*. New York: Oxford UP.

Block, Greg. 2003. "Trade and Environment in the Western Hemisphere: Expanding the North American Agreement on Environmental Cooperation into the Americas." *Environmental Law* 33,3: 501–46.

CEC. 1997. *NAFTA's Institutions: The Environmental Potential and Performance of the NAFTA Free Trade Commission and Related Bodies*. Montreal: Commission for Environmental Cooperation.

Charnovitz, Steve. 1994. "The North American Free Trade Agreement: Green Law or Green Spin?" *Law and Policy in International Business* 26: 1–77.

Devine, Robert S. 2004. *Bush versus the Environment*. New York: Anchor Books.

Dowie, Mark. 1995. *Losing Ground: American Environmentalism at the Close of the Twentieth Century*. Cambridge: The MIT Press.

Esty, Daniel C., and Damien Geradin. 1997. "Market Access, Competitiveness, and Harmonization: Environmental Protection in Regional Trade Agreements." *Harvard Environmental Law Review* 21: 265–336.

Gallagher, Kevin. 2004. *Free Trade and the Environment: Mexico, NAFTA, and Beyond*. Stanford, CA: Stanford UP.

Godshall, Lauren. 2003. "In the Cold Shadow of *Metalclad*: The Potential for Change to NAFTA's Chapter 11." *New York University Environmental Law Journal* 11: 264–316.

International Institute for Sustainable Development and the World Wildlife Fund. 2001. *Private Rights, Public Problems: A Guide to NAFTA's Controversial Chapter on Investor Rights*. Winnipeg: IISD.

Jayadevappa, R., and S. Chhatre. 2000. "International Trade and Environmental Quality: A Survey." *Ecological Economics* 32: 77–95.

Johnson, Pierre-Marc, and André Beaulieu. 1996. *The Environment and NAFTA: Understanding and Implementing the New Continental Law*. Washington, DC: Island Press.

Juillet, Luc. 2001. "Regional Models of Environmental Governance in the Context of Market Integration." In Edward A. Parson (ed.), *Governing the Environment: Persistent Challenges, Uncertain Innovations*. Toronto: U of Toronto P. 125–68.

——. 2005. "La politica ambiental canadiense en el cambio de siglo." in A. Hristoulas, C. Denis, and Duncan Wood (eds.), *Canada: Politica y gobierno en el siglo XXI*. Mexico: Instituto Technologico Autonomo de Mexico. 105–23.

Kennedy, Jr., Robert F. 2004. *Crimes Against Nature*. New York: HarperCollins.

Kraft, Michael E. 2000. "US Environmental Policy and Politics: From the 1960s to the 1990s." *Journal of Policy History* 12,1: 17–42.

OECD. 1998. *Environmental Performance Review for Mexico*. Paris: Organization for Economic Cooperation and Development.

Poirier, Marc. 2003. "The NAFTA Chapter 11 Expropriation Debate through the Eyes of a Property Theorist." *Environmental Law* 33,4: 851–928.

Ritchie, Mark. 1993. "Trading Away the Environment: Free-Trade Agreements and Environmental Degradation." In Richard Hofrichter (ed.), *Toxic Struggles: The Theory and Practice of Environmental Justice*. Philadelphia, PA: New Society Publishers. 209–18.

Steinberg, Richard H. 1997. "Trade-Environment Negotiations in the EU, NAFTA, and WTO: Regional Trajectories of Rule Development." *American Journal of International Law* 91: 231–67.

TRAC (Ten-year Review and Assessment Committee). 2004. *Ten Years of North American Environmental Cooperation—Report of the Ten-year Review and Assessment Committee to the Council of the Commission for Environmental Cooperation*. Montreal: Commission for Environmental Cooperation.

Vaughan, Scott. 2003. "The Greenest Trade Agreement Ever? Measuring the Environmental Impacts of Agricultural Liberalization." In John Audley *et al.* (eds.), *NAFTA's Promise and Reality: Lessons from Mexico for the Hemisphere*. Washington, DC: Carnegie Endowment for International Peace. 61–87.

Vogel, David. 2000. "The Environment and International Trade." *Journal of Policy History* 12,1: 72–100.

PART FOUR

Redefining Spatial Relations: Post-9/11 Borders, Migration, and National Security

The fourth section deals with themes relating to borders, migration, and national security. While these issues have been of long-standing relevance in North America, they have taken on renewed saliency since 9/11.

Yasmeen Abu-Laban analyzes migration and the politicization of borders in this era of continental economic integration in Chapter 15, "Migration in North America." Whereas the EU model of integration has meant relatively free movement of citizens of member countries, the North American model has led to free movement of capital, goods, and services, rather than the free movement of people. Abu-Laban reviews the NAFTA debate and the final agreement, arguing that they have served to reinforce existing class, gender, and national inequities in migration between member countries through, for example, the temporary business and professional entry provision, which is biased in favour of class-privileged males in certain occupations. As a result, NAFTA reflected the very different relations Mexico and Canada had with the US around migration, and this continues to the present in the way that border accords have taken bilateral (US-Canada or US-Mexico) rather than trilateral forms.

Chapter 15 also highlights the politicization of the US's northern and southern borders, and how American national security since 9/11 has increasingly trumped human security (or human rights). As Abu-Laban shows, this is especially evident in the areas of refugee asylum rights (where Canada and the US have merged their refugee systems), in increased practices of detention (for example, in Mexico, where undocumented migrants/refugees from Asia, Africa, and the Middle East trying to reach the US may be detained in centres funded by the US), and in racial profiling of various people of colour in the name of combating terrorism. The latter has implications for citizens too, since, as Abu-Laban argues, such features as place of birth; race, ethnicity, or religion; presumed race, ethnicity, or religion; and holding more than one citizenship can be grounds for differentiation irrespective of the passport one holds.

Christina Gabriel and Laura Macdonald take a rather different view of the implications of 9/11 for North American borders in Chapter 16, "From the 49th Parallel to the Río Grande: US Homeland Security and North American Borders." Rejecting the traditional realist conception of borders as hard lines delineating the territorial space of state sovereignty, they draw upon constructivist and critical geo-political approaches to understand the reconstruction of both "imagined communities" and the continental geo-political space of North America since the 9/11 attacks. Their brief account of the evolution of US power in North America begins with eighteenth- and nineteenth-century assertions of the "Manifest Destiny" of the US to fill the entire continent (its seizure of Indigenous lands, the annexation of Texas from Mexico, and similar attempts to invade Canada) and examines the role of borders in defining relationships with its two neighbours. While the US and Canada cooperated extensively on the "security perimeter" during the Cold War, the predatory behaviour of the US led Mexico to see that country as the greatest external threat to its security. However, the US's largely unilateral fortification of its borders and the Bush Administration's adoption of the "homeland security" frame since the 9/11 attacks have induced such accommodative responses from Canada and Mexico as the Smart Border agreements aimed at maintaining access to US markets. Finally, Gabriel and Macdonald analyze the complex position of borders in contemporary and future "imaginings" as new "deterritorialized threats" such as terrorism, narco-trafficking, illegal migration, refugee, and environmental conflicts challenge pre-existing assumptions about the nature of borders in the North American region.

Athanasios Hristoulas and Stéphane Roussel begin Chapter 17, "North American Security and Foreign Policy: Does a Trilateral Community Exist?" with the observation that 9/11 radically changed the priorities of the US administration so that security now trumps trade. This development gives Mexicans and Canadians no choice but to comply with the US agenda or face economic and political consequences. "Security" encompasses everything from "smart borders" to immigration law and cooperative law enforcement agencies charged with protecting "Fortress North America." After an historical analysis of the very different emphases of the foreign and security policies of the three NAFTA partners, the authors outline their positions on the issue of security cooperation and examine the main obstacles to further cooperation. They reveal the logic behind the bilateral model preferred by Canada versus the comprehensive trilateral security cooperation favoured by the US and Mexico. Finally, Hristoulas and Roussel discuss some of the effects on and the implicit demotion of human rights by the various security measures taken by the three countries, including the US Patriot Act, Canada's Anti-Terrorism Act, and Mexico's increased attention to its southern border. They conclude that, as far as foreign and security policies are concerned, for the time being it is not possible to conceive of North America as a single unified region.

CHAPTER FIFTEEN

Migration in North America

Yasmeen Abu-Laban

Writing of the period between World War I and World War II, Hannah Arendt (2004) poignantly highlighted the connection between stateless-ness and rightlessness: a person's "right to have rights" was contingent on membership in a state. In the decades following World War II, a strong discourse developed around human rights, and international agreements, including some on the rights of migrants, were concluded (Soysal 1994). Tellingly however, even in the 1948 United Nations Universal Declaration of Human Rights, the right to emigrate (leave a country) is not backed by a right to immigrate (enter a country) (Benhabib 2004: 11). Legally, the UN has played a critical role in determining who is entitled to asylum and the responsibility of states through the 1951 Convention Relating to the Status of Refugees, which defined who was a refugee and outlined the rights of refugees and the obligations of states, and the 1967 Protocol, which removed the geographic and temporal restrictions of the 1951 Convention. Yet, the fact remains that international agreements are only binding on signatory states and, moreover, can even be ignored by signatories. As a consequence, the problem identified by Arendt 50 years ago of statelessness, and possible rightlessness, remains in the twenty-first century, though it plays out in geographically specific ways.

The purpose of this chapter is to analyze migration, rights, and the politicization of borders in North America in light of the deepening patterns of regional economic integration that have linked Canada, the US, and Mexico more closely since the 1990s. When analysts address international migration today, they have to grapple with a global phenomenon that implicates states. By definition, international migration involves the movement of people for temporary or permanent settlement across state boundaries. The UN estimates that worldwide there are about 150 million people (2.5 per cent of the earth's population) who are migrants, that is, whose nationality does not coincide with their country of residence (Commission of the European Communities 2002: 9). Given this, it is also clear why those interested in globalization are interested in migration. The term "globalization" as used here refers to a world-scale reorientation of economic, technological, and cultural processes and activities that transcend the nation-state. Global cultural and economic flows include the movement of peoples, such as tourists, immigrants, guest workers, and refugees (Appadurai 1990: 295–310).

Analysts of contemporary globalization, such as sociologist David Held and his colleagues, have pointed out that migratory flows today are really qualitatively different from those of the past. In the processes associated with European imperialism and colonialism in the nineteenth century, migration tended to be from metropoles to colonies; however, since World War II, migration patterns have become more complex, with the result that all major world regions both send and receive migrants (Held *et al.* 1999: 425). Contemporary globalization has also gone hand in hand with growing regional economic integration. Particularly since the 1990s, we have witnessed interesting developments at regional levels. This is most graphically the case with the EU. It is also the case with Asia, through APEC (Asia-Pacific Economic Cooperation) and ASEAN (Association of South-East Asian Nations), and Latin America, through MERCOSUR (the *Mercado del Sur*, a common market between Argentina, Brazil, Paraguay, and Uruguay), and not least North America through NAFTA.

The North American region, however, has been shaped not only by economic integration but by a re-constitution of security around the threat posed by terrorism after 9/11. While the US-led "war on terrorism" has been approached as geographically boundless, in many ways the discourse underpinning terrorism is racialized. Within North America, the popular image of a "terrorist" is someone who is dark, who is Arab, and/or who is Muslim. The resurgence in popularity of "the clash of civilizations" also speaks to the tenacity of essentialist ways of viewing the world and its peoples in the post-9/11 environment. This helps to explain why immigration policies and practices and new or revamped anti-terrorist legislation across many polities are coming now to be analyzed with renewed concern for profiling, civil liberties, and human rights, especially with respect to racialized minorities (Abu-Laban 2005).

Keeping these dimensions in mind, I argue that the NAFTA provisions and their implementation have served to reinforce existing class, gender, and national inequities in migration between member countries. Moreover, since NAFTA was passed, and increasingly since 9/11, human security has been trumped by re-articulations of national security, particularly though not exclusively, US national security, with negative consequences for both human and citizen rights. Judging from this history and recent developments, it would seem that North America is more clearly marked by two sets of bilateral relations (US-Mexico and US-Canada) rather than trilateralism, making the emergence of a "Fortress North America" that allows for the free movement of all Mexican nationals unlikely.

To illustrate this argument, I will precede in three parts. First, I will review the debate, the text, and the application of NAFTA to illustrate its biases in relation to specific groups. Second, I will examine how, in the name of national security, the US southern and more recently northern borders have been politicized since NAFTA was passed and the consequences for citizens and non-citizens of NAFTA member states. Third, I will address how North America has been shaped, at best, by bilateralism.

Migration and NAFTA

Many comparisons between the EU and NAFTA as regions suggest that the former is fundamentally different because, over the 1980s and 1990s, European regionalism was premised on facilitating the movement of goods, capital, services, and also people. In the case of NAFTA, the focus was primarily on goods, capital, and services. In practice, in the case of the EU, the way the right to move is actually taken up can be extremely variable. Nevertheless, there is a long-standing discourse about European workers being able to move that dates back to the foundation of the EU in the 1950s; by the 1990s the focus on workers expanded into the idea of "EU citizens" being able to move between member states not only for purposes of employment but for family reasons, study, or even retirement.

In contrast, there is no foreseeable regional political union in the North American arrangement, nothing analogous to EU citizenship developing in North America, and nothing like the social dimension, however fragile, one finds in Europe (see also the Chapter 5 in this volume). In the NAFTA arrangement, as exemplified by the emphasis on "free trade" with labour simply relegated to "side deals," there is a strong neo-liberal underpinning.

NAFTA has been aptly described by Grinspun and Kreklewich (1994) as a conditioning framework insofar as it fosters the continued pursuit of neo-liberal policies at the domestic level in the countries party to the agreement, in a context where the US is dominant. NAFTA flowed—both in inspiration and form—from the 1989 Canada-US Free Trade Agreement. Provisions carried over from that agreement to NAFTA simply allow for the expedited temporary entry of business visitors, professionals, intra-company transferees, and traders and investors; moreover, this temporary entry provision for business people and professionals carries a discernable national bias. Since the mid-twentieth century, flows—especially short-term ones between Canada and the US—tended to be primarily of so-called skilled workers, professionals, and managers. Moreover, because of the special relationship between these two countries, such people enjoyed visa-free entry, often for unspecified periods (Papademetriou 2003: 41). Indeed, according to the 2000 US Census, Canadians comprise one of the larger groups of immigrants into that country, standing at 2.2 per cent of the foreign-born population, though Mexicans form the largest at 29.8 per cent (Meyers and O'Neil 2004: 46).

In both Canada and the US, issues about migration between the two countries have not been contentious for policy-makers or for publics in negotiating trade agreements. However, the twentieth century was marked by a much more tumultuous relationship between Mexico and the US in terms of immigration policy and politics. On the one hand, major sectors of the US economy such as agriculture, industry, and increasingly the service sector demanded and indeed benefited from so-called unskilled labour from Mexico, and the US state complied with these demands. On the other hand, the terms of entry for Mexicans were not the same as those for Canadians. Consequently, the focus of US policy-makers on the issue of "illegal" immigration from Mexico has been recurrent throughout the twentieth century, from the Depression in the 1920s and 1930s, during the 1950s with what the

US Immigration and Naturalization Service (INS) derogatorily termed "Operation Wetback," and once again during the 1980s and 1990s.

Thus, rather than opening legal channels for labour migration, the NAFTA discussions were dominated by issues of "illegal immigration" from Mexico. In the face of opposition by Mexican officials, including former Mexican President Salinas, US officials explicitly kept labour mobility off the NAFTA agenda, instead holding up the agreement as a panacea for Mexican development; with such development would come the end to the problem of illegal Mexican immigration into the US. Indeed, some US politicians in the administration of George H. Bush even suggested that trade could succeed where the 1986 Immigration Reform and Control Act (IRCA) failed (IRCA was the legislation that targeted illegal immigration through the introduction of employer sanctions and enhanced border control).

In addition to national bias, the temporary business and professional entry provisions introduce other points of differentiation that affect specific groups. For instance, in comparison with their male counterparts, female executives who are married and have children typically face distinct obstacles in seeking global assignments (Gabriel and Macdonald 2004). To make use of the NAFTA provisions, one has to mobilize class privilege, which discriminates against specific groups—such as women and many ethnic minorities in all three countries—who may have differential access to the networks, educational institutions, or resources required to be a businessperson or professional. These groups frequently fall in the unskilled category, itself a distinction intimately connected with the sexual division of labour. As feminist analysts have stressed, the kinds of work that women perform in the private sphere—such as domestic work or care work—are not considered skilled when applied in the labour market. In short, the NAFTA provisions served to reinforce existing class, gender, and national inequities between the member countries through a valorization of professionals and business people.

Table 15.1: Flow of NAFTA Professionals

		1994	2001
TO THE US (ADMISSIONS)	From Canada	24,826	92,915
	From Mexico	11	2,571
TO CANADA (INDIVIDUALS)	From the US	6,385	8,236
	From Mexico	34	101
TO MEXICO (INDIVIDUALS)	From the US	2,628	46,335
	From Canada	240	3,890

Source: Adapted from Papademetriou 2003: 43–44.

Moreover, the implementation of these provisions after NAFTA came into force clearly suggest a continued national bias. As Christina Gabriel and Laura Macdonald (2004: 78) have demonstrated, a review of NAFTA's ten-year record with respect to migration shows that, even within its limited mobility provisions, Mexicans did not enjoy the same access to the US labour market as Canadians, because, unlike

Canadians, Mexicans were required to get visas to enter the US. In addition, a cap was put on NAFTA flows from Mexico by the US, although no cap was put on flows from Canada. Gabriel and Macdonald's findings are numerically demonstrated in Table 15.1.

This table shows that admissions to the US from Canada increased to close to 93,000 by 2001 from less than 25,000 in 1994. Those coming to the US from Mexico, while they increased over time, numbered less than 2,600 in 2001. Considering the relative population size makes these figures even starker. Canada's population in 2001 was approximately 30 million, whereas Mexico's numbered over 100 million.

As a result, many seeking to migrate from Mexico to the US had to find other channels to do so. As Demetrious Papademetriou (2003: 53) has shown, despite the way in which the NAFTA agreement was sold in the US, migration from Mexico continued to grow after the agreement was passed, especially through illegal channels. Indeed, by 2005, the undocumented population in the US was by some estimates as large as 11.5 million, with more than half (6.2 million) from Mexico (Passell 2006: 4). Undocumented ("illegal") immigrants are vulnerable not only to discrimination but to abuse by employers and are unable to access many basic social provisions in the US. However, it has proven difficult to change this situation. In 2006, the conflicted politics surrounding "illegal migration" was revealed in dramatic fashion in Congress, in the streets, and at the border over a proposed draconian measure passed in the House of Representatives. Tellingly entitled the Border Protection, Antiterrorism and Illegal Immigration Control Act of 2005, the proposed bill sought to classify "illegal aliens" and anyone who aids them (such as medical doctors) as felons. Opposing it were President George W. Bush, the Democrats, and some Republicans in the Senate, who favoured finding ways of opening possibilities of US citizenship for the "illegal" population. The bill ignited both a series of large demonstrations across the US by immigrants and their allies, which culminated in a May Day boycott of work and spending as a way of symbolizing the value of immigrants to the US economy (BBC News 2006), and some counter-protests by groups, such as the Minutemen, which oppose any path to citizenship/amnesty. Various Minutemen branches, sometimes armed, patrol the US border with Mexico in an attempt to catch "illegal immigrants" and turn them over to American officials (Fox News 2005).

Of course the border is not without state personnel. In fact, between 1993 and the end of the decade, the number of guards and surveillance equipment along the southern US border doubled (Andreas 1998–99: 594–98). This is one of the ways that the politics of re-bordering has taken place in North America, and this process also has implications for the rights of citizens and non-citizens of countries party to the NAFTA arrangement.

Rights in the Age of Re-bordering

Historically and currently Indigenous peoples use the motif of Turtle Island to refer to the whole North American continent, rejecting the demarcations of settler colonies that became Canada, the US, and Mexico. This serves to remind us that state borders are in fact not natural but the outcome of history, politics, power, and violence. However, much of the popular commentary on borders in North America has a tendency implicitly, if not explicitly, to take them literally. Likely this is because the Westphalian ideal of the sovereign state with clear lines of authority, clear territorial space, and a homogeneous population is still a powerful idea. However, the Westphalian nation-state is a historically specific form of organization, and we know the boundaries of such states can change. Indeed, at one point, Texas, New Mexico, Arizona, Colorado, California, and Nevada were Mexican territory.

THE BORDERS BETWEEN THE NATION-STATES OF NORTH AMERICA

Borders are not clear lines as on a map, least of all in this era of globalization when much state security screening takes place before people even arrive in the geographic space of a state (e.g., in airports around the world). Yet, there is good reason to address borders as specific kinds of territorial spaces that are particularly prone to violence and human rights abuses. In North America, as noted, the border between Mexico and the US has seen a dramatic growth in the number of border police, surveillance equipment, and fencing since the 1990s. A further militarization of the border emerged in conjunction with the war on drugs, which posited illegal drug production as a threat to US national security and US citizens. People crossing from Mexico into the US risk being beaten, raped, and shot at the border, not only by criminals who prey on them but even by some US border patrol agents (Nermaier 1990: 256; Dunn 2001; Falcón 2001). David Spenser (2004) suggests that many Mexicans rely on small-scale smugglers who have deep ties in the Mexican migrant community itself, to get them across the border, but others depend on hired smugglers who may rob them or leave them stranded in remote areas. Perhaps it is not surprising, although it is horrifying, that an average of two people a day die while attempting to cross the border from Mexico into the US in the early years of this new century (*Migration News* 2002).

Although there has been somewhat less focus on it by both the media and academic writers, Mexico's southern border is also of interest. Under pressure from the US, this border was also increasingly militarized in the 1990s in an effort to deport Central Americans who were crossing illegally into Mexico and who were deemed a "security problem" by state officials (Custred 2003: 6–7). Not only is the discourse similar but so also are issues relating to human rights abuses. Moreover, Michael Flynn (2002) observes that it is no longer just Mexicans and Central Americans but also increasing numbers of undocumented immigrants from such diverse places as China, Iraq, Yemen, India, and Pakistan who use Mexico as a way of gaining access to the US, thus underscoring the complexity of migration in this era of globalization. Because of this, the US has begun to fund migrant detention centres in countries south of the border—what Flynn (2002: 28) has referred to as the INS (now the Customs and Border Protection) going global. Thus, both the Mexican and the US southern borders are sites where human security and human rights are precarious.

Additionally, in the wake of 9/11, and speaking to the racialized nature of the threat of terrorism, the Mexican government detained and questioned hundreds of people of Middle Eastern origin, restricted the entry of citizens from a number of Central Asian and Middle Eastern countries, and provided US authorities with intelligence information on possible suspects based in Mexico (Andreas 2003: 12). These steps were taken despite the lack of any evidence whatsoever that the 9/11 hijackers came through Mexico.

In contrast to the US's southern border, the northern one, with Canada, was for much of the twentieth century viewed with pride on both sides as the "world's longest undefended border." It is true that even prior to 9/11 there were discussions about border issues. These involved not only drug, alcohol, and cigarette smuggling but the case of an Algerian national who was caught in 1999 trying to enter Washington state from British Columbia with explosives in his car. There were also concerns, especially voiced by business, about bureaucratic delays at the border (see Chapters 16 and 17 in this volume). However, the US-Canada border was not a major political issue.

Since 9/11, the US has put more money into fortifying the northern border, increasing the number of Border Patrol agents from about 300 before 2001 to 1,000 in 2003. This has created new interest in themes of border control and cross-border integration between Canada and the US among political elites, the media, and academic commentators. For example, by 2003, Canada's then ambassador to the US, Michael Kergin, flagged as *the* top priority for Canada-US relations issues around the border and mobility, especially the desire to exempt Canadian citizens and permanent residents from proposed US legislation that would require logging the arrival and departure of all persons entering the US from Canada (Walker 2003: A17).

The shift in focus may in part be attributed to how the future of the "world's longest undefended border" is at stake in the post 9/11 order. Specifically, Canada has been portrayed by US media and political elites as a "haven for terrorists" due to its immigration policy (Clarkson 2002: 12; Gabriel and Macdonald 2003: 223–24). Such a representation is misleading not only because none of the 9/11 hijackers came through Canada but also because among the roughly 18 per cent of Canadians who are immigrants there are very few instances of criminal behaviour (Abu-Laban and Gabriel 2003: 291). The evidence therefore does not back the new portrayal of Canada's borders as presenting a risk to the US. Nonetheless, the politicization of the US-Canada border continues. For example, the 2005 Border Protection, Antiterrorism and Illegal Immigration Control Act mentioned earlier highlighted the possibility of introducing "physical barriers" along the northern border.

BORDERS BASED ON RACE/ETHNICITY AND BELONGING

A long tradition of work in the area of race/ethnicity studies has uncovered how US immigration and border policies, practices, and debates have targeted both Mexican nationals and US citizens of Mexican descent or appearance. For example, during "Operation Wetback" in the 1950s, some 3.8 million Mexicans were deported over a five-year period, and "Mexican-looking" Americans were required to prove their legitimate status in identity checks (Marger 1985: 173). The post-9/11 period is serving in a new way as a reminder of how one's citizenship may be irrelevant in light of one's perceived ethnicity, religion, or country of birth. Newly passed anti-terrorist legislation in Canada and the US Patriot Act carry considerable implications not only for migrants but for citizens from minority groups, and there is evidence in both countries of profiling those who are or look "Arab" and/or "Muslim" (Abu-Laban

2004). Since 2001, Canadian media stories about the mistreatment of Canadian citizens entering the US have been so numerous that it has become possible to talk about a new segmentation of Canadian citizenship in the post-9/11 order (Abu-Laban 2004). "Segmented citizenship" is a phrase that describes how state actions—both nationally *and* internationally—can inscribe hierarchies onto citizenship based variously on actual or presumed place of birth, race, ethnicity, or religion and on dual citizenship. For example, one of Canada's internationally acclaimed novelists, Rohinton Mistry, cancelled a US book tour in November 2002 on the grounds of the "unbearable humiliation" (*Ottawa Citizen* 2002: A5) of being constantly profiled in US airports. Born in India—a country not officially targeted by the US—and not a Muslim, Mistry's experience shows how profiling may implicate all racial minorities irrespective of place of birth, religion, or formal citizenship.

Perhaps the most graphic instance of the abrogation of due process and constitutional rights of citizens in the post-9/11 order is in the case of Maher Arar, a Canadian citizen born in Syria who immigrated to Canada at the age of 17 and also retained Syrian citizenship. En route to Canada via New York's Kennedy Airport in October 2002, Arar was detained and interrogated by US officials and accused of being a member of Al-Qaeda. He was then deported to Jordan and ultimately Syria, a country known for extensive human rights abuses. Arar languished in a Syrian prison for over one year, although any connection with Al Qaeda was not proven. Under increasing public pressure in Canada, the Canadian government pushed for his release. Arar returned to Canada in late 2003, where he detailed how he was tortured in Syria. The fallout from this case has raised questions concerning the role not only of the US, but also of the Canadian state—particularly the Royal Canadian Mounted Police. Due to the public outcry, the federal government in Canada was compelled to form a commission of inquiry to investigate his case. It reported in 2006 that Arar was completely innocent of all connections with terrorism, posed no threat to Canadian security, and that the RCMP provided inaccurate information to US authorities about him (Commission of Inquiry 2006). To avoid a lawsuit, in 2007 the Canadian government extended a formal apology and offered him a financial settlement, however the US government continues to keep Arar on its watch list and bars him from entering or even passing through its territory.

Thus, in spite of the Canadian acceptance of fault, the debate remains in the US over the legality of deporting a naturalized Canadian citizen to the country of his origin. Thus, as NAFTA underscored the importance of citizenship in being able to cross borders, with Canadians and Americans favoured over Mexicans, post-9/11 underscores the limitations of citizenship in the face of a racialized terrorist threat. For example, holding formal Canadian citizenship is no guarantee because it can be limited on grounds of:

» profiling and differential treatment on the basis of race/ethnicity or religion;
» profiling and differential treatment on the basis of perceived ethnicity, race, or religion;
» profiling and differential treatment on the basis of place of birth;

» profiling and differential treatment on the basis of dual citizenship;

» abrogation of rights or due process of the law in the name of combating terrorism. (Abu-Laban 2004: 33)

As US legal scholar David Cole (2002–03) has also noted, profiling migrants or non-citizens can quickly turn into profiling citizens. This was graphically shown in December 2004 when the US Customs and Border Protection officers fingerprinted and photographed dozens of US citizens who attended a religious conference in Toronto when they returned to the US. The Council on American-Islamic Relations is now accusing US Customs and Border Protection officials of religious profiling (*Migration News* 2005). In various ways then, the politicization and re-bordering of the US's northern border since 9/11 has carried negative consequences for human rights and the civil rights associated with citizenship.

The Emerging North American Migration Regime

There are ongoing debates about whether we are witnessing the creation of a "Fortress America"—a unilateral fortification of US border controls—or whether the NAFTA countries, or at least Canada and the US, will have a "Europeanization" of border controls akin to the Schengen arrangement—the removal of internal checkpoints (in relation to EU citizens) and the fortification of external borders—among most EU countries (Andreas 2003: 14–15).

For migration specialists, "Fortress Europe" has for many years been the phrase used to signal the difficulty non EU citizens have increasingly had in entering Europe (especially asylum seekers and nationals from many Third World countries). A "Fortress North America" involving Canada, the US, and Mexico would also create boundaries of inclusion and exclusion. Nonetheless, that a security perimeter is on the agenda for public and policy discussion at all relates heavily to economic developments. Between 1994 (when NAFTA was signed) and 2000, trade between Canada and the US more than doubled, and trade between Mexico and the US tripled (it has also grown, though much less spectacularly, between Canada and Mexico) (Hufbauer and Vega-Cánovas 2003: 130). The virtual closure of the US border in the days following 9/11 was in essence analogous to the US imposing "a blockade on its own economy" (Flynn 2003: 117) and therefore carried significant economic consequences for all three countries. Indeed, major business interests in all three countries have been applying pressure to ensure that security post-9/11 does not trump trade flows (Biersteker 2003: 155). Considering the history of NAFTA and its exclusionary logic with respect to Mexico, it seems unlikely that there will be a North American perimeter that includes mobility for all Mexican nationals.

The "Fortress America" image neglects the way that both the Canadian and Mexican governments have worked and negotiated with the US around borders and how they may also pursue their own version of national security. It also ignores the fact that there are major interests in the US that do not want closed borders, especially for wealthy individuals. For instance, in February 2005, US Travel and Tourism executives, including those who run Disneyland and Walt Disney World, expressed concern that even three years later the number of international visitors to the US had not returned to pre-2001 levels. They were critical of the way homeland security measures had been implemented since they felt that tourists should be greeted as "customers" not potential "invaders" (Foss 2005).

Reflecting these various tensions, North America is developing a "series of incremental, piecemeal initiatives, involving a mixture of enhanced cross-border security coordination and collaboration, partial and uneven policy convergence, and ... new inspection methods" (Andreas 2003: 14–15). This is contained in the idea of "smart borders," although these arrangements have taken bilateral, rather than trilateral forms and have been more extensive between Canada and the US than between that country and Mexico. According to Commissioner Robert C. Bonner (2003: 4–5) of the US Customs and Border Protection Agency of the new Department of Homeland Security, in contrast to trying to "search, inspect and question everyone and everything that presents itself at the border," a smart border requires "adding personnel, detection equipment and getting advance information in automated form to risk manage who you question and what you inspect."

Smart border agreements were signed between Canada and the US in December 2001 and between Mexico and the US in March 2002. The "US-Canada Smart Border Declaration" is a 30-point plan to review and possibly change everything from refugee determination processes to visa policies, as well as share passenger information and immigration databases and develop common border policing teams (Abu-Laban and Gabriel 2003: 300). The "US-Mexico Border Partnership Agreement" is a 22-point agreement that focuses on fostering bilateral cooperation to enhance the "secure flow of people, goods and infrastructure" (Meyers 2003: 9). Movement on the Mexico-US agreement has been much slower than on that with Canada, in part because Mexico does not have the same budget and resources for such initiatives as Canada (in fact US$25 million was given by the State Department in 2002 to aid Mexico to implement the agreement) (Meyers 2003: 9). This emphasis on smart borders, primarily through bilateral measures, has also been continued in the agenda stemming from the 2005 Security and Prosperity Partnership of North America.

New patterns of exclusion are emerging in the budding refugee regime that developed out of the US-Canada border initiatives. The US-Canada Safe Third Country Agreement, which went into effect in December 2004, deals with refugee determination. The Safe Third Country Agreement says that an asylum seeker must make his/her claim in the country where he or she first arrives (i.e., Canada or the US). This applies to land border ports of entry only, with certain specified exceptions (e.g., relating to a family member being present in the other state or being an unaccompanied minor). The critics of this move have been refugee advocacy groups on both sides of the border "who challenged the contention that the US is always a safe country for refugees, denounced the purpose and effect of reducing the number of refugees who can seek Canada's protection, and predicted that the Agreement would lead to an increase in smuggling and irregular crossing at the border" (Canadian Council for Refugees 2005: ii). Additionally, the agreement has been criticized for not sufficiently taking into account gender and the vulnerable position of female refugees in particular. As it stands, Canada's guidelines regarding gender-based persecution in determining refugee status may be more liberally applied than those in the US (Macklin 2003: 15–17). Not least, this agreement does nothing to respond more to the ongoing plight of refugees in camps, mainly in countries of the global South.

Notably, there is considerable evidence that the Canadian government was the one that pushed for this provision relating to refugees (DeVoretz and Hanson 2003: 2). In light of the charges that the Safe Third Country Agreement makes it more difficult for refugee claims to be heard in Canada, it is worth recalling that Canada's response to refugees began to shift in the 1980s. A primary way in which refugee exclusion has been enacted discursively by the Canadian state relates to the more frequent use of themes of security, public safety, crime, and fraud—what Anna Pratt (2005) terms "criminality." This is a tendency that has found further sustenance since 9/11. As Pratt (2005: 220) has shown in her extensive examination of the evolution of the Canadian immigration system, the invocation of "criminality" to justify the exclusion of refugees (via both detention and deportation) moved from being one of many justifications historically, to becoming the single guiding rationale of policy by the 1990s. This characterization serves to "construct the state and the public, not the refugee, as the victim" (Pratt 2005: 221). Portraying the public as a victim may allow for a level of comfort in not welcoming the stateless Other. Such a portrayal also presents seemingly reasonable grounds for not honouring international instruments such as the 1951 UN Convention. The Safe Third Country Agreement likewise carries implications for Canada's ability to act upon the UN Convention and Protocol.

Of course, it will take some time to know what the full impact of the Safe Third Country Agreement will be. In strictly numerical terms, it is clear that prior to the Safe Third Country Agreement there were more refugee claimants arriving from the US to Canada to make claims than the inverse, which is precisely why Canadian supporters of the agreement—such as James Bissett, former Canadian ambassador to the Balkans—suggested it would reduce the number of asylum seekers and save Canadian taxpayers money (2002: 36–38). It appears that there has been a drop in the number of refugee claims in Canada since the agreement went into effect. A report by the Canadian Council for Refugees (2005: ii) suggests that based on the first year of operation in 2005, Canada received the lowest number of claims it has had since the mid-1980s, with numbers at only 51 per cent of what they were in 2004. In this way, refugees destined for either Canada or the US may experience a "Fortress North America."

Conclusion

The NAFTA provisions and their implementation have not radically challenged existing migration patterns between the three countries; rather, they have served to reinforce existing class, gender, and national inequities in migration between them. Moreover, since 9/11, human security has moved further to the shadows. The US, with the creation of the Department of Homeland Security, is focused, as the name suggests, on national security in the US especially in relation to terrorism, not with human security at borders of NAFTA countries. The smart border accords, forged through bilateralism, also reflect this focus, with negative consequences for both human and citizen rights. North America is more clearly marked by two sets of bilateral relations (US-Mexico and US-Canada) rather than by trilateralism, making unlikely the emergence of a "Fortress North America" that includes the free movement of Mexicans. In this context, both Canada and Mexico have also reinforced their own discourses and policies of national security with implications for those who move as tourists, migrants, and refugees. Thus, while NAFTA left much to be desired when it came to the mobility of labour, the emerging migration regime in North America leaves much to be desired from the standpoint of human rights and citizen rights.

As noted at the beginning of this chapter, over 50 years ago Hannah Arendt identified the way lack of membership in a state can serve to deny some "the right to have rights." Since the refugee problem shows no signs of disappearing in the twenty-first century, since at the same time states of both the South and the North have been increasingly erecting barriers to the entrance and rights of refugees fleeing persecution and other migrants, and since states still form the basic organizing unit of our world, the problem Arendt identified is still with us.

References

Abu-Laban, Yasmeen. 2004. "The New North America and the Segmentation of Canadian Citizenship." *International Journal of Canadian Studies* 29: 17–40.

——. 2005. "Regionalism, Migration, and Fortress (North) America." *Review of Constitutional Studies* 10,1/2: 135–62.

Abu-Laban, Yasmeen, and Christina Gabriel. 2003. "Security, Immigration and Post-September 11 Canada." In Janine Brodie and Linda Trimble (eds.), *Reinventing Canada: Politics of the 21st Century*. Toronto: Prentice Hall. 290–306.

Andreas, Peter. 1998–99. "The Escalation of US Immigration Control in the Post-NAFTA Era." *Political Science Quarterly* 113,4: 591–615.

——. 2003. "A Tale of Two Borders: The US-Canada and US-Mexico Lines After 9-11." In Peter Andreas and Thomas J. Biersteker (eds.), *The Rebordering of North America*. New York and London: Routledge. 1–23.

Appadurai, Arjun. 1990. "Disjuncture and Difference in the Global Cultural Economy." In Mike Featherstone (ed.), *Global Culture: Nationalism, Globalization, and Modernity*. London: Sage. 295–310.

Arendt, Hannah. 2004. *The Origins of Totalitarianism*. New York: Schocken Books.

BBC News. 2006. "US Immigrants Stage Boycott Day," 2 May. <http://news.bbc.co.uk/go/pr/fr/-/2/hi/americas/4961734.stm>.

Benhabib, Seyla. 2004. *The Rights of Others: Aliens, Residents and Citizens*. Cambridge: Cambridge UP.

Biersteker, Thomas J. 2003. "The Rebordering of North America? Implications for Conceptualizing Borders After September 11." In Peter Andreas and Thomas J. Biersteker (eds.), *The Rebordering of North America*. New York and London: Routledge. 153–65.

Bissett, James. 2002. "A Defense of the 'Safe Country' Concept for Refugees." *Policy Options* (September): 36–38.

Bonner, Robert C. 2003. "Remarks of Commissioner Robert C. Bonner, Customs and Border Protection." Keynote Address at the Conference on "Safety and Security in North American Trade," Center for Strategic and International Studies, 16 July.

Canadian Council for Refugees. 2005. "Closing the Front Door on Refugees: Report on the First Year of the Safe Third Country Agreement." Ottawa: Canadian Council for Refugees, December.

Chase, Steven. 2003. "US Border Plan is Unfair, Manley Says." *Globe and Mail*, 6 May: A4.

Clarkson, Stephen. 2002. *Lockstep in the Continental Ranks: Redrawing the American Perimeter After September 11th*. Ottawa: Canadian Centre for Policy Alternatives.

Cole, David. 2002–03. "Their Liberties, Our Security: Democracy and Double Standards." *Boston Review* (December/January): 1–17.

Commission of the European Communities. 2002. "Communication from the Commission to the Council and the European Parliament: Integrating Migration Issues in the European Union's Relations with Third Countries." Brussels: CEC, 12 March.

Commission of Inquiry into the Actions of Canadian Officials in Relation to Maher Arar. 2006. "Press Release: Arar Commission Releases its Findings on the Handling of the Arar Case." Ottawa: Commission of Inquiry, 18 September.

Custred, Glynn. 2003. "North American Borders: Why They Matter." *Backgrounder* Center for Immigration Studies (May): 1–12.

DeVoretz, Don J., and Philip Hanson. 2003. "Sourcing Out Canada's Refugee Policy: The Safe Third Country Agreement." *Commentary Series* No. 03–06. Vancouver: Vancouver Centre of Excellence for Research on Immigration and Integration in the Metropolis, November.

Dunn, Timothy J. 2001. "Border Militarization via Drug and Immigration Enforcement: Human Rights Implications." *Social Justice* 28,2: 7–30.

Falcón, Sylvanna. 2001. "Rape as a Weapon of War: Advancing Human Rights for Women at the US-Mexico Border." *Social Justice* 28,2: 31–50.

Flynn, Michael. 2002. "Dónde está la Frontera?" *The Bulletin of Atomic Scientists* 58,4: 24–35.

Flynn, Stephen E. 2003. "The False Conundrum: Continental Integration versus Homeland Security." In Peter Andreas and Thomas J. Biersteker (eds.), *The Rebordering of North America*. New York and London: Routledge. 110–27.

Foss, Brad. 2005. "Foreign Travel to US Still Lagging." Associated Press, 17 February.

Fox News. 2005. "James Gilchrist, Minuteman Project on Defending the US Border." On "Hannity and Colmes," 16 January. <http://www.foxnews.com/story/0,2933,145630,00.html>.

Gabriel, Christina, and Laura Macdonald. 2003. "Beyond the Continentalist Divide: Politics in a North America 'Without Borders.'" In Wallace Clement and Leah F. Vosco (eds.), *Changing Canada: Political Economy as Transformation*. Montreal and Kingston: McGill-Queen's UP. 213–40.

———. 2004. "The Hypermobile, the Mobile, and the Rest: Patterns of Inclusion and Exclusion in an Emerging North American Migration Regime." *Canadian Journal of Latin American and Caribbean Studies* 29: 57–58, 67–91.

Grinspun, Ricardo, and Robert Kreklewich. 1994. "Consolidating Neo-liberal Reforms: Free Trade as a Conditioning Framework." *Studies in Political Economy* 43 (Spring): 33–61.

Held, David, Anthony G. McGrew, David Goldblatt, and Jonathan Perraton. 1999. *Global Transformations: Politics, Economics, and Culture*. Stanford, CA: Stanford UP.

Hufbauer, Gary Clyde, and Gustavo Vega-Cánovas. 2003. "Whither NAFTA: A Common Frontier." In Peter Andreas and Thomas J. Biersteker (eds.), *The Rebordering of North America*. New York and London: Routledge. 128–52.

Macklin, Audrey. 2003. "The Value(s) of the Canada-US Safe Third Country Agreement." Paper prepared for the Caledon Institute of Social Policy (November).

Marger, Martin M. 1985. *Race and Ethnic Relations: American and Global Perspectives*. Belmont, CA: Wadsworth.

Meyers, Deborah Waller. 2003. "Does 'Smarter' Lead to Safer? An Assessment of the Border Accords with Canada and Mexico." *Migration Policy Institute Insight* 2: 1–24.

Meyers, Deborah W., and Kevin O'Neil. 2004. "Immigration: Mapping the New North American Reality." *Policy Options* (June/July): 45–49.

Migration News. 2002 (September). Cited in Peter Andreas, "A Tale of Two Borders: The US-Canada and US-Mexico Lines After 9-11." In Peter Andreas and Thomas J. Biersteker (eds.), *The Rebordering of North America.* New York and London: Routledge. 5.

Migration News. 2005 (January). <http://migration.ucdavis.edu/mn/archives/php>.

Nermaier, Diane. 1990. "Judy Baca: Our People are the Internal Exiles." In Gloria Anzaldúa (ed.), *Making Face, Making Soul: Creative and Critical Perspectives by Feminists of Color.* San Francisco, CA: Aunt Lutte Books. 256–70.

Ottawa Citizen. 2002. "Celebrated Author Cancels US Book Tour over Racial Profiling: Indian-born Mistry Faced 'Unbearable Humiliation.'" 3 November: A5.

Papademetriou, Demetrios G. 2003. "The Shifting Expectations of Free Trade and Migration." In John J. Audley *et al.* (eds.), *NAFTA's Promise and Reality: Lessons from Mexico for the Hemisphere.* Washington, DC: Carnegie Endowment for International Peace. 39–59.

Passel, Jeffrey S. 2006. "The Size and Characteristics of the Unauthorized Migrant Population in the US: Estimates Based on the March 2005 Current Population Survey." Research Report. Pew Hispanic Center, 7 March.

Pratt, Anna. 2005. *Securing Borders: Detention and Deportation in Canada.* Vancouver: U of British Columbia P.

Soysal, Yasemin Nuhoglu. 1994. *Limits of Citizenship: Migrants and Postnational Membership in Europe.* Chicago, IL: U of Chicago P.

Spenser, David. 2004. "Mexican Migrant-Smuggling: A Cross-Border Cottage Industry." *Journal of International Migration and Integration* 5,3 (Summer): 295–320.

Walker, William. 2003. "US Border Exemption Sought—Log-in, Log-out Law will Snarl Traffic." *Toronto Star*, 4 January: A17. [University of Alberta Library Systems, *Dow Jones Interactive.*]

CHAPTER SIXTEEN

From the 49th Parallel to the Río Grande
US Homeland Security and North American Borders[1]

Christina Gabriel and Laura Macdonald

Regional economic integration has prompted discussions of whether a North American community (modeled, in part, on the European Union) is a viable project. Within these discussions North American borders were generally seen as of declining importance. However, in the last few years, borders have become increasingly visible and problematic. The bordering of North America is an ongoing, contentious, and contradictory process.

In this chapter, we argue that an understanding of the historical evolution in the borders that separate Canada and the US and the US and Mexico is necessary for a true appreciation of the nature of political changes in the North American continent. We argue that what has been apparent since 9/11 is the reconstruction of continental geopolitical space. In this process of reconstruction, the redefinition of national borders plays a critical role. The pattern of change does not follow that of the European Community, however, where frontier controls are being gradually eliminated. In North America, borders are being redefined as the result of conflicting tensions between aspirations for territorial control based on US reassertion of national control at the "49th parallel" and the "Río Grande,"[2] and other actors' aspirations for more deterritorialized forms of security and identity, reflected in such ideas as a "North American security perimeter."

Traditional realist international relations theories depict state borders as a unilateral and unproblematic imposition by a centralized rational state actor. For realists, borders are clearly demarcated lines that separate one state from another and within which states establish their claims for sovereignty and identity. In contrast, newer theories, such as constructivism and critical geopolitics, highlight the importance of subjectivity and the shifting character of national identities in the delineation of territorial space. Adopting this approach, we argue that realist conceptions of impermeable state borders and sovereignty fail to capture much of the historical experience of North America. As well, we indicate how shifts in "imagined communities" in Canada, the US, and Mexico in the period following 9/11 shape and interact with nation-state projects of border control and security policies.

We begin by providing a theoretical and historical background on how US power in North America has evolved over time and what role borders have traditionally played in defining the relationship between the US and its two neighbours. In the second section, we examine the immediate aftermath of the 9/11 attacks and outline the impact on border control policies at the Canada-US and US-Mexico border. The adoption of "Homeland Security" doctrine under the Bush administration marks a critical redefinition of US hegemony in the region and a rethinking of continental space. Canada and Mexico are not, however, passive pawns of US foreign policy. We will argue that both countries have attempted to mould US homeland security policies to be more compatible with their own national interests. In the final section, we discuss the implication for Canadian foreign policy of the US reassertion of continental hegemony, and prospects for greater Canada-Mexico cooperation on North American border and security policies.

The Evolution of North American Borders

Globalization, in all its dimensions, is destabilizing and reshaping how we see the world: borders, boundaries, national identities, and sovereignty are all being dramatically recast in a world of flows of money, ideas, people, and goods. As numerous students of critical geopolitics have pointed out, however, globalization is not just about the erasure of national borders but also involves their selective re-enforcement. As states move to open up borders to the free movement of goods and capital (and those groups of people constructed as desired, such as investors and high-skilled workers), they are also increasingly acting to restrict the movement of people (particularly low-skilled labour) across national borders. This fundamental contradiction in the logic of neo-liberalism creates clear practical dilemmas: how do we police our borders to keep out threats while also opening up borders to the movement of "licit" substances and migrants? The contradiction, we argue, also evokes deep fears and anxieties among both states and populations about national identity and sovereignty that affect our ability to resolve these practical dilemmas.

The process of negotiation and signing of NAFTA apparently signified the formal equality of the three North American partners, since each country had a seat at the table. Canada and Mexico hoped that establishing a rules-based system for the management of regional trade would diminish the historical asymmetries between the US and its two neighbours and restrain US unilateralist behaviour in the region. Some analysts even spoke of the emergence of a North American Community (Wirth 1997; Pastor 2001). While it could be argued that the equality of the three partners within the trade agreement was always rather illusory,[3] the resurgence of US security concerns since 9/11 has led to the US's reassertion of its regional hegemony, creating dilemmas for both Canada and Mexico. In this context, the redefinition of the role of borders is critical.

Students of critical geopolitics have contributed significantly to our understanding of the diverse impact of globalization on state boundaries. As David Newman notes, the idea that globalization has led to the end of the nation-state ignores the complexity of current processes of territorial reordering. Boundaries' functions and roles have indeed changed, but "as they become more permeable to trans-boundary movements and flows, they continue to display a powerful impact on the world map" (1999: 3). Reflecting on the Finnish-Russian border, Anssi Paasi argues that the current confusion about boundaries is easier to understand if we consider the roles of boundaries "as *institutions* and *symbols*" (1999: 72, author's emphasis). Similarly, changes in borders across North America can be better understood if we, like Paasi, remember that the "same symbolizing element may have variegated meanings for different people in different contexts" (1999: 72).

In the North American context, Peter Andreas's work on policing at the US-Mexico border illustrates the importance of myth-making and image construction in the activities of US border control strategists. Andreas emphasizes the apparent ineffectiveness of US attempts to reduce illegal migration in the south despite dramatic measures to militarize the border. This suggests, he argues, that border control strategy is designed primarily to reassure US residents and project an image of strength and control rather than to really clamp down on Mexican migrants who play an important role in the US economy (Andreas 2000). Similar tendencies are now at work at the US-Canadian border, which in the days after the 9/11 attacks, was pointed to by many in the US as the way in which terrorists had entered their country. This impression has proved stubbornly resistant to the lack of any evidence to support this view. Critical geopolitics approaches thus highlight the need to pay attention to how borders are socially constructed and how this process of social construction varies across time and space.

Benedict Anderson defines the nation as an "imagined community—and imagined as both inherently limited and sovereign" (1983: 15). The limited character of national identity has required reliance on the security and reliability of state borders. In the North American context, traditional nationalism and imperatives of border construction were somewhat obscured in the era of the negotiation of NAFTA, when the rhetoric of leaders of all three states emphasized the openness of North American borders to the flow of goods. Even just before 9/11, when President Vicente Fox of Mexico was in the US negotiating changes in the latter's immigration law, President Bush proclaimed, "I want to remind people, fearful people build walls. Confident people tear them down" (cited in Croucher 2004). This cheerful and confident rhetoric was replaced by a shift toward erecting barriers to the flow of "high risk" goods and people in the days following September 11 attacks. Nationalism was resurgent throughout the region.

The shift in US thinking about its North American location and its implications for national security are apparent in the *National Strategy for Homeland Security*, released by the US Office of Homeland Security in July 2002:

> America historically has relied heavily on two vast oceans and two friendly neighbors for border security, and on the private sector for most forms of domestic transportation security. The increasing mobility and destructive potential of modern terrorism has required the United States to rethink and rearrange fundamentally its systems for border and transportation security. (US Office of Homeland Security 2002: 21)

However, the *Strategy* insists:

> Our future border management system will be radically different from today's which focuses on linear borders. It will create a "border of the

future" that will be a continuum framed by land, sea, and air dimensions, where a layered management system enables greater visibility of vehicles, people, and goods coming to and departing from our country. (US Office of Homeland Security 2002: 22)

This concept of the "border of the future" involves a shift away from realist one-dimensional concepts of border security to two-dimensional security systems such as pre-clearance of cargo and a reliance on intelligence systems that permeate national and regional territories.

The *Strategy*'s reference to "two friendly neighbours" points to the heavy reliance the US has traditionally had on its geopolitical location. The high degree of security that the US is assured in its North American setting was not achieved automatically or peacefully, however. Throughout much of the nineteenth century, the US drive to expand its territorial control westward, southward, and northward throughout the North American continent created anxiety among both Mexicans and the British colonies that became Canada, not to mention the Aboriginal peoples who were often violently displaced. The US's right to territorial expansion into Aboriginal lands was justified by the (specious) argument that "Indians" were nomads and that the land could be considered empty (Stephanson 1995: 25). Expansion throughout the whole North American continent was justified in the name of the concept of "manifest destiny," a term coined in 1845 by John O'Sullivan to refer to the mission of the US, as a nation chosen by God, to "overspread the continent allotted by Providence for the free development of our yearly multiplying millions" (Stephanson 1995: xi). The "imagined community" established in the early nineteenth century in the US thus rested on a sense that this was a new kind of country, marked by "social, economic, and spatial *openness*," in contrast to the emphasis on permanency and continuity of the sovereign state in European nationalism (Stephanson 1995: 28; author's emphasis).

The US was able to expand rapidly throughout the nineteenth century through the eventual "re-annexation" of Texas and the Louisiana Purchase. In his presidential campaign of 1844, Henry Polk also called for the "reoccupation" of the whole Oregon territory, which covered an ill-defined area on the Pacific between the 42nd parallel by what is now the California border to as far north as Alaska. In 1818, Britain and the US had agreed to a "joint occupancy" policy, which gave neither power exclusive rights to the territory. Polk recklessly proclaimed the slogan "54–40 or Fight!," claiming the whole of the Oregon Territory up to Alaska. After he was elected, he secretly reached a compromise with Britain on the 49th parallel as the border, and his eyes turned to Mexico (Stephanson 1995: 36).

Unlike Canada, which enjoyed the protection of the British Empire, the newly independent Mexican state faced the territorial ambitions of the US alone. As a result it was a much easier target. Confrontation between the two countries erupted into war, and US troops marched through Mexico in 1847, eventually occupying Mexico City. In 1848, Sam Houston attributed the success of the US army in Mexico to a "mandate from God" and claimed that "Americans regard this continent as their birthright" (Weeks 1996: 128). He also claimed, "the Mexicans are no better than Indians, and I see no reason why we should not go on in the same course now, and take their lands" (Weeks 1996: 128). Whig opponents to the war criticized Polk's policy on the basis of the "ignorant and degraded population" that would be brought into the US if Mexico were conquered (Weeks 1996: 129). On 2 February 1848, the Treaty of Guadalupe Hidalgo was signed; it ceded California and New Mexico to the US and confirmed the annexation of Texas, with the border established at the Río Grande. In exchange, the US paid $15 million to Mexico. Mexico lost more than half of its national territory and suffered widespread destruction. This event continues to mark Mexican perceptions of the US and to fuel fears of US intentions.

Throughout the twentieth century, once continental borders were firmly established, the US was able to extend its global reach, secure in the notion that neither neighbouring country would present a military challenge and that they would also insulate the US from more hostile nations and peoples. In the next section we discuss in more detail the historical development of the two land borders.

THE 49TH PARALLEL

The early history and pre-history of Canada-US relations are replete with border disputes ranging from that of the Strait of Juan de Fuca (1872) to the Alaskan boundary dispute (1908). Throughout the nineteenth century, many believed that Manifest Destiny would eventually bring Canada into the US's embrace without the need for open conflict.

> As Representative William Munger of Ohio told the House in 1870, now that "England's star has passed its zenith ... Canada will fall into our lap like a ripe apple." To help shake the tree, throughout the late nineteenth century the United States tested Canadian national sovereignty in boundary, fisheries and sealing disputes.... No one yet spoke of an "undefended border" ... (Thompson and Randall 2002: 42)

During this period and for much of the early twentieth century, as Kim Richard Nossal points out, English Canadians maintained a hybrid identity, loyal both to Canada and to the British Empire: "... most English-speaking Canadians, while they might have had a love for 'Canada' as a nascent nation, did not embrace the core nationalist goal of establishing a separate and sovereign government to protect and nurture the nation" (Nossal 2004: 507). This hybrid identity is consistent with constructivist accounts of international relations, which emphasize the existence of overlapping and sometimes multiple national identities, and the lack of fixity of nation-state borders. Canada's imperial connection gradually faded in the course of the twentieth century with the decline of British and the rise of US power, permitting a more robust sense of national identity to emerge.

During the twentieth century, the 5,526 mile-long Canada-US border was largely characterized by a calm and consensual approach to the management of shared problems. Americans largely ignored or took for granted their northern border. According to Canadian historian Robert Bothwell, "Canada exists, where the US is concerned, in a state of sovereign ambiguity" (2000: 166). Both Canada and the US historically celebrated the 49th parallel as "the longest undefended border in the world." While the northern border was largely absent in the US construction of an "imagined community," it occupied a much more central place in the Canadian imagination. This symbolic centrality partly results from the fact that 90 per cent of the Canadian population lives within 200 miles of the border. For Canadians, borderlands and "the" border are a central part of how national identity is constructed. In his book *Borderlands: How We Talk About Canada*, Canadian Studies theorist W.H. New states:

> Consider Martin Kuester's evocative phrase that "Canada is unthinkable without its border with the U.S.A." ... True. The 49th parallel—itself a synecdoche, a rhetorical part standing for the rhetorical whole—at once joins and divides two nation-states, permits contact, influence, choice, trade (hypothetically in two directions), and difference as well. (New 1998: 6)[4]

Changes in border control and border management are thus central to Canadians' self-conception in a way they are not to Americans. Throughout most of the twentieth century, Canada-US relations have been marked by increasing cooperation. Early border disputes came under the purview of a joint bilateral institution, the International Boundary Commission (IBC), established in 1908. The peaceful and non-controversial character of the Canada-US border was a result of a broad consensus reached between the two countries about the management of foreign policy and the nature of common threats from the region (particularly during the Cold War era when Canadian territory was seen as the front line of defence from potential Soviet aggression). Both countries adopted a strong isolationism during the inter-war period.

However, World War II brought about a new shift in Canada-US relations. Statements by President Franklin Roosevelt and Prime Minister Mackenzie King constituted what Fortmann and Haglund call the "Kingston Dispensation": "Each country understood that it had a 'neighbourly' obligation to the other, not only to refrain from any activities that might imperil the security of the other, but also to demonstrate nearly as much solicitude for the other's physical security needs as for its own" (2002: 18). The strategic ties between Canada and the US were formalized in the 1940 agreement signed at Ogdensburg, New York, creating a de facto "security community."

The early years of the Cold War led to an even tighter security alliance between Canada and the US and a blurring of continental geopolitical space, with the formation of the North American Air Defence (NORAD) and a joint Canada-US command of continental air defences. The emergence of the threat of Soviet long-range manned bombers led to the building of extensive radar lines in northern Canada. During the 1960s, NORAD took on the role of warning system for possible attacks by Soviet nuclear-equipped intercontinental ballistic missiles. Nossal argues that NORAD "was not only a pragmatic response to the defence requirements of the US, but also a manifestation of the willingness of Canadians to draw their security perimeter and their definition of what was 'inside' more widely than simply Canadian borders" (2004: 8). The exigencies of the Cold War thus led to definitions of national security in both Canada and the US that in some ways predated the concept of a North American security perimeter that emerged after 9/11. However, strategic changes by the late

1950s made obsolete the Distant Early Warning (DEW) system, and as Fortmann and Haglund note, the North American "heartland" "tumbled into deep eclipse" as a theatre of operations (2002: 18).

From the 1960s onward, changes in both the global geopolitical situation and Canadian domestic politics encouraged the construction of a sturdy Canadian imagined community. The 49th parallel took on a strong symbolic resonance for Canadians. Successive Canadian administrations, particularly those of Trudeau and Chrétien, emphasized Canadian distance from US foreign policy positions. At the same time, economic integration proceeded apace, particularly after the signing of CUFTA in 1989. Moreover, both Canadians and Americans remained complacent and self-congratulatory about the undefended character of their shared border. Border residents became accustomed to frequent and easy cross-border travel, and North American production systems became increasingly integrated.

THE RÍO GRANDE

While the 49th parallel dimmed in significance in US strategic calculations throughout the twentieth century, the Río Grande assumed growing importance. This importance stemmed not from the presence of hostile troops on the other side of the border but from growing fears, particularly in the southern states, of an influx of Mexican migrants. On the Mexican side, US predatory behaviour in the nineteenth and early twentieth centuries loomed large in the popular imagination and continued to shape the Mexican imagined community. Mexican foreign policy was limited by constitutional provisions that committed the country to non-interventionism in foreign affairs, preventing substantial military collaboration between the two countries.

Thus, in contrast to the US-Canada relationship, no security community existed between the US and Mexico in the form of shared institutions, beliefs, and values. The two countries were divided by distinct, if not hostile, conceptions of national identity and by different perceptions of relevant threats to national interests. While the US focused on trans-Atlantic threats, it was seen as the only real external threat to Mexican security. However, since the US was not perceived as a true military threat, the Mexican security apparatus was primarily designed to counter internal threats to domestic order. In contrast with other Latin American states, the Mexican military remained relatively small and under tight civilian control (Mares 1996).

Despite these differences, behaviour on both sides of the border was regulated by recognition by both parties of the desirability of avoiding open confrontation. According to former CIA Latin American specialist Brian Latell, "between 1941 and 1989, a special strategic relationship continued, perhaps without serious interruptions, as successions of Mexican and US administrations quietly collaborated on security issues" (2002: 284). This relationship was never institutionalized and relied upon behind-the-scenes diplomacy and collaboration, which were never publicly acknowledged by either government. Mexico collaborated with the US in a variety of spheres, including World War II (which Mexico entered reluctantly after Nazi U-boats sank two Mexican freighters), intelligence sharing (particularly regarding Cuban activity in Mexico), and other matters (Latell 2002: 285–88). For the US, the main benefits of this relationship lay in the continued political stability of its south-

ern neighbour, in contrast with the considerable political instability that characterized most other Latin American countries. As Latell puts it:

> There was never a time during the Cold War when U.S. officials
> really had to worry about chaos or challenges on its southern border.
> Administrations did not have to seek large military appropriations from
> Congress to better secure the southern border, and the Department of
> Defense was able almost entirely to ignore Mexico in its strategic plan-
> ning. (Latell 2002: 290)

The US's apparent disinterest in the lack of democracy in Mexico can largely be
attributed to geopolitical interest in order and stability at its southern flank (Mazza
2001). While more of a "distant" than a "friendly" neighbour (Riding 1984), Mexico
was nonetheless quiet and predictable for the entire Cold War period.

In recent years, the realist perspective has been destabilized by the end of the
Cold War and the changes associated with globalization. In response, realists have
identified new transnational threats that are seen as combining with traditional ones
to create an even more unstable, anarchical global environment. For example, the
December 2000 "Global Trends 2015" report, produced under the authority of the
Director of the US Central Intelligence Agency, identified serious new types of threats
on the horizon:

> States will continue to be the dominant players on the world stage, but
> governments will have less and less control over flows of information,
> technology, diseases, migrants, arms, and financial transactions, whether
> licit or illicit, across their borders. Non-state actors ranging from business
> firms to nonprofit organizations will play increasingly larger roles in both
> national and international affairs. The quality of governance, both nation-
> ally and internationally, will substantially determine how well states and
> societies cope with these global forces. (National Intelligence Council
> 2000: 10)

In response to these threats, the report claimed US foreign policy priorities will
become more transnational:

> International or multilateral arrangements increasingly will be called upon
> in 2015 to deal with growing transnational problems from economic and
> financial volatility; to legal and illegal migration; to competition for scarce
> natural resources such as water; to humanitarian, refugee and environ-
> mental crises; to terrorism, narcotrafficking, and weapons proliferation;
> and to both regional conflicts and cyber threats. (National Intelligence
> Council 2000: 18)[5]

In the waning years of the Cold War, then, a series of "deterritorialized threats"
associated with the US-Mexican border, such as undocumented workers and the drug
trade, assumed new prominence. An economic downturn in the early 1990s and the

rise of angry citizens groups in the southern US states led to a crackdown. Large numbers of Immigration and Naturalization Service workers were assigned to the US-Mexican border, and efforts such as "Operation Gatekeeper" attempted to assure Americans that the US remained in control of it (Nevins 2000: 104–06). The border became a major irritant in US-Mexican relations, in contrast to the "benign neglect" that characterized US policy toward its northern border.

While the continental vision that the Manifest Destiny articulated did not survive through the twentieth century, continental imaginings remain at the fore today. However, whereas Manifest Destiny underwrote explicit US expansionism that secured the nation's geographic borders, today continental imaginings are of a different order. Within these visions, borders, as outlined below, occupy a very complex position.

North America or America

Benedict Anderson's *Imagined Communities* suggests that a nation is imagined as a community "because, regardless of the actual inequality and exploitation that may prevail in each, the nation is always conceived as a deep and horizontal comradeship" (1983: 16). This claim implies that processes of identity construction involve a strategic determination of how "the people"—be they Canadians, Americans, Mexicans, or North Americans—will be constituted. Such determinations and processes of imagining are contentious, problematic, and contradictory. Consider, for example, that in the postwar period the term North American was (and is) used to define for the most part the bilateral relationship between Canada and the US, while in Mexico the term *norteamericano* signifies a citizen of the US. NAFTA provided a reminder to many Canadians that Mexico was a part of the continent as well.[6]

In this section we consider how North American space has been "imagined" by its three member states. In particular, two visions have emerged in recent debates. The first takes economic integration as an unproblematic starting point for a teleological path toward a North American community in which there would be some measure of convergence. In this case, borders appear to matter less. To some extent, this idea of an evolutionary unfolding, which downplays the asymmetrical nature of the partnership, has been severely tested by the events of 9/11. The second tendency, which became more pronounced in the post-9/11 period, sees a re-assertion of strong territorial borders encasing a bounded national territory. This realist understanding of the role of borders is clearly articulated in the Office of Homeland Security's *National Strategy for Homeland Security* (2002). It signals an emerging robust vision of US homeland security that in many ways challenges the more nascent and idealistic conceptualizations of North American community. The strategy would appear to validate a realist perspective.

These developments have led some to proclaim that "borders do in fact matter" (see Drache 2004), but the rebordering of North American space defies easy characterization. That is, as we argue, borders do matter, but they matter in ways that are distinctly different from conventional realist understandings of borders and border functions. Despite the pre-eminent position of the US in the continent, the process of bordering and border control requires that we move beyond what Agnew (1994) has characterized as the "territorial trap" and consider the ways in which the three member states are responding to the challenges of border management. Canada and Mexico, the two peripheral partners, have attempted to advance their own positions to counter US tendencies toward hardening of the border by proposing Smart Border Accords. The Accords offer an example of a counter imagining of North American space. Moreover, they defy easy characterization insofar as they embrace a conception of shared border management and regional space. In this respect they would appear to belie realist conceptualizations of absolute territorial integrity and state power.

Continental spatial imaginings are not new in North America. As we saw above, the nineteenth-century conception of Manifest Destiny allowed the US to appoint itself as the guarantor of the continent's security and rights on "behalf of democracy and free enterprise" and in so doing secured its current continental borders. As outlined above, this belief guided US annexation of large portions of Mexican territory.

NAFTA (1993) marked a new period of continental imagining. The three partners—albeit to different degrees—were prompted to reflect upon their positioning within the continent and in relation to each other. Under its terms, each member country agreed to a number of provisions, including the removal of barriers to the cross-border trade of goods and services and the recognition of a disputes resolution mechanism. The growing economic relationship between Canada, the US, and Mexico put pressure on the three countries to facilitate cross-border traffic, since the border is viewed as an unnecessary impediment to trade. This pressure has been counteracted by equally vocal demands that borders be "secure" and "policed" against threats such as drugs, crime, alien-smuggling, and terrorism. In this respect, even predating 9/11, North American borders became a site of insecurity and anxiety. Simultaneously, increasing cross-border trade raised concerns about the efficiency of the border itself and lack of investment in infrastructure. These twin concerns led Canada and the US to take steps in the 1990s toward the management of a shared border in the form of the 1995 US-Canada Shared Accord on our Border and the 1999 Canada-US Partnership Initiative (CUSP) (Meyers 2000). These developments and subsequent ones after 9/11 signal that the border can no longer be treated as that emblematic fixed line that delimits a sovereign territory and population.

The signing of NAFTA also prompted some soul-searching about the future of the continent. To some extent these reflections also raised questions about the nature of the northern and southern borders. For the most part, prior to 9/11 NAFTA-related issues focused on trade and access to US markets. Not surprisingly, reviews of the efficacy of NAFTA frequently focused on the growth of trade flows between the three countries:

> From 1993 to 2001, Canadian merchandise exports to Mexico and the United States grew from $117 billion to $229 billion. Mexico exported $139 billion to its NAFTA partners in 2001, a 225 per cent increase from 1993. U.S. merchandise exports to Canada and Mexico grew from $142

billion in 1993 to $265 billion in 2001. (*Foreign Policy* 2002: 61, citing US Census Bureau and NAFTA Secretariat)

There were some important exceptions to this trade-focused tendency. In the popular press, for example, both *Time Magazine* and *Macleans* called the Canada-US border into question with covers that referred to "What Border?" and the "Vanishing Border" (*Time Magazine* 2000; *Maclean's* 1999). Academic studies also examined the extent to which values in the three countries were converging (see Inglehart, Nevitte, and Basañez 1996) and/or the prospects for a new North American community. Two important interventions came from the US. Robert Pastor called for a deepening of NAFTA and the creation of a North American community. He argued that, through NAFTA, "North America became more than a term of geography; it defined a new entity and offered the citizens of its three countries the possibility of a new and unique relationship" (Pastor 2001: xi). In a similar vein, *New York Times* journalist Anthony DePalma wrote *Here: A Biography of the New North American Continent*. In it he stated:

> From 1993–2000, North America evolved from being defined solely as three separate nations divided by two borders on one continent to being recognized as a community of shared interest, common dreams, and coordinated responses to problems that have no regard for borders. If we are lucky, in years to come the kinship formed during this initial era of the new American continent will be emulated and deepened. Our borders will not disappear, not any time soon. But what may fade away are the misunderstanding and ignorance that have plagued North American for so long. (DePalma 2002: 354)

We highlight these accounts, not because we believe they provide a blueprint to a future North American trajectory, or even because they have widespread currency, but rather because they are attempts to think about the position of a nation-state in a globalizing and some would suggest post-national world. Importantly, neither Pastor nor DePalma is suggesting that national boundaries will disappear, but rather their work emphasizes that it may be possible in the future that the citizens of the three member states of North America may have multiple identifications. One of these would be to membership in a North American community.

Another, more influential, vision for a new North America with a different conception of North American borders came from Mexican President Vicente Fox. Upon his election in July 2000, Fox and his foreign minister, Jorge Castañeda, sought to change the direction of Mexican foreign policy by embracing a number of priorities. Chief among these was an emphasis on opening a dialogue with both the US and Canada about the future of North American regional integration (Rozental 2004: 88). Fox's vision saw future integration as the outcome of a deliberate trilateral decision-making process that would embrace not just closer economic ties but freedom of movement for citizens in the three countries across land borders. He unveiled this plan at the 2000 Summit of the Americas in Ottawa, where he called for "improved policy co-ordination, a common monetary policy, a common external tariff, mobile pools of labour and fiscal transfers from the industrialized North (i.e., the US and Canada) to the developing South (i.e., Mexico)" (Purcell 2004: 149). Ultimately, this proposal met with a cool reception in both Ottawa and Washington, but it is nonetheless significant. Within it is a view that the destinies of the peoples of North America are ultimately linked. That is, as citizens of a continent, we have responsibilities and obligations to each other. This particular vision of common destiny was difficult to sell in Ottawa and Washington, but it became even harder to sustain in the post-9/11 period as homeland security came to the fore and Washington under President George W. Bush adopted an increasing unilateral position.

POST-9/11 NORTH AMERICA

The 9/11 attacks prompted the newly elected Bush government to focus squarely on security of the US nation. This priority was clearly signaled through the construction of new administrative architecture and the deployment of considerable expenditure to support it. This "domestic" architecture included the Patriot Act (2001) and the National Strategy for Homeland Security (2002), while on the foreign policy front the administration has made it clear that it will pursue unilateral and pre-emptive action against those identified as threats. It is not our intent to provide an exhaustive review of the administration's initiatives and the debate surrounding them. However, each of the initiatives, as the terms "homeland" and "patriot" underscore, embraces a very particular view of home, the nation, its people, and way of life. Thus, in a 16 July 2002 letter to Americans that accompanies the National Strategy for Homeland Security, Bush stated:

> We are today a Nation at risk to a new and changing threat. The terrorist threat to America takes many forms, has many places to hide, and is often invisible. Yet the need for homeland security is not tied solely to today's terrorist threat. The need for homeland security is tied to our enduring vulnerability. Terrorists wish to attack us and exploit our vulnerabilities because of the freedoms we hold dear.
>
> Our enemy is smart and resolute. We are smarter and more resolute. We will prevail against all who believe they can stand in the way of America's commitment to freedom, liberty, and our way of life. (US Office of Homeland Security 2002)

The centrepiece of this new architecture is the National Strategy for Homeland Security (2002), which also included the call for a creation of the Department of Homeland Security. As outlined in the Strategy, the new department's mission was to:

» prevent terrorist attacks within the United States;
» reduce America's vulnerability to terrorism; and
» minimize the damage and recover from attacks that do occur.
   (US Office of Homeland Security 2002: vii)

Accordingly, the new department brought together a number of departments and agencies under one umbrella. For example, border and transportation security was identified as one of four key priority areas. The latter would incorporate the "Immigration and Naturalization Service, the US Customs Service, the US Coast Guard, the Animal and Plant Health Inspection Service" (US Office of Homeland Security 2002: viii).

For the most part, the actions of the US government from the hours following 9/11 (when the US put the Canada-US border on high alert and closed its airspace to commercial traffic) to the present, with some exceptions, have been unilateral. That is, although Canada and Mexico are its closest neighbours, are supposedly equal trade partners in NAFTA, and will feel the effects of homeland security measures, there has been little space for negotiation or discussion. As Daniel Drache has flatly argued:

> Homeland security is a bare-knuckled, unilateral policy framework that is not rules-based and negotiated like NAFTA. There is no hint of partnership somewhere down the road, nor is the idea of political integration contemplated. Homeland security is based on American self-interest and the unilateral exercise of power. The US does not ask if its allies or even its closest neighbour approves of boarding the security train. They are expected to be on it.

The homeland security doctrine is the embodiment of undivided sovereignty—the US sets down the rules for others (Drache 2004: 11).

On the one hand, these actions emphasize the US nation-state and the territorial integrity of its borders. There are few if any gestures to a vision of North America or, for that matter, partnerships with Canada and Mexico. But an examination of attempts to reassert the mechanisms of conventional control at the site of the border are more complex than this. That is, the border is implicated in US control points in major Canadian airports, in the granting of visas abroad and the coordination of the visa regime, and in proposals for truck inspection away from the border itself (Gabriel and Macdonald 2004a: 9–10).

CANADIAN AND MEXICAN RESPONSES TO 9/11

The asymmetrical economic relationship between Canada and Mexico, on the one hand, and between both of these countries and the US, on the other, has meant that access to the US market is of critical importance to the two peripheral partners. The 9/11 attacks shifted the Bush administration's focus to the Middle East and other countries and away from Mexico and Latin America. Yet, the top foreign policy issue for Mexico (and Canada) was its relationship with the US (Purcell 2004: 156). Fox's proposals for immigration reform and a deepening of NAFTA were also victims of the outcome of the 9/11 attacks.

In Canada, the immediate outcome of the events of 9/11 was to make Canadians more aware of the importance of Canada-US bilateral trade and issues of border control. Canadian officials had to address widespread perceptions that the Canada-US border was too porous and would let in those constructed as threats—undocumented migrants, terrorists, people smugglers, drug smugglers—into the US. Hillary Clinton, for example, stated: "We need to look to our friends in the north to crack down on some of these false documents and illegals getting in" (Kennedy 2003: E5). While there was no evidence to suggest a link between the entry of the 19 hijackers into the US from Canada, the widespread currency of these perceptions and fears forced Canadian policy makers to look for ways to reassure Americans and the Bush administration (Gabriel and Macdonald 2004b: 84–85).

Prime Minister Chrétien's immediate response in the days after 9/11 was to move cautiously. However, under increasing pressure from a number of stakeholders, provincial premiers, business groups, and the media, he tried to address US concerns. Measures included the establishment of a high-profile cabinet committee on anti-terrorism, the introduction of an Anti-Terrorism Act (Bill C-36), and increased spending commitments for border infrastructure and technology (Clarkson 2003: 80). All were designed to keep the Canada-US border open while addressing US security concerns.

While Canada struggled with the US perception that it could not control its border and that its immigration and refugee policies were too lax, Mexico's immediate actions in the autumn of 2001 were characterized as unfriendly. That is, while Chrétien immediately offered sympathetic words and there was an outpouring of public Canadian solidarity with their US neighbours, the same was not true in Mexico. Fox did not quickly visit the US, and the US media carried stories of anti-US comments "on the part of the Mexican public and expressions of support for, or justification of the behavior of, the terrorists" (Purcell 2004: 157).

The importance of the Mexico-US bilateral relationship prompted Fox to respond to US security concerns by becoming more proactive. Consequently Mexico, like Canada, moved to address the security concerns of its stronger neighbour and in so doing preserve access to its market. Almost immediately, Fox further secured the US-Mexican border and went further than Canada insofar as the government stopped and interrogated hundreds of people of Middle Eastern heritage and banned the entrance of citizens from particular countries (Andreas 2003: 12). This step was taken despite the fact that there was no evidence to suggest that the hijackers had arrived from Mexico.

Smart Borders: A Perimeter Strategy

As noted above, in the wake of 9/11, both Canada and Mexico pursued smart border agreements with the US. The roots of these agreements are located in Canada's bilateral relationship with the US. In December 2001, the Canadian and US governments announced the "Joint Statement on Cooperation on Border Security and Regional Migration Issues" in which the two countries seek to cooperate and collaborate in immigration matters. The most sweeping action in this respect came in the form of the Smart Border Declaration.

The Declaration covered four key action areas: secure flow of people, secure flows of goods, secure infrastructure, and coordination and information sharing in the enforcement of these areas. As we have outlined elsewhere (Gabriel, Jimenez, and Macdonald 2006) the Canada-US Smart Border Action Plan focused on matters that had been of long standing concern to both countries, such as visa harmonization and hastened the implementation of action to address these concerns. For example, by December 2002, Canada's Department of Foreign Affairs and International Trade (DFAIT) reported that the two countries have common visa policies for 144 countries and they "have agreed to formally consult one another during the process of reviewing a third country for the purpose of visa imposition or exemption" (Canada 2002: 4). Both countries also signed a Safe Third Country Agreement to cover asylum claims made at the land border ports of entry (Gabriel, Jimenez, and Macdonald 2006).

The Declaration is indicative of the ongoing political process of rebordering North American space to address trade-related concerns around access and US border anxieties that focused on security. But more than this, while it is congruent with the intent of the US Homeland Security initiative, it also belies the unilateralism embodied by the latter insofar as the deterritorialized issues that need to be addressed—whether more efficient truck traffic, refugees, shared information measures, etc.—require a degree of regional cooperation. Mexico followed this bilateral declaration by proposing its own smart border initiative.

Initially, the Fox government favoured trilateral cooperation in terms that cast Mexico within a North American security area. He hoped that building a security perimeter would lead to progress on its "NAFTA +" agenda as well as permit a return to discussion on immigration policy. Consequently, he viewed the Canada-US bilateral agreement as "disappointing and exclusionary" and negotiated his own US-Mexico Border Partnership Action Plan in March 2002. This 22-point plan includes the same objectives as that of the Canada-US agreement in that it stresses secure infrastructure, secure flow of people, and secure flow of goods. However, it has been suggested that the Mexican plan expresses a set of aspirations in contrast to the 30-point action plan of Canada and the US (Gabriel, Jimenez, and Macdonald 2006). The two smart border agreements represented the first steps toward a North American common security perimeter.

The movement toward a perimeter strategy was pushed further in March 2005 when Presidents Bush and Fox and Prime Minister Martin announced the Security and Prosperity Partnership of North America (SPP) at their meeting in Waco, Texas. In their Joint Statement at that meeting, the leaders stated that "our security and prosperity are mutually dependent and complementary." There was a heavy emphasis on security imperatives in the leaders' pledge to "... establish a common approach to security to protect North America from external threats, prevent and respond to threats within North America, and further streamline the secure and efficient movement of legitimate, low-risk traffic across our shared borders."[7] In the SPP, the three governments created ministerial-level working groups on key security and economic issues, and established a short deadline of June 2005 for these working groups to report back on their progress.[8]

The version of a perimeter strategy first promoted in the smart border accords and taken further in the SPP does not, however, involve the erasure of existing state boundaries but rather the simultaneous reinforcement of borders accompanied by additional measures carried out far away from them. These agreements raise questions about the nature of national borders and the way in which they are regulated. The form of the perimeter is still dependent on the extent to which the three states actually move forward on all the points enumerated in their plans. Canada's and Mexico's ability to secure favourable terms rests on the extent to which the US can and will pursue unilateral action regarding "homeland security" vis-à-vis border control. The tendency for Canadian officials is to fall back to a vision of North America that is largely bilateral. That is, Canada has been seeking exemptions from a number of new US border control measures, such as exemption from entry and exit rules for all visitors and advance notification of the deportation of Canadian citizens to other countries.

Conclusion

In an era of North American continental economic integration, borders have not disappeared but have become increasingly visible and contentious. Contemporary debates about border control policy often lack a regional perspective on the issue, and also fail to take into account the historical evolution of borders on the North American continent. As we have seen, the realist view of borders as fixed and stable may have adequately described aspects of border control in North America during the Cold War period. A longer historical perspective, however, suggests that borders are, as critical geography perspectives argue, social constructions that shift over time, reflecting shifts in power relations. In the nineteenth century, US territorial expansionism was central to the construction of imagined communities in all three states of the region. In the contemporary period, new territorial imaginings have been presented by competing interests, reflecting the competing claims of security and market access. The US has put forward a particular vision of homeland security that relies heavily on the fortification of nation-state boundaries, while its peripheral partners have countered with alternative approaches that attempt to reconcile US security interests with their own economic requirements for access to US markets. The future of North American borders is unclear, as various visions of the North American space compete. Whatever the outcome, it is clear that changes in economic and security relations have destabilized pre-existing assumptions about the nature of borders in the North American region.

Notes

1   An earlier version of this paper was presented at the May 2004 conference of the Organization for the History of Canada. This research was supported by the Social Sciences and Humanities Federation (SSHRC) #410 2000 1466. Thanks as well to William Walters for comments.

2   We follow popular usage in using these geographic references to represent the entire geographic extension of both of the US's land borders.

3   On the asymmetries in the negotiation of NAFTA, see Cameron and Tomlin 2000.

4   He continues, "Though it's perhaps salutary to remember Ambrose Bierce's [a fictional character of renowned Canadian novelist, Robertson Davies] definition of boundary in 'The Devil's Dictionary' that 'In political geography [it is] an imaginary line between two nations, separating the imaginary rights of one from the imaginary rights of the other'" (New 1998).

5   The report also warns that "[d]ivergent demographic trends, the globalization of labor markets, and political instability and conflict will fuel a dramatic increase in the global movement of people through 2015" (National Intelligence Council 2000: 20, 23).

6   Similarly, the term "American" is commonly used to refer to citizens of the US, while Latin Americans view the term as applying to all residents of the Americas.

7   See <http://www.pm.gc.ca/eng/news.asp?id=443>.

8   See <http://www.fac.gc.ca/spp/spp-menu-en.asp>.

References

Agnew, John. 1994. "The Territorial Trap: The Geographic Assumptions of International Relations Theory." *Review of International Political Economy* 1,1: 53–80.

Anderson, Benedict. 1983. *Imagined Communities: Reflections on the Origin and Spread of Nationalism*. London: Verso.

Andreas, Peter. 2000. *Border Games: Policing the US-Mexico Divide*. Ithaca, NY: Cornell UP.

——. 2003. "A Tale of Two Borders: The US-Canada and US-Mexico Lines after 9-11." In Peter Andreas and Thomas J. Biersteker (eds.), *The Rebordering of North America*. New York: Routledge. 1–23.

Bothwell, Robert. 2000. "Friendly, Familiar, Foreign, and Near." In Maureen Appel Molot and Fen Hampson (eds.), *Canada Among Nations 2000: Vanishing Borders*. Don Mills, ON: Oxford. 165–80.

Cameron, Maxwell A., and Brian W. Tomlin. 2000. *The Making of NAFTA: How the Deal Was Done*. Ithaca, NY: Cornell UP.

Canada. 2002. *Governor Ridge and Deputy Prime Minister Manley Issue One Year Status Report on the Smart Border Action Plan*. Ottawa: Department of Foreign Affairs and International Trade Canada.

Clarkson, Stephen. 2003. "The View From the Attic: Toward a Gated Continental Community?" In Peter Andreas and Thomas J. Biersteker (eds.), *The Rebordering of North America*. New York: Routledge. 68–89.

Croucher, Sheila. 2004. "Homeland Insecurity: Ambivalent Attachments and Hegemonic Narratives of American Nationhood Post 9/11." Paper presented at the Annual Meeting of the International Studies Association, Montreal, 17 March–20 March.

DePalma, Anthony. 2002. *Here: A Biography of a New American Continent*. Toronto: HarperCollins.

Drache, Daniel. 2004. *Borders Matter: Homeland Security and the Search for North America*. Halifax: Fernwood.

Foreign Policy. 2002. Debate: "Happily Ever NAFTA." September/October: 58–65.

Fortmann, Michel, and David G. Haglund. 2002. "Canada and the Issue of Homeland Security: Does the 'Kingston Dispensation' Still Hold?" *Canadian Military Journal* (Spring): 17–22.

Gabriel, Christina, and Laura Macdonald. 2004a. "Canada in North America: Farewell to the 'Special Relationship.'" International Studies Association Meetings, Montreal, 17 March–20 March.

——. 2004b. "Chrétien and North America: Between Integration and Autonomy." *Review of Constitutional Studies* 9,1/2: 71–91.

Gabriel, Christina, Jimena Jimenez, and Laura Macdonald. 2006. "Hacia Las 'Fronteras Inteligentes' Norteamericanas: Convergencia o Divergencia en las Políticas de Control de Fronteras?" *Foro Internacional* XLV 1,3: 549–79.

Inglehart, Ronald F., Neil Nevitte, and Miguel Basañez. 1996. *The North American Trajectory*. New York: Aldine de Gruyter.

Kennedy, Janice. 2003. "Blame Canada. Hillary Clinton Does It Again." *Ottawa Citizen*, 23 August: E5.

Latell, Brian. 2002. "US Foreign Intelligence and Mexico: The Evolving Relationship." In John Bailey and Jorge Chabat (eds.), *Transnational Crime and Public Security: Challenges to Mexico and the United States*. La Jolla, CA: Center for US-Mexican Studies. 279–95.

Maclean's. 1999. "The Vanishing Border." 20 December.

Mares, David. 1996. "Strategic Interests in the US-Mexican Relationship." In John Bailey and Sergio Aguayo Quezada (eds.), *Strategy and Security in US-Mexican Relations Beyond the Cold War*. La Jolla: Center for US-Mexican Studies, UCSD. 19–39.

Mazza, Jacqueline. 2001. *Don't Disturb the Neighbors: The United States and Democracy in Mexico, 1980–1995*. New York: Routledge.

Meyers, Deborah. 2000. "Border Management at the Millennium." *American Review of Canadian Studies* 30,2 (Summer): 255–68.

National Intelligence Council. 2000. "Global Trends 2015: A Dialogue About the Future with Nongovernment Experts." <http://www.cia.gov/cia/reports/globaltrends2015/>.

Nevins, Joseph. 2000. "The Remaking of the California-Mexico Boundary in the Age of NAFTA." In Peter Andreas and Timothy Snyder (eds.), *The Wall Around the West: State Borders and Immigration Controls in North America and Europe*. Lanham: Rowman and Littlefield. 99–114.

New, W.H. 1998. *Borderlands: How We Talk About Canada*. Vancouver: U of British Columbia P.

Newman, David (Ed.). 1999. *Boundaries, Territory and Postmodernity*. London: Frank Cass.

Nossal, Kim Richard. 2004. "Defending the 'Realm': Canadian Strategic Culture Revisited." *International Journal* 59,3 (Summer): 503–20.

Paasi, Anssi. 1999. "Boundaries As Social Processes: Territoriality in the World of Flows." In David Newman (ed.), *Boundaries, Territory and Postmodernity*. London: Frank Cass. 69–88.

Pastor, Robert A. 2001. *Toward a North American Community: Lessons from the Old World for the New*. Washington, DC: Institute for International Economics.

Purcell, Susan Kaufman. 2004. "The Changing Bilateral Relationship: A US View." In Luis Rubio and Susan Kaufman Purcell (eds.), *Mexico under Fox*. Boulder, CO: Lynne Reinner. 143–64.

Riding, Alan. 1984. *Distant Neighbors: Portrait of the Mexicans*. New York: Knopf.

Rozental, Andrés. 2004. "Fox's Foreign Policy Agenda: Global and Regional Priorities." In Luis Rubio and Susan Kaufman Purcell (eds.), *Mexico under Fox*. Boulder, CO: Lynne Reinner. 87–114.

Stephanson, Anders, 1995. *Manifest Destiny: American Expansionism and the Empire of Right*. New York: Hill and Wang.

Thompson, John Herd, and Stephen J. Randall. 2002. *Canada and the United States: Ambivalent Allies*. 3rd ed. Montreal and Kingston: McGill-Queen's UP.

Time Magazine. 2000. Special Report: "What Border?" 156 (2 July): 10, 20–29.

US, Office of Homeland Security. 2002. *National Strategy for Homeland Security*. 16 July. <http://www.whitehouse.gov/homeland/book/>.

Weeks, William Earl. 1996. *Building the Continental Empire: American Expansion from the Revolution to the Civil War*. Chicago, IL: Ivan R. Dee.

Wirth, John D. 1997. "Advancing the North American Community." *American Review of Canadian Studies* 27,2 (Summer): 261–73.

CHAPTER SEVENTEEN

North American Security and Foreign Policy
Does a Trilateral Community Exist?[1]

Athanasios Hristoulas and Stéphane Roussel

September 11, 2001 dramatically changed the context of North America. What all three North American trade partners came to realize was that "security essentially trumps trade" and that new bilateral and trilateral security measures would have to be implemented in order for the business of North America to continue. Given their economic dependence on the US, Canada and Mexico really had no choice in the matter; both countries must comply or else suffer the economic and political consequences of a US now worried for its own territorial security.

North American security means different things to different analysts and policy-makers. It runs the gamut of exchange of information and intelligence to the harmonization of immigration policy all the way to (possible) integration of military and public security policy and forces. The Conference Board of Canada (2001) has outlined three ways in which North American security can be conceived:

1. Enhancing border efficiency by exploiting more intelligent methods of processing border examinations to identify and facilitate the passage of secure commerce, trade, and other types of cross-border transactions (including travelers). Border agencies from the three countries could then focus on the minority of border transactions that are "unknown" and potentially dangerous. This most basic form of North American security would turn the frontiers between Canada and the US and Mexico and the US into "smart borders."

2. Enhancing cooperation between Canadian, Mexican, and US law enforcement agencies. Presumably, this would reduce the need for inspection at the physical borders themselves.

3. Harmonizing immigration and refugee policy, customs clearance, and even national and public security policy in order to remove border inspections altogether. Often referred to as Fortress North America, this final scenario postulates that Canada, Mexico, and the US should mimic the EU in its attempts to foster a common foreign and security policy.

Mexico favours a much more comprehensive approach to North American security, preferring to link it to other forms of cooperation within the context of an expanded and renegotiated NAFTA, the so-called "NAFTA +" option. The government's willingness to entertain this option is based on a belief that a comprehensive security arrangement will also necessarily imply secondary benefits for Mexico, such as a migration accord (Leiken 2002; Hristoulas 2003). For this reason, Mexico also prefers a trilateral approach to cooperation in the North American region. Canadian policy-makers, on the other hand, have taken a much more cautious line, preferring an incremental "baby steps" approach. Predictably, this has led them to push bilateral rather than trilateral mechanisms for security cooperation. They have argued that the threats facing Canada and the US are qualitatively different from those of the US-Mexico relationship and that, therefore, lumping North America into one single "security zone" is not necessarily the best option. The US position on North American security is similar to that of Mexico's. The recent creation of US Northern Command (NORTHCOM) essentially signals that Washington treats North America as a singular geographic area and would like to take security cooperation with Canada and Mexico as far as possible.

This chapter seeks to achieve a number of interrelated goals. Paying particular attention to the foreign security policies of the three North American states, the chapter examines the logic behind bilateral and trilateral security cooperation in North America. It first presents a historical analysis of the three countries' foreign security policies, then outlines their positions with regard to the issue of North American security cooperation. Next, it identifies the main obstacles to further cooperation. A discussion of the impact of these policies on human rights practices then follows. The chapter concludes that, for the time being, it is still difficult to conceive of North America as a single unified region, at least with respect to foreign and security policy.

Contrasting Foreign Security Policies: The US, Canada, and Mexico

THE US

Throughout most of its history, the US felt that its territory was invulnerable to the military struggles taking place in other parts of the globe. In great part, this explains why Washington pursued a policy of isolationism and/or neutrality until the end of World War II. During the Cold War, US foreign security policy focused almost exclusively on the threat posed by the Soviet Union to "export" the socialist revolution. With some notable exceptions that will be discussed shortly, the focus of these US concerns was on Europe and Asia. The American hemisphere more generally and the North American sub-region more specifically were generally ignored. This US foreign security policy, often referred to as "containment" of the Soviet Union, was used to justify its political and military actions, first in the Middle East, then in Asia, and finally in Central America in the 1980s.

The invention of the nuclear bomb and the intercontinental ballistic missile (ICBM) for the first time implied a direct and serious threat to the US homeland. In response, the US and Canada established the North American Aerospace Defence system (NORAD) to deal with the potential threat posed by the Soviet Union and its missile and bomber capability. In many instances during the Cold War, Canadian fighter pilots under the auspices of NORAD intercepted Soviet bombers and other types of aircraft on the margins of Canada's northern border. The US also installed and maintained an "over the horizon" early warning radar system on Canadian territory. Given the similarity in terrain between Canada and the Soviet Union, Ottawa provided military training facilities to the US and other allied countries. Finally, and with much controversy in Canada, during the 1980s, the US tested a new type of sub-sonic, radar-evading weapon system, called the cruise missile, over Canadian territory.

CANADA

The single most important idea in the making of Canadian foreign policy has been *internationalism*, whose main goals are the avoidance of interstate war and instability in the international system (Nossal 1997). To achieve these related goals, an internationalist state seeks the political, social, and economic engagement of other actors in the international system because only through constructive dialogue can problems between them be resolved. Beyond the emphasis on cooperation, internationalist states believe that peace and stability are indivisible. In other words, "internationalists hold that the fate of any one state and the peace of the international system as a whole are interconnected" (Nossal 1997: 53).

With the end of the Cold War, Canadian internationalism shifted its attention away from the management of interstate conflict to other threats to international security (Nossal 1997). However, it is important to note that multilateralism has remained a central pillar of Canadian foreign policy, which actively supports, participates, and contributes to a wide range of multilateral international institutions. However, it now also emphasizes the idea that the main threats to the stability of the international system are no longer only state-based but rather "people-based." Known as "human security" and adopted in the middle of the 1990s, this is defined as "safety for people from both violent and non-violent threats. It is a condition or state of being characterized by freedom from pervasive threats to people's rights, their safety, or even their lives."

A central feature of Canada's foreign policy is a common belief among officials at the Department of Foreign Affairs and International Trade Canada (DFAIT) that economics and security are strongly linked in today's globalized world. In other words, global human security is a prerequisite for economic growth and development. What makes Canadian foreign policy innovative in this respect is the belief that the country's security depends on the security of others. Canadian policy-makers argue that Canada's national interest necessarily intersects and depends on the national interests of other states. Broadly defined, Canadian national security *is* global security. For these reasons, Canada has essentially become a *post-national* state,[2] which views its national interests in the following ways:

1. Economic issues are considered security issues, and security issues are economic in nature; in other words, the fundamental cause of global security problems can be traced to economic instability.

2. International relations are a positive sum game: cooperation rather than competition between states is the only way to deal with global security threats.

3. A more flexible definition of sovereignty allows other states and non-state actors to actively participate in the resolution of national and international problems.

Canadian policy-makers even go so far as to argue that it is the right and obligation of states to interfere in the affairs of another state—even to violate its sovereignty—if the need arises. Such an occurrence, however, can only take place under the auspices of an international organization such as the OAS or the UN. Indeed, Canada has identified these two institutions as key vehicles for the pursuit of its security objectives.

MEXICO

Mexico's foreign policy is based on the constitutional principles of self-determination, non-intervention, and the peaceful resolution of conflict (Benítez Manaut 1996). These legal requirements have manifested themselves in a foreign policy that historically can be characterized as one almost opposite to that of Canada, namely, a foreign policy that emphasizes independence and autonomy in foreign policy-making, especially with respect to security matters. Of particular importance here has been the specific impact of US-Mexico bilateral relations. Indeed, as argued by one Mexican scholar, "the direct vicinity with such a colossus has cost Mexico ... the loss of more than half of its original territory, several military interventions, constant interference in internal political affairs, and economic penetration at all levels.... In few countries, as is the case in Mexico, has the phenomenon of geographical situation operated as a major factor in foreign policy" (Ojeda 1981: 87–88).

The lesson the Cold War taught Mexico was the need to avoid superpower politics, and this led to a somewhat unsuccessful attempt to maintain the foreign policy orientation of *non-alignment* (Smith 1996). Mexico attempted to balance the influence of superpower politics in general, and US influence in particular, by taking a more active and independent role in international relations. Examples included attempts to establish solidarity with Arab and other Third World nations by openly supporting many of their causes, such as openly criticizing Israel throughout the 1970s and 1980s. Similarly, President Jose López Portillo (1976–82) supported the Sandinistas in Nicaragua by withdrawing diplomatic recognition from the Somoza regime in 1979. And in 1980, after the Sandinistas had succeeded in overthrowing Somoza's dictatorship, Mexico began shipping petroleum on preferential terms to Nicaragua. Perhaps the most blatant attempt at distancing Mexican foreign policy from that of the US was the recognition of El Salvador's rebel group—the *Frente Farabundo Marti para la Liberacion Nacional* (Farabundo Marti Front for National Liberation or FMLN in Spanish)—as a "legitimate political force." Along similar lines, in February 1982, Portillo unilaterally issued a plan to negotiate an end to the conflict in Central America whereby Mexico would serve as a bridge between the different parties involved. The Reagan administration dismissed the Mexican initiative with annoyance and contempt (Smith 1996).

For Mexico, the first multilateral security organization in the hemisphere, the Inter-American Treaty of Reciprocal Assistance (ITRA), signed in 1947, proved to be a non-starter. Most Latin American governments assumed that ITRA would serve as a hemispheric collective security arrangement against external aggression, but it quickly expanded its role to include dealing with threats, such as communism, originating inside states, including Guatemala and Cuba (Connel Smith 1966). The Mexican delegation sent to negotiate the treaty was interested first and foremost in minimizing its military commitments and organizational capacity in order to limit the capacity of the US to project influence and interfere in the domestic affairs of Latin American countries (Torres 2000: 83).

Yet another regional institution—the Organization of American States (OAS)— was supported wholeheartedly by Mexico in its early years, since it believed that the new institution might have a chance of balancing the influence of the US within the context of hemispheric-only issues. Given the fact that the US had only one vote (and no veto power), this idea did not seem all that unrealistic in 1948 when the OAS was founded. However, the same events that led Mexico to attempt to undermine the goals of the ITRA also suggested that the utility of the OAS as an instrument of Mexican foreign policy was minimal. As noted by Torres (2000), in 1954 Mexico began to argue that the OAS had been converted into an instrument of US intervention in countries like Guatemala where political reform was perceived as a communist threat against US national security. Mexico saw its purpose within the OAS as maintaining an essentially "defensive" posture against the potential for intervention. This defensive posture turned into outright hostility, however, when Cuba was expelled from the organization in 1958. From then on, and for the remainder of the Cold War, Mexico was extremely critical of the OAS's intentions.

A number of recent developments suggest that Mexican foreign policy is in a transition phase. As argued by Covarrubias (1999), Mexican policy-makers seem to have abandoned strict definitions of defence of sovereignty and nationalism in favour of a policy that emphasizes "pragmatism" and recognizes its own limitations vis-à-vis the US. Successive economic crises have resulted in a slow but definite evolution, which has highlighted the fact that autonomy in foreign policy and economic growth may not necessarily be compatible goals (Heredia 1997). The apex of this radical reorientation occurred in the early 1990s when Mexico, Canada, and the US entered into negotiation to sign NAFTA. Heredia (1997) argues that NAFTA signalled three fundamental changes in Mexican foreign policy: a new openness towards the US, a dominance of economic themes in foreign policy, and a strategic reorientation towards participation in multilateral institutions. Given the fact that, historically, Mexican ambivalence with respect to multilateral institutions was the result of less than friendly US-Mexico bilateral relations, this suggests that Mexico might take a participatory role in multilateral security institutions in the future. The strongest sign of change has occurred since 9/11; with the negotiations now taking place to "securitize" North America, Mexico appears to have wholeheartedly accepted and even encouraged a multilateral security mechanism between the three NAFTA partners.

SUMMARY

The security partnership between Canada and the US during the Cold War has often been characterized as a "special relationship." US homeland security directly depended on how cooperative Canada was in the struggle against the Soviet Union, and for the most part Canada was more than willing to satisfy US requests for security cooperation. The same was not the case with respect to the relationship between the US and Mexico. In fact, Mexico attempted to distance itself as much as possible from US Cold War policy. And as will be discussed shortly, this distancing often led to significant differences and specific focal points of conflict between the two countries. To say the least, Mexico was definitely not an ally of the US in its struggle against global communism. There were severe policy differences, especially over Cuba in the 1960s and 1970s, and Central America in the 1980s. Indeed, Mexico was not even considered to be a North American country until after the signing of NAFTA in 1993, well after the end of the Cold War.

Therefore, Canadian and Mexican foreign security policy traditions can be characterized as being essentially polar opposites. Canada has always looked to multilateral and bilateral institutions for its security requirements, while Mexico has preferred a more autonomous or independent course of action. And while Canada has since the end of World War II characterized its bilateral relationship with the US as being positive-sum, Mexican policy-makers have, on many occasions, emphasized the historically conflicted relationship between the two countries.

Finally, for the greater part of the last 60 years or so, US foreign security policy has focused on geographic areas outside of the North American space, the essential goal being the containment of the Soviet Union. Even after the end of the Cold War, North America was not considered relevant from a security perspective. This did not mean that Canada and Mexico were not considered important. Indeed, the signing of NAFTA in 1993 attested to the fact that North America was important, but only with respect to economic issues. The terrorist attacks dramatically altered US foreign security policy orientation towards North America. It signalled that the region was vulnerable from a security standpoint and therefore needed to be protected with the help of Canada and Mexico.

The Logic of Cooperation

As noted in the introduction to this the chapter, Mexican President Vicente Fox's government liked the idea of North American security cooperation. Indeed, in October 2001, Fox stated that Mexico "considers the struggle against terrorism to be part of the commitment of Mexico with Canada and the United States to build within the framework of the North American free trade agreement a shared space of development, well-being and integral security" (Canadian Press 2002). Similarly, the then Mexican undersecretary of foreign relations, Enrique Berruga, argued that Canada, Mexico, and the US face common threats, and that the [Mexican government thinks] the room is wide open now to the development of a North American community (Taber 2001). Long-time observers of Mexican foreign policy note how astonishing such statements are, given the complicated and sometimes less than friendly historical US-Mexico bilateral relationship (see, for example, Benítez Manaut 1996; Ojeda 1981; Smith 1996; Torres 2000; and Heredia 1997).

So why the change? Beyond the economic element driving cooperation, Mexican officials see North American security cooperation as offering opportunities as well. In other words, Mexico's interests go beyond trade and security. Mexico's strategy has been one of issue *linkage* or the attempt to trade security for other types of benefits (Hristoulas 2003). The first such issue linkage is in the area of law enforcement cooperation and technology transfer for efficient border management, an area where Mexico desperately needs assistance. A second and more important issue linkage directly relates to the expansion of NAFTA to include other non-trade related issues (often referred to as the NAFTA + option by academics and policy-makers alike). The Fox administration repeatedly argued that as long as Mexico is a place where 40 per cent of the population makes less than $2 a day, US borders and, by extension, the US homeland will never be secure. The solution is either a migration agreement whereby the US *legally* absorbs a substantial number of Mexican migrant workers, or a North American social cohesion program similar to that in existence in the EU, or preferably *both*. Pushing this linkage idea even further, Mexican officials have gone so far as to argue that it is in the national security interests of the US to legalize millions of undocumented Mexican workers because it is better to know who they are. Oddly enough, and although migrants had been crossing over to the US for many decades, the issue only began to receive public attention in Mexico in the context of new anti-immigrant legislation in the US during the 1990s. Thus, the desire for a migration deal with the US is motivated by Mexican domestic politics. Fox wishes to appear as a defender of migrant rights for purely domestic electoral reasons.

Thus, migration is the key to understanding Mexico's strong support for a NAFTA + continental and security scenario. Yet in practical terms, Mexico only requires the support of the US. Canada is not relevant here because the number of Mexican migrants to Canada pales in comparison, totalling approximately only 10,000 people every year. Mexico's interest in a trilateral security arrangement is purely institutional: NAFTA must become something more than a trade agreement because it did not deliver on its promise to raise the living standard of ordinary Mexicans as promised by President Salinas in 1994.

Fox, however, has had to finely tune his approach to security cooperation with the US because of an almost stubbornly anti-US domestic political environment. Mainly due to cultural and historical reasons, Mexican public opinion is vehemently anti-American, and this is reflected strongly in the Mexican Congress. For this reason, it took Fox about two weeks to officially respond with condolences to the 9/11 attacks. Thereafter, the Mexican Congress repeatedly accused Fox of "selling" the nation to the Americans. It even prevented Fox from visiting the US on one occasion.[3] Similarly, basic and long-standing forms of cooperation between Canada and the US, such as US immigration and customs officials being stationed at Canadian airports, are viscerally rejected by Mexican pundits as a blatant violation of Mexican sovereignty.

Fox not only faced resistance to his vision from public opinion and his Congress, but elements of his own administration saw security cooperation with the US as a threat to Mexico's interests. Minister of the Interior Santiago Creel sees himself as

a future candidate for president and therefore had to finesse his discourse on cooperation with the US in order to appease potential voters. The Minister of Defense,
General Vega Garcia, is a staunch nationalist who also considers further foreign
security cooperation with the US a threat to Mexico. Finally, Jorge Castaneda, the
foreign minister at the time of the 9/11 attacks, and probably Mexico's strongest
supporter of foreign security cooperation with the US, resigned and was replaced
by the minister of the economy, Ernesto Derbez. For many, this change signaled a
moderation in diplomatic engagement with the US.

To further complicate the issue for Fox, the border between the US and Mexico
has always been one of the most important areas of conflict and cooperation between
the two countries, as it has been the scene of violence against unauthorized Mexican
and third country migrants and the smuggling of drugs, arms, sex slaves, stolen
cars, and other contraband. Moreover, "the prospect of cross-border collaboration
bears the baggage of nearly three decades of misgivings and suspicions from both US
and Mexican officials resulting from divergent objectives and perceived failures of
cooperation in the war on drugs. Further, the lack of shared mutual goals on immigration and narcotics have been major obstacles to cooperation in the past" (Shirk
2003). More recently, and within the context of the creation of NORTHCOM, US
officials believe that the most efficient line of communication should be between
the NORTHCOM commander and Mexican Secretary of Defence Vega Garcia. The
general has repeatedly insisted, however, that given the fact that he is a government
minister, he should only speak directly with his US counterpart, namely, Secretary of
Defence Donald Rumsfeld.

These diplomatic quagmires are often made worse by difficulties at the operational
or tactical level. US law enforcement officials often find themselves in frustrating
situations, unable to deal with the inefficiency that often characterizes Mexican offi-
cialdom, while Mexican authorities are overly sensitive to US unilateralism. Further,
they lack the technical expertise to create the kinds of cooperative mechanisms that
exist along the Canada-US border. The end effect is that no "security confidence"
exists along the Mexico-US border, and "bi-national cooperation is typically focused
on reducing cross-border interagency irritants and misunderstandings rather than on
coordinated operations, and while occasionally stronger at the local level of interagency cooperation—tends to vary from place to place and time to time" (Garcia
2002: 117). A final operational area of concern relates to incompatible and competing administrative structures. The experience of state and local authorities along the
border region has not been fully taken into account in designing policy responses in
both Mexico and the US.

As far as Canada is concerned, security and border cooperation obviously makes
good economic sense. Early on in the debate over perimeter security (immediately following 9/11) the then Canadian Foreign Minister, John Manley, highlighted this fact
clearly by stating that Canada must be inside any such security perimeter because
87 per cent of the country's exports go to the US (Hristoulas 2003). Yet in a policy
shift, within weeks Canadian officials were arguing against a common continental
defence. Manley later expressed reservations, telling a parliamentary committee that
the notion that somehow or other Canada can solve a perceived problem by something called a perimeter is "simplistic" (McCarthy 2001).

Mexico's potential participation in North American security mechanisms is one of the central reasons for Canada's ambivalence. The government of former Prime Minister Jean Chrétien began to argue that the security issues along the Canada-US border are fundamentally different from those along the Mexico-US border. The issue facing Canada and the US is to ensure the efficient flow of legitimate goods and travelers within the context of heightened US security concerns. On the other hand, the Mexico-US border is far more complex, characterized not only by a high level of trade but also by the significantly greater existence of illegal migration and drug trafficking. The negotiation of a trilateral security mechanism would require much more time and the introduction of a third actor—from a Canadian perspective—would unnecessarily delay the entire process or possibly stall it completely. Moreover, "smart border" technology at the Canada-US border has been in place for a while, predating the terrorist attacks by a number of years. The same is not the case along the Mexico-US border.

Therefore, and by way of contrast to the Mexican approach, Canada has attempted to stick to the status quo. Unenthusiastic about explicit or implicit modes of trilateralism, Canada prefers to deal with the US strictly on a one-to-one basis. By design, it has chosen to differentiate itself (both in terms of issues and solutions) from Mexico. While this stance can be justified on the technical grounds already discussed, it also underscores important symbolic political factors, which depict Mexico not so much as partner but as a complicating ingredient in the neighbourhood (Cooper and Hristoulas 2007).

A second explanation has to do with the specific terminology of a "security perimeter." Any overt endorsement of the phrase was explicitly rejected by key elements of Canada's former Liberal government. One problem is that by its tone the concept of a perimeter in the North American context plainly privileges security over economic/commercial matters. As such it conditions (and legitimizes) a shift in perception—in conceptual terms—that sees the Canada-US relationship increasing through a realist self-help model of national interest rather than through the vantage point of complex interdependence between states. Through this lens, Canada has the disadvantage of remaining stuck in the US mindset as a source or conduit of danger—a mindset exploited by the US media (Cooper and Hristoulas 2007).

For all of the reasons outlined above, it is understandable why Canadian politicians and officials have tried to re-brand the frontier, not as part of a North American security perimeter, but as part of a set of initiatives that reassure the US that Canada takes security concerns seriously while not forgetting either its commercial interests or wider foreign policy identity.

The US position on security cooperation is probably the most straightforward: the US Office of Homeland Security, as well as the new NORTHCOM, would like to engage both Canada and Mexico in discussions to enhance cooperation either at a bilateral or a trilateral basis. Indeed, about two months after the terrorist attacks Bush ordered the US government to pursue bilateral and trilateral compatibility of immigration, customs, and visa policies (Freedberg 2001) with both Canada and Mexico. US policy-makers recognize that Canada and the US have a much stronger and more long-standing security relationship; however, given the fact that in the US the Latino vote has become increasingly important in recent years, Mexico cannot easily be excluded from the discussions.

The US desire for increased security cooperation with Canada and Mexico stems from a partly justified belief that both Canada and Mexico might serve as platforms from which further terrorist attacks might be launched. Indeed, the US media has portrayed Canada as a hotbed for terrorist activity with special emphasis being placed on its refugee laws, which purportedly allow terrorists to operate within the country with relative ease (see, for example, DePalma 2001; Clayton and Chaddock 2001; and Regan 2002). Second and probably more importantly, Canada has been viewed as slow in dealing with known terrorist groups operating within the country. The case of Ahmed Ressam—the "millennium bomber" captured by US Customs and Immigration officials trying to cross over to the US from Canada with a trunk-load of explosives on 14 December 1999—has served as the rallying point with respect to criticisms against the country in this regard. Ressam, an Algerian, lived in Montreal for five years as a political refugee even though a Canadian judge had ordered his deportation from the country because he had falsified travel documentation. Yet he was able to move around the country because Canada's law enforcement agencies admit that they simply do not have the resources to track down individuals who have been ordered deported.

It is this specific area where concerns on the part of US officials seem most warranted because, unlike refugee law—which most Canadians would vehemently defend even in light of 9/11—the underfunding of security agencies is to blame. Ward Elcock, the former director of the Canadian Security and Intelligence Agency (CSIS), stated that "with perhaps the singular exception of the United States, there are more international terrorist groups active [in Canada] than any other country in the world." He also said that the Counter-Terrorism Branch of CSIS was investigating the existence of over 50 terrorist organizations and 350 individuals for links to groups deemed by the Canadian government to be terrorist. Among the most active groups, Elcock listed Hezbollah, Hamas, the Provisional IRA, the Tamil Tigers, and the Kurdistan Worker's Party (PKK). None of these groups directly target Canadian interests; rather, they use Canada as a "venue of opportunity to support, plan, or mount attacks elsewhere" (Elcock 1998; Kelly 2001).

Alternatively, the US concern with respect to Mexico is that the country *might* become a terrorist risk in the future. Mexico does not have a large Muslim community where Islamic terrorists can easily "blend in" as is the case in Canada. Yet the fear is that Al Qaeda and other terrorist organizations might somehow take advantage of the chronic weakness characteristic of many of the country's security institutions. A more serious concern is that illicit transnational routes employed by migrants and drug dealers might someday be used by international terrorist groups. Finally, US officials have also voiced concern over the porous nature of the southern Mexican border with Central America.

Why Go Trilateral

Irrespective of the positions of the three countries, there are essentially three reasons why trilateral security cooperation in the North American context is necessary (Hristoulas and Roussel 2004). The first argument is economic in nature: the increasing levels of trade between the three states create a situation where security cooperation is inevitable, especially with regard to the Canada-US and Mexico-US border regions. Between 1988, when the first North American free trade agreement was signed, and 2000, Canada's exports to the US grew from 75 per cent to 87 per cent of total exports (Report of the Standing Committee on Foreign Affairs and International Trade 2002). Similarly, trade between Mexico and the US has expanded by 428 per cent since the signing of NAFTA. The US accounts for 89 per cent of all of Mexico's exports worldwide.

As early as the mid-1990s it became evident that border controls had to be somehow modified or "updated" in some very profound manner in order to be able to handle the dramatically increasing level of commercial traffic. The process of reforming border procedures therefore, predates 9/11 by almost six years. The logic in favour of border reform is simple and is often employed by those in the business community: strengthen border control along the perimeter of North America in order to convert the subregional borders into "zones of confidence." Within a context of "just in time" production schedules, every hour lost at a border inspection translates into important financial losses for transnational firms.

Increased trade between the three NAFTA partners tends to confirm the idea that increased security cooperation is necessary and inevitable, and to this day this increased security cooperation has evolved on a parallel bilateral and independent basis. The two smart border agreements signed between Canada and the US on the one hand, and Mexico and the US on the other, are similar in many respects; however, they are not linked to each other in any way. This twin bilateral process has saved substantial time and thus has satisfied the three states: all three recognize that border differences make a trilateral deal difficult. However, increasing trade between Mexico and Canada, as well as the "trilateralization" of North American industry, will eventually render harmonization necessary. In other words, if NAFTA eventually provokes the emergence of a real trilateralization of commerce (as opposed to twin bilateral relationships), it will become necessary to think of the security relationship in similar terms.

The second argument in favour of security cooperation relations rests on the fact that the three states are all potentially affected by the same threats. Without a doubt, the US is the central target, but both Canada and Mexico are also directly involved for three central reasons.

1. Another terrorist attack on the US will have a direct impact on both Canada and Mexico as occurred on 9/11, when the US essentially imposed a trade embargo on itself by shutting down its borders. Thus, US security concerns are of prime interest to Canada and Mexico because both countries' economic prosperity depends directly on how "safe" US policy-makers feel. Canada

and Mexico must therefore not only take the necessary steps in order to assure that their territories are not being used as bases of operation for international terrorist groups, they must also make sure the US knows that its neighbours to the north and to the south are doing so.

2. The destruction of Canadian or Mexican industrial and/or commercial infrastructure (gas pipelines, electrical grids, bridges, etc.) could have a direct impact on the daily lives of not only Mexicans and Canadians but also Americans. This scenario became a reality with the transnational power blackout of August 2003, which left large populated areas in Canada and the US without electricity.

3. Within the context of this second reason, Canada and Mexico could potentially become indirect targets for enemies of the US.

For these three reasons, the threat is to the region as a whole, not only to the US.

The third factor justifying a trilateral approach to North American security is the multifaceted nature of the terrorist threat. The ways in which terrorism can manifest itself are manifold: they can target transportation routes, such as border crossings, rail lines, gas lines, maritime ports, containers, etc., as well as visible and public objects, such as critical infrastructure and symbolic monuments. What may prove to be even more alarming are the weapons they may employ in the future. No one is willing to rule out the possible use of biological, chemical, and maybe even nuclear terrorist attacks against the North American continent.

A large number of efficient anti-terrorist measures exist at the national and even local level in all three states, but most analysts agree that to truly succeed against terrorism, regional and even global interagency cooperation is necessary. The same logic that led to the creation of the US Office of Homeland Security—the need for interagency cooperation in the form of intelligence sharing and joint operations—can be applied at the North American subregional level. Alternatively, the proper protection of the North American region requires the proper surveillance of its aerial, maritime, and territorial space. Such a task is impossible without a minimum level of regional coordination, which could imply, but is not necessarily limited to, joint training operations, shared surveillance "zones," and even coordinated and joint operations.

What Has Been Done

Canada has taken some steps towards changing its immigration and refugee policies and procedures. With respect to anti-terrorism measures, the government introduced Bill C-36, which provides for additional resources and police powers to identify and punish terrorists and terrorist support groups. More specifically, the bill makes it illegal to raise funds on behalf of terrorists, allows the government to seize assets of terrorist organizations, and expands the police authority to pursue suspected terrorists. Similarly, on an operational level, Canada-US border and defence cooperation has been unprecedented in the areas of intelligence and police cooperation and coordination. Moreover, Canadian and US officials presently are discussing ways in which to coordinate further in the areas of customs, immigration, and refugee policy. Finally, the Canadian government has earmarked about US$5 billion towards enhanced security, which includes but is not limited to the areas of intelligence and policing, emergency preparedness, military deployment, air security, and border infrastructure.

The Fox government also signalled its intention to strongly support the US in its war against terror. In the days following 9/11, Mexico detained and interrogated dozens of people of Middle Eastern origin. Moreover, the Fox government deployed police and military across the country to protect strategic facilities, public transportation, and border points. Finally, Mexico has begun to pay much more attention to its southern borders with Central America, deploying military troops to assist immigration and customs officials. Operation Sentinel, a large-scale military operation designed to protect strategic infrastructure, was also launched in the wake of the war in Iraq.

Perhaps the most significant progress toward North American security cooperation has been the signing of the two Smart Border agreements between Canada and the US in October 2001 and between Mexico and the US in March 2002. Both promise to develop further bilateral mechanisms with regard to border infrastructure. The documents also placed special emphasis on the twin principles of coordination and information sharing as critical components of a secure common border.

Challenges to Deepening Cooperation

Although some important progress has been made in "securing" North America from further terrorist attacks, many obstacles remain. The first obstacle—the one most frequently mentioned in the literature—is the asymmetric distribution of power in the North American subsystem (Hristoulas and Roussel 2004). The logic here is that differences of power provoke mistrust between the actors, and the weakest are at the mercy of the strongest. The latter are least inclined to give up the privilege that this power superiority gives them, the ability to act unilaterally. Equally important is the fact that the most powerful tend to have global interests, while smaller states tend to limit their reach to their particular region. Thus, "asymmetric cooperation" becomes a difficult objective to achieve.

This scenario can be applied to the relations among the three North American states. The difference of power that separates the US and Canada on one side and Mexico and the US on the other is probably the element that best differentiates the North American integration process from that of the EU. There, the power asymmetry is much less pronounced, and the increased number of state actors allows for a greater balancing act. Nothing like that exists in the North American context, and even the extremely unlikely scenario of a Canadian-Mexican coalition cannot serve as a counterweight to the US.

A second obstacle is the place that security has in the priorities of the three governments. Oversimplifying the issue, one can argue that Washington is mainly worried about the security of the US homeland, while Mexicans want some kind of substantial migration agreement, and Ottawa is preoccupied by trade concerns. To make matters worse, when the three states deal with security issues, they do so from different starting points, mainly because they have developed distinct strategic cultures. Each partner perceives differently the nature of the threats coming from outside of the continent and the means necessary to face them, especially with regard to the use of force.

The Canadian government is generally in favour of a multilateral approach, which by its very nature tends to privilege negotiation (Nossal 1997). The "human security" doctrine probably constitutes one of the best illustrations of this approach. On the other hand, the Bush administration seems to prefer direct confrontation, as demonstrated by the Afghanistan and Iraq wars. Lastly, Mexico, mainly because of historical experience, has evolved a policy of isolation and of non-participation in military operations abroad, even if these operations are purely peace-keeping in nature. It goes without saying that in comparing the three states, the US is much more likely to resort to the use of force in the management of its security threats.

The issue of resources is the third, yet often overlooked obstacle to trilateral solutions to North America's security threats. Washington has at its disposal financial, technological, and material resources far beyond the reach of its two NAFTA partners. This disparity, often not recognized by policy-makers in the US, places pressure on Mexico and Canada to meet US security demands that are simply out of the reach of the two countries. The inevitable outcome is that US policy-makers (and especially US public opinion) feel that Canada and Mexico are not doing enough in the war against terrorism. Collaboration between the police and military forces of Mexico and those of Canada and US is also hindered by a lack of confidence. Mexican security forces suffer from their reputation for being corrupt and inefficient, which limits the possibilities of information exchange and for joint operations. More generally, the absence of large-scale and permanent programs of cooperation between Mexico and the two other states (except perhaps between certain agencies in charge of supervising the Mexico-US border) has not allowed the development of inter-institutional bonds as close as those that link Canadian and US officials. It should be noted that since 9/11, there has been a dramatic increase in the level of cooperation between US and Mexican officials. However, confidence-building is generally the result of a very long process, and the bilateral Mexico-US experience simply cannot be compared to that of Canada and the US.

Human Rights

One of the central challenges facing all three nations in their search for a safer North American space is the issue of human rights. All three governments have been accused in recent years of violating human rights in the pursuit of terrorists, from racial profiling (suspicion based on actual or perceived race and religion) at airports and by immigration officials, to legislation—such as the US Patriot Act—which, for many legal experts, violates many of the principles of the US Constitution. A recent Amnesty International report has argued that "the USA Patriot Act undermines the human rights of Americans and non-citizens, and weakens the framework for promoting human rights internationally" (Amnesty International 2004). First, the report argues that the concept of terrorism has been broadened extensively, with the potential for loose interpretation. Second, the law allows for non-US citizens to be detained without being formally charged and held indefinitely once charged. Third, the law removes many of the existing judicial controls over the ability of government authorities to "spy" on citizens. Specifically, it allows for "sneak and peak" tactics such as physical search of property and computers, wiretapping and monitoring of email, and access to financial and educational records. These activities contradict the right to be free from arbitrary interference with individual privacy, as protected in the US Constitution.

Perhaps the most blatant violation of human rights on the part of the Bush administration has been the establishment and maintenance of a prison compound in Guantanamo, Cuba for so-called enemy combatants, most of whom were arrested in Afghanistan during the early days of the war there. These prisoners have not been afforded the rights prisoners of war should receive as defined in the international Geneva Conventions. Of the literally hundreds of prisoners in the camp, only a few dozen have actually been charged with any crime; most of the others have been held without trial for several years.

Thus, George W. Bush's government has set a dangerous international precedent with regard to human rights. Its message is that respect for human rights is second to issues of national security. The impact of this policy has been felt on a global level, with many countries loosening their human rights legislation in the name of the war against terrorism. Indeed, "opportunistic governments have been co opting the US 'war on terrorism,' citing support for US counter-terrorism polices as a basis for internal repression of domestic opponents. In some instances, US actions have encouraged other countries to disregard domestic and international law when such protections stand in the way of US counter-terrorism efforts" (Lawyers Committee for Human Rights 2003: 73).

Washington's anti-terrorist policy has also had a direct and negative impact on the human rights of Mexican migrants to the US. Mexican illegal migrants make an important contribution to the US economy and they do not represent a threat to US national security. Yet the Bush administration has chosen to deal with the issue of illegal migrants within the context of the Office of Homeland Security. Conceptualizing migrants in this manner has led to two distinct but related policy options. First, US controls have dramatically increased along the Mexico-US border, forcing migrants to use much more dangerous routes through mountain ranges and deserts. Accordingly, the number of Mexicans dying during the process of migrating to the US has increased dramatically since the militarization of the border. Second, US policy towards illegal workers within the US has also changed dramatically. Irrespective of the fact that these illegal residents overwhelmingly contribute more to US society than they take, the Bush administration has chosen to consider these individuals (approximately 10 million in total) as a threat to national security. The combined effect of changes along the border as well as changes within the US has made the life of illegal migrants and residents much more dangerous.

The "war on terrorism" has also led to new laws and policies in Canada. In the wake of 9/11, Canada introduced a range of legislation—including Bill C-36, the

Anti-terrorism Act. Some aspects of the legislation undermine basic human rights. First, similar to US legislation, the definition of "terrorism" remains broad and includes a number of undefined terms. Preventative detention and secret evidence provisions raise concerns about due process and abuse of power. Second, the listing procedure for "entities" considered to support "terrorism" does not allow any opportunity to refute the decision before it is made public (Amnesty International 2004). This new Canadian legislation stands in sharp contrast to the country's human security agenda. Over the last ten years or so, Canadian officials have been quick to criticize other governments, especially in the American hemisphere, for their less than stellar records on human rights protection. Indeed, on many occasions, Mexico has been the target of many of these criticisms, primarily in respect to the treatment of Indigenous populations and especially in the state of Chiapas. Many Latin American countries have accused Canada of being hypocritical (Hristoulas 2004). This criticism seems even more warranted now.

In the case of Mexico, the Miguel Agustín Pro Juárez Center for Human Rights has argued that the war against terrorism has had an important impact on the protection of human rights in the country. First, there has been a dramatic increase in the use of the military in police roles such as in airport security and border control. Second, the Center worries that as long as the war against terrorism remains paramount in the international agenda, there might be a blurring of the distinction between terrorist and legitimate political opposition (Miguel Agustín Pro Juárez Center for Human Rights 2004). Finally, prior to the events of 9/11, human rights issues were considered a central pillar in the foreign policies of all three North American states. The terrorist attacks and subsequent responses by Canada, Mexico, and the US have relegated them to the backburner. Canada's human security agenda has been modified to place much more importance on economic security, while Mexico's attempt to champion human rights issues in multilateral fora has, at least for the time being, stalled. Finally, the US has clearly demoted human rights vis-à-vis the global anti-terrorist crusade. As noted earlier, this has led to human rights violations within and outside the US as well as turning a blind eye to the human rights violations of other countries involved in the war against terrorism.

The most obvious impact of these developments is that civil society as an actor has been systematically excluded from the process of developing foreign (and domestic) policy in response to 9/11. Thus, citizens in all three countries are perplexed by the measures taken in the name of protecting North America against future terrorist attacks.

Conclusion

Confronted with such obstacles, it is not surprising that the political leaders of the three North American states are not rushing to engage in a more thorough integration process. The benefits from this process remain vague or remote, while the problems appear immediate. Further, with the exception of border communities and business, there is little or no civil society pressure to encourage the governments to engage in a trilateral process. Of primary importance here is the lack of communication between Canadians and Mexicans. Canadian public opinion sees Mexico as a place to vacation and not much more than that, while Mexican public opinion often stereotypes Canada as simply an extension of the US. Thus, although a sense of community and shared goals exists along the bilateral border regions, the same cannot be said at national levels and even less so at the regional level. Adapting a now famous quotation from former Canadian Prime Minister Pierre Elliot Trudeau to the present context, Canada and Mexico are two very different mice living in separate parts of the house trying to avoid being stepped on by a rather large (and now nervous) elephant.

Security integration will continue, but in an incremental and ad hoc manner. Canadian and Mexican policy-makers cannot avoid the pressure being placed on them by US authorities (Kraus 2002). Consequently, the double bilateral approach adopted by each government meets the least resistance, and it is likely that for the foreseeable future, the three governments will continue the hub and spoke process typically characteristic of the Warsaw Pact rather than that of multilateralism more characteristic of the Atlantic Alliance or the EU.

Notes

1 The authors would like to thank the editors for their helpful comments on an earlier draft of this paper. Ongoing financial assistance has been provided for by the Asociacion Mexicana de Cultura, A.C.

2 For a more thorough explanation of this terminology, see Buzan and Segal 1996; Hellman 1996.

3 In early 2002, the Mexican Congress claimed that President Fox had been traveling excessively and thus ignoring Mexico's internal problems. The Congress subsequently froze the President's visits abroad.

References

Amnesty International. 2004. "At Home and Abroad." *Amnesty International's Human Rights Agenda for Canada*. <http://www.amnesty.ca/canada/>.

Benítez Manaut, Raúl. 1996. "Sovereignty, Foreign Policy, and National Security in México, 1821–1989." In Hal Klepak (ed.), *Natural Allies? Canadian and Mexican Perspectives on International Security*. Ottawa, ON: Carleton UP and FOCAL.

Buzan, Barry, and Gerald Segal. 1996. "The Rise of Lite Powers: A Strategy for the Postmodern State." *World Policy Journal* 13,3: 127–69.

Canadian Press. 2002. "Mexico Would Support Shift to Security Perimeter with US and Canada." 2 February. <http://www.cp.org/english/hp.htm>.

Clayton, Mark, and Gail Russell Chaddock. 2001. "Terrorists Aided by a Leaky US-Canada Line." *Christian Science Monitor*, 19 September: 12–13.

Conference Board of Canada. 2001. "Border Choices: Balancing the Need for Trade and Security." <http://www.conferenceboard.ca/pubs/borderchoices.10.01.pdf>.

Connel Smith, Gordon. 1996. *The Inter-American System*. Oxford: Oxford UP.

Cooper, Andrew, and Athanasios Hristoulas. 2007 "Relating the Powerful One: Security and Efficiency at the Borders." In Maureen Molot (ed.), *Relating to the Powerful One: Security and Efficiency at the Borders*. Mexico City: Porrua.

Covarrubias, Ana. 1999. "El problema de los derechos humanos y los cambios en la política exterior." *Foro Internacional* 39,4: 34–72.

DePalma, Anthony. 2001. "Canada Altering Its System Of Vigilance Against Terror." *New York Times*, 3 December: 11.

Elcock, Ward. 1998. "Submission to the Special Committee of the Senate on Security and Intelligence." <http://www.csis-scrs.gc.ca/eng/misdocs/kelly_2.html>.

Freedberg, Louis. 2001. "US Advocating Continent Wide Security Blanket." *San Francisco Chronicle*. October 7: 3.

Garcia, J.Z. 2002. "Security Regimes on the US-Mexican Border." In Jorge Chabat (ed.), *In Transnational Crime and Public Security: Challenges to Mexico and the United States*. La Jolla, CA: Center for US-Mexican Studies.

Hellman, Gunther. 1996. "Goodbye Bismark? The Foreign Policy of Contemporary Germany." *Mershon International Studies Review* 40, Supp. 1 (April): 13–38.

Heredia, Blanca. 1997. "El dilema entre crecimiento y autonomía: reforma económica y reestructuración de la política exterior en México." *La política exterior de México: enfoques para su análisis*. México: El Colegio de México-Instituto Matías Romero.

Hristoulas, Athanasios. 2003. "Trading Places: Canada, Mexico, and North American Security." In Peter Andreas and Thomas Biersteker (eds.), *The Rebordering of North America*. New York: Routledge.

——. 2004. "Canada y México: Visones encontradas." *Foreign Affairs en español* 2,3: 12–22.

Hristoulas, Athanasios, and Stéphane Roussel. 2004. "Le trilatéralisme sécuritaire en Amérique du Nord: Revue ou réalité?" In Albert Legault (ed.), *Le Canada dans l'orbite américaine: Mort des théories intégrationnistes?* Quebec: Presses de l'Université Laval. 41–59.

Kelly, Jack. 2001. "Quick, Easy Crossing a Thing of the Past at Canadian Border." <http://www.post-Gazette.cm/headlines/20011014canadabordernat5p5.asp>.

Kraus, Clifford. 2002. "Canada Alters Security Policies to Ease Concerns of US." *New York Times*. February 22: 7.

Lawyers Committee for Human Rights. 2003. *Assessing the New Normal: Liberty and Security for the post September 11 United States*. <http://www.humanrightsfirst.org/pubs/descriptions/Assessing/AssessingtheNewNormal.pdf>.

Leiken, Robert. 2002. "Enchilada Lite: A Post 9/11 Mexican Migration Agreement." *Center for Immigration Studies*. <http://cis.org/articles/2002/leiken.html>.

McCarthy, Shawn. 2001. "Manley Doubts Perimeter Idea: Minister Tells Commons Committee Security Proposal is 'Simplistic' Solution." *The Globe and Mail*. 10 May.

Miguel Agustín Pro Juárez Center for Human Rights. 2004. <http://www.centroprodh.org.mx/Sala%20de%20prensa/index_prensa.htm>.

Nossal, Kim Richard. 1997. *The Politics of Canadian Foreign Policy*. Scarborough, ON: Prentice Hall.

Ojeda, Mario. 1981. *Alcances y límites de la política exterior de México*. México City: El Colegio de México.

Regan, Tom. 2002. "Security and the Canadian Way." *Christian Science Monitor*, 17 February.

Report of the Standing Committee on Foreign Affairs and International Trade. 2002. *Partners in North America: Advancing Canada's Relations with the United States and Mexico*. Ottawa: House of Commons.

Shirk, David. 2003. "Nafta Plus: US Mexican Security Relations After the 9/11 Terrorist Attacks." Paper presented at the Conference on Reforming the Administration of Justice in Mexico, Mexico City. April 17.

Smith, Peter. 1996. *Talons of the Eagle*. Oxford: Oxford UP.

Taber, Jane. 2001. "Security Perimeter on Agenda for PM, Fox," *National Post*. November 13: 7.

Torres, Blanca. 2000. *De la Guerra al mundo bipolar: México y el mundo*. México City: Senado de la República.

PART FIVE

Redefining Cultural Relations: Towards a North American Community?

Among social and political philosophers the concept of "community" has been one of the most discussed as well as contested notions. The purpose of this section is to explore the future of North America as an integrated region, not only by drawing on empirical findings, but by thinking critically and theoretically about the idea of "community" as applied to the territory. How appropriate is it to think of North America as a "community"? The lines of conflict and cooperation within North America and possible futures of the North American partnership are also considered in this section.

Taking up the themes of globalization, democracy, identity, and representation, Stephen White and Neil Nevitte examine the mutual effects of North American economic integration and political culture in the three states in Chapter 18, "Economic Integration and North American Political Cultures." After describing the very different political cultures of each country, they use data from the 1981, 1990, and 2000 World Values Survey to test a number of hypotheses purporting to explain the extent and direction of change in core values among the Mexican, Canadian, and US mass publics. The data suggest that these core values have indeed changed: globalization has led to the fragmentation of cultural and communal identities but has also strengthened national ones; and, despite the dominance of neo-liberal ideology, North Americans overall express a "diminished enthusiasm for free markets" and would prefer less privatization and a greater role for government in income support, redistribution, regulation, and welfare. It is not clear, however, whether such shifts have been caused by general globalization, transformation in domestic economic structures, the rise in post-materialism in industrialized states, or North American economic integration per se.

Greater integration across North America has not only affected state and business sector activities, it has also affected the strategies of civil society groups organizing across the continent, the subject of Chapter 19, "Civil Society Organizing Under Continental Integration: The Promise and Limits of Community-Building 'From Below,'" by Jeffrey M. Ayres. Ayres assesses the progress and limits to civic community building in North America from a social movement perspective. He focuses particularly on oppositional popular sector organizations that have mobilized against continental economic integration. Ironically, in the process, they have fostered more of a sense of community, at least among activists and citizens participating in such organizations, and have contributed to the construction of a continent-wide sense of citizenship and community across North America.

Just as European states lost their monopoly on the structuring of popular contention as the EU developed, transnational collaboration between Canadian, US, and Mexican civil society groups has increased as limited authority and decision-making processes have become more embedded in regional and global institutions. Ayres identifies three key factors that have conditioned civil society responses: the availability of organizational resources for mobilizing campaigns (such as labour movements and umbrella coalitions of various groups united in opposition to NAFTA, for instance); the existence of political opportunities for collective action (varying with the election of particular political parties); and the dissemination and limited consolidation of an anti-NAFTA collective action frame. Given the many divisions within and between civil society groups in each country, arriving at such a frame (or interpretation of socio-political conditions) was a formidable challenge that eventually gelled around concerns about social justice, labour mobility and worker migration, and environmental standards. However, Ayres is skeptical as to whether such transnational civic exchanges will translate into "a more interdependent, continental civil society increasingly embracing shared cultural and political norms," as the asymmetries of bargaining power between lower and middle income groups and capital persist. Moreover, the battening down of the US hatches post-9/11 and the absence of thicker institutional structures of governance for the continent that would be efficacious targets for policy lobbying make it unlikely that the North American civic project will advance much in the near future.

In Chapter 20, "Performing North America as Community the Canadian Way," Janine Brodie analyzes the allure of the concept of a "North American community" as a distinct geopolitical space with shared values and interests to the (primarily) business and government elites in Canada who have been "performing" it of late (performance understood more as a conjuring trick than as a description of a reality), though opinion leaders in the US and Mexico are notably less enthusiastic about it. Brodie rejects the tendency among such elites to naturalize and render inevitable continental integration, which is in fact driven by the pursuit of the "holy grail" of secure access to the US market. The eventual instruments created, CUFTA and NAFTA, did not deliver such access, however, especially after the shift to a security- rather than trade-dominated mindset in the US after 9/11. The two agreements' records on the promised "more and better jobs," increased productivity and diversification, knitting of the social safety net, and prosperity to disadvantaged individuals and regions are mixed. Brodie analyzes the performance by Canadian economic and political elites of North America as a political community, as an economic community, and as a security community. Despite the "North American" rhetoric, all of these "communities" essentially exclude Mexico, however, and envision closer integration of Canada and the US in a common market within a secure perimeter. As Brodie points out, "community" not only describes the "in" group but also the "out" group: what deeper continental integration offers Canadians, she argues, is a choice between the gated "community" of North America (with increased vulnerability to "the shifting economic and political fortunes of the United States"), versus a stronger place among the international community of nations in view of the rise of other powerful economic centres in Europe and Asia.

To Robert A. Pastor goes the last word in the volume. In Chapter 21, "Beyond NAFTA: The Emergence and Future of North America," he provides a rather more up-beat and optimistic assessment of the NAFTA period to date and proposes an agenda for NAFTA's second decade. He begins by observing that the negotiation of NAFTA was almost a reversal of policy for each of the three signatories, each of which had its reasons for resisting the idea of a regional trading bloc. The histories of Canada-US and Mexico-US relations reveal the causes of distrust of the US by each of its neighbours—its attempts to invade and annex them both, with considerable success in the case of Mexico—and also the subsequent conditions in each country that led their governments to initiate free trade with the US and eventually with each other. His review of NAFTA institutions such as dispute settlement mechanisms, the Commission for Labor Cooperation, the Commission for Environmental Cooperation, the North American Development Bank, and the Border Environment Cooperation Commission suggests moderate successes for each as the three economies have become more integrated in one decade than the EU has in five. However, Pastor notes that NAFTA's relatively simple purpose of dismantling barriers to trade and investment was not supported by the expansion of infrastructure that turned out to be needed. Nor did it deal with critical issues such as the North-South gap in development, immigration and energy, and trilateral institutions that might have made for more continental governance in what is a deeply asymmetrical set of inter-state relations. Thus, in view of the sins of commission and omission in the NAFTA agreement, Pastor boldly sets out to craft an agenda for its second decade.

Arguing that North America needs to be supported by appropriate supranational institutions, Pastor draws lessons from the EU's over-institutionalization and its commitment to channel resources in the form of aid to poorer regions. North America cannot truly become a community, he argues, with such a skewed distribution of wealth between Mexico and the other two states. He advocates the creation of a range of institutions, from a North American Investment Fund to bring infrastructure up to par, to a North American Commission as an advisory body to the three national leaders, to a Permanent Court on Trade and Investment to replace today's ad hoc dispute panels. North American policy would focus on areas such as transportation and infrastructure, a customs union, and immigration and refugee policy. The chapter concludes with brief assessments of the legitimacy of some concerns about further integration, as well as its feasibility in terms of both public opinion and governments' willingness to relinquish their sovereignty somewhat. Meeting the challenges of further integration, in Pastor's view, will reverberate well beyond the boundaries of North America to infuse the world with hope.

CHAPTER EIGHTEEN

Economic Integration and North American Political Cultures

Stephen White and Neil Nevitte

C anada, the US, and Mexico now have more than a decade's worth of experience with NAFTA, an agreement that is sometimes seen as reflecting one face of globalization, namely, the internationalization of trade. Trading countries have strong incentives to participate in agreements that give them secure access to key export markets. At the same time, some worry that the pressures of globalization and international economic integration can constrain significantly the ability of governments to pursue autonomous domestic policy-making, particularly in those policy areas that have to do with income redistribution and social welfare (Cerny 1995; Strange 1996; Evans 1997).

There is no consensus about what are the catalysts of, and the barriers to, economic integration. By focusing on economic and political interests, economic, rational choice, and institutionalist theoretical perspectives provide important insights into how domestic policy-makers can guide and respond to the forces of economic integration. These interest-based perspectives suggest that even though international trade agreements constrain domestic social and economic policy-making to some extent, states still have at their disposal different instruments for managing welfare and macro-economic policy (Esping-Anderson 1996). Economic interests are undoubtedly an important factor to consider because trade expansion can re-adjust the domestic alignment of political interests in trade sensitive economies by creating new economic "winners" and "losers" (Rogowski 1989). And the balance of re-aligned economic interests can, in turn, decisively shape the dynamics of integration and of domestic social and economic policy (Milner and Keohane 1996). If powerful domestic interests are threatened by the internationalization of trade, income redistribution and welfare policies may not be impaired by international agreements. From a different vantage point, research from the institutionalist perspective suggests that welfare state policies can also create their own institutional interests that cannot be readily dismantled (Pierson 1996).

This chapter argues that explanations of the dynamics of continental integration, and the impact of integration on welfare and economic policies, should take into account the influence of political cultures as well as economic and institutional interests. Political culture is concerned with core values; core values, as well as economic interests, are the foundation of public preferences. Political cultures are relatively enduring, and shifts in the core values of publics tend to take place gradually.

Determining precisely what role political culture plays in the dynamics of integration has received little sustained attention, but it is reasonable to speculate that the core values of citizens might intersect with the forces of integration in at least two ways. First, there are those core values that have to do with communal identities. The strength of communal identities might influence the pace of integration. That line of speculation produces the expectation that experience with NAFTA might weaken citizen communal identifications with the state and encourage supranational ones. Secondly, there is the possibility that citizens' basic orientations towards free markets, the welfare state, and the role of the state in the economy more generally might predispose them to be more, or less, open to those forces that enable or resist continental economic integration.

Drawing on systematic and comparable empirical data this chapter explores two questions: first, have the core political values of mass publics in Mexico, the US, and Canada changed during the first decade of NAFTA? Second, are these changes consistent with speculations about the links between political culture and integration? The discussion is divided into four parts. The first provides an overview of the political cultures of Mexico, the US, and Canada; it both lays the theoretical groundwork for examining questions about North American political cultures in an era of globalization and develops some hypotheses concerning communal identifications and orientations toward the role of the state in the economy. The second presents some baseline data concerning core values in the three countries in a comparative perspective. The indications are that value changes do seem to have taken place among North American publics. The third attempts to account for the shifts in core values. The conclusion summarizes the key findings and speculates about what these may mean for the future.

Political Cultures in North America: Historical Images

Following Feldman and Zaller (1992: 271), political culture can be defined as "a set of values that are widely endorsed by politicians, educators, and other opinion leaders and that animate the principal political institutions of a society." These core values are fundamental to the shaping of people's preferences: they filter political information, encourage people to accept or reject certain ideas, and predispose people to act in certain ways (Eckstein 1988; Zaller 1992).[1]

There a number of different ways to study political culture. For some scholars, the thoughts and beliefs of individuals are impossible to separate from their behaviours; as such, behaviours are indicators of culture (Stewart 2002). According to this view, the political beliefs of a mass public can be inferred, for example, from the kinds of political parties they support. We argue that equating culture with behaviour has a considerable disadvantage: it is hard to determine the effects of culture when its empirical definition is constructed to encompass all thoughts and actions. An alternative way to gauge beliefs, then, is by directly asking people what they believe (Nevitte 1996: 20).

This chapter explicitly focuses on the core values and political orientations that characterize aggregate populations within the nation-state. Nearly all states have significant subcultures (Elazar 1966, 1970; Elkins and Simeon 1980; Grabb and Curtis 2004), but analyzing subcultures with survey data designed to analyze entire states is potentially problematical because there are too few observations of individuals in any one "subculture" to draw any reliable conclusions.

Our approach is also explicitly comparative; we use similar questions across time and across nations. The main advantage of the comparative approach is that it puts findings from any single country in context: are core values changing in North America, and, if so, how do they compare with other countries that have undergone a similar internationalization of trade?

There are a number of long-standing conventional wisdoms about the central features of the political cultures of the US, Canada, and Mexico. Historically, for example, the US has been widely regarded as a highly participatory political culture with a strong commitment to economic individualism. In their pioneering five-nation study of political cultures, Almond and Verba described America in the 1960s as the closest approximation to the "civic culture." Basing their interpretations on public opinion data, they observed that political culture in the US exhibited a balance of political attitudes that was conducive to democratic stability. Americans held a sense of duty towards political activity, expressed high levels of political efficacy, and reported positive orientations toward their political system (Almond and Verba 1963). Along with these uncommonly high levels of efficacy, US core beliefs about the role of the state in society and the economy were also regarded as exceptional. There is, as Verba and Orren put it, a "consensus against redistribution" in the US (1985: 253). Feldman and Zaller express the same idea in a slightly more expansive way: Americans' orientations towards the welfare state, they contend, are guided by "suspicion of big government, humanitarianism, the protestant ethic, and, above all, economic individualism" (1992: 292). Indeed, even those who justify economic redistribution rarely employ an explicitly egalitarian rationale for holding that position (Feldman and Zaller 1992).

By contrast, the historical image of Canadian political culture is of a deferential society, one that combines a mixture of liberal and collectivist political values. According to Lipset (1990), the origins of these variations are attributable to different responses to the same formative event, the American War of Independence. While Americans embraced their revolution, Canadians resisted the principles upon which it was founded, and Canada provided a new political homeland for the influx of British Empire Loyalist refugees from the US. Lipset and others suggest that, as a result, Canadians are more deferential to political authority—indeed, authority of any kind—and that they are more elitist (Porter 1965) than their US counterparts. This tendency toward deference to authority and elitism is pervasive. Van Loon's (1970) observation that Canadian political behaviour is best characterized as "spectator-participant" is entirely consistent with that long-standing interpretation: Canadian citizens are interested in politics, but they are inclined to leave activities beyond voting to political elites. Moreover, Canadian political culture contains both a collectivist and liberal strain when it comes to what role they see for governments in the economy and society. Like their US counterparts, Canadians support free market values, but unlike them, they also place greater reliance on state involvement in the economy and society (Horowitz 1966; Lipset 1990).

More than 40 years ago, Almond and Verba described Mexico's political culture as alienated but aspiring to democratic stability. According to their data, Mexican citizens felt politically competent, but the other elements conducive to full democratic citizenship were in shorter supply. Mexican survey respondents, for instance, exhibited low levels of political participation and knowledge. And although they expressed pride in their political system, they also evaluated such specific political objects as the bureaucracy and police quite negatively (Almond and Verba 1963). Together, these findings seemed to suggest that the Mexico of the 1960s was still navigating the uncertain waters of democratic transition and that the processes of democratic consolidation remained far from complete. Indeed, the evidence is that Mexicans continued to exhibit an inclination toward centralized authority well into the 1960s and 1970s (Craig and Cornelius 1980).

More contemporary analyses of these North American countries suggest that some of this inherited conventional wisdom requires revision. Contemporary evidence from the US, for example, suggests that the US "civic culture" may well be eroding. Trust in government, trust in other people, group memberships, and participation in such political activities as voting are all in decline (see Putnam 2000; Pharr and Putnam 2000).[2] Some of these phenomena have been evident elsewhere, though the declines in the US have been steeper than in most other states. Hardin, for instance, notes that declining civic voluntarism and interpersonal trust may be "perhaps unique to the United States" (2000: 38). But similar patterns are evident in the Canadian setting. Trust in government and voting turnout, for example, have both fallen during the last two decades (see Roese 2002). These patterns may be symptomatic of broader shifts in authority orientations across nearly all advanced industrial states. Respect for political and social authority is waning, particularly among younger generations. Participation in such conventional political behaviours as voting, contacting public officials, and working on election campaigns is declining; at the same time, participation in such unconventional forms of political activity as joining in protests and boycotts, attending unlawful demonstrations, and joining unofficial strikes is rising (Nevitte 1996). Canada has also experienced a shift in authority orientations, and that finding challenges the idea that deference remains a defining characteristic of Canadian political culture.

There is also evidence of significant and systematic shifts in other orientations as well. Canadians and Americans are becoming more tolerant of others and less restrictive when it comes to matters of personal morality (Nevitte 1996). These changes appear to be closely related not only to the rising levels of formal education and the growing secularization of advanced industrial societies but also to another sustained and well-documented trend, namely, the shift towards postmaterialist values in Europe and North America.

Inglehart (1990) contends that older segments of populations in Canada, the US, and Europe, who have had direct experience with social and economic upheaval such as World War II and the Great Depression, place a high priority on such "material" goals as economic and physical security. More recent generations who were socialized during sustained periods of peace and economic prosperity, by contrast, are more likely to take for granted their economic and physical security. Younger generations place a greater priority on "postmaterial" goals, both for themselves and others. These goals include protection of the environment, greater independence, and more autonomy over those matters affecting their lives (see Figure 18.1). Using repeated, cross-national survey data, Inglehart demonstrates that postmaterialists constitute an increasing proportion of the population as a result of generational replacement. These value changes are not limited to the US and Canada. There are also increasing signs of cultural change in Mexico. While the rise of postmaterialism has been less substantial there than in the other North American countries, there does appear to be growing support for civil rights and freedoms (Coleman and Davis 1988) and a rise in levels of unconventional political action (Inglehart *et al.* 1996). After some largely unsuccessful electoral reforms early in the decade (McCann and Dominguez 1998), new electoral rules in the late 1990s equalized political parties' access to money and the media, and enhanced autonomy to independent elections authorities (Wallis 2001). The defeat of the Institutional Revolutionary Party (PRI) after more than 70 years of rule in the elections of 2000 suggests that Mexico is now an electoral democracy (Casillas and Mujica 2003). Moreover, there may have been substantial change in orientations towards the role of the state. Prior to the 1980s, the idea of strong state involvement in the Mexican economy was a mainstay of political culture: the idea that state ownership quelled social divisions and promoted national unity was central in Mexican political beliefs (see O'Toole 2003). But following the 1982 debt crisis, the Salinas government instituted an ambitious program of privatization and trade liberalization, and the government justified these reforms by also promoting the core values of liberal individualism (O'Toole 2003). What is less clear are the effects of these reforms on mass beliefs.

Figure 18.1: Material and Postmaterial Values

Higher-Order Values (Postmaterialist)	• Seeing that people have more say about how things are done in their jobs and in their communities. • Giving people more say in important government decisions. • Protecting freedom of speech. • Trying to make our cities and countryside more beautiful. • Progress towards a less impersonal society. • Progress toward a society in which ideas count more than money.
Basic Values (Materialist)	Security: • Making sure this country has strong defense forces. • Maintaining order in the nation. • The fight against crime. Sustenance: • Fighting rising prices. • A stable economy. • A high level of economic growth.

Source: Adapted from Dalton 1996.

Theoretical Orientations

There are at least four possible expectations to explore concerning the dynamics of core values in an era of globalization. These expectations correspond to four phenomena that may affect core values related to the role of government in the economy.

THE IMPACT OF SHIFTING COMMUNAL IDENTIFICATIONS

A prominent line of reasoning suggests that globalization, particularly as a result of an emerging worldwide media and increasing cross-border travel, causes fragmentation of communal and cultural identities and thereby weakens the traditional bonds of citizenship in the nation-state (see Castells 1997; Held *et al.* 1999; Benhabib 2002). Mass publics across different states increasingly identify with local or, conversely, global communities.

THE IMPACT OF THE NEO-LIBERAL PARADIGM

A second possibility concerns economic values, namely, that the neo-liberal paradigm of economic integration has become so pervasive that it has influenced the core values of mass publics in Mexico, the US, and Canada. The roots of this set of expectations come from our understanding of socialization and the impact of institutions. Norms and values certainly influence the development of social and political institutions, but political cultures are also influenced by political institutions. At the heart of the concept of political socialization is the idea that people learn the rules of the political game (Easton and Dennis 1969), and often those rules are embedded within institutions. Thus, institutional variation influences norms and values concerning everything from generalized support for the system of government (Easton 1965) to partisanship (Westholm and Niemi 1992). One possibility, then, is that the core values of North Americans have shifted towards less state intervention as a result of a top-down diffusion of neo-liberal values.

Publics throughout North America witnessed an apparent ideological "shift to the right" during the course of the 1990s when North American governments embraced policies that reduced the role of the state in society and the economy. Thus, a second possibility is that North American publics could now be reacting against the consequences of a shrinking interventionist state. People who think that state retrenchment went too far in the 1990s might now be more inclined to support greater state intervention in the economy. In Canada and the US, for example, public social expenditures as a percentage of GDP first grew, and then shrank substantially, during the course of the 1990s. But this argument seems most plausible in Mexico. Social expenditures in Mexico continued to grow throughout the decade, but remained substantially smaller than in Canada and the US (OECD 2001). Mexico's economic crisis in the mid-1990s may have significantly weakened support for neo-liberal economic reforms in that country. Kaufman and Zuckermann (1998) show that opposition to economic reforms in Mexico grew from 10 per cent in 1992 to 47 per cent at the height of the economic crisis in 1995. That finding is consistent with Katzenstein's (1985) theory that citizens of "small states"—that is, less economically powerful nations—are more susceptible to, and so more likely than citizens of larger states to feel the effects of, the reverberations of expanding economic environments.

THE IMPACT OF BROAD VALUE CHANGE

Another possibility that cannot be discounted is that core values concerning the role of the state in the economy may have shifted but that the shifts are unrelated to globalization. As we have already noted, Canada, the US, and Mexico have experienced broad changes in political orientations and values during the last two decades or more. These may have led to shifts in core values about the role of government. Some argue that the role of the state in the economy is less important than it once was. Inglehart and others posit that the materialist/postmaterialist value cleavage is gradually displacing the classic "Left-Right" debate about economic distribution and the role of government in the economy (see Inglehart 1987). Kitschelt and Hellmans put the case succinctly:

> As concerns with political control over the economy and redistribution of incomes lose salience in advanced industrial society, so it is argued, new politics parties contribute to the semantic transformation of the [Left-Right] dimension. They constitute the most clear-cut instances in which the meaning of left and right has been dissociated from economic issues and, instead, is related to postmaterialist concerns with the quality of life. (1990: 213–14)

An alternative interpretation, proposed by Knutsen (1995: 163), is that materialist and postmaterialist values are distinct from core values about the role of the state and that "individuals of a postmaterialist orientation have to take a standpoint regarding left-right materialism because it still appears to be central to political conflict in most Western democracies."

Another possibility cannot be ruled out, namely, that the materialist/postmaterialist and state intervention value cleavages are reinforcing rather than cross-cutting. Feldman and Zaller (1992) argue that people can and do hold conflicting values. And there is empirical evidence demonstrating that postmaterialist orientations do coincide with support for state involvement in the economy and income redistribution. Inglehart and Abramson (1999) unexpectedly found such a relationship when examining the US component of the 1990 World Values Survey (WVS), and Erickson and Laycock (2002) show that social democrats in Canada hold both postmaterialist and egalitarian values.

The second important dimension of value change concerns the growth of "moral permissiveness" and a decline in intolerance. There are theoretical and empirical reasons for the expectation that moral permissiveness is positively and intolerance is negatively related to core values favouring government intervention. When it comes to social welfare and redistributive policies for others and not for themselves, citizens who are tolerant and less restrictive on matters of personal morality are less likely to question whether or not state intervention for certain members of society is merited. Goren (2003), for example, provides evidence that government spending is not perceived as a single issue by citizens in the US Rather, people distinguish between the spending on the "deserving poor" and the "undeserving poor." Citizens in a variety of advanced industrial states are more likely to support spending on the "deserving poor," such as the elderly and disabled, who are seen as not responsible for their economic situation, rather than the "undeserving poor," whose economic situation is seen as a consequence of the poor choices they have made in life (Applebaum 2001; Kangas 2003).[3] There is also evidence that levels of prejudice and intolerance may affect perceptions of whether certain members of some social groups are less deserving of social support than others (see Gilens 1995, 1996; Peffley, Hurwitz, and Sniderman 1997).

THE IMPACT OF STRUCTURAL ECONOMIC CHANGE

Finally, there are broader changes in the economic structure to consider. One important economic transformation in Canada, the US, and Mexico concerns income distribution. All three North American countries experienced a significant growth in income inequalities between the mid-1980s and 2000. In Mexico and the US, the growth in income inequality was more pronounced from the 1980s to the early 1990s, after which income differences stabilized (US Census Bureau 2004; Corbacho and Schwartz 2002).[4] In Canada, income inequalities widened in the mid-1990s (Statistics Canada 2002). The second important change is a decline in job security associated with advanced industrialism. According to Wilensky, this "spread of 'contingent labor'—part-time, temporary, or subcontracted workers in both services and manufacturing.... is a new source of instability and insecurity—not confined to low-paid, low-skilled workers—that will play out in the politics of labor and public policy" (Wilensky 2003: 4–5). The desire for job security, and comfortable hours and pay, might also shape value shifts among North American publics.

With these theoretical and empirical considerations in mind, we turn to consider the basic findings regarding value orientations.

Findings

To examine the plausibility of arguments concerning value change, we use data from the 1981, 1990, and 2000 WVS in Canada, the US, and Mexico (see Appendix A). The WVS data are useful because they are comparable in important respects. The surveys ask the same core battery of questions and follow the same coding protocols in all participating countries. This means that their data are likely to be as reliable and comparable as any other evidence of this sort. The first possibility was that North American communal identifications are fragmenting, which might weaken nation-states in Canada, Mexico, and the US. The evidence indicates that communal identities have changed in North America, but the changes are not shifting in the expected direction. To be sure, there is evidence of weakening local identifications. But, at the same time, publics in all three North American countries increasingly identify with the nation-state. The data in Figure 18.2 demonstrate that the proportion of Canadians who identify with "Canada as a whole" rose from 30 to 40 per cent between 1981 and 1990, and remained at 39 per cent in 2000. The trend is similar among Americans and is even more pronounced among Mexicans. Moreover, this growth in national identities came primarily at the expense of local identities, which declined in all three countries. The WVS data provide no evidence that ties to the nation-state have weakened.

Figure 18.2: Percentage Belonging to Given Geographical Units, by Year

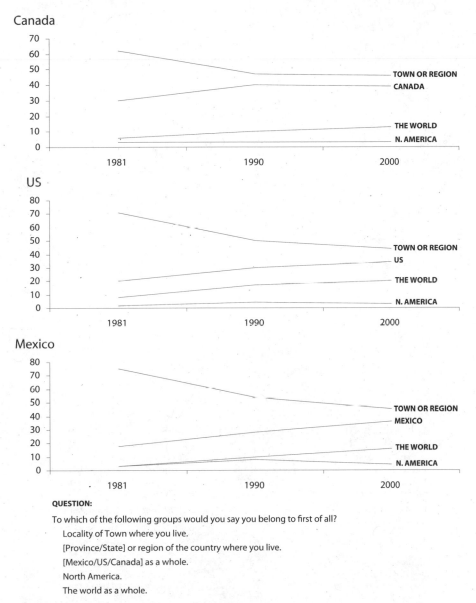

QUESTION:

To which of the following groups would you say you belong to first of all?

    Locality of Town where you live.

    [Province/State] or region of the country where you live.

    [Mexico/US/Canada] as a whole.

    North America.

    The world as a whole.

Sources: 1981, 1990, 2000 WVS (Canada, US, Mexico).

But what about other shifts in core values? How, for example, have views about the role of the state in the economy changed? On these value dimensions, a cross-national perspective is particularly useful because it places the North American evidence in context. If the internationalization of trade has significant effects on core values, then we would expect these effects to also be evident in Europe where cross-border trade has also flourished.[5] Four WVS items clearly measure value orientations

Figure 18.3: Orientations towards Economic Equality, 1991–2000

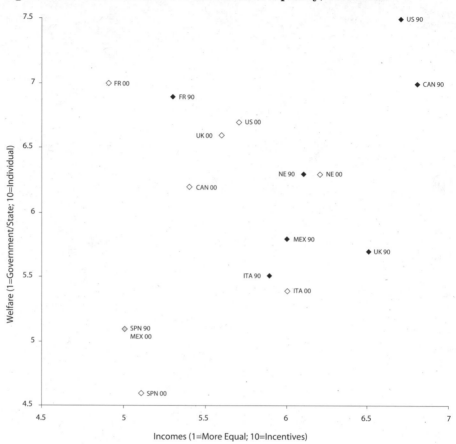

QUESTION:

Now I'd like you to tell me your views on various issues. How would you place your views on this scale? 1 means you agree completely with the statement on the left; 10 means you agree completely with the statement on the right; and if your views fall somewhere in between, you can choose any number in between.

Incomes should be made more equal.								We need [larger income differences as/more] incentives for individual effort.	
1	2	3	4	5	6	7	8	9	10

The [government/state] should take more responsibility to ensure that everyone is provided for.								People should take more responsibility to provide for themselves.	
1	2	3	4	5	6	7	8	9	10

concerning government intervention in the economy. Two of these survey items tap egalitarian and social welfare values. One captures respondents' beliefs about income distribution, asking them whether they believe "Incomes should be made more equal" or "We need larger income differences as incentives for individual effort." The other item measures beliefs about who should ensure the welfare of individuals within society, asking whether "The government should take more responsibility to ensure that everyone is provided for" or "People should take responsibility to provide for themselves."[6] The second pair of survey items taps liberal market values. The third measures orientations toward capital and the free market, asking whether "Private ownership of business and industry should be increased" or "Government ownership of business and industry should be increased." The final item in the socioeconomic dimension measures whether people believe "Competition is good. It stimulates people to work hard and develop new ideas" or "Competition is harmful. It brings out the worst in people."

How do North American publics compare with their European counterparts? On these dimensions, the place to begin is with egalitarian and social welfare values. The data in Figure 18.3 show the mean scores on the 10-point income equality and welfare scales for eight countries in 1990 and 2000. Countries with low scores on both scales, indicating support for greater income equality and government responsibility for welfare, respectively, appear in the bottom left corner of the figure. Countries with high scores suggest negative orientations to government effort and appear in the top right corner of the figure. Canadians and Americans, particularly in 1990, clearly occupy a value space that is different from their Mexican and European counterparts. Notice both the direction and strength of the shift in Canada, the US, and Mexico from 1990 to 2000. All three North American countries clearly move towards more government effort on both dimensions. Publics in Western Europe, by contrast, exhibit greater value stability over the same period. Indeed, in some cases, European publics move towards less government effort during the decade.

The results illustrated in Figure 18.4 show that there was a similar dynamic when it comes to orientations toward liberal market values. On both the ownership and competition dimensions, Canadians, Americans, and Mexicans shifted away from support for more private ownership and competition between 1990 and 2000. And, once again, the Mexican public is far less supportive of more private ownership and competition than are their counterpart publics in Canada and the US. Moreover, on the ownership dimension, the gap between Mexico and the rest of North America widened between 1990 and 2000 as Mexicans came to see public ownership much more positively. The pattern in Western Europe is once again uneven. On the one hand, publics in France, the Netherlands, and Britain become more supportive of competition but are relatively stable on the ownership dimension. On the other hand, publics in Italy and Spain become more supportive of public ownership, but their outlooks on competition were stable.

These shifts may appear small, but they are noteworthy. What is impressive is the consistency of the pattern of value transformation in North America. The comparisons between North American and European values between 1990 and 2000 illuminates just how dynamic orientations concerning the economic function of government are in Canada, Mexico and the US. We can further demonstrate this point by looking at just how much more North American publics value government intervention with a concrete example. Recall that high scores on our four government intervention survey items indicate negative orientations to government involvement in the economy. Here, the data show that approximately 28 per cent of Canadians and 19 per cent of Americans moved down from the highest points (8 to 10) on the 10-point income distribution scale between 1990 and 2000. Among Mexicans, there

Figure 18.4: Orientations towards the Market, 1990–2000

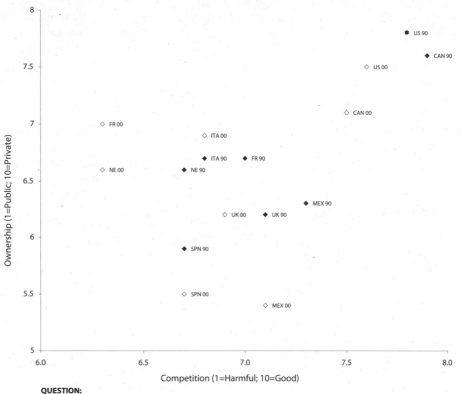

QUESTION:
Now I'd like you to tell me your views on various issues. How would you place your views on this scale? 1 means you agree completely with the statement on the left; 10 means you agree completely with the statement on the right; and if your views fall somewhere in between, you can choose any number in between.

Private ownership of business and industry should be increased.							Government ownership of business and industry should be increased.		
1	2	3	4	5	6	7	8	9	10

Competition is good. It stimulates people to work hard and develop new ideas.							Competition is harmful. It brings out the worst in people.		
1	2	3	4	5	6	7	8	9	10

was a 16 per cent shift towards the lowest points (1 to 3) on the same scale between 1990 and 2000.

These changes, and their possible linkages to the evolution of values during the 1990s are worth considering in more detail. First, consider the case of the shift towards postmaterialist values, which was first observed in Canada and the US between 1981 and 1990 (Nevitte 1996; Inglehart *et al*. 1996). The available evidence suggests that similar changes have been occurring among European publics since at least the early 1970s (Inglehart 1977, 1990). Postmaterialist values have continued to increase among publics in North America (see Table 18.1), though the momentum of the shift has slowed. Fewer Canadians and Americans share materialist orientations, and more share postmaterialist values, in 2000 than in 1990.[7] The percentage difference between materialists and postmaterialists (bottom row in Table 18.1) shrank in both countries during the 1990s. By contrast, Mexicans appear to have shifted towards materialism, a change that may well reflect a public reaction to Mexico's economic turmoil in the 1990s.

Table 18.1: Materialism and Postmaterialism in North America, 1990–2000

	CANADA		US		MEXICO	
	1990	2000	1990	2000	1990	2000
% Materialist (M)	39	34	49	45	45	52
% Postmaterialist (PM)	16	17	12	16	8	8
% M minus PM	23	17	37	29	37	44

See Appendix 18.B for Variable Coding.
Sources: 1981, 1990, 2000 WVS (Canada, US, Mexico).

Second, orientations towards moral permissiveness and intolerance were also changing. In 2000, all North American publics were less restrictive on matters of personal morality than they were two decades ago. They were also less intolerant towards a variety of social and racial/ethnic out-groups. The data in Figure 18.5 show the proportion of citizens between 1981 and 2000 in Canada, the US, and Mexico who think that six different behaviours (homosexuality, prostitution, abortion, divorce, euthanasia, and suicide) are in some way "justifiable." In the US, the

Figure 18.5: Moral Permissiveness in North America, 1981–2000

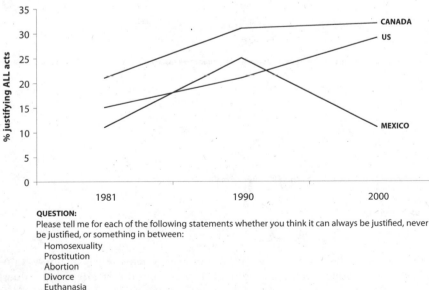

QUESTION:
Please tell me for each of the following statements whether you think it can always be justified, never be justified, or something in between:
   Homosexuality
   Prostitution
   Abortion
   Divorce
   Euthanasia
   Suicide

Sources: 1981, 1990, 2000 WVS (Canada, US, Mexico).

proportion of people willing to justify all six behaviours nearly doubled (from 15 to 29 per cent) between 1981 and 2000. The proportion of those Canadians who qualified as morally permissive grew from 21 per cent to 31 per cent between 1981 and 1990 and leveled off at 32 per cent in 2000. Once again, Mexico turns out to be an outlier: in that country moral permissiveness increased substantially from 1981 to 1990, but the trend reversed during the 1990s.

North Americans exhibit similar trends on racial/ethnic and social intolerance.[8] There has been a general shift away from intolerant orientations towards racial and ethnic groups in Canada and the US. Between 1990 and 2000, the proportion of respondents who did not mention any racial or ethnic group they would *not* like to have as neighbours rose from 77 to 84 per cent in the US and from 85 to 91 per cent in Canada. There was no change in Mexico, where the proportion went from 62 to 61 per cent. Results are more mixed on social intolerance in Canada and the US: fewer people are highly intolerant, but also fewer people are very tolerant. The Mexican data indicate that levels of social intolerance are lower in that country.

According to the WVS data, it appears that several years of experience with NAFTA has not resulted in a movement towards more neo-liberal values; there is also evidence of a broader shift in values. One possibility is that the value shifts relating to income distribution, welfare, and control of the economy among all three North American publics could be connected to broader value changes. They may also reflect transformations in domestic economic structures. Or they could be related to other aspects of globalization.

Table 18.2: Intolerance in North America, 1990–2000

	US		MEXICO		CANADA	
	1990	2000	1990	2000	1990	2000
% Ethnic/Racial Intolerance	23	16	38	39	15	9
% High Social Intolerance	21	12	39	27	14	8

QUESTION:
On this list are various groups of people. Could you please sort out any that you would not like to have as neighbours? High Social Intolerance is indicated by choosing any five or six of the following groups:
  People with a criminal record
  Heavy drinkers
  Emotionally unstable people
  People who have AIDS
  Drug addicts
  Homosexuals

Ethnic/Racial Intolerance is indicated by choosing any one of the following groups:
  People of a different race
  Muslims
  Immigrants/foreign workers
  Jews

Sources: 1990, 2000 WVS (Canada, US, Mexico).

This latter possibility is more difficult to confirm conclusively. The internation-alization of trade could well have indirect, rather than direct effects on values. Nonetheless, we can conduct a plausibility probe; if the theories of structural and broad cultural change are weak, or are ruled out, when squared against the empirical evidence, then the idea that the value shift is a reaction to the effects of globalization is still plausible.

A MULTIVARIATE APPROACH

The best way to assess the independent effects of structural change, intolerance, moral permissiveness, and postmaterialism on orientations toward the role of government in the economy is to resort to a multivariate approach. A number of different variables, or factors, may influence orientations toward income distribution, welfare, and control of the economy at the same time but do so in different ways. A multivariate approach has the advantage of allowing us to isolate the independent effects of a single variable net the effects of all other factors.[9] Multivariate analysis is useful for two reasons. First, all of the possibilities outlined so far may hold some merit, and it is unlikely that any single factor will account for the shift in values relating to income distribution, welfare, and control of the economy to the exclusion of all other factors. Second, it is entirely possible that some of the factors mentioned above are strongly related to one another.[10]

Standard ordinary least squares regression was used to analyze the independent impact of a variety of factors on all four value dimensions concerning the role of government in the economy, and separate analyses were conducted for the US, Canadian, and Mexican respondents. (The results of the Canadian and American analyses are presented in detail in Appendix 18.C.) Regression analysis is a statistical strategy that allows us to determine how well the values on one variable (for example, education) "fit" with the variable the researcher is trying to explain (for example, support for welfare policies). Thus, if people with higher levels of education are generally more supportive of welfare policies, we can say there is a positive relationship between education and support for welfare policies. Three categories of variables are included in our analyses. First, there are socio-demographic variables, including gender, year of birth (in generational categories), employment status, education and income, and an indicator of visible minority status. Including these variables controls for the varying composition of the survey samples from 1990 to 2000. The second category of variables measures the impact of orientations and values, including items that gauge materialist/postmaterialist orientations, moral permissiveness, social and ethnic/racial intolerance, the desire for job comfort and security, and political engagement. The third group measures how some variables interact with others. The three interactive variables capture interactions with timing, or period effects, and these allow us to test whether that part of the shift in values concerning the role of government in the economy has to do with the *evolution* of values and structural economic conditions: factors that did not matter much in 1990 mattered much more in 2000.[11]

MULTIVARIATE RESULTS

What accounts for the value shift in the US? Americans shifted considerably on the income distribution and responsibility dimensions, less on the ownership and competition dimensions. The multivariate results clearly show that broader values mattered. Postmaterialists were significantly less likely to believe individuals should be responsible for providing for themselves or that competition is a good thing (see Appendix 18.B for variable coding). But the most significant finding concerns orientations towards income equality. Postmaterialists shifted substantially towards support for greater income equality between 1990 and 2000.

Second, moral permissiveness also has a significant impact on orientations towards welfare, but its effect varies by birth cohort, and it is stronger in 2000. Among the youngest generation of survey respondents, Americans born between 1964 and 1970, those who were morally permissive were substantially more supportive of government providing for people's welfare than morally permissive respondents from previous generations. Moral permissiveness influences orientations towards welfare, but that influence is stronger in 2000, and it is strongest for the youngest generation of Americans.

An intriguing generational finding emerges with regard to moral permissiveness. The direction of the relationship contradicts our expectations when it comes to government control of the economy. The youngest generation of Americans who were morally permissive actually supported more private ownership of the economy, rather than more government ownership. Whether this finding indicates growing salience of libertarian values among the public in the US is hard to tell, but this finding does go some distance towards explaining why orientations towards market values changed less between 1990 and 2000 than did orientations towards income equality and welfare. And yet another reason income equality and welfare orientations seem to be diverging from market values might have to do with the relative importance of such other social values as tolerance. As expected, social and ethnic/racial intolerance are significantly related to support for more unequal incomes and positive orientations towards personal responsibility for welfare.

Changes in the economic structure also have a marked effect on core values relating to the role of government in the economy. But some of the results are surprising. In 2000 in particular, Americans with both high education and low incomes are much more supportive of income equality than other people, including other people with low incomes.

One possible explanation for this finding concerns the expansion of post-secondary education during the last half-century. While rising levels of formal education has a positive economic impact, the economic returns of higher education appear to be diminishing: fewer and fewer people are able to find work that they believe is proportionate to their level of education. And much of the available evidence suggests they are correct in this assessment. The positive impact of schooling—especially attainment of a university degree—on income and occupational status has weakened considerably since the 1950s (Wanner 2000; Van der Ploeg 1994).

The effect of a growing group of well-educated, low income earners is likely to be a shift in core values towards a greater role for the government in the economy. People with lower incomes are the beneficiaries of redistributive policies. But, traditionally, low income earners lack the resources of political knowledge and engagement because they are also usually less educated than wealthier citizens (see Verba *et al.* 1995; Nie *et al.* 1996). People with more education, by contrast, are better equipped to identify and articulate their interests clearly. It stands to reason that well-educated, low income earners are more likely to hold positive orientations towards government intervention. They may also be among the least likely to hold notions of "deserving" and "undeserving poor," suggesting that growing dissatisfaction with the diminishing financial returns of education have taken root during the 1990s. Moreover, the desire for a comfortable job—one with good hours, good wages, and job security—is also related to positive attitudes towards welfare.

Canadian evidence is broadly similar to findings from the US. Transformations in other value dimensions such as moral permissiveness, postmaterialism, and tolerance influence Canadian orientations towards the role of government in the economy. Post materialists, in particular, are significantly more likely than materialists to support income equality and government provision of welfare, as well as more government ownership in the economy. They are also far more inclined to believe competition is harmful.

Orientations towards moral permissiveness and social and ethnic/racial intolerance are also related to support for income equality and government provision of welfare. Canadians who are more morally permissive are more likely than others to believe incomes should be made more equal and that the government should be responsible for ensuring people are provided for. The same pattern holds for Canadians who are more tolerant than others.

In contrast with the US, interaction effects are generally unimportant in explaining value change in the Canadian setting. There is, however, one major exception. People with high education and low incomes were substantially more likely to support government provision of welfare than other people. This relationship emerges only in 2000 and is similar to the relationship between education, income, and support for income equality that we found in the US. The growth of an increasingly dissatisfied cohort of well-educated but economically disadvantaged people turns out not to be an isolated phenomenon.

Theories concerning structural economic change suggest that increases in education have outpaced the growth of skill requirements in the labour market. Post-industrial societies have experienced a growth in the service economy, with a mix of both highly skilled/high-wage jobs and low-skill/low-wage jobs, and a general growth in levels of education (Wilensky 2003). This situation creates a growing number of people who are underemployed in the sense that they work in jobs for which they are overqualified.

Both broad value and structural change go some distance towards explaining the shift in orientations among publics in Canada and the US towards a greater role for government in the economy. The growing salience of social orientations, particularly in the US, suggests a value realignment may be occurring; postmaterialism, for example, is an increasingly important determinant of support for greater income equality among Americans.

This value/structural change model seems to at least partially explain the transformation of core values concerning income equality and government provision of welfare. The easiest way to calculate their effectiveness is by examining the change in the "period effect" before and after entering in all the other variables in the model. The basic period effect indicates the difference between the mean scores on each 10-point scale from 1990 to 2000. An advantage of multivariate analysis is that this difference can be calculated *assuming that value and structural changes have no effect*. Thus, a basic period effect of -1.08 on the income equality scale means that people became more supportive of income equality between 1990 and 2000. When all other factors are taken into account, however, the period effect falls to -.03. In effect, the other factors account for 97 per cent of the shift; thus, were it not for these other factors, orientations towards income equality would not have changed at all. On the income equality dimension, 97 per cent of the US shift and 19 per cent of the Canadian shift between 1990 and 2000 is explained by economic and sociodemographic factors, along with changes in moral permissiveness, intolerance, and materialism/postmaterialism. On the welfare dimension, 47 per cent of the US shift and 91 per cent of the Canadian shift is explained by these same factors.

The value/structural change model has a comparatively modest impact when it comes to accounting for the shift in orientations toward ownership and competition, however. On the ownership dimension, 29 per cent of the Canadian shift from 1990 to 2000 can be accounted for with structural and cultural factors. In the case of the US public, however, the difference on this dimension actually *increases* over the decade once these structural and cultural factors are controlled. In other words, if cultural and structural factors had not mattered, US support for government ownership would have increased even more. On the competition dimension, the model accounts for 46 per cent of the shift towards the view that "competition is harmful" in the US but only 13 per cent of the movement towards that view in Canada.

The value/structural change model, then, explains most of the change in US and Canadian orientations toward income equality and welfare. In the absence of value and structural effects, these shifts would have been much smaller. However, the evidence also suggests that something other than value change and structural change caused the move towards greater support for government ownership in the economy and less support for competition among US and Canadian publics.

The multivariate results for Mexico are less clear. The difference between the core values of Mexicans in 1990 and 2000 do not diminish after we take into account values and structural variables. In fact, the gap in core beliefs about state intervention actually *widens* when value orientations and social and demographic variables are controlled. This finding implies that sociodemographic changes and broader value change actually suppress an even greater shift towards support for state intervention in the economy.

It is quite possible that the Mexican shift in orientations can be attributed to a negative reaction to the neo-liberal economic restructuring in Mexico during the 1990s. There were already indications in the mid-1990s that public opinion had turned against the economic reforms of the PRI government (Kaufman and Zuckermann 1998; Morris and Passé-Smith 2001); a growing number of Mexicans felt that the country was not better off as a result of the restructuring.

Conclusion

Political culture has not occupied a prominent place in the contemporary empirical research on globalization. Our goal in this chapter has been to draw on the available literature to develop empirically testable hypotheses about how values and value change might be linked to the dynamics of integration. Long-standing functionalist theories produce the expectation that increased trade flows and greater contact between peoples will result in value convergence (Deustch *et al.* 1957; Haas 1958). That perspective is certainly plausible. What is missing is the empirical evidence supporting that expectation. Earlier efforts to probe that hypothesis systematically indicated that value changes have taken place among these publics in North America, but there is no clear pattern of convergence (Inglehart *et al.* 1996). Nor does the empirical evidence unequivocally show that the values held by the US public are leading the value changes taking place among Canadians and Mexicans (Nevitte 1996).

This chapter has examined two other lines of speculation that have received little attention. First, is there evidence, after more than a decade of closer economic ties, that communal identities are eroding? And, second, are the pathways of value change consistent with the expectations that greater economic integration has been accompanied by value shifts that signal a stronger embrace of free market values that, in turn, weaken public support for the role of government in the economy?

The answer to the first question is clearly "no." Canadians, Americans, and Mexicans have not abandoned their national identities in favour of North American or global outlooks. Nor is there any evidence that they have turned to local identities. Indeed, the systematic evidence indicates the proportion of Canadians, Americans, and Mexicans identifying with their country increased substantially between 1981 and 2000.

The answer to the second question is a qualified "yes." Political, social, and economic outlooks, particularly among Canadians and Americans, have changed. And viewed from a broader cross-national vantage point, it becomes clear that these shifts over the last decade have been more emphatic among these North American publics than comparable West European publics experiencing greater economic integration on that continent. However, these shifts reflect a diminished enthusiasm for, rather than a stronger embrace of, free market values.

There is reason, however, to be cautious about attributing these value changes to the dynamics of globalization. Because globalization is itself conceptually amorphous (see Skogstad 2000), providing a definitive test of the links between value change and the dynamics of globalization remains a challenge. Furthermore, to suppose that all value change following NAFTA, for example, is a consequence of NAFTA is also problematic. That said, the empirical evidence is that views about the economy have changed and that these changes are related to broader structural and value change. Shifting orientations towards the role of government in the economy in Canada and the US are significantly related to rising postmaterialism and moral permissiveness and declining intolerance. That these same patterns do not hold for Mexico may be less surprising. The surge in postmaterialist outlooks among publics, after all, is usually associated with the kinds of stable economic prosperity that most Mexicans have yet to experience. Nonetheless, Mexicans do exhibit a substantial increase in support for government intervention in the economy.

One implication that emerges from this analysis is that arguments about the erosion of the state in an era of globalization need to be examined more closely (Strange 1996). The evidence assembled here suggests that regardless of which forces are driving the internationalization of economies, there is no reason to suppose that these necessarily signal a shift in *laissez-faire* values among publics. The crafting of such policies as NAFTA is rarely led by publics; they are elite-led endeavours. But public values nonetheless constrain what leaders can and cannot do. Levels of public support for closer economic and political ties between countries clearly do vary when publics are asked to consider what implications closer economic ties might have (Inglehart *et al.* 1996).

The fact that orientations towards freer trade are shaped by other considerations, as this chapter has shown, raises other broad questions. It is reasonable to suppose that the changing salience of other considerations, such as security in the wake of 9/11, may influence political orientations. However, it is difficult to speculate on how increased concerns about terrorism might affect political culture in the US, Canada, or Mexico. Some research has shown that 9/11 may have contributed to public support for the curtailment of civil liberties in the US (see Davis and Silver 2004), and there is also evidence of a substantial increase in Americans' trust in their national government in the months following the attack (Chanley 2002). Other public opinion data suggest the attacks led to only a modest increase in fear and anxiety among the US public (Huddy *et al.* 2003). The effects of 9/11 on political orientations in Canada and Mexico are even less clear.

Notes

1   Political culture is usually distinguished from public opinion *per se*: the core values that constitute a political culture are general principles that structure opinions and beliefs about political institutions and actors and public policies (Conover and Feldman 1984).

2   Turnout was unusually high in the 2004 presidential election, but the sources for it are not entirely clear, and it may be exceptional. It was a close presidential race, and it has been empirically demonstrated that closeness tends to lead to higher turnout (Blais 2000).

3   The distinction between those for whom income redistribution and social spending is justified and those for whom it is not important is related to what Feldman and Steenbergen (2001) call the "humanitarian foundation" of support for welfare: US citizens are more likely to support social welfare programs on the basis of *humanitarian*, rather than *egalitarian*, values.

4   Some of the large rise in the GINI coefficient, a measure of income inequality within states, between 1992 and 1993 in the US may have been the result of a change in data collection methods from paper and pencil to computer-assisted telephone interviewing.

5   The data on which the following analysis is based come from the 1990 and 1999–2000 World Values Surveys (WVS) and European Value Studies (EVS) in Canada, the US, Mexico, Britain, France, the Netherlands, Spain, and Italy. The five European countries were selected for comparison because their surveys all include the same battery of items that gauge values concerning state intervention.

6   These first two items are worded slightly differently in the EVS. For the first measure regarding income distribution, EVS respondents were given the statement "There should be greater incentives for individual effort" rather than "We need larger income differences as incentives for individual effort." For the second item concerning welfare, the word "government" is replace with "state," and the word "people" is replaced with "individuals." These minor variations are unlikely to have a substantive impact on the results, particularly for the second item, given that "the government" holds similar meaning for North Americans as "the state" does for Europeans.

7   We use a 12-point index as our measure of postmaterial values. Inglehart and Abramson demonstrate that the 12-item index is a better measure of postmaterialist value orientations than the original 4-item index (1999: 671). The 12-item index of postmaterialism used here

ranges from 0 (fully materialist) to 6 (fully postmaterialist). See Appendix 18.A for details on the construction of this variable, including the survey items used to gauge value orientations. For ease of presentation in Table 18.1, "postmaterialists" are those who scored 4 to 6, and "materialists" are those who scored 0 to 1.5 on the index.

8   The measures of racial and social intolerance used here ask respondents to sort out any groups "you would *not* like to have as neighbours." We use the concept of *in*tolerance deliberately. The concept of tolerance, Sullivan and his colleagues observe, "implies a willingness to 'put up with' those things that one rejects" (1979: 784). The WVS survey items capture intolerance: if respondents would not like various groups of people as neighbours, they are both rejecting members of that group and saying they will not "put up with" them.

9   Our intent is to explain as fully as possible the changes in values. For example, consider Figure 18.2, which shows that US respondents had mean scores of 7.5 and 6.7 on the 10-point welfare scale in 1990 and 2000, respectively, for a difference of -0.8 points. It could be that Americans shifted towards valuing government intervention in welfare because they became more postmaterialist during the course of the 1990s. Under this scenario, we would expect the difference between 1990 and 2000 to shrink from -0.8 to zero once we take into account the independent effects of postmaterialism.

10 Consequently, what might appear as a relationship between high levels of moral permissiveness, for instance, and positive orientations towards government intervention may be an artifact of a relationship between postmaterialist values and positive orientations towards government intervention. An analysis of the interrelationships between ethnic/racial tolerance, social tolerance, moral permissiveness, postmaterialism, and a number of other factors confirmed the suspicion that a number of these factors are significantly associated with one another.

11 Other values such as postmaterialism and moral permissiveness, for example, might have been weakly related to values concerning the role of government in the economy in 1990 simply because issues regarding income equality, welfare, and the free market were less salient to postmaterialists in 1990 than they are in 2000.

References

Almond, G.A., and S. Verba. 1963. *The Civic Culture: Political Attitudes and Democracy in Five Nations*. Toronto: Little, Brown and Company.

Appelbaum, L.D. 2001. "The Influence of Perceived Deservingness on Policy Decisions Regarding Aid to the Poor." *Political Psychology* 22: 419–42.

Benhabib, S. 2002. "Political Theory and Political Membership in a Changing World." In I. Katznelson and H.V. Milner (eds.), *Political Science: The State of the Discipline*. New York: Norton. 404–32.

Blais, A. 2000. *To Vote or Not to Vote: The Merits and Limits of Rational Choice Theory*. Pittsburgh, PA: U of Pittsburgh P.

Casillas, C.E., and A. Mujica, A. 2003. "Mexico: New Democracy with Old Parties?" *Politics* 23: 172–80.

Castells, M. 1997. *The Information Age: Economy, Society, and Culture, Volume 2: The Power of Identity*. Oxford: Blackwell.

Cerny, P. 1995. "Globalization and the Changing Logic of Collective Action." *International* 9: 595–625.

Chanley, V.A. 2002. "Trust in Government in the Aftermath of 9/11: Determinants and Consequences." *Political Psychology* 23: 469–83.

Coleman, K.M., and C.L. Davis. 1988. *Politics and Culture in Mexico*. Ann Arbor, MI: Institute for Social Research.

Conover, P., and S. Feldman. 1984. "How People Organize the Political World." *American Journal of Political Science* 28: 95–126.

Corbacho, A., and G. Schwartz. 2002. "Income Distribution and Social Expenditure Policies in Mexico: What Can We Learn from the Data?" *Latinamerika Analysen* 1: 5–64.

Craig, A.L., and W. Cornelius. 1980. "Political Culture in Mexico: Continuities and Revisionist Interpretations." In G.A. Almond and S. Verba (eds.), *The Civic Culture Revisited*. Boston: Little Brown. 325–93.

Dalton, R.J. 1996. *Citizen Politics: Public Opinion and Political Parties in Advanced Industrial Democracies*. Chatham, NJ: Chatham House.

Davis, D.W., and B.D. Silver. 2004. "Civil Liberties vs. Security: Public Opinion in the Context of the Terrorist Attacks on America." *American Journal of Political Science* 48: 28–46.

Deutsch, K., S.A. Burrell, R.A. Kann, M. Lee, Jr., M. Lichterman, R.E. Lindgren, F. Loewenheim, and R.W. Van Wagenen. 1957. *Political Community and the North Atlantic Area: International Organization in the Light of Historical Experience*. Princeton, NJ: Princeton UP.

Easton, D. 1965. *A Systems Analysis of Political Life*. New York: Wiley.

Easton, D., and J. Dennis. 1969. *Children and the Political System: Origins of Political Legitimacy*. New York: McGraw-Hill.

Eckstein, H. 1988. "A Culturalist Theory of Political Change." *American Political Science Review* 82: 789–804.

Elazar, D. 1966. *American Federalism: A View from the States*. New York: Crowell.

——. 1970. *Cities of the Prairies: The Metropolitan Frontier in American Politics*. New York: Basic Books.

Elkins, D.J., and R. Simeon. 1980. *Small Worlds: Provinces and Parties in Canadian Political Life*. Toronto: Methuen.

Erickson, L., and D. Laycock. 2002. "Postmaterialism versus the Welfare State? Opinion Among English Canadian Social Democrats." *Party Politics* 8: 301–25.

Esping-Andersen, G. 1996. "After the Golden Age? Welfare State Dilemmas in a Global Economy." In G. Esping-Andersen (ed.), *Welfare States in Transition. National Adaptations in Global Economies*. London: Sage. 1–31.

Evans, P. 1997. "The Eclipse of the State? Reflections on Stateness in an Era of Welfare." *American Journal of Political Science* 45: 658–77.

Feldman, S., and M.R. Steenbergen. 2001. "The Humanitarian Foundation of Public Support for Social Welfare." *American Journal of Political Science* 45,3: 658–77.

Feldman, S., and J. Zaller. 1992. "The Political Culture of Ambivalence: Ideological Responses to the Welfare State." *American Journal of Political Science* 36: 268–307.

Gilens, M. 1995. "Racial Attitudes and Opposition to Welfare." *Journal of Politics* 57: 994–1014.

——. 1996. "'Race Coding' and White Opposition to Welfare." *American Political Science Review* 90: 593–604.

Goren, P. 2003. "Race, Sophistication, and White Opinion on Government Spending." *Political Behaviour* 25: 201–20.

Grabb, E., and J. Curtis. 2004. *Regions Apart: The Four Societies of Canada and the United States*. Toronto: Oxford UP.

Haas, E. 1958. *The Uniting of Europe*. Stanford, CA: Stanford UP.

Hardin, R. 2000. "The Public Trust." In S.J. Pharr and R.D. Putnam (eds.), *Disaffected Democracies: What's Troubling the Trilateral Countries?* Princeton, NJ: Princeton UP.

Held, D., A. McGrew, D. Goldblatt, and J. Perraton. 1999. *Global Transformations*. Stanford, CA: Stanford UP.

Horowitz, G. 1966. "Conservatism, Liberalism, and Socialism in Canada: An Interpretation." *Canadian Journal of Economic and Political Science* 32: 143–70.

Huddy, L., S. Feldman, G. Lhav, and C. Taber. 2003. "Fear and Terrorism: Psychological Reactions to 9/11." In P. Norris, M. Kern, and M. Just (eds.), *Framing Terrorism: The News Media, the Government, and the Public*. New York: Routledge. 255–78.

Inglehart, R.F. 1977. *The Silent Revolution: Changing Values and Political Styles Among Western Publics*. Princeton, NJ: Princeton UP.

——. 1987. "Value Change in Industrial Societies." *American Political Science Review* 81: 1289–1303.

——. 1990. *Culture Shift in Advanced Industrial Democracy*. Princeton, NJ: Princeton UP.

Inglehart, R.F., and P.R. Abramson. 1999. "Measuring Postmaterialism." *American Political Science Review* 93: 665–77.

Inglehart, R.F., N. Nevitte, and M Basañez. 1996. *The North American Trajectory: Cultural, Economic, and Political Ties among the United States, Canada, and Mexico*. New York: Aldine de Gruyter.

Kangas, O. 2003. "The Grasshopper and the Ants: Popular Opinions of Just Distribution in Australia and Finland." *Journal of Socioeconomics* 31: 721–43.

Katzenstein, P.J. 1985. *Small States in World Markets: Industrial Policy in Europe*. Ithaca, NY: Cornell UP.

Kaufman, R.R., and L. Zuckermann. 1998. "Attitudes Towards Economic Reform in Mexico: The Role of Political Orientations." *American Political Science Review* 92: 359–75.

Kitschelt, H., and S. Hellmans. 1990. "The Left-Right Semantics and the New Politics Cleavage." *Comparative Political Studies* 23: 210–38.

Knutsen, O. 1995. "Left-Right Materialist Value Orientations." In J.W. Van Deth and E. Scarbrough (eds.), *The Impact of Values*. New York: Oxford UP. 160–96.

Lipset , S.M. 1990. *Continental Divide: The Values and Institutions of the United States and Canada*. Ottawa: C.D. Howe Institute.

McCann, J., and J. Dominguez. 1998. "Mexicans React to Electoral Fraud and Political Corruption: An Assessment of Public Opinion and Voting Behaviour." *Electoral Studies* 17: 483–503.

Milner, H.V., and R.O. Keohane. 1996. "Internationalization and Domestic Politics: An Introduction." In H.V. Milner and R.O. Keohane (eds.), *Internationalization and Domestic Politics*. Cambridge: Cambridge UP. 3–47.

Morris, S.D., and J. Passé-Smith. 2001. "What a Difference a Crisis Makes: NAFTA, Mexico, and the United States." *Latin American Perspectives* 28,3: 124–49.

Nevitte, N. 1996. *The Decline of Deference: Canadian Value Change in Cross-national Perspective*. Peterborough, ON: Broadview.

Nie, N.H., J. Junn, and K. Stehlik-Barry. 1996. *Education and Democratic Citizenship in America*. Chicago, IL: U of Chicago P.

OECD (Organization for Economic Cooperation and Development). 2001. *Social Expenditure Database, 1980–1998*. <http://www.oecd.org/dataoecd/43/14/2087083.xls>.

O'Toole, G. 2003. "A New Nationalism for a New Era: The Political Ideology of Mexican Liberalism." *Bulletin of Latin American Research* 22: 269–90.

Peffley, M., J. Hurwitz, and P.M. Sniderman. 1997. "Racial Stereotypes and Whites' Political Views of Blacks in the Context of Welfare and Crime." *American Journal of Political Science* 41: 30–60.

Pharr, S.J., and R.D. Putnam (Eds.). 2000. *Disaffected Democracies: What's Troubling the Trilateral Countries?* Princeton, NJ: Princeton UP.

Pierson, P. 1996. "The New Politics of the Welfare State." *World Politics* 48: 143–79.

Porter, J. 1965. *The Vertical Mosaic: An Analysis of Social Class and Power in Canada*. Toronto: U of Toronto P.

Putnam, R.D. 2000. *Bowling Alone: The Collapse and Revival of American Community*. Toronto: Touchstone.

Roese, N.J. 2002. "Canadians' Shrinking Trust in Government: Causes and Consequences." In N. Nevitte (ed.), *Value Change and Government in Canada*. Toronto: U of Toronto P. 149–64.

Rogowski, R. 1989. *Commerce and Coalitions: How Trade Affects Domestic Political Alignments*. Princeton, NJ: Princeton UP.

Skogstad, G. 2000. "Globalization and Public Policy: Situating Canadian Analyses." *Canadian Journal of Political Science* 33: 805–28.

Statistics Canada. 2002. *Income Trends in Canada, 1980–2000*. Cat. No. 13F0022XCB.

Stewart, I. 2002. "Vanishing Points: Three Paradoxes of Canadian Political Culture Research." In J. Everitt and B. O'Neill (eds.), *Citizen Politics: Research and Theory in Canadian Political Behaviour*. Don Mills, ON: Oxford UP. 21–39.

Strange, Susan. 1996. *The Retreat of the State: The Diffusion of Power in the World Economy*. Cambridge: Cambridge UP.

Sullivan, S.L., J. Pierson, and G.E. Marcus. 1979. "A Reconceptualization of Political Tolerance: Illusory Increases, 1950s–1970s." *American Political Science Review* 73: 781–94.

US Census Bureau. 2004. "Historical Incomes Tables—Households, Table H-4. Gini Ratios for Households, by Race and Hispanic Origin of Householder: 1967 to 2002." <http://www.census.gov/hhes/income/histinc/ho4.html>.

Van der Ploeg, S. 1994. "Educational Expansion and Returns on Credentials." *European Sociological Review* 10: 63–78.

Van Loon, R. 1970. "Political Participation in Canada: The 1965 Election." *Canadian Journal of Political Science* 3: 376–99.

Verba, S., and G.R. Orren. 1985. *Equality in America: The View from the Top*. Cambridge, MA: Harvard UP.

Verba, S., K. Lehman Schlozman, and H.E. Brady. 1995. *Voice and Equality: Civic Voluntarism in American Politics*. Cambridge, MA: Harvard UP.

Wallis, D. 2001. "The Mexican Presidential and Congressional Elections of 2000 and Democratic Transition." *Bulletin of Latin American Research* 20: 304–23.

Wanner, R.A. 2000. "A Matter of Degree(s): Twentieth-Century Trends in Occupational Status Returns to Educational Credentials in Canada." *Canadian Review of Sociology and Anthropology*. 37: 313–43.

Westholm, A., and R.G. Niemi. 1992. "Political Institutions and Political Socialization: A Cross-National Study." *Comparative Politics* 25: 25–41.

Wilensky, H.L. 2003. "Post-industrialism and Postmaterialism? A Critical View of the 'New Economy,' the 'Information Age,' the 'High Tech Society,' and All That." Discussion Paper, Social Science Research Centre Berlin, Order No. SP 03–201.

Zaller, J. 1992. *The Nature and Origins of Mass Opinion*. Cambridge: Cambridge UP.

Appendix 18.A: The World Values Surveys and European Values Studies

Below is a list of each survey used in this analysis. More information about the World Values Surveys and European Values Studies can be found at <http://www.worldvaluessurvey.org>.

COUNTRY	SURVEY DATE	SURVEY TYPE	SAMPLE SIZE
Canada	1981	WVS	1254
	May–June 1990	WVS	1730
	Aug–Sept 2000	WVS	1931
US	1982	WVS	2325
	May–June 1990	WVS	1839
	Nov–Dec 1999 and Aug–Sept 2000	WVS	1200
Mexico	1981	WVS	1837
	May 1990	WVS	1531
	Jan–Feb 2000	WVS	1510
Britain	June–Sept 1990	EVS	1484
	1999	EVS	1000
France	June–July 1990	EVS	1002
	1999	EVS	1615
Italy	Oct–Nov 1990	EVS	2018
	1999	EVS	2000
Netherlands	June–Aug 1990	EVS	1017
	1999	EVS	1003
Spain	May 1990	EVS	1510
	Nov 2000	WVS	1200

Appendix 18.B: Variable Construction for Regression

1. MATERIALIST/POSTMATERIALIST INDEX

The Materialist/Postmaterialist measure (Cronbach's Alpha= .48) is a composite index ranging from 0, "materialist," to 6, "postmaterialist," and is based on the *combined* responses to the *three* sets of questions below. For each set of questions: respondents whose first and second choices were postmaterialist (indicated by an *) scored 2; respondents whose first choice only was postmaterialist scored 1; and respondents whose second choice only was postmaterialist scored 0.5.

> **Question:** People sometimes talk about what the aims of this country should be for the next ten years. On this card are listed some of the goals which different people would give top priority. Would you please say which one of these you, yourself, consider the most important? And which would be the next most important?
>> A high level of economic growth.
>> Making sure this country has strong defence forces.
>> *Seeing that people have more say about how things are done in their jobs and in their communities.
>> *Trying to make our cities and countryside more beautiful.

> If you had to choose, which one of the things on this card would you say is most important? And which would be next most important?
>> Maintaining order in the nation.
>> *Giving people more say in important government decisions.
>> Fighting rising prices.
>> *Protecting freedom of speech.

> Here is another list. In your opinion, which one of these is most important? And what would be the next most important?
>> A stable economy.
>> *Progress towards a less impersonal society.
>> *Progress toward a society in which ideas count more than money.
>> The fight against crime.

2. MORAL PERMISSIVENESS INDEX

The Moral Permissiveness measure (Cronbach's Alpha= .82) is a composite index ranging from 0 to 6, and is based on the combined responses from six survey items.

> **Question:** Please tell me for each of the following statements whether you think it can always be justified, never be justified, or something in between:
>> Homosexuality
>> Prostitution
>> Abortion
>> Divorce
>> Euthanasia
>> Suicide

For each act, respondents who stated that it could "never be justified" were coded 0, and respondents who stated that it could "always be justified" or something in between were coded 1.

3. INTOLERANCE

The indexes of social and racial/ethnic intolerance are based on responses to the following battery of survey items.

> **Question:** On this list are various groups of people. Could you please sort out any that you would not like to have as neighbours?
>> People with a criminal record
>> *People of a different race
>> Heavy drinkers
>> Emotionally unstable people
>> *Muslims
>> *Immigrants/foreign workers
>> People who have AIDS
>> Drug addicts
>> Homosexuals
>> *Jews

The Racial/Ethnic intolerance index (Cronbach's Alpha= .73) ranges from 0 to 4, and combines the responses to the four items with an *. For each item, respondents who mentioned the group were coded 1, and respondents who did not mention the group were coded 0.

The Social intolerance index (Cronbach's Alpha= .68) ranges from 0 to 6, and combines the responses to the remaining six items. For each item, respondents who mentioned the group were coded 1, and respondents who did not mention the group were coded 0.

4. POLITICAL ENGAGEMENT

The political engagement index (Cronbach's Alpha= .65) ranges from 0 to 3, and combines the responses to the three items below. Responses that indicated engagement with politics were coded 1, and responses that indicated disengagement from politics were coded 0.

> How interested would you say you are in politics?
>> 1 Very interested
>> 1 Somewhat interested
>> 0 Not very interested
>> 0 Not at all interested

> When you get together with your friends, would you say you discuss political matters frequently, occasionally, or never?
>> 1 Frequently
>> 1 Occasionally
>> 0 Never

> Would you say politics is very important, rather important, not very important, or not at all important in your life?
>> 1 Very important
>> 1 Rather important
>> 0 Not very important
>> 0 Not important at all

5. DESIRE FOR JOB SECURITY/COMFORT

The Job Security/Comfort index (Cronbach's Alpha= .66) ranges from 0 to 5 and is based on responses to the following question:

> Here are some aspects of a job that people say are important. Please look at them and tell me which ones you think are personally important in a job?
> Good pay
> Not too much pressure
> Good job security
> Good hours
> Generous holidays

For each of the five job aspects listed above, respondents who mentioned the aspect were coded 1, and respondents who did not mention the group were coded 0.

6. EDUCATION

The education measure is a scale running from 1 to 10, and is based on responses to the following question:

> At what age did you (or will you) complete your full time education, either at school or at an institution of higher education? Please exclude apprenticeships.

Respondents who completed their education at age 12 years or younger were coded 1, 13 years were coded 2, and so on. Respondents who completed their education at age 21 years or older were coded 10.

7. INCOME

The incomes were divided into quartiles in each country, for both 1990 and 2000. Responses are based on the following question:

> Here is a scale of incomes. We would like to know in what group your *household* is, counting all wages, salaries, pensions, and other incomes that come in. Just give the letter of the group your *household* falls into, before taxes and other deductions.

8. BIRTH COHORT

Respondents were grouped into four categories based on their year of birth:
Cohort 1: Born before 1929
Cohort 2: Born 1930–45
Cohort 3: Born 1946–64
Cohort 4: Born 1965–72

9. GENDER AND VISIBLE MINORITY STATUS

These were coded by the interviewer.

Appendix 18.C

Table C.1: Canadian Predictors of Orientations towards the Role of Government in the Economy

	INCOMES		WELFARE		OWNERSHIP		COMPETITION	
	β	(S.E.)	β	(S.E.)	β	(S.E.)	β	(S.E.)
ZERO ORDER								
Constant	6.78	(.08)**	7.03	(.08)**	7.65	(.07)**	7.91	(.07)**
Period Effect (2000)	-1.25	(.11)**	-.71	(.11)**	-.51	(.09)**	-.38	(.09)**
MULTIVARIATE								
Constant	6.44	(.41)**	6.17	(.38)**	7.94	(.33)**	7.55	(.34)**
Period Effect (2000)	-1.01	(.26)**	-.06	(.24)	-.36	(.21)	-.33	(.21)
Sociodemographic								
Female	-.31	(.11)**	-.07	(.11)	-.27	(.09)**	-.38	(.09)**
Visible Minority	.27	(.22)	-.61	(.21)**	.62	(.18)**	.26	(.18)
High Education	.04	(.03)	.04	(.03)	-.04	(.03)	.02	(.03)
Low Income	-.17	(.06)**	-.12	(.06)**	-.14	(.05)**	-.14	(.05)**
Employed	-.07	(.14)	.29	(.13)	.09	(.12)	.09	(.12)
Birth Cohort (vs. 1946–64):								
Born Before 1930	.30	(.23)	.83	(.21)**	.01	(.19)	.48	(.19)*
Born 1930–45	.02	(.20)	.89	(.19)**	.35	(.16)**	.44	(.16)**
Born After 1964	-.10	(.22)	-.27	(.20)	-.12	(.18)	.05	(.18)
Orientations								
Postmaterialist	-.15	(.06)*	-.12	(.06)*	-.15	(.05)**	-.20	(.05)**
Morally Permissive	.10	(.04)**	.02	(.03)	-.04	(.03)	-.01	(.03)
Socially Intolerant	.11	(.04)**	-.01	(.03)	-.02	(.03)	.03	(.03)
Racially Intolerant	.03	(.08)	.16	(.08)*	.00	(.07)	-.03	(.07)
High Desire for Job Security	-.16	(.04)	-.18	(.04)**	-.09	(.03)**	-.09	(.03)**
High Political Engagement	.10	(.05)*	-.07	(.05)	-.07	(.04)	.12	(.04)**
Interactions								
Postmaterialism × Period	-.06	(.09)	-.12	(.08)	.00	(.07)	.05	(.07)
High Education × Low	-.03	(.07)	-.19	(.07)**	-.04	(.06)	.01	(.06)
Income × Period								
Morally Permissive × Period								
× Birth Cohort:								
Born Before 1930	-.08	(.08)	-.08	(.08)	.08	(.07)	-.05	(.07)
Born 1930–45	-.03	(.06)	-.10	(.06)	-.09	(.05)	-.10	(.05)**
Born After 1964	.00	(.06)	.10	(.06)	-.02	(.05)	-.01	(.05)
N	2406		2404		2395		2405	

** $p \leq .01$; * $p \leq .05$ (Unstandardized OLS Regression coefficients—standard errors in parentheses)

Table C.2: US Predictors of Orientations towards the Role of Government in the Economy

	INCOMES		WELFARE		OWNERSHIP		COMPETITION	
	β	(S.E.)	β	(S.E.)	β	(S.E.)	β	(S.E.)
ZERO ORDER								
Constant	6.88	(.07)**	7.57	(.07)**	7.75	(.06)**	7.88	(.06)**
Period Effect (2000)	-1.08	(.11)**	-.78	(.12)**	-.24	(.10)*	-.28	(.10)**
MULTIVARIATE								
Constant	6.11	(.38)**	7.59	(.38)**	6.57	(.33)**	6.94	(.34)**
Period Effect (2000)	-.03	(.25)	-.41	(.25)	-.61	(.22)**	-.15	(.22)
Sociodemographic								
Female	-.38	(.11)**	-.26	(.11)*	-.14	(.10)	-.27	(.10)**
Visible Minority	-.06	(.15)	-.41	(.15)**	-.99	(.13)**	-.64	(.13)**
High Education	.08	(.03)**	.06	(.03)	.08	(.03)**	.04	(.03)
Low Income	-.07	(.06)	-.06	(.06)	-.15	(.05)**	-.18	(.06)**
Employed	-.12	(.14)	.05	(.14)	-.13	(.12)	-.29	(.12)*
Birth Cohort (vs. 1946–64):								
Born Before 1930	.51	(.20)*	.04	(.20)	.16	(.17)	.22	(.18)
Born 1930–45	.23	(.18)	.22	(.17)	-.20	(.15)	.02	(.16)
Born After 1964	-.12	(.19)	-.13	(.19)	-.77	(.16)**	.17	(.17)
Orientations								
Postmaterialist	-.05	(.05)	-.28	(.05)**	-.09	(.05)	-.13	(.05)**
Morally Permissive	-.05	(.03)	-.09	(.03)**	-.03	(.03)	-.03	(.03)
Socially Intolerant	.01	(.04)	.10	(.04)**	-.01	(.03)	.02	(.03)
Racially Intolerant	.16	(.07)*	-.11	(.07)	-.04	(.06)	-.11	(.06)
High Desire for Job Security	-.05	(.04)	-.12	(.04)**	-.06	(.03)	-.08	(.04)**
High Political Engagement	.10	(.05)	.03	(.05)	-.01	(.04)	.02	(.05)
Interactions								
Postmaterialism × Period	-.25	(.08)**	.01	(.09)	.11	(.07)	-.05	(.08)
High Education × Low Income × Period	-.22	(.08)**	-.04	(.08)	.03	(.07)	.03	(.07)
Morally Permissive × Period × Birth Cohort:								
Born Before 1930	-.12	(.09)	.01	(.09)	.04	(.07)	.09	(.08)
Born 1930–45	-.06	(.07)	-.09	(.07)	.08	(.06)	.13	(.06)*
Born After 1964	-.02	(.06)	-.15	(.06)**	.14	(.05)**	-.09	(.05)
N	2096		2090		2092		2097	

** p ≤ .01; * p ≤ .05   (Unstandardized OLS Regression coefficients—standard errors in parentheses)

CHAPTER NINETEEN

Civil Society Organizing Under Continental Integration

The Promise and Limits of Community-Building "From Below"

Jeffrey M. Ayres

To what extent has the move towards greater integration across North America affected the strategies of civil society group organizing across the continent? Or, to put it differently, how can approaching North America as a regional unit of analysis help to explain the upsurge in contentious national and transnational civic behaviour across the societies of Canada, the US, and Mexico? This chapter explores the puzzle of what might be called the regional structuring of contentious politics, a phenomenon that has accompanied the now decade-long process of North American economic integration. It is clear that the three state partners to NAFTA still shape a considerable amount of civic activity. Nonetheless, it is increasingly apparent as well that regional economic and political arrangements under NAFTA are affecting the styles and strategies civil society groups have adopted.

This chapter adopts a social movement perspective, borrowing especially from the political process approach, which is helpful for understanding how actors mobilize resources, exploit political opportunities, and frame episodes of collective action and protest. The political process approach is useful in particular for both assessing the available body of empirical evidence on what can be called contentious civil society organizing across North America and for conceptualizing the progress and continued limits to civic community-building across the continent. Civil society can be understood as that "arena of organized political activity between the private sphere (the household and the firm) and the formal political institutions of governance (the parliament, political parties, the judiciary, etc)" (Macdonald 1994).[1] Moreover, contentious political activity undertaken by civil society groups includes a variety of forms of sustained collective action that draw particularly from non-institutionalized forms of protest, campaigns, petitions, and other acts of claims-making (Tarrow 1996).

Therefore, the focus in this chapter in particular is on those more aggrieved social groups, sometimes referred to as popular sector organizations,[2] who, unlike those largely business associations involved in pro-economic integration campaigns in alliance with government officials and other state authorities, have undertaken campaigns of both national and transnational contentious claims-making against state authorities and the broader continental economic integration agenda. Research on the social dimensions of North American integration has traditionally received less attention than work that focuses on explicitly trade and investment issues under NAFTA and has ignored in particular those actors opposed to the largely market-based model of integration which has unfolded in NAFTA. Yet, there is a growing body of work that documents a significant increase in collaboration between Canadian, US, and Mexican civil society groups. This resulting mix of ongoing national and transnational collaboration ultimately raises interesting questions about the role being played by popular civic groups in the construction of a continent-wide sense of citizenship and community across North America.

North American Integration from a Social Movement Perspective

The emergence and political fortunes of national social movements and those related civil society groups engaged in collective action are clearly linked to the centuries-long process of modern state building. Specifically, research continues to document that "state building created an opportunity structure for collective action of which ordinary people take advantage" (Tarrow 1998: 56). There is now a long record of state political processes and institutions shaping the dynamics of popular protest: from the 1960s US civil rights movement, to the European anti-nuclear and peace movements of the 1970s and 1980s, and even to the more recent mobilizations in Canada against trade liberalization (McAdam 1982; Rochon 1988; Ayres 1998). In these instances, for example, strategically placed political elites, sympathetic political parties, electoral volatility, and public opinion created opportunities for effective mobilization and protest campaigns. However, what increasingly intrigues observers of social movements and civic protest is how the rise of more regional and global institutions and political processes is affecting the dynamics of popular organizing (Tarrow 2001; Khagram *et al.* 2002). In particular, it seems increasingly clear that many social groups are "going transnational" as limited authority and decision-making processes become more embedded in regional and global institutions (Smith 2001).

The growth of international institutions, the unfolding process of global economic restructuring, and the rise of regional and global trade and investment regimes has encouraged national social actors and movements to develop transnational ties and mobilize and intervene in transnational political processes (della Porta, Kriesi, and Rucht 1999; O'Brien 2000; Smith and Johnston 2002). Neo-liberal economics, with its prescriptions for unfettered free trade and capital flows, deregulation, and privatization—and realized in such regional and global regimes and institutions as NAFTA, the IMF, and the WTO—has especially encouraged a proliferation in new forms of contentious political behaviour (Ayres 2001). A host of constituencies across different national settings have mobilized against the perceived hierarchical, non-transparent character of multilateral trade negotiations and the lack of attention to labour, human rights, or environmental concerns in the resulting agreements as well as over concerns about the purported negative impact of these accords on democracy and popular sovereignty. In particular, the annual ministerial meetings and regulatory prescriptions integral to neo-liberal globalization have stimulated innovative responses by activists who have consciously rescripted their popular strategies to contend with constraints that have been placed on national-level opportunities for collective action.

The regional institutional arrangements buttressing the EU have already been linked to the spread of this type of contentious popular politics. However, in this case, it is deep supranational institutions and international trends that have begun to structure protest and transnational cooperation that target European institutions and policies (Imig and Tarrow 2001). The rise of a European polity, then, has encouraged increased incidences of cross-border collaboration by social actors, a redirection of some national-level protest to the supranational level, and the tentative development of European-wide transnational social movements. Thus, European states no longer have a monopoly on the structuring of popular contention, as opportunities and threats have arisen at the supranational level to reshape the style of protest across that continent.

Compared to its European counterpart, the North American integration model, rooted primarily in NAFTA, is institutionally light, with only limited political initiative existing towards the deepening of the political-institutional relationship between Canada, the US, and Mexico.[3] The European model also has the benefit of a 40-year head-start over North America, the former also prompted by the deep and historic antagonisms of numerous European conflicts stretching back through the nineteenth century. Finally, the North American integration model is clearly more asymmetrical than the European model, with Germany's renewed power counterbalanced by other medium-sized European states and the continued admission of new members into the EU. Meanwhile, the US remains the economic giant (as well as the global hegemon) in the North American relationship, less inclined to dilute its sovereignty through the adoption of any new North American initiative, such as a common market or common currency, for example. Clearly then, if the European and North American integration processes are so different, the rise of North American contentious politics should seem that much more remarkable.

In fact, despite these differences in history, policy substance, and power, a pattern of North American-centred contentious activity has arisen over the past 15 years. Across North America civil society groups mobilized against NAFTA for many of the same reasons that have provoked other regional and global episodes of contentious civic action. NAFTA's negotiation process, the substance of the agreement, and ultimately its results have at different times been found to be objectionable by a wide variety and cross-section of groups. Civil society groups criticized the lack of civic input into the negotiations, the privileging of trade and investment liberalization, the absence of enforceable labour and environmental standards, and the perceived negative economic and social fallout from the accord for lower and middle income people across Canada, the US, and Mexico. These same groups responded to the shifting political-economic terrain under NAFTA with transformations in organization and political strategy. Three important factors have conditioned these civil society responses: the availability of organizational resources for mobilizing campaigns, the existence of political opportunities for collective action, and the dissemination and limited consolidation of an anti-NAFTA collective action frame.

ORGANIZATIONAL CHARACTERISTICS: NORTH AMERICAN MOBILIZING STRUCTURES

The ability of North American civil society groups to mount campaigns and mobilize constituencies has heavily depended on the pre-existence of available resources and organizations. Such organizational infrastructures, which are critical for sustaining contentious activity over time, have been conceptualized as "mobilizing structures." National mobilizing structures can be understood as "those collective vehicles, informal, as well as formal, through which people mobilize and engage in collective action" (McAdam, McCarthy, and Zald 1996: 3). Transnational mobilizing structures incorporate organizations, resources, and membership from two or more countries and encourage collective action and communication across national borders (Smith, Chatfield, and Pagnucco 1997: 61). There have been numerous examples where national and transnational mobilizing structures have facilitated popular action against North American continental integration.

The most important precursor to more widespread continental organizing around NAFTA occurred during the national campaign in Canada against the CUFTA. In particular, the emergence in April 1987 of the Pro-Canada Network (PCN) marked a milestone in contentious political activity in Canada. The PCN was a pan-Canadian, cross-sectoral coalition of women's, church, labour, farmer, Aboriginal, and other self-described popular sector groups opposed to the proposed agreement. Nationalist groups were also active in the formation and activities of the PCN, especially the newly emerged Council of Canadians (COC). This combination of popular sector and nationalist groups constituted the national mobilizing structure for the PCN-led anti-free trade movement in Canada.

The PCN's strength arose from its umbrella-like coalition, and this innovative structure would prove to be the model for similar creative developments in the national mobilizing structures of similar organizations in the US and Mexico during the negotiations over NAFTA. For instance, it was chosen to be the model by Mexican activists in the creation of the Red Mexicana de Acción Frente al Libre Comercio (Mexican Action Network on Free Trade or RMALC) in April 1991. Through cross-border political exchanges and meetings, Canadian activists shared their lessons in critiquing and mobilizing against trade liberalization with those Mexican civil society groups skeptical of the purported benefits of the type of integration accord embodied in the proposed NAFTA. Again, similar to the PCN, RMALC emerged as a national cross-sectoral coalition of Mexican civic organizations, representing a variety of independent labour, peasant, women's, environmental, human rights, and urban organizations, as well as education and research groups (Massicotte 2003: 108). RMALC was less critical of the proposal to enhance Mexican access to the US market but was still opposed to the NAFTA model. At the same time, RMALC became a catalyst for transformative change in Mexico, agitating for the democratization of the Mexican state and for greater input into policy debates by Mexican civil society groups (Massicotte 2003: 109).

Similarly, in the US, the NAFTA debate encouraged the coming together of a broad cross-section of organizations opposed to economic integration with Mexico. For example, a significant part of the US national mobilizing structure was divided more clearly into two coalitions: the Citizen's Trade Coalition (CTC) and the Alliance for Responsible Trade (ART). Both of these umbrella-style networks emerged during the NAFTA negotiations—ART in 1991 and the CTC in 1992—yet each had a different strategic orientation and resource base. ART emerged with a greater grassroots approach, drawing support from a multi-sectoral coalition of unions, environmental groups, social justice and religious groups, and policy and research organizations. ART took an explicitly internationalist position on the trade debate, working closely with Canadian and Mexican coalitions to develop a series of trinational citizens' statements that both critiqued the official NAFTA text, and offered alternatives to generate a vision of North American integration that would promote equitable and sustainable trade and development.[4] ART lacked the capacity for effective lobbying, but its transnationalist orientation laid the groundwork for continued cross-border collaboration between Canadian, US, and Mexican groups even after the implementation of NAFTA in 1994.

The CTC, on the other hand, emerged as a national multi-sectoral coalition with significant lobbying clout within the US Congress. Buttressed by larger unions and environmental groups, the CTC largely mobilized as an interest group and commanded, in comparison to ART, the majority of activist resources devoted to the anti-NAFTA campaign (Dreiling 1999: 6). It could much more effectively scrutinize trade votes by members of Congress and carried considerable clout as an active lobbying group in Washington to promote an alternative vision on trade. By 1993, with ART focused on its mobilization capacity as a smaller more transnational networking group, the CTC had constructed a broad national network linking 52 million Americans with 38 state-level coalitions and a field staff in 43 states (Dreiling 1999).

When NAFTA came into effect on 1 January 1994, the organizational infrastructure remained for a continuation of anti-NAFTA activity. The most innovative and attention-grabbing developments have occurred as groups stepped up cross-border cooperation. In fact, much is now known about the increase in cross-border activity that transpired between Canadian, US, and Mexican groups during the NAFTA negotiations and in the first years after its implementation (Thorup 1991; Sinclair 1992; Alexander and Gilmore 1994; Ronfeldt and Thorup 1994). This pooling of resources created a multi-level continental mobilizing structure. That is, civil society groups from Canada, the US, and Mexico, through information and communication exchange, continued to draw resources, expertise, and membership from pre-existing national anti-NAFTA organizations. Yet, at the same time, incidents of cross-border action and organizational innovation gradually emerged from the experience of transnational cooperation during the NAFTA negotiations.

On the one hand, civil society groups continued to be involved in national campaigns against the perceived negative social and economic fallout from NAFTA. For example, by the mid-1990s the COC effectively had replaced the Action Canada Network[5] as the most active and visible national progressive organization in Canada committed to both continuing to critique NAFTA while opposing further Canadian involvement in trade and investment liberalization (Ayres 1997). Through petitions, boycotts, and advocacy campaigns, the COC monitored NAFTA's impact on social programs and cultural industries and highlighted its investor rights provisions and the potential for resource-depleting bulk water exports to the US. While increasingly engaging in international campaigns against neo-liberal globalization, the COC has more recently become involved in another domestic campaign with over two dozen Canadian civil society groups in the "Our Canada Project" against proposals to deepen North American integration.[6]

Throughout the second half of the 1990s, US and Mexican civil society groups continued to mobilize in a political climate significantly more politicized around international trade policy following the NAFTA debate (Rupert 2000; Wise, Salazar, and Carleson 2003; Otero 2004). The CTC, for example, continued to lobby the US Congress against further NAFTA-style trade liberalization and played an important role in the defeat of then US President Clinton's request for the renewal of fast-track trade negotiating authority in 1997 and 1998. In Mexico, RMALC had by the latter half of the 1990s grown to represent dozens of Mexican civil society organizations. It continued to engage in national education campaigns to promote discussions on economic justice, democratization, and the social and economic repercussions of NAFTA for the average Mexican worker. Drawing expertise from its cross-sectoral coalition structure, RMALC directed research and resources to support grassroots education on NAFTA's long-term impact on Mexico's agricultural sector and environment, as well as the lack of serious attention to migration issues in the accord (Salazar and Carleson 2001).

The pre-existence within Mexico of a grassroots civil society infrastructure also played a role in the emergence of the Zapatista Army of National Liberation. The Zapatistas began their armed uprising timed to coincide with the 1 January 1994 implementation of NAFTA. Centred in the remote, southern, and extremely poor Mexican state of Chiapas, the uprising was begun in part as a direct criticism of NAFTA's neo-liberal orientation, which the Zapatistas feared would have an especially negative impact on the region's mostly Indigenous population. The uprising had long-term roots in the early 1980s, when peasant and Indigenous groups, especially in Chiapas, struggled in the face of Mexico's growing debt crisis, the gradual abandonment of its historic state-led industrial model, and the loss of state support for the peasant and agricultural sector (Johnston 2000). While the actual armed uprising lasted little more than a few weeks, the Zapatistas evolved throughout the decade into an active and influential force within Mexican civil society, both in pressuring the Mexican government for democratic reform and Indigenous rights as well as in the development of a broader critique of the socio-economic implications of neo-liberalism.[7]

Aside from the much publicized Zapatista campaign, considerable attention in the post-NAFTA era has been focused on the emergence of varied forms of cross-border activity (Hunter 1995; Kidder and McGinn 1995; Carr 1996; Cook 1997; MacDonald 2003). In the decade since NAFTA's implementation there has been an increase in the number of Canadian, US, and Mexican groups becoming partners in sectoral or cross-sectoral coalitions. Cross-border networking and information-sharing across North America preceded NAFTA, for example, between human rights, social justice, and church groups. However, NAFTA contributed to a deepening of sectoral cooperation across borders between those groups whose interests seemed certain to be most directly affected by economic restructuring.

Labour union collaboration has received the most attention and the most enthusiastic reviews (Hathaway 2000; Bacon 2001; Cohen and Early 2001; Stevis and

Boswell 2001). As one keen observer of this budding North American labour transnationalism has noted, "NAFTA has brought the issue of continental labor cooperation to the fore of labor union strategy, not as a well-meaning moral duty or empty political slogan, but as a necessary and concrete tactic in the neoliberal era of the regionalized production system" (MacDonald 2003: 173). Other examples of sectoral cross-border collaboration have involved women's, environmental, Indigenous peoples, and church group collaboration, although none of these groups seem to have experienced the same degree of deepening cross-border collaboration as labour groups, a testament to labour's advantages in resources and political power (Gabriel and Macdonald 1993; Bowles, MacDonald, and Mullen 2002; Macdonald 2002).

A considerable amount of transnational activity has been located along the US-Mexico border region (Brooks and Fox 2002). US and Mexican groups, in part due to their proximity to each other but also due to the growth in border *maquila* employment, began to collaborate in earnest after NAFTA came into effect in 1994. Examples include the US-based Mexico Solidarity Network, a coalition of dozens of organizations that seeks to strengthen links between US and Mexican civil society groups engaged in a campaign for democracy, economic justice, and human rights along the border. Other such networks include the Coalition for Justice in the Maquiladoras, which draws membership from social justice and civic advocacy groups from Canada, the US, and Mexico (Kamel and Hoffman 1999).

There have been other types of cross-border solidarity actions that have involved North American civil society groups but that have not been limited to close border collaboration. These efforts include the work of the Workers Rights Consortium and the United Students Against Sweatshops in the backing of striking Mexican workers at the Mexmode assembly plant in Atlinxco, Mexico. In the fall of 2000, roughly 900 workers at this factory—a key supplier of college sweatshirts to Nike and Reebok— boycotted the company cafeteria to protest unsanitary conditions. This action was followed in early 2001 by a walkout and sit-in by Mexmode workers, partly in solidarity with those fired over the cafeteria boycott and subsequent attempts by workers to form an independent union. In response, the Workers Rights Consortium, a US-based activist coalition with over 90 members on US college and university campuses, traveled to Atlinxco to hear workers' complaints and returned to the US to undertake a high-profile publicity campaign and consumer boycott against Nike. At the same time, activists involved in the United Students Against Sweatshops, an organization active on over 200 US campuses, conducted a similar investigation and staged protests outside Nike offices and stores across the US. The negative publicity and cross-border campaigns resulted in wage and workplace gains for Mexmode workers, the reinstatement of ousted workers, improved cafeteria conditions, and the creation at the time of one of the only independent unions at a *maquiladora* factory (Thompson 2001). The explosive growth in such foreign-owned, low-wage assembly plants in Mexico since the implementation of NAFTA has subsequently encouraged further campaigns to stretch corporate codes of conduct across borders.

The employment of transnational collective activity has not been limited to sectoral resistance by assembly-line workers or environmental advocates. Concerns surrounding NAFTA's possible impact beyond trade issues has also encouraged cross-border solidarity actions by education experts, teachers, and students (Howard 1998). For instance, educators from all three NAFTA countries created the Trinational Coalition to Defend Public Education in February 1995. This coalition has drawn together concerned Canadian, US, and Mexican educators to conferences and workshops to exchange information and personnel and to engage in solidarity actions with unions, students, and concerned families in an effort to monitor and defend public education and union rights against feared NAFTA-inspired budget cuts to public education. Coalition members have participated in events in all three countries, including supporting Mexican student protests in 1996 against the Mexican government's proposed standardized testing and in solidarity actions with teachers' unions on strike in Ontario in 1997 (Lemus 1999). The activist and education work of the more formal trinational coalition continues to be complemented by sometimes episodic but more often coordinated incidences of national and cross-border collective protest.

In short, a state-level view of civil society organizing across North America under NAFTA provides an incomplete picture. Rather, it is clear that the years since NAFTA was negotiated and passed have witnessed what might be called a regional structuring of contentious collective action. Continental integration has dramatically increased the numbers of possible groups who have converged and collaborated on oppositional tactics and organizational innovations to challenge the record of social and economic restructuring. These continent-wide interactions have helped to build mutually beneficial organizational skills; have furthered a shared understanding of the labour, environmental, and other social challenges facing civil society groups; and strengthened communication networks and the dissemination of strategic information across the continent.

EXPANDED POLITICAL OPPORTUNITY FOR CROSS-BORDER COLLABORATION

Organizational innovations alone do not fully explain the record of North American civil society activities. In fact, the push for NAFTA and its eventual implementation shaped not only domestic alignments and institutions but created new international opportunities for cross-border civil society activism. On the one hand, the more traditionally conceptualized national political opportunity structure of the US was clearly a factor in allowing groups to apply pressure on US congressional members to oppose NAFTA. A divided Democratic majority in the US House of Representatives, for example, created strategic openings for anti-NAFTA mobilization in the fall of 1993. For groups affiliated with the Citizen's Trade Campaign, waffling House Democrats became important, vulnerable, and ultimately effective targets of anti-NAFTA campaigns. Faced with the increasing likelihood of defeat, due to opposition from within his own party, Democratic President Bill Clinton proposed NAFTA side-agreements on labour and the environment. These side-agreements convinced enough Democratic law-makers to support NAFTA and were key to its eventual implementation.

While NAFTA shaped openings for concerted popular mobilization in the US, it had less of an effect in encouraging an opening of domestic political opportunities in Canada and Mexico. In fact, throughout the 1990s the Canadian political environment became less hospitable to civil society organizing. The election of the federal Liberal Party to majority government status in 1993, in an election that witnessed the shattering of Canada's traditional two-party system, dramatically reduced the lever-age of the anti-free trade coalition that had outlasted the CUFTA debate. After 1993, and throughout the rest of the decade, with the governing Liberals abandoning their election campaign pledge to renegotiate if not pull out of NAFTA, groups in Canada were left with few effective political allies to support the anti-free trade campaign. By the mid-1990s many of those actors involved in the anti-CUFTA or NAFTA campaigns began to focus on global justice issues and challenged the negotiations over the proposed Multilateral Agreement on Investment, the WTO, and the Free Trade Area of the Americas (FTAA). Moreover, during this same time period, while Canada's governing Liberal Party evolved to become a leading advocate for neo-liberal trade and investment policies worldwide, Mexican civil society groups similarly found few political allies in a political system still constrained through the year 2000 by the hegemonic control of the governing Institutional Revolutionary Party.

However, despite these domestic political constraints, the process of North American economic integration created new international opportunities for cross-border collective action. On one level, NAFTA represented a common target, increasingly affecting the strategy and availability of civic allies who found solidarity in mobilizing across borders. Yet, more substantially, the NAFTA side-agreements on labour and the environment inadvertently provoked examples of formal and informal claims-making and popular sector transnational alliance building.

Both the North American Agreement on Environmental Cooperation (NAAEC) and the North American Agreement on Labour Cooperation (NAALC) provide a review process for civic groups to register complaints about alleged failures by one of the NAFTA state governments to uphold existing environmental or labour laws. While these agreements have no mechanism to punish states that lower environmental or labour standards in an effort to attract investment, civil society groups have still exploited them to highlight perceived weaknesses in labour or environmental rights enforcement. Citizen groups have had some success in this manner through the submission process in gaining media publicity and scrutiny of their concerns. Thus, again, the most unexpected result of these agreements has been the emergence and deepening of cross-border ties and cooperation between North American citizen groups (Compa 2001).

Specifically, these side-agreements and their corresponding institutions—the Commission for Environmental Cooperation, its Secretariat and Joint Advisory Public Committee; the Commission for Labour Cooperation and its three National Administrative Offices (NAO) in Canada, the US, and Mexico—have surprisingly emerged, in effect, as formal channels through which citizen groups can direct claims against state governments regarding the effects of NAFTA (Graubart 2002). The procedural demands of the submission process have encouraged a deepening of trinational civic ties. For the labour side-agreement, civic groups must direct concerns about violations of labour rights in one country to the NAO of a different NAFTA country, and this logic has provoked groups to reach across borders and form links with other groups to more quickly come to grips with foreign political, legal, and social norms. In the case of the environmental side-agreement, civic groups have similarly networked across borders to demand national enforcement of environmental regulations as well as more transparent and inclusive means for engaging the NAFTA publics in environmental oversight (Tollefson 2002).

Since 1994, citizens groups have filed dozens of complaints with either the labour or environmental institutions (Katz 1999). The cases have brought together a variety of groups, from the level of bureaucratic labour leaders to the grassroots. Workers and environmental activists have visited different NAFTA states to help in publicity events, petitions, or union drives and have engaged in both the formal institutionalized process of complaints submissions and more contentious parallel protests and picketing (Alexander 1999; Rosen 1999). From ad hoc and temporary protests to more formalized, multi-sectoral coalitions, these submission procedures have helped to develop a somewhat more routinized pattern of interaction between civil society actors and the limited structures of North American regional governance.

THE LIMITS TO FRAMING OPPOSITION TO CONTINENTAL INTEGRATION

The way in which civil society activists have interpreted the process of North American integration has also played an important role in the shaping of continent-wide popular action. Broadly speaking, the mediating role of what are called "framing processes" continues to be shown to play at least as important a function as a supportive political-economic environment in the successful structuring of protest. Framing involves "meaning work," a dynamic and conflicted process wherein activists engage in the production and distribution of interpretations that challenge existing understandings of socio-political conditions (Benford and Snow 2000). So-called "collective action frames" are produced from this active meaning production and aid in the identification and resolution of problems and challenges facing a certain subset of an agitated population. Collective action frames are developed when actors "negotiate a shared understanding of some problematic condition or situation they define as in need of change, make attributions regarding who or what to blame, articulate an alternative set of arrangements and urge others to act in concert to affect change" (Benford and Snow 2000: 613).

Negotiations over and ultimately the difficult arrival at shared understandings of the neo-liberal character of North American integration contributed to the development of an anti-NAFTA collective action frame between civil society groups. NAFTA, of course, was the instigator of this "meaning work" as it became a target for oppositional tactics undertaken by the wide cross-section of civil society groups across Canada, the US, and Mexico. Yet, a frame critical of the neo-liberal underpinnings of NAFTA was not widely shared at first between national groups. At the early stage of negotiations, between 1990 and 1993, many divisions existed both within and between national civil society configurations. Canadian groups largely opposed NAFTA, bringing lessons from the CUFTA battle to the debate. Many groups across the US betrayed a strong nationalist orientation and were divided in their intensity of opposition to the deal (Dreiling 2001). Similarly, Mexican civil society groups were divided on the proposed agreement (Brooks and Fox 2004), with the trade union movement largely supportive, whereas a budding grassroots critique embodied in the RMALC was more critical.

By the fall of 1993, a collective action frame critical of NAFTA had sufficiently taken shape to embolden groups across Canada, the US, and Mexico to engage in varied incidents of cross-border political exchange, lobbying, and protests against the deal. It was not a completely hegemonic counter-frame to the arguments put forth by NAFTA's proponents, and national-level variations persisted. Yet the contents of a more continent-wide frame coalesced around similar concerns: NAFTA's inattention to social justice, labour mobility, worker migration, and environmental standards. This is not to suggest that national and sectoral variations of a NAFTA critique melted away, but there seemed to have developed among North American civil society groups a common diagnostic frame that implicated NAFTA in many of the social and economic upheavals facing lower and middle income communities. Organizational developments towards transnational exchange, networking, and alliance-building helped to disseminate if not strengthen a continental conceptual consensus against the effects of NAFTA. The increased availability and use of the Internet—through activist websites, email, and listservs—also aided in the consolidation of an anti-NAFTA frame. The largely ignored if not unknown investor-state provision in NAFTA's Chapter 11 has also increasingly become a target of civil society complaints and mobilizations, helping to sustain anti-NAFTA framing (Gonzalez 2003; Liptak 2004).

However, the post-NAFTA context for the continued production and dissemination of a collective action frame against North American integration was in fact quite complicated. As early as 1994, the emerging negotiations over a possible FTAA began to expose the limits of the continental collective action frame. The drive for trade and investment liberalization across the hemisphere, while modeled after NAFTA, often pushed activists conceptually and organizationally outside the geographic political contours of North America. This fractured focus in part has mirrored the preoccupations in business and trade bureaucracy circles, which have been busy pushing for further liberalizations in hemispheric and global trade and investment regulations.

A significant amount of time, energy, and resources, therefore, has gone into such civil society projects as the anti-FTAA Hemispheric Social Alliance and anti-WTO coalitions, robbing emergent North American civil society projects of the full attention of citizen groups across the continent. In fact, framing has increasingly "gone global" with much more energy directed towards targeting, for example, unjust labour practices of multinational corporations, instances of child or sweatshop labour, environmental destruction, or debt relief for some of the world's most heavily indebted states. All of these issues are arguably tied together as products of neo-liberal free trade and investment policies. Yet, it has still become much more difficult to stitch together a geographically consistent collective action frame against global neo-liberalism or continental integration.

Conclusion: Towards a Continental Civil Society?

The difficulties facing North American civil society groups as they struggle to develop and particularly to sustain a continent-centred collective action frame are but one example of the many barriers inhibiting the development of a transnational community "from below." In addition to lacking a common project, other impediments to any widely consolidated transnational citizens' cooperation loom large. These include the persistence of asymmetries of power and resources between national groups and between the three NAFTA states, as well as the residual built-in conflicts of interest between and across sectors within the three civil societies (Bensusán 2002; Bowles, MacDonald, and Mullen 2002; Macdonald 2002). The persistent limits to transnational civil society cooperation are significant enough to raise questions about the permanence and future sustainability of these cross-border organizations and interactions.

Again, within the North American space, there is little evidence to suggest that transnational civic exchanges portend the emergence of a more interdependent continental civil society increasingly embracing shared cultural and political norms. Much of the membership base in many of the groups that would be considered to fall within the so-called popular sector rubric remains strongly nationalist in outlook, regardless of the sector. In truth, even cross-border labour cooperation remains limited—no North American umbrella federation exists, and there is little sustained contact between the three national labour federations. Trade is also increasingly becoming a more politicized issue in the US, with growing fears over the outsourcing of jobs and the broad decline in the manufacturing sector feeding nationalist and protectionist concerns (Becker 2004). Nationalists in Canada appear poised to oppose deepening integration proposals, while Mexicans grapple with growing manufacturing job losses, particularly to China (Malkin 2002), and the increased scepticism of the Mexican labour movement and farmers over further trade liberalization initiatives (Thompson 2002). Moreover, the growing income differentials across the continent and the persisting asymmetries of bargaining power between lower and middle income groups and capital,[8] suggest that the innovative transformations in political practices across the continent have not translated into transformations in political power relations (Ayres 2004).

Thus, while new transnational opportunities for popular sector collaboration across North America have indeed emerged, it is much less clear whether these opportunities for interaction have produced desired results. In other words, to what extent have these NAFTA institutions assisted civil society groups in the exercise of political and economic leverage across the continent? Recent evidence suggests a fall-off in citizen submissions, and questions have grown about the longer term possibilities for advancing civil society concerns through the toothless side-agreement mechanisms that have little capacity for punishing government failures to abide by existing environmental or labour standards (Finbow 2002; Markell and Knox 2003). Moreover, these NAFTA institutions are clearly poor shadows of the sorts of supranational governance structures that have provoked contentious politics across Europe. There is little pooling of sovereignty or accountability in the NAALC and NAAEC, and the more recent loss of enthusiasm for participating in these mechanisms highlights the constantly shifting contours of the multi-layered continental opportunity structure for popular sector activism across North America.

The resurgent statism following the 9/11 terrorist attacks on the US also has presented a more immediate challenge to further deepening the North American civic project (Ayres and Tarrow 2002). The vision of a modern North America, as a community of three countries recently drawn into a more tightly integrated relationship through NAFTA, has become strained. A defensive and agitated US has become much more conscious of the potential vulnerability of its borders, and tri-lateral relations have, at least in current Washington policy circles, taken a backseat to enhancing bilateral security, military, trade, and immigration ties between the US and Canada (Andreas and Beirsteker 2003). Despite efforts by President Fox of Mexico to sustain Washington's interest in deepening Mexican-US relations—an interest that had been apparently shared early on by the George W. Bush administra-tion—the events of 9/11 have currently lessened incentives in the US for deepening NAFTA and developing a more robust set of North American political institutions. The growing chorus within Canada's business community to push for some sort of "grand bargain" involving deeper integration with the US is also of limited interest to a country increasingly bogged down in the war on terror and ongoing instabilities in Afghanistan and Iraq.

What North America lacks, then, are the sorts of deep structures of governance and supranational decision-making procedures that would convince civil society groups that cooperative activity is an exercise in efficacious politics. Any moves undertaken to harmonize regulations to ease business transactions, with an eye towards prevent-ing the border gridlock in evidence after 9/11, will not be enough to generate a sense among civil society groups that they have a valued role to play in building the North American community. What is needed, albeit clearly not on the political agenda at this point, are dramatic moves towards the creation of a North American citizens' assembly that could at a minimum serve some type of advisory role to legislative and executive leaders in the three NAFTA states. A North American parliament with any effective authority over the national legislatures, however, is beyond political contem plation at this still early stage of the continental integration process.

Nonetheless, it would be foolish to ignore the activities, concerns, and goals of North American civil society groups, as any further moves to deepen North American integration from above would be necessarily a flawed process and project. Discussion on deepening North American integration has remained a top-down affair, largely discounting alternative popular sector scenarios for continental integration and fail-ing to represent the full diversity of voices that could be brought to discussions about North America's future. There are valid normative considerations involved in includ-ing the concerns and potential contributions of civil society actors in these larger debates. Yet, because the domestic effects of North American integration continue to unfold, it is likely that more episodes of politically significant contentious activity across the three civil societies will transpire, providing a more instrumental reason for considering the perspectives of civil society groups.

The goals and continuing dynamics of North American civil society group activity may be summarized as follows:

> 1. *Civil society actors across North America continue to target for conten-tious actions the most accessible institutions and structures of authority.* A look at the record of civil society contentious politics over the past decade reveals that civil society actors direct their protests predominantly at national governments. With the recent further removal of agricultural import tariffs in Mexico, continued controversy over the NAFTA Chapter 11 investor-state provision, and rising alarm in the US and Mexico over

the loss of manufacturing jobs, there remains a pool of potential griev-ances to fuel continued episodes of contentious claims-making against political authorities in the NAFTA states. Such state-centred targeting may encourage an increased role for the state in mediating between citizen groups as they demand that their governments act on their behalf.

2. *Instances of civil society transnationalism will continue albeit in lim-ited episodic forms in the absence of a further institutional deepening of North American integration.* Transnational protest remains an empiri-cally interesting component of North American civil society activity, yet the lack of North American political authority structures undercuts any possible move towards a more politically and socially coherent North American civil society. Transnational cooperation between Canadian, US, and Mexican civil society groups is certainly not indicative of a shift in habits of the broader North American population, much less does it her-ald any moves towards any transnational progressive social movement.

3. *Civil society actors remain a force for potentially shaping moves to deepen North American integration.* While debates over deepening North American integration continue to maintain a narrow focus, civil soci-ety groups may yet play an important role in shaping this discussion. If civic actors within the three NAFTA states begin to see that the source of more of their claims becomes increasingly located in the integrated North American marketplace, civil society groups may begin a more concerted push "from below" for more formalized and authoritative grievance-resolution processes and institutions.

In short, transnational North American civil society remains for many more wish-ful thinking than reality. That there remain significant impediments to sustained examples of transnational collaboration after a mere decade of shallow, largely eco-nomic integration is really not that surprising. What is perhaps surprising is the extent to which regional integration has affected national civil society groups, which have engaged in significant cross-border dialogue and constructed unique vehicles to defend their interests and pursue related social and political goals. Moreover, these changing patterns of North American-based civil society interactions speak directly to those who have asked "what's next?" in the study of North American integration, or, rather, just what are North Americans "doing together" that they are not doing elsewhere?[9] Developing cross-border relationships has at times proven more difficult than expected, and the impact of this contentious transnationalism has more often than not been limited. Yet, the ongoing record of exchanges between North American civil society groups does represent an important case illustrating the inability of states to contain all forms of collective action today under conditions of regional and global integration.

Notes

1 As quoted in Draimin and Plewes 1995: 79.

2 Cameron and Drache (1985) refer to popular sector organizations as those civil society groups that, under neo-liberal conditions, are progressively marginalized from economic and political decision-making institutions.

3 The push for deepening North American integration has received limited play in the US, with Mexican but especially Canadian political and business circles pressing the subject. See Canada 2002 and a number of the studies on deepening North American integration on the Institute for Research on Public Policy website, <http://www.irpp.org>.

4 See <http://www.art-us.org> for information on various campaigns in which the ART has been involved since it emerged during the NAFTA debate.

5 The Pro-Canada Network was renamed the Action Canada Network shortly after the CUFTA campaign.

6 See the Council of Canadians website for more information on the Our Canada Project and other campaigns, <http://www.canadians.org>.

7 A number of retrospective reports have analyzed the Zapatista's campaign at year ten. See, for example, the stories by Willis 2004, Sanchez 2004, and Weinberg 2004.

8 For examples of recent tenth anniversary reports that are critical of NAFTA, see the Hemispheric Social Alliance 2003, Audley 2004, and Public Citizen 2004.

9 See Molot 2002 for an interesting discussion of the need for a more creative research agenda on North American integration.

References

Alexander, Robin. 1999. "Experience and Reflections on the Use of the NAALC." In *Memorias: Encuentro trinacional de Laboralistas Democraticos*, Ciudad Universitaria. Mexico: Universidad Nacional Autonoma de Mexico. 136–66.

Alexander, Robin, and Peter Gilmore. 1994. "The Emergence of Cross-Border Labor Solidarity." *NACLA Report on the Americas* 28,1: 42–51.

Andreas, Peter, and Thomas Biersteker (Eds.). 2003. *The Rebordering of North America: Integration and Exclusion in a New Security Context*. New York: Routledge.

Audley, John, *et al.* (Eds.). 2004. *NAFTA's Promise and Reality: Lessons from Mexico for the Hemisphere*. New York: Carnegie Endowment for International Peace. <http://www.ceip.org/pubs>.

Ayres, Jeffrey. 1997. "From National to Popular Sovereignty: the Evolving Globalization of Protest Activity in Canada." *International Journal of Canadian Studies* 16: 107–23.

——. 1998. *Defying Conventional Wisdom: Political Movements and Popular Contention Against North American Free Trade*. Toronto: U of Toronto P.

——. 2001. "Transnational Political Processes and Contention Against the Global Economy." *Mobilization: An International Journal* 6: 55–69.

——. 2004. "Power Relations Under NAFTA: Reassessing the Efficacy of Contentious Transnationalism." *Studies in Political Economy* 74 (Autumn): 79–100.

Ayres, Jeffrey, and Sidney Tarrow. 2002. "The Shifting Grounds for Transnational Civic Activity." *After September 11: Perspectives from the Social Sciences*. <http://www.ssrc.org/sept11>.

Bacon, David. 2001. "Unions Without Borders." *The Nation* 272,3: 20–24.

Becker, Elizabeth. 2004. "Globalism Minus Jobs Equals Campaign Issue." *New York Times*, 30 January.

Benford, Robert, and David Snow. 2000. "Framing Processes and Social Movements: An Overview and Assessment." *Annual Review of Sociology* 26: 611–39.

Bensusán, Graciela. 2002. "NAFTA and Labor: Impacts and Outlooks." In Edward Chambers and Peter Smith (eds.), *NAFTA in the New Millennium*. La Jolla, CA: U of California P. 243–64.

Bowles, Stefanie, Ian Thomas MacDonald, and Jennifer Leah Mullen. 2002. "Continentalism from Below: Variations in Tri-National Mobilization Among Labour Unions, Environmental Organizations and Indigenous Peoples." Paper presented at the Annual Meeting of the Canadian Political Science Association, Toronto, Canada, 28–31 May.

Brooks, David, and Jonathan Fox (Eds.). 2002. *Cross-Border Dialogues: US-Mexican Social Movement Networking*. La Jolla, CA: U of California P.

———. 2004. "NAFTA: Ten Years of Cross-Border Dialogue." Americas Program, Interhemispheric Resource Center. <http://www.americaspolicy.org/reports/2004/0403nafta.html>.

Cameron, Duncan, and Daniel Drache (Eds.). 1985. *The Other Macdonald Report: The Consensus on Canada's Future that the Macdonald Commission Left Out*. Toronto: James Lorimer.

Canada. 2002. *Partners in North America: Advancing Canada's Relations with the United States and Mexico*. Report on the House of Commons Standing Committee on Foreign Affairs and International Trade. Ottawa: Public Works and Government Services.

Carr, Barry. 1996. "Crossing Borders: Labor Internationalism in the Era of NAFTA." In Gerardo Otero (ed.), *Neoliberalism Revisited: Economic Restructuring and Mexico's Political Future*. Boulder, CO: Westview Press. 209–32.

Cohen, Larry, and Steve Early. 2001 "Globalization and De-Unionization in Telecommunications: Three Case Studies in Resistance." In Michael Gordon and Lowell Turner (eds.), *Transnational Cooperation Among Labor Unions*. Ithaca, NY: Cornell UP. 202–22.

Compa, Lance. 2001. "NAFTA's Labor Side Agreement and International Labor Solidarity." *Antipode* 33,3: 451–67.

Cook, Maria Lorena. 1997. "Regional Integration and Transnational Politics: Popular Sector Strategies in the NAFTA Era." In Douglas Chalmers *et al.* (eds.), *The New Politics of Inequality in Latin America*. Oxford: Oxford UP.

della Porta, Donatell, Hanspeter Kriesi, and Dieter Rucht (Eds.). 1999. *Social Movements in a Globalizing World*. New York: St. Martin's Press.

Draimin, Tim, and Betty Plewes. 1995. "Civil Society and the Democratization of Canadian Foreign Policy." In Maxwell Cameron and Maureen Molot (eds.), *Democracy and Foreign Policy: Canada Among Nations 1995*. Ottawa: Carleton UP. 63–82.

Dreiling, Michael. 1999. "Unionism in Transnational America: Divergent Practices and Contending Visions in Labor's Fight with NAFTA." Paper presented at the Annual Meeting of the American Sociological Association, Chicago, IL, 6–10 August.

———. 2001. *Solidarity and Contention: The Politics of Sustainability and Security in the NAFTA Conflict*. New York: Garland Publishing.

Finbow, Robert. 2002. "NAFTA's Labour Side Accord: The Limits of Regionalism." Paper presented at the Annual Meeting of the Canadian Political Science Association, Toronto, Canada, 28–31 May.

Gabriel, Christina, and Laura Macdonald. 1993. "NAFTA, Women, and Organizing in Canada and Mexico: Forging a Feminist Internationality." *Millennium: Journal of International Affairs* 23,3: 535–62.

Gonzalez, Fernando Bejarano. 2003. "Investment, Sovereignty, and the Environment: The Metalclad Case and NAFTA's Chapter 11." In Timothy Wise *et al.* (eds.), *Confronting Globalization: Economic Integration and Popular Resistance in Mexico*. Bloomfield Hills, CT: Kumarian Press.

Graubart, Jonathan. 2002. "Emerging Soft Law Channels for Mobilization under Globalization: How Activists Exploit Labour and Environmental Side Agreements." In John Kirton and Virginia Maclaren (eds.), *Linking Trade, Environment, and Social Cohesion: NAFTA Experiences, Global Challenges*. Burlington, VT: Ashgate.

Hathaway, Dale. 2000. *Allies Across the Border: Mexico's "Authentic Labor Front" and Global Solidarity*. Cambridge, MA: South End Press.

Hemispheric Social Alliance. 2003. *Lessons from NAFTA: The High Cost of "Free" Trade.* <http://www.asc-hsa.org>.

Howard, Leslie. 1998. "Transnational Civil Society, Neoliberal Hegemony, and Resistance: The Role of Mexican-Canadian Civil Linkages." Paper presented at the Joint Conference of the Canadian Association of Latin American and Caribbean Studies and Canadian Association for Mexican Studies, Vancouver, British Columbia, 19–22 March.

Hunter, Allen. 1995. "Globalization from Below? Promises and Perils of the New Internationalism." *Social Policy* 6: 6–13.

Imig, Doug, and Sidney Tarrow (Eds.). 2001. *Contentious Europeans: Protest and Politics in an Emerging Polity.* Lanham, MD: Rowman and Littlefield.

Johnston, Josée. 2000. "Pedagogical Guerrillas, Armed Democrats, and Revolutionary Counterpublics: Examining Paradox in the Zapatista Uprising in Chiapas Mexico." *Theory and Society* 29: 463–505.

Kamel, Rachel, and Anya Hoffman (Eds.). 1999. *The Maquiladora Reader: Cross-Border Organizing Since NAFTA.* Philadelphia, PA: American Friends Service Committee.

Katz, Sheila. 1999. "NAALC in Canada." In *Memorias: Encuentro Trinacional de Laboralistas Democraticos*, Ciudad Universitaria. Mexico: Universidad Nacional Autonoma de Mexico. 167–83.

Khagram, Sanjeev, James Riker, and Kathryn Sikkink (Eds.). 2002. *Restructuring World Politics: Transnational Social Movements, Networks, and Norms.* Minneapolis, MN: U of Minnesota P.

Kidder, Thalia, and Mary McGinn. 1995. "In the Wake of NAFTA: Transnational Workers Networks." *Social Policy* (Summer): 14–21.

Lemus, María de la Lux Arriaga. 1999. "NAFTA and the Trinational Coalition to Defend Public Education." *Social Justice* 26,3: 145–55.

Liptak, Adam. 2004. "NAFTA Tribunals Stir US Worries." *New York Times*, 18 April: A1.

MacDonald, Ian Thomas. 2003. "NAFTA and the Emergence of Continental Labor Cooperation." *American Review of Canadian Studies* 33,2: 173–96.

Macdonald, Laura. 1994. "Non-governmental Organizations: Agents of a 'New Development'?" Ottawa: Canadian Council for International Cooperation.

——. 2002. "Globalization and Social Movements: Comparing Women's Movements' Responses to NAFTA in Mexico, the USA, and Canada." *International Feminist Journal of Politics* 4,2: 151–72.

Malkin, Elisabeth. 2002. "Manufacturing Jobs are Exiting Mexico." *New York Times*, 5 November: W1.

Markell, David, and John Knox (Eds.). 2003. *Greening NAFTA: The North American Commission on Environmental Cooperation.* Palo Alto, CA: Stanford UP.

Massicotte, Marie-Josée. 2003. "Local Organizing and Global Struggles: Coalition-Building for Social Justice in the Americas." In Gordon Laxer and Sandra Halperin (eds.), *Global Civil Society and Its Limits.* Basingstoke, UK: Palgrave. 105–25.

McAdam, Doug. 1982. *Political Process and the Development of Black Insurgency.* Chicago, IL: U of Chicago P.

McAdam, Doug, John McCarthy, and Mayer Zald. 1996. "Introduction: Opportunities, Mobilizing Structures, and Framing Processes—Towards a Synthetic, Comparative Perspective on Social Movements." In Doug McAdam, John McCarthy, and Mayer Zald (eds.), *Comparative Perspectives on Social Movements: Political Opportunities, Mobilizing Structures, and Cultural Framings.* New York: Cambridge UP. 1–20.

Molot, Maureen. 2002. "Review of Guy Poitras, *Inventing North America: Canada, Mexico and the United States.* Boulder: Lynne Rienner, 2001." *Canadian Journal of Political Science* 35,4: 914–15.

O'Brien, Robert. 2000. "The Agency of Labor in a Changing Global Order." In Richard Stubbs and Geoffrey Underhill (eds.), *Political Economy and the Changing Global Order.* 2nd ed. Toronto: Oxford UP. 38–47.

Otero, Gerardo (Ed.). 2004. *Mexico in Transition: Neoliberal Globalism, the State, and Civil Society*. London: Zed Books.

Public Citizen. 2004. "NAFTA at Ten Series." <http://www.citizen.org/trade/nafta>.

Rochon, Thomas. 1988. *Mobilizing for Peace: The Antinuclear Movements in Western Europe*. Princeton, NJ: Princeton UP.

Ronfeldt, D., and Cathryn Thorup. 1994. "NGOs, Civil Society Networks, and the Future of North America." In R. Dobell and Mark Neufeld (eds.), *Transborder Citizens: Networks and New Institutions in North America*. Lantzville, BC: Oolichan Books. 21–39.

Rosen, Fred. 1999. "The Underside of NAFTA: A Budding Cross-Border Resistance." *NACLA Report on the Americas* 32,4: 37–39.

Rupert, Mark. 2000. *Ideologies of Globalization: Contending Visions of a New World Order*. New York: Routledge.

Salazar, Hilda, and Laura Carlsen (Eds.). 2001. *The Social and Environmental Impacts of NAFTA: Grassroots Responses to Economic Integration*. Mexico: Red Mexicana de Acción Frente al Libre Comercio.

Sanchez, Mary Ann Tenuto. 2004. "The Zapatistas Construct Another World." *Left Turn* 12 (March/April): 50–52.

Sinclair, Jim (Ed.). 1992. *Crossing the Line: Canada and Free Trade with Mexico*. Vancouver: New Star Books.

Smith, Jackie. 2001. "Globalizing Resistance: The Battle of Seattle and the Future of Social Movements." *Mobilization* 6,1: 1–20.

Smith, Jackie, Charles Chatfield, and Ron Pagnucco (Eds.). 1997. *Transnational Social Movements and World Politics: Solidarity Beyond the State*. Syracuse, NY: Syracuse UP.

Smith, Jackie, and Hank Johnston (Eds.). 2002. *Globalization and Resistance: Transnational Dimensions of Social Movements*. Lanham, MD: Rowman and Littlefield.

Stevis, Dimitris, and Terry Boswell. 2001. "From National Resistance to International Labor Politics." In Barry Gills (ed.), *Globalization and the Politics of Resistance*. Basingstoke, UK: Palgrave. 150–70.

Tarrow, Sidney. 1996. "Social Movements in Contentious Politics: A Review Article." *American Political Science Review* 90,1: 1–10.

——. 1998. *Power in Movement: Social Movements and Contentious Politics*. 2nd ed. Cambridge: Cambridge UP.

——. 2001. "Transnational Politics: Contention and Institutions in International Politics." *Annual Review of Political Science* 4: 1–20.

Thompson, Ginger. 2001. "Mexican Labor Protest Gets Results: Workers at Nike-Reebok Contractor Attract Activists from the US." *New York Times*, 8 October.

——. 2002. "NAFTA to Open Floodgates, Engulfing Rural Mexico." *New York Times*, 19 December: A3.

Thorup, Cathryn. 1991. "The Politics of Free Trade and the Dynamics of Cross-Border Coalitions in US-Mexican Relations." *The Columbia Journal of World Business* 26,11: 12–26.

Tollefson, Chris. 2002. "Stormy Weather: The Recent History of the Citizen Submission Process of the North American Agreement on Environmental Cooperation." In John Kirton and Virginia Maclaren (eds.), *Linking Trade, Environment and Social Cohesion: NAFTA Experiences, Global Challenges*. Burlington, VT: Ashgate.

Weinberg, Bill. 2004. "Zapatistas and the Globalization of Resistance." <http://www.futurenet.org/29globalhope/weinberg.htm>.

Willis, Andrew. 2004. "Zapatista Retrospective: Rebellion for the Possibility of Tomorrow." *Left Turn* 12 (March/April): 42–48.

Wise, Timothy, Hilda Salazar, and Laura Carlsen (Eds.). 2003. *Confronting Globalization: Economic Integration and Popular Resistance in Mexico*. Bloomfield, CT: Kumarian Press.

CHAPTER TWENTY

Performing North America as Community[1]

Janine Brodie

In March 2005, Mexican President Vicente Fox, US President George W. Bush, and Canadian Prime Minister Paul Martin met in Waco, Texas to sign the Security and Prosperity Partnership of North America (SPP). The SPP initiative had been spearheaded by a powerful coalition of Canadian business leaders, key actors in the Canadian federal government, and influential think tanks that mounted a concerted campaign to push for deeper continental integration with the US after 9/11. Unlike the periods leading up to the implementation of CUFTA (1989) and NAFTA (1994), both of which were sold to the public solely as trade deals, this twenty-first-century drive for deeper continental integration involves a much broader policy terrain and is cast in the language of community, especially North America as a security community. This chapter argues that the flurry of conferences, reports, and government initiatives, which invite us to "think North American," are largely performative. By this I mean that contemporary references to North America as a distinct geopolitical space, with shared values and interests, aim to create this entity rather than describe it. As this chapter explains, these concerted attempts to forge a vision of a North American community have congealed around a particular performance of North America—one which conflates economic security with secure borders and equates security with anti-terrorist initiatives. However flawed, this vision is realizing a far deeper form of economic integration than ever was envisioned by NAFTA or sanctioned by the Canadian public.

The signing of the SPP and the series of integration initiatives that it has set in motion followed on the heels of an unprecedented deluge of appeals in Canada to "think North American," beginning in late 2001. In 2002, for example, the C.D. Howe Institute, a business-funded neo-liberal think tank, launched its *Border Papers* series to examine a broad range of economic and security issues affecting the NAFTA partnership. Later that year, the Canadian Council of Chief Executives (CCCE), a premier flagship organization of corporate Canada, announced that "redefining Canada's role and responsibility in North America [was] the country's most urgent priority" and launched its *North American Security Initiative* (SPI). The CCCE actively campaigned for "a common North American vision" and, in 2004, published a comprehensive report, *New Frontiers*, which, among many other things, called for a "reinvented border" between Canada and the United States" (CCCE 2004). In October 2003, the Montreal-based Institute for Research in Public Policy, headed by Hugh Segal, a former advisor to Brian Mulroney, launched a research agenda entitled "Thinking North America," which was published as a boxed set in 2005 (Courchene *et al.* 2005). At the same time, other corporate-funded researchers called for a "reshaping of North American economic space" (Dobson 2003) and for thinking about a "deeper and broader" North American citizenship (Schwanen 2004: 1).

Similarly, the federal government's Standing Committee on Foreign Affairs and International Trade held cross-country hearings and issued a report entitled "Partners in North America" (Canada 2002), while the Policy Research Initiative (PRI), then an influential research arm of the Privy Council Office, launched a research theme on North American integration in 2001, hosted conferences, and published a series of reports on the benefits of deeper continental integration (Horizons 2003, 2004). These initiatives were buttressed by the 2005 report of a trilateral Independent Task Force, sponsored by the US-based Council of Foreign Relations, entitled "Building a North American Community" (ITF 2005). As this chapter explains, each of these initiatives variously evoked North America as a coherent entity—as community—but this descriptor represents much more than literary licence. These images both prescribe and underlie an aggressive continentalist agenda that reaches well beyond the ever-illusive goals of securing open markets and achieving economic efficiencies for Canadian business. They are designed to construct North America as a securitized transnational region within the contemporary global political economy.

Before outlining the ways in which a North American community has been variously performed on the Canadian stage, the chapter first reviews the history of North American integration and critiques streams of thinking that represent continentalization as somehow natural or inevitable. Instead, I argue that the deepening of North American economic integration during the past century embodies the strategic calculations of political and business elites to secure export markets for Canadian resources, goods, and services. Such calculations, as we will see, are always partial, temporary, and vulnerable to resistance and unintended consequences, if not outright failure (Jessop 2002). Contemporary representations of North America as community thus can be understood as yet another attempt to grasp the "holy grail" that has eluded Canadian policy-makers since before Confederation, namely, economic certainty understood as secure access to the US market.

In Search of the Holy Grail

In 1910, Sir Wilfrid Laurier's federal Liberal Party negotiated a new trading agreement with the US, which opened that market to Canadian resources and considerably reduced tariffs on US-manufactured goods entering Canada. During the federal election the following year, Laurier promised that there would be "no more pilgrimages to Washington" (quoted in Randall 2000: 34). Despite this sincere assurance, Laurier's government and his free trade proposal were roundly defeated by the Conservatives who had rallied the electorate under the banner of "no truck nor trade with the Yankees." The 1911 free trade election thereafter entered the collective Canadian memory as a reminder of the fate that awaited any political party that dared to place free trade with the US at the centre of their electoral platform.

Of course, Laurier was not the first Canadian prime minister to seek a secure and open market for Canadian exports in the US. Neither would he be the last. Canadian politicians made pilgrimages to Washington to gain secure access to the US market twice before Confederation, twice during Canada's first decade, again in 1911 and 1935, and during World War II. None of these adventures, however, resulted in sustained or secure access. The successful negotiation of the 1989 CUFTA was thus a rather unique moment in the history of relations between the two countries.

The CUFTA found its genesis in the economic crisis of the 1970s. Throughout the decade, rising oil prices, competition from newly industrializing countries, the economic revival of Japan and Europe, and stagflation (inflation + unemployment) combined to erode the efficacy of postwar economic strategies in both the US and Canada. Growth stalled, and, facing a growing balance-of-payments deficit, the US increased tariffs and offered its multinational corporations tax concessions to bring investment and jobs back to US soil. In response, Canadian officials quickly began to search for new international trading partners, but proponents of the so-called "Third Option" soon discovered that there was little room in the increasingly powerful trading blocs of Europe and the Asia-Pacific for Canadian goods. Seemingly without alternatives, in 1982, the Trudeau government appointed Donald Macdonald, a former Liberal finance minister, to head the Royal Commission on the Economic Union and Development Prospects for Canada (hereafter the Macdonald Commission) and charged it with recommending "appropriate national goals and policies for economic development" (Canada 1985: Appendix A).

As alternatives to the status quo of "Canada's increasingly isolated position in the international economy," the Macdonald Commission assessed the costs and benefits of three potential development strategies—import substitution, enhanced multilateral trade liberalization, and free trade with the US. The commissioners rejected "unequivocally a general policy of import substitution" while casting doubts as to whether the necessarily protracted and uncertain multilateral approach would achieve reductions in non-tariff barriers or increase foreign trade. Instead, the commission opted for freer trade with the US, reasoning that "Canadians are wealthier because of the Americans, but we are also vulnerable to changes in their fortunes" (Canada 1985: 271–82). A comprehensive free trade agreement, it was argued, need not compromise Canadian political and social norms. Rather, a trade deal promised to reduce the exposure of Canadian exporters to non-tariff barriers and countervailing duties in the US, maintain and increase access to the US market, and increase the productivity and competitiveness of Canadian firms in North America and globally (Canada 1985: 313, 323–24).

The Macdonald Commission also explored the relative merits of different kinds of free trade arrangements, among them a common market, a customs union, and sectoral free trade. The first two options were considered to be a threat to Canadian sovereignty, while the last was judged to be insufficient (Canada 1985: 305–06). It recommended that only broad-based free trade negotiation would promote productive bargaining with the US and reiterated that freer trade with the US was the only viable development strategy left to Canada in the late twentieth century. A bilateral free trade agreement promised to realize the ever-elusive goal of increasing and securing access to the US market. Even before the release of its report, the commission's chairman, Donald Macdonald, frequently dared the public to take "a leap of faith" and support the idea of free trade as the key to Canada's future economic security and prosperity (Drache and Cameron 1985: xx).

This is not the place to review the politics of CUFTA or of NAFTA, negotiated five years later. Suffice it to say that a significant segment of Canadian business leaders and corporate-funded think tanks had been agitating for just such a deal for some time. The Business Council on National Issues (BCNI, later to become the Canadian Council of Chief Executives, CCCE) and the Conference Board of Canada, for example, were convinced that free trade would strengthen productivity and open markets, while the Progressive Conservative Party, under neo-liberal leader Brian Mulroney, embraced the plan as a central plank in its successful 1988 electoral campaign. All the while, the CUFTA was represented solely as a trading deal that would not impinge on Canadian sovereignty, social policy, or cultural values.

The crafting of NAFTA was very much an encore performance. Canada, it was argued, needed to be at the negotiating table with Mexico and the US to ensure that the gains achieved in CUFTA were not compromised with the inclusion of an additional trading partner. Neither CUFTA nor NAFTA were celebrated as the foundations for deepening cultural or political integration or for the eventual creation of a North American Community. A very broad coalition of civil society organizations and the weight of public opinion also firmly opposed the idea of continental integration. They were assured that the goals of NAFTA, as stated in its preamble, were solely "to create an expanded and secure market," "reduce trade distortions," and "enhance the competitiveness" of firms (quoted in Pastor 2001: 96).

In many ways, CUFTA and NAFTA were to end the pilgrimages to Washington by Canadian officials seeking secure markets. These comprehensive trade deals were celebrated as the gateway to a level playing field in the US market. Yet, as with all public policies, large and small, these agreements have brought both intended and unintended effects, as well as partial victories and outright defeats. The report card on CUFTA/NAFTA is thus mixed with respect to economic prosperity, productivity, and security. Canadian export trade has grown far faster than "the advocates (and critics) of the FTA ever envisaged"—from 25 per cent of GDP in 1989 to 45 per cent in 2000 (43 per cent in 2001).[2] The proportion of these exports going to the US also has increased substantially, from 73 per cent in 1989 to approximately 85 per cent in the early 2000s (Jackson 2003: 12). Moreover, Canada has reversed its chronic trade deficit with the US.

However, there is also a general consensus that free trade has failed to deliver on its other ambitious promises such as providing more and better jobs, increasing the productivity and diversity of Canadian industry, sustaining the social safety net, and delivering prosperity to the average Canadian or to disadvantaged regions. Most glaring, however, free trade failed to deliver on its central promise and motivating force— gaining secure access to the US market. As Jackson aptly summarizes, "from lumber to agriculture, the US still actively uses its countervailing and anti-dumping trade laws to selectively harass and penalize Canadian exporters" (2003: 23). Even when NAFTA and WTO dispute settlement mechanisms have determined that US trade barriers are ungrounded or excessive, they persist, leaving Canada without further avenues to seek redress. Under free trade, Canada has not been exempt from self-interested US trade laws or the parochial political deals struck in Congress that shape them. In fact, the partial resolution of the softwood lumber dispute in 2006 did not result from formal NAFTA processes but rather from high-level political bargaining. Many suspected that President Bush gave some ground to newly elected Canadian Prime Minister, Stephen Harper, to signal a new era in US-Canadian relations.

In recent years, the US has negotiated a number of other bilateral free trade deals that appear to displace or threaten its historically "special" relationship with Canada. The well-grounded apprehension that Canada was rapidly losing its special status in Washington accelerated after the election of George W. Bush in 2000, especially after 9/11. Immediately after taking office, Bush turned south to Mexico rather than north to Canada, extending an invitation first to President Fox rather than to Prime Minister Chrétien to visit the White House. Bush also incorrectly identified Mexico, rather than Canada, as the US's largest trading partner. Concerns that Canada might be relegated to the backseat in NAFTA only intensified when Bush and Fox, meeting on Fox's expansive ranch, signed a bilateral deal on labour and migration—the Guanajuato Agreement in February 2001. These developments gave substance to earlier concerns among Canadian business leaders that Mexico would prove to be a competitor rather than a partner under NAFTA.

If the shifting political sands in Washington raised Canadian insecurities about NAFTA, 9/11 consolidated them. It was one thing to have countervailing duties placed on Canadian lumber and quite another to have the flow of exports from Canada shut down at the border or slowed to a trickle. Moreover, after the attack, US politicians and media pundits pointed accusing fingers at Canada, condemning it for having porous borders and for being a haven for terrorists. Even though none of the 9/11 terrorists had entered the US from Canada, business and political leaders quickly tried to ease these fears. Almost immediately, the business community formed the Coalition for Secure Trade and Efficient borders and released a plan of action in December 2001 (Gabriel and Macdonald 2004: 88–89). This document bore a distinct resemblance to the Smart Border Declaration, negotiated between the Canadian and US governments, which appeared in the same month. This 30-point plan, much of which was already in the works before 9/11, included coordinating strategies to better secure the flow of people and goods across the border, safeguard infrastructures, and facilitate information sharing and law enforcement. It soon became apparent, however, that these measures were insufficient to allay US security concerns, which increasingly have constituted what is in effect a new kind of non-tariff barrier (Andreas 2002: 199). While Canadian elites were still preoccupied with economic issues, the US mindset clearly had shifted to a securitized-militarized paradigm (Golob 2002). The contemporary campaign to think North American must be placed within this context.

The Inevitable North America

Contrary to the assertions of neo-liberal fundamentalists, the creation of markets and the regulations that govern economic activity are decided through political processes. Over the course of Canadian history, the type and degree of interrelationships between Canada and the US have embodied the calculations and perceived interests of strategic actors in both countries. Increasingly, however, Canada's place within the North American continent is variously framed as merely transitional because of the natural and inevitable pull of continentalization, or the progressive logic of economic integration, or the irresistible forces of economic globalization. North America is a geographical space—one way to map physical space—but it also has been represented as an integral social or geopolitical entity, often through metaphors of nature. For example, in the vintage study, *The North American Triangle*, Brebner compares Canada and the US to Siamese Twins (1945: xi). This image conveys the idea that, while each country is distinct, they are, at the same time, mutually inter-dependent and share the same body—the North American continent. Importantly, Brebner, similar to many contemporary advocates of a North American community, omits Mexico as an integral part of the continent.

Appeals to the natural also are evident in more recent work such as Orme's study of "the New North America." He argues that "to be 'for' or 'against' greater North American trade is much like being for or against the weather." "Like it or not," he contends, "the continent's economic integration is fast becoming a reality" (Orme 1996: 1). The reference to weather, in this case, implies that continentalization is an immutable force beyond the imagination or actions of mere mortals. And, as we all know, it is folly to mess with Mother Nature! Finally, the naturalization of North America has been cast in terms of evolution and the attendant idea of natural selec-tion. We are encouraged to understand trade agreements such as CUFTA and NAFTA "not so much as radical departures" but, instead, "as additional steps in a long-term evolution" (Randall 2000: 33). In other words, trading agreements represent a stage in the eventual unfolding of North America as an adaptive organic entity with a destiny that outshines that of single national states in the competitive struggle for survival.

The naturalization of North America is closely aligned with integration theory, long a staple of the social sciences, which also predicts the inevitability of a North American entity. Integration theory contends that economic integration nurtures shared tastes, cultural icons, and values which, in turn, provide the foundation and motivation for political union (Hoberg 2002: 8). In the case of North America, grow-ing trade interdependence and the fusion of production processes are said to blur national economic boundaries, rendering the process of continentalization irrevers-ible (Cooper and Drummond 2002: 5; CCCE 2004: i). Integrationists remind us that, among other critical factors, the vast majority of Canadians (80 per cent) live within 50 miles of the US border, overwhelmingly consume US cultural products (95 per cent of feature films, 85 per cent of sound recordings, 60 per cent of television programming, 70 per cent of books) and, of course, are dependent on trade with the US (Hoberg 2002: 162; Randall 2000: 33).

Multiple and increasingly diverse cross-border linkages, Depalma confidently asserts in his book, *Here: A Biography of the New American Continent*, "are leading inevitably toward the integration of North America into a single, seamless entity" (2001: 14). Paul Tellier, then CEO of Canadian National, similarly noted that "our economy is increasingly integrated with the United States. This integration will continue. It is inevitable. It is irreversible" (quoted in Hurtig 2002: 133). Thomas d'Aquino, head of the CCCE, repeats what has rapidly become the mantra of contemporary continentalists: "North American integration is now well advanced and is irreversible" (CCCE 2004: i). The underlying trope of the integrationist thesis is that North Americans have grown so similar that they might as well erase the border and integrate on a deeper and broader basis.

Integration theorists predict that increased economic and other forms of contact between two countries builds trust and nurtures shared values which, in turn, provide the foundations for deeper forms of integration. And, indeed, the history of the development of the EU since World War II, beginning first with sector integration and then moving to economic and political union, appears to confirm this prediction. To date, however, there is little evidence that NAFTA is shaping common values or building bridges to deeper cultural or political integration. Such obvious examples of value divergence as same sex marriage, the legalization of marijuana, safe injections sites, the International Criminal Court, the Kyoto Accord, and the Iraq War seem to underline, in the words of US historian Gil Troy, that "the two countries are sounding more different—after 9/11 dramatically more different." A 2003 *New York Times* article concludes that "the nations remain like-minded in pocket, but the centre of gravity in each has changed" (both quoted in Krauss 2003).

If the initiators of CUFTA anticipated that popular resistance to continental integration would erode with time as the new normal became lodged in public perceptions, they have been disappointed. By all indicators, the values structuring Canadian and US public opinion are diverging, not converging. In his popular book, *Fire and Ice* (2003), Canadian pollster Michael Adams compared Canadian and US public opinion during the 1990s on a broad range of issues that tap key underlying values. He concluded that "Canadian social values are not becoming indistinguishable from the United States. Rather ... we find a picture of startling dissimilitude, and—even more startling—ongoing divergence. The two countries are actually becoming more disparate" (2003: 72–73). Adams attributes this difference to the US "society's absolute failure or refusal to postmodernize" (2003: 45). Both Adams and a similar study of the World Values Survey (1990–2000) found Canadians, in contrast to their US counterparts, to be more socially liberal, collectivist, morally permissive, and tolerant of difference.

This latter study underlines that, with respect to public values, the US is growing more unlike, not just Canada, but all industrialized countries (Boucher 2004: 47). The minority of Canadians wanting to become more like the US identify with the far right of the political spectrum (Nevitte 2003: 26) or are themselves economic elites. A 2000 Ekos poll, for example, reported that 37 per cent of Canadian private sector elites wanted Canada to be become more like the US, compared to only 14 per cent of the general public (Canada 2002: 43, note 14). The sum of these findings amounts to what Alain Noel has called the "paradox of integration": Canada has never been so economically integrated with the US yet, at least on the cultural/value plane, it has never been so different (quoted in Macdonald and Rounce 2003: 51).

Performing Globalization/Continentalization

Selective interpretations of the implications of globalization are similarly weighed down with a heavy load of inevitability. Sherri Cooper, chief economist for an influential Bay Street (Toronto) brokerage house, for example, supports her case for deeper continental integration by declaring that "globalization is accelerating and irreversible" (Cooper and Drummond 2002: D5). A necessary part of this argument is the conflation of continentalism with globalization. Hoberg, for example, considers North American integration as an integral part of the more general phenomenon of globalization. For Canada, he suggests, "globalization is 80% Americanization" (2002: 4). This convenient, if inaccurate, formulation positions the US outside of and unaffected by the multifaceted and ongoing processes subsumed under the broad conceptual umbrella of globalization, while stifling questions about whether Canada should look outward to global markets. As important, it ignores the influence of emerging economic giants on long-standing continental inter-relationships themselves. In 2006, for example, China displaced Mexico as the US's second largest trading partner and economic analysts project that China will replace Canada as the US's largest trading partner within the next decade.

Globalization is an inclusive and persuasive term that increasingly shapes the social and political imagination of the twenty-first century. As Massey explains, the term nurtures visions of "total unfettered mobility," "free and unbounded space," "instantaneousness," and the "annihilation of space by time" (1999: 33). Although these and other attributes increasingly resonate with some of our lived experiences (or perhaps more accurately, the lived experience of some), Urry argues that there are a number of distinct discourses on globalization that, for both analytic and political reasons, should be clearly distinguished from one another (2003: 3). For one, globalization is frequently aligned with the concepts of structure and flows, that is, with the growing density of international trade and production as well as with trans-border movements of people, objects, information, and images (Urry 2003: 4).

There has been widespread and uncritical acceptance of this account of globalization even though it is not particularly accurate (Massey 1999: 36). Capital and information may indeed flow instantaneously through and above national boundaries, but borders remain formidable barriers for people, especially for those in the South seeking to escape abject poverty, insecurity, and exploitation (Gabriel and Macdonald 2003). The vast majority of the poor, both within and between countries, do not experience free and open space but, instead, are increasingly locked down onto local terrains by poverty, restrictions on migration and refugee status, and intense border surveillance (Brodie 2004). Sassen similarly observes that two sets of rules govern globalization—one set regulates the flow of capital while another set regulates the flow of people (1998: 60).

Massey contends that it is not simply sloppy social science that explains the many discrepancies between, on the one hand, accounts of globalization as the irreversible transcendence of national borders and, on the other, the reality of fortified borders, especially in the prosperous North. Instead, she argues that the neo-liberal vision of globalization as inevitable transnational flows is "not so much a description of how the world is, as an image in which the world is being made." Having been raised and installed, this powerful imaginative geography legitimizes "in the name of (though of course without saying so) the powerful and justifies the actions of those who promulgate it." Moreover, this geographical imagination ignores "the structured divides, the necessary ruptures and inequalities, on which the successful projection of the vision itself depends" (Massey 1999: 40, 36–37).

These critical observations about the imagination and production of globalized space correspond with Urry's depiction of globalization discourses grounded in the concepts of ideology and performance. Understanding globalization as an ideology focuses on the role of economic interests, transnational corporations, and international financial institutions (such as the IMF and WTO) in promoting the idea that globalization is both inevitable and irreversible. More important for our purposes, the concept of performance understands globalization *as an effect rather than as a condition*, that is, as a project to be achieved instead of an entity or process to be described. For Urry, "the global is not so much a 'cause' of other effects but an effect.... It is continuously reconstituted through various material and semiotic processes.... It is something that is made" (2003: 6).

The idea of the global as performance, as part of the geographical imaginations of identifiable material and political interests, draws our attention to the fact that development strategies promote specific assumptions about how to achieve economic growth (through political philosophies and regulatory practices) as well as where, in real geopolitical space, that growth will occur and at what scale the rules governing the economy will be decided (e.g., local, national, global). The use of scale here refers to more than the familiar levels of economic and political organization that have been handed down to us through centuries of political practices and conflict. The scale where economic and political agendas are set is itself "the outcome of social struggle for power and control" and is always negotiated, contested, and regulated (Swyngedouw 1997: 140–41). Put differently, neither the spaces of economic activity nor the political mechanisms that regulate these spaces pre-exist or occur naturally (Jessop 2002: 179). They are the products of political imaginations and material struggles.

For many decades, struggles over space and scale have been neglected in thinking about national development strategies. This is because, for much of the history of the national state, both geographical space and scale were usually imagined and performed as national, that is, as coterminous with the territorial boundaries of the national state. The logic of the postwar Keynesian state, in particular, assumed congruence between national economy, national state, national citizenship, and national society (Jessop 2002: 54, 74; Beck 2000). Jessop calls this kind of congruence a spatio-temporal fix (STF) and argues that all accumulation/development strategies, implicitly or explicitly, advance one. Although such STFs vary over time, they act to delimit the administrative, spatial, and temporal boundaries within which economic development is anticipated and pursued, while externalizing certain costs beyond these boundaries (Jessop 2002: 48–49).

Development strategies are always partial, provisional, and unstable; and their inevitable failure to sustain conditions for economic growth provokes a search for new strategies, new institutional compromises, and new STFs (Jessop 2002: 74). During such periods of transition, alternative models of development (and the material interests embedded within them) compete to realize a new and "better" STF.

These alternatives are invariably cast in terms of an "imagined general interest" which, by definition, privileges some identities and spatio-temporal horizons and marginalizes others (Jessop 2002: 30). The contemporary era, as Jessop argues, is marked by the very absence of an embracing strategy or primary scale upon which capitalist accumulation and social stability can be secured. In fact, development strategies in the contemporary era of globalization involve a number of experiments in governance, among them:

>> *debordering*: the emergence of new political spaces that transcend territorially defined spaces;
>> *denationalization*: state capacities are reorganized territorially and functionally on local, regional, and national scales;
>> *destatization*: shifting public goods and regulatory capacities to the economy, third sector, private sphere;
>> *internationalization* of policy regimes and regulatory capacities. (Jessop 2002: 181–200)

Each of these experiments, as discussed in the next section, informs the contemporary campaign to "think North American."

In summary, the research discussed in this section reminds us that neither continentalization nor globalization is a natural or inevitable way to organize contemporary economic and political life. Instead, this work invites us to think about North America as an "imagined geography" that is performed by and through the discourses, practices, and political manoeuvres of powerful public and private actors. This imagination reflects a specific understanding of a natural economic territory within an uncertain and increasingly competitive international economy. More tangibly, performing North America can be read as yet another attempt to seize the "holy grail" of access to a secure market, not this time through bilateral or multilateral trade agreements, but instead by shifting the scale of Canada's development strategy from the national to the continental, from interdependent economies to an economic region within the global economy.

Performing North America as Community

Although business elites and corporate-sponsored think tanks have underwritten an orchestrated campaign to "think North American," the idea of a North American community has not yet been widely debated in either Canada or the US (Golob 2002). Indeed, after an extensive cross-country consultation in 2001–02, the Canadian House of Commons Standing Committee on Foreign Affairs and International Trade concluded that "the North American project, whatever it turns out to be, is still to be defined" (Canada 2002: 21). In many ways, then, the flurry of reports, described earlier in this chapter, represent attempts by interested actors to promote a new STF—the debordering of the continent—as being in the general interest and to give meaning to the idea of a North American community that might resonate in the public imagination.

Community is a complex and contested term that attaches itself to diverse meanings and associations. The Oxford Dictionary defines community as "a *common position* in relation to something" such as a "body of persons" (e.g., a religious community) or "life on a scale" (e.g., all members of a country or a town). As Bauman points out, however, besides having a specific meaning, some words such as community also generate a particular "feel": "It feels good, whatever the word 'community' may mean, it is good 'to have a community,' 'to be in a community'.... In a community we can relax, we are safe, we all understand each other well, we are never strangers" (2001: 1–3).

For over two centuries, this feeling of community has been attached to a particular STF—the nation-state. Anderson persuasively argues that nations are "imagined communities"—they are "never natural" occurrences (1991: 6, 205). But, Anderson also makes a more fundamental point that is germane to our discussion—notably, that nations have been imagined *as community*. This imaginary performs community as being limited (with boundaries that separate the same from the different, as having members and non-members), as sovereign (with control over its destiny), and as knit by "a deep, horizontal comradeship," "regardless of the actual inequality and exploitation that may prevail" (Anderson 1991: 6). Imagining geographical entities as community thus transmits a series of coded messages that implicitly identify who are the insiders and outsiders, what the insiders share in common, how they are threatened, and by whom (Golob 2002: 1). As Anderson is often quoted, "communities are to be distinguished, not by their falsity/genuineness, but by the style in which they are imagined" (Anderson 1991: 7).

The orchestrated campaign, after 9/11, to give content to the idea of a North American community is a case study in public policy agenda setting, consensus-building, and implementation. The rest of this chapter describes three different visions of North America as (1) political community, (2) economic community, and (3) security community. As will be discussed, the latter two visions were progressively fused in the years leading up to the 2005 SPP, and it is this fused vision that is now being written into public policy.

1. NORTH AMERICA AS POLITICAL COMMUNITY

The idea of North America as a political community finds its genesis in a particular understanding of the formation of the EU. Over the past half century, the EU has developed from a modest sectoral integration to an elaborate transnational state, complete with constitutional guarantees of citizenship rights and political representation. Advocates of North America as political community assume that this specific and evolving story of de-bordering and re-bordering can be transported and replicated in different geopolitical spaces that have very different histories and configurations of political and economic power.

The US academic, Robert Pastor, is perhaps the most widely cited advocate of the project of constructing a North American political community. According to Pastor, NAFTA is fundamentally flawed because of its failure to provide either "a compelling vision" that defines the new North America or continental institutions that could translate this vision into politics. Following from the experience of the EU, which "did begin with an idea," Pastor laments the fact that North American leaders have not articulated "what the idea of a community is intended to evoke" (2001: 2, 98). The solution to remedy these flaws, he suggests, is trilateral cooperation in continental institution-building. Central to this process would be the creation of a North American Commission, comprised of distinguished individuals appointed by the leaders of the three countries; a North American Parliamentary Group, comprised of elected representatives from each of the three countries; a permanent North American Court on Trade and Investment, a proliferation of trilateral exchanges among cabinet ministers and senior bureaucrats; and, again miming the EU model, the creation of a North American Development Fund. These concrete initiatives, involving representative institutions of each country, would help construct "a concept of community" in the North American context (Pastor 2001: 99–107; see also Chapter 21 in this volume). As described below, the vision of North America as a security community explicitly rejects the EU model, especially the development of transnational democratic institutions.

2. NORTH AMERICA AS ECONOMIC COMMUNITY

The non-negotiable goal of most Canadian corporate leaders in the early twenty-first century has been to expand and deepen NAFTA in ways that would create "seamless borders" for the movement of goods within North America and, in doing so, prevent any future border closings, whether for security or other reasons. In other words, the drive behind this push for deeper continental integration has been unrepentantly driven by economic interests. As the CCCE underlined, "Canadian business leaders believe that our country's economic prosperity and global influence can best be served by forging competitive advantages within a vibrant North American economic space" (2004: 31). But, initially at least, there were differing views about how this could be achieved, especially in light of the US preoccupation with border security after 9/11.

Early on, Wendy Dobson's controversial April 2002 contribution to the C.D. Howe Institute's *Border Papers* series generated the most attention. Dobson, then Director of the Institute for International Business at the University of Toronto, argued that, however much Canadian business might want to reduce border effects, "Canada risks a dialogue of the deaf if it pursues an economic goal of deeper bilateral integration without taking account of US security preoccupations" (2002: 5). In a macabre twist in logic, Dobson proposed that the terrorist attacks opened a "door of opportunity" for Canada to realize deep integration, whether in the form of a customs union, common market or harmonized regulatory regimes, if it was willing to seize the initiative and present the US with a deal that they could not refuse (2002: 18). Dobson's "Big Idea" was that the Canadian government should enter into a "strategic bargain" with the US, pandering to the latter's concerns about borders, terrorism, and energy security in exchange for harmonization policies that would ease the flow of Canadian goods and services into the US market (2002: 24).

Dobson's proposal was deceptively simple: to keep the US from shutting its border, there should be no border (Pickard 2005). The US preoccupation with its physical security following 9/11 simultaneously threatened Canadian economic security and provided a rationale for implementing a deep integration agenda that otherwise seemed beyond the political reach of Canadian business interests. The security-harmonization nexus was quickly embraced and embroidered by the CCCE when, at its January 2003 annual meeting, Thomas d'Aquino told the gladiators of Canadian capital that "North American economic and physical security are indivisible." "Building the idea of a North American community," he announced, required Canada to take the lead in promoting a "five-part strategy for a new Canada-US partnership within a common North American vision" (CCCE 2003). This CCCE initiative, as we will see, effectively set the agenda for two intense years of lobbying, which culminated with the signing of the SPP in March 2005. The CCCE five-point agenda included:

» Reinventing the border: e.g., a shared North American identity card, shared systems of commercial processing, shared policing;
» Maximizing economic efficiencies: e.g., regulatory harmonization, once tested product standards, open skies agreements;
» Building Resource Security: e.g., further continental integration of oil, natural gas, electricity, coal, uranium, primary metals, forest products, agriculture;
» Sharing Continental and Global Security: e.g., cooperation with the US in defence and security of continent, rebuild the Canadian armed forces to enhance its capabilities in "confronting the terrorist challenge and promoting world order";
» Developing 21st Century Institutions: e.g., a rejection of European-style supranational institutions in favour of appointed joint commissions and bureaucratic regulatory process (CCCE 2003).

3. NORTH AMERICA AS SECURITY COMMUNITY

After setting the agenda, the CCCE took the lead in building consensus around its plan. Throughout 2003–04, it consulted business and government officials in the three NAFTA countries, meeting privately with a number of key members of the Bush administration. In April 2003, for example, the CCCE met in Washington, DC with Tom Ridge and John Manley, the authors of the 2001 Smart Border Initiative, in which Ridge had clearly articulated precisely how the US imagined a reinvented border with Canada:

> The border of the future is not simply a straight line between nations; it is a continuum that includes the airspace above it, the economic zones that surround it, the international ports of origin that serve it and the network of intelligence and law enforcement professionals who monitor and administer laws to protect it. (Quoted in d'Aquino 2003: 34)

In April 2004, the CCCE released the results of its consultations on its North American Security and Prosperity Initiative in the form of a discussion paper, entitled *New Frontiers*. The working document proposed a "comprehensive" new partnership with the US that would fuse together the CCCE's deep integration agenda with US security concerns and that would broaden the sphere of continental policy harmonization to include a continental energy strategy, a defence policy review, investment in a "credible military capacity," and North American defence institutions (CCCE 2004: 26–28).

Shortly after releasing *New Frontiers*, d'Aquino took Canada's corporate elite to Washington to engage in private meetings with its US counterpart, the Business Roundtable, along with leading members of the US Senate and such key Bush administration insiders as Tom Ridge, first Director of Homeland Security, and Richard Pearle, one the architects of Bush's pre-emptive strike doctrine and the Iraq War. According to press accounts, the Bush team told the CCCE delegation that security was their non-negotiable priority and that any new trade initiatives would have to mesh with and advance this priority (Clarke 2004). Moreover, apparently still stinging from Canada's refusal to join the "Coalition of the Willing," Richard Perle reportedly warned the blue chip CEOs that "in the future Canada had better realize where its best interests lie." US officials, including the US ambassador to Canada, made it clear that henceforth "security trumps trade" (Staples 2004).

The CCCE's intense lobbying around its agenda was followed in October 2004 with the launch of the Independent Task Force on the Future of North America (ITF) by the Washington-based conservative think tank, the Council of Foreign Relations (CFR). While it was represented as an autonomous research and consultative effort, the ITF was, in effect, a collection of deep integrationists from all three NAFTA countries that gathered under the guise of objectivity to pronounce on the future of the continent. Indeed, only one member (from Mexico) of the 31-member task force was widely recognized as an opponent of NAFTA (Pickard 2005: 8). The ITF was chaired by John Manley (former Canadian deputy prime minister charged with security after 9/11), Pedro Aspe (a former Mexican finance minister), and William Weld (a former governor of Massachusetts with close ties to the Bush camp), while co-chairs included Thomas d'Aquino, Robert Pastor, and Andre Rozental (President of the Mexican Council of Foreign Relations). Canadian members of the ITF included Michael Wilson, the former Progressive Conservative finance minister who had negotiated NAFTA (and who was later appointed by the new Harper government as Canadian ambassador to the US), and Jim Dinning, a former finance minister in Alberta and oil patch executive who, at the time, was widely considered to become the next premier of the oil rich province.

A month later, and with very little fanfare, Prime Minister Martin and President Bush entered into a "new partnership agenda" in which both governments agreed to cooperate in harmonizing standards, regulations, and security. This bilateral agreement, in turn, provided the groundwork for the much celebrated Waco Summit between the leaders of the three NAFTA countries held in late March 2005 (Canada PRI 2005: 20). In the resulting SPP, the leaders agreed to work toward:

» greater regulatory cooperation, including standard testing;
» strengthening North American energy markets;
» building a North American security strategy, including common screening of overseas travellers;
» creating inter-ministerial working groups to report within three months and regularly thereafter work on a "rolling harvest of accomplishments" (or ongoing regulatory harmonization).

In effect, the key themes of the CCCE's integrationist agenda, launched in 2003, had been transformed and legitimized as a formal international partnership, the SPP, by 2005. The fit between the two was not a coincidence. Throughout March 2005, d'Aquino had been criss-crossing the US on a ten-city speaking tour designed to convince the US corporate sector of the benefits of deep integration. In fact, d'Aquino took some credit for the SPP: "The comprehensive agenda laid out by the three leaders," he boosted, "represents a quantum leap forward for the continent" (CCCE 2005). The only difference between the agenda and the SPP was that the latter included Mexico in its performance of North America as security community. This fact was not lost on President Vincente Fox who, on the flight home from the Waco Summit, explained to the press that "I would like you to understand the magnitude of what this [the SPP] means. It is transcendent, it's something that goes well beyond the relationship we have had up to now" (quoted in Pickard 2005: 1).

The release of the final report of the ITF, *Building a North American Community*, in May 2005, following a year of research and consultations, was somewhat of an anticlimax. However, it pushed the deep integration agenda even further than the SPP, calling for "the establishment by 2010 of a North American economic and security community, the boundaries of which would be defined by a common external tariff and an outer security perimeter" (ITF 2005: vii). Not surprisingly, considering its neoliberal bloodline, the ITF recommended that this new North American community should rely on market forces rather than representative bodies, and that a trinational competition committee be established by 2010 to "promote healthy competition" (ITF 2005: 22). Other recommendations included the creation a North American border pass with biometric identifiers, preferential migration, harmonization of visa and asylum regulations, data sharing on foreign nationals, and additional border measures. As the report emphasized, "the three governments should strive toward a situation in which a terrorist trying to penetrate our borders will have an equally hard time doing so, no matter which country he elects to enter first" (ITF 2005: 8).

The ITF had held three meetings in preparation of its report—in Toronto (October 2004), New York (December 2004), and Monterrey (February 2005). Importantly, for our purposes, an internal memo leaked from the Toronto meeting showed that the task force members were clearly cognizant of the importance of performing North America as a security community. This first meeting agreed that, unlike previous trade negotiations, they should consider nothing to be "off the table" but also recognized that "contentious or intractable issues will simply require more time to ripen politically" (Pickard 2005: 8). The leaked Toronto memo also indicated that "members generally agreed that Task Force *recommendations will be taken most seriously to the extent that they are placed in the context of heightened concern about security*: for example, increasing regional cooperation on energy could be presented as addressing security-related concerns" (Pickard 2005: 8; my emphasis). The confidential memo also underlined the importance of creating a "shared North American identity" and the need to develop a "North American brand name—a discourse and a set of symbols designed to distinguish the region from the rest of the world" (Pickard 2005: 10; see also CIEPAC 2005).

The fashioning of North America as security community already has been played out in Canada through a series of executive decrees and bureaucratic initiatives, which have only intensified since the Waco Summit. During the past five years, the Smart Border Initiative has been refined and elaborated, most recently after the implementation of the SPP. The Smart Border Action Plan now:

> ... calls for common biometric standards for identity cards that can be used across different modes of travel, coordinated visa and refugee policy, coordinated risk assessment of travellers, integrated border and marine enforcement teams, integrated national security intelligence teams, coordinated terrorist list, new counter-terrorism legislation, increased intelligence sharing, and joint efforts to promote the Canada-US model internationally. (Webb 2006: 13)

Moreover, the implementation of a safe third country refugee agreement in December 2004, for example, which requires Canada to turn back political and economic refugees that arrive at its border from the US, is a direct result of the post-9/11 "smart border" regime. Although Canada prides itself as being open to the plight of refugees, this agreement effectively closes the door to those, many from Central and South America, who have to make their way through the US in order to apply for refugee status in Canada. This practice has been challenged in the Supreme Court of Canada.

The performance of North America as a seamless economic space is now commonly termed as "smart regulation" and has been advanced, as the ITF recommended, under the veil of or along side of security discourses. The SPP both formalized and accelerated the momentum to create a common North American regulatory regime. The trilateral agreement called for "regulatory cooperation"; "sectoral collaboration in energy, transportation, financial services, technology, and other areas to facilitate business"; and "to reduce the costs of trade through the efficient movement of goods and people." "This work," the agreement noted, "will be *based on the principle that our security and prosperity are mutually dependent*" (ITF 2005: 6; my emphasis). To this end, the SPP set in motion a series of working groups that were directed to consult with stakeholders and develop a harmonized "smart" regulatory regime. As requested in Waco, a Progress Report to the Leaders was released in June 2005 (Canada FAC 2005). The report identified approximately 300 initiatives relating to smart borders and smart regulations, including liberalized rules of origin, information sharing regarding product safety, textile labeling, temporary work entry, aviation safety, and harmonized air navigation systems. While this process of regulatory cooperation is ongoing, bureaucratic working groups are expected to introduce a Trilateral Regulatory Cooperation Framework in 2007.

Conclusion

During the early years of the new millennium, a powerful coalition of economic and political actors have begun to fashion a new North American geopolitical and economic space through a process of deep integration by stealth. Although the Canadian public has consistently opposed the idea of deeper integration with the US, this agenda has been both imagined and performed by fusing economic integration with the insecurities generated by an unstable world order, especially, the 9/11 terrorist attacks.

The proponents of this development strategy invite us to "think North American" and to imagine North America as a community with shared values, interests, and common threats. But, while the term community conjures feelings of safety and certainty, it can also stand for isolation, separation, protective walls, and guarded gates (Bauman 2001: 144). And, indeed, this latter image is a more accurate depiction of the North American security community that is currently taking shape. It is doubtful, however, whether this particular imaginary can foster either physical or economic security for Canadians. Closer ties with an increasingly isolated, unilateralist, and belligerent "American Empire," to the contrary, promises increased security risks for Canada. In this sense, the performance of North America as a security community has elements of self-fulfilment—deeper continental integration will likely increase external risks to Canada and, in turn, reinforce the walls of a continental security perimeter. As this process intensifies, as surely it will, Canadians have to engage in an informed debate about the kind of community they want and whether this community must or should be contained within a North American security perimeter. They may very well prefer to situate themselves in an evolving and more expansive geographic imagination of a global community, which is concerned with more pressing definitions of security, including human security and environmental security. Ultimately, I would argue, this is where Canada's "zone of security" should be performed.

Notes

1   I wish to thank Isabel Altamirano, Jason Bisanz, and Mel Hurtig for their helpful contributions to this chapter. This research has been supported by the Canada Research Chair Program in which I hold a Tier 1 Chair in Political Economy and Social Governance. An earlier version of parts of this paper appeared in "North American Deep Integration: Canadian Perspectives," *Asia-Pacific Panorama* 4:1 (June 2006).

2   There is considerable debate about whether these indicators of integration are inflated because these figures often double or triple count the value of manufactured goods, especially in the automotive sector, that frequently move back and forth across the border in the production process. See a useful discussion in Hurtig 2002: 390–97.

References

Adams, Michael. 2003. *Fire and Ice: The United States, Canada, and the Myth of Converging Values*. Toronto: Penguin Canada.

Anderson, Benedict. 1991. *Imagined Communities*. Rev. ed. London: Verso.

Andreas, Peter. 2002. "The Re-Bordering of America After 11 September." *World Affairs* 8,1: 195–202.

Bauman, Zygmunt. 2001. *Community: Seeking Safety in an Insecure World*. London: Polity.

Beck, Ulrich. 2000. *What is Globalization?* London: Polity.

Boucher, Christian. 2004. "Canada-US Values: Distinct, Inevitably Carbon Copy, or Narcissism of Small Differences." *Horizons: Policy Research Initiative* 7,1 (June): 42–47.

Brebner, John. 1945. *The North American Triangle: The Interplay of Canada, the United States, and Great Britain.* New York: Yale UP.

Brodie, Janine. 2004. "Globalization and Citizenship Beyond the National State." *Citizenship Studies* 8,4: 323–31.

Canada. 1985. *Report of the Royal Commission on the Economic Union and Development Prospects for Canada. Volume One.* Ottawa: Minister of Supply and Services Canada.

——. 2002. *Report of the Standing Committee on Foreign Affairs and International Trade. Partners in North America: Advancing Canada's Relations with the United States and Mexico.* Ottawa: Public Works and Government Services Canada.

Canada, Foreign Affairs Canada (FAC). 2005. Security and Prosperity Partnership of North America. Report to Leaders. June. <http://www.fac.gc.ca/spp/sppmenu-en.asp>.

Canada, Policy Research Initiative (PRI). 2005. *North American Regulatory Cooperation: A Results Agenda.* Symposium Report. Prepared by James Martin, AMC Consulting Group. December. <http://policyresearch.gc.ca>.

CCCE (Canadian Council of Chief Executives). 2003. "Security and Prosperity: The Dynamics of a New Canada-United States Partnership in North America." Presentation by Thomas d'Aquino to Annual Meeting of CCCE. 14 January. <http://www.ceocoucil.ca>.

——. 2004. *New Frontiers: Building a 21st Century Canada-US Partnership in North America.* <http://www.ceocoucil.ca>.

——. 2005. *Security and Prosperity Partnership of North America.* March 23. <http://www.ceocouncil.ca/en/view?>.

CIEPAC. 2005. "Summary of Toronto Meeting." <http://www.cipac.org/otras%20temas/nafta-plus/index.htm>.

Clarke, Tony. 2004. "Big Business Pushing Security Agenda." *Toronto Star*, 29 November. <http://www.thestar.com>.

Cooper, Sheri, and Don Drummond. 2002. "Lament for the Loonie: Duelling Over Dollars." *Edmonton Journal*, February 15: D5.

Courchene, Thomas, Savoie, Donald and Daniel Schwanen (Eds.). 2005. *The Art of the State, Volume II: Thinking North America.* Montreal: Institute for Research on Public Policy.

d'Aquino, Thomas. 2003. "Coaxing the Elephant: Can Canada Best Support Multilateralism by Cozying Up to the United States?" *Policy Options*, May.

Depalma, Anthony. 2001. *Here: A Biography of the New American Continent.* New York: Public Affairs.

Dobson, Wendy. 2002. *Shaping the Future of North American Economic Space: A Framework for Action.* C.D. Howe Institute. The Border Papers. April. <http://www.cd.ca (FIX)>.

——. 2003. "The North American Economic Space." *Borderlines* 2,4: 23–29.

Drache, Daniel, and Duncan Cameron (Eds.). 1985. *The Other Macdonald Report.* Toronto: James Lorimer.

Gabriel, Christina, and Laura Macdonald. 2003. "Beyond the Continental/Nationalist Divide: Politics in a North America 'Without Borders.'" In Wallace Clement and Leah Vosko (eds.), *Changing Canada: Political Economy as Transformation.* Toronto: U of Toronto P. 213–40.

——. 2004. "Of Borders and Business: Canadian Corporate Proposals for North American 'Deep Integration.'" *Studies in Political Economy* 74: 79–100.

Golob, Stephanie. 2002. "North American Beyond NAFTA? Sovereignty, Identity, and Security in Canada-US Relations." *Canadian American Public Policy* 52: 1–50.

Hoberg, George (Ed.). 2002. *Capacity for Change: Canada in a New North America.* Toronto: U of Toronto P.

Horizons. 2003. Policy Research Initiative 6,1.

——. 2004. Policy Research Initiative 7,1.

Hurtig, Mel. 2002. *The Vanishing Country*. Toronto: McClelland and Stewart.

ITF (Independent Task Force). 2005. *Building a North American Community*. Report No. 53. New York: Council of Foreign Relations.

Jackson, Andrew. 2003. "Why the 'Big Idea' is a Bad Idea: A Critical Perspective on Deeper Economic Integration with the United States." Ottawa: Canadian Centre for Policy Alternatives, June. <http://www.policyalternatives.ca>.

Jessop, Bob. 2002. *The Future of the Capitalist State*. Cambridge: Polity Press.

Krauss, Clifford. 2003. "Canada's View on Social Issues is Opening Rifts with the US." <http://www. nytimes.com/2003/12/02/international/americas/02CANA.html?>.

Macdonald, Laura, and Andrea Rounce. 2003. "Federalism and Transborder Integration in North America." *Horizons* 6,2: 50–51.

Massey, Doreen. 1999. "Imagining Globalization: Power-Geometries of Time-Space." In Autar Brah, Mary Hickman, and Mairtin Mac an Ghail (eds.), *Global Futures: Migration, Environment, and Globalization*. London: Macmillan. 27–44.

Nevitte, Neil. 2003. "North American Integration: Evidence from the World Values Survey, 1990–2000." *Horizons: Policy Research Initiative* 6,1: 24–26.

Orme, William. 1996. *Understanding NAFTA, Mexico, Free Trade, and the New North America*. Austin, TX: U of Texas P.

Pastor, Robert. 2001. *Toward a North American Community: Lessons from the Old World for the New*. Washington, DC: Institute for International Economics.

Pickard, Miguel. 2005. "Trinational Elites Map North American Future." <http://www. Americanspolicy.org>.

Randall, Stephen. 2000. "Integrating Canada and the United States: The Historical Framework." *Isuma: Canadian Journal of Policy Research* 1,1: 32–38.

Sassen, Saskia. 1998. "The Transnationalization of Immigration Policy." In Frank Bonilla, Edwin Melendez Rebecca Morales, and Maria de los Angeles (eds.), *Borderless Borders*. Philadelphia: Temple Press. 53–67.

Schwanen, Daniel. 2004. *Thinking North America*. Montreal: Institute for Research on Public Policy, April. <http://www.irpp.org>.

Staples, Steve. 2004. "Paul Marin, George W. Bush, and Fortress North America." <http://www. polarisinstitute.org>.

Swyngedouw, E. 1997. "Neither Global Nor Local: Glocalization and the Politics of Scale." In K.R. Cox (ed.), *Spaces of Globalization: Reasserting the Power of the Local*. New York: Guilford. 137–66.

Urry, John. 2003. *Global Complexity*. Cambridge, UK: Polity Press.

Webb, Maureen. 2006. "Security Overtaking Trade as Driver of Deep Integration." Canadian Centre for Policy Alternatives *Monitor* 12,10 (April). 12–16.

CHAPTER TWENTY-ONE

Beyond NAFTA

The Emergence and Future of North America[1]

Robert A. Pastor

For each of the three nations of North America, the decision to negotiate and sign NAFTA represented a sharp turn—almost a reversal—from previous policy. Canada and Mexico had long defined their vital interests in terms of autonomy from the great power next door. Both tried to keep their relationship with the US at arm's-length for fear that a close embrace would be suffocating. Mexico constructed trade and investment barriers and championed a political doctrine of non-intervention to keep the US from interfering in its internal affairs. Canada considered free trade at several moments in the twentieth century but each time retreated from the idea, fearful that US investment would purchase the country's assets. The US also resisted the idea of a regional free trading area because it believed that the optimal trading system was a global one, and as the world's wealthiest country and the initiator of the GATT after World War II, the US government wanted to prevent any initiative that could undermine the global trading system.

While NAFTA was a departure from past policy for the three governments, in a paradoxical way it also represented a wholly natural response to the logic of integration. The three nations already were major trading partners of each other, and the international trading system had evolved in an unusual way. Instead of one world, there were actually three distinct trading regions: the EU, East Asia, and North America. Most of each region's trade with the world was actually within each region. Sixty-one per cent of the EU's trade with the world was intra-regional, and 58 per cent of North America's trade with the world was among the three nations. Together, however, all three trading regions were responsible for about 80 per cent of the world's gross product and trade (Pastor 2001: 21). In other words, the world trading system had rediscovered the benefits of proximity, and the three countries of North America recognized that their competitiveness in the world required a higher level of integration. NAFTA was a framework to achieve that goal.

NAFTA's purpose was to dismantle trade and investment barriers, and that explains why it reads like a business contract. Its architects planned neither for its success nor the crises that would confront it. Trade expanded as its proponents had hoped, but the three governments failed to build new roads, bridges, and border entry points, and thus the costs of delays exceeded the tariffs that were eliminated. Although NAFTA fueled the train of continental integration, it did not provide conductors to guide it. As a result, two setbacks—the Mexican peso crisis of 1995 and

9/11—threatened to derail the integration experiment by disillusioning its members and erecting new barriers. In addition, NAFTA did not address many key issues—including the development gap separating Mexico from its northern neighbours, immigration, and energy. Moreover, the absence of any credible trinational institutions or any mode of North American governance has meant that the advantages of the continent were untapped and NAFTA's competitive edge eroded.

In this chapter, I will first explore the origins of NAFTA and the characteristics of the North American region. Then, I will evaluate NAFTA's impact on the region and its flaws of commission and omission. Finally, I shall propose an agenda for North America's second decade.

Origins and Characteristics

In 1990, when Mexico's President Carlos Salinas proposed a free trade agreement with the US, two years after CUFTA came into force, the GDP of the US was about 20 times larger than Mexico's and ten times larger than Canada's. Asymmetry, whether in size of the economy or power of the military, is the defining characteristic of the relationship of North America's three states, and history has provided reinforcement of this unevenness. In contrast to Europe, where its catastrophic wars propelled its post-World War II leaders to unify, North America has been divided by its history and, more precisely, by its memory of nineteenth-century conflicts.

"Americans do not know, but Canadians cannot forget," writes Seymour Martin Lipset, "that two nations, not one, came out of the American Revolution." The US emerged confident and proud of its revolution, whereas Canada defined itself to a considerable extent as "that part of British North America that did not support the [American] Revolution" (Lipset 1991). In 1812, the US tried, but failed, to annex Canada, and the fear in 1865 that the formidable Union army might trek north to try again to expel the British was the principal reason why Canadians sought independence, and why the British accepted it in 1867 in the form of Dominion within the British Empire. Both judged correctly that the US was less likely to make war against an independent Canada (Howlett, Netherton, and Ramesh 1999: 163).

Canadians remained wary of a close relationship with its southern neighbour. In 1911, Canadian Prime Minister Wilfrid Laurier lost an election for concluding a free trade agreement with the US. Thirty-seven years later, Prime Minister William Lyon McKenzie King refused, at the last minute, to approve a freer trade agreement, evidently fearing a similar political result.

Having lost its war and one-third of its territory to the US in the nineteenth century and having suffered several military interventions in the early twentieth century, Mexico's distrust of its powerful neighbour was deeper than Canada's. Because it has been less stable, prosperous, and democratic, Mexico also bears a heavier sense of inferiority and thus was averse to any proposal that would bring it into closer contact with the US. For this reason, any proposal from the US to reduce trade or investment barriers was usually met with a curt rejection when officials deigned to respond.

Given this history and the imbalance in power, perhaps the only way for NAFTA to be implemented was for the smaller countries to take the lead. And, of course, that is what occurred, starting in the mid-1980s by Canada. In the 1970s, the Liberal Party under Pierre Trudeau had given Canadian nationalism an edge that made many Canadians proud and others very uneasy. In 1984, a national election brought the Progressive Conservative Party under Brian Mulroney to power with a large majority. Although his party had also opposed free trade with the US, Mulroney recognized a change in the public mood in favour of experimenting with more open trade. Not only had trade already increased, but a second reason for pursuing an agreement was to prevent the US from arbitrarily shutting down trade in a particular competitive sector. President Ronald Reagan responded positively, and the two governments negotiated and signed a free trade agreement in 1988.[2] In the same year, Mulroney called an election, and the free trade agreement was hotly debated, with the Liberals strongly opposed. Mulroney won re-election, but by a narrower margin.

The reversal on free trade by Mexico and its President Carlos Salinas was even more startling than Mulroney's. However, when the debt crisis threatened to bankrupt the country in 1982, Mexico's leaders reassessed their development strategy and embarked on an export-oriented policy. The government imposed fiscal discipline, sharply reduced tariffs and limitations on foreign investment, and privatized state corporations. When Salinas took office in December 1988, he understood that the success of the Mexican economy depended on whether it could attract large sums of private investment, and neither Europe nor Japan were prepared to invest. He turned to Washington for a free trade agreement and for the key that he hoped would unlock the door of foreign investment.[3] The agreement was signed in December 1992 and came into force on 1 January 1994.

Evaluating NAFTA

NAFTA aimed to eliminate all trade and investment barriers and level the playing field on procurement, telecommunications, banking, services, and other sectors.[4] To secure the market, the three governments created a state-of-the-art dispute-settlement mechanism. Instead of trying to establish an institution for negotiating the reduction or harmonization of regulations, as the EU did, NAFTA selected a few sectors and harmonized the policies. The agreement was a minimum one that reflected the Canadian and Mexican fear of being dominated by the US and the US antipathy toward bureaucracy and supra-national organizations. It was an "invisible hand," classical liberal framework whose principal shared goal was the elimination of impediments to trade.

The vast literature on the consequences of NAFTA reflects to a certain extent the debate that preceded it.[5] In an astute review of the debate, Sidney Weintraub shows that many of the arguments of both advocates and opponents use similar criteria, which are related to the balance of payments or the gain and loss of jobs. Weintraub argues persuasively that these criteria are misleading and that a more useful assessment of NAFTA's progress would be based on its effect on total trade, productivity, intra-industry specialization, industrial competitiveness, the environment, and institution-building (Weintraub 1997).

With regard to NAFTA's principal goals on trade and investment, the agreement has been a resounding success. In 1993, Mexican tariffs averaged about 10 per cent, 2.5 times those of the US. By 1999, they had fallen to 2 per cent while import licensing and other non-tariff barriers were eliminated. Today, nearly all goods traded between the US, Mexico, and Canada enter each country duty-free. Agricultural products are the most sensitive, and thus freer trade in this area is delayed until 2008.

As barriers declined, trade and investment soared in all three directions. US exports to Mexico increased almost fourfold, from $36 billion in 1990 to $140 billion in 2005, and exports to Canada more than doubled, from $100 billion in 1990 to $244 billion in 2005. Annual flows of US direct investment to Mexico went from $1.3 billion in 1992 to $15 billion in 2001. US investment flows in Canada increased from $2 billion in 1994 to $16 billion in 2000, while Canadian investment flows to the US grew from $4.6 billion to $27 billion over the same period. More than 36 per cent of the total energy imports of the US now come from its two neighbours. Travel and immigration among the three countries also increased dramatically. In 2000 alone, people crossed the two borders legally 500 million times. But the most profound impact came from those people who crossed and stayed. The 2000 census estimated that there were 22 million people of Mexican origin living in the US. Nearly two-thirds of them arrived in the last two decades. As many as 600,000 Americans living in Canada were eligible to vote in the 2004 US election, which is more than those voting in six US states (Brautigam 2004).

Intra-regional exports as a percentage of total exports—an index of integration—climbed from around 30 per cent in 1982 to 58 per cent in 2002. As in the auto industry, which makes up nearly 40 per cent of North American trade, much of this exchange is either intra-industry or intra-firm, two other indicators of an increasingly integrated economy. Many industries and firms have become truly North American.

There are still other signs of an increasingly integrated community. After 75 years of single-party rule in Mexico, in the year 2000 a highly professional electoral service, trained in part by Canadian election officials, conducted an election that was very closely contested. The result was an unprecedented acceptance of the process and outcome by all Mexican parties and the international community and a peaceful transfer of power. Indeed, the Mexican election was much more effectively administered than the one in the US in the same year.[6]

The signatories of NAFTA deliberately wanted to avoid establishing any bureaucratic or supranational institutions. The core of the agreement was therefore self-executing or designed to be implemented by *each* government. With regard to the dispute-settlement mechanism, William Davey, a Canadian scholar, concluded that it "worked reasonably well ... the basic goal of trade dispute settlement ... is to enforce the agreed-upon rules. By and large, these dispute settlement mechanisms have done that" (Davey 1996: 288–89).

Both the Commission for Labour Cooperation (CLC) and the Commission for Environmental Cooperation (CEC) provide citizens, corporations, unions, and NGOs an avenue for presenting their complaints. Since 1994, the CLC has received 23 complaints—14 were directed against Mexico, seven against the US, and two against

Canada.[7] Both commissions have done some useful work, and NGOs from the US and Canada have helped their counterparts in Mexico to develop and pursue complaints. Both commissions reflect the caution of their governments. No one has criticized them for being too aggressive or trying to forge common responses on difficult questions such as pollution on the border or labour rights in the apparel industry (McFadyen 1998; Hufbauer, Orejas, and Schott 2000). Nonetheless, Mexico's environmental standards and capacity have actually improved faster than those of the US or Canada, not surprising given the initial level, but encouraging nonetheless.

Another institution established under NAFTA was the North American Development Bank (NADBank), which has channeled funds into the border area to improve the environment. On a parallel track, the US and Mexico negotiated the establishment of a Border Environment Cooperation Commission (BECC) to assist border states and local communities to design and coordinate environmental infrastructure projects. The BECC, based in Ciudad Juarez, Chihuahua, involves local communities in the development of projects and then seeks financing from the private sector and NADBank, which is based in San Antonio, Texas. Mexico and the US have each contributed $225 million of paid-in capital, which gives the bank a lending capacity of $2 billion. The combination of chronic poverty and rapid urbanization and industrialization on the border have created a multiplicity of health problems involving water and waste treatment, solid and toxic wastes, and air pollution. The two institutions were very slow in getting organized, but by 2000, 29 projects had begun or been completed.

During the past decade, Mexico has changed from an oil-dependent economy to an urban one based on manufactured exports. The impact on Canada was also quite pronounced. NAFTA deepened Canada's dependence on the US market, but it also helped diversify and internationalize its economy. Canada's trade as a percentage of its GDP expanded from 52.4 per cent in 1990 to 89 per cent in 2002, making it the most trade-oriented country with the best economic performance in the G-7/8 (DFAIT 1999: 1).

As for the US, its total trade as a per cent of GDP increased by 25 per cent during the 1990s. Those who predicted substantial job losses were wrong as the 1990s witnessed the fastest expansion of US employment in decades. While Mexico and Canada grew more dependent on the US—up to 90 per cent of its trade and with exports accounting for roughly 35 per cent of each GDP—the US also grew more dependent on its two neighbours, with whom it does more than one-third of its total trade. More broadly, many firms became continental and more competitive.

An evaluation of NAFTA should not be confined just to trade and investment criteria or the side-agreements. One needs to view NAFTA as the centre of a unique social and economic integration process and of an effort to redefine the relationship between two advanced countries and a developing one.

The flows of people, cultures, food, music, and sports across the two borders have accelerated even more than the trade in goods and services. In 1996, the first destination for most US tourists abroad was Mexico; 20 million Americans went there. The second most popular destination for US tourists was Canada; 13 million traveled there. In 2003, the same pattern held, although fewer Americans traveled abroad—only 15.8 million to Mexico. Of the millions of tourists who visit the US each year, the vast majority—20 million—come from Canada. The second source is Mexico—7.5 million in 1996 and 10 million in 2003 (Crosette 1998: IV5; Fry 1992: 78; Chicago Council on Foreign Relations *et al*. 2004: 14).

The increase in numbers of immigrants understates their social impact. While the overall population of the US grew by 13.2 per cent in the last decade of the twentieth century, the Hispanic population increased 57.9 per cent (from 22.4 million to 35.3 million) and the Mexican population by 52.9 per cent (from 13.5 million to 20.6 million). About 30 per cent of the immigrants living in the US today are from Mexico (Martin and Midgley 2003: 31). While half of all Hispanics live in California and Texas, during the past decade, the Hispanic population in Oregon doubled; in Minnesota, tripled; in Georgia, quadrupled; and in North Carolina, quintupled (Guzman 2001).

Remittances have played an increasingly important role in the relationship between Mexicans in the US and their relatives. The most recent Mexican government report estimates that Mexican workers send their families about $17 million a day; in 2000, that amounted to $6.2 billion; and in the last decade, it totaled $45 billion (*La Jornada* 2000).[8] A recent survey found that 61 per cent of Mexicans had relatives living outside the country, mostly in the US, and 21 per cent received remittances from family members working in the US (Chicago Council on Foreign Relations *et al*. 2004: 14).

The result of the social and economic integration of North America is that the region now represents the largest free-trade area in the world in terms of gross product and territory. In addition, North America is almost as integrated after one decade as the EU is after five decades. There has been a lack of compliance in some areas—notably, the US imposes limitations on Mexican trucks, vegetables, and sugar and duties on Canadian softwood lumber and wheat. Mexico restricts high-fructose corn syrup from the US. The principal problem with NAFTA, however, is not the lack of compliance but the lack of imagination or rather political will to address some difficult questions.

First, NAFTA was silent on the development gap separating Mexico from its two northern neighbours, and that gap has widened. Second, NAFTA did not plan for its success; as a result, inadequate roads and infrastructure cannot cope with the increased traffic. The resulting delays have raised the transaction costs of regional trade more than the elimination of tariffs has reduced them. Third, NAFTA did not address immigration, and the number of undocumented workers in the US jumped. Fourth, NAFTA did not address energy issues, and eastern Canada and northeastern US suffered a catastrophic power black-out in August 2003, even while Mexico imports natural gas from the US. Fifth, NAFTA made no attempt to coordinate macro-economic policy, leaving the region with no way to prevent market catastrophes such as the Mexican peso crisis. Finally, NAFTA was silent about security, and 9/11 threatens to cripple the North American integration process by placing new and formidable barriers in the path of trade and movement of people.

An Agenda for North America's Second Decade

The thread that connects many of these omissions is the lack of institutions. Meetings of the three leaders of North America are "photo opportunities" because there are no institutions to prepare a common North American agenda (Pastor 2004). North America is not a trilateral partnership; it is characterized by dual-bilateralism (US-Mexico and US-Canada). Even when the governments negotiated a so-called "smart" border strategy, they duplicated virtually the same agreements.

This failure to construct North American institutions was deliberate. Canada thinks it can get a better deal bilaterally, though there is substantial evidence to question that. The US is not exactly in a multilateral mood during the administration of George W. Bush. Mexico has been pursuing this, but no one else is paying attention. The architects of NAFTA also seemed determined to make the opposite mistake to that of the EU—which they viewed as being over-institutionalized, excessively bureaucratic, and interventionist—by creating no institutions.

There are good reasons to avoid the European example, but there is little chance of this happening. The two models of integration are quite different. In contrast to Europe, North America's model has been more market-driven, resistant to bureaucratic answers, pragmatic, and deferential to national autonomy. Nonetheless, North America should learn from the EU's 50 years of experience not only what it should try to avoid but what it should try to adapt. It should avoid excessive bureaucracy and a common agricultural policy, but if the three countries of North America are to become genuine partners, and if illegal migration from Mexico is to be curtailed, there is no goal more important than reducing the development gap, and the European experience is valuable in this area.

During the last 15 years, the income gap between the poorest and the richest countries of Europe shrank substantially, and migration was reduced. From 1986–2002, the per capita GDP of the four poorest countries of the EU—Spain, Portugal, Ireland, and Greece—rose from 65 per cent to 80 per cent of the EU average. The progress was due to free trade, foreign investment, and a huge transfer of aid at a level that ranged from 2 to 4 per cent of the recipient's GDP. Good policies by the recipients, and conditioning aid on these policies, also made a substantial difference, as one can see in comparing the spectacular success of Ireland with the mediocre progress of Greece.

Among the lessons to be learned are, first, that the number of institutions for providing aid should be limited and have a "sunset" provision. Second, the most effective projects were in infrastructure and post-secondary education (community colleges in rural areas). Third, funds should be concentrated in the poorer countries (half went to the poor regions of the richer EU countries). Fourth, macro-economic policy coordination and resources are essential to cushion the effects of volatility of the poorer countries. Finally, a community requires that all members assist each other because problems cannot be contained, and growth in one can help others.

There was a moment at the beginning of the Fox and Bush administrations when the two leaders appeared to accept these points. In February 2001, President Vicente Fox invited President George W. Bush to his home, and together they endorsed the "Guanajuato Proposal," which read: "After consultation with our Canadian partners, we will strive to consolidate a North American economic community whose benefits reach the lesser-developed areas of the region and extend to the most vulnerable social groups in our countries" (Gobierno de la Republica de Mexico 2001). Unfortunately, they never translated that sentiment into policy.

A true partnership in North America is simply not possible while the people of one of the nations earn, on average, one-sixth of the income of people living next door. Actually, the gap is much wider because one-third of the people of Mexico live in deep poverty. Mexico's underdevelopment is not only a threat to its stability and, therefore, to its neighbours, but its growth offers its neighbours the most promising market.

In the absence of an explicit development strategy, 90 per cent of new foreign investment in Mexico went to just four states, three of them in the north, which grew roughly ten times faster than the south.[9] The border became a magnet for emigrants from the southern part of Mexico. Why do companies invest in the border area where labour is three times as expensive as in the south, labor turnover is 100 per cent after a year, and congestion and pollution is chronic? The answer: the roads to the south are poor, and infrastructure (roads, communications) is worse. The World Bank estimates that Mexico needs to spend $20 billion per year for at least ten years to meet the infrastructural deficit. This lack of infrastructure, combined with a Third World fiscal system, an energy sector that is inefficient and unreliable, and rigid labour laws, has resulted in a drop in Mexico's competitiveness, and a diversion of foreign investment to China.

Mexico needs to grow at 6 per cent per year for ten years in order to reduce the development gap with the US by 20 per cent. A long journey would still be needed to close the gap, but just a consistent strategy that reduces it each year would alter the perceptions of Mexico and by Mexicans. A North American Investment Fund is needed to fill this infrastructural gap by investing $20 billion per year for ten years. The US would provide $9 billion; Canada, $1 billion; and Mexico, $10 billion by gradually increasing its tax revenues from 11 per cent to 16 per cent of its GDP during the course of the decade. This is less than half of what the Europeans have been investing in the south of their continent. Fox, of course, tried unsuccessfully to persuade the Mexican Congress to approve fiscal reform, but if he had the leverage of a promise of $10 billion per year from the US and Canada, the Mexican Congress might be more amenable. A new agency is not needed. The money could be managed by the World Bank. If roads were built, then investors would come to the centre and the south of the country, and immigration levels and disparities in income would decline.

The weakest link in North America is the lack of credible institutions, and the three governments should begin to fix that by establishing a North American Commission (NAC). Unlike the sprawling and intrusive European Commission, which manages and administers European policy, the NAC would be lean and advisory, consisting of just 15 distinguished individuals, five from each country. Its principal purpose would be to prepare an agenda on "North American issues" for the three leaders to consider at annual summits and then to monitor the implementation of the decisions and plans. The NAC would have an office that would gather statistics from the three governments, and it would commission studies of different sectors, like transportation, electricity, or technology. These studies would ask what could be done to facilitate economic integration in these sectors on a continental basis; it would submit these analyses with specific options to the prime minister and the two presidents. The NAC would encourage the three governments to respond to a continental vision. For example, in agriculture, farmers in a few areas cannot compete, and their representatives use all the legal and political channels possible to protect themselves. The three countries can continue aggravating each other, and subverting NAFTA, or they could negotiate a set of North American rules that modify their individual regulatory schemes.

A second institution would represent a merging of two bilateral legislative groups into a North American Parliamentary Group. The US Congress is the most insular and clearly the most powerful and autonomous of the three legislatures. The approval in July 2001 of legislation to ban Mexican trucks from US highways and a Congressional Resolution aimed at prying open Mexico's nationalized oil industry are just two examples of many that offend the US's neighbours. It is possible that a North American Parliamentary Group might become a mechanism for the three parliaments to deal with each other differently than they have in the past.

The third institution should be a Permanent Court on Trade and Investment. The dispute panels established under NAFTA are ad hoc, and it is proving difficult to recruit experts who do not have a conflict of interest. The hearings have finally been opened to the public. Some narrowing or clarification of the scope of Chapter 11 panels on foreign investment is also needed to prevent the erosion of environmental rules.

Canada and Mexico have long organized their governments to give priority to bilateral-issues with the US, and Canada has recently established a Director-General for North American Affairs. Only the US is poorly organized to address North American issues. In 1997, the Canada office was finally moved out of the Bureau of European Affairs and into the Bureau of Western Hemisphere Affairs in the Department of State, and in 2002, a Deputy Assistant Secretary was appointed to handle North American Affairs, but this official cannot negotiate on a par with domestic cabinet officers or congressional leaders. The US needs to establish a White House Advisor to the President for North American Affairs. That person would need to bridge the National Security, Domestic Policy, and Homeland Security Councils and chair a cabinet-level Inter-Agency Task Force on North America. No president can have much of an effect on US policy toward North America without such a wholesale reorganization.

Institutions are key to structuring the way governments function and address issues on a routine basis, but what would a North American policy look like? The first set of issues that the NAC should consider relates to transportation. "Crossing the border," concludes a May 2000 report by a Canadian Member of Parliament, "has actually gotten more difficult over the past five years." The causes are two-fold: "While continental trade has skyrocketed, the physical infrastructure enabling the movement of these goods has not." And second, the bureaucratic barriers that confront cross-border business make the infrastructural problems seem "minor in comparison" (Pastor 2001: 104). While some people have been critical of the US for imposing US safety standards on Mexican trucks, the true problem is that there are 64 different sets of safety regulations in North America, 51 of which are in the US. A

NAFTA subcommittee struggled to propose a uniform standard and concluded that *"there is no prospect"* of accomplishing that (Pastor 2001: 104; emphasis added). The elected leaders of the three countries should have been embarrassed and would have been, if anyone had been paying attention.

The North American Commission should review this issue and develop an integrated continental plan for transportation and infrastructure. The first step is for the US and Canada each to develop national standards on weight, safety, and configuration of trucking and then negotiate with Mexico on a single set of standards. Second, the governments should eliminate feather-bedding schemes that increase the cost of transporting goods across the borders. Third, the governments should plan and finance new highway corridors on the Pacific Coast and into Mexico. Fourth, the regulatory agencies should negotiate a plan that would permit mergers of the railroads and development of high-speed rail corridors between Canada and the US.

The establishment of the US Department of Homeland Security represents as great a threat to North American integration as does the terrorism it is designed to confront. In the immediate aftermath of 9/11, the US responded by virtually shutting down the border. Within hours, trucks on the Canadian side were backed up as far as 25 miles. Companies that relied on "just-in-time" production began to shut their plants. Canada responded first, by negotiating a 30-point "smart border" agreement with the US. The essence of the strategy, which had been developing before 9/11, is to separate low-risk goods and people; expedite their transit with transponders, sealed containers, pre-clearance, and other techniques; and concentrate inspection resources on the high-risk traffic. Mexico followed a few months later with a similar agreement with the US.

This strategy is too narrow to be a serious or enduring solution to what is fundamentally the same integration dilemma: how to facilitate the legitimate flows of people while protecting ourselves from terrorists and smugglers. What is needed is a broader approach to continental integration, first, by negotiating a customs union with a Common External Tariff (CET). This would significantly reduce inspections at the border and would eliminate the cumbersome rules-of-origin provisions. Mexico will have the most difficulty because its tariffs are the highest, but, fortunately, President Fox, the most visionary of North America's leaders, proposed a customs union and more. The negotiations would be very difficult, but not beyond the reach of the three countries, and it would accelerate integration.

The problem of transaction costs reaches beyond the issue of trucks and transportation. As the three countries deepen their integration, their three regulatory regimes have raised additional impediments, which are evident in the divergent approaches to trade in pharmaceuticals, mad cow disease, and softwood lumber. Part of the problem stems from the many regulations that customs officials need to administer on the border. The Canadians, for example, have to enforce 96 statutory regulations on the border, while US customs inspectors are responsible for 400 separate statutory requirements. Regulatory standards—from product safety to pollution to business competition—all affect the flow of goods. New approaches are needed to reduce the protectionist dimension while assuring health, safety, and security. These might involve new North American regulatory agencies or coordinated subcommittees of existing national agencies. The second decade of NAFTA will need to address the emerging regulatory agenda.

The US and Canada should also negotiate a convergence of their immigration and refugee policies. It will not be possible to expand this to include Mexico until the development gap is reduced, but in the meantime, all three governments could negotiate a "North American Passport," which could be extended to a wider group of citizens of the three countries each year.

For security reasons, all three governments need to focus more on the continental perimeter, and one way to do that, while at the same time eliminating the duplication of documents that comes with crossing the border, would be to establish a single "North American Customs and Immigration Force." This force would be composed of officials from the three governments and trained together in a North American professional school. Most important, if the Department of Homeland Security is not to become a fortress and insult to its neighbours, Mexican and Canadian perspectives and personnel need to be incorporated in some way.

Finally, our three governments could learn from the EU's project to fund five EU Centres in the U.S to stimulate research and awareness in the US of the EU. The three governments of North America should sponsor Centres for North American Studies in each of the countries to help all understand the problems and the potential of North America and view each other as both nationals of each country and also as North Americans.

Is any of this feasible? Since NAFTA came into effect, the opposition to free trade agreements has grown. Some people fear that they could lose their jobs to countries with low wages. Others fear that global development will have an adverse effect on the environment. Still others fear that a free trading system will be dominated by US-based multinational corporations. Efforts to deepen North American integration will undoubtedly provoke the same groups plus others in Canada and Mexico who worry that steps toward a community could diminish each country's identity or accentuate their vulnerability. The chapters in this book by Janine Brodie (Chapter 20) and Cristina Gabriel and Laura Macdonald (Chapter 16) capture and articulate such fears.

Are these concerns legitimate? Some stem from a fear of globalization. Certainly, as global competition increases, wealthier countries will lose unskilled or manufacturing jobs to China, India, and other middle-income countries. To the extent that workers cannot move up the value ladder, they will lose out as "producers," even while they benefit as consumers. Of course, the essence of globalization in the modern world is that there is nowhere to hide. Canada and the US did not lose many jobs to Mexico though they gained some higher value jobs. At the same time, all three countries have probably lost more jobs to China. The fear of cultural domination that one hears in Canada has a similar ring, though in this case, the workers want to be free to consume products from around the world, and a part of the intellectual elite, supported by those magazine and movie producers that seek protection for old-fashioned economic reasons, resist freer trade.

In an age of increasing integration, national governments should make sure that the gains of trade are redistributed to those who lose the competition and that regulations protect their people. Not all do that. Still, the premise of the "North American idea" is that the public of all three countries would be far better off forging rules to deepen integration than to rebuild barriers to trade.

Are the three governments prepared to give up their sovereignty for a wider community? The term "sovereignty" is one of the most widely used, abused, and least understood in the diplomatic lexicon. "Sovereignty" is not a fixed or immutable concept. Three decades ago, Canada interpreted sovereignty to restrict US oil companies from investing in Canada. Mexico used it to ban international election monitors, and the US used it to insist on "states rights" rather than human rights. In each case, sovereignty was used to defend bad policies, and yet changing these policies enhanced the prestige and prosperity of the country. Sovereignty, in brief, is a misleading if not a mistaken defence against an increasingly open and integrated world.

The question is whether the people of the three countries are ready for a different relationship, and public opinion surveys suggest that the answer is affirmative and, indeed, that the people are way ahead of their leaders. A survey of the attitudes of people in the three countries during the past 20 years demonstrates an extraordinary convergence of values—on personal and family issues as well as public policy. Each nation has very positive feelings about their neighbours (although this has changed somewhat since the war in Iraq). In all three countries, the public's views on NAFTA shifted in the 1990s. There is now modest net support, but a neat consensus: each nation agrees that the others benefited more than they have!

The most interesting surveys, however, show that a majority of the public in all three countries is prepared to join a larger North American country if they thought it would improve their standard of living and environment and not threaten their culture. Mexicans and Canadians do not want to be incorporated into the US, and they are ambivalent about adopting the US dollar, but they are more willing to become part of a single country of North America and of a unified currency, like the "Amero," proposed by Herbert Grubel (Grubel 1999).[10] The "Amero" would be equivalent of the US dollar, and the two other currencies would be exchanged at the rate in which they are then traded for the US dollar. In other words, at the outset, the wealth of all three countries would be unchanged, and the power to manage the currency would be roughly proportional to the existing wealth. The three governments remain zealous defenders of an aging conception of sovereignty whereas the people seem ready to entertain new approaches.

Other surveys by EKOS of Canada suggest that people in all three countries have begun to think of themselves as part of a larger community. In Europe, instead of renouncing nationhood, Frenchmen and Germans also think of themselves as Europeans. Similarly, 58 per cent of Canadians and 69 per cent of the US public feel a "strong" attachment to North America, and, most surprising, 34 per cent of Mexicans consider themselves "North American," though that term in Spanish has referred to the US alone. The surveys also outline a "North American model" that is quite different from that of the EU. For example, in considering 12 values, people in all three countries gave the highest priority to "freedom" and the lowest to government size and "redistribution of wealth" (Public Policy Forum and EKOS 2002).

The October 2003 survey by EKOS found that a clear majority (56–62 per cent) believe that a North American Economic Union is likely to be established in the next ten years. An overwhelming majority of the public in all three countries favoured more integrated North American—rather than separate—policies on the environment, transportation, and defence, with more modest majorities in favour of common policies on energy and banking. And on the issue of whether to develop a common security perimeter for North America, both Americans and Canadians favoured it by 3:1 and Mexicans by 2:1.

Despite this convergence and a popular desire to experiment, the three governments have devoted so much effort to defining differences that they have not found the time or energy to expand what they have in common. The market has advanced integration; it is time for the political leaders to address its externalities—including currency crises, development gaps, environmental degradation, terrorist threats, and infrastructural impediments. That is the challenge of the North American Commission—to sketch an alternative future for the entire continent that the people will embrace and the politicians will feel obligated to accept.

NAFTA built an economic foundation under a formidable regional entity. North America needs leaders who can articulate and pursue a broader vision. North America's second decade poses three distinct challenges—one for each country to take the lead. The first is for Canada to take the lead in replacing the dual-bilateralism of the past with rule-based North American institutions. If Canada leads, Mexico will support it, and the US will accept it. The second challenge is for Mexico to demonstrate how it would contribute to and use a North American Investment Fund to double its growth rate and lift its economy. If Mexico and North America succeed, then Latin America would have reason to ride the train toward a Free Trade Area of the Americas, but if we cannot narrow the development gap in North America, then the prospects are bleak for other middle-income countries. The third challenge is for the US to redefine its leadership in the twenty-first century to inspire support rather than resentment, fear, or unease. If the US can adjust its interests to those of its neighbours, the world will look to the US in more positive ways than it has since the invasion of Iraq.

These three challenges constitute an agenda of the greatest consequence for North America in its second decade. Success will not only energize the continent, it will infuse hope throughout the world.

Notes

1 I wish to express my gratitude to Vassia Gueorguieva for research assistance on this paper.

2 For two analyses of the issues and the agreement, see Wonnacott 1987 and Schott and Smith 1988. Both were published by the Institute for International Economics in Washington, DC.

3 This summary of Carlos Salinas's views on trade is derived from numerous interviews that the author had with Salinas from 1979 through 1994 and particularly during the period 1989–92, when his views on NAFTA took shape.

4 For a description and preliminary analysis of NAFTA, see Pastor 1993; see also Hufbauer and Schott 1993.

5 For a review of that literature, see Pastor 2001: Chapter 4. For an excellent assessment of the original agreement, see Hufbauer and Schott 1993, Grayson 1995, and Orme 1996.

6 For a detailed analysis of the electoral systems in the three countries and the ways in which each has and can learn from each other, see Pastor 2004.

7   For the submissions, see <http://www.dol.gov/dol/ilab/public/programmes/nao>; also see <http://www.naalc.org>.

8   For the more recent estimate, see Ferriss 2001.

9   The estimates on the gap between northern and southern Mexico vary. Luis Ernesto Derbez, a World Bank economist, who became Mexico's minister of the economy and then of foreign relations, estimated that during the 1990s the export-oriented North grew at annual rates of 5.9 per cent, while the South barely grew at .4 per cent—more than 10 times faster (cited in Tricks 2001). Tamayo-Flores also concluded that the gap in income between northern and southern Mexico had widened significantly since NAFTA even while the population in the poorer part of Mexico declined vis-à-vis the North (2001: 405–07). Based on data from INEGI and CONAPO, the North American Development Bank estimated that the northern part of Mexico was growing more than twice as fast as the south or centre.

10 An October 2001 survey in Canada found that 55 per cent favoured the same currency as the US, but 59 per cent opposed adopting the US dollar (see Dunfield 2001).

References

Brautigam, Tara. 2004. "As Many As 600,000 American Living in Canada Eligible to Vote in US Election." *Canadian Press*, Canada.Com News, 18 October.

Chicago Council on Foreign Relations, CIDE, and Consejo Mexicano de Asuntos Internacionales. 2004. "Comparing Mexican and American Public Opinion and Foreign Policy." Chicago: Council of Foreign Relations.

Crosette, B. 1998. "Surprises in the Global Tourist Boom." *New York Times*, 12 April.

Davey, W. 1996. *Pine and Swine: Canada-United States Trade Dispute Settlement—the FTA Experience and NAFTA Prospects*. Ottawa: Centre for Trade Policy and Law.

DFAIT (Department of Foreign Affairs and International Trade of Canada). 1999. *Opening Doors to the World: Canada's Market Access Priorities, 1999*. Ottawa: DFAIT.

Dunfield, Allison. 2001. "Canadians Feel Closer to the US, but Reject Currency." *Globe and Mail*, 6 November.

Ferriss, Susan. 2001. "An Altered View of Mexican Immigrants." *Atlanta Journal-Constitution*, 12 July.

Fry, E.H. 1992. *Canada's Unity Crisis: Implications for US-Canadian Economic Relations*. New York.: Twentieth Century Fund Press.

Gobierno de la Republica de Mexico. 2001. "Towards a Partnership for Prosperity: The Guanajuato Proposal." Press Release, 16 February. <http://www.presidencia.gob.mx/?P=42 orden=Leer&Tipo=Pe&Art-548>.

Grayson, G. 1995. *The North American Free Trade Agreement: Regional Community and the New World Order*. Lanham, MD: UP of America.

Grubel, Herbert. 1999. *The Case for the Amero: The Economics and Politics of a North American Monetary Union*. Vancouver: Simon Fraser Institute.

Guzman, B.. 2001. "The Hispanic Population: Census 2000 Brief." US Census Bureau and US Department of Commerce. May. <http://www.census.gov/prod/2001pubs/c2kbr01-3.pdf>.

Howlett, M., A. Netherton, and M. Ramesh. 1999. *The Political Economy of Canada: An Introduction*. 2nd ed. New York: Oxford UP.

Hufbauer, G.C., D. Orejas, and J.J. Schott. 2000. "NAFTA and the Environment: Seven Years Later." October. Washington, DC: Institute for International Economics.

Hufbauer, G.C., and J.J. Schott. 1993. *NAFTA: An Assessment*. Rev. ed. Washington, DC: Institute for International Economics.

La Jornada. 2000. "Remesas de Migrantes Equivalen a 83 per cent de la Inversion de EU en Mexico." 30 October.

Lipset, S.M. 1991. *Continental Divide: The Values and Institutions of the United States and Canada*. New York: Routledge.

Martin, P., and E. Midgley. 2003. "Immigration: Shaping and Reshaping America." Population Reference Bureau. *Population Bulletin* 58,2 (June).

McFadyen, J. 1998. *NAFTA Supplemental Agreements: Four Year Review*. Working Paper Series No. 98–4. Washington, DC: Institute for International Economics.

Orme, W.A. Jr. 1996. *Understanding NAFTA*. Austin. TX: U of Texas P.

Pastor, Robert A. 1993. *Integration with Mexico: Options for US Policy*. Washington, DC: Twentieth Century Fund.

———. 2001. *Toward a North American Community: Lessons from the Old World For the New*. Washington, DC: Institute for International Economics. Chapter 1.

———. 2004. "North America's Second Decade," *Foreign Affairs*, 83, 1, January/February.

Public Policy Forum and EKOS. 2002. "Rethinking North American Integration: Report from the PPF/EKOS Conference." Toronto, 18 June.

Schott, J.J., and M.G. Smith (Eds.). 1988. *The Canada-United States Free Trade Agreement: The Global Impact*. Washington, DC: Institute for International Economics; and Montreal: Institute for Research on Public Policy.

Tamayo-Flores, Rafael. 2001. "Mexico in the Context of the North American Integration: Major Regional Trends and Performance of Backward Regions." *Journal of Latin American Studies* 33, 377–407.

Tricks, Henry. 2001. "Free Trade Still Rules in Mexico." *Financial Times*, 27 February: 6.

Weintraub, S. 1997. *NAFTA at Three: A Progress Report*. Washington, DC: Center for Strategic and International Studies. Chapter 2.

Wonnacott, P. 1987. *The United States and Canada: The Quest for Free Trade*. Washington, DC: Institute for International Economics.

Notes on Contributors

YASMEEN ABU-LABAN is Associate Professor in the Department of Political Science at the University of Alberta. She was a Visiting Scholar (2004–05) at the University of Washington and a McCalla Research Professor (2006–07) at the University of Alberta. Her research centres on gender and ethnic politics, nationalism and globalization, immigration policies and politics, and citizenship theory. As well as publishing over 40 articles, chapters, and book reviews, she is the co-author (with Christina Gabriel) of *Selling Diversity: Immigration, Multiculturalism and Employment Equity* (2002) and editor of *Gendering the Nation-State: Canadian and Comparative Perspectives* (forthcoming 2008).

GREGORY ALBO teaches in the Department of Political Science at York University. He is editor of *Canadian Dimension*, *Relay* and *Socialist Register*, all of which regularly cover North American politics. He is currently working on a study on neo-liberalism in Canada.

ISABEL ALTAMIRANO-JIMÉNEZ is Assistant Professor in the Department of Political Science and the Faculty of Native Studies at the University of Alberta. Her area of specialization is Indigenous comparative politics, and she has published on the subject in both edited texts and journals.

JEFFREY AYRES is Associate Professor and Chair of the Department of Political Science at Saint Michael's College in Burlington, Vermont. He is the author of *Defying Conventional Wisdom: Political Movements and Popular Contention Against North American Free Trade* (1998) as well as numerous articles, chapters, and reviews on Canadian and North American political economy, social movements, and transnational contention. In winter/spring 2004 he was the Fulbright Research Chair in North American Studies at the Centre for North American Politics and Society, Carleton University, Ottawa, Canada. His current research interests include the link between neo-liberal globalization and civil society protests, including the impact of NAFTA on contentious politics across North America.

NORMA BORREGO is Researcher and Professor at University of Sinaloa, Mexico. She has served as Coordinator of the Graduate Program on American and Canadian Studies (2002–05) and General Secretary for the Mexican Association on Canadian

Studies (2005–07); she was a Visiting Professor at the University of Massachusetts for the Fulbright Seminar Series (2005). She is currently developing research in conjunction with the PhD Program on Environment and Development at the National Polytechnic Institute. Her particular interests relate to comparative environmental policy (between Mexico, Canada, and the US post-NAFTA), as well as accountability and transparency and North American comparative politics. Recent publications include *Organizations and Public Management* (2006) and "The North American Environmental Policies" (*Mexican Review on Canadian Studies* 11, June 2006).

SAMUEL BOTTOMLEY is Assistant Professor of Political Science at Carleton University. His doctoral thesis examined the role of the Canadian Parliament on the policy-making process, focusing on gun control policy and the passage of the Firearms Act. His other research interests include Canadian parliamentary government, federalism, and public policy. He is currently researching how leadership selection methods influence federal politics, with particular concern for the relationship between the prime minister and his or her parliamentary caucus.

JANINE BRODIE is a Professor of Political Science and Canada Research Chair in Political Economy and Social Governance at the University of Alberta, where she served as Chair of Political Science from 1997 to 2003. She was elected as a Fellow of the Royal Society of Canada in 2002. Before joining the University of Alberta in 1996, she was a Professor of Political Science at York University, where she also served as Faculty Fellow of the Institute for Social Research, Director of the York Centre for Feminist Research, and John Robarts Chair in Canadian Studies. Her publication and research foci are North American political economy and politics, gender and politics, social theory and policy, and governance in an era of globalization.

ROSS E. BURKHART is Associate Professor and Chair of the Department of Political Science, Boise State University. His main research interests are in the areas of cross-national democratization patterns, Canada-US environmental policy relations, and US political culture. His research has been published in several journals, including *American Political Science Review*, *International Journal of Canadian Studies*, and *Social Science Quarterly*.

JULIÁN CASTRO-REA is Associate Professor at the Department of Political Science, University of Alberta. He is also Adjunct Professor, Facultad de Estudios Internacionales y Políticas Públicas, Universidad Autónoma de Sinaloa, Mexico. His broad research interest is North American politics, both from comparative and trilateral perspectives, with a focus on federalism, nationalism, Aboriginal peoples, elections, and foreign policy. He has written and published extensively on these issues.

STEPHEN CLARKSON, while teaching Political Economy at the University of Toronto, has devoted much time to trilateral continental integration. Among his principal publications are *An Independent Foreign Policy for Canada?* (1968); *Canada and the Reagan Challenge* (1982), which won the John Porter Prize; *Trudeau and Our Times. Volume 1: The Magnificent Obsession* (1990) and *Trudeau and Our Times. Volume 2: The Heroic Delusion* (1994) with Christina McCall; *Uncle Sam and Us: Globalization, Neoconservatism, and the Canadian State* (2002). He is now writing a study of continental governance: *Does North America Exist? Transborder Governance under NAFTA and the War on Terror.* In 2004, he was elected Fellow of the Royal Society of Canada.

CLAUDE COUTURE is Professor at Campus Saint-Jean and Director of the Canadian Studies Institute of the University of Alberta. He is the recipient of the University of Alberta Rutherford Award of Excellence for Teaching (2006) and serves as Editor in Chief of the *International Journal of Canadian Studies.* In 2004–05 he was a Fulbright Scholar at the University of Washington, and is currently Principal Investigator of a Social Sciences and Humanities Research Council grant which addresses the impact of the social sciences in Canada. He has published widely on issues relating to nationalism, minorities, and the French in North America, including *Pierre E. Trudeau et le libéralisme canadien* (1996), *Paddling with the Current* (1998), *Espace et différences: Histoire du Canada* (1996), *L'Alberta et le multiculturalisme francophone* (2002), and *Discours d'Étienne Parent* (2000).

JOSÉ A. CRESPO is Senior Scholar and Researcher of the Political Studies Area at the CIDE (Centro de Investigación y Docencia Economica) based in Mexico City. He has been visiting professor at University of California in San Diego (UCSD) and is a member of the National System of Researchers (SNI). A journalist and author of several books about the Mexican political system and comparative politics, his publications include *Votar en los Estados* (1996), *¿Tiene futuro el PRI* (1998), *Fronteras Democráticas en México* (1999), *PRI. De la hegemonía a la oposición* (2001), *La democracia real, explicada a niños y jóvenes* (2004), and *El fracaso histórico del Presidencialismo Mexicano* (2006).

DAN CROW teaches in the Political Science Department at York University and is president of CUPE 4207 at Brock University. His current research is a comparative study of the effects of neo-liberal state and economic restructuring on unions in Canada, the US, and Mexico, with a particular emphasis on unions in steel.

VINCENT DELLA SALA is Associate Professor of Political Science at the University of Trento (Italy). He has held similar positions at the University of Durham and Carleton University. His research and publications have concentrated on the changing role of the state and new forms of governing in industrialized societies. He has examined these questions with respect to a range of issues, from the European Union to the legalization of gambling. He has most recently edited, with Carlo Ruzza, two volumes on *Governance and Civil Society in the European Union* (2007).

GORDON DIGIACOMO is a doctoral candidate in Political Science at Carleton University in Ottawa. He also teaches on a part-time basis at Carleton and the University of Ottawa. His area of concentration has been Canadian government and politics, specifically, federalism, the Constitution, and public policy. His articles on federalism and the constitution have appeared in the *Journal of Canadian Studies,* the *Canadian Labour and Employment Law Journal,* and as part of the working papers series of the Queen's Institute of Intergovernmental Relations and the Saskatchewan

Institute of Public Policy. His dissertation is generally about the federal approach to intergovernmental policy-making.

CHRISTINA GABRIEL is Associate Professor in the Department of Political Science and the Pauline Jewett Institute of Women's Studies at Carleton University. She has published on issues related to gender, citizenship, and migration as well as North American regional integration. In 2002 she co-authored with Yasmeen Abu-Laban *Selling Diversity: Immigration, Multiculturalism, Employment Equity and Globalization* (2002). She is currently completing an edited volume on international labour migration. She is also a co-applicant (with Laura Macdonald and Rianne Mahon) in a SSHRC-funded project entititled "Social Citizenship in North America."

TERESA GUTIÉRREZ-HACES is Research Professor at the Instituto de Investigaciones Económicas of the Universidad Nacional Autónoma de México (UNAM) and Professor at the Political Sciences Faculty at UNAM. She is currently the head of the project "The US Foreign Economic Policy towards Mexico and Canada." In 1992 she founded the Mexican Association on Canadian Studies, and she has been visiting professor at the University of Quebec in Montreal (1987), Carleton University (1994), the University of Ottawa (2000), the University of Barcelona (2002), and the University of Gerona (2002). In recognition of her outstanding work in Canadian studies in 2007 she received the highest honour the Canadian government gives a foreign academic, the Governor General Prize in Canadian Studies.

LOIS HARDER is an Associate Professor of Political Science at the University of Alberta. She is the author, co-author, and editor of three books, including *Women, Democracy and Globalization in North America* (2006). She has also published several book chapters and journal articles on various dimensions of Canadian social policy and is currently working on a project concerning state regulation of families in Canada and the US.

ATHANASIOS HRISTOULAS is a Professor of International Relations at the Instituto Tecnológico Autónomo de México (ITAM) as well as the Director of the National Security Program at the same institution. He also regularly teaches at the Mexican Naval and Army Staff colleges. Before moving to México from Canada, he was the Military and Strategic Post Doctoral Fellow at the Norman Paterson School of International Affairs, Carleton University. His research interests include civil-military relations, Mexican defence and national security policy, and Canada-Mexico-US relations. He has published extensively on North American security affairs.

RADHA JHAPPAN is an Associate Professor in the Department of Political Science, Carleton University, Ottawa. Her publications and teaching interests include Indigenous politics, human rights and constitutional law, law and morality, feminist legal theory, critical race theory, and Canadian politics. She has published a number of journal articles and book chapters on Indigenous politics of North America in Canada and in Mexico. She is currently writing a book on child pornography and sex tourism in seven countries.

LUC JUILLET is an Associate Professor at the School of Political Studies at the University of Ottawa. His research on North American environmental politics has mainly explored the impact of NAFTA on environmental policy-making as well as US-Canada relations in the field of conservation policy. Recent publications on these issues include a chapter entitled "National Institutional Veto Points and Continental Policy Change: Failing to Amend the U.S.-Canada *Migratory Birds Convention*" (A. Lecours, ed., *New Institutionalism: Theory and Analysis* [2005]).

LAURA MACDONALD is a Professor in the Department of Political Science and the Institute of Political Economy at Carleton University and the Director of the Centre on North American Politics and Society. She has published numerous articles in journals and edited collections on such issues as the role of NGOs in development, global civil society, citizenship struggles in Latin America, Canadian development assistance, and the political impact of NAFTA on human rights and democracy in the three member states. She is currently principal investigator on a project funded by SSHRC on social citizenship in North America (with Christina Gabriel and Rianne Mahon).

NEIL NEVITTE is Professor of Political Science at the University of Toronto. He is a co-investigator of the Canadian Election Study and the principal investigator of the Canadian World Values Surveys. His books include *Anatomy of a Liberal Victory* (2002), *Value Change and Governance* (1998), and *The Decline of Deference* (1996). He has contributed to *The Journal of Democracy*, *Comparative Political Studies*, *Electoral Studies*, *Public Opinion Quarterly*, and *Political Methodology*.

ROBERT A. PASTOR is Director of the Center for North American Studies (which he established), Vice-President of International Affairs, and Professor of International Relations at American University. He was Vice Chair of the Council on Foreign Relations Task Force on the Future of North America, which issued a report "Building a North American Community" in May 2005. From 1985–2002, he was Professor at Emory University and Fellow and Founding Director of the Latin American Program and the Democracy Project at The Carter Center. He was also Director of Latin American and Caribbean affairs on the National Security Council (1977–81) and was Consultant to the State and Defense Departments. He is the author or editor of 16 books, including *Toward a North American Community: Lessons from the Old World for the New* (2001) and *Democracy and Elections in North America: What Can We Learn From Our Neighbors?* (2004).

ROOPA RANGASWAMI is currently pursuing a combined JD/MA in International Relations at the University of Toronto. Her areas of interest include international trade, political economy, and development, which she has explored through work with the UN and the International Labour Organization. Upon completing her studies, she plans to work in both public and private international law.

FRANÇOIS ROCHER is Professor of Political Science at the University of Ottawa. He held a similar position at Carleton University, where he was also Director of the School of Canadian Studies (2003–06). He served as President of the Société québécoise de science politique (2001–02) and co-editor of the *Canadian Journal of*

Political Science (1996–99). His research centres on Canadian federalism, citizenship, and inter-ethnic relations policies in Canada. He is the co-editor of *New Trends in Canadian Federalism* (with Miriam Smith, 2003), *The Conditions of Diversity in Multinational Democracies* (with Alain-G. Gagnon and Montserrat Guibernau, 2003) and *Contestation transnationale, diversité et citoyenneté dans l'espace québécois* (with Micheline Labelle, 2004).

STÉPHANE ROUSSEL is currently Associate Professor, Department of Political Science, Université du Québec à Montréal (UQAM) and Canada Research Chair in Canadian Foreign and Defence Policy. From 2000–02, he was Professor at Glendon College (York University) in Toronto where he taught international relations and security studies. His most recent publications include *The North American Democratic Peace: Absence of War and Security Institution-Building in Canada-US Relations, 1867–1958* (2004). He is currently directing three research programs on the subject of North American security.

ANA LUZ RUELAS is Professor of Constitutional Law at Facultad de Estudios Internacionales y Políticas Públicas at Universidad Autónoma de Sinaloa México. Her research interests include telecommunications regulation, new information and communication technologies and social issues, and the digital divide. She is author of *La reconversión regulatoria de las telecomunicaciones* (2006) and is co-editor and co-author of *Mexico y Canada en la globalization* (2000). She is the current director of the *Mexican Journal of Canadian Studies*.

DAVID SCHNEIDERMAN is Professor of Law and Political Science at the University of Toronto and Visiting Faculty at Georgetown University Law Center. He has authored numerous articles and book chapters on Canadian constitutional law and history, comparative constitutional law, and economic globalization in a wide variety of journals and books. He recently co-authored *The Last Word: Media Coverage of the Supreme Court of Canada* (2005) and has forthcoming the book *Constitutionalizing Economic Globalization: Investment Rules and Democracy's Promise*. His current research interests concern those matters that distinguish Canadian constitutional culture from the US, and the constitutional impacts of economic globalization in various places around the world.

MARCUS TAYLOR is an Assistant Professor in the Department of Development Studies at Queen's University. His work focuses on the theory and practice of reforming labour and social policies in Latin America, with specific emphasis on the role of the World Bank. He recently published *From Pinochet to the Third Way: Neoliberalism and Social Transformation in Chile* (2006) and is the contributing editor of *Global Economy Contested: Production, Finance, and the International Division of Labour* (2007).

STEPHEN WHITE is a PhD candidate in the Department of Political Science at the University of Toronto. His research focuses on political socialization and comparative electoral behaviour.

Index

Aboriginal peoples. *See* Indigenous peoples
Aboriginal rights. *See* Indigenous rights
Abu Ghraib prison, Iraq, 253
Abu-Laban, Yasmeen, 337, 477
Acteal, Mexico, 65
Action Canada Network, 427
Adams, Michael, *Fire and Ice*, 447
AFL-CIO, 276–78, 285–86, 290
African Americans
    tenancy and sharecropping, 38
    in US Bureaucracy, 169–70
African slaves, 34–36, 38
Agreement on Internal Trade (Canada), 210
agriculture, 79, 116
    agribusiness, 14
    common policies (EEC), 116
    New France, 35
    subsistence, 14, 41, 329
al-Quaeda, 21, 380
Alberta, 63, 140, 208
Alberta Act, 135
Albo, Gregory, 222, 477
Alfred, Taiaiake, 234, 237–38
Alliance for Responsible Trade (ART), 426–27
Altamirano-Jiménez, Isabel, 221–22, 477
American environmental movement, 316–17, 321
"American exceptionalism," 25, 51–53, 67
American federalism. *See* US federalism
American Independence, 80, 190
American Indians. *See* Indigenous peoples
American Iron and Steel Institute, 108

American political culture, 53, 58, 395–96, 407–08
American Revolution, 53, 58
"Amero" (single currency), 472
amicus curiae, 45
amparo, writ of, 187, 262
Anderson, Benedict, 355
    Imagined Communities, 361
Andreas, Peter, 355
anti-CUFTA campaign. *See* CUFTA
anti-NAFTA campaign. *See* NAFTA
Anti-Reciprocity League, 88
Anti-Terrorism Act (Canada), 21, 338, 345, 366, 382
    human rights and, 385
Anton, Thomas J., 195, 197
APEC (Asia-Pacific Economic Cooperation), 340
Arar, Maher, 346
Arendt, Hannah, 339, 350
ASEAN (Association of South-East Asian Nations), 340
Asian-Americans, 340
    in US Bureaucracy, 169–70
Aspe, Pedro, 454
asylum, 339, 367, 455. *See also* refugees
"asymmetric cooperation," 383
asymmetrical distribution of power in North America, 13–14, 26, 128, 130, 383, 434, 462. *See also* US power
asymmetrical federalism, 130
asymmetries in economic development, 71, 190
Atlantic fisheries, 82
Aubry, Andrés, 244
authoritarianism, 99, 175, 177
auto industry, 275

labour-management cooperation, 283
    shift to Mexico, 280
    TNCs, 108
Auto Pact (1965), 108
Ayres, Jeffrey M., 389–90, 477

Baker v. Carr, 161
Basel Convention, 327
Bentsen, Lloyd, 165
Berruga, Enrique, 376
bilateral relations, 71
    Canada US, 12, 361, 372, 379, 441, 467, 473
    double bilateralism, 387
    federal-provincial, 209–10
    Mexico and US, 13, 445
bilateralism *vs.* trilateralism, 340, 350, 372
Bill C-36. *See* Anti-Terrorism Act (Canada)
Bissett, James, 349
Black Civil Rights Movement, 38
Bloc Québécois, 32, 63
Boldt, Menno, 240
Bonner, Robert C., 348
Border Environment Cooperation Commission (BECC), 465
Border Papers (C.D. Howe Institute), 441, 452
Border Protection, Antiterrorism and Illegal Immigration Control Act (2005), 343, 345
Borderlands: How We Talk About Canada (New), 358
borders, 11, 16, 27, 107, 337, 353–68, 441. *See also* national security; North American security community
barriers for people, 448

Canada-US, 13, 111, 345, 348, 357, 362, 382
    Canadian national identity and, 358
    Coalition for Secure Trade and Efficient borders, 445
    common policies regarding migration and border-security, 13
    debordering, 450
    disempowering by, 237, 241, 243
    Mexico's southern border, 338, 344, 380, 383
    politicization of, 339, 347
    re-bordering, 343, 361, 367
    Secure Fence Act, 11
    Smart Border Accords, 13, 111, 338, 348, 350, 362, 366, 371, 379, 383, 445, 456, 470
    socially constructed, 355, 368
    trans-border environmental questions, 128
    unclear future, 368
    US-Canada Shared Accord on our Border, 362
    US-Canada Smart Border Declaration, 13, 348
    US-Mexico border, 11, 13, 317, 344, 348, 357, 359–61, 366, 378, 429, 465
    US-Mexico Border Partnership Action Plan, 13, 366
    "US-Mexico Border Partnership Agreement," 348
    violence and human rights abuses, 344
    water issues, 105–06
Borrego, Norma, 99, 477
Bothwell, Robert, 357
Bottomley, Samuel, 98, 478
boundaries. *See* borders
Brebner, John Bartlett, *The North American Triangle*, 446
Britain, 28, 71, 116, 123
    free trade with US and Mexico, 80
    imperial preferences system, 87
    influence in Mexico, 73, 84
    treaty making, 226–28
Britain's Enabling Act of 1846, 82
British American League of Upper Canada, 81
British Columbia, 44–45, 63, 140
    electoral reform, 141
    Indigenous land claims, 43–44

British Empire, 74, 79, 90, 226
Brodie, Janine, 390, 471, 478
Brown vs. Board of Education of Topeka, 38, 254–55
Brubaker, Rogers, 52
Building a North American Community, 442, 455
Bureau of Indian Affairs (US), 31
Burkhart, Ross, 99, 478
Bush, George Sr., 166
Bush, George W., 42, 303, 467
    Commission to Strengthen Social Security, 302, 305
    conservative movement, 57
    Department of Homeland Security, 171
    direct confrontation approach, 384
    Guanajuato Agreement, 445
    human rights under, 385
    "Iraq's weapons of mass destruction" scandal, 163
    "new partnership agenda," 454
    parallel track approach, 318–19
    powers acquired post 9/11, 158
    presidential injunction, 285
    proposal for temporary work permits, 17
    Secure Fence Act, 11
    at Special Summit of the Americas, 17
    Security and Prosperity Partnership of North America (SPP), 367, 441
    on undocumented immigrants, 343
    veto, 162
    war on terrorism, 111
Business Council on National Issues (BCNI), 444
business unionism, 223, 277, 285

C.D. Howe Institute, *Border Papers*, 441, 452
cabinet (Canada), 144–45
    cabinet solidarity, 142
    dominated by PM, 142
Cahokia (hub of Native North America), 27
Cairns, Alan, 138, 240
Calder Case, 62, 238
Calderón, Felipe, 42–43, 66, 99–100, 191
    on Secure Fence Act, 11
Calvo, Carlos, 258
Camin, Aguilar, 184
Canada, 28, 52, 57
    annexation (support for), 81

bilateral approach, 12, 361, 372, 379, 467, 473
centre-left ideologies, 63
colonial period, 72–73, 81–83
Commercial Reciprocity Agreement of 1854, 82–83
conservatism, 58, 63
Constitution (*See* Canadian Constitution)
"democratic deficit," 98, 134, 145
Dominion in British Empire, 80
drive for deeper continental integration with US, 18, 441–42, 452
economic dependency on US, 71–72, 83, 85, 87–88, 371
election 1911, 88
ethnic hierarchies, 36
Executive (*See* Canada's Executive)
export trade post CUFTA/ NAFTA, 444
federalism (*See* Canadian federalism)
First Nations nationalism, 52, 62–63
first trade agreement with US, 85–87
foreign policy (*See* Canada's foreign policy)
"haven for terrorists," 31, 345, 355, 379–80, 445
human rights, 21 (*See also* Charter of Rights and Freedoms)
independence movements, 31–32, 52–53, 59, 62–63, 208–09
Indian Act, 36, 230–31 (*See also* Canada's First Nations policies)
Indigenous lands, 31, 43–45
Loyalists, 58
Mexican professionals and refugees, 13
migration patterns, 58
multilateral approach, 384
National Policy, 83, 90
nationalism, 359, 463
political institutions, 133–53
position in NAFTA, 12–13, 445
post-national state, 373
prime minister (*See* prime minister [Canada])
property rights, 252, 256–57

provinces, 83, 136, 208
(*See also* Canadian
federalism)
Quebec nationalism, 53 (*See
also* Québec)
race/ethnicity and income
inequality, 36, 39, 58
Rand Formula, 28
reciprocity, 81–83
refusal to join the "Coalition of
the Willing," 454
resource hinterland, 26, 74
role of the courts (*See* Canadian
Judiciary)
social policy (*See* Canada's
social policy)
social unionism, 277
"staples theory," 35, 73–74, 88
subnational and regional
minorities, 26,
62–63, 230–31 (*See also*
Québec)
universal health care (*See*
Canada's social policy)
Canada Health and Social Transfer
(CHST), 298–99
Canada-US border, 111, 357, 382
border disputes, 357
longest undefended border,
345, 357, 366
new portrayal as risk to US,
345, 355, 379–80, 445
politicization, 345
US-Canada Shared Accord on
our Border, 362
US-Canada Smart Border
Declaration, 13, 348
Canada-US Free Trade Agreement.
See CUFTA
Canada-US Partnership Initiative
(CUSP), 362
Canada-US security partnership
during Cold War
"special relationship," 376–77
Canada-Wide Accord on
Environmental
Harmonization, 210
Canada's electoral system, 139–41
"artificial" parliamentary
majorities, 140
call for reform, 139
single-member plurality (SMP),
139–40
Canada's Executive, 141–45
cabinet, 144–45
different from NAFTA partners,
141
Governor General, 141–42

prime minister, 99, 141–44,
150, 152
Canada's First Nations policies
assimilation policies, 231
Canada Aboriginal Action Plan
(1998), 240
Christian churches, 230
co-optation strategy, 238
Constitution Act (1982), 231,
239
Hawthorne Report, 238
Indian Act, 36, 230–31
institutional bias, 230
isolating self-government from
territorial rights, 241
paradigm of domestication, 230
promoting Aboriginal economic
development, 239
reserve system, 230
residential schools, 230–31
Royal Proclamation, 230
Supreme Court, 238
White Paper, 237–38
Canada's foreign policy
global security, 373–74, 376
"human security" doctrine,
373, 384
internationalism, 373
multilateralism, 373
Canada's social policy, 297–301
Canada Health and Social
Transfer (CHST),
298–99
CPP/QPP, 299
Employment Insurance
program, 300
family allowance, 298
health care, 58, 206, 210,
297–98
income support programs,
299–301
link between social well-being
and paid work (post-
NAFTA), 301
National Child Benefit (NCB),
299–300
Old Age Security (OAS), 299
primary and secondary
education, 298
shared cost programs, 207
Social Union Framework
Agreement, 209
universal social programs, 58,
297–98
Canadian Auto Workers (CAW),
282, 284, 289
Canadian Bill of Rights (1959),
255–56

Canadian Bureaucracy (federal
civil service)
bilingualism, 151
democratic control, 152
Employment Equity Act, 152
professional, permanent, and
non-partisan, 151
Canadian Confederation, 87, 90
Canadian Constitution, 32, 99,
135–39, 198, 208
Aboriginal rights, 135, 138,
256
amending formula, 135, 138
amendment for old age
pensions, 207
amendment for unemployment
insurance, 207
Charlottetown Accord, 139
Constitution Act (1867), 135,
138, 198
Constitution Act (1982), 135,
138, 198, 256
constitutional battles (1987–
1995), 208–09
constitutional conventions,
135–36
constitutional rights, 255–57
constitutional supremacy, 138
conventions, 135–36
divided authority, 255 (*See also*
federalism)
entrenched bill of rights (*See*
Charter of Rights and
Freedoms)
federal powers under (residual
power), 199
federal statutes, 135
federalism (*See* Canadian
federalism)
flexibility, 136–37
longstanding source of tension,
137
Meech Lake Accord, 139
ongoing debate, 138–39
patriation, 208
provincial powers under, 199
Canadian Council for Refugees,
349
Canadian Council of Chief
Executives (CCCE), 18,
441, 444
deep integration agenda, 453,
455
Canadian Economist, The, 81
Canadian federalism, 99–100,
195, 198
accommodating French and
English, 136, 198

central government's residual
power, 203
court judgments, 202–03
effect of international trade
agreements, 137
fear of US expansionism, 198
provincial fiscal and political
autonomy, 195
similarity to EC, 122
strong central government
(intended), 198–99, 202
Canadian federalism (post WW II)
Agreement on Internal Trade,
210
bilateral agreements, 209–10
Canada-Wide Accord on
Environmental
Harmonization, 210
cooperative federalism, 207
decentralized, 136–37, 210
emerging confederalism, 210
equalization program, 207
executive federalism, 208
NAFTA's impact on, 215–16
province-building, 208
shared-cost programs, 207
Social Union Framework
Agreement, 209
Canadian International
Development Agency, 284
Canadian Judiciary, 149
Federal Court of Canada, 150
increased power from NAFTA,
134
Supreme Court, 44, 150–51,
203, 209, 238, 257, 456
Canadian Labour Congress (CLC),
276
Canadian labour law
back-to work legislation, 282
decertification of unions, 282
Industrial Relations and
Dispute Act (1948), 275
Canadian military policy
American dominance, 110–11
Canadian National League, 88
Canadian political culture, 395–96,
409
Canadian political party system.
See party system (Canada)
Canadian Security and Intelligence
Agency (CSIS), 380
Canadian Union of Postal
Workers, 150
Canadian Union of Public
Employees, 289
Canadian unions
concession bargaining, 283

"Days of Action" (Ontario
1995–97), 283
internationalism, 278, 284
opposition to FTAA, 283–84
partnerships with employees,
283
response to neo-liberalism and
free trade, 281–84
social movement unionism, 283
strike rates, 282–83
Canadian welfare state, 58, 297
neo-liberal reformation, 298
capital mobility. See international
capital mobility
Cárdenas, Lazáro, 63, 185, 210,
233, 259
Cardinal, Harold, 238
Carnacho, Avila, 64
Carr, Barry, 64
Carter, Jimmy, 166
"Carter Doctrine," 166
Cartier, Georges Etienne, 74
Cartier, Jacques, 35, 74
Casanova, Pablo Gonzalez, 66
Castaneda, Jorge, 378
Castro-Rea, Julián, 221–22, 478
Catholic Church, 58–61, 64–65
CAW, 282, 289
educational programs for
Mexican workers, 284
CCCE. See Canadian Council of
Chief Executives
CEC, 223, 315, 320, 431, 464
binding dispute resolution
process, 321
citizen and NGO participation,
330
citizens' submission process,
330–31
development of Mexico's
policy capacity, 323,
330, 332
dispute resolution process,
331–32
Central American free trading
zone, 157
centre/periphery division, 52
Centres for North American
Studies, 471
Chamber of Deputies (Mexico)
electoral system, 182
functions, 182
Charlottetown Accord, 139, 208
Aboriginal participation, 239
Charter Committee on Poverty
Issues, 150

Charter of Rights and Freedoms
(1982), 36, 135, 198, 208,
255–57
Americanizing influence, 138
collective rights, 256
constitutional supremacy, 138,
149
ended parliamentary
supremacy, 138, 149
increased role of courts, 139,
150
Quebec opposition, 256
Cherokees, 55
Chiapas uprising. See Zapatista
uprising
Chicago School, 59
Chrétien, Jean, 239, 319, 379
distancing Canada from US
foreign policy, 359
NAFTA negotiations, 144
response to 9/11, 366
Churchill, Ward, 29–30
Cistero Revolt, 65
citizen committees, 431, 434, 464
Citizen's Trade Coalition (CTC),
426, 430
lobbying clout within US
Congress, 427–28
citizenship, 346
European, 124, 341
racial profiling and, 345–47
"segmented citizenship," 346
civil rights, 347. See also human
rights
Civil Rights Act (1964), 38
civil society organizing. See
transnational mobilization
of civil society
Civil War (US), 160
Civilian Conservation Corps, 160
Clark PC government, 146
Clarkson, Stephen, 97, 478
Clinton, Bill, 163, 167, 304–05,
430
Lewinsky, Monica, scandal, 163
NAFTA side deal
(environment), 315, 319
NAFTA side deal (labour), 290
passage of NAFTA bill, 162
proposed devolution of powers
towards states, 206
Clinton, Hillary, 365
Coalition for Justice in the
Maquiladoras, 429
Coalition for Secure Trade and
Efficient borders, 445
COCOPA, 42, 212, 243
Codinach, Jiménez, 79

Cold War, 61, 116–17, 166, 375–76
　security alliance between Canada and the US, 358, 376–77
Cole, David, 347
collective rights, 98, 251, 256
Collier, John, 228
colonialism. *See* European colonialism
Columbus, Christopher, 27, 33
Columbus, Diego, 34
Comisión Federal de Electricidad, 109
commercial reciprocity, 81
Commercial Reciprocity Agreement of 1854, 82–83
Commission for Environmental Cooperation (CEC). *See* CEC
Commission for Labour Cooperation (CLC), 431, 464
Commission on Concordance and Pacification (COCOPA), 42, 212, 243
Commission to Strengthen Social Security (US), 302, 305
Committee of Permanent Representation (COREPER), 122
Common External Tariff (CET), 470
Common Foreign and Security Policy (CFSP), 117
common market, 116
communal lands. *See ejido* lands
Communications, Energy and Paper Workers of Canada (CEP), 283–84
　concession bargaining, 283
community, 16, 54, 390. *See also* EU; North American community
　civic community building, 130, 389
　definition, 451
　"imagined communities," 353, 355–56
　language of, 441
concession bargaining, 223, 283, 285
condominium model, 129–30
　relevance to North America, 130–31
Confederacion de Trabajadores de Mexico (CTM), 276, 287

Confederación Regional Obrera Mexicana (CROM), 287
Confederación Revolucionaria de Obreros y Campesinos (CROC), 287
confederalism, 210
Confederation of National Trade Unions, 275
Conference Board of Canada, 444
Congreso del Trabajo (CT), 287
Consejo Mexicano de Asuntos Internacionales, 18
conservatism, 25, 51, 53–54
　British North America, 58
Conservative Party. *See also* names of Conservative PMs
　on institutional reform, 134
Conservative Party (Quebec), 61
consortium, 129
continental energy strategy, 454
continental governance, 101–13
　air, 106
　epistemic communities, 105
　FERC, 112
　informal networks of civil society groups, 105
　interest-based, asymmetrical and US-driven, 97, 112
　labour, 107
　market-led institutions, 102, 107–10
　NAFTA, 102–04, 111
　North American Competitiveness Council (NACC), 112
　security, 102, 111–12
　Security and Prosperity Partnership of North America (SPP), 112
　state-generated security institutions, 110–11
　water, 105–06
continental integration. *See* EU; NAFTA; North American integration
continentalism, 88, 448, 453
　portrayed as natural or inevitable, 442, 450
contingent and informal sector work, 278–79, 306, 400
"Contract with America," 162
Convention Relating to the Status of Refugees, 339
convergence
　"default convergence," 253
　immigration and refugee policies, 471

rights and freedoms protection, 252–53
　of values, 472
Cooper, Sherri, 448
Cortés, Hernán, 33, 74
cosmopolitanism, 25, 51
Costilla, Hidalgo y, 63
Côté c. La Reine, 62
COTERIN, 262–64
Council of Canadians (COC), 150, 426–27
Council of Foreign Relations (CFR), 454
Council of Ministers, 122
Courchene, Thomas, 19
Couture, Claude, 23–26, 479
Cree, 32, 46
Creel, Santiago, 377
Crespo, José, 99, 479
critical geopolitics, 353–55
cross-border solidarity. *See* trans-national mobilization of civil society
Crow, Dan, 222, 479
Cruise missile, 111
Cuba, 55, 375–76
CUFTA, 12, 21, 41, 102, 359, 443
　anti-CUFTA campaign, 426
　democracy and, 20
　enabling legislation, 144
　prohibition of Canadian government intervention, 109
　Senate's treatment of, 143
　temporary entry of business visitors and professionals, 341
"cult of *mestizaie*." *See mestizo* national culture
currency crises, 308–09, 461, 473
Curtis, James, 56, 59
customs union, 71, 470

d'Aquino, Thomas, 446, 453–55
Davey, William, 464
De la Madrid, Miguel, 188
　Municipal Reform (1984), 210
De Tocqueville, Alexis, 176
De Vattel, Emmerich, 29
De Vitoria, Francisco, 29
decentralization and privatization. *See* neo-liberal reforms
Delgamuukw v. British Columbia, 44, 62, 257
Della Sala, Vincent, 479
Delors, Jacques, 119
democracy, 19–20, 42–43, 98, 152, 395–97, 429

definition, 20
democratic legitimacy, 120, 130
direct democracy, 148
Mexico, 99, 177, 179, 191
NAFTA and, 16
neo-liberalism and, 273
"democratic deficit," 98, 134, 145
Democratic Party (US), 162
Democratic Revolution Party, 42
denationalization, 450
DePalma, Anthony, Here: A
    Biography of the New North
    American Continent, 363,
    446
Department of Homeland Security,
    99, 169, 171–72, 364
deregulation, 17, 109, 112, 191
destatization, 450
"deterritorialized threats," 338,
    360
development gap
Mexico, 462, 466–67, 473
Dewey, John, 56
Diaz, Porfirio, 63, 89–90, 179, 200
    modernization of Mexico, 91
Diaz-Cayeros, Alberto, 202
DiGiacomo, Gordon, 99–100, 479
Dinning, Jim, 454
Director General for North
    American Affairs (Canada),
    469
Distant Early Warning (DEW)
    system, 359
Dobson, Wendy, 19, 452
doctrine of discovery (international
    law), 29
dollar diplomacy, 87
Dominican Republic, 55
downward equalization, 14. See
    also "race to the bottom"
    argument
Drache, Daniel, 365
drugs and drug trade, 18, 190,
    360, 462
Duffy, Diane, 237
Duguit, Léon, 258
Dukakis, Michael, 165
Duplessis, Maurice, 61

Earned Income Tax Credit (EITC),
    303–04
Economic Communities, 117
Edwards, John, 165
EEC. See European Economic
    Community
Eisenhower, Dwight, 56
ejido lands, 30, 41, 65, 233

abolishment of, 242–43,
    259–60
Elcock, Ward, 380
electoral frauds, 20, 42, 99,
    191–92
Mexico, 180
Elgin-Marcy agreement, 86
"Empire of Freedom," 54
Employment Equity Act, 152
EMU (economic and monetary
    union), 117
encomienda system, 33–34, 41
energy, 190, 462, 473
    balance between market
        autonomy and state
        intervention, 109
    continental energy strategy, 454
    electricity, 109
    FERC (Federal Energy
        Regulatory
        Commission), 109
    on Indigenous lands, 234, 241
    oil and gas, 45, 109, 191
    US energy imports, 464
environment, 16, 126, 191, 221,
    469, 473
    air, 106
    American environmental
        movement, 316–17, 321
    Canada-Wide Accord on
        Environmental
        Harmonization, 210
    Integrated Border
        Environmental Plan
        (IBEP), 319
    NAAEC, 319–20, 330–31,
        341, 434
    NACEC, 106
    NAFTA side deal, 290, 315,
        319, 332
    NAFTA's impact, 223–24,
        264–66
    "pollution haven" scenarios,
        321, 328–30
    trans-border environmental
        questions, 128
    US domestic policies and, 332
    US government's "parallel
        track" proposal, 223,
        321, 324
    water, 105–06
    wildlife conservation, 330
Environmental Defence Fund, 318
environmental governance, 107
environmental law enforcement,
    320–21
environmental regulations

NAFTA Chapter 11 and, 104,
    264–66, 316, 327
US Supreme Court and, 255
voluntary withdrawal, 326, 328
environmental security, 457
environmental standards, 390
    harmonization of, 322
    scientific evidence and risk
        assessment, 322–23
Equal Employment Opportunity
    Act, 170
Ethyl Corporation case, 104, 326
EU, 13, 21, 98, 117, 340, 447, 451
    creation of, 97
    debate between
        supranationalism and
        intergovernmentalism,
        128
    democracy, 131
    historical context, 115–18
    institutional and policy
        "thickness," 118
    lessons for North America, 115,
        120–21, 123, 129
    reduction of income gap, 467
    sense of belonging to "Europe,"
        131
EU Centres, 471
euro, 117
European citizenship, 124, 341
European Coal and Steel
    Community (ECSC), 21,
    116
European colonialism, 12, 221
    boundaries and, 27, 226
    economic motivation, 28
    legacies of, 16, 27–47, 99
    unequal development, 28
European Commission, 98
    College of Commissioners,
        118–20
    democratic legitimacy and,
        120–21
    institutional "thickness," 119
    links with interest groups
        and sub-national
        governments, 119
European Council, 98, 122
European Court of Justice (ECJ),
    98, 119
    trumps national courts, 123
European Economic Community
    (EEC), 116
European foreign policy, 118
European integration process,
    98, 126
European Parliament (EP), 98, 120

co-decision-making procedure, 122
decision-making role, 121
European social model (ESM), 98, 124–26
Europeanization
offsetting effects of globalization, 126

Fair Vote Canada, 139
Falardeau, Jean-Charles, 59
FAT, 276, 288
Federal Court of Canada, 150
Federal Electoral Institute (IFE), 192
Federal Judicature Council (FJC) (Mexico), 187–88
federalism, 100, 128–29, 133, 195 217
Canada (See Canadian federalism)
collaborative, 216
coordinate, 212–13
definition, 195
executive, 208
Mexico (See Mexican federalism)
opportunistic, 207
US (See US federalism)
FERC (Federal Energy Regulatory Commission), 109, 112
FET (Federal Election Tribunal), 42–43
Fire and Ice (Adams), 447
First Nations. See Indigenous peoples
First Nations Governance Act (FNGA), 226, 240–41, 245
Flanagan, Tom, 62
Fleras, Augie, 238
flexible work. See labour market flexibility
Florescano, Enrique, 66
Florida vote recount (2000), 43
Flynn, Michael, 344
foreign investment, 72, 85–86, 116, 260, 467
China, 468
maquiladora zones, 287
Mexican Constitution's "Calvo clause," 259
Mexico, 64, 89–92, 287, 463, 468
Multilateral Agreement on Investment, 431
foreign investment protection, 316. See also NAFTA Chapter 11

"regulatory chill" danger, 324–27, 332
Forsyth-Montes Agreement, 86
"Fortress America," 347
"Fortress Europe," 347
"Fortress North America," 340, 349–50, 371
49th parallel, 357
Fowler, Will, 177
Fox, Vicente, 213, 307, 355, 377
advocate of EU type institutions, 103
anti-poverty policy, 309
customs union proposal, 470
election (2000), 99, 181
favoured trilateral cooperation, 367, 435
on freedom of movement of citizens, 363
Guanajuato Agreement, 445, 467
Indigenous peoples and, 243–44
lowered protection for workers, 107
response to 9/11, 366
on Secure Fence Act, 11
security cooperation, 377
at Special Summit of the Americas, 17
SPP, 441, 455
support for US war on terror, 383
trilateral approach to security, 376
France, 28, 116, 123
Franklin, Benjamin, 158
Franks, C.E.S., 145
free trade, 80, 222, 395, 442 44, 462. See also CUFTA; NAFTA
access to US market and, 444
anti-free trade coalition, 431
diminished enthusiasm for, 389, 411
impact on federalism, 136
opposition (post NAFTA), 471
prosperity of average Canadian and, 444
Free Trade Area of the Americas (FTAA), 431
protests, 17, 283, 433, 473
Free Trade Association (1846), 81
French Revolution, 175, 253
Frideres, James, 240
Friends of the Earth, 317

"Friendship, Trade, and Navigation Agreement between Mexico and the United States," 85
Fur Trade, 31, 35, 74

G8, 17
Gabriel, Christina, 337–38, 342–43, 471, 480
Garcia, Vega, 378
Garcia v. San Antonio Metropolitan Transit Authority, 203
GATS, 172
GATT, 317–18
Gellner, Ernst, 51–52, 57
General Congress (Mexico), 178, 181–82, 185
General Motors, 283
General Motors of Canada Ltd. v. City National Leasing, 203
Geneva Convention, 21
Germany, 116, 119, 123
Gingrich, Newt, 162
"Global Trends 2015," 360
globalization, 126, 134, 223, 339–40
as an ideology, 449
benefits for rich at expense of poor, 42
challenges to state sovereignty, 16, 18, 172
challenges to US court system, 169
consistent with American values, 216
corporate nature, 21
definitions, 157
European imperialism as, 161
fear of job losses, 471
impact on US institutions, 158
as inevitable and irreversible, 448–49
not inevitable, 450
restricting movement of people, 354
selective re-enforcement of borders, 354
shifting communal identifications, 389, 398
and US federalism, 160
Globerman, Steven, 241
Godbour, Adélard, 61
Godina, Tejada y, 185
gold, 55, 74–75, 78
Grabb, Edward, 59
Regions Apart, 56
Gran, Peer, 64
Great Depression, 160–61

Great Divide theory, 56
Great Lakes Commission, 129
Great Society programs (Lyndon
    Johnson), 171, 302
Greenfeld, Leah, 53
group accommodation. *See* collec-
    tive rights
Growth and Stability Pact, 117–18
Grubel, Herbert, 472
Guadalcazar (town), 262, 264
Guanajuato Agreement, 445, 467
Guantanamo Bay, Cuba, 21
Guaranteed Income Supplement,
    299
Guatemala, 375
Guérin c. la Reine, 62
Guibernau, Monserrat, 226
Guindon, Hubert, 59
Gulf of Tonkin Resolution, 165
Gutiérrez-Haces, Teresa, 26, 480
Gutiérrez González, Juan Marcos,
    201

Haass, Richard N., 18
Haida Nation v. British Columbia,
    44
Hamas, 380
Hamilton, Alexander, 158, 254
Harder, Lois, 223, 480
Harper, Stephen, 43, 134, 144,
    148, 445
    cabinet, 145
    on Secure Fence Act, 11
Harris, Mike, 107
Hartz, Louis, 54, 57–58
    *Liberal Tradition in America,
    The*, 53
Hawaiian Independence
    Movement, 32
Health Council of Canada, 210
Held, David, 340
*Here: A Biography of the New
    North American Continent*
    (DePalma), 363, 446
Hezbollah, 380
Hobsbawm, Eric, 51, 57
Holland, Kenneth, 202
Holmes, Oliver Wendell, 255, 260
homeland security. *See* US
    Department of Homeland
    Security
Hormel, James, 167
Hospital Employees Union (BC)
    concession bargaining, 283
House of Representatives (US),
    161–62
Hristoulas, Athanasios, 338, 480
Huerta, Carla, 214

Hull, Cordell, 259
Human Resources Development
    Canada, 152
human rights, 20, 251–68, 337–40,
    347, 372
    Anti-Terrorism Act (Canada)
        and, 385–86
    campaigns, 429
    Canadian Bill of Rights,
        255–56
    Charter of Rights and
        Freedoms, 36, 135,
        138, 149–50, 198, 208,
        255–57
    illegal immigrants, 21, 385
    "individual rights" *vs.* "states
        rights," 54
    international human rights, 21
    NAFTA and, 16, 221
    National Equal Rights League,
        37
    National Human Rights
        Commission (Mexico),
        259
    post-9/11, 21
    racial profiling, 384
    smart borders and, 350
    trumped by national security,
        385
    UN Universal Declaration of
        Human Rights, 251, 339
    US Bill of Rights, 254
    US Patriot Act, 384
    by virtue of membership in
        community, 222
    vs. property rights, 222
    "war on terrorism" and, 385,
        387
human rights violations, 253
    Guantanamo prison, 385
    Mexico, 259
human security, 340, 384, 457
Hutchinson, Tim, 167

illegal immigrants, 17, 341, 343,
    355, 360, 466–67. *See also*
    undocumented workers
    human rights, 21
    important contribution to US
        economy, 385
    "Operation Wetback," 342, 345
ILO, 234, 243
"imagined communities," 353,
    355–56
Imagined Communities
    (Anderson), 361
IMF, 17, 103, 306
Imhofe, James, 167

immigration, 98, 190–91, 462,
    464, 468. *See also* illegal
    immigrants; migration
    common policies regarding
        migration and border-
        security, 13
    harmonization of regulations,
        355, 371
    US-Mexico bilateral deal, 445,
        467
Immigration Reform and Control
    Act (IRCA), 342
imperialism, 12, 26, 28, 81.
    See also British Empire;
    European colonialism
    economic underdevelopment of
        colonies, 78
income disparities, 17, 39–40, 310,
    400, 434, 467–68
    within and between states,
        14–15
    US, 39
income equality, 408, 410
income support programs, 223,
    297. *See also* Canada's
    social policy; social safety
    net; welfare
    Mexico, 307–10
income support (US)
    Earned Income Tax Credit
        (EITC), 303
    Food Stamps, 303
    Social Security, 303–06
    Temporary Aid to Needy
        Families (TANF), 303
    Unemployment Insurance
        Benefits (UIB), 303
Independent Task Force on the
    Future of North America
    (ITF), 454–55
Indian Act, 36, 230–31
Indian Allotment Act (1887)
    (US), 31
"Indian laws." *See Leyes de Indias*
Indian Reorganization Act (1934)
    (US), 31, 229
Indian Self-Determination and
    Education Assistance Act
    (US), 226, 236, 245
indigenismo, 242
Indigenous lands, 41
    Canada, 31, 199, 241, 257
    economic development and,
        240
    energy resources and, 236, 241
    exploitation of natural
        resources and, 43
    international law, 31

Mexico, 30, 35, 41–42, 76, 226, 232, 242, 245
  opening to private investment and development, 245
  territorial integrity of states and, 19, 25, 28–29, 43, 45
US, 30–31, 54–55
WTO and NAFTA tribunals, 25, 45
Indigenous Law. *See also* Canada's First Nations policies; US Tribal policies
Mexico, 226, 244–45
Indigenous peoples, 26, 62–63, 199, 225–46, 343
  Accords on Indigenous Rights and Culture, 212
  amicus curiae submissions, 45
  assimilation, 223, 225, 231, 242 (*See also* mestizo national culture)
  challenges to territorial integrity of states, 19, 25, 28–31, 43, 45
  "citizens plus," 238
  colonial mining sector, 78–79
  corporate/Aboriginal relations, 241
  economic development and, 239, 241
  economic integration, 225
  exploitation of, 79
  federal civil service (Canada), 151–52
  federalism, 159
  human rights abuses (Canada), 253
  international organizations and, 234
  land conflict with settlers, 228
  Mexico, 44, 64–65, 76, 211–12, 223, 231–33, 243, 259–60
  modern treaties, 239–40
  nation-to-nation treaty relations, 227–28
  North America as an integrated continent, 25, 27
  poverty, 245
  role in international trade issues, 45
  self-determination, 221, 225–26, 234–35, 237, 243
  self-government, 46, 222, 237, 239, 241, 244–45
  slavery, 34–36
  stateless nations, 226
  traders of knowledge, technologies, and goods, 27
  in US Bureaucracy, 169–70
  US constitution on, 197
  violence against, 28
  zero-sum choices, 222
Indigenous peoples resurgence, 221, 225–26, 233–35, 242–43
  American Indian Movement (AIM), 235
  Assembly of First Nations, 238
  Canada's response, 237–41
  Fourth World, 235
  Mexico's response to, 241–44
  National Indian Brotherhood, 238
  Native American movement, 235–37
  pan-Indian movement, 221, 233
  Red Power movement, 235
  US response, 235–37
  Zapatista movement, 41–42, 242–43, 259, 309, 428
Indigenous rights, 16, 21, 44, 199, 212
  in Canadian Constitution, 128, 135, 256
  international law, 29, 221
  relevance to international trade, 45
  in US Constitution, 197
Indigenous title as *sui generis*, 44
individualism, 53–55
Industrial Revolution, 37, 74, 79–80
industry. *See* manufacturing
infant mortality rates, 14
informal sector. *See* contingent and informal sector work
Innis, Harold, 73–74
Institute for Public Policy, 441
Institutional Revolutionary Party. *See* PRI
Integrated Border Environmental Plan (IBEP), 319
integration theory, 446–47
Inter-American Treaty of Reciprocal Assistance (ITRA), 375
intercontinental ballistic missile (ICBM), 372
interest groups, 40, 119, 172
intergovernmentalism, 127–28
International Boundary Commission (IBC), 358
international capital mobility, 278–80, 291
International Joint Commission (IJC), 105
International Labour Organization (ILO), 234, 243
International Longshore and Warehouse Union, 285
internationalism (unions), 277, 286, 289–91
internationalization, 450
intolerance, changes in, 399, 406, 410–11
Inuit, 46, 231
Investors' rights. *See* NAFTA Chapter 11
Iran-Contra scandal, 163
Iraq. *See* Persian Gulf Wars
"Iraq's weapons of mass destruction" scandal, 163
"iron triangles," 172
"issue networks," 172
Italy, 64, 116, 123, 125
ITF, 454–55
Iturbide, Agustin de, 85

Japanese Canadians and Americans, 253
Jefferson, Thomas, 30, 37, 158
Jhappan, Radha, 25, 199, 480
"Jobs with Justice," 289
Johnson, Lyndon, 236
  Great Society programs, 171
  Gulf of Tonkin Resolution, 165
Johnson, Samuel, 37
"Joint Statement on Cooperation on Border Security and Regional Migration Issues," 366
Juárez, Benito, 63, 76, 178
Judicial Committee of the Privy Council (JCPC)
  impact on Canadian federalism, 203
Judicial Research Institute of the National Autonomous University, 189
Juillet, Luc, 223–24, 481
Justice and Home Affairs, 117
"Justice for Janitors," 289

Karpa v. Mexico, 150
Kedourie, Elie, 52
Kennedy, John F., 236
Kerry, John, 165
Kincaid, John, 216
King, Mackenzie, 358, 462
"Kingston Dispensation," 358

Kurdistan Worker's Party (PKK), 380

labour, 14, 16, 55, 64, 107, 191, 275
  Canada's labour legislation, 275, 282
  changed nature of work, 223, 295–96
  Commission for Labour Cooperation (CLC), 431, 464
  contingent and informal sector, 278–79, 306, 400
  job migration, 40
  manufacturing, 276, 280, 296
  maquiladora section, 40–41, 106, 279, 287–89, 296, 310, 317, 429
  "McJobs," 296
  Mexican Federal Labour Law, 275
  Mexican labour movement, 287–89
  NAALC, 43, 215, 290, 434
  NAFTA side deal, 290
  national labour movements, 276, 281
  neo-liberal labour market policies, 273–74, 279–80
  North American Commission on Labour Cooperation (NACLC), 107
  private sector service jobs, 276, 278
  search for cheaper, 41
  temporary entry provisions for business and professional workers, 41
  undocumented workers, 17, 41, 360, 466 (*See also* illegal immigrants)
  US labour law, 275, 284–85
  US labour movement, 284–86
  US-Mexico bilateral deal, 445
  wage compression and wage inequalities, 279
labour market flexibility, 280, 302
labour mobility, 390
  EU *vs.* NAFTA, 341–42
labour unions, 40, 150, 222, 274–76, 278, 281–84, 289
  anti-unionism, 277, 285
  business unionism, 275, 277
  capital mobility and, 278–91
  collaboration, 428–29
  concession bargaining, 223, 283

corporatist unionism, 223, 277
de-unionization, 281
democracy, 223, 273
economic slowdown, 278
global trends toward weakening unions, 282
international solidarity, 277, 286, 289–91
labour-management cooperation, 283
national federations, 276
neo-liberal labour market policies, 278–80, 289
partnerships, 223, 283
sectoral bargaining, 291
social movement unionism, 277
social partnership, 277
transnationalism among, 40, 107, 429
union density, 281–82, 285, 287
l'Action Libérale Nationale (ALN), 61
Land Management Act (Canada), 241
Latell, Brian, 359–60
Laurier, Wilfrid, 61, 87, 442
  free trade agreement with US, 462
  reciprocity agreement, 88
Lauterpacht, Eli, 263
"Law Regarding the Making of Treaties" (Mexico), 259
Lesage, Jean, 61
Lewinsky, Monica, scandal, 163
Ley de Expropiaction (1936) (Mexico), 265
Leyes de Indias, 30, 232
Liberal party (Canada), 430. *See also* names of Liberal PMs
  leading advocate for neo-liberal trade policies, 431
Liberal Party (Quebec), 61
Liberal Tradition in America, The (Hartz), 53
liberalism, 25, 51, 54, 57, 60
  liberal-democratic rebellions in Upper and Lower Canada, 58
  of US political culture, 53, 55
Lincoln, Abraham, 38
Lipset, Seymour Martin, 53–54, 58, 138, 462
  Great Divide theory, 56
Lochner Era, 254
"London Debt," 84
Louisiana Purchase, 54
Lujambio, Alonso, 214

Maastricht Treaty, 98, 117, 121
MacArthur, Douglas, 165
Macdonald, Donald, 443–44
Macdonald, John A., 83, 87, 198
Macdonald, Laura, 337–38, 342–43, 471, 481
Macdonald Commission, 443
Mackenzie Gas Project, 46
Maclean's, 363
Madero, Francisco I., 179
Madison, James, 158
"Manifest Destiny," 54, 338, 356, 362
Manley, John, 453–54
manufacturing
  decline in, 296
  move to Mexico, 108, 278 (*See also maquiladora* sector in Mexico)
maquiladora sector in Mexico, 41, 279, 289, 296, 429
  environmental issues, 106, 317
  ethnic pecking order in, 40
  flight to China, 310
  health problems, 288
  low-wage labour market, 287
market-led institutions, 102
  automobile industry, 108
  energy, 109
  steel industry, 108–09
  stock exchanges, 110
  textile industries, 108
Martin, Paul, 133–34, 144, 241, 367, 441
  cabinet, 145
  "new partnership agenda," 454
  at Special Summit of the Americas, 17
Marx, Karl, 19
McCarthy years, 56
McKinley Tariff, 89
McLane-Ocampo Agreement, 86
media, 21, 41
  attention to prime minister, 142–44
  Canada as haven for terrorists, 379–80, 445
  Mexico, 181
Meech Lake Accord, 139, 208–09
mercantilism, 73–75. *See also* European colonialism
MERCOSUR (the *Mercado del Sur*), 340
mestizo national culture, 35, 241
Metalclad case, 221, 253, 261–66, 326–27
Methanex case, 326

Métis, 35, 231
Mexican civil society groups, 431
Mexican Constitution, 30, 65, 179,
     183, 242–43, 259–60
     "Calvo clause," 259
     elected Senate, 200
     strong executive, 200
Mexican Constitution (1824),
     181, 258
Mexican Constitution (1857), 258
Mexican Constitution (1917), 181,
     257, 259
Mexican election 2000, 464
Mexican election July 2006, 42
Mexican federalism, 99–100,
     188–91, 195
     centralization, 200–202, 210
     decentralization, 211
     division of powers, 196
     Indigenous peoples' self-
          government aspirations,
          212
     moving toward coordinate
          federalism, 212–13
     municipalities, 201–02
     NAFTA's effect on, 214–15
     "New Federalism," 211
     political devolution, 211
     residual powers to the states,
          200
Mexican Indigenous policies,
     231–33
     communal land and ejidos, 233
     indigenismo or Indigenous
          assimilation policies,
          233, 242
     "Law Regarding the Making of
          Treaties," 259
     Leyes de Indias, 30, 232
Mexican judicial branch, 186–90
     amparo, writ of, 187
     corruption, 189
     Federal Judicature Council
          (FJC), 187–88
     lower circuit courts, 187
     reforms, 187–88, 202
     upper circuit courts, 187
     weakness, 201–02
Mexican labour movement. See
     also Mexican unions
     attitude toward NAFTA,
          288–89
     response to neo-liberalism,
          287–89
Mexican labour relations system,
     275
     Federal Labour Law (1931),
          275

Mexican party system. See party
     system (Mexico)
Mexican peso crisis, 273, 308–09,
     461
Mexican presidential election
     (2006), 66, 191
Mexican presidential system
     "divided government," 177–78
     presidential power, 177–79,
          201–02
     principle of presidential non
          re-election, 179
     "unified government," 177–78
     US-style system, 175–77
Mexican revolution, 30, 63, 65,
     73, 179
Mexican states, 195
Mexican unions, 289
     corporatist structures, 277, 287
     corruption, 287
     democracy, 276, 287–88
     independent, 288
     instruments of state policy, 277
     strike action, 287–88
Mexico, 28, 52
     Agrarian Law, 242
     agricultural production, 79
     agricultural workers, 14
     annexation ideas, 81
     authoritarian political and
          cultural legacy, 175–77
     branch-plant economy, 89
     British Empire and, 73, 84
     civil society trends, 191
     commercial agreements, 82
     conservatism, 66
     constitutional rights, 257–60
     counter-revolutionary element,
          73
     crisis of Mexican Catholicism,
          65
     customs union proposal, 89
     democracy, 43, 99, 177, 179,
          191
     development gap, 462, 466–67,
          473
     direct foreign investment,
          89–92, 468
     distrust of US, 357, 359, 462
     economic dependency on US
          market and investment,
          85, 87, 371
     economic development, 71–72,
          74, 76
     electoral reform, 180
     environmental protection,
          317–18, 329, 465

     export-oriented economy,
          64, 73
     federalism (See Mexican
          federalism)
     first trade agreement with US,
          85–87
     Fiscal Coordination Act (1980),
          201
     foreign-born residents, 13
     General Congress, 181–82
     hegemonic classes, 64
     human rights, 20–21, 253,
          257–60
     IMF and World Bank
          prescriptions, 103
     income distribution, 14, 39
     independence from Spain, 20,
          32, 63, 72, 80
     Indigenous lands, 30, 35,
          41–42, 76, 245 (See also
          ejido lands)
     Indigenous Law, 30, 226,
          244–45
     Indigenous peoples, 34, 64, 76,
          211–12, 221–33
     infant mortality rates, 14
     labour force (See labour)
     legislative branch, 181–85
     legislative process, 184
     liberalism, 64, 66, 76
     lobbying, 185
     maquiladora sector in, 40
     mestizo national culture, 35
     migration, 64, 377, 384 (See
          also illegal immigrants;
          immigration)
     mining, 34
     miscegenation, 34, 76–77 (See
          also mestizo national
          culture)
     modernization, 86, 90–91, 242
     NAFTA + option, 18, 372, 377
     neo-liberal reforms, 242, 307,
          309
     oil and gas protection, 109
     opposition to economic
          reforms, 398
     per capita income, 14
     political culture, 396–97, 410
     political institutions, 175–92
     Porfirista Dictatorship, 73
     position in NAFTA, 12–13, 445
     poverty, 14, 306, 308–09, 329
     precious metals, 74, 76
     property rights, 252, 257
     public opinion, 188–90, 377,
          408–09 (See also value
          changes)

public sector employees, 288
pursuing trilateralism, 467
race/ethnicity and income
        inequality, 39
regional inequality, 191, 211
resource hinterland, 26, 74
revisionist historiography,
        65–66
slavery, 33–34, 77
social inequality, 306
southern border, 338, 344,
        380, 383
sovereignty issues, 191
subnational and regional
        minorities, 26
subsistence farmers, 41, 329
trade with Canada, 381
trilateral approach to
        cooperation, 372, 467
trucking dispute with US, 103,
        469
US/Britain rivalries, 84
US dominance, 73, 80
US territorial ambitions and,
        356
viceroyalty period, 175–77
war against the US, 63
War of Independence, 84
as way of gaining access to
        US, 344
Yucatan nationalism, 53
Mexico City, 66, 90
Mexico presidential election
        (2006), 20
Mexico's foreign policy
    attempts to maintain distance
            from US, 374, 376
    isolation and non-participation,
            384
    NAFTA's effect on, 375
    new openness towards US, 375
    pragmatism, 375
    recognition of El Salvador's
            rebel group, 374
    solidarity with Arab and other
            Third World nations, 374
Mexico's social policy
    Mexico's income support, 306
    OPORTUNIDADES, 309–10
    PROGRESA (Program for
            Education, Health, and
            Food), 308–09
    PRONASOL (National
            Solidarity Program),
            307–08
    SEDESOL, 307–08
Mexmode workers, 429
Meyer, Lorenzo, 189

migrant detention centres (US
        funded), 344
migration, 16, 64, 66, 337, 340,
        384. See also illegal immi-
        grants; immigration
    Canada/US visa-free entry, 341
    "EU citizens," 341
    inequities, 340, 342–43, 347,
            349, 466
    investors and skilled workers,
            354
    job, 40
    "Operation Wetback," 342, 345
mining (Mexico), 34, 78–79
Minutemen, 343
miscegenation, 34–35, 37, 76–77
Mistry, Rohinton, 346
Mizrahi, Yemile, 210
modernists, 51–52, 57
modernity, 51–54, 57, 65, 67
modernization theories, 67
modernization "winners" and "los-
        ers," 52
Monnet, Jean, 116
"Monroe Doctrine," 80
Monsivais, Carlos, 189
Monterrey, 66
moral permissiveness, 399, 410
    changing views on, 405
    and orientation toward welfare,
            408–09
    role of state and, 411
Mulroney, Brian, 144, 208, 442
    free trade, 463
multi-level governance, 98, 128
multiculturalism, 36
Multilateral Agreement on
        Investment, 431
multinational corporations. See
        (TNCs) transnational
        corporations

NAAEC, 319, 330–31, 341
    on enforcement of
            environmental laws, 320
    loss of enthusiasm for, 434
NAALC, 43, 215, 290
    loss of enthusiasm for, 434
NAFTA, 21, 118, 158, 162, 172,
        288
    agenda for second decade, 391
    anti-NAFTA campaign, 36, 40,
            191, 315–21, 426–30
    Canada's dependence on US
            market, 465
    Canadian court rulings under,
            149–50

challenge for trade unions,
        273–75, 278, 280
"convergence," 190–91, 252,
        447
democracy and, 16, 20
departure from past policy, 461
dispute-settlement mechanisms,
        17, 97, 99, 104, 464
effect on Mexico's foreign
        policy, 375
effect on poverty, 14, 223
energy provisions, 109
environmental legacy, 223–24,
        315–33
environmental provisions, 316,
        322
environmentalist opposition to,
        315–21
failure to create genuine free
        trade, 108
flaws of commission and
        omission, 462
flows of people, cultures, food,
        music, and sports, 465
focus on trade and access to US
        markets, 362
human rights and, 16, 20
impact on American federalism,
        161, 216–17
impact on Canadian federalism,
        215–16
impact on Canadian
        institutions, 98, 133–34
impact on Mexican federalism,
        214–15
impact on political culture,
        393–412
impact on social policies, 295,
        310
impact on subnational
        governments, 97, 137,
        215–16
implementation, 101–03, 466
Indigenous populations, 41–42,
        65
inequities in migration, 340,
        342–43, 347, 349, 466
labour mobility and, 342
lack of compliance, 444, 466
Mexico's modernization for,
        41–42, 242, 259, 265
new period of continental
        imagining, 361–62
North American Commission
        for Environmental
        Cooperation (NACEC),
        106
not a "new" relationship, 26

origins and characteristics,
462–63
possibility of expansion, 157
power asymmetries, 12–14,
40, 71, 98, 103–04, 111,
354, 425
pre-NAFTA trade negotiations,
71, 92–93
rules of origin, 108
shift of jobs to Mexico, 280,
429
softwood lumber dispute, 43,
104
state sovereignty and, 16, 18,
103–04
success (goals on trade and
investment), 464
trade expansion after, 461
and transnational civil society
alliances, 191
trucking dispute, 104
US Courts and, 168
Zapatista movement, 41–42,
211, 242–43, 259, 309
NAFTA + option, 18, 372, 377
NAFTA Chapter 11, 46, 99,
149–50, 324
adverse findings under, 46, 255,
263, 325–27
bill of rights for investors, 222,
253, 260–61, 267, 280
environmental regulations and,
104, 264–66, 316, 327
Ethyl Corporation case, 104
Metalclad Case, 261–66
regulatory taking, 260, 263,
325–26
S.D. Myers, 104
subnational governments and,
263
NAFTA Free Trade Commission
(FTC), 103
NAFTA side agreements, 97, 104,
290, 430–31
formal channels (citizen
committees), 431, 434,
464
National Action Party (PAN), 42,
66, 99–100, 181, 185
National Child Benefit (NCB), 300
National Democratic Plan
(1995–2000), 188
National Equal Rights League, 37
National Human Rights
Commission (Mexico), 259
national identities, 400, 411
National Indigenous Institute
(INI), 242

National Labour Relations Board
(NLRB) (US), 284–85
National Policy, 87, 90
National Public Safety System,
189–90
National Revolutionary Party
(PNR), 184
national security, 16, 337. See also
borders; security
national sovereignty. See state
sovereignty
National Strategy for Homeland
Security, 364
National Strategy for Homeland
Security, 355, 361
National Wildlife Federation,
317–19
nationalism, 16, 51–67
expressed by minorities, 51–52
nationalism/modernity relationship, 52
nationalism theory, 26
nationalism vs. continentalism, 88
Native American movement,
235–37
Native Americans. See Indigenous
peoples
Native Women's Association of
Canada, 239
naturalization of North America,
446
negative liberties, 251
neo-conservatism, 112
neo-functionalism, 128
"spillover," 127–28
neo-liberal ideology, 17, 42, 223
neo-liberal labour market policies,
273–74
anti-union legal restrictions,
279
flexibility, 279–80
right-to-work laws, 279–80
neo-liberal paradigm
impact on political culture, 398
role of state, 398
neo-liberal promise, 310
neo-liberal reforms, 265
decentralization, 296–97, 303
expanded "working poor," 296
Mexico, 242, 307, 309
privatization, 303
reductions in social spending,
296
social costs, 42
targeting social groups,
296–97, 303
neo-liberalism, 14, 16, 222, 424

challenges for social justice and
democracy, 273
contradictions, 354
Nevitte, Neil, 389, 481
New, W.H., Borderlands, 358
New Brunswick, 82, 136, 141
New Democrat Party, 63, 149
back-to-work legislation, 282
"New Federalism," 160, 236
general revenue-sharing, 206
New Frontiers, 441, 453–54
New Mexico, 357
New Orleans, 39
New Spain, 75. See also Mexico
Newman, David, 354
NGO amicus curiae briefs, 45, 464
NGOs, 102, 106, 119
Nicaragua, 55, 374
Nike, 429
9/11, 111, 169, 337–38, 364, 371,
462
Canada's response, 365–66
effect on political orientations,
412
impact on border control
policies, 354–55, 361
impact on human rights, 385
Mexico's response, 366
new barriers for trade and
movement of people,
365, 445, 466
redefinition of national borders,
353
US reassertion of hegemony,
354, 361
Nisga'a Agreement, 240
Nixon, Richard, 163, 236
drift toward "Imperial
Presidency," 158
"New Federalism," 206
secret bombing of Cambodia,
166
Noel, Alain, 447
NORAD, 111, 358
North America
colonial period, 72 (See also
European colonialism)
dual-bilateralism, 467
imagined geographic
boundaries, 11–12, 450
(See also Turtle Island)
institutional and policy
"thinness," 118
as interconnected, 226
understood as community
(See North American
community)

North America as political community, 451
North America as security community. *See* North American security community
North America Energy Working Group (NAEWG), 109
North American Agreement for Environmental Cooperation. *See* NAAEC
North American Agreement on Labour Cooperation. *See* NAALC
North American Air Defence Organization. *See* NORAD
North American citizens' assembly need for, 435
North American Commission for Environmental Cooperation (NACEC), 106
North American Commission (NAC), 452, 468–70, 473
North American community, 21, 71, 354, 450–51
  agenda for second decade, 467–73
  attempts to forge, 441
  concept of, 190
  as distinct geopolitical space, 390
  viability, 353, 363
North American Competitiveness Council (NACC), 112
North American Court on Trade and Investment, 452
"North American Customs and Immigration Force," 471
North American Development Bank (NADBank), 465
North American Development Fund, 452
North American Economic Union, 472
North American governance, 462
North American institutions, 473
  failure to construct, 467–68
North American integration. *See also* NAFTA
  asymmetries of power, 128
  deeper integration, 18–19, 448, 453, 455–56
  as part of globalization, 448
North American Investment Fund, 468, 473
North American Parliamentary Group, 452, 469
"North American Passport," 471

North American security, 191, 371, 376
  Canada-US security partnership during Cold War, 376
  Canada's position, 378–79
  double bilateral approach, 387
  human rights issues, 384–86
  Mexico's NAFTA + option, 18, 372, 377
  obstacles to trilateral solutions, 383–84
  trilateral cooperation, 381–82
  US position on, 372, 379, 389
North American security community, 441, 452–57
North American Security Initiative (SPI), 441
North American security perimeter, 353, 358, 367, 379, 457
North American Triangle (Brebner), 446
NORTHCOM (Northern Command), 111, 378–79
Nossal, Kim Richard, 357
Nova Scotia, 35, 82, 136
nuclear bomb, 372
nuclear family, 223, 295–96

OAS, 17, 234, 374–75
Obrador, Andrés Manuel López, 42–43, 66, 99–100, 189, 191
Obregon, Albaro, 187
OECD, 71
Official Languages Act (Canada), 32, 151
O'Gorman, Edmondo, 66
oil and gas, 45, 109
  First Nations, 241
  Mexico, 191
Old Age, Survivors and Disability Insurance (OASDI). *See* Social Security
Ontario, 52, 136, 140
  electoral reform, 141
  human rights instruments, 255
  opposition to Secure Fence Act, 11
  statutory protection for workers, 107
Ontario Court of Appeal, 150
Ontario Superior Court, 150
Operation Sentinel, 383
"Operation Wetback," 342, 345
"opportunistic federalism," 207
Oregon Territory, 356
Organization of American States. *See* OAS

Otter, Butch, 164
"Our Canada Project," 428

Paasi, Anssi, 354–55
Pacific Salmon Treaty (1985), 45
Palerm, Angel, 79
PAN (National Action Party), 42, 66, 99–100, 181, 185
Papademetriou, Demetrious, 343
Parliament (Canada)
  dominated by PM, 142
  House of Commons, 145–48
  NAFTA's impact on, 134
parliamentary supremacy, 138
part-time work. *See* contingent and informal sector work
Parti Québécois, 32
Partido Revolucionario Institucional. See PRI
"Partners in North America," 442
Party of the Democratic Revolution (PRD), 66
Party of the Mexican Revolution (PRM), 185
party system, 145
party system (Canada), 146–48
  party discipline, 142, 146–48
party system (Mexico), 179–81, 214–15
  democratic legitimacy, 180–81
  multiparty system, 181, 202
  polarization, 177
party system (US), 163
Pastor, Robert, 363, 391, 451, 454, 481
Paz, Octavio, 66
Pearle, Richard, 454
Pearson, Lester, 146
Pemex, 109
Pereyra, Carlos, 66
Permanent Commission (Mexico), 183
Permanent Court on Trade and Investment, 469
Persian Gulf Wars, 166
Personal Responsibility and Work Opportunity Reconciliation Act (US), 303
petty nationalism, 57. *See also* regionalism
Platt Amendment, 55
Plessey vs. Ferguson, 38
Poinsett, J.R., 85
Policy Research Institute (PRI), 442
political community, 124–25
political culture, 257, 389, 393–412

definitions, 394
  role in dynamics of integration,
    394
political institutions
  Canada, 133–53
  Mexico, 175–92
  US, 157–73
political party system. *See* party
  system
political process approach, 423
political socialization, 398
Polk, Henry, 356–57
"pollution haven" scenarios, 321,
  328–30
Porfirista Dictatorship, 73
Portillo, Jose López, 374
Portugal, 28, 80
  in EU, 116, 125
postmaterialism, 396–97, 399,
  404, 410
  role of state and, 409, 411
  shift toward income equality,
    407–08
postmodernists, 51–52
postwar economic slowdown,
  278–79
poverty, 14, 17–18, 39, 237, 310,
  465
  anti-poverty groups, 40, 50
  Indigenous peoples, 228, 231,
    233, 245
  NAFTA and, 223
Pratt, Anna, 349
PRI, 99, 180–81, 185
  dominance, 202
  stifling of Mexican federalism,
    214
prime minister (Canada), 99,
  141–44
  authority to negotiate treaties,
    143
  double democratic legitimacy,
    143
  foreign affairs and, 143–44,
    152
  government party leader, 142
  leadership selection process,
    143
  media attention, 142–44
  political executive, 141–42
  power of appointment, 143,
    150
  powers of, 99, 133–34, 142–44,
    150, 152
  public opinion as check, 144
Prince Edward Island, 82, 141
private investors. *See also* foreign
  investment

Aboriginal land, 237, 240
privatization, 223, 296–97, 303
Pro-Canada Network (PCN), 426
property
  social function of, 258, 266
property rights, 222, 253, 255, 284
  Canada, 256–57
  common law, 256
  in constitutions, 252
  convergence of standards, 267
  Mexico, 257–58, 265–66
  NAFTA chapter 11, 267
property rights *vs.* human rights,
  21
Protestantism, 74
province-building, 208
provincial governments, 83, 136
provincial rights movement, 136
provincial/state jurisdictions, 20,
  136
Provisional IRA, 380
public opinion, 144
  anti-American, 377
  Canada *vs.* US, 447
  on free markets, 389, 411 (*See
    also* CUFTA; NAFTA)
  Mexican judicial branch and,
    188–90
  opposition to deeper
    integration, 457
  recent trends, 51
Public Service Human Resources
  Management Agency
  (PSHRMA), 152
Puebla Panamá Plan, 244
Puerto Rico, 26, 32, 53, 55

Québec, 61, 136, 141, 255
  Aboriginal title, 31
  constitutional concerns, 138–39
  diversity, 60
  ideological stand, 56, 61, 63
  liberalism, 60
  modernity, 61–62
  Quiet Revolution, 59–61, 208
  referendums, 32, 208–09
Québec exceptionalism, 59
Québec Federation of Labour, 275
Québec nationalism, 31, 52–53,
  59, 208–09
  First Nations on, 32
  seeking constitutional
    recognition, 137
Québécois, 26
Queen Charlotte Islands, 44–45
Queen v. Sparrow, 62

*R. v. Crown Zellerbach Canada
  Ltd.*, 203
race, class, and gender politics, 28,
  38–40, 254, 303, 406
race mixing. *See mestizo* national
  culture; miscegenation
"race to the bottom" argument,
  206, 317, 321
racial profiling, 337, 340, 345,
  347, 384
Rand Formula, 28, 280
Rangaswami, Roopa, 97, 481
Reagan, Ronald, 163, 206
  firing of striking air traffic
    controllers, 284
  "Indian" policy, 236
  welfare reforms, 303
"Reagan Revolution," 160
Reaganomics, 221
Real de a Ocho (Mexican coin), 75
reciprocity, 81–83, 87
Red Mexican de Acción Frente al
  Libre Comercio (Mexican
  Action Network on Free
  Trade) (RMALC), 426, 428
redistribution of income. *See*
  income support programs;
  welfare
Reform Party, 134
refugees, 337, 348–49, 456. *See
  also* immigration
  harmonization of regulations,
    355, 371
  Safe Third Country Agreement,
    348–49, 367
regionalism, 51–52, 430
Regions Apart (Grabb), 56
religion, 51
religiosity, 25
religious right, 57
remittances in Mexican economy,
  17, 466
repartimiento (system of forced
  labour), 34. *See also* slavery
República de Indios, 232
Republican Party, 164
residential schools, 230-31
  cultural genocide, 231
responsible government, 135, 144,
  146, 148
  confidence convention, 146
Ressam, Ahmed, 380
Ridge, Tom, 453–54
right-to-work laws, 279–80
Rio Grande, 357, 359
Rioux, Marcel, 59
Rocher, François, 99–100, 481
Rodríguez, Victoria, 210–11

Roosevelt, Franklin D., 171, 358
    New Deal, 55, 304
    veto, 162
Roosevelt, Theodore
    "Big Stick" policy, 55
    New Nationalism, 55
Roosevelt-Wilson-Roosevelt
    period, 56–57
Roussel, Stéphane, 338, 482
Royal Canadian Mounted Police
    Maher Arar affair, 346
Royal Commission on
    Bilingualism and
    Biculturalism, 31
Royal Commission on the
    Economic Union and
    Development Prospects for
    Canada, 443
Royal Commission Report on
    Aboriginal Peoples, 240
Royal Proclamation of 1763, 31,
    44, 63, 230
    Aboriginal rights, 199, 256
Rozental, Andre, 454
Rudin, Ronald, 60
Ruelas, Ana Luz, 99, 482
Rumsfeld, Donald, 378
Russel, Peter, 203
Rynard, Paul, 240

S.D. Myers v. Canada, 104, 149,
    326–27
Safe Third Country Agreement,
    348–49, 367
Sala, Vincent Della, 98
Salinas, Carlos, 188, 306, 308,
    342, 377, 462–63
    decentralization of education,
    211
    ejidos, 65, 260
    NAFTA negotiations, 103, 259
    neo-liberal reforms, 242, 307
Samoa, 32
San Andrés Accords, 243
Sánchez, Consuelo, 241
Sandinistas, 374
Saskatchewan, 255
Saskatchewan Act, 135
Savoie, Donald J., 142, 144
Schleshinger, Arthur, 158
Schmitter, Philippe, 129
Schneiderman, David, 222, 482
Schuman Plan, 116
SEA, 117, 121
secularism, 25, 51
Secure Fence Act (2006), 11

security, 110–11, 190, 441. See
    also North American secu-
    rity community
    human security, 373, 384
    as new non-tariff barrier, 445
    "security trumps trade," 371,
    454
    trilateral cooperation, 381–83
    US-Canada cooperation, 111,
    358, 376–77
    US-Mexico security
    cooperation, 111, 359
Security and Prosperity
    Partnership (SPP), 13, 112,
    348, 441, 452
security-harmonization nexus,
    452–53
"security perimeter" during Cold
    War, 338
SEDESOL. See under Mexico's
    income support
Segal, Hugh, "Thinking North
    America," 442
self-determination for Indigenous
    peoples, 221, 226, 234–35,
    237, 243
    economic development and,
    225
self-government, 46, 222, 239
    devolution of government-
    designed programs, 237
    separation from land base, 241,
    244–45
Senate (Canada), 148
    legitimacy, 149
    "Triple-E Senate," 149
Senate (Mexico), 183
Senate (US), 30, 161, 166
    election, 161
    Senate confirmation process,
    167
separation of powers, 161–62, 181
September 11, 2001. See 9/11
Service Employees International
    Union, 285, 289
Shays' Rebellion, 159
Siemerling, Winfried, 12
silver, 75–76, 78, 80, 82
Simeon, Richard, 216
single currency, 130, 472
    "Amero," 472
    euro, 117, 125
    unlikely in North America, 173
Single European Act (SEA), 98,
    117, 121
single market, 122, 125
Skogstad, Grace, 215

slavery, 28, 38, 41, 77, 254. See
    also repartimiento (system
    of forced labour)
    Africans, 34–36
    chattel slavery, 37
    encomienda system, 33–34, 41
    Mexico, 33–35
    reproduction of slave labour, 37
    US, 33
Smart Border Accords, 13, 338,
    348, 362, 366, 371, 379,
    383, 445, 456, 470
    human rights and, 350
    visa harmonization, 366
"social accords," 275
social constructivists, 51–52
"social Europe." See European
    social model (ESM)
social justice, 273, 390
social movement unionism, 277,
    283, 289
social movements, 21, 36, 40, 389,
    423–24
social partnership unionism, 277
social polarization, 279, 309
social policy, 16, 126. See also
    Canada's social policy;
    Mexico's income support;
    US social policies
    labour market attachment, 295
    post-NAFTA changes, 295–311
    private sector involvement, 310
social rights, 251, 257. See also
    human rights
    Mexico, 257–58
social safety net, 17, 55. See also
    welfare
Social Security (US), 303–06
Social Union Framework
    Agreement, 209
softwood lumber, 21, 43–45, 104,
    445
sovereignty, 130, 235, 472. See
    also state sovereignty
    meaning of, 19
Spain, 28, 71–72, 80
    in EU, 116, 123, 125
    golden age of, 78–79
Spanish colonization, 74, 175. See
    also European colonialism
    Indigenous peoples and, 76, 78
    repartimiento (system of forced
    labour), 34
Spanish conquistadores, 30, 76
    slavery, 33
Spanish milled dollar, 75
"special" relationship (US with
    Canada), 376, 445

Special Summit of the Americas (Monterey, Mexico), 17
Spenser, David, 344
sponsorship scandal, 152
SPP, 13, 112, 348, 441, 452
St. Catharines Milling and Lumber Co.v. R., 62
stagflation, 443
"staples theory," 73–74
state, role of, 58, 259, 401, 408
    broad value change, 399
    NAFTA's limitations on, 267
    neo-liberal paradigm, 398
    neoliberalism and, 16–17
    North American views of, 402–03, 409, 411
    shrinking state, 17
    US, 55
state sovereignty, 19, 98, 123
    challenges to, 20
    globalization, 18
    NAFTA and, 16, 103–04
statelessness, 339
Stem Cell Research Enhancement Act (2005), 162
Strategic Arms Limitation Treaty II (SALT II), 166
Stubben, Jerry, 237
sub-state regionalism. *See* regionalism
subnational jurisdictions, 20, 25–26, 119, 195, 263. *See also* provincial governments
Summit of the Americas in Ottawa (2000), 363
supranationalism, 20, 128
Supreme Court (Canada), 44, 203, 238, 257, 456
    appointment of judges, 150–51
    reference on Quebec secession, 209
Supreme Court of Justice of the Nation (SCJN) (Mexico), 186, 262
    reform, 187–88
Supreme Court (US), 30, 161, 197
    advisory opinions, 167
    Boldt decision, 45
    Florida vote recount (2000), 43, 167
    on interventions into the marketplace, 254
    on Mexican-US trucking dispute, 103–04
    "New Deal" rulings, 168
    political influence, 168
    on racial segregation, 38

"regulatory takings"
    jurisprudence, 255
    state power, 203
    support for federal power, 203
sustainable development, 321, 324, 330
Sweeney, John, 285

Taft-Hartley Act (1947), 275
Taking Stock (CEC), 330
Taku River Tlingit First Nation v. British Columbia, 44–45
Taliban, 21
Tamil Tigers, 380
targeting social benefits, 297, 303, 310
Taylor, Marcus, 223, 482
telecommunications shift to Mexico, 280
Tellier, Paul, 446
Temporary Aid to Needy Families (TANF), 304
    labour force attachment, 303
    promoting marriage and responsible fatherhood, 303
    reduction of out-of-wedlock pregnancies, 303
    reflection of race politics, 303
    single mothers, 303
temporary business and professional entry provisions (NAFTA), 342
Tennessee Valley Authority, 160
territorial integrity, 29, 41, 221
    Canada, 31–32, 43
    Indigenous challenges to, 19, 25, 28–29, 45
    Mexico, 30, 43
    US, 30–31
terrorism, 190, 362, 376, 473
    Canada's Anti-Terrorism Act, 21, 338, 345, 366, 382, 385
    racialized, 340, 344
    US Patriot Act, 21, 158, 172, 338, 345, 364, 384
Texas
    annexed to US, 85
    independence from Mexico, 200
"Thinking North America" (Segal), 442
"Third Option," 443
Time Magazine, 363
Tlingit Nation, 32, 45
TNCs (transnational corporations), 41, 108, 216, 280

Toscano, Alejandra Moreno, 66
trade re-liberalization, 25, 28
trade unions. *See* labour unions
traditionalism, 25, 51–52
transnational mobilization of civil society, 20–21, 40, 99–100, 191, 308, 390, 434
    anti-CUFTA campaign, 426
    anti-NAFTA, 423–26
    anti-WTO coalitions, 433
    Coalition for Justice in the Maquiladoras, 429
    Coalition for Secure Trade and Efficient borders, 445
    education experts, teachers, and students, 429
    labour unions, 40, 107, 277, 286, 289–91
    pan-Indian movement, 221, 233
transnational social movements (European), 425
transportation and infrastructure need for integrated plan, 468–70, 473
treaties, 30–31, 55
    nation to nation, 227–28
treaties (modern treaties), 240
Treaty of Amsterdam, 121
Treaty of Guadalupe Hidalgo, 357
Treaty of Rome, 98, 116
Treaty on European Union (TEU). *See* Maastricht Treaty
Treaty Relating to the Utilization of Waters of the Colorado and Tijuana Rivers and of the Rio, 106
Trente Autentico del Trabajo (FAT), 276, 288
Trilateral Regulatory Cooperation Framework, 456
trilateralism, 381–83, 435, 452, 467. *See also* bilateralism *vs.* trilateralism
Trinational Coalition to Defend Public Education, 430
Troy, Gil, 447
Trudeau, Pierre, 110, 146, 208, 237, 387, 443
    Canadian nationalism, 359, 463
Truman, Harry S., 162
Tuna-Dolphin decision, 317–18
Turpel, Mary Ellen, 239
Turtle Island, 12, 27, 343
    as US, Canada, and Mexico, 226
Tushnet, Mark, 216
Tutino, John, 232

United Auto Workers (UAW), 283, 286
United Nations (UN), 20, 234, 374
UN Commissioners on Justice Administration and Human Rights, 189
UN Convention (1951), 349
UN Convention Relating to the Status of Refugees (Protocol [1967]), 339
UN Universal Declaration of Human Rights, 251, 339
undocumented workers, 17, 41, 360, 466. *See also* illegal immigrants
unemployment, 278–79
    Employment Insurance program, 300
    Unemployment Insurance Benefits (UIB), 303
unequal power relations. *See* asymmetrical distribution of power in North America
UNESCO, 234
Union Nacional de Trabajadores (UNT), 276
Union Nationale party, 61
Union of Needletrades, Industrial and Textile Employees, 285–86
unions. *See* labour unions
United Electrical, Radio and Machine Workers of America, 286
United Food and Commercial Workers (UFCW), 283
United Mexican States. *See* Mexico
United Steelworkers of America (USWA), 108, 276, 282, 286
    concession bargaining, 283
United Students Against Sweatshops, 429
universal health care. *See* Canada's social policy
UN's International Experts Commission, 189
urban (modern)/regional (conservative) split, 53
United States (US), 28, 52–53, 71
    Articles of Confederation, 159
    bilateral trade, 12–13
    Bill of Rights, 254
    business unionism, 277, 284–85
    central position in NAFTA, 12
    Civil Rights Act (1964), 38
    Civil War, 80

Congress (*See* US Congress)
conservatism, 54, 56–57
Constitution (*See* US Constitution)
"Empire of Freedom," 54
expansionism, 55, 81–82, 356, 359
federalism (*See* US federalism)
Great Divide theory, 56
hegemonic power, 3, 13, 15, 18, 38, 92, 128, 338, 354, 425, 473
human rights, 21, 254
immigration, 13, 55, 355 (*See also* illegal immigrants)
income disparities, 39–40
independence movements, 32
indigenous land rights, 30–31
Indigenous legislation (*See* US Tribal policies)
individualism, 54
industrialization, 55
influence on globalization, 158
liberalism, 54–55
Lochner Era, 254
Louisiana Purchase, 54
"Manifest Destiny," 54, 362
miscegenation, laws against, 37
modernity, 25–26, 51, 53–54, 67
"Monroe Doctrine," 80
nation-building, 54
old age pensions (*See* US social policies)
Platt Amendment, 55
political institutions, 99, 157–73
population, 55
poverty rate, 38
Presidents (*See* US Presidency)
property rights, 252, 255
Puerto Rico nationalism, 53
purchase of Alaska, 54
race/ethnicity inequality, 38–40
re-annexation of Texas, 356
religion, 57–58
role of the state, 55
Secure Fence Act (2006), 11
Senate (*See* Senate [US])
separation of powers, 161–62
slavery, 33, 36–38, 77
state autonomy, 195
subnational and regional minorities, 26
trade harassment measures, 108
trade with China, 448
traditionalism, 52
urbanization, 55

wars against Indigenous peoples, 55
wars against Mexico, 54, 85, 356
wars against Spain, 54
welfare reform law (1996), 160
welfare state, 55–56, 302, 304 (*See also* US social policies)
US-based Mexico Solidarity Network, 429
US Bill of Rights, 254
US Bureaucracy, 158, 169–72
    affirmative action, 169–70
    Equal Employment Opportunity Act (1972), 170
    "iron triangles," 172
    permanence or security of tenure, 172
US-Canada Shared Accord on our Border, 362
US-Canada Smart Border Declaration, 13, 348
US Census Bureau, 38
US Central Intelligence Agency, 360
US "civic culture," 396
US colonial governments, 159
US Congress, 30, 161–64, 166
    autonomous from executive branch, 161
    committee structure, 162–64
    declaration on Indigenous rights, 31
    "elastic clause," 161
    House of Representatives, 161–62
    increasing partisanship, 163
    legislation, 161
    norms of conduct, 162–64
    prominence in Constitution, 158
    Senate, 161, 166
    War Powers Act, 166
US Constitution, 158–59, 168, 253–55
    constitutional rights, 253–55
    division of powers under, 161, 196–97, 203, 254
    Fourteenth Amendment, 254
    "Great Compromise," 160
    sovereignty of American Indian, 197
    supremacy clause, 197
    Tenth Amendment (residual powers to states), 197, 203, 254

Thirteenth Amendment, 254
US Council on Foreign Relations, 18
US Courts, 167–69
    Supreme Court, 30, 38, 43, 45, 103–04, 161, 254–55
US Declaration of Independence, 80, 196
US Department of Homeland Security, 338, 349, 354, 379
    threat to North American integration, 470
    unilateralism, 365–66
US federalism, 159–61, 195
    adaptability, 161
    centralist tendency, 207
    during Civil War, 160
    under F.D. Roosevelt, 160
    federal pre-emption power, 217
    NAFTA's impact on, 216–17
    New Federation, 160
    "permissive federalism," 207
    during Reagan Revolution, 160
    state power, 160
    Supreme Court rulings, 203
US federalism (post WW II)
    centralization, 204, 206
    fiscal dominance of federal government, 205
    "New Federalism," 206
US foreign security policy. See also North American security community
    containment of the Soviet Union, 372
    cruise missile, 373
    early warning radar system, 373
    isolationism and/or neutrality, 372
    North American Aerospace Defence system (NORAD), 373
US foreign trade policy, 260
US Indian Education Assistance Act, 226, 236, 245
US labour law, 284–85
    affirmative action, 169–70
    Industrial Relations and Dispute Act (1948), 275
    right-to-work legislation, 284
    Taft-Hartley Act (1947), 275, 284
    Wagner Act of 1935, 275
US labour movement
    drive toward organizing, 285
    internationalism, 286
    opposition to NAFTA, 286

    response to neo-liberalism, 284–86
US-led invasion of Iraq, 17
US-led "war on terrorism," 340
US-Mexico border, 11, 357, 359–61, 366
    border police, surveillance equipment, and fencing, 344
    conflict and cooperation, 378
    "deterritorialized threats," 360
    environmental problems, 317, 465
    "Operation Gatekeeper," 361
US-Mexico Border Partnership Action Plan, 13, 366
"US-Mexico Border Partnership Agreement," 348
US Northern Command (NORTHCOM), 372
US Patriot Act, 21, 158, 172, 338, 345, 364
    human rights and, 384
US political culture. See American political culture
US power, 3, 13, 18, 38, 92, 128, 338, 354, 425
US Presidency, 165–67
    "Commander in Chief" of military, 165–66
    Electoral College mechanism, 165
    foreign affairs, 166
    power of appointment, 165, 167
    scandals, 163
    veto, 162
US social policies, 302–06
    income support, 303–06
    market-based solutions, 302
    welfare reforms, 303
US Supreme Court. See Supreme Court (US)
US Tribal policies, 227–29
    disempowering by boundaries, 229
    emphasis on economic development, 229, 235
    General Allotment Act (1887), 228
    Indian Removal Act (1830), 228
    Indian Reorganization Act (1934), 31, 229
    Indian Self-determination and Education Act, 226, 236, 245
    institutional bias, 228

    Meriam Report (1928), 229
    paradigm of domestication, 227–29
    Termination Policy, 229, 235
    Tribal Self-Determination Act, 237
    Tribal Self-Governance Act, 237
US unions
    concession bargaining, 285
    partnership with management, 285–86
    strike rates, 285

value changes, 399–400, 407, 447. See also political culture
Veblen, Thorstein, 56
Veracruz, 66
Verrazano, Juan, 35
Victoria, G., 84
Vidal, Gore, 53
Vietnam War, 165
visible minorities in federal civil service, 151–52
"Volcker shock," 273

Waco Summit, 367, 441, 454–56
Wagner Act of 1935, 275
War of 1812, 58
War Powers Act (US), 166
Washington, George, 37
"Washington consensus," 17
water, 105
Watergate scandal, 163
Weatherford, Jack, 27
Weber, Max, 171
Weintraub, Sidney, 463
Weld, William, 454
welfare, 160, 393, 395, 408–09
    decentralization, 297, 303, 310
welfare state, 55, 58, 98, 171, 302, 304
    conservative resistance to, 56
"Welfare to Work" legislation (1996), 39
Westminster system of government, 133, 135, 142
Weyerhaeuser, 44–45
White, Stephen, 389, 482
White House Advisor to the President for North American Affairs, 469
Wilson, Michael, 454
Wilson, Woodrow, 162
    New Freedom, 55
women, 37–38, 40, 42, 429
    black, 37

cabinet representation
    (Canada), 144–45
federal civil service, 151–52
female refugees, 348
Indigenous, 41
murdered women of Ciudad
    Juarez, 189
negative effects of NAFTA, 40
paid work, 296
poverty, 39
temporary business and
    professional entry
    provisions (NAFTA),
    342
in US Bureaucracy, 170

women of colour, 40
work. See labour
Workers Rights Consortiums, 429
working classes, 64, 274, 281,
    288, 296
World Bank, 17, 103, 189, 296,
    468
World Values Survey (1990), 399,
    447
World Wildlife Fund, 317
WTO, 17, 43, 99, 169, 172, 431

Yucatan, 53

Zapata, Emiliano, 41, 65

Zapatista Army of National
    Liberation, 42, 428
Zapatista uprising, 41–42, 211,
    242–43, 259, 309
Zedillo, Ernesto, 188, 202, 211,
    306